The ROTARY CLUB OF PLEASANTON

is pleased to present this book to the

PLEASANTON CITY LIBRARY in appreciation of

Tim Ragusa

from Coane Ridge 4H

our guest speaker on 1 / 21 / 2010

Caitlin Marta   Katelynn Bradford

Livermore FFA

Right Here on Our Stage Tonight!

The publisher gratefully acknowledges the generous support of the Art Endowment Fund of the University of California Press Foundation, which was established by a major gift from the Ahmanson Foundation.

Gerald Nachman

Right Here on Our Stage Tonight!

Ed Sullivan's America

UNIVERSITY OF CALIFORNIA PRESS
Berkeley · Los Angeles · London

University of California Press, one of the most distinguished university presses in the United States, enriches
lives around the world by advancing scholarship in the
humanities, social sciences, and natural sciences. Its
activities are supported by the UC Press Foundation
and by philanthropic contributions from individuals
and institutions. For more information, visit www
.ucpress.edu.

University of California Press
Berkeley and Los Angeles, California

University of California Press, Ltd.
London, England

Library of Congress Cataloging-in-Publication Data

Nachman, Gerald.
    Right here on our stage tonight! : Ed Sullivan's
America / Gerald Nachman.
        p.   cm.
    Includes bibliographical references and index.
    ISBN 978-0-520-25867-9 (cloth : alk. paper)
    1. Ed Sullivan show (Television program).
2. Sullivan, Ed, 1902–   3. Television personalities—
United States—Biography.   I. Title.
PN1992.77.E35N33   2009
791.45'75—dc22   2009003351

Manufactured in the United States of America

18   17   16   15   14   13   12   11   10   09
10   9   8   7   6   5   4   3   2   1

This book is printed on Cascades Enviro 100, a 100%
post consumer waste, recycled, de-inked fiber. FSC
recycled certified and processed chlorine free. It is acid
free, Ecologo certified, and manufactured by BioGas
energy.

*In memory of Marshall Jacobs and
Ray Golden, two talented lovers of talent*

Ed . . . is so aware of talent—so struck with the splendor of it—so altogether stage struck, in the true sense of the phrase, that one can actually *feel* it.

Helen Hayes in Collier's, 1956

Contents

Photographs follow page 182

Theme Music

You can tell a lot about a people by how they choose to amuse themselves. "The Ed Sullivan Show," for millions of otherwise culturally deprived Americans, was the prime source of pure entertainment, television's most powerful, influential show for 23 years, between 1948 and 1971.

Popular culture is a quick, reliable barometer of the national spirit at a moment in time, and for nearly a quarter century "The Ed Sullivan Show"—and Sullivan himself—produced and nurtured America's cultural life. Not just pop culture but haute culture, art with a capital *A*. The hot, the new, the old and cold, the classic, the fleeting, the frivolous, the serious, the bizarre—all of it came tumbling out of Ed Sullivan's flickering tube of plenty each Sunday night. This is a biography of that show and, to an extent, the man who made it happen, which is to say a memoir of pop culture in mid-20th-century America.

Ed and I share a fuzzy history. The first review I ever wrote, in 1953, was of "The Ed Sullivan Show"—or "Toast of the Town," as it was then called. I was 15 years old and wrote the review, for myself, in my bedroom on a secondhand Underwood typewriter. I gave the show a mixed notice, my debut as an entertainment critic.

I gradually settled into watching Ed Sullivan, Milton Berle, "Masquerade Party," Arthur Godfrey, Hopalong Cassidy, "Martin Kane, Private Eye," and "What's My Line?"—gray images cast on our neighbors' seven-inch porthole screen. My father, a community theater actor, refused at first to buy a TV set. He eventually relented and purchased one—a massive Packard-Bell console encased in walnut—in 1953, when I was in high school, mainly to watch dramatic series with original plays such as "Playhouse 90," "Studio One," "The Hallmark Hall of Fame," and "The Kraft Television Theater." On Sunday nights, while nibbling cold cuts off spindly wooden TV tables in our new knotty-pine den, we, like most 1950s families, watched "Toast of the Town."

Seven years later, in my senior year of college, I was hired to write about television three days a week for the *San Jose Mercury-News*. Having watched TV so rarely in college that I had to rent a TV set, at three dollars a week, in order to write my reviews, I was clearly well qualified for the position. My first review was of, yes, "The Ed Sullivan Show," a fat, sitting duck for young smart-ass critics. Hoping to make an impression as a witty fellow, I packed the review with wisecracks; naturally, I kidded the dog acts and jugglers and mocked the host's garbled introductions. When I was hired full-time by the paper in 1960, TV was still so new and insignificant that the job of reviewing shows could be dumped on a 22-year-old kid who didn't own a TV set and had reviewed nothing professionally. Most newspapers in 1960 didn't even have their own TV critics, satisfied to dismiss television with cursory wire service reviews.

When I first glimpsed Sullivan's show in 1948, I was ten years old. That was the year network television expanded to fill up the evening TV log and our quiet nights, and the year that "Toast of the Town" debuted. Only a year earlier, TV had been a true wasteland, with clowns, puppets, and local cooking shows popping up willy-nilly; between shows, a blank window tried out test patterns on us. Most stations said good night by 10:30.

So, although television, Ed Sullivan, and my TV-viewing life all started out together, in 1948 I was still deeply immersed in radio, watching TV haphazardly and never at my house. TV struck me as a mechanical gimmick, a cousin of wire recorders and home movie projectors, then also in vogue. Television was something you watched at other people's houses. My main escape route was still comic books. "Superman," "Captain Marvel," "Batman," "Little Lulu," and "Archie" enticed me far more than old Johnny Mack Brown westerns, fake wrestling matches, Roller Derby marathons, and nitwit game shows.

Early TV was a drowsy, timid, inept, primitive giant that few took seriously or grasped, until it stirred from its sleepy infancy and turned, within ten years, into the crazed, ravenous, out-of-control, lumbering beast we know today. What nobody realized at the time is that we were witnessing the start of a mighty, mind-altering medium. That grainy herky-jerky gizmo reinvented show business and gobbled up most of popular culture not nailed down.

Television began life in a defensive crouch, sneered at and snubbed by the movie industry, ignored and insulted on radio, whose headliners—Fred Allen, Henry Morgan, Bob Hope, Jack Benny—regularly slandered television. Privately, however, movie and radio moguls fretted that TV would destroy them. Movie magazines regarded TV personalities as tacky, tainted figures. A kind of telephobia infected Hollywood; television then was beamed mainly from New York. Once America began watching TV in serious numbers, and movies played to half-full houses, frantic theater owners had to begin bribing people to show up by offering free dinnerware. Radio countered with giveaway shows—"Break the Bank," "Queen for a Day," "Stop the Music"—sending listeners to their phones to compete for hefty prize money.

Nobody in America in 1948—not the networks, agents, advertisers, or performers—foresaw television's rapid development, greedy grasp, and influence. But they caught on fast. In 1948, when "Toast of the Town" began, the entertainment industry was a conservative, autocratic enterprise. Radio had settled into a cozy habit, like reading the funny papers and nestling into the neighborhood movie house. Television changed all that forever, with "The Ed Sullivan Show" steering much of the change.

Once television moved west to take advantage of slick movie technology and a new talent pool, TV became a film industry subsidiary, where it stands (or squats) today. What gave TV its original literary and theatrical flavor, its creative flair, brisk pace, and high-risk crackling energy, was its gritty New York–ness. In Hollywood, gloss soon trumped grit. Within a very few years, TV had slid from "Requiem for a Heavyweight," "Days of Wine and Roses," and "12 Angry Men" to "The Beverly Hillbillies," "Mister Ed," and "The Donna Reed Show." While much early TV was drivel, much was also exciting, and Ed Sullivan's show was a major reason for that early tingle.

My main memory of the show was not of Elvis, the Beatles, Señor Wences, or Topo Gigio. It was, rather, of beholding the aging vaudevillians Ed Sullivan doted on, as did my father, but who had been only billboard names to me: Maurice Chevalier, Sophie Tucker, Ted Lewis, Joe Frisco, Harry Richman, Blossom Seeley, Fanny Brice, George Jessel. They had all been on radio, but now seemed magnified many times in vivid black-and-white flesh on the Sullivan show, granted renewed theatrical lives on a weekly national stage where they could strut their stuff for the next generation—mine.

Sullivan's show was where most Americans—like the notorious baby boomers—got their rudimentary education about pop culture and the finer arts, past and present. Today, there is no commercial TV showcase even remotely similar that exists solely for the arts, pop and otherwise, as Sullivan's show did. Even the early bright hope of cable TV—the Bravo and Arts & Entertainment channels—soon dimmed, both networks reduced to airing mainly movie and TV reruns.

Sullivan's show was something beyond even what it first envisioned for itself: it became the great equalizer, relentlessly democratic, cutting across all age, class, cultural, and ethnic boundaries—elitist one moment (a Helen Hayes dramatic reading) and lowbrow the next (performing poodles), now ethnic (Harry Belafonte) and now white bread (Kate Smith). Sullivan drew no distinction between Bible readings and juggling seals. The show appealed to Republicans, Democrats, and Independents, everyone from taxi drivers to tycoons.

On a normal Sunday night in 1955, the show drew 47 million viewers (the "American Idol" finale attracted 35 million viewers in 2008, when America had about twice as many people as it did in 1955. "What's right about 'American Idol,' " said *New York Times* critic Stephen Holden in 2008, "is the way it holds up a mirror to American mass culture. Not since the heyday of Ed Sullivan has a variety show cast such a wide net." But there's a major difference between the two: "American Idol" is not a real variety show, nor does it claim to be; but it's the closest we have to one.

Ed Sullivan, a middlebrow with highbrow pretensions, revered the fine arts, though only from afar (like most of his audience), but he knew it was good for us. Without him, many Americans might never have seen or heard Andrés Segovia, Margot Fonteyn, or Maria Callas. Even if you never saw another ballet or heard another aria, you understood the basics and knew what you were missing. And if you happened to love what you saw, you were transfixed, transported, transformed—and on your way. Unwittingly, Sullivan broke ripe, fertile ground for public broadcasting.

Even when we beheld a Chinese guy twirling platters on bamboo sticks, we knew he was the best twirler money could buy. Sullivan was driven to present the greatest performers in the world. He revered talent, *any* talent, maybe because he had none himself. But he longed to be on a stage, even if it meant standing at the far edge, basking in the talent of a grand opera singer or a petite Polish tumbler.

Through pure dogged ambition, Sullivan survived his own stage incompetence, vile attacks by critics, and the disapproval of grammarians everywhere. His mangled introductions became the stuff of legend: "How about a hand for Jose Feliciano—he's not only blind, he's also Puerto Rican!," "Out in our audience tonight is Dolores Grey, now starving on Broadway!," "Let's really hear it for 'The Lord's Prayer'!" Unlike most TV performer-hosts, Sullivan had no agenda, but how he did quiver at the sound of clapping hands!

The show was campy even in its own time, all of it keenly captured by mimic Will Jordan in his early-1950s record parody, "The Roast of the Town." When Jordan's Ed Sullivan announced, "Next week, on our stage—17,000 Polish dentists . . . drilling!," it didn't seem all that preposterous. Ed was awed by precision and, thus, all drill teams. He also had a lustful eye for the rare and exotic—leaping Russian dancers, a 12-year-old Israeli violin prodigy (Itzhak Perlman)—as well as for the curious or innocuous: a singing nun from Belgium, a guy who read sentences backward. And he stood at attention for all theatrical patriotic salutes—the West Point Glee Club, singing Irish cops, a Marine drill squad, prancing horses.

"When we have a real hero like this," he explained after introducing a fireman who had pulled two children from a burning building, and who was part of a band of bagpipers, "risking his life to save little children, people should be told. It's good for firemen, and it's good for America." A waiter at Danny's Hideaway in New York City, Sullivan's favorite retreat, once verified Ed's Americanism: "He's a right guy, Ed. He's America. He will never be destroyed. The way I feel about my country is the way I feel about Ed." Or in the words of Martha Weinman Lear, in a 1968 *Life* magazine piece, "Ed Sullivan, although he lives light-years away from where the grass roots grow, reflects exquisitely the best and worst of the national character."

By "worst," she was likely hinting at Sullivan's emotional pleas, his nationalistic fervor, his love of American apple-pie sentiments—respect your elders, help thy neighbor, buy war bonds—but Ed was hardly alone. He lived in a time of the kind of solid, unquestioned values still yearned for today by many and loudly trumpeted across red-state America. Despite all the social, political, and cultural upheaval since the show left the air in 1971, millions of folks *still* reside, steadfastly and terminally, in Ed

Sullivan's America. And dammit, many want it back, a time and place where seldom was heard a discouraging word—about abortions, homosexuals, drugs, and classroom prayers.

Sullivan's show became, apart from unquestioned entertainment, both a prism and a promoter of traditional American values of the 1950s and 1960s. While the show featured an astonishing 10,000 acts, it is now, alas, mainly remembered for four or five momentous events: for Elvis Presley in his first national TV exposure (which it wasn't); for the Beatles, in their first dynamic American TV appearances; and for two of its most beloved recurring novelty acts—Topo Gigio, the artificially sweetened mouse-puppet that signed off in a weentsy Italian accent ("Kees-a-me goo' night, Eddie!"), and an even stranger Spanish ventriloquist, Señor Wences, who spoke through a mouth scrawled in red lipstick on his fist and through a wooden head in a box. And finally, to be sure, for Ed Sullivan himself, in all of his eventually endearing on-screen ineptitude. As author David McCullough said of Teddy Roosevelt, "They came to love him for the very things they had laughed at him for earlier."

The show's towering 23-year layer cake of entertainment provided career opportunities for performers, who had seven minutes to captivate the country. This book explores the transcendent Sullivan experience through the eyes of some 75 performers—famous, infamous, and long forgotten—who appeared on the show. Some artists became like relatives in our homes: Roberta Peters (41 appearances), Jerry Stiller and Anne Meara (36), the McGuire Sisters (22). But many had only one chance at fame, and saw it snatched away at the last minute—performers like Lou Alexander and Larry Wilde, and the team of Charley Brill and Mitzi McCall, which was flattened by the hoopla surrounding the first Beatles show. For some, the Sullivan show meant fame, posterity, and a golden annuity. For many, though, it was a fast exit back onto Broadway and West 53rd Street.

They were all part of what was, undeniably, the authentic "greatest show on earth." If Ringling Bros. Circus could lay claim to that title, what did this make "The Ed Sullivan Show," which swallowed entire circuses and spat out their prize acts each week? Pre-Sullivan, being the toast of the town meant playing New York's Palace Theatre; but Sullivan's "Toast of the Town" dwarfed every vaudeville palace. Performers reached virtually all of America in an instant. As Joan Rivers said, "Johnny Carson gave you the cities. Ed Sullivan gave you the country."

Before the rock revolution declared war on traditional pre-1960s pop culture, Sullivan's show was the gold standard for what mattered in show business. Ed was the gatekeeper, booker, barker, and CEO. He turned Times Square into the showbiz capital of the universe—not Hollywood, not Las Vegas, not Detroit, not Nashville. As the show's announcer cried each Sunday night: "*And now, from New York City, the nationally syndicated* New York Daily News *columnist—Ed Sullivan!*" If a nationally syndicated New York columnist was not plugged into America's pop culture, who the hell was?

Sullivan himself had the heart of an autograph collector and the soul of a mogul. To his credit, he gave as many boosts to performers on their way down as on their way up. Stars he had once revered later clung to him, and their legend, for dear life—Buster Keaton, Blossom Seeley, Bert Lahr, Sophie Tucker, Maurice Chevalier. He even tried to ignite the hoofing career of ex-fighter Sugar Ray Robinson by booking him seven times. It didn't help.

Sullivan's personal story, largely played out during the late hours of New York nightlife, holds its own fascination for me. It was a romantic, roistering Big Apple era I've always wished I'd had a bite of. While I never met Sullivan, we did brush columns at the *New York Daily News,* where I was hired in 1972, two years before he died. His by then doddering column, "Little Old New York," ran twice a week in the entertainment section, where I covered nightclubs and reviewed and interviewed stars—just as he had for 30 glittering years.

Sullivan lived through three majestic golden ages in America—the gilded age of sports in the 1920s, which he covered intensely; Broadway's heyday, which included not just theater but also the New York nightclub scene; and finally, TV's own golden age in the 1950s, when he was a towering figure. During the first era, he roamed through the greatest, most dramatic period of sports in America, chronicled by Sullivan and his sportswriting comrades, who invented the athletic Paul Bunyons of his time—Babe Ruth, Jack Dempsey, Red Grange, Ben Hogan, Knute Rockne, Bill Tilden, Jesse Owens, Gene Tunney, and Joe DiMaggio, whom he knew and later proudly paraded on his show. Ed was a huge, authentic, unembarrassed fanatic. Like most other fans, Sullivan saw great athletes as absolute heroes, no matter how decadent their off-field adventures. He was an evangelist for the Frank Merriwell–Bill Stern academy of jock iconography that remains a bedrock of American sports lore.

Ed had a sweaty sweet spot for sports and could never quite bond with show folks as comfortably as he did with athletes. A multisport high-school letterman, briefly a semipro catcher, and an intense life-long golfer, Sullivan instinctively loved and protected fellow jocks. But he was aloof, unsure, and wary around entertainers. Never more than a stage-door Eddie to singers, comics, and actors, he had few performer pals but many sports cronies. His TV stage was in part a colorful weekly sports page, a primitive ESPN without the attitude. Athletes' exploits were extolled as they took bows in the audience or were invited onstage for verbal victory laps, handshakes, or a stilted exchange with Sullivan. Sports heroes then were even more media-shy and uneasy on camera than the host.

He had consummately eclectic tastes. While his primary passions (girl singers aside) were boxing and golf, he even loved harness racing. Well, you figured, if trotters—or soapbox derby winners or horseshoe champions—were featured on "The Ed Sullivan Show," they must be a big deal. He shared all his enthusiasms with us. After winning a big game, athletes didn't announce they were off to Disneyland—instead, they headed straight for "The Ed Sullivan Show."

Sullivan's early life as sportswriter and then Broadway columnist gave him the confidence, the contacts, and the bravado to take on television. He lucked into both good timing and destiny. He was thrust into the reluctant role of gossipmonger after the *Evening Graphic*'s Broadway columnist moved to a rival paper, opening a prize slot for Sullivan. It wasn't a job he wanted. He was drafted by a desperate editor with a gi-ant hole to fill. During the 1930s and 1940s, Broadway columnists were monarchs at the New York tabloids, more vital than city hall reporters and on the same pedestal as crime reporters.

While Sullivan was never in Walter Winchell's league as a writer, phrasemaker, snoop, or, to be sure, newspaper terrorist, he learned to mount his soapbox as aggressively as any media orator. His dramatic sense of outrage and indignation, a survival tool among gossip merchants, was useful for hanging scarlet letters on the celebrities who stepped over his own blurred moral lines. Sullivan's easily bruised temperament and Irish temper flared famously and often, but quickly subsided. Unlike Winchell, he bore few grudges—except against Winchell, his lifelong goad and nemesis.

Although he reveled in his role as big shot Broadway columnist, Sulli-van rarely used his newspaper column as a blunt instrument, as Winchell and the right-wing vigilante Westbrook Pegler did. He seldom picked public fights, as they did, but he had his share of serial feuds, with Arthur Godfrey, Jack Paar, Jackie Mason, Ingrid Bergman, Joan Crawford, and Frank Sinatra, as well as with Winchell and other fellow columnists. When indignant, he could wield a poison pen.

In retracing Sullivan's giant footprints, you discover rich strains of pure Americana, a lusty, often lurid, lore now gone. Sullivan, for better or worse, lived and publicly championed the majority values of his times— all reflected in his show's broad stripes and bright stars, the sprawling unruly country Sullivan stuffed in that glass box every Sunday night. Unlike anyone else on television, Sullivan directly channeled America's funhouse essence into our homes.

There was never a more alien star in all of show business than Ed Sullivan—nor any that loomed larger or more influentially. Before CBS knew what to do with him, or even whether to dump him, Sullivan became a habit, a fixture, a power broker, a star, and finally a legend who walked like a man (kind of). Simultaneously a titan and a joke, he was TV's first "reality" star 50 years before glorifying the mundane became a 21st-century plague. Nobody on TV was more real, with more warts, than Ed Sullivan.

Even so, Sullivan rides on that great American float of impresarios— Florenz Ziegfeld, the Shubert brothers, Billy Minsky, Sol Hurok, Mike Todd, David Merrick, P. T. Barnum. But he rides as an onstage star as well, unlike any other impresario. Despite his many defects, only Sullivan could have made his show work the way he did. He didn't just handpick performers he loved: an inner faith in his own taste buds told him we would love them too. For 52 weeks a year, he produced an electronic *Time* magazine, but it was also the *Good Housekeeping* of show business, where Sullivan's imprimatur was the ultimate seal of approval. And if Ed also bestowed an awkward pat on a performer's back, this meant even more money in the bank for that entertainer. If he rejected an act or failed to invite someone back, it could be career-damaging, almost worse than being banned by the FCC.

Sullivan wielded his awesome power for both good and not so good— rolling out the red carpet Sunday nights for those he felt deserved a national spotlight, but also rolling up the "Red" carpet quickly when a performer was merely suspected of being a Communist. Although never a shrill right-wing patriot like Winchell, Sullivan made sure we knew that his true colors were red, white, and blue. And yet this same man casually, matter-of-factly, presented scores of great black performers (overriding race-frightened sponsors), who often appeared on TV for the first time when they stepped onto his stage.

Everything Sullivan stood for—his taste in entertainment, his addiction to celebrities, his adoration of athletes, his racial attitudes—radiated from our sets. Even if Sullivan himself hardly glowed, he also was never a mere grinning front man in the tradition of hosts like Perry Como, Dinah Shore, Andy Williams, and Garry Moore. Ed Sullivan was his own show. It was his idea, his chosen performers onstage whom he bent into his own image of entertainment. Sullivan is a case study in perseverance and bottomless ego, which allowed him to conquer viperish critics, timid sponsors, and even CBS boss William Paley, who kept waiting for Sullivan to crumple so he could be replaced by a more polished host.

Sullivan's chronic addiction to new or unusual acts, plus his own severe attention-span disorder and compulsive need for variety, prodded him to order up a vast array of magicians, animal acts, acrobats, dancers, and scenes from musical and serious theater, right alongside flag-wavers, do-gooders, sports legends, and bowing celebrities. His aim each Sunday was to serve up a cultural TV dinner that would please everyone. As Alan King, Sullivan's go-to comedian, said, "In a sense, what he was doing was using his talent as a newspaperman, scooping everyone. When he heard there was a singing nun in Brussels, he was on the next plane to bring back Sister Sourire."

He was never satisfied with the show, forever doodling and fiddling and second-guessing himself. In search of headlines, he added hour-long celebrity tributes (an early blueprint for A&E's "Biography"), scenes from upcoming movies, and rare onstage interviews with TV-leery film stars (primitive, stand-up talk shows). He regularly toured Europe, inspecting new acts, ultimately camping out with the stars in Las Vegas versions of the TV show. His paid talent scouts lurked everywhere, but he relied as well on tips from bartenders, barbers, waiters, and doormen. Even the poet Carl Sandburg found acts for Sullivan, who boasted to *Time* magazine in 1967, "He got us the Australian woodchopper act . . . and the fellow who stitches his fingers together with a needle and thread." Sullivan fought censors and his own network before heading to Russia to stage a jubilant Moscow show, and later defiantly flew to Havana, hoping to scoop CBS News, to interview Castro.

If he couldn't bag a big-name performer for the stage, Sullivan would sprinkle the house with some—plopping them on the fifth-row aisle to take a celebratory wave during the show, deftly changing the pace and stopping his own show. The audience plants were not just performers and athletes ("right here in our town") but also priests, social reformers, politicians, writers, artists, heads of state, Boy Scouts, and mine-disaster survivors: anyone in the news that week, from Salvador Dalí to the Dalai Lama. This revealed both that Sullivan was on top of the news and that, should you have any doubt, "The Ed Sullivan Show" was, for millions, the only place to be that night, no matter where you lived.

Sullivan's own story was living, weekly proof that anybody could make it in America, as Sullivan himself did. A shambling nobody from Port Chester, New York, a middle-class Irish Catholic kid with no performing skills, became a star—and better still, a star-maker.

He artfully wove his modest toastmaster talents, booster mentality, and Broadway columnist credentials into a major TV career. Sullivan was reborn in the spring of 1947, the night he emceed his newspaper's annual Harvest Moon Ball finals, a local dance contest that was televised and seen by a CBS programming executive who had been searching for someone to host a new TV variety show. To the CBS executive, Sullivan seemed a self-assured, even suave, emcee during the broadcast. Sullivan always claimed he thought he was looking into newsreel cameras. TV cameras later terrorized him, causing him to freeze. It took him years on the air to thaw out even a little.

Sullivan, a hack $50-a-week sportswriter who became an American icon by dint of pluck and luck, reveled in his TV success. He invented himself as the Henry Ford of television, rolling out an assembly line of entertainment by building a highly efficient factory of affordable big-name singers, comics, dancers, actors, and divas.

When Sullivan insisted the audience give a performer a Really Big Hand, he meant it—it was his method of generating applause for both the performer and himself, a way of confirming that he had earned his salary that week. He had a habit, which he was told to curb, of asking audiences at the end of a show, *"Tell me, didja all have a good time here tonight?"* He could never hear enough, or loud enough, applause. Albeit a self-confessed no-talent, like any performer he craved constant approval. High ratings were nice, and he studied them closely in search of microscopic signs of audience ennui, but the sound of 1,400 hands applauding propelled him into next week's program.

Because of its cozy presence as a daily houseguest, television gave rise to the vaguely qualified "host." Sullivan, Arthur Godfrey, and Dave Garroway begat the Jack Paars and Dick Cavetts, the Arlene Francises and Faye Emersons, the Merv Griffins and Mike Douglases, the Regis Philbins and Phil Donahues, the Hugh Downses and Ed McMahons, the Kathie Lee Giffords, Charlie Roses, and Larry Kings—quasi performers-cum-announcers-cum-newscasters, personalities who became huge TV stars, forces even. At a time when television was up for grabs, anyone who grabbed our attention was a nascent star, from Pinky Lee to Bishop Sheen to Julia Child to, well, Ed Sullivan.

Ed was the guy at the end of the lunch counter, a face in the crowd. His entire manner—his neighborly name, his hangdog Irish mug, his slouching body language, and, to be sure, his rambling, mumbly introductions—contained an implicit message, partly the secret of his lengthy tenure: if Ed Sullivan can host a show, anyone can (and many did). But as he always pointed out, often to deaf ears, hosting was the least of his tasks. Producing was his huge, hidden, lifesaving talent.

Sullivan was show business's most brilliant nonperformer. If he had been, as often charged, lethally dull, he would have died an early TV death. Always resourceful, he learned to use, and sell, his awkward image, and he parlayed it into a persona as indelible as any movie star's. His accumulation of grimaces, a deadpan gaze, contorted body language, non sequiturs, and snarled sentences added mesmerizing depths to his supposed nonpersona. Making fun of Sullivan became a national pastime. Almost anybody could "do" Ed Sullivan, even if only a lame imitation of Will Jordan's original creation, or a pale copy of John Byner's, Jack Carter's, Rich Little's, or Jackie Mason's version. Making fun of Sullivan, which comedians did on the show as a rite of passage, was an indication of the public's affection for him.

Sullivan never tired of his original forum—hosting benefits for all causes, perhaps to justify his own fluky celebrity. When he didn't host an event, he was honored at it, the subject of countless adoring tributes that kept him draped in medals and ribbons. Sullivan, like Willie Loman, liked being well-liked; indeed, he craved it. Ultimately, as a critic once observed, "The Sullivan saga is stuffed with irony, miracle, and wonder enough to make 'The Great Gatsby' small potatoes."

By the time the saga ended, in 1971, "The Ed Sullivan Show" had become a gigantic telescope through which we could—and still can—view America's violent pop culture eruption and the changing taste in entertainment: in a decade, the spotlight swung from Joni James to Janis Joplin, from wistful moonlit songs to wild sexual yowls. "The Ed Sullivan Show" was both the staging area and the stunned victim of the revolt. In shows that gradually featured more rock acts and fewer divas, dancers, and Broadway stars, Sullivan's show unknowingly, but inevitably, sowed the seeds of its own destruction.

"The Ed Sullivan Show" became both a final resting place for America's biggest headliners in their twilight years and the nursery for rock-and-roll rebels. The onetime legends with long careers represented traditional showbiz standards (time-tested artistry, charm, humor, style) that Sullivan—and most of the country—took for granted. When the legends retired or died, his world died and with it much of the show's original spirit. As the show, defying all the early odds, entered its third decade, the writer Martha Weinman Lear proclaimed, "Twenty years! And where are the Berles of yesteryear? And the Godfreys and George Gobels and Red Buttonses? And the Caesars and Cocas, the Philco Playhouses. And all the little $64,000 questions? Gone, all gone. And still Ed Sullivan drifts on, immortal."

Sullivan ultimately triumphed over everyone—CBS's dubious network hierarchy, his first disgruntled sponsor (the Emerson Radio and Phonograph Corporation), and all his sniping critics. The only prime-time network entertainment show to outlive Sullivan's was Walt Disney's show, under various titles, which premiered in 1954. That other immovable CBS Sunday night colossus, "60 Minutes," has run since 1968, but it's a news show and not in prime time.

After Elvis blasted a hole in the carefully guarded Sullivan format in 1956, the host held out against the pop music revolution as long as he could. Sullivan was prodded into booking rockers against his better judgment by his young coproducer and new son-in-law, Robert Precht. Ed always boasted of being a newspaperman with a finger on the public pulse, so when that pulse suddenly showed a wildly erratic rhythm and a blues or rock-and-roll beat, he could only grimace, grin through clenched teeth, obey his instincts, and make good on his promise to introduce hot new performers, however painfully it rubbed against his conservative grain.

It could be argued that Ed Sullivan, ensconced in a velvet sinecure with a seeming lifetime appointment as America's impresario in chief, simply sold out so he could keep the store open Sunday nights. He gave the public what it wanted, instead of, as he had for so many years, *telling* the public what it wanted—what he wanted. But if the bold yet pragmatic leader had turned follower, even panderer, to youth-cult tastes, teenagers were the newly prized demographic, of which he was an early victim. Rock and roll was not really what the public wanted at all—it was what the "youngsters" wanted. When rock arrived, Sullivan, like most of the show business establishment, treated it like a novelty, a fad, that year's mambo or cha-cha craze.

Rock and roll was not, of course, simply about the music or even sex and drugs. It was about social values, politics, fashion, food, language—and what would soon constitute "entertainment." Rock changed the definition, the climate, the entire show business fabric and framework, destroying and remaking comedy, movies, TV, radio, and even theater. The decline of the Broadway musical can be traced to the rise of the Beatles—indeed, to their four landmark Sullivan shows in 1964 and 1965.

Like no other TV program, "The Ed Sullivan Show," both pre- and post-Beatles, resonated far beyond television and even showbiz. It was a measure of mid-20th-century America, a direct result of its time and of Ed Sullivan's own personal history. It arrived during an era when New York (that is to say, Broadway and the chic supper clubs) still ran the pop culture show.

For decades, Ed had sat in on countless opening nights and floor-shows during his rounds of the city's gaudiest entertainment palaces—El Morocco, the Copacabana, the Cotton Club, the Empire Room, the Latin Quarter, the Persian Room. He had a visceral, almost born-again sensation when a performer powerfully connected with people, and with him. In the 1930s he had even produced Broadway shows, including a Harlem revue, anticipating the day when he would bring black perform-ers to lily-white 1950s television. Nobody presented nearly as many black entertainers in prime-time TV, from Moms Mabley and Pigmeat Markham to James Brown and Aretha Franklin.

Sooner or later, just about every important figure in American life turned up on "The Ed Sullivan Show." Even Miss America began her global tour with a prim curtsy on Sullivan's stage, to be followed a week later by, say, the new world dominoes champ and a recent Oscar winner grinning at us from an aisle seat. Today, Super Bowl victors might swap a few jokes with Jay Leno, Conan O'Brien, or David Letterman, whose shows are boutique versions of Sullivan's weekly spectacle, but in the 1950s and 1960s all major, semiofficial bows by national heroes were first taken on "The Ed Sullivan Show."

Ed Sullivan had a box seat or a front-row table at some of the most exhilarating turning points in American life. But he was a lively partici-pant as well, an eyewitness to the "Front Page" era of manic tabloid jour-nalism, the Jazz Age of subterranean speakeasies and sleek clubs, the Broadway renaissance of the 1930s and 1940s—and, most of all, television's own golden age, which he feverishly burnished. Sullivan saw it all, reported much of it, and lived it intensely—it was part of the untold backstage story that leads into his career as the bumbling but brilliant television host and producer of what became an American archive of 20th-century entertainment.

PART I

No-Talent Host Tames the One-Eyed Beast

CHAPTER I

Out of the Paley-ozoic Ooze

The Columbia Broadcasting System is preparing—for presentation over its television network—a full-hour Sunday revue series and tentatively has scheduled the first performance for June 20 from 9 to 10 p.m. The show has been given the title of "You're the Top," and Ed Sullivan has been signed to be master of ceremonies and producer. According to the network, it will adhere to a format which avoids a vaudeville or variety-type routine.

New York Times, May 22, 1948

When Ed Sullivan welcomed America to watch the premiere of a new CBS television show called "Toast of the Town," at 9 P.M. on Sunday, June 20, 1948, World War II had been over for only three years, the boys were back, babies were booming, and everything was bountiful—bubblegum, nylon stockings, gasoline, jugglers, acrobats.

In the spring of 1948, the country was in a contented, conservative mood following the turmoil of a world war, even if the memory of Hiroshima had been replaced by a silent mushroom cloud that hovered over the globe and instilled a chilly new interior turmoil—a "cold war." Outwardly, peace and prosperity had descended on America and created the appearance of a population eager to forget the past and have a good time. As John Updike said in an interview with Jeffrey A. Trachtenberg of the *Wall Street Journal* in 2005, "The U.S. in the wake of World War II was a naïve, innocent country looking to be led."

Radio had united, and helped cheer up, the nation during the war and, by the late 1940s, was in its middle-age prime, but several of its major programs had overstayed their welcome. A new broadcasting menace, the "giveaway show," knocked off the air such beloved veterans as Fred Allen and Edgar Bergen. CBS president William Paley, desperate to rejuvenate his radio network, went on the march in what were called "the Paley raids," enticing Jack Benny, George Burns and Gracie Allen, "Amos 'n' Andy" (Freeman Gosden and Charles Correll), and other loyal longtime NBC radio stars to defect to CBS. For Paley, it was insurance against the slim chance that television might succeed. Movies were still popular, though their huge wartime attendance dipped after 1945, when moviegoing became less a diversion from wartime angst. To help pull people into movies in their new streamlined Oldsmobiles and Stude-bakers, the drive-in theater was invented; older movie houses played to smaller audiences.

It was time for some serious nest building and cocooning. Finally, everyone was home together again, and TV was there to welcome them. The first hit show that kept people at home was "Texaco Star Theater," whose star was a used-up radio comic and battered ex–slapstick vaude-villian named Milton Berle. Berle debuted on TV only 12 days before Sullivan's TV debut and shortly after the emergence of TV's other early major megastar, Arthur Godfrey, a radio-bred personality as relaxed as the brassy Berle was in-your-face. Neither a brash Berle nor a folksy God-frey, Ed Sullivan somehow managed to squeeze himself into a niche between these two reigning TV giants of 1948.

Berle, though he didn't know it yet, was about to become old news. As fresh as he was on TV in 1948, he wore out his comic welcome in a few years, whereas Godfrey, with his homespun, guy-next-door style, was the wave of TV's future. Together, Berle and Godfrey ruled those primitive video airwaves. Godfrey had an all-time high of *four* CBS shows on the air at once: one telecast every morning ("Arthur Godfrey and His Friends") and one seen weekly ("Arthur Godfrey's Talent Scouts"), and both programs were also simulcast on radio. Godfrey wore a radio headset on-screen, as if treating TV as a branch of radio; he could wing an entire show, often arriving at the studio five minutes be-fore airtime. An unidentified Milwaukee broadcaster said, "The only thing a person could turn on in his house without getting Godfrey was the faucet."

Viewers doted upon the ubiquitous Godfrey, who managed to be si-multaneously wry, folksy, and mildly risqué. He was surrounded by his circle of "friends"—a chummy, worshipful showbiz family that included the basso profundo announcer Tony Marvin ("That's right, Ah-thuh"), singers Frank Parker, Marian Marlow, and Jeanette Davis, plus a rain-bow coalition: a cheery Hawaiian named Haleloke; a black quartet, the Mariners; two trios of wholesome girl singers, the Chordettes and the McGuire Sisters; and a spunky Irish lass, Carmel Quinn.

Others would come and go, most visibly Julius La Rosa, a cuddly, twinkly-eyed baritone just out of the navy and one of the proudest discoveries of former navy radioman Godfrey. La Rosa left the show more spectacularly than anyone ever had or ever would, after Godfrey fired him on the air, much to La Rosa's and listeners' utter shock, a page-one news story that made both of them famous beyond their talents. It was the start of Godfrey's own swoon, revealing the petty, vengeful, tyrannical reality behind his chatty, chuckly fatherly facade and mellow, clogged-up voice that someone described as "butterscotch."

Milton Berle may have been dubbed "Mr. Tuesday Night," but Godfrey was all over the place every weekday. With his four broadcasts, Godfrey all by himself was responsible for 17 percent of CBS's total advertising revenue. But Berle had the lead in one crucial respect: in the words of historian Bruce Dumont, in the PBS documentary "Pioneers of Primetime," "Berle was 'must-buy' TV. He sold television sets." And on Tuesday night he had a phenomenal 95 percent share of the audience, unequalled even by Super Bowl broadcasts. A TV set was now a necessity, not a luxury. Just as "Amos 'n' Andy" had transformed radio into an essential aspect of life and a viable commercial commodity in the 1930s, Berle sold TV sets in the late 1940s and 1950s. He helped make TV indispensable, as did two other TV curiosities—Roller Derby and "professional" wrestling, two "sports" created totally for television.

TV reception was terrible—as radio had been in the 1920s—but it was the novelty of *any* reception at all that thrilled people. That little round seven-inch screen with the greenish glow came from another planet, another time. Reception was actually determined by where people sat around the set. If you moved two inches, the picture could flop over, go into a diagonal zigzag dance, or, worse, turn into "snow." To bring an image back into focus, everyone frantically waved their arms like semaphore operators.

But TV or no TV, radio still controlled the airwaves in 1948. The nation's ears were stuck, almost genetically programmed, to "The Jack Benny Program," "The Pepsodent Show" with Bob Hope, Walter Winchell's "Jergens Journal," "Fibber McGee & Molly," "My Friend Irma," "Duffy's Tavern," "Arthur Godfrey's Talent Scouts," and "The Phil Harris–Alice Faye Show"—not to mention radio's most addictive soap operas: "When a Girl Marries," "Backstage Wife," "Stella Dallas," "Portia Faces Life," "Young Widow Brown," "Pepper Young's Family," and "The Romance of Helen Trent." In 1948, when CBS's William Paley lured away two of NBC's most entrenched radio shows, "Amos 'n'

Andy" and Jack Benny, Benny's defection created an entertainment
revolution that continues today—artists, not networks, suddenly could
control their futures.

Still, only a few favored radio shows made the leap to early TV—
"The Goldbergs," "The Original Amateur Hour," "Our Miss Brooks,"
and "Ozzie and Harriet." Many invincible radio stars, leery of TV and
hedging their bets, tiptoed timidly into camera range. Jack Benny began
with two shows in 1950. He did four in 1951. Not until 1960 did he
commit himself to a bimonthly TV show. The walls of entertainment's
Jericho began to crumble. Huge stars were devoured—Fred Allen, Edgar
Bergen and Charlie McCarthy, Henry Morgan, Ed Gardner (of "Duffy's
Tavern"), and Marian and Jim Jordan ("Fibber McGee & Molly"). Radio was malleable and manageable, a known commodity; television was
a vast, scary unknown. Radio was one-dimensional—sound—whereas
mixing sound and sight created a jungle of not just wires but also creative
and logistical problems. Nobody really understood it except the engineers
(just barely). It was like shifting in the 1980s from typewriters to computers.

Fred Allen, who detested TV and failed miserably at it, said, "Television is much too blunt. Radio is more subtle and lets each listener enjoy
it on his own intellectual level." Allen's brand of topical satire would not
be welcomed on TV until the 1970s, with the troubled "Smothers Brothers Comedy Hour" and with "Saturday Night Live," which aired safely
at midnight. Radio shows, especially comedies, had familiar aesthetic
boundaries that needed to be redrawn in visual terms. Jokes for the ear
had to be spelled out for the camera, which often squelched them in the
process: when Jack Benny descended into his vault on radio, you heard
echoing footsteps that drew instant laughs; somehow it just wasn't as
funny to *watch* him actually walk down those same steps.

Radio formats contained the DNA of TV, but radio stardom was
hardly a guarantee of TV success; often it was a warning. TV was a no-
man's-land, the shark-infested Bermuda Triangle of traditional entertainment. Television was not just radio with pictures, despite all of Fred
Allen's zingers ("TV is called a medium because so little of it is well
done"). Great or gruesome, it was a fresh, unexplored form all its own.

Most radio people disdained the new medium and figured (even
prayed) it was a fad—much as vaudeville and the movie industry had fretted about radio 30 years before. For one thing, it was live at a time when
radio had gone to transcriptions, a safety net. Richard Kiley, who began
acting in live TV dramas, recalled, "If you screwed up, Charley, it was

curtains." Dead bodies were caught ducking off camera, sets collapsed, and phones failed to ring, doors to open, and guns to go off—all of radio's early horrors were now fully visible, like moments out of the backstage farce "Noises Off."

The exciting new visual medium with infinite potential was all ready to go, but—apart from Berle, Sid Caesar, and a few shadow Berles (Jerry Lester, Jack Carter, Morey Amsterdam, Henny Youngman)—there were no stars, no vivid TV personalities. The networks were forced to scrounge up hosts and headliners wherever they could, unearthing television performers under the most unlikely rocks.

TV, again like old radio and, before that, movies, was making itself up every night, and anybody with enough moxie (Berle), or a good enough gimmick (pretty-boy blond wrestler Gorgeous George), or just an ample bosom (Dagmar) could catch the camera's eye and that of desperate network programming bosses, who had no idea what made good TV. As the movie and early TV director John Frankenheimer put it, "There wasn't any history. We *were* the old days." In a sketch on Jack Benny's 1954 TV show, Fred Allen applies for a job in television and the director asks him, "Do you have any experience in television?" Allen replies, "Nobody in television has any experience."

The former television writer Max Wilk recalled in *The Golden Age of Television*, "It was all new and terrifyingly complex. Until now no one had ever tried to do it before, nobody really knew how to do anything." In 1949, the director Delbert Mann was hired as a floor manager by NBC even though he had never seen a TV program before; Mann soon became a TV director. Wilk said, "An 'old hand' was somebody who'd worked on the show last week. Scripts were often written overnight and rewritten before breakfast; it was no business for anyone over 35 with even a vaguely nervous stomach [Ed Sullivan was then 47 with an erratic ulcer]. Improvisation, angst, tension were the daily diet, along with endless deliveries of delicatessen sandwiches, black coffee, and hourly doses of what every CBS secretary kept in her desk drawer—aspirin and uppers in large bottles, referred to as 'CBS candy.'"

TV was far more suspect, more foreign, and trickier than radio had been. Not only wasn't television really radio; it also was not exactly movies, nor was it quite theater. It stole a little from each, in varying degrees. Radio was portable but TV was stationary and demanded your undivided attention—it was the appliance that came to dinner. Television made more grandiose claims on its audience than radio did. You could go about your life—mopping the kitchen floor, mowing the lawn, washing the car, driving to work, fixing dinner—with radio in your ear or in the background, but TV required you to stop everything and focus on a fixed screen.

For physical comics, TV was a godsend. Milton Berle, who had been a severely straitjacketed radio star, a nightclub comic dependent solely on vocal slapstick for laughs, and a failed film actor, suddenly burst anew on-screen in an explosion of medieval burlesque shtick that—because it was now on TV—*appeared* new, hilarious, irresistible. Television was treading air in those days, trying frantically to come up with something that would captivate an easily hypnotized nation of 150 million potential, willing subjects.

In those days, it didn't take a genius to come up with a new TV show. As one video pioneer remembered, "You could say, 'I've got a great idea for a show: Robert Montgomery.' Period. It was bought. Nobody asked: Robert Montgomery doing *what?* You could buy 'Toast of the Town' for $7000. 'Arthur Godfrey and His Friends' cost $10,000. 'Texaco Star Theater' cost $15,000." He added, "Shows were dreamed up in men's rooms and sold moments later over a couple of martinis." No focus groups, audience-testing devices, or market surveys. It was seat-of-the-pants show business.

Radio was still vital and omnipotent, while television was given so little serious attention in those first days that CBS-TV consisted of a few cubicles at 485 Madison Avenue, a few makeshift studios above Grand Central Terminal, and rented rehearsal spaces around town. Warily, the networks responded with the trite and true—dramatic series ("Ford Television Theater Hour," "ABC Television Players"), private eyes ("Martin Kane, Private Eye," "Barney Blake, Police Reporter"), game shows ("Break the Bank," "Winner Takes All"), sportscasts ("The Gillette Cavalcade of Sports," "Wrestling from Park Arena"), newscasts ("The Camel Newsreel," "Douglas Edwards with the News"), variety shows ("The Original Amateur Hour," "Super Circus"), and the first TV situation comedy ("Mary Kay and Johnny"). It was no coincidence that the first TV stars were puppets, not people—Kukla and Ollie, Beanie, and Howdy Doody, plus the animated "Crusader Rabbit." Flesh-and-blood performers weren't quite ready to risk their careers.

So while the new gee-whiz technology was there—TV was hailed everywhere as a "miracle"—where were all the miraculous gee-whiz performers?

In the dawn of the Television Age, all the old showbiz rules no longer applied. TV lacked any stars of its own. Anyone could apply for stardom, and all sorts of performing misfits wound up as TV stars: Arthur Godfrey, most visibly, a chatty Washington, D.C., radio announcer; but also a burned-out burlesque comic reborn as a kiddie star—Pinky Lee, the Pee Wee Herman of his day; an ex–carnival barker with a freckle-faced marionette named Howdy Doody—Bob Smith; a bald, aging dance instructor—Arthur Murray; a grinning lounge pianist—Liberace; a forgotten movie cowboy—William Boyd (Hopalong Cassidy); an ex–science teacher with a roomful of gadgets—"Mr. Wizard"; an itinerant dance bandleader from North Dakota who spoke broken English—Lawrence Welk; and a priest with a Count Dracula cape, dark gleaming eyes, and serene sermons—Bishop Fulton J. Sheen (Berle's major rival, preaching on the show "Life Is Worth Living," on the DuMont network).

The most highly praised program in 1948, cited by critics for its whimsical charm and sophistication, was a grown-up Punch & Judy show, "Kukla, Fran and Ollie." There had been no puppets on radio, of course, except for Charlie McCarthy and Mortimer Snerd, whom ventriloquist Edgar Bergen fashioned into quasi-human figures; the idea of puppets on radio was such a bizarre concept that the show was a huge hit.

Out of this primitive talent tar pit in 1948, in television's Paley-ozoic era, crawled a hunched, slightly Neanderthal figure named Ed Sullivan, by then a slightly frayed Broadway gossip columnist, a veteran of World War II benefits, and the sometime host of vaudeville's last hurrah. Fumblingly, he found a toehold on the screen, then a niche, then a devoted mass audience, and eventually a lifelong position as TV's cultural commissar. So, full-time network television and Ed Sullivan were hatched the same year, 1948, and, after a struggle to live under the same roof, spent 23 happy seasons together.

The story of Ed Sullivan's show is a window on early television. Sullivan's show arrived at a time when America was in a mood for whatever a makeshift TV host decided to serve up for dessert after Sunday dinner. The country's postwar defenses were down, and TV was a wide-open showbiz frontier, with formats fluid and unsettled. It was an ideal climate for show business mavericks, hustlers, has-beens, and never-weres, a hothouse in which all ancient and emerging forms could flourish.

Perhaps the prospect of returning to a prewar theatrical form, vaudeville, carried a subtle sentimental appeal—old wine now served in a new square bottle. The variety show had been a reliable radio format, with its hosts, guests, banter, songs, and comedy sketches, first hammered out on Rudy Vallee's "Fleischmann Hour" in 1928 and molded into radio

art on Bing Crosby and Al Jolson's "Kraft Music Hall" in the 1940s and
1950s.

Vaudeville was basic rock-bottom, no-frills entertainment, and Ed Sullivan was the perfect no-frills guy to get it up and running again. Berle's
show was a kind of rough-and-tumble neovaudeville, but closer in spirit
to burlesque, without the seedy strippers and raunchy gags. The manic
hub of Berle's show was, of course, Uncle Milty, whose guests were just
excuses for him to burst in and further ham it up.

Vaudeville was in vogue again, reinvented out of sheer desperation. In
1949, Berle wrote, "Despite the really arduous task of putting on a full-
hour video show each week, it really has been a pleasure to have had a
part in bringing back to the people of the United States what I consider
one of the greatest forms of entertainment we've ever seen. America has
been the poorer since old vaudeville passed away, and it makes a lot of
us troupers, who made our start and were weaned in the wings of the old
Palace and other theaters, feel darn good to have television—the newest
of all media—be the means of bringing back one of the happiest phases
of American life."

John Lahr, the New Yorker theater critic, noted as late as 1997, "We're
still living off the energy of vaudeville." And as David Kehr wrote in a
New York Times review of a DVD featuring restored Vitaphone vaudeville shorts, "To watch [a classic act] soft-shoe their way through . . . the
turn that had sustained them as vaudeville headliners for years, is to be
transported back in time to an orchestra seat at the Palace." Vaudeville,
recalled the ex–vaudeville hoofer Buddy Ebsen, "produced a feeling of
well-being." And as Margo Jefferson pointed out in her New York Times
review of a 2006 vaudeville history, "In the late 19th century, vaudeville's
managers decided to divorce it from bawdy saloons and low-life clubs
patronized only by men. They stressed the pure and wholesome to attract
women and children."

This was Ed Sullivan's concept exactly—to capture the whole family,
from grandkids to granny, to drag everyone into his vast elastic television tent, creating global entertainment before "global" got fashionable.
Sullivan may have invented the TV variety show, but he was simply
repackaging and reclaiming shows he had reveled in while growing up.
He was creating a form of restoration theater. His acts recalled performers in music halls like Tony Pastor's Opera House on 14th Street in New
York, and the sumptuous uptown Olympia Theatre at Broadway and
44th Street, where Oscar Hammerstein (lyricist Oscar Hammerstein II's

impresario grandfather) erected a music-hall-cum-movie-house that booked every sort of act. Hammerstein hired not just pop singers and comics but also—as Sullivan later did—literal headliners like heavy-weight Jack Johnson, Captain Cook (who claimed he discovered the North Pole), Lady Hope (displaying her enormous diamond), and a mur-deress on probation, Florence Burns (she danced).

For Hammerstein's enterprising son, Willie, who booked the Olympia, the more sensational the act, the better—creating a bill that was a fizzy, intoxicating blend of show business and tabloid journalism. Sullivan modeled his own "Toast of the Town" on the revered shows at the Palace Theatre, the entertainment mecca whose stars became, yes, the toast of the town. Sullivan's version became a video Palace Theatre; a later 1964 TV rip-off called itself "The Hollywood Palace," hoping to steal the thunder from Sullivan's version of the revered music hall. So when Sulli-van's show arrived in 1948, vaudeville was still stirring—or, in the words of critic Stefan Kanfer, "a lively ghost."

Sullivan once wrote that, for all its gaudiness and appeal, old-time vaudeville lacked a lively pace—and he sped up the pace for his viewers. "Acts that did 17 minutes in vaudeville found themselves equally effec-tive when cut to six minutes on TV," he said. "A singer singing one song can be just as effective as if he or she sang six songs. And the singer learns that it extends his lifetime on TV, too." He would fly an act in from Eu-rope and unapologetically cut it to three minutes, explaining, "But that three minutes was the real core of their specialty."

Sullivan observed sagely, "You were a willing captive in vaudeville. In TV, there is no captive audience. All that listeners have to do in their living room is lean over and turn the dial, to release themselves from captiv-ity." He insisted, "Vaudeville never died. Vaudeville was coldly and de-liberately murdered by the owners of theater circuits. The assassination occurred at the exact minute when theater chain operators discovered that a Clark Gable or a Jean Harlow, teamed in a picture, could pack a the-ater to capacity without any help from live performers. Eagerly and hap-pily, theater chain operators killed vaudeville, shuttered the dressing rooms, and pocketed the additional weekly receipts."

Television was neovaudeville's resurrection, granting once-popular old-timers like Bill Robinson a potential rebirth, a chance to revive their classic but aging acts and add a few years to decaying careers. The bad news was that many old-timers' routines would be old after a single coast-to-coast outing. One-trick vaudeville ponies and supper club warhorses—

comedians with a finely tuned 27 minutes of material, or whose hook was a catchphrase and a few dog-eared shticks—were played out in a few weeks on TV.

The most resourceful ex-vaudevillians—Berle, Red Skelton, Burns & Allen, Jack Carter, Bud Abbott and Lou Costello, Danny Thomas, George Gobel, Bob Hope, Martha Raye, Morey Amsterdam, Jackie Gleason— found a way to recycle themselves on TV after years of running in place in radio, clubs, or films. The more resilient comics found a refuge, and rerun annuity, in situation comedies, which remains the most efficient way for a hot new comedian to burn up material and still cook without flaming out as a personality.

Video variety shows were electronic vaudeville. When Sullivan's version came along, it was naively dismissed as simply the spirit of vaudeville past, but he had more ambitious plans for the newly reborn form. Yes, he would have animal acts, acrobats, comics, singers, and an emcee— but no banter, no sketches, no mingling. He would cram the stage with acts of every kind—lowbrow, highbrow, middlebrow, no-brow.

Sullivan had come of age watching true theatrical vaudeville and had a passion for it, a feel for it, but it served merely as the starter dough for what would become "Toast of the Town," the show's first title, which people often confused with "Talk of the Town" (from the *New Yorker*'s lead section) or even "Little Old New York" (the title of Ed's own column). Sullivan, considered an anachronism himself, not only revived but, more significantly, streamlined a dead art form. As Jeffrey Hart commented in his book about the 1950s, *When the Going Was Good!*, "Vaudeville rose from the dead on 'Toast of the Town.'" Or as Bob Hope more memorably put it, "TV is the box that vaudeville was buried in."

"TV *became* vaudeville," said onetime baby vaudevillian Rose Marie, herself resurrected on 1960's "Dick Van Dyke Show." It was the simplest format to reproduce in TV's awkward, unformed infancy. As Berle said, "TV needed to establish itself quickly in 1948," and vaudeville was an old, recognizable friend. Vaudeville also was the ultimate family entertainment, thus ideal for TV, which was custom-made for knockabout physical comics like Berle, Skelton, Raye, Ed Wynn, and Bobby Clark. However, Clark and Wynn quickly washed out, throwbacks to a too-distant showbiz past; two years after he won an Emmy for best show in 1949, Ed Wynn was history, segueing out of comedy and into acting.

"The Ed Sullivan Show" was always hailed, or ridiculed, as merely televised vaudeville, and this is far too facile a reading of its secret. While Sullivan famously, compulsively, cannily peppered the show with vaudeville acts, traditional vaudeville had the luxury of time, whereas he had to edit and alternate acts so viewers weren't tempted to change channels. He was able to jam eight acts into 60 minutes (less commercials). Few acts ran beyond seven minutes, and each had to prove itself airworthy at an afternoon audience run-through. Here, Sullivan might hurriedly, ruthlessly, yank an act for reasons of time or flatness, editing by instinct. Only hours before airtime, he would pull apart his running order to create a faster, livelier show. He was a wizard at such showbiz calculus.

Sullivan didn't merely erect his empire on vaudeville's ruins; he improved on vaudeville and rebuilt it to suit himself. As Jeff Kisseloff noted in his book *The Box,* the veteran TV producer-director Joseph Cates pointed out that, "in vaudeville, you start with an opening act and build to the closing. Ed said, 'It's television. You think people are gonna wait to see what you got at the end? This isn't vaudeville. People flip that knob.' He changed 'routine-ing,' he front-loaded. He would start with Elvis or the Beatles and say, 'They'll be back later in the program.' Then he'd bury the weak acts in the back." Cates added, "He knew that a variety show meant novelties. He worked even harder to get a balloon act than he did to get a star, because he knew the public tuned in for the novelty. He also recognized the contemporary nature of TV. If a guy pitched a no-hit game, he had him there in the audience to be introduced. Ed Sullivan was the Ziegfeld of our era. He didn't have a personality, but he didn't need one. He got the acts, and to get the acts you have to understand the country and the times. He did, and he was better at it than anybody else."

Theatrical vaudeville had often featured newsmakers torn from the tabloids—the flamboyant heavyweight champ Jack Johnson had an act, as did Evelyn Nesbitt, "The Girl on the Red Velvet Swing," whose husband, Harry Thaw, had murdered architect Stanford White, leading to the O. J. Simpson trial of the 1920s. John L. Sullivan starred in a cut-down version of "Uncle Tom's Cabin"; Helen Keller answered questions written into her palm; and Prohibitionist Carrie Nation gave speeches. Ed Sullivan refined this newsmaker-as-theater concept by seating front-page figures out front to take a bow on camera (at $1,000 per wave).

As a result, Sullivan's show became a parade of one-hit wonders like Johnny Horton, singing "The Battle of New Orleans" as soldiers marched off to, and then mimed, an onstage battle, thus allowing Horton and other surprise hit-makers to keep working for years. The show also presented video scrapbooks of the era, or future time capsules, such as Nat King Cole crooning the no. 1 record of 1950, "Orange Colored Sky," with

two black showgirls from (Ed explained) "a great Negro show" at
Small's Paradise. On another show, Ed asked Buster Keaton to join him
onstage before beginning a sketch, "Goin' Fishin'," first carefully explaining to young 1950s viewers exactly who Buster Keaton was.

As simple an idea as "vaudeo" seemed to be, it was really a totally
new dimension in entertainment: before TV, before radio put vaudeville
out of business, you paid cash at the local vaudeville house to watch a
variety show. But Sullivan brought an entire vaudeville troupe to *your*
house—not just now and then, but every Sunday night, free of charge,
52 weeks a year (not until the last years did it trail off to 39 weeks, of
which 15 were reruns). Radio had done that, too, but you had to be satisfied with just voices. On radio, there were no whirling acrobats, ca-
vorting poodles, magicians, jugglers, or dancers.

In her *New York Times* review of a vaudeville history, critic Margo
Jefferson observed, "After all, isn't America a kind of ethnic, social, and
political variety show?" Sullivan understood the American taste for the
spectacular, because he was so totally, intensely, American. Even if he
wasn't truly typical, he considered himself to be.

Now consider this: we are today four times further away from the first
Ed Sullivan show (which took place some 60 years ago) than his first TV
broadcast was from vaudeville's heyday. Only 16 years separated vaudeville's official death—the closing of the Palace Theatre, in 1932—from
the debut of "Toast of the Town," in 1948. Sullivan could book the historic, legendary vaudevillians Smith & Dale in 1957, because they were
still alive and kicking.

The late 1940s seem not only a very different but also a vastly distant
age, another galaxy away. The mood during this pretelevision era was
sunny: College, a house, and a car were suddenly affordable dreams for
everyone, thanks to the GI Bill and a robust economy. After the disrup-
tions and uncertainties of a harrowing war, domestic life in America
glowed (at least on the surface) with a long-postponed warmth. The war
was over, people were planning careers, starting families, and buying
washing machines and deep freezers. Another prized appliance was a
newfangled box with a small window, a sort of radio gadget that flashed
pictures.

But despite how the decade is always portrayed, especially on TV, the
1950s were not a warm and fuzzy period for everyone. "Father Knows
Best," "Make Room for Daddy," and "The Adventures of Ozzie and
Harriet" to the contrary, there were still lynchings in the South, mostly

menial work for minorities, and few jobs for women beyond that of housewife, nurse, secretary, or teacher. Patriotic Americans were summoned to Washington to swear their official allegiance to the country, and many, such as teachers, were required to take loyalty oaths. While America's WASP power structure and a rigid class system had loosened, they remained basically intact. Once the war was all over, most people fell back into their prewar roles.

Americans, in a wild upset, elected as president a no-nonsense, down-to-earth Missourian, Harry Truman, over a sleek New York district attorney, Thomas Dewey . . . scanned the scandalous Kinsey report on male sexuality . . . worried how many Communists were in the State Department, in Hollywood, and on the air . . . bought new long-playing records . . . first heard an impassioned North Carolina preacher named Billy Graham . . . and grudgingly accepted the first black player in baseball, Jackie Robinson. And Bostonians sent to Congress a shy, skinny navy vet, a rich political heir from Massachusetts with big hair, teeth, and ambition, and a big libido, named John F. Kennedy.

In 1948, newspapers headlined these major events: Israel becomes a state . . . President Truman asks Congress to adopt a civil rights program . . . the Supreme Court rules against teaching religion in public schools . . . three atomic bombs are tested . . . General Dwight Eisenhower becomes head of Columbia University . . . the Soviet Union closes its consulates in New York and San Francisco . . . the State Department's Alger Hiss, addressing the House Un-American Activities Committee (whose members include the somber, intense California congressman Richard Nixon), denies Whittaker Chambers's charge that he's a Communist . . . a California court rules that anti–interracial marriage laws are unconstitutional . . . Queen Elizabeth II gives birth to a boy named Charles . . . and the United Nations outlaws genocide and draws up a Declaration of Human Rights. Death in 1948 claimed Mohandas Gandhi, Babe Ruth, Sergey Eisenstein, Charles Evans Hughes, Franz Lehar, General John Pershing, Hideki Tojo, and Dame May Whitty.

Serious readers' noses were stuck in *The Naked and the Dead, How to Stop Worrying and Start Living, Raintree County, The Young Lions,* and *The Life and Times of the Shmoo.* James Michener won a Pulitzer Prize for *Tales of the South Pacific.* Moviegoers lined up to see "Treasure of the Sierra Madre," "I Remember Mama," "The Snake Pit," "Johnny Belinda," "Sitting Pretty," "Sorry, Wrong Number," "Red River," and "Easter Parade." Bing Crosby was the no. 1 box office attraction for the fifth straight year, "Gentleman's Agreement" won the

Oscar for Best Picture of 1947, Howard Hughes bought RKO Studios, and Dalton Trumbo, John Howard Lawson, and Lester Cole of the Hollywood Ten refused to testify before the House Un-American Activities Committee.

Staunchly all-American activities that year included the "Hit Parade" songs "Buttons and Bows," "Nature Boy," "I'm Looking Over a Four-Leaf Clover," "It's Magic," "You Call Everybody Darling," "The Woody Woodpecker Song," "Mañana," "On a Slow Boat to China," and a stocking stuffer, "All I Want for Christmas Is My Two Front Teeth." Be-bop was hip. On Broadway, the hottest tickets were "Mister Roberts," "Brigadoon," "A Streetcar Named Desire," "Carousel," "Life with Mother," "Anne of the Thousand Days," "Light Up the Sky," "Death of a Salesman," "Where's Charley?," "Kiss Me, Kate," "Tonight at 8:30," "Inside U.S.A.," and "Lend an Ear," starring a quirky new face named Carol Channing.

Television's prewar commercial future had been interrupted by Hitler and Hirohito, but in 1948 the box began popping up in taverns, store windows, and a few homes. Those first tentative, flickering TV shows were sparse in 1947 and filled with "ghosts" and slanting images. Between 1947 and 1951, the number of TV sets soared from 6,000 to 12 million, but in 1948 there were a quarter million sets—not a lot, but enough to be taken seriously by the entertainment, news, communications, and advertising industries. That year, every hour of the networks' logs was finally filled in.

Nothing thrilled Americans more in 1948 than staring at a zany called "Uncle Milty" on a squat, square brown box whose other lead attraction was a tall, unknown young comic with a sour expression and frantic eyes, Sid Caesar. The star of a fresh, inventive satirical Saturday night revue called "Your Show of Shows," Caesar was the cutting-edge opposite of Berle's ancient, anarchic clowning.

Meanwhile, crouched over his typewriter at the New York Daily News, a used-up Broadway columnist and wannabe radio star named Ed Sullivan was about to seize the day.

CHAPTER 2

Battle of the Videoville Titans— Berle, Godfrey, and Sullivan

Sullivan was about the longest shot ever to have paid off in show business.

Time magazine

In the spring of 1948, Milton Berle had instantly grabbed the television ratings—and America—by the throat, and he refused to let go until the nation cried uncle, or in this case Uncle Milty. Berle's early colossal impact on TV only underscores what the nonperforming, unpolished Ed Sullivan and his new, civilized variety show were up against.

Berle set the tone and made up the rules in television's crucial first years. His rise and fall on the tube were totally in synch with the trajectory of TV in America. Established comics like Jack Benny and Bob Hope were leery of TV, edging into it throughout the 1950s; Benny didn't begin a regular show until 1960. Both men still timidly hedged their bets on radio. Milton Berle, meanwhile, desperate for fame and a new life, flung himself into TV, literally—he was a comic tornado. He had no shame and an outlaw gambler's bravado. Like Ed Sullivan, Berle, at 42, knew TV was his last, best shot. Like Sullivan, Berle had little to lose when, in 1948, he plunged into a new, untried thing called television, becoming the star of "Texaco Star Theater." Like Sullivan, he deftly repackaged and exploited vaudeville.

Berle's blockbuster new show on NBC was TV's first smash, so huge that it put Berle—and TV itself—on magazine covers, on the showbiz map. Imagine "Seinfeld," "Sex and the City," and "The Sopranos"— now multiply by ten, and you have Milton Berle's impact on TV in 1948. His Tuesday night show became a weekly event, the first example of "appointment TV."

People without sets cadged invitations to friends' houses to guffaw at Berle, or gathered in saloons and outside TV store windows to stare in wonder as Berle raced through the audience snipping off men's neckties, stuck his hand into a fellow comic's mouth, cracked up on cue at his own screwball antics, and horned in on singers. Amid the flying wigs and dropped trousers, the blackened teeth and lisping fag jokes, the flying glass and busted furniture, a swaggering TV legend arose from the ashes of vaudeville.

One reason Sullivan seemed a critical dud in his first months on "Toast of the Town" was the unfair comparison made between him and the manic Berle, which was like comparing Larry King to Robin Williams. CBS chief William Paley wrote in his memoir, "The critics' reaction to Sullivan's show was devastating. They had committed themselves to Berle. Berle's great public was kids and barflies; that was not what Ed Sullivan was about. I made a bet, a very small bet, that the Sullivan show would outlast Milton Berle. Berle lasted seven years. NBC signed a contract whereby Berle was on salary for life, a massive mistake. Ed Sullivan produced shows for 23 years."

Milton Berle was much more than a mere comedian. In 1948, he simultaneously defined TV, defied it, and defiled it. He arrived on the screen like a man on fire, announcing his presence in the loudest, most brutish, and outlandish ways, often in drag. Sixty years ago, he set the goofy slam-bang tone for television comedy that persists today—raucous, silly, dopey, juvenile, crude, lunatic. Berle established the standard and the boundaries; he wrote TV's first law of comedy: anything goes.

Television was graduate school for old-school knockabout comics like Berle—Jimmy Durante, Jackie Gleason, Buddy Lester, Morey Amsterdam, Phil Silvers, Red Skelton. Supposedly forgotten names were welcomed by TV as long-lost prodigal sons come home at last. They didn't have to be clever or rely on verbal humor like the great radio comics— Benny, Allen, Burns & Allen, Edgar Bergen and Charlie McCarthy. Berle could go bananas, and he did, becoming TV's loudest "top banana" (and the subject of a 1951 musical by that name, with Phil Silvers as a thinly veiled Berle).

All the broadcasting pioneers who harbored high hopes that TV could elevate public taste saw their giddy dreams dashed the night of June 8, 1948, when "Texaco Star Theater"—the name of Berle's former radio show—debuted. A mere 12 days later, Ed Sullivan's traditional variety show, "Toast of the Town," politely arrived in Berle's frenzied dust, to muted, mixed, and disappointed reviews by critics still shell-shocked by Berle's comic convulsion.

Berle on TV struck many as a tired throwback, a hack, a caveman comic—but he was the best comedian TV could dig up during its infancy. Berle wasn't as funny as he was frenetic, which was just as good in TV's undemanding early days, when anything on a screen that moved, even a squiggly test pattern, was viewed as a miracle. "People who say Milton is too manic miss the point," wrote Steve Allen in *Hi-Ho, Steverino!* "His manic spirit is what *makes* him funny." He appealed to America's insatiable craving for action, for broad, dumb, noisy visual comedy: a direct line might be extended from Berle dropping his pants to Sponge-Bob SquarePants.

Like TV's other great early physical comics—Caesar, Skelton, Ed Wynn, Jerry Lewis, Gleason, Ball, and later Carol Burnett—he was more clown than comedian. Berle struck the perfect note as a pure *television* comic: you needed to look funny, not just tell funny jokes, to get laughs on TV. The utterly unfettered, unafraid Berle was precisely what new TV owners wished to see—totally different from the tightly formatted, heavily scripted radio comedy shows they were used to. He didn't need a laugh track to goose guffaws. Within weeks, Berle fever had infected America, emptying movie houses and restaurants on Tuesday nights; he was watched on 87 percent of all 150,000 sets in use then, numbers any dictator would kill for. In 1949, *Time* and *Newsweek* put him on their covers the same week. People had to watch, if only out of curiosity, to see what all the fuss was about.

What was so magical about Berle that he should become TV's first great star virtually overnight? Nothing, really. As a *New Yorker* critic pointed out, Berle wasn't doing anything that you couldn't then find in any third-rate nightclub. But he was doing it on *television,* right in your house and before millions. Suddenly Berle (and then Sullivan) was significant, just by his presence. Their actual talent level almost seemed irrelevant.

Nobody was more amazed by his total TV triumph than Berle. He had been a flop in films, a mediocre star of various radio shows, and an also-ran on Broadway, but a rousing success in nightclubs. His problem in movies was that they didn't let Berle be Berle. But on TV, they would. His show was pure Berlesque. He set a new high for low comedy. Berle convinced you he wasn't just funny, he was hysterical, via any means at hand—pratfalls, spit-takes, pies in the face, women's wigs and dresses, rubber chickens, the kitchen sink. He was above nothing, determinedly

crude and crazy. Berle browbeat laughs out of audiences, and if that
failed he'd beat up on his own jokes and shred his shopworn material.
Milton Berle came to personify the word *comedian,* his name synony-
mous with a steamroller stand-up style.

But Berle's sizzling comic comet fizzled fast. He slid from no. 1 to
no. 20 between January and June of 1952, when Texaco pulled out and
Berle tried to remake himself into a more satirical comedian, a lowbrow
Sid Caesar. *Variety* reported, "The Berle craze has subsided as the Lucille Balls and the rival CBS situation comedy formula took hold."
Viewers loved Uncle Milty, but they loved Lucy more. This was before
comedians discovered sitcoms as a way to rescue stalled stand-up careers. Berle not only was finished at NBC but also had outsmarted himself by signing a landmark 30-year, $250,000-a-year contract in 1951
that kept him from appearing on rival networks. When the show was
canceled in 1955, he went from king of comedy to legend without a
camera. By 1960, the mightiest star of 1950s TV was hosting "Jackpot
Bowling." He spent the rest of his life, almost half a century, coasting
on his early TV banana skins.

Berle felt blindsided by NBC: "Right out of left field I got the word
I wouldn't be doing it anymore," he recalled in his memoir, *Milton Berle,*
by Haskel Frankel. "Ed Sullivan was taking over." He offered a flimsy
excuse: "Well, Sullivan had the column and he had the juice." Berle was
wounded not by Sullivan but by television, the medium that had crowned
him. Bob Hope said, "Milton Berle has used up so much material he's
stealing from himself." As TV spread via coaxial cable, linking cities beyond eastern markets, Berle's urban-based comedy, with its inside jokes
and fast-paced gags and characters (nerdy sidekick Arnold Stang, mo-
tormouth pitchman Sid Stone: "Tell ya what I'm gonna do!"), was too
New York (read: too Jewish) for most of America. Of the 5 million
people who watched him, 35 percent lived in New York City.

This was the same fate that felled Sid Caesar, the other major TV comedian of the era. Caesar's smartly satirical "Your Show of Shows,"
with its parodies of Broadway shows and foreign films, lost impact every
mile it moved west. But Ed Sullivan, with his middle-American sensibility and Everyman demeanor, grew *more* popular as TV was hooked up to
the hinterlands. A TV anomaly, he was a New York creature who played
beautifully in Kokomo. Starstruck Ed, a Manhattanite with a midwestern soul, never missed a chance to drop a New York name.

Before his demise, Milton Berle was dubbed "Mr. Television" because, like "Amos 'n' Andy" on radio, he proved the viability of TV as a

commercial enterprise that could master two American musts: appeal to multitudes and push products. Before Berle, TV was simply a novelty, an amusing gadget. When Berle departed, TV was a global economic force. Sullivan, with his own vaudeville redux format, inherited that audience.

It was useless to try to combat the Berle juggernaut. So CBS had only a modest "revue-type show" in mind when its founding father, William Paley, ordered his new network program development manager, a creative and cultured guy named Worthington (Tony) Miner, considered one of TV's most innovative executives, to devise a first-rate dramatic show, a half-hour situation comedy, a children's show—and a variety show.

Tony Miner was CBS's in-house genius, the answer to NBC's inventive Pat Weaver, who created the "Today" and "Tonight" shows and the "TV spectacular," among many innovations. Miner created "Studio One," TV's most prestigious early dramatic series; "The Goldbergs" (a rare successful radio transfer); and the much-honored "Mr. I. Magination" for kids. He had directed plays on Broadway by Robert Sherwood with the Lunts, a Maxwell Anderson drama, and "Jane Eyre" with Katharine Hepburn, and later produced "The Play of the Week" for the fledgling PBS. An original idea for a CBS variety show, however, eluded Miner's usually fertile mind.

Precisely who came up with the unlikely concept of a middle-age newspaper guy fronting a major TV variety show depends on whose memoir you read. At least five people take credit for the show's existence. Paley, Miner, and ad executive Marlo Lewis all claimed to be the father of the show. In his book, Lewis, Sullivan's first coproducer, insisted that he "sold the idea to CBS and that Miner had nothing to do with the show until it was already on the air, and that Ed concocted the 'Miner-discovered-me' story because Tony was a big wheel at CBS and Ed wanted his support."

Edward Slater, author of a CBS history, traced the show's origins to an idea Sullivan had for a golfing series. Sullivan mentioned the idea to Lewis, then an executive at a big New York advertising agency (in the day when ad agencies packaged shows), who passed it along to CBS. Sullivan didn't know Lewis but, though married, was hotly pursuing a sexy young singer, Monica Lewis, Marlo's sister. She volunteered to introduce Ed to her brother—the spark that ignited the show. In appreciation, and no doubt to further ingratiate himself with her, Sullivan booked Monica on the first show, where she performed with a microphone hidden in her bouquet.

That is the official version of how the show was born, but Sullivan offered a more dramatic, apocryphal variation in *Variety* in 1953, when he wrote that, while he was emceeing the Harvest Moon Ball finals at the Roxy Theater, Marlo Lewis suddenly "charged through the dressing room door. 'Do you want to do a TV show for CBS? I hope you do, Ed, because I brought Tony Miner with me.' And that's how it all started."

Sally Bedell Smith, in her biography of Paley, claimed that the Sullivan show was really "the brainchild" of Charlie Underhill, CBS's chief of programming, who hired Sullivan as a master of ceremonies when no Berle-like performer could be found to host the network's new variety show. Smith said that, while the show was intended as a summer replacement, CBS hoped it would run in the fall.

"Ed Sullivan was hired as a temporary master of ceremonies for a variety program I wanted in 1948, because the CBS programming department could not find anyone like Milton Berle," Paley noted in his memoir—although Berle's show debuted less than two weeks before Sullivan's. "Ed Sullivan certainly had no personal performing talent that any of us could discern when we hired him." Paley went along with him because "Sullivan promised he could produce a good show cheaply," starring big names; he used his Broadway column as both a bargaining chip and a promotional tool. But Paley added, ominously, "We planned to replace him as soon as we could afford a professional master of ceremonies for the program." Sullivan apparently had no idea he was viewed as merely an expendable CBS-TV lab rat.

Paley figured, rightly, that the columnist's Broadway connections would guarantee plenty of star power, so he wanted Sullivan as a producer, not host. But to land Sullivan, Paley allowed him to host the show temporarily and was dismayed when Ed didn't go away. "His popularity was magical—beyond explanation," Paley wrote. "He could not perform in any way. He never tried. All he had to do was talk, and he did very little of that." Paley, his heart still in radio, had scant contact with Sullivan.

Miner told Sullivan that his first priority was to find new talent. "He brought back a very limp list of tired performers—stale acts that were second-string all the way down the line," wrote Marlo Lewis. "Ed couldn't talk any of the top headliners into coming on the show. They wouldn't go near it. So I said, 'Ed, you've missed the point. You're in there to *discover* talent. Nothing will sell this show as much as the stars of tomorrow, not yesterday." Sullivan, devoted to the stars of yesterday, was temporarily puzzled.

Miner was simply aping Arthur Godfrey's "Talent Scouts" and Major Bowes's "Original Amateur Hour." Miner told Sullivan, "You find me two great bets for tomorrow—and we will have a great opening show. And that's what he did." The two great bets were a silky Italian crooner and a Jewish adenoidal adolescent whose infantile routines died on radio but scored high in clubs—Dean Martin and Jerry Lewis. "They came on and were dynamite," said Miner, suddenly a Sullivan convert.

When he first presented the idea of Sullivan hosting a show at a CBS executive meeting, Miner recalled, "they were bored stiff. Everyone thought I had gone off my rocker. Frank Stanton, executive vice president, said, 'Well, let's move on to some other matters we have to cover.' At that moment, Paley walked in and said, 'How do we stand on Berle?' Embarrassed, Mr. Stanton said, 'Tony Miner has given us an idea. We don't think it's adequate to compete with Berle. But I've asked him if he has an alternative suggestion. He said, "No, none as good as that," so there we sit.' Paley said, 'I want to hear [the idea].' I relayed the concept and the reasoning. . . . There was a long pause as I finished. And unexpectedly, Mr. Paley said, 'I like it.'" The issue was decided. On June 20, 1948, hot on the heels of Berle's blockbuster show, "Toast of the Town" debuted.

Throughout all the later critical sniping, Miner remained Sullivan's one-man support group at CBS and a key to the show's success. Miner, though he conceded Sullivan was "not the most attractive of men," stuck by the mush-mouthed host, whom he had chosen because he was *not* a performer or a wacky character like Berle. (A year later, Paley finally found his ideal Berle: a comic bit movie actor named Jackie Gleason, whose TV debut was on Sullivan's show.) "Ed was my choice to be emcee—he seemed relaxed and likable," Miner later recalled. "I based my theory on not wanting a performing emcee. I didn't think a performing emcee would last long, but that a non-performing emcee would."

Sullivan, Miner wisely figured, had no "act" to tire of; *he* was the act, such as it was. "He had the type of manner we wanted for a Sunday night audience. . . . I believe in Ed. He doesn't compete or interfere with the acts. He just gets them on and off and lets the audience enjoy itself. On the TV screen, Sullivan comes off just like the guy next door. The viewer can identify with him. Let the critics remember—Major Bowes [host of 'The Original Amateur Hour'] made a tremendous success with a monotone delivery and a deadpan face. . . . Ed's performance is good enough." It turned out that good enough was just enough. Had Sullivan come along five years later, he likely would have been laughed off TV.

As it was, he was laughed at but tolerated; he refused to knuckle under, and stuck it out.

Miner had imagined the show as a sort of 1940s "Star Search" or "American Idol," later telling Max Wilk, author of *The Golden Age of Television,* "I determined that a weekly variety show depended upon talent, and also that a performing emcee generally had spent years polishing his act, which he lived off for years, [and] would be gobbled up in one TV week, and no great performer was going to survive under those conditions. So I said, 'I'm going to conceive of a variety show where the emcee is a *discoverer* of talent.' "

Sullivan perfectly fit the bill of nonperforming (if not antiperforming) onstage producer, and he knew it—maybe the only one in television, indeed in all of show business history (apart from Dick Clark). He said, "I don't think you can ever get anybody but me content to introduce an act and get off. The most difficult thing in the world is to shut up." Peter Noone, of Herman's Hermits, said in the BBC documentary "Ed Sullivan and the Gateway to America," "Ed was the first guy on TV who didn't do ten minutes of shtick before he brought you on." Sullivan's later rival Steve Allen, who grew up watching his parents in vaudeville, once said, a bit dismissively, "Ed didn't care what the acts were—he'd just get four or five great acts and cram them into an hour. It was great TV because vaudeville was great."

Although Miner felt that the average American would identify with Ed Sullivan and cut him much-needed slack, the newly appointed CBS programming chief was not about to entrust the show to Sullivan entirely. Without Marlo Lewis's talent for fusing all the elements of a complex show, it is doubtful the show would have survived. Lewis—charming, affable, handsome, adept—was a skilled, respected advertising whiz who wanted Sullivan out front because Ed Sullivan had credibility with the public, or at least the New York public that knew him from his column in the *Daily News,* "Little Old New York." The title is revealing—it speaks of Sullivan's wish to paint America's mightiest city as a lovable small town. In 1948, there was nothing little or old-timey about New York City, world capital of the big and the new and exciting, which Ed Sullivan was about to exploit for all America to behold.

CHAPTER 3

A Live Broadway Column
Every Sunday Night

He was a shameless celebrity worshipper.
.Mina Bess Lewis, writer

In 1948, to be a syndicated New York gossip columnist was to enter into the literati as a major mover and shaker. Ed Sullivan wasn't the first of his swaggering breed to be awarded a broadcast of his own. He followed in the footsteps of the gabby Louella Parsons, Hedda Hopper, and Jimmy Fidler of Hollywood, Irv Kupcinet out of Chicago, and Dorothy Kilgallen and Hy Gardner of New York. None of them were on TV as yet, but each one had a popular radio program with a large, avid following.

Sullivan, in fact, was following in his own radio footprints: he had a fling with radio in 1932, hosting a variety show, "Broadway's Greatest Thrills" (later changed to "Ed Sullivan Entertains"), where his first scoop was introducing Jack Benny to listeners, as well as a 1943–1944 interview show that originated at the 21 Club, "The Ed Sullivan Program." Sullivan went on to also introduce to the air Jimmy Durante, Frances Langford, Jack Pearl, Irving Berlin, and Florence Ziegfeld. "I decided radio was ready for me," he much later recalled. "It was easy so I stepped in. I was on the ground floor of radio but I dropped out like a dope before making my real rich strike. Now I'm on the ground floor of TV and I'm not giving up my lease until the landlord evicts me. I'm determined not to let that happen again."

Even worse, he had to bear gossip rival Walter Winchell's spectacular radio success, a constant prod: "No wonder I was always tense and moody," he said once. "I would have a radio show, have it get canceled, then I would turn on my radio on Sunday night and there he was, that staccato voice calling to 'Mr. and Mrs. America and all the ships at sea,' and me realizing that America was listening. I didn't even have the comfort of telling myself he was lousy. He wasn't good. He was simply great. I would grow another small ulcer and start planning another radio show. I'd get it on. And somebody would quickly get it off."

Ever resilient, he returned to the air with a weekly 15-minute commentary in the mid-1940s. For one of the shows, Sullivan dared mimic Winchell's famed chattering telegraph key with his own version—a clacking Remington typewriter and the ratchety sound of a carriage return. But nobody could duplicate the frenzied Winchell at full cry. Sullivan's show didn't last.

Despite his mediocre radio career, when Sullivan finally was tapped by CBS's Tony Miner to emcee his own network TV show, it was—to Sullivan, if nobody else at the time—a totally logical progression. It was not, as everyone else thought, a horrible and bizarre accident. Sullivan had been waiting for this moment all his life. The more you learn of the wartime benefit shows he produced and emceed at Radio City Music Hall, Madison Square Garden, and other theatrical palaces, the more you realize that choosing Ed Sullivan to host and produce a new vaudeville-style TV show seemed an inevitable, obvious decision.

As it did for Winchell, a former vaudeville hoofer, greasepaint coursed through Sullivan's veins. He produced several vaudeville minishows, as Winchell had earlier, earning big money in the early 1930s ($3,750 a week) for rounding up acts and bringing them out onstage between movie showings at so-called presentation houses. It was vaudeville's last gasp. Later, before radio, Sullivan hosted his first of many benefits as a Broadway columnist in 1932, emceeing a $100-a-plate United Jewish Federation dinner at the Plaza Hotel that led to an offer to produce a variety show at the Paramount Theatre, a revue called "Gems of the Town." This was followed by a series of stage shows at Loew's State Theatre, so-called Dawn Patrol revues accompanying the films. This is when Sullivan first began introducing celebrities in the house. In 1936 he hosted his first Harvest Moon Ball, a major, widely publicized dance contest. Several balls later, Sullivan found himself on television.

He was always scrambling for a show business niche, busily working the theatrical fringes, looking to make a name beyond newspapers and yearning to break into showbiz himself. He even appeared in two B movie cameo roles, playing Ed Sullivan—famous Broadway columnist—and, when he worked in Hollywood from 1937 to 1940, he sold an original story, "There Goes My Heart," to Hal Roach Studios, and another original screenplay, "Ma, He's Making Eyes at Me," to Universal. B. R. Crisler, reviewing the latter for the *New York Times,* labeled it "limp and foolish" and "bargain basement." Sullivan narrated "Big Town Czar," a 1939 film adapted from a Frank Capra–esque story he had written about a mobster who undergoes a change of heart. Frank Nugent of the *New York Times* called it "extremely first-personal, quite sentimental and edifyingly moralistic."

But Sullivan remained undaunted, even emboldened. He began producing Broadway revues—"Harlem Cavalcade" in 1942, with the songwriter Noble Sissle (his credit reads "assembled by Ed Sullivan"), and a floor show at the Paramount Theatre called "Take a Chance," with Lillian Roth, Buddy Rogers, and Cliff Edwards. A year earlier, he had resuscitated a dying revue, "Crazy with the Heat," by hiring a new director and two hot dance teams, and adding a faddish South American dance number, all of which helped keep the show running for 99 performances. In his review of the revised "Crazy with the Heat," Brooks Atkinson of the *New York Times* wrote, "Being a person of unusual compassion, Mr. Sullivan, the celebrated columnist, hated to see all the good things going to waste. . . . [He] improved the second half"—though not enough to turn it around. Even so, Sullivan's stock was rising on the Rialto.

Thus Ed Sullivan was eager, ready, and waiting when TV beckoned in the spring of 1948, doubtless telling himself (like the dancer in "A Chorus Line"), "I can do that!" Mina Bess Lewis, Marlo's widow, told me in 2005, while in her nineties: "He was ambitious. He wanted to become prominent, noted, and famous. That's not a good or a bad thing. That's just the Holy Grail for some men. He was never satisfied with being lower-middle class; his own background was ordinary and mundane." He wanted to flee his ordinary suburban origins, although he later extolled his hometown's virtues in print and on camera.

Sullivan liked to say that he stumbled into emceeing by accident, but he was far too canny and ambitious a guy to leave a shot at theatrical fame to chance. He once told a *Holiday* writer, "I'd done some benefits, but I didn't have any stage ambitions. They talk about 'stage-struck Sullivan,' but that's not so. Boris Morros called me. He was running the Paramount Theatre and I guess they had a real stinker of a picture coming up. They wanted a hot stage show in a hurry. And would I emcee it? I said no. Morros said it paid $1500. I still said no and goodbye. He called me back and raised it to $2000. I explained I wasn't trying to run up his price, but this just wasn't my racket. I said no again. He called back again, and again. Well, when the price hit $3700, I was dazed and said yes."

Of the resulting show, Sullivan later wryly said, when reviewing himself: "It was a great show and I was a great actor. No 'Frozen Face' in that appearance. I wrote myself what I thought were screamingly funny lines and delivered them, I thought, beautifully." He arranged for a big buffet for friends after the show, "and I was ready for them to tell me that Alfred Lunt should move over. Some of them did tell me that, too." But actors Victor Moore and William Gaxton told him he was lousy and to forget about a future onstage.

Unlike today's paparazzi pygmies, gossip columnists in the 1940s and 1950s were media giants in an era when scandal truly scandalized readers. Columnists then could create or wreck careers in one headline, one line. Hedda Hopper called her Beverly Hills estate "The House that Fear Built." Gossip columnists were self-appointed ministers of showbiz. They doled out advice and shook their inky fingers at misbehaving stars. They were coddled and kowtowed to at a time when readers both depended on and believed what major columnists reported. Mina Bess Lewis, in the Lewises' joint memoir, called Parsons and Hopper "unlikable harpies—ruthless. They became little Caesars—pugnacious, uncooperative."

Mina Bess's sister-in-law, the singer Monica Lewis, told me, "In those days, columnists had tremendous power. But Ed was benign compared to Winchell." Winchell was ten times the power broker after he began broadcasting his column on radio, but he later flopped on TV. Will Jordan, the famous Sullivan impressionist, commented to me, "By everything that's holy, Winchell, not Sullivan, should have been the TV star."

Mina Bess wrote, "Only a world steeped in show business, dependent on public whims and personality cults, could have spawned a breed like the gossip columnists. These journalists were sought after, catered to, and cuffed [that is, given free meals, hotel rooms, women]. The motion picture companies spent millions of dollars a year servicing them. The columnists were kings." Damon Runyon, Leonard Lyons, Winchell, and their ilk, aided by *Variety* founder Sime Silverman, invented Broadway (to swipe John Mosedale's book title, *The Men Who Invented Broadway*).

In the 1930s and 1940s, cynical, wisecracking newspaper guys and gals (portrayed by Jimmy Cagney, Lee Tracy, Ann Southern, Rosalind

Russell, Joan Blondell, Cary Grant) were standard movie types. Fast-talking newspaper films were a beloved genre—besides "The Front Page," there was "Gentlemen of the Press," "Picture Snatcher," "Platinum Blonde," "She Wanted a Millionaire," and "His Girl Friday," in 1940, the replated "Front Page."

In Sullivan's own 1939 newspaper movie, "Big Town Czar," based on his story "Czar of Broadway," he plays himself, mixing it up with real actors (a young Eve Arden, for one). Movie-TV critic Ron Miller told me, "The movie demonstrates how celebrated big New York columnists were in the 1930s. He's treated like a superstar, wielding heavy influence, apparently immune from gangster retaliation."

As "Big Town Czar" opens, Sullivan is reading from his own column, narrating the tale of a New York mobster who wants to quit the mob for a farm. He asks Sullivan for makeover advice—"How do I meet the right class of people?" Sullivan, looking remarkably dapper—slicked down hair, three-piece suit—replies, "You need polish. You need new clothes, you have to learn how to talk" (yes!). After he departs, forgetting his hat, a mobster picks it up and says, "Columnists have big heads."

Ego-bloated reporters in Sullivan's day were glamorous figures—cocky, funny, bantering, crime-busting, skirt-chasing, hard-drinking, hat-wearing hotshots and fearless crusaders. It's no wonder Jerry Siegel and Joe Shuster chose a reporter as Superman's undercover guise and set their comic book at the *Daily Planet,* a name inspired by the *New York Daily News*'s massive revolving globe in its old East 42nd Street lobby. Radio's newsroom heroes included Steve Wilson on "The Big Story," "Front Page Farrell," and "Casey, Crime Photographer." During the 1930s and 1940s, Winchell appeared as himself in three films; even society columnist Elsa Maxwell played herself in a few movies.

This was also the golden age of the media junket, when critics, entertainment writers, and editors went on free cruises and were flown around the world by publicity agencies to movie locations, lavishly wined and dined "for all the whoopee they could make," in one flack's phrase. Marlo Lewis's background as an executive at Blaine Thompson Advertising, which created much entertainment advertising in 1940s New York, had taught him the rudiments of glad-handing. To promote a Warner Bros. movie, Lewis's agency packed up a trainload of merry media junketeers from Grand Central Terminal, with two well-stocked bar cars, for a summer holiday in the Maine countryside. On board were Errol Flynn, Ann Sheridan, and Jack Carson, should anyone in the rolling media caravan care to talk to them about their new movie.

Showbiz columnists, a ravenous part of the entertainment family, rode up front in the Payola Express. While cash was not exchanged, gifts, tickets, liquor, and showgirls were laid at the doorsteps of major columnists. The quid pro quo: weeks of protective flattering and fawning over upcoming movies, TV shows, or stage shows. Sullivan biographer Jerry Bowles wrote, "The Hollywood studio powers had discovered an interesting truth: newspapermen might not be easily bought, but they could be rented."

The hustling publisher Lyle Stuart, who got his start as a press agent, remembered not only that Sullivan was hospitable to publicists but also that "the press agents would play poker with him once a week at the Warwick Hotel and deliberately lose to him. It was understood you'd lose $150 that night to Ed. He wasn't taking any bribes but he was always a winner, and he pretended total innocence of the whole scam. He always won $150, $200. I didn't play but I attended one or two games." Stuart recalled that Sullivan would send him incriminating notes about Winchell. "Every one of them said, 'Please do not tell anyone that I've written you.' He was a total coward with Winchell."

The Broadway columnists—the regal title itself no longer exists—had life-or-death power over shows, books, songs, and celebrities. Their realms were financial and cultural fiefdoms, media empires within newspapers. Darryl Zanuck, head of 20th Century-Fox, built a bungalow on the studio grounds for Winchell's trysts and equipped it with servants, food, drink, and a chauffeur; Winchell paid Zanuck off in news and gossip items. Years later, on his show, Sullivan allocated an hour to a shimmering tribute to Zanuck, a back-scratching payoff for services rendered. Miami's Roney Plaza Hotel was Winchell's home away from home, where he reigned in a royal, secluded beach house. For Winchell, as for Sullivan and other Broadways studs, flashy gifts, personal favors, and public recognition (not to mention the available girls) were potent aphrodisiacs.

Sullivan, likewise, was treated as visiting royalty at Miami's Eden Roc and Fontainebleau hotels, residing in the presidential suites, which had poolside cabanas, and he had a private box at Hialeah Race Track. Miami was dedicated to courting Sullivan (even naming a major street Ed Sullivan Plaza) in exchange for casual mentions on the air ("When Sylvia and I were recently down in Miami, staying at the gorgeous Eden Roc Hotel . . ."). He even did shows from Miami, including the second historic Beatles broadcast. Sullivan, like Winchell and later Jackie Gleason, was attached at the hip to the Miami Chamber of Commerce. Although Sullivan was forced to walk in Winchell's shadow, he was avidly wooed, largely because his column ran in the nation's largest paper—the *New York Daily News*. It was read by a million readers, twice as many on Sundays. Sullivan cherished his reporter status above his TV stardom. In conversation, he often spelled out names in anecdotes as if talking to a rewrite man. He lacked the journalistic clout of Winchell, Hopper, and Parsons (given his skimpy syndication of about 25 newspapers), but his circulation in New York had the publicity establishment at his feet.

The *Daily News* dutifully chronicled its Broadway gossip star's own comings and goings ("Chicago Tribune–New York News Syndicate columnist Ed Sullivan and his wife flew from New York Oct. 4 for Miami from where they will Clipper to Rio de Janeiro for a month tour of South America."). And it touted his faithful appearances at fund-raising and charitable events: "The Main Stem's favorite historian, Ed Sullivan, Broadway columnist of *The News,* will move over to Eighth Avenue next Monday night to emcee the finals of the 19th annual Silver Skates contest at Madison Square Garden." When he and his wife returned from a European vacation celebrating his 35th birthday, aboard the *Normandie,* Sullivan was greeted by two tugboats filled with celebrities and a band playing "Happy Birthday," as a plane circled overhead bearing a welcome-home placard on its tail. Nice work if you can get it.

Such was the pampered, plush-lined world in which Ed Sullivan moved nightly during the 1930s and 1940s. Far less feared and brazen than Winchell, he was lionized anyway. Heads swiveled when he entered a theater lobby, a nightclub, or a restaurant. Each day, theater press agents like Sy Presten, Max Eisen, Alan Eichler, and Harvey Sabinson would turn up at the *Daily News* office, clutching manila envelopes, tentative grins on their faces, hoping to get an actual word with The Columnist himself. This sort of ritual was all methodically and melodramatically chronicled in the film "The Sweet Smell of Success," with Tony Curtis as the obsequious press agent to Burt Lancaster's icy, bare-knuckles gossip columnist based on Winchell.

A brief flash-forward: In 1960, 12 years into his TV show, Sullivan told Marlo Lewis he wanted to quit his daily column, which had become a chore he now felt was behind, even beneath, him. As Lewis described in his book, he wisely talked him out of it, realizing "that byline of his, over the years, was the unacknowledged source of our strength, the big stick that allowed us to walk softly. It was the key to Ed's power with important people in the entertainment world, who would always want his printed boasts, his scoops." If the TV show was the carrot, the column was the stick. Lewis's widow told me that Sullivan used his column as leverage to bag stars for his show ("Everyone knew it was a quid pro quo arrangement"), but Sullivan forever denied it, remarking that the sniping came "not from the critics so much but from entertainers who either couldn't get on TV or had failed at it."

Lewis slyly flattered Sullivan, telling him he was the only journalist ever to achieve such stature in television, and that he must hang on to the column out of respect for the profession that had catapulted him to fame and that was now so proud of him: "The Fourth Estate was too important and honorable a profession to abandon summarily." Ed not only bought it but also kept cranking out showbiz items until his death. He was born again, newly aware that the column was his lifeline to TV fame and fortune.

Sullivan never passed up a chance to identify himself as a newspaperman first and foremost. Most of the press corps rolled its eyes at his lifeless, old-fashioned column, which became a showbiz bulletin board, a celebrity service written in a verbless shorthand, like those news-ticker flashes today that crawl across the bottom of CNN news shows ("The Jack Warners honeymooning in Catalina . . . Barbara Stanwyck ailing . . . Joe Louis honored by Friars"). It was rumored that his assistant, Carmine Santullo, really wrote the column after Sullivan lost interest, but Santullo denied it: "I may have put together the notes and the items and talked to people on the phone," he said, "but Ed always looked at it and usually changed things. He really wrote it."

People had always underestimated Sullivan, misjudged him, mocked him, attacked him, and refused to take him seriously, but in retrospect a pattern emerges. Ed carefully climbed from one platform to the next: he used a mediocre sports column to get to New York, a beat he quickly abandoned when an opportunity opened up to become a Broadway columnist. He parlayed that column into a job hosting a radio show and charity shindigs, also popping up in screen cameos and producing Broadway stage revues. These were baby steps in his career; his strategy ended with him landing a network television hosting job in 1948.

It was your classic up-from-the-streets saga that Sullivan often featured on his show—America's favorite fairy tale, a national mythology of success, especially in show business, which never tires of its own backstage fables. And Ed Sullivan embodied it. He always cloaked his ambitions for national stardom in the gray, grim, fella-next-door disguise that served him so well for so long in print—that of the mild-mannered reporter who seemingly had ducked into a CBS studio phone booth and emerged a TV superhero.

He was approaching 50 when TV beckoned, and was weary of cranking out a daily gossip column about people he didn't much admire or feel comfortable around, a world full of the "phonies" he regularly disparaged in his column and in person. A meat-and-potatoes guy, he was never truly comfortable on the caviar-and-champagne circuit with show folks, much as he loved dining among them. Mina Bess Lewis recalled, "The column gave him the prestige he wanted. He was tireless and frankly stage struck, which gave him an affinity with the public. He was a shameless celebrity worshipper."

While Sullivan wrote a column for New York's biggest tabloid, it lacked the wallop of Winchell's or even Dorothy Kilgallen's column; few beyond New York read it. Even in New York, Sullivan's column was skimmed out of habit, not avidly read out of love or need. Not only was his archfoe, Winchell, widely read, quoted, copied, and chronicled, but he also became the excited, nattering, self-appointed spokesman for "Mr. and Mrs. North America," heard over the air Sunday nights, one of radio's hottest, must-hear shows and regularly in the top ten. Mina Bess Lewis recalled each man well: "They were both very ambitious, ruthless men." Sullivan didn't merely "envy" Winchell, noted Lewis— "That's too cozy a term." He loathed him. Sullivan "didn't have the power of Winchell, but they were both in the same boat, pulling different oars. Winchell was the designated driver."

When Winchell was an icon in 1948, Ed Sullivan considered himself a has-been or at least at a dead-end. Nearing 47, he felt it was all over for him. After writing a Broadway column for 16 years, he had not become a household name and wasn't likely to be one in the future. As Jim Bishop wrote in an in-depth *New York Journal-American* series on Sullivan in 1957, "The column wasn't enough. He had unreasoning ambition perched on one shoulder and an ulcer on the other. The column would have been enough for the average egomaniac. But Sullivan, like Winchell, wanted to be known and respected by everyone. After the first few years, he knew that he was not going to make himself a national figure with three dots and a dash of Winchell."

Even in his youth, Sullivan had worried about becoming an anachronism, once telling an interviewer, "As a young newspaperman, I always had the fear that some day an efficiency expert would come into the office and point to a character huddled in a corner. He'd ask, 'Who's

that?' and they'd say, 'Oh, that's old Sullivan. Been with us 30 years.'
And the efficiency man would say, 'That's too long. Get rid of him.'"
Sullivan once moaned to his wife, "Where am I headed for? The copy
desk? Working in a morgue [newspaper library], digging up old clippings?" Sullivan had a recurring dream of going into the *News*'s morgue
and asking a gray-haired old man for some clippings, only to realize that
the gray-haired old man was himself.

This midlife fear of winding up a discarded newsman, he claimed,
was the real reason he "decided to try my hand at a sideline—first vaudeville, then radio and TV. Stagestruck, nuts! I was money struck. I went
into show business to make dough I needed." Only half-true; he needed
fame far more than money. (Ironically, Sullivan became one of TV's first
major victims of demographics, when CBS discarded him at 71 as a
Sunday-night fixture, but he wrote his newspaper column until the bitter
end.)

Despite private fears that he was washed up, Sullivan was an unabashed
optimist, a can-do self-starter whose athletic background made him a
fierce competitor. He was a worrier, a brooder, but he was also bullheaded, with more faith in himself than others had, and much more than
was warranted. When Marlo Lewis returned from his first meeting at
CBS with news that the network had given their proposed show a nod,
he was afraid to tell Sullivan the bad news: the total weekly budget was
a hefty $375.

Before his jaw had dropped, Lewis had assumed CBS's negotiator
Merritt Coleman meant $375 for him and $375 for Sullivan, but Coleman had said, "No—375 total." Lewis: "And how much more for the
stars, the performers, [conductor] Ray Bloch, and the dancing girls?"
Coleman: "No more. That's it. That pays for you and Sullivan and all
the rest. Split it any way you like—that's the deal." It seems a bad joke
now, or even in 1948—and Lewis was sure Sullivan would laugh in his
face and say forget it. But Sullivan wasn't insulted, just disappointed that
CBS hadn't shown more financial confidence in the show—in him.

The network didn't call the new venture "The Ed Sullivan Show,"
should the host walk out, change networks, die, or, more likely, be replaced, which was always in the back of William Paley's mind. The titles
CBS suggested were "Tops in Town," "Talk of the Town," "You're the
Top," and "Toast of the Town"—Sullivan owned the final choice, even
after the name was changed in 1955 to "The Ed Sullivan Show"; at his
death, his estate still owned the original title.

For CBS, the show was a huge gamble—as was all television, which in 1948 was like an electronic off-Broadway or early cable show. As Lewis recalled from the meeting, Coleman explained, "You know how undeveloped, how downright experimental television is at this stage. The way we read it, anyone who wants in now has got to play along, and work for practically nothing." Lewis was stunned. Coleman added, "I don't know what to tell you. You were the guys who wanted TV. You came to us. We didn't come to you. And if you still want it, we're prepared to start the first show on June 20th. Take it or leave it."

Many performers would have walked away, humiliated and angry, but the fact that Sullivan was *not* a performer, a star with a reputation to uphold, and was used to relatively modest newspaper wages (even as a syndicated columnist) worked in his favor. He saw it as an opportunity to get a foot in the TV door, and, because of his previous failures in radio, he was determined to squeeze his way inside any way he could.

This clearly would be his last stab at a future beyond churning out inane show business minutiae, a final chance at something more substantial— coast-to-coast fame, which he wasn't sure he deserved. But at this point in his life, in 1948, Ed Sullivan would have taken the job for nothing. Which is exactly what he did—indeed for less than nothing. He and Lewis subsidized the show's first 26 weeks, paying the office expenses out of their own pockets. So what? Ed was hosting a huge TV show. He was *on the air.*

CHAPTER 4

The $375 Extravaganza

You couldn't keep Ed Sullivan out of show business.

Burns Mantle, critic

From his first days in New York City, Ed Sullivan had skillfully maneuvered himself into place as journalism's ambassador to show business. He produced and hosted charity bashes and emceed the *Daily News*'s annual Harvest Moon Ball for 12 years, lining up names like Jimmy Stewart, Jack Benny, Lucille Ball, Risë Stevens, Ronald Colman, Bill Robinson, and Lena Horne. Sullivan boasted that, to put on a benefit, "you had to be a bookkeeper, a showman, and a manager, and you didn't have time to freeze"—precisely the gifts needed to produce a weekly TV show on a laughably tight budget.

In a promotional piece for the 1947 Harvest Moon Ball, his paper referred to him as "the *News*' own columnist-showman," twittering, "The Ball certainly wouldn't seem the same without Ed expertly pacing the show." It credited him with being "one of the first to recognize the dancing talents of such luminaries as Ginger Rogers, Eleanor Powell and Ray Bolger," adding that "when Sullivan likes something he shouts it from the housetops."

The Harvest Moon Ball was a big deal in New York, the "Dancing with the Stars" of its day, featuring amateurs in a kind of dance-off left over from the marathon dances of the 1930s. It played off the Latin dance fads of the 1940s, and was also sparked by the dreamy Astaire-Rogers musicals. The finale was held in Madison Square Garden over several nights, and the crowds often totaled more than 50,000 people. Mainly, the ball was a showcase for big bands. The Benny Goodman, Harry

James, Tommy Dorsey, Glenn Miller, and Guy Lombardo orchestras accompanied dancers who were fresh off the floors of the Waldorf-Astoria
Starlight Room and Roseland, as well as from Chicago's Drake Hotel
and Aragon ballrooms.

It wasn't unusual for columnists to emcee events in New York, but
one reviewer of the 1947 Harvest Moon Ball observed, "Newspaper
columnists as Broadway stage personalities have long since become a
passing vogue, and of these only Ed Sullivan of the New York *Daily
News* has managed to survive the field." So even before he got the TV
gig, Ed Sullivan was a showbiz luminary within New York.

Sullivan, a hustling showman who, in his early thirties, had created and
hosted the *New York Evening Graphic*'s All-Sports Dinners, found a way
to cash in on all the Harvest Moon Ball publicity by packaging contest
winners and professional acts and persuading M-G-M to back a 1947
show at Loew's State Theatre on Broadway. Two pros that he booked
were a young ventriloquist, Paul Winchell, and the popular singer, Monica
Lewis, whom he was chasing. That 1947 production, significantly, turned
out to be the last vaudeville show at Loew's, a neat stage-to-TV segue that
Sullivan produced just a year before "Toast of the Town" debuted.

Recounting his TV show's genesis in a 1953 *Variety* article, Sullivan
said that, to get a Heart Fund charity event off the ground, he'd needed a
big advertising campaign but hadn't had the money, and had hoped to get
the radio industry to donate airtime as a public service. "The singing star
of our bill, Monica Lewis, piped up with a suggestion. 'Lord,' said Monica, 'my big brother Marlo and his wife Mina Bess could do that in a
minute.'" The television world in 1948 was "like a small family," Sherwin Bash, the son-in-law of longtime Sullivan conductor Ray Bloch, told
me. "Monica recorded for Signature Records, which Ray owned part of,
and he was very fond of her." Sullivan wrote, "Within 48 hours, the city
began learning about the Heart Fund campaign. They lined up 30 spots a
day on every radio station, and they arrayed the disc jockeys."

Neither Marlo nor Mina (pronounced "Minna"), who worked at the
Blaine Thompson ad agency owned by her father, had ever met Sullivan
when the columnist first called. The conversation as remembered by
Mina in the Lewises' memoir, *Prime Time:* "Hello? Mina Bess? This is Ed
Sullivan. Monica thinks it would be a good idea if we all got together."
Ed had just been appointed chairman of the New York Heart Fund and
wanted their help to snag name performers. Mina recounted to me that
she told her husband "the last thing we needed was another gossip columnist in our lives," and wanted to wriggle out of Sullivan's request, but

Sullivan played on their sympathies until Lewis agreed to meet him at their office that afternoon.

Mina, the warier, tougher minded of the two, shook her head and told her husband, "You don't know how to say no." He pleaded, "I couldn't help it. It's for a very good cause." Mina: "You could have sent a check." Marlo: "I wasn't referring to the Heart Fund. I meant Monica. Sullivan gave her a tremendous break when he booked her into Loew's State with him. He could have hired any of the top singers—Rosemary Clooney, Betty Hutton, Kitty Kallen. The kid's grateful to him and so am I. Anyway, he's nothing like Winchell . . . maybe he's different." Mina wasn't buying it: "When you know one [gossip columnist], you hate 'em all," she said, and 50 years later explained to me, "I almost put a halt to the whole process. I didn't want to talk to Sullivan. Newspaper [gossip] columnists were about as low as you can get. They were creeps."

Monica, still bright and peppy in her mid-80s, told me of her own pivotal role in the show's creation: "The basic fact, which has never come out, is that in 1947 I was recording for Signature Records and had been in the top ten for a very long time [and was also the voice of Chiquita Banana], and Ed wanted me on the stage show" at Loew's State Theatre with the Harvest Moon Dancers. Sullivan had neatly converted the contest he hosted as a *Daily News* promotional event into a full stage show that also showcased him.

"Ed had a reputation for having girls and girl friends—they all did. They all had chinks in the armor," Monica said of Sullivan's interest in her. "I was hot as a rocket. . . . Anyway, at one point backstage, my brother picked me up. Ed sees this guy talking to me and walking out with me, and he's fuming. The next day, he says to me, 'Who was that guy you were with last night?' I said, 'That's my brother.' He said, 'No kidding! What does he do?' "

She told Sullivan that her brother was an advertising man about to move to CBS as head of music, variety, and comedy. In those days, the ad agencies packaged radio and TV shows. Suddenly, "Ed was very interested, and very interested in my family. I said, 'You oughta talk to Marlo, he might have something interesting. Television is here now.' They formulated some ideas of what would become 'Toast of the Town.' "

Monica Lewis noted, "TV was in such a primitive stage. When they say 'golden years,' they mean years later, when the big dramas came on. This was *before* the golden years. This was really the creation. It was a time of such innovation." The Sullivan show succeeded, she thought, for a simple reason: "What else was there? The Sid Caesar show and Milton

Berle. Sunday nights, people were home; they'd sit around their one TV set, just like in the days during the war when people sat around one radio, listening to vaudeville, FDR's fireside chats. Now, every kid has a TV in his room, every kid has the Internet computer in his room. We only had three channels—a whole different world."

Of her brother's alliance with Sullivan, she remembered, "Half the people said Marlo Lewis is a genius who recognized what was happening in TV, and the other half said, 'What the hell is Marlo bothering with *him* for?'" Lewis was a cultured, charming glamour-puss. He and Gregory Peck were once walking down Fifth Avenue, and they looked like twins, related Monica, "except Marlo looked a little better." He was also a congenial, calming influence, unlike the tightly wired, brooding, explosive Sullivan. "Everyone said when Marlo put his hand on your shoulder, you felt not jittery but ready to go. Your nerves disappeared, you knew you weren't going to vomit, you were going to heaven." If Sullivan put a hand on your shoulder, you shuddered.

Asked about Sullivan's major contribution to creating the show, she shrugged: "Ed showed up on time." His greatest gift? She paused, laughed, and said, "Being in the right place at the right moment and seeing me meet my brother!" Monica added that, if Sullivan hadn't met Marlo, "he would have remained a gossip columnist—and then they [gossip columnists] all disappeared. Ed could talk, but he wasn't compelling or at ease. Matt Lauer he wasn't."

Marlo liked Sullivan from their first meeting. "He was different. He wore no hat, he came alone, his voice was low and unobtrusive, he looked and dressed like a conservative businessman, and there wasn't a rumpled spot on him. Moreover, he had the time and taste for the amenities. Before long, we found ourselves deep into a discussion of the ways and means of planning the Heart Fund campaign." Sullivan told him, "And I'll guarantee to deliver every big name in town—Martin & Lewis, Berle, Durante . . . they'll all join us."

Lewis said he might be able to get radio stations to donate airtime, the recording studios to donate technicians and space, and the announcers, musicians, and performers to contribute their fees to the fund. "I was relieved to see Mina warming up to Ed," Marlo noted. Sullivan suggested they go downstairs to Sardi's for dinner, saying, "I have an ulcer waiting to be fed." Lewis noticed that "Sullivan displayed a marked civility to the waiters, and, although it was obvious that he had taken note of everyone in the room, he allowed nothing to divert his attention from our conversation. Like all good reporters, he had the knack of making people willing to talk, to say more than they intended. He reacted, asked leading questions, and he hung on my every word."

Over dinner at Sardi's, Sullivan tried to charm the skeptical Mina and got her talking about the family's history in early Hollywood—her father had been head of Warner Bros. advertising in the 1920s and a close friend of Harry Warner, which fascinated Sullivan. When Lewis related his own family showbiz history (his father, a classical violinist, was musical creative director at Chicago's United Artists Theatre), and told of his boyhood memories of the animal acts Fink's Mules and Power's Elephants, Sullivan grinned and said, "And how about Potash and Perlmutter? Smith and Dale? Willie West and McGinty? I used to play hooky from school anytime I got a chance to see any of them." A bond was formed, built on Ed's and Marlo's mutual passion for ancient animal acts.

Finally, Lewis steered the conversation to the Heart Fund benefit, but when he mentioned that there was likely to be resistance from the musicians union (due to a recording industry strike), he got a flash of Sullivan's tough, hardball spirit: "The smile faded from his face and a kind of gold glint iced over his eyes," Lewis recalled. "His jaw jutted out a little and his shoulders stiffened. It was apparent that he could be ticked off very easily." Sullivan muttered, "Christ! Petrillo [the hardnosed boss of the musicians' union]! He's the one union leader I'm not close to. I've done him a dozen favors, but I've never been able to get close to the little czar." Lewis, a can-do guy himself, suggested they call Petrillo on the spot and, to their great surprise, the music czar gave the benefit show a begrudging okay ("Go ahead, make your *forkakta* [crazy] announcements, but no replays or other use . . . ever! And don't make this request a habit").

On such spur-of-the-moment phone calls is showbiz history made. Ed Sullivan and Marlo Lewis were on their way: the Heart Fund benefit was a huge success, and Sullivan had found a partner who could sweet-talk anybody, from Petrillo to Paley, laying the first bricks in the edifice that became "Toast of the Town."

Marlo was impressed with Sullivan—not just by his amiability but also by his ability to deliver the hottest names in show business, including Hope, Benny, Durante, Crosby, Berle, and Louis Armstrong. Wrote Mina Bess, "As a grand finale to the entire drive, Sullivan gathered these same entertainers and put on a remarkable, star-studded, blockbuster of a show. For three hours, the jam-packed audience at the Copacabana cheered the songs and antics of this incredible roster of stars"—and the money raised broke Heart Fund records.

After the show, on their stroll back to Sullivan's home at the Delmonico Hotel, full of themselves and inflated by their triumph, Lewis told Sullivan, "What a shame that a million-dollar show was only seen by a saloon full of people." Lewis added on sheer impulse, "That kind of vaudeville would be a sensation on television. It's too damn bad that TV isn't big enough to handle it yet. Well . . . maybe someday."

Lewis recalled, "It was as though I'd pulled a trigger. Stopping dead in his tracks, Sullivan's lantern jaw jutted forward and one stiffened finger jabbed out at me. 'Kiddo,' he snapped, 'what's to stop us? If I can deliver the bodies free to every charity that comes along, I can do it for television! We could bring vaudeville back so big nobody will ever remember it died! So what if TV's still in its infancy? It'll grow, and we'll grow with it. Let's jump into this thing with both feet. . . . Once we get in, they'll never get us out!'" Even allowing for retroactive embellishment and dramatic revisionism, it's safe to say the idea was planted that night at Park Avenue and 59th Street.

"I already knew Ed well enough," Lewis went on, "to recognize that such immediate enthusiasm and quickness to act was typical of him. Right there on the spot, he urged me to get moving, be his partner, make a deal with one of the networks. He promised, 'Everybody who's anybody will come to our show. All the big ones. You can count on it! You'll handle the production, I'll emcee. We're a winning team, kiddo! We just proved it!" Sullivan stuck out his hand. "Partners?" he asked Lewis, who later wrote, "It was more a statement than a question. 'Don't let the idea cool off. Light a fire under the network boys . . . you know 'em all. Get us a deal!'"

A few days after the Heart Fund drive, Lewis got a scribbled memo from Sullivan: "Did you light that fire under the network brass? Your lovin' cousin, Ed." Lewis said that Sullivan's "enthusiasm for the show far exceeded my own." Sullivan was firmly convinced he was the only guy for the job. "In his own mind, he was a professional showman," Lewis recalled. "It mattered to him not at all that he had no training or special skills in the arts of show business." Not so: Sullivan had mastered the basic intricacies of staging events, which boiled down to luring superstars to appear. Lewis, swept up by Sullivan's excitement, recognized that this would-be TV host had something in common with other successful people he had known, notably "a stubborn drive to accomplish, coupled with an ability to dream and accompanied by a refusal to admit to any personal weakness—[he was] a man who believed that if you could think it, you could do it."

No slouch himself, Lewis became Sullivan's crucial key to TV. Lewis was then executive vice president at a major ad agency and producer of a six-day-a-week radio series, "Luncheon at Sardi's," one of Mutual Radio's most popular shows. But he had recurrent second thoughts about the whole scheme and about TV itself. Lewis had dabbled in producing a few early TV shows, without success, and called television "a primitive toy," one that the stars, nightclubs, and concert bookers all snubbed. He recalled, "There was no money in it and technically it was so underdeveloped—with out-of-synch kinescopes, streaked images, heads cut off—that performers came through looking like Dracula on a bad night." Film studios banned stars from appearing on TV, fearful it might destroy the movie industry and the stars' carefully manicured images.

TV networks in 1947 were a little like the garages that computer supergeeks would first tinker in 40 years later. CBS's jerry-rigged studio in a Grand Central Terminal annex above the train station was so primitive that, whenever a train pulled into or out of the station, static electricity from sound waves ruined the picture. Makeshift studios went up in deserted Broadway theaters. The struggling DuMont network was headquartered in a basement of Wanamaker's Department Store, which was located in a damp, rat-infested area peopled by winos, hookers, drug addicts, and panhandlers. A desk, a chair, a couch, and a few klieg lights constituted the entire DuMont studio; there was no air conditioning to provide relief from the hot, blazing TV lights. Early TV, said Sullivan associate director Marvin Silbersher in the BBC documentary "Ed Sullivan and the Gateway to America," "was just above the circus then."

DuMont's big show was "Charade Quiz," on which Mina Bess Lewis was a regular panelist. According to the Lewises, one of its first guests was Lucille Ball, making her TV debut. After ten minutes, bathed in perspiration, Ball shouted, "This is ridiculous! Haven't these TV clowns ever heard of motion picture studios? Why don't they visit one to see how things are done? This isn't show business. This is madness! Never again!" Only NBC, whose ruthless founder, David Sarnoff, pioneered the development of TV before and during the war, had anything close to a respectable television operation. CBS, by contrast, was still trying to master TV's basic technology.

Marlo Lewis sensed that Sullivan's enthusiasm for TV was mainly fueled "by the need to be universally recognized." Observed Lewis, "He wanted to make the multitudes love him, to hear the sound of applause, to meet the celebrated on an equal footing. He wanted, in short, to be a star!" Lewis, despite misgivings about his new partner's TV appeal, and much to his own surprise, dialed CBS-TV program director Jerry Danzig and said, "Jerry, this is Marlo. I'd like to come up and see you about a program idea that Ed Sullivan and I own. Believe me—television is ready for this one!"

Sullivan was uneasy, despite his bravado. "He was desperate," recalled Mina Bess, who says the variety show concept didn't directly grow out of the Heart Fund benefit, as Marlo Lewis claimed. Early Sullivan biographer and ex–CBS publicist Michael David Harris maintains that Ed first approached Marlo Lewis with the idea of hosting a TV interview show with golf pros dispensing advice, to be called "Pros and Cons," which CBS quickly turned down.

But CBS's visionary program chief Worthington Miner told Lewis that CBS *was* looking for someone to host a variety show, but not a bravura Berle-like "personality." According to the Lewises, Miner said that Sullivan had "the type of manner we want for a Sunday-night audience"—that of a genial traffic cop, basically. Miner felt that Ed Sullivan could handle the basics, based on his efficient handling of the annual Harvest Moon Ball, which revealed his slick producing and primal emcee skills in presenting performers like Bill Robinson, Lena Horne, and the famed Tony and Sally De Marco dance team. And, yes, ladies and gentlemen, out in the audience, Sullivan introduced a batch of luminaries he had corralled to attend the ball: Jack Benny, Lucille Ball, Jimmy Stewart, Risë Stevens, Patsy Kelly, Ronald Colman, and Alan Ladd. It was a veritable future Ed Sullivan TV show.

At the end, Sullivan called Ladd to the Garden stage and asked the crowd of 18,000 to sing "Happy Birthday" to him. No wonder Miner was impressed when he saw it all unfold on TV. Sullivan claimed he was unaware that it had been televised until Jack Benny called the next day and said, "You should have told me the Garden show was being televised." Knowing Sullivan's hands-on controlling style, it's hard to imagine he didn't know a camera was present televising the show, now part of the Sullivan-produced legend.

As Sullivan explained when describing the new show's concept, "Miner outlined what the network had in mind, said it would be the type of thing I'd done at Madison Square Garden and presently was doing in vaudeville. I signed the contract a week later for a 13-week series." Peter Miner, Tony's son, gives his contemporary version, quoted in Jeff Kisseloff's *The Box:* "My father knew Berle was gonna burn out, and he knew just what he needed: a variety show with a nonperforming emcee

as host. The idea was that the acts would change. And all the host
should do is introduce the acts. That way he wouldn't burn out. He sat
my mother and me down in front of the set to watch the Harvest Moon
Ball at Madison Square Garden. He was always looking to steal talent
from anywhere, and here was Ed Sullivan, hosting the Ball and getting
all the top stars."

The original title for the new show, "You're the Top," was history before the ink was dry on the first press release. The show had a staff of 35,
including Ray Bloch's ten-piece orchestra, a crew of six, and six dancers,
and the paltry $375 talent budget. The Milton Berle show's budget, ac-
cording to Berle, was $15,000. Ten years later the Sullivan show had 200
staffers and cost $372,000 a week. "When the show first hit the air,"
conductor Ray Bloch once recalled, "I can't say I thought very much of it.
I wasn't sure it would last a second week. I was a nervous wreck." Bloch
rode out that anxious first week and wound up staying with the show its
entire run, a familiar bald presence at the bottom of the screen ("Take it
awaaay, Ramondo!" Sullivan liked to say, cuing him).

Although privately Sullivan was worried that the show wouldn't survive any longer than his early radio efforts had, that the meager budget
would make it impossible to attract the names he needed and pay for decent production values, he became its head cheerleader, writing in a trade
magazine, "The sky is the limit in this new field. There are no limits to
what can happen because there are no limits to the eye and the ear."

After Marlo Lewis informed Sullivan that his initial suggested lineup
of guests was old hat, the host came up with a second list. That premiere
hour included a hot new nightclub act—Martin & Lewis making their
TV debut; a sports figure—Ruby Goldstein, referee of a big upcoming
fight between Joe Louis and Jersey Joe Wolcott (Ed interviewed Goldstein
while leaning against the ropes of a fake ring); a pretty girl singer—
Monica Lewis, who reminded Marlo she had been the instigator of the
show; a dash of culture—pianist Eugene List and dancer Kathryn Lee;
and two big Broadway names—Richard Rodgers and Oscar Hammerstein II, for a TV chat with Ed and (in lieu of a fee) a chance to plug their
struggling new musical, "Allegro."

If you had schemed to design the template for the entire run of "The
Ed Sullivan Show," you could not have found a more prototypical guest
list (give or take a juggler and animal act). It contained most of Sullivan's
favorite elements—big names, sports, high culture, hero worship, and
three news hooks: not just the fighters discussing the impending heavyweight championship fight but also pianist List, who had just made

headlines when he performed at the Potsdam Conference before Truman, Churchill, and Stalin; and a touch of pure Sullivanesque hometown pride and sentiment—a heroic Bronx fireman named John Kokoman, winner of a citywide singing contest. For a pinch of sex, Ed borrowed six "Copa Girls," Copacabana dancers, at eight bucks each, and their choreographer. They evolved into a minichorus line of six "Toastettes" and, eventually, became part of what came to be called the June Taylor Dancers, who more memorably later decorated Jackie Gleason's show.

An announcement of the new CBS series got plenty of media attention, not just in the *Daily News* ("Dean and Jerry to appear with Sullivan on TV") but also in *Variety* ("Rodgers & Hammerstein snagged for new Sullivan TV'er") and the trade magazines (*Radio Daily* blared, "TV takes a giant step forward"). Martin & Lewis had already been discovered and were, in fact, red hot from a sold-out run at the Copa, were on the verge of getting their own radio show, and had just signed to star in their first film.

CBS was impressed that Sullivan could round up so many major personalities so cheaply, but as Copa choreographer Wally Wanger told Marlo Lewis, only half-jokingly, "This television is a new kind of swindle. You've got Dean and Jerry, me and the kids [dancers], and your sister—the whole Copa show—for peanuts! If it weren't for Ed Sullivan, we wouldn't touch this deal with a ten-foot pole!" Wanger had put his finger on a sensitive subject that fueled ugly rumors for decades: that Sullivan could snag big names only because of the power of his column, which he strenuously denied. It sounds fishy anyway: the opportunity to appear on a big new CBS TV show was not exactly anathema to performers; for many, it was a new staircase to stardom. Sullivan didn't need to blackmail anyone.

Capturing Martin & Lewis on the cusp of superstardom was Sullivan's first TV coup. While they were a sensation in nightclubs, they were wasted on radio. Marlo went to the Copa to closely observe them. He saw people lined up outside the club. His gut said to grab them for the premiere. He met with Jerry after the show in a hotel suite above the Copa, and found him much like he was onstage—"Irrepressible, breezy, brash, he kidded his way through our conversation." Jerry kept referring to Ed as "the smiling Irishman." (More recently, recalling Sullivan on that very first show, Jerry said, "He was as dull then as he was on his 400th show.")

When Marlo tried to get down to business, Jerry said, "Marlo, boychik—just tell me how many minutes you want." He was insulted when Lewis the elder told him 20 to 25 minutes, a third of the show. "That's all? Dean and I *bow* for 25 minutes. Don't worry, just have the cameras ready to pick me up wherever I go—in the aisles, the bandstand . . ." Dismayed to learn that the band would be sequestered backstage, Jerry shrugged and said, "Dean and I have worked in worse places," put his hand on a Gideon bible, and vowed, "Tell Abe Solomon we do jokes, we dance and we sing, and we're really pretty good. We promise to give him a very nice show." Meeting over. Marlo then headed downstairs into an airless, windowless room that Mina called the "Copacabasement" to meet with the club's choreographer to choose chorus girls to open and close the "Toast of the Town." They couldn't sing or dance very well, but they were sexy, flexible, and camera ready, truly Copacetic. Lewis purchased six girls to go, for $48 a week.

Despite all the advance hype for "Toast of the Town" within the television industry, the opening broadcast barely made it to the air, on June 20, 1948. The show took over the abandoned Maxine Elliott Theatre on West 39th Street. Sullivan had four weeks to convert this decaying cavern into a TV studio, which meant tearing out the entire orchestra pit, installing a control room, connecting all the cables and power lines, and installing lights and sound equipment. (Radio shows, by comparison, required only a few microphones, an engineer, an organist, and a sound effects guy.)

When Lewis arrived at the theater at 6:30 the morning of the first show, he was met by a petrified stage manager, who told him that the cyclorama (backdrop) wouldn't cover the stage, leaving gaps on either side piled with furniture that the camera would show the world. A penthouse set had been too tall to squeeze through the stage door, forcing the crew to saw it into segments to reassemble inside. A panicked head cameraman reported that the stage lights were so bright they would flood the screen, blinding viewers; curtain sequins were flashing into the camera so that performers in front of it vanished—a skilled spotlight operator was needed. The sound man panicked too, fearing that many of the 16 microphones hanging above the stage would be visible on TV, as well as that the large number would make it impossible to balance the sound mix. He needed a mike boom, but that would interfere with Jerry Lewis running amok around the stage tearing things up.

Marlo Lewis, as unflappable under pressure as the ulcer-ridden Sullivan was excitable, calmed everyone down. He was Ed's Mr. Fix-It. Mina Bess Lewis says Sullivan was the "hunter" who found the talent and did

all the negotiating, dumping all the messy production details in her husband's lap. Ray Bloch, the veteran CBS conductor, had warned Marlo,
"If there's any way to fuck up a show, CBS will find it." Bloch had his
own problems. His accomplished orchestra had been stuffed into a
backstage storage area out of view of the performers ("We might as well
be out of town," he moaned), forcing him to rely on a crude headset; in
his left ear he heard camera directions from the control room, in the
right ear he heard the performers onstage, a confusing cacophony
("Camera two, dolly in, Camera three, go to a 90-milimeter lens. Camera one, focus on a medium shot. Get Monica ready for her entrance").

Fire inspectors showed up and instantly gave Bloch a $50 fine for
smoking his pipe in the theater. After firemen inspected the curtain and
scenery, they informed Marlo, "There will be no show tonight." Neither
the curtain nor the sets were protected with flame retardant. Sullivan,
undaunted, said, "I've done plenty of benefits for those boys, and the
chief's a good friend of mine." Sullivan arranged a compromise.

Lewis didn't burden the host with all the other technical snafus, so
when Sullivan asked how everything else was going, Marlo just said,
"Great crew! You'll love 'em," and Ed replied, "Can't wait to get down
there. I've invited a score of celebs to sit in the audience. I'll make 'em
take a bow. We'll do it every week; should give the show a really big look.
You know: those in the know love the show!" (Walter Winchell claimed
Sullivan stole the idea of introducing audience celebrities from him when
Winchell toured with a show that featured a mock radio broadcast and
intros of stars out front.)

Sullivan was in a jubilant mood when he got to the theater, shaking
hands with everyone in the crew, porters, stagehands, and musicians, hoping to establish "just the right mixture of confidence and camaraderie,"
wrote Lewis, telling everyone that they were about to take part in "a
blockbuster of a show." Lewis noted, "Morale was visibly boosted as he
moved toward the stage-right proscenium arch, perched on a high stool,
and observed the proceedings. He called for a pad and a pencil and began working out the running order, consulting with me as to any staging
problems. Within minutes, a final list was established and we were ready
for the dress rehearsal."

Lewis, also now keyed up and poised for the show's premiere, went
upstairs to Sullivan's dressing room 30 minutes before airtime, but when
he opened the door he was stunned. "I stopped cold at the sight of him,"
he wrote. "His face, ashen and glassy-eyed, stared back at me from a
mirror over the sink. A plastic tube hung out of his mouth like a piece of

thick linguini and was attached to a rubber syringe in his hand. He tried to allay my shock. 'It's nothing,' he gurgled, half choking. 'I'm just pumping my stomach—acid's too high, ulcer's killing me.' He waved me to a chair and minutes later downed a large dose of medicine. 'Belladonna,' he explained. 'The stuff the eye doctors give you in an exam that expands the pupils.' "

All of which helps explain Sullivan's famous glassy-eyed look on camera. After he pumped his stomach before a show, the belladonna he took for his duodenal ulcer also blurred his vision and made the cue cards hard to read, leading to his famous garbled introductions, meandering ad-libs, and mangled names. When he went onstage that first night in 1948, Sullivan's hands were shaking. Recounted Lewis, "He seemed a far different person from the confident, congenial man who had walked into the theater just a few hours before. When I was leaving, I could only think of one thing to say: Remember . . . when your camera light goes on, look into it! That's your cue to start talking. Don't forget—the red light means go. . . . Only in two places did that statement hold true—a TV studio and a whorehouse."

At 9 P.M., announcer Art Hannes shouted, *"Ladies and gentlemen, the Columbia Broadcasting System is proud to present its star-studded revue, the 'Toast of the Town,' with the nationally known newspaper columnist Ed Sullivan!"* Despite the ponderous sets, the blinding lights, the jungle of microphones, the hostile fire inspectors, and the emcee's defiant ulcer, the show—broadcast to only six stations—was beamed without a noticeable hitch. Lewis later recalled, though, that the host's hands "trembled like leaves in the wind, he forgot to look into the cameras, and he grimaced and fidgeted like a man in torment"—Ed Sullivan's on-air persona for the next 23 years. A star was stillborn.

CHAPTER 5

Very Critical Condition

For a variety revue, where a dominant personality is so helpful
in tying up the loose ends, the choice of Ed Sullivan as master
of ceremonies seems ill-advised.

Jack Gould, *New York Times* television critic

Critics' first and unanimous verdict on "Toast of the Town" was that its
master of ceremonies, Ed Sullivan, was unable to master the ceremonies.
One wrote, "If you did not know who Sullivan was and simply tuned
into 'Toast of the Town' Sunday at 8 P.M., you might plausibly conclude
that the star had suddenly taken ill and that the producers in desperation
had pressed a security guard into a suit and shoved him onstage."

None of several rival New York newspapers were eager to plug a TV
debut by a columnist from a competing paper, and not even Sullivan's
own *Daily News* reviewed the first shows. The paper was irked that
WPIX, the station the *News* had just bought, hadn't acquired the new
show. When the critics got around to reviewing "Toast of the Town,"
the news was not good, mainly due to Sullivan, considered to be a gloomy
albatross about to kill vaudeville all over again.

"By today's standards," conceded coproducer Marlo Lewis in 1979,
"the first 'Toast of the Town' was a crude shambles—the pictures were
gray and muddy, heads were lopped off by the cameras, the voices and
music were uneven and unbalanced—not that much more was expected
from television in 1948." The critics, he added, "seized the opportunity
to knock the brains out of their fellow newspaperman. Although they
liked the show for the most part, they called Ed everything from 'inept'
to 'ridiculous.'"

Sullivan's deepest wound was inflicted by John Crosby, the widely
read *New York Herald Tribune* critic, a master of vitriol, who, six

months after the show premiered, delivered in his column—still called
"Radio in Review" (later collected in his book *Out of the Blue*)—a body
blow that bruised the show's chronic soft spot and bloodied its host in
one wicked swoop: "One of the small but vexing questions confronting
anyone with a television set is, 'Why is Ed Sullivan on it every Sunday
night?' "

Crosby nailed him with deadly accuracy: "After a few opening bars
of music, Mr. Sullivan wanders out on the stage, his eyes fixed on the
ceiling as if imploring the help of God, and begins to talk about his 'very
good friends.' Sullivan's very good friends include virtually everyone in
show business. . . . One of them—let's say Connee Boswell, who was on
the show last Sunday—then comes onstage and the pair of them discuss
how enormously fond of each other they are, how profoundly each ad-
mires the work of the other, and how wonderful it is to be able to meet
on this wonderful show in front of this wonderful audience."

Crosby continued his amusingly lethal attack: "The entertainer usually hints to the audience that, without the help of Ed Sullivan, he or she
would still be slinging hash on Eighth Avenue. Miss Boswell then goes
on with her song. . . . 'Let's have a nice hand for that wonderful girl!,'
says the nationally syndicated columnist. 'Connee, come out and take a
bow. How do you like that, eh? Wasn't that wonderful?' Sullivan at this
point halts the operations to introduce some of his very dear friends in
the audience. If the dear friends are show people, Mr. Sullivan may request
them, with rather steely insistence, to come up and amuse the folks."

Crosby concluded his clubbing by noting, "Mr. Sullivan is a persuasive fellow. If he has any other qualifications for the job, they're not visible on my small screen. Sullivan has been hopelessly fascinated by show
business for years. He has been in vaudeville, on the radio, and now on
television. He remains totally innocent of any of the tricks of stage presence, and it seems clear by now that his talents lie elsewhere." But
Crosby unwittingly buried a compliment in the diatribe—"He remains
totally innocent of any of the tricks of stage presence," Ed's eventual
key to success, as things turned out. Years later, once these old wounds
had healed, Sullivan boasted, "I think my awkwardness on camera is the
real reason I am still here today. It has aroused the mother instinct in
America."

As soon as Crosby's piece appeared, Sullivan ripped off an angry
response—something he never would have done had he been an established star. Treating Crosby as just another ill-tempered, rumpled fellow
journalist, he pulled no punches in his lawyerly defense: "Your review of

my CBS 'Toast of the Town' television show, in last Sunday's issue, is in
error on so many points that I must challenge it. You object to 'Ed Sullivan's predilection for introducing his friends in the audience,' on the
grounds that it 'slows up the show.' If the introductions were of nonde-
script characters, or of my grocer or butcher, you'd be on firm ground,
but when the introductions bring to the television camera the retired un-
defeated heavyweight champion, Joe Louis; the manager of the Brooklyn Dodgers, Leo Durocher; Tin Pan Alley's Richard Rodgers, I seriously
question that your reaction is shared by the video audience.

"Perhaps a newspaperman is bored by seeing these celebs. But to the
television public, names make news and faces make news. The mail
proves that you are wrong, if proof were needed, and the studio audience underscored it." Sullivan then cited early audience surveys and a
rare rave that said "Toast of the Town" had advanced television by five
years, plus OKs from such celebrities as Oscar Hammerstein and Eddie
Cantor, before adding, "Your conclusions are at such variance to the expressions of expert showmen, and so opposed to public reaction, that I
feel very strong that you are in error. So much for the overall show."

Just warming up, Sullivan told Crosby he didn't have to like him, but
that comparing him to Berle was unfair: "You misunderstand my position on our show. They wanted a working newspaperman [his favorite
fallback position], sufficiently versed in show business, to nominate acts
that could live up to a 'Toast of the Town' designation. . . . They wanted
a certain measure of dignity and restraint, rather than a vain attempt to
work with acrobats, tumblers, etc., which Berle does brilliantly."

No stranger to tussling with adversaries, Sullivan went after Crosby,
both guns blazing, in tones that few seasoned performers would have
dared. His famous Irish temper up and boiling, he drilled Crosby with a
second indignant letter: "Public opinion, I'm certain, would agree that
I've contributed more to television in its embryonic state than you have
contributed with your reckless and uninformed back-seat driving. You
belt away at performers and producers as a means of earning a weekly
salary. At least I give them a gracious introduction and showmanly presentation that enhances their earning power. Your column acquires a
tremendous importance. When it is employed to recommend that a man
be thrown out of his job, it becomes quite an evil instrument."

The less nasty, more measured Val Adams, a TV reporter and critic at
the *New York Times,* wrote in 1952, under a headline reading "Not on
TV: The Ed Sullivan Story," that all the new show needed was a reliable
host. Jack Gould noted in a July 4, 1948, review in the *Times* that the

acts' "order of presentation was far from happy and most of them ran too long. . . . CBS has all necessary ingredients for a successful program of variety. Once it appreciates more fully the need for knowing hands to guide the proceedings—both onstage and off—it . . . should have an enjoyable hit."

Months later, reviewing both Sullivan and the local WPIX variety show hosted by Sullivan's fellow Broadway columnist Danton Walker, Gould remarked that "life in front of the footlights is different from the anonymous existence behind the typewriter. . . . Put bluntly: do newspapermen make good performers?" Not yet. Gould hadn't changed his mind the following year, when, in a roundup review of TV variety programs in the *New York Times* in April 1949, he uttered a swift dismissal: " 'Toast of the Town,' another hour-long variety show, suffers from the listless job of Ed Sullivan as master of ceremonies."

Ben Gross, the radio and TV critic at Sullivan's own *Daily News,* said in his memoir: "During his early days in broadcasting, I had regarded [Sullivan] as a nice, friendly, sentimental Irishman, but so cold in his personality, so utterly lacking in the exuberance commonly attributed to Gaels, that he would have been the last person I should have named as a future television star." Gross added, "His detractors said . . . that here was merely another instance of a columnist who had used the prestige of his position to 'blackjack' his way into a job that scores of professionals could have filled more adequately"—a common rap.

Gross then praised Sullivan's perseverance: "But these critics did not know Ed Sullivan. They failed to realize that they had taken on a tough opponent. He swung back at his critics and pointed out that he did not pretend to be a professional emcee [which in fact he pretty much was, after years of hosting charity events]. He was not a gag man or a wisecracker; he was merely a newspaperman introducing various acts." Ruminating on that rugged period, Sullivan told Gross in 1963, "From the very beginning, I was determined, regardless of any critical comment—good or bad—to make a success of it."

Fred Allen, unwilling to adapt to—and terrified of—television, regularly took shots at Sullivan in interviews: "What does Sullivan do? He points at people. Rub meat on actors and dogs will do the same" (to which Sullivan snidely countered, "Maybe Fred should rub some meat on a sponsor"). Allen later relented a little: "All he does is point but he's here to stay because he does a nice simple job of running his show. Hit-you-over-the-head performers aren't going to wind up making the money in television." One oft-quoted jibe, attributed to Allen (also to Oscar

Levant): "Ed Sullivan will be a success as long as other people have talent." Sullivan was crushed, saying, "I always admired him [Allen] so tremendously, and because I did, it hurt. But one day, years later, I was sitting in a restaurant and his widow, Portland Hoffa, came up to me and said, 'You know, they're twisting what he said around. He only meant it jokingly.' " Perhaps.

Comics had a field day. Joe E. Lewis got off a prime Oscar Wildean wisecrack, afterward attributed to platoons of others: "Ed Sullivan is the only man who brightens up a room by leaving it." Jack Carter told Ed onstage, "I'd mail you a present, but what do you give to a man who has nothing? . . . Ed, don't cross your arms or they may bury you." Alan King came up with the ultimate put-down, close critical analysis, and backhanded compliment all in one: "Ed does nothing, but he does it better than anyone else on television."

Over the years, descriptions of Ed Sullivan became a can-you-top-this? game of wits, as one critic or comic after the other vied to hurl the wickedest bon mot: "Forest Lawn Cemetery is trying to buy commercials on his show" (Hal Humphrey, *Los Angeles Mirror-News*). "Ed has personality but not for a human being" (Joe E. Lewis). "While he doesn't sing, dance, or tell jokes, he does them all equally well" (Bing Crosby). Everybody got into the beat-up-Ed-Sullivan act, an unending critical riff.

Few major figures in entertainment ever endured such a thorough and steady lambasting—and prevailed. Atra Baer wrote of Sullivan in a *New York World Journal Tribune* series on him in 1967, "It is a carefully documented fact that in all the history of modern show business no man

We didn't have television until 1954 or '55, and prior to that we normally spent Sunday evenings at my uncle's farm ten miles outside of Delphi, Indiana. Being a farmer, he had more money. He owned a big black-and-white TV set in a huge mahogany box with doors on the front that snapped shut (God knows why), and we used to gather 'round in a semicircle and stare at the Sullivan show like the Middle Americans that we were. I was too young to know why, but something about this Sunday evening routine bored me stiff. On Sunday evening, I was experiencing American cultural stagnation at its worst. Sullivan's "nonverbal communication" was agonizing to watch. This probably endeared him to audiences that mistrusted too much New York slickness on TV.

Michael Johnson, Bordeaux, France

has taken a beating from professional critics that has been as rough and as constant and survived. If critics could kill, Ed Sullivan would be a corpse."

John Crosby ragged Sullivan about Bob Hope's supposedly unplanned 1948 TV debut on "Toast of the Town" (in a day, said Ed, "when a movie star in a TV theater was page-one news"), after Hope was introduced in the audience and seemingly coerced into performing. Sullivan sent a seething two-page letter demanding Crosby correct the false assumption that he didn't pay entertainers. Crosby had written, "One entertainer I know who gets from $1500 to $2000 a week in nightclubs was talked into doing his cherished routines on the show for $55. Mr. Sullivan is a persuasive fellow." Sullivan later recalled, "Crosby never acknowledged the letter, never made any retraction. From that one column of his stemmed the legend that our show didn't pay performers."

Four years after the show's debut, Crosby still refused to get off Sullivan's back, bashing him for his cheap applause-milking tactics: "After the singer finishes her song, Mr. Sullivan heaves into view, exclaiming, 'How do you like that? Wasn't that wonderful?' Then the cameras pan the audience and we see them applauding. Sullivan is credited with having invented the audience-participation shot. The idea that an audience at home can be entertained by watching an audience in the theater pounding its palms together may be the greatest shill game in show business since Barnum exhibited the Fiji Mermaids back in 1842." Eight years after his first review, Crosby was still peppering Sullivan, whose scorn for the *Herald Tribune* TV critic matched Crosby's own disdain for Sullivan. On one poisonous Crosby review he kept on file, Ed scrawled, "I'd like to meet this fella some dark night when I'm learning to drive the largest Mack truck ever made!"

Sullivan inspired television critics to new heights of vitriol: Harriet Van Horne wrote in the *World Telegram,* beating a by-now-bedraggled dead horse: "He got where he is not by having a personality but by having no personality." To this, Sullivan, unversed in the fine points of making nice with (or ignoring) critics, dashed off a telegram: "Dear Miss Van Horne: You bitch. Sincerely, Ed Sullivan." He later said he was ashamed of what he'd done. Val Adams wrote in the *Times* in 1952, "Probably some of the most scathing long letters ever received by television critics have come from Mr. Sullivan." In a lighter mood, Ed once chortled to *Time,* "They really burn after they get one of my letters."

In a 1955 cover story on Sullivan, "Big as All Outdoors," *Time*'s critic wrote, "He moves like a sleepwalker; his smile is that of a man sucking a lemon; his eyes pop from their sockets or sink so deep in their bags that they seem to be peering up at the camera from the bottom of twin wells." *Newsweek* chimed in on the chorus: "Stony-faced, baggy-eyed, so stiff through his bull neck and shoulders that he is frequently assumed to have broken his back, a mangler of thought and language, a stumbling, bungling, fumbling perpetual amateur who has yet to master the smallest gesture, the simplest phrase, Sullivan is the most painfully unlikely stage figure in all of the bizarre history of vaudeville."

"Some of the criticism used to tear my guts out," Sullivan told biographer Michael David Harris in 1968. "Here I was working for nothing. In 1948, networks and advertising agencies knew little about the medium and so could be influenced easily by writers in important papers. Small wonder that I couldn't smile into the TV cameras."

The easily injured Sullivan simply didn't get it, all this hurtful personalized abuse after a lifetime of adulation for emceeing charity events and being fawned over as a powerful big-city columnist. He confronted critics with phone calls and snarling letters, and even demanded personal meetings. He accused them of professional jealousy. When Jack Gould wrote to complain about a hostile note Sullivan had sent him in response to what he felt was an honest review, the TV host told him, "What are you so hot about? I just put my opinion of you in a personal letter. You spread your opinions of me all over the Sunday *Times*."

What Gould had dumped across the Sunday paper in July, three weeks after the show's debut, was this: "In terms of lavishness and expense, ['Toast of the Town'] is on a par with 'Texaco Star Theatre' but suffers badly if the comparison is extended to such matters as routining and general professional know-how. . . . As it works out, 'The Toast of the Town' bears more resemblance to a radio program than to a live stage show." Then Gould plunged in his dagger and twisted the blade: "Since [Sullivan] is a newspaperman, there is no reason to expect him to be an actor, but his extreme matter-of-factness, plus his predilection for introducing his friends in the audience, does not add up to very sparkling entertainment."

When Helen Dudar of the *New York Post* asked Sullivan in 1963 what form of criticism upset him most, he said, "All of it. You don't get any more hardened to criticism." In her story "Ed Sullivan: Always on Sunday," she wrote of him, "He loves and hates in primary colors and cannot quite fathom those who fancy pastels," and penned her own tone poem to her subject's glorious ineptitude: "As he ushers acts on and off, Sullivan's hands still hover helplessly about the region of his tie and

nose, and his eyes shift restlessly toward some distant field beyond camera range. . . . He starts involved sentences he can't really finish; he sum-
mons guests from the audience and then doesn't know what to do with
them once they're there; and he will, when there's time to fill toward the
end, persist in asking those out front, 'Well, how did you like our show
tonight? Did you have a good time?'" As Sullivan badgered audiences
into applause, he sounded like an anxious hostess inquiring of her dinner guests, "Did you all enjoy what I prepared tonight?"

Ed's showbiz crony Abel Greene wrote in *Variety,* "He gives a non-
professional facade to his highly professional show." Sullivan lashed out
at Greene, whose paper had long lauded Sullivan's selfless work organiz-
ing and hosting benefits, when Greene stated, "Sullivan, as an emcee, is
a good newspaper columnist." Marlo Lewis overheard Sullivan snapping at Greene, "What the hell is it with you and your writers? Here I'm
giving exposure to the greatest names in show business, and your staff is
taking delight in knocking the crap out of me. What are you people
anyway—a bunch of Communists?" Sullivan saw assaults on him as almost un-American, subversive acts committed against the nation—or at
the very least, unsporting.

Over the years, TV critics everywhere piled on, ridiculing Sullivan as
the Great Stone Face, Liver Lips, Smiley, Old Granite Jaw, the Toast of
the Tomb, Cod-Eyed, Mr. Rigor Mortis, the Cardiff Giant, the Nights
of the Living Ed, the Rock of Ages, the Milltown Maestro, the Unsmiling Irishman, and an Artistic Basket Case. Sullivan inspired TV critics to
withering heights of disdain. In 1951, *Time* magazine, when it finally
got around to reviewing the show, noted in a review titled "Toast of the
Town": "The TV Sullivan is a strange contrast to the bumptious, know-
it-all of Sullivan's Broadway column in New York's *Daily News.* His TV
expression—or lack of expression—is a cross between that of Joe Louis
and a cigar-store Indian. When he walks out to introduce an act he looks
as if someone had wound him up with a key—located somewhere under
the coat hanger that seems to have been built into the broad shoulders of
his double-breasted jacket."

Long after the show's debut, when it had become a lucrative, iconic
hit, the New York critics still couldn't digest Sullivan's triumph. John
Crosby refused to back off, writing on the show's eighth anniversary,
"Mr. Sullivan, of course, is notoriously and admittedly without any talent." Sullivan moaned, "This same chorus still yowls at me." He harbored lasting resentment toward all his early and constant foes, writing

in "My Story," a multipart life story that appeared in *Collier's* magazine in 1956: "My sober conduct of a show affronted the critics."

Sullivan quickly acquired a reputation as a prickly, tempestuous character. Mina Bess Lewis wrote, "If he was in the right mood he'd ignore the criticism, but he could easily get incensed. He had a hair-trigger temper. I saw it evidenced. Push him a little too far and he'd go off. People were intimidated by him. I got along with him fine—I think he respected me—but he enjoyed a fight. Marlo used to say that when Sullivan woke up he didn't brush his teeth but wondered who he could fight with today." Marlo recalled being cut off in midsentence at one point during the show's first preproduction meeting, and later noted, "Certain aspects of Sullivan's personality had now begun to show. He had demonstrated no interest in anything that was on my mind and seemed concerned only with discussing what he had accomplished."

When riled up over a review, Sullivan had to finesse his wife, who tried to keep him from dispatching hostile replies to critics. He told a biographer, "I used to sit down in the evening and write a letter. Sylvia would come in and say, 'Type it up, put it in an envelope, seal it, put a stamp on it and then, when you're all done, tear it up.' I would do everything except tear it up, and then, when she went inside, I would slip out of the room, run out to the mailbox and mail it. She would come back and ask me what I had done with the letter, and I would say that I had torn it up."

John Crosby finally relented a little in a 1954 column where he praised Sullivan (after noting he "was elected least likely to succeed when he went on the air") for his tenacity: "From the outset, people whose opinions he respected told him that a variety show would never go on TV and was as dated as vaudeville. He didn't believe it and statistics seem to prove he was right. He has always believed there is nothing too highbrow for a TV audience." Crosby singled out Sullivan's hour-long tributes to Oscar Hammerstein, Helen Hayes, Robert Sherwood, and Joshua Logan, citing "their indefinable human quality," and lauded Sullivan for resisting formulaic shows "by putting interesting people in unusual settings, getting them to do something they've never done before, and changing his show all around so the viewers never know what to expect"—such as dressing 20 jockeys in top hats and tails for a song-and-dance number, or featuring boxer Sugar Ray Robinson skipping rope to jazz. "Some of these novelties come off, some don't. But they keep the audience off-balance."

Ultimately, begrudgingly, Crosby changed his mind, realizing Sullivan was not going away anytime soon, and in a 1957 column, as the
show headed into its tenth year, the critic wrote, rather sheepishly:
"He's been there nine years and he'll probably be there another nine,
and I must say I have enjoyed many of the shows." He noted, "Through
the years, Mr. Sullivan has grown no more skillful with his hands or his
face or his prose. But he is still there, which is more than you can say
about a lot of people who are enormously skillful in all these depart-
ments. There is a great lesson in this for all of us. But I'm damned if I
know what it is."

The insult volleys never fully ended. In its July 14, 1962, issue, the
New Yorker published one in its "Talk of the Town" section: "People
celebrate anniversaries in different ways. Mr. Ed Sullivan recently sol-
emnized the fourteenth anniversary of his TV show by arranging to have
Steve Allen, Lucille Ball, Jack Benny, Teresa Brewer, Red Buttons,
Johnny Carson, Jack Carter, Bing Crosby, George Gobel, Jerry Lewis,
Ted Mack, the Arthur Murrays, Phil Silvers, and Kate Smith rally round
and tell everyone what a great fellow Mr. Sullivan is."

Helen Hayes, a Sullivan heroine, staunchly rose to his defense, and he
duly quoted her in his *Collier's* series: "Surely all the people who have
worked with Ed on his stage know what he's got. Appreciation! It's one
of the rarest, most wondrous of God's gifts when it's real—and Ed's is."

At my family home in El Cerrito [California], we ate dinner just in time to
finish and watch Sullivan. It was such a ritual on Sundays. Always roast
chicken with trimmings. Ed Sullivan at 8 P.M., and Mom would buy a box
of See's Victoria toffee, which we would finish off by the end of the show.
It is a wonderful memory. Life was so simple in those years. No matter
what, we would never miss Sullivan. I loved the comedians Jack Carter,
Alan King, Newhart, and Myron Cohen (wasn't he the one with the gimmick of [an] eyelid that would get stuck closed?). I saw Eartha Kitt for the
first time on Sullivan and was enthralled by her[,] . . . and Sammy Davis
when he was still with the Will Mastin Trio. We didn't like Wayne &
Shuster and hated that whiney Topo Gigio mouse. However, when the
Beatles were on, my father argued that we should not be watching such
music, and it was totally forbidden when Elvis was on (my God, I loved
Elvis!).

Diane Shields, Portland, Oregon

Sullivan, without honor in his hometown, took on the New York critics en masse in the *Collier's* series: "TV writers in other cities and towns,
remote from New York, do a much better and more literate job day in
and day out than those to be found on the staffs of Manhattan dailies."
With bitter, almost Nixonian disgust, he said critics from out of town
actually came to the show, but that, in eight years, only one New York
critic had ever deigned to watch the show in person—loyal old Ben Gross
of the *Daily News*.

Sullivan's chronic telephobia was the result of never learning to approach
the camera as a friend, as did Arthur Godfrey and Dave Garroway, instinctive 1950s masters of the medium who caressed the camera like a
lover. He neglected TV's first commandment: ignore the multitudes and
speak to one person. Ed saw the camera as a loudspeaker, addressing the
lens as he might an auditorium at a bond rally. He addressed, rather than
conversed with, the studio audience—not his home audience—breaking
yet another broadcasting rule. But he was only comfortable with live bodies, not invisible beings beyond the camera.

And yet he had been praised as a poised New York banquet emcee by
his journalistic peers. A 1941 advance piece in the *Daily News* about the
Harvest Moon Ball gushed, "Ed's strong, clear voice, cleverness and
pleasing personality have been important factors in five consecutive
Harvest Moon Ball successes. To watch Ed handle the mike and hear
him ad-lib is a treat you'll long remember."

William Paley, his CBS underlings, and the sponsor were all horrified
by Sullivan's dangerously inept, lurching, on-air hosting style. These
may have seemed tolerable behind a dais or at a local stage show, but
under TV's glare, he looked laughably small-time, like the dithering
schnook drafted to deliver Robert Benchley's classic stage monologue
"The Treasurer's Report."

While the press was happily heaping scorn on him, Sullivan's TV public was worried about his future. "I don't know why, but people get ma-
ternal about it," he once said. Sympathetic viewers began asking what
was wrong with his neck, what specific disease did he suffer from. They
related. As Sullivan liked to recall in interviews, one fan even wrote to
praise his courage, saying, "It takes a real man to get up there week after week with that silver plate in your head" (he didn't have one). Sullivan was simply not sculpted for TV—he had a large head on a thick
neck and huge, rounded shoulders, which tapered abruptly into a trim
torso. TV critic Kay Gardella, his *Daily News* colleague, told me that

when Ed came to the office his entire body moved like a military unit, or a toy soldier. "He didn't move flexibly like we all move." On the show, he tried moving his neck more but gave up: "By this time people would think there was something wrong if I suddenly began moving like everybody else."

He also photographed badly, and people, including women like the gossip columnist Liz Smith, who later inherited his place at the *Daily News,* said he was far better looking in person. Monica Lewis agreed: "He looked sick on television." In early photos, Sullivan appears even handsome—a classic black Irishman with thick dark hair, big intense blue eyes, and a manly jaw that had not yet turned to quartz. He had a deep, hunky smile that he flashed sparingly on camera. His teeth, later dentures, were too large for his mouth, which exaggerated his jaw line. "When I walk onstage I apparently look as if I'd been embalmed," he acknowledged. Early viewers rudely mugged him. "The better the show became, the worse I looked, and people got sore at me," he told *TV Guide.* "I knew I wasn't getting through to them, but I honestly couldn't understand why they got so sore about it. It was very discouraging."

Charles Underhill, the CBS programming chief who helped Sullivan make the show a reality, told Marlo Lewis after its debut, "Sullivan certainly stumbled his way through, but do you think he can possibly book enough big names to keep the thing going another six weeks? This thing won't make it with Sullivan. The man is a total disaster. He's got no stage presence. He's scared to death up there! My God, I'm embarrassed just watching him."

Six weeks after "Toast of the Town" premiered, Ben Abrams, the president and CEO of the show's sponsor, the Emerson Radio and Phonograph Corporation, panicked. He couldn't take it any longer. At a meeting with Lewis at Abrams's office, he snapped, "Frankly, Marlo—Sullivan stinks! Even from here and holding my nose. He stinks." As Lewis recalled the conversation years later, Abrams said, "I'll admit Ed delivered the stars he promised. But what good is that? He fouled the whole thing up. I wouldn't let Sullivan host a garbage collectors' convention at the city dump. For more than a month now I've watched the damn show—and with him up there it can't last. He's a rank amateur and getting worse."

Abrams had signed up to sponsor the show for six months, but he wanted to pull out after six weeks, mortifying Lewis: "I was reeling, in a state of shock, as though a sand bag had landed on my head." Abrams and Lewis's oral agreement had persuaded CBS to give the show a green light. Strangely, there was no written contract. Lewis wrote that oral agreements between networks and sponsors were common practice then, as binding as written contracts—which cut no ice with Abrams. "Don't give me any of that shit," Abrams told Lewis. "You should have protected me. That's your first job. Instead, you and CBS gave me a pretty fast shuffle with this Sullivan, and I'm not about to underwrite your mistakes. I'm running a big company here . . . and a bumbler like Sullivan is not going to represent my product." Fuming, Abrams argued that Lewis's arrangement with Sullivan and the sponsor was a legal conflict of interest.

"To give it to you fast," Lewis remembers Abrams barking, "I'm through with your agency, CBS, and Mr. Ed Sullivan. Go find yourself another client and another sucker to support your lousy show." Lewis calculated that the cost of the remaining 20 weeks would come to $160,000, a lost fortune in those early days of do-it-yourself TV—about $1.4 million in 2008 dollars. "Up to that moment, I'd thought of myself as a pioneer," wrote Lewis, "clear eyes fixed on far horizons, setting out to conquer the new frontier of television. A half hour with Abrams had changed that romantic self-portrait."

Frantically, Lewis called Frank Stanton, Paley's second in command, and broke the news to him "with a chill in my spine and a quiver in my voice." He envisioned bankruptcy, lawsuits, media and business ridicule, a second mortgage on his home, his finely planned new TV career gone—and worse, the swift death of "Toast of the Town." Stanton, cool under pressure, asked Lewis why Abrams had canceled. "Abrams thinks we all took him by selling him Sullivan as a host." Stanton, in his unshakable corporate voice, said, "Tell Abrams the boat has sailed. He's in for 26 weeks. CBS honors its deals. He had better honor his."

CBS held Emerson to their 13-week oral contract, but after that, Emerson pulled the plug, forcing CBS to hustle new sponsors for the show—"with or without Sullivan," in the chilling words of CBS executive Jack Van Volkenburg. According to Lewis, Van Volkenburg said the CBS Sales Department claimed the specter of Sullivan as host was frightening off advertisers. Sullivan's daughter, Betty, said that Van Volkenburg's "with or without Sullivan" insult just galvanized her father, "making him more of a fighter," so much so that he rudely confronted Paley and Stanton. Both apologized for Van Volkenburg's ill-chosen phrase. As more than one loyal staffer said, Sullivan was a guy who just didn't know how to give up.

For weeks, Sullivan labored in limbo. He called it the lowest point of his life—"I couldn't believe what had happened. I've never been so hurt or angry before or since." His professional life was endangered. His personal reputation was collapsing. His TV dream show was dying, almost hourly it seemed. But Sullivan was rescued by an unlikely angel, one with deeper pockets and longer patience, who descended in the form of Benson Ford, Henry Ford II's brother. Benson loved the show and asked the Ford ad agency to sponsor it. Stanton called Lewis to tell him he didn't owe CBS his life savings, after all. As Lewis recalled, Stanton said, "We've decided to wipe the slate clean. The Ford Motor Company is going to sponsor 'Toast of the Town' immediately."

Ford had been looking for a TV show that its upscale Lincoln division could sponsor. Ford's ad department liked "Toast of the Town" because it came cheap, it was seen in New York, Boston, and Philadelphia (and was about to be available in Baltimore and Washington, D.C.), and it was a family show with an early Sunday night slot. Moreover, the program was available with or without its problematic host. Ed now had a new deadline—precisely 91 days to prove he could attract an audience and sell Lincolns. To pacify his dubious newspaper bosses, he asked to be introduced on the air as the "nationally syndicated columnist for the *New York Daily News*." Even so, somebody in the *News* hierarchy, figuring Sullivan's fling with TV was about finished, wrote him a note asking, "When are you coming back to us?"

Joe Bayne, a Ford general sales manager who had worked with Major Bowes in the heyday of "The Original Amateur Hour," told me, "It took us less than 20 minutes to decide on Ed Sullivan. It was crystal clear— Ed was a second Major Bowes [a dour monotonal host]. Bowes used to muff the English language. Ed does, too, but the thing about the two of them is their genuineness and truthfulness. So we said, 'We'll buy the Sullivan show for 13 weeks.'" With Sullivan.

CHAPTER 6

The Magic of Sullivision

If someone walked into my office and said he wanted to be just like Ed Sullivan, I'd throw him out. *Nobody* should want to be like Ed Sullivan. He is all wrong for television. He just happens to be great.

Mike Dann, former CBS programming head

Approval of Sullivan's "Toast of the Town" came gradually and grudgingly, usually with a zinger directed at its hapless host. News magazines didn't review the show for years, and the *New Yorker* didn't even deign to recognize its existence until December 18, 1954, when Philip Hamburger at last reviewed it, referring to "Mr. Ed Sullivan and his monstrously lavish, all-network, all-glamour variety show."

Hamburger noted its big budget ("must be equal to that of many of the larger municipalities in this country. . . . Sullivan and his weekly guests spend money with an almost thoughtless and arrogant abandon") and its endless and shameless variety of guests: "A dog in Racine can recite the opening lines of 'Il Penseroso'? He will be grabbed up for the Ed Sullivan show. A man in New Orleans can faultlessly render 'La Marseillaise' on a kazoo stuck in his ear? He'll turn up right after the dog act."

The show had the cultural distinction of being one of those things that nobody but the people loved, yet Sullivan labored mightily to get not just ratings but critical respect from his fellow journalists. His TV presence never failed to elicit critical wisecracks verging on poetry. You can almost envision Hamburger gleefully licking his chops while writing, "This Mr. Sullivan is a study. He's always impeccably dressed, wearing neat and what I take to be lightweight suits, with padded shoulders. His dark hair is greased to a fine, but not too fine, gloss. His smile is a mixed smile, betraying a good deal of sorrow, and even suffering, as though aware of the struggle the performers had to go through to reach perfection. He seems to be saying that his only wish is that they, and he, and you, could do better. He is obviously a theater buff—a performer at heart—and after all these years he still stands in awe of the notion that human beings, not to mention dogs, seals, and horses, can display so damned much ability in public." Moreover, concluded Hamburger, "He can really whip himself up over a new Lincoln or Mercury! If I were Mr. Lincoln, or Mr. Mercury—or even Mr. Ford—I would certainly hold on to this fellow, for his faith is the faith that can sell a million cars."

Even if people liked the show, it (or Sullivan) seemed too grandiose, too self-important, for critics to resist taking potshots at it. Sullivan presented a huge, irresistible stationary target. Maybe if he hadn't insisted each week that every act was stupendous, and hadn't browbeat the audience into wild applause, the press might have gone easier on the show and its host. But critics couldn't stop pitching poison darts at Ed.

Eventually, Sullivan gave up sending nasty responses to critics, learned to live with his fumbling image, and made it work for him, though he never grew a protective skin. As he told the *World Journal Tribune*'s Atra Baer in April 1967, "I hate adverse criticism. I loathe it and will never get used to it. Furthermore, I suspect anyone who says he's immune to it of being a really big liar." He kept a file of personal attacks, arranged alphabetically by assailant. Now and then he would reread them, growing as livid at long-ago knocks as he had originally, which cannot have calmed his ulcer. Baer called this exercise in autoantagonism Ed's "toning up exercise"—a way to pump up his psychic muscles and stay in shape to kick sand in his critics' faces.

At some point, he realized that his much-maligned antipersonality was as good as any standard "personality"—on TV anyway. Sullivan thought his great lack of "personality" was in fact a huge plus. In time, he harnessed all the nasty digs and put them to work. "My 'great stone face' was a good identifiable gimmick, so I kept it," he later said; he attributed the moniker to Philadelphia writer Merrill Pannitt (later editor of *TV Guide*). He was, it finally appeared, a totally different breed of TV cat, which goes a long way in show business: Ed Sullivan was himself, such as he was, an admired American virtue. And being yourself, unless you're a bore, works wonders on television. If you can withstand the withering gibes, you may emerge as a beloved figure, exactly as Ed Sullivan did (Liberace and Lawrence Welk did the same). In his case, longevity was also on his side: the years piled up and he became an established, invincible icon. In 1958, he was famous enough to confess to columnist Hy Gardner in a TV interview, "If I'd been reviewing those early kinescopes, I'd have teed off on me, too."

Early television was an open invitation to every kind of performing misfit, has-been, and wannabe, many of whom wound up as TV stars; the trend continues unabated today. (Andrew Peek, in his 2007 book *The Cult of the Amateur,* trounces the Internet for elevating amateur writers and Wikipedia experts to professional status, but the first great TV pro-am was Ed Sullivan.) Radio stars on camera were washing out in droves, unable to make the transfer to a visual medium. These were performers whose appeal had been based on their vocal skills or on pure radio appeal, such as soap opera heroines, crooners, and comics who relied on puns and verbal wit (such as Fred Allen and Henry Morgan).

Movie and theater stars sneered at TV and refused to show their faces on it for years. In the 1950s, it was a minor event when a film star appeared in Sullivan's audience for a much-heralded bow. For decades, even into the 1980s, it was considered a coup for a talk-show host like Dick Cavett or Merv Griffin to snag real movie stars—Katharine Hepburn, Bette Davis, Orson Welles, Laurence Olivier—and get them to show their revered faces on TV. Only over-the-hill film stars were forced to back into TV, like Barbara Stanwyck on "The Big Valley" or Jane Wyman on "Falcon Crest."

Among its pioneering traits, television had discovered amateurism—polished it, exploited it, and now had the power to promote it to professional status. In a 1952 *Saturday Evening Post* article, "The Amateurs Take Over TV," John Crosby began by quoting Sullivan's admission that he had no talent, and then wrote, "He has avoided learning even the rudiments of his trade. He has trouble even smiling. Many amateurs have broken into show business, but most have turned pro through the pressures of experience. Sullivan has remained a triumphant amateur." Crosby called TV "a haven of amateurs," and added that, because Sullivan had no talent to burn, he "can go on forever, and probably will." Many writers echoed Crosby's sentiments—sometimes as caustic comment, other times as left-handed praise. TV became the ultimate democratic medium, where anyone could become the equal of a president—a star.

And of course Sullivan did go on, and on, and on, forcing the smart money and the smart alecks to eat their collective hat. Crosby added, "Talent, as Mr. Sullivan has unconsciously expressed it, is a handicap." He cited Godfrey and Mrs. Arthur Murray as serious rivals for Sullivan's amateur-night crown, closely followed by nonperforming game show panelists on "I've Got a Secret," "To Tell the Truth," and "What's My Line?" Next on the list were attractive quasi celebrities with fuzzy credentials, like Faye Emerson, Hal March, Kitty Carlisle, Garry Moore, and Bess Myerson, who all became big TV stars, along with endless, modestly gifted "hosts"—the Mike Stokeys, Alan Luddens, Bill Cullens, Gene Rayburns, Bud Collyers, and Art Linkletters of TV's infancy. Linkletter once called Sullivan "one of the strangest men ever to appear on TV. He had absolutely no business being on television." But he was popular with viewers in spite of his glum visage and awkwardness, "where a more overpowering personality might drive them away," conceded Crosby, suggesting Marshall McLuhan's famous decree that TV was a "hot medium" where a cold fish could flourish and, eventually, survive on land.

As a corollary to the Rise of the Amateur, polished stage and screen stars who did stoop to appear on the denigrated "tube" often fared poorly on TV, too grand and theatrical for a small screen to contain. "The television screen has a personal, perhaps unfair, preference for folksy people who look as if they might live next door," said Crosby. "TV has a positive, rather old-fashioned, horror of glamour. Some of the great names of the theater have not been exactly sensational on television"— Laurence Olivier, John Gielgud, Orson Welles, Gertrude Lawrence, Katharine Cornell, Tallulah Bankhead.

"Glamour, in short, is not meant to be displayed on television," he went on, even if "it is discussed on television," as on Sherman Billingsley's Stork Club TV talk show, whose snobby host Crosby dubbed "the most conspicuous all-around amateur of them all. Amateurism pays such high dividends on television that some professionals have tried it. Generally the results have been disastrous."

Syracuse University's Robert J. Thompson, director of the Bleier Center for Television and Popular Culture, discussing Sullivan's success, told me, "It was TV, so he could get away with it. It would have been a lot more difficult if Ed Sullivan had tried to be a movie star. Television perfectly contained and absorbed him—this domestic medium coming out of a very small screen right in the middle of our living space, and we're likely looking at the screen over stacks of laundry. There wasn't a demand for perfection of presentation." Thompson added, "He seemed stiff and robotic, but by being so stiff and robotic it made a guy who normally you wouldn't have thought of as warm and fuzzy come off as warm and fuzzy, because we felt for his clearly nonslick performance. That was enough for us to cut him some slack. Once it started, it was clear he was the guy with the Rolodex that, week after week, was gonna fill the stage with stars." -

Our own era's most conspicuous TV amateur would be Vanna White. Where else but on TV could a woman be transformed from game show flunky to star by clapping her hands and flipping letters? Vanna's minimalist performance on "Wheel of Fortune" made her 1950s counterpart, the blonde and bodacious Dagmar, look like Meryl Streep.

Fifties game show panels were packed with sometime actors (Kitty Carlisle, Arlene Francis, Betsy Palmer) and ex–beauty queens (Bess Myerson, Lee Ann Meriwether, Mary Ann Mobley). A prime-time example, Faye Emerson, was a Warner Bros. contract player in the 1940s who left Hollywood when nothing was happening for her, did a Broadway play, and interned as hostess of local interview TV shows in New York, before becoming a national TV "personality" most famous for her plunging necklines. Emerson was a constant game show panelist and—well, "personality." A little cleavage on network TV in the 1950s went a long way and could ignite a major career.

Nobody could have known it at the time, but Ed Sullivan was TV's first major "reality" star, in the sense that he was what he was, warts and all, forcing viewers to like him or lump him. If anybody ever proved that TV was the medium of the common man, it was Sullivan, who reveled in his common-man status. No matter how long he was on TV, his ad-libbed chats with performers and athletes were stilted and embarrassing, even laughable—and all too real. When Sullivan engaged anyone in conversation, it usually sounded as if it had been filtered through a U.N. interpreter. Gracie Allen remarked, "When Ed introduces the performers, he sounds like he never heard of them before."

Arthur Godfrey, with his corn-fed facade, folksy chuckle, and reliance on personality over talent, is often singled out as the guy who changed broadcasting's tradition of orotund announcers, hosts, and commercial spokesmen. But it was really Ed Sullivan who made it possible for newly minted TV hosts to parlay a lack of easily quantifiable talent into a TV career—people like Ed McMahon, Tom Snyder, Merv Griffin, Dick Cavett, even Mike Wallace, all hybrid showbiz creatures: part announcer or newsman, part singer or comic, part faded actor, part you-name-it. A "host" could be anything or anyone. Radio employed few "hosts" in the TV sense; radio demanded solid up-front performing skills—an actual resume. Al Jolson, watching Godfrey's show, exclaimed, "That son of a bitch proves one thing about show business today—in order to be a success, all you have to do is show up!"

Godfrey was a proven radio commodity when he moved to TV, and Sullivan clearly was not (indeed, Sullivan was a proven radio failure). Godfrey was utterly at ease on camera, and Sullivan was a nervous wreck. Godfrey could beguile viewers with relaxed banter with his hired, on-camera "friends," and Sullivan could not; Ed had no TV pals, sidekicks, gang, or genial patter. He was strictly business: bring on the big star, or the bicycling bear, and step back.

As Sullivan often said in his own defense, it was impossible to find any performer willing to clam up and relinquish the spotlight to others. Ed's nontalent was ideal for his show: he had a unique gift for bringing on an act and happily getting out of their way—a small-town traffic cop who became a big-city star. Even though Sullivan had emceed scores of benefits and banquets and hosted many war relief and charity shows, the bar for such events was not set terribly high; you were awarded points just for, yep, showing up.

Godfrey, what's more, had an innate sense of comic and dramatic timing. He was skilled at using his voice and manner to convey a jolly or somber mood, most of which was lost on Sullivan, who had all the verbal skills and charisma of an Elk's Club officer. Jayne Meadows told me, "If you didn't know who he was and had never met him—well, you know a 'star walk'? A star like Bob Hope walks through the door and it's like the parting of the Red Sea. With Sullivan, it was the opposite! If he came in the room, you would think, 'Who's that old man?' In fact, you wouldn't even think that." You wouldn't notice him at all.

While Godfrey was not really a singer or a comedian, he was a jaunty, self-made performer and a formidable, beloved presence on-camera—off-camera, of course, he could be a vindictive Captain Queeg. Godfrey's shows felt like a kaffeeklatsch (or tea klatch—Lipton was his longtime sponsor). Godfrey could strap on his neighborly "ol' redhead" costume and charm the country—telling stories, reading funny news squibs, razzing his cast and sponsors, and discussing his hobbies (horses, flying) while munching on goodies sent him by admirers. Sullivan was neither a likable nor even an unlikable presence on-camera; he was just Ed Sullivan, a traveling salesman from Port Chester, New York—the bloke at the end of the bar.

John Moffitt, associate director of the show for many years, told me he remembers giving Sullivan a ride home one night. "So he got in, and he was directing traffic! It was a typical busy New York street, and he says [imitating Sullivan], 'Excuse me, can we get by?' People were able to talk to him. I remember being on location with him and people would yell out, truck drivers honking their horn, 'Hey, Ed, how ya doin'?' [Again as Sullivan:] 'I'm fine, young man, how are you? Where ya hail from? . . . Well, you're a long way from home, aren'tcha?' He wasn't doing that to get people to watch the show. He was just very accessible."

Godfrey and Sullivan, however, shared one crucial quality—a sure sense of their audience, of what the folks at home liked, what amused and moved Americans. Both knew instinctively the country's sense of itself and could accurately read its patriotic pulse, with an unerring feel for what used to be called "human interest" stories. They also each had huge egos that let them believe that what they loved we would love too, and they were usually right. When Sullivan talked up the Michigan–Ohio State game, he assumed we all cared. He told Sydney Fields, in his April 11, 1968, *New York Daily News* column, "Only Human," "If a comic, an actor, a singer, opera star, ballet dancer, or a lady who knits with her toes pleases me, the chances are she'll please everybody in town or the country." As TV critic Harriet Van Horne wrote in 1955, "He's the commonest common denominator. He got where he is not by having a personality—but by having *no* personality." But a canny New York cab driver who once drove Sullivan wasn't buying it: "For a guy with no poisonality, he's got a lot of poisonality."

What Sullivan did, unwittingly, was open wide the front door to the Era of the Everyman, which would finally find full plastic flower in our own "reality TV" age, even if "reality" shows are scripted, rehearsed, produced, and hyped, and bear no resemblance to real life. But Sullivan was real, virtually unrehearsed, unpackaged, and utterly himself, for better or worse. He personified the amiable amateur. He made it OK to be mediocre on TV and succeed—as opposed to purposely bad, like "American Idol" basket cases or "Gong Show" bozos. He was naturally, instinctively, bad on his own, and in time people grew to love him for it. As Wikipedia's Ed Sullivan entry put it in 2008, "That high discomfort factor helped develop the Cult of Ed. There was something novel about an awkward TV host, and like [passing] a fender bender on the side of the highway, people couldn't avert their gaze."

In time, even his antagonists grew accustomed to his face, his contortions, and his halting delivery that often ended in a verbal pileup— his inimitable Ed Sullivan–ness. "There was a time when I thought the show would be immeasurably improved if Sullivan simply lined up the talent each week and then found a good game of seven-card stud to keep him from the studio Sunday evenings," wrote Philip Minoff in *Cue* in 1954. "A couple of seasons later I found myself becoming used to his self-conscious mannerisms and groping elocution. Still later, I found myself actually liking him."

Publicly, Sullivan responded to criticism by hiring a Yiddish vaudeville comedian named Patsy Flick to sit in a box seat on TV and heckle him. "I'm not myself tonight," Ed apologized on cue. "Are we lucky!" cried Flick, the first of many comedians to call him "Ed Solomon" (others included Minerva Pious's "Mrs. Nussbaum," Myron Cohen, Rickie Layne's dummy "Velvel," and Molly Goldberg), as in, "For God's sake, Solomon, smile! Did you look dat vay ven you ver alive?" In late 1948, before mimic Will Jordan re-created him, Sullivan hired Frank Fontaine to imitate him on the show—as usual, Ed was ahead of the curve.

In 1962, a veteran gag writer, Buddy Arnold, was hired to write for Sullivan and integrate the host into occasional sketches with performers, producer Bob Precht's idea. Arnold was ordered to write material for all nonperformers on the show—repartee for Mickey Mantle, a funny song for Alfred Hitchcock—anything to avoid the mindless blather between the host and the special guests he invited onstage for a chat and, much like a small-town mayor, smothered with accolades for a recent honor. Yet Sullivan was, in a sense, the mayor of Broadway. Until (and after) Arnold, John Moffitt told me, "there were no writers on the show. It was all concepts." Precht told me he wasn't trying to make a Garry Moore or Perry Como out of him but wanted Sullivan to have more interplay with some of the guests. Some guests even played off each other, as when Rudy Vallee talked to puppets. Cute idea, but it pretty much died there, and a good thing. Forced banter would have made the show look and sound like every other variety show.

Sullivan's intros soon assumed legendary proportions, one more measure of his stature. At first, the mixed-up intros were shameful and embarrassing, but over time, as Sullivan's fame grew, the botched intros became funny and famous, as fondly quoted as the best of Yogi Berra and Sam Goldwyn—some of whose funniest malapropisms were not actually uttered (as Berra even said, "I never said everything I said"). Like Jimmy Durante's mangled verbiage, Ed's gaffes were too idiosyncratic to make up.

Many were actual glitches, such as his introduction of classical guitarist Andrés Segovia: "Now let's hear it for Andrés Segovia! Ray Bloch—strike up the band!" Or his cue to Nat King Cole: "King—take a bow out here!" Some were apocryphal yet all too conceivable, like his alleged introduction of legend Eddie Peabody: "And now let's hear it for the greatest banjo player in the world—Eddie Playbody, who will now pee for us!"). Or his supposedly asking a paraplegic war hero in the audience to stand up and take a bow. Such stories were not hard to imagine and only further enhanced the Sullivan image and lore.

"Sullivanisms," as they came to be called, were badges of honor, with performers proudly boasting how Sullivan had butchered their names or intros. Half a dozen performers (Yul Brynner and Dolores Gray, to name just two) noted that Sullivan once introduced them as "now starving on Broadway." He often cracked up at his own gaffes, and he doubled over with laughter after a matronly Gray stood up. He added, "Well, if you look at her you can see she's not starving!" After the laughter died down, Sullivan said, "Sylvia's gonna kill me when I get home."

A few of his better, authenticated faux pas include the time he asked Jose Feliciano to perform without his seeing-eye dog. When Feliciano said no, Ed asked, "Well, can the dog do any tricks?" Unable to remember singer Sergio Franchi's name correctly on a 1965 Christmas show, Sullivan gave up and instead brought him on with: "Now let's hear it for the Ave Maria!'"—although some remember it as, "Let's really hear it for 'The Lord's Prayer!'" He also once proudly announced his Sunday lineup as: "Next week, the Beatles and the Pietà!" Yet another time, he introduced three nuns in the audience and cried, "Come on—let's hear it for the nuns!"

He regularly blanked on names. Forgetting Rosemary Clooney's name (it scarcely mattered that she had been on the show a dozen times), he announced, "And now, a young lady who has two top ten songs in America . . . We're happy to have her here, and she's a good friend of ours—Miss . . . come on out here, honey!" Rip Taylor played the show 13 times. He told me, "He forgot my name. He said, 'He's just wonderful! The latest thing! He's so different!' He couldn't read the cue card, so they pushed me onstage, and I said, 'Rip Taylor!' And he said, 'Of course you are!'" Dionne Warwick told me, "Out of all the five times I did the show, I think he only pronounced my [first] name correctly once. The one time he got it right, I almost got whiplash."

Other classic Sullivanisms: "Good night now, and help stamp out TV!"; wishing his co-producer Bob Precht a speedy recovery, he said, "I hope my son-in-law, Bob Hope, feels better"; "Now I'd like to prevent Robert Merrill"; and, introducing mimic Rich Little, "Let's hear it for this fine young comedian, Buddy Rich!" He is said to have once introduced the Supremes with: "And now, the Supremes from Detroit! Come out here, girls, and tell us where you're from!" He introduced dancers Marge and Gower Champion as "Gower and Champion!" He brought out a dance troupe from New Zealand while stating they were part of "the fierce Maori tribe from New England!," referred to Benny Goodman as "a great trumpeter," presented "the Samoans from Samoa!," and asked "the late Irving Berlin" to take a bow.

When a French knife-throwing act appeared on the show, Sullivan was told not to invite the performers to chat because they only spoke French. Sullivan promptly forgot and asked them to tell the children watching not to try to duplicate their act at home. When the knife-thrower gestured helplessly, "No English! No English!," Sullivan said, "Well, then, tell them in French."

Among the lesser-known mishaps: On a Christmas show, Sullivan introduced Frankie Lyman not once but twice as "Frankie Robinson," telling Lyman on the show that he was thinking of Sugar Ray Robinson. Obeying a cue card identifying Omar Bradley as a "World War II hero," Sullivan shouted, "Let's hear it for Omar Bradley, the great hero of World War One One!" Shelley Winters was introduced as "Shelley Berman." He mentioned that Marty Allen and Steve Rossi were "currently starring at the Copabanana." Comedian Jeremy Vernon told me he was on the show the night Sullivan said to the audience, "Let's really hear it for Melba Moore! Let's hear it for this fine black singer!" Connie Francis told me, "After my performance, I would often go into the control booth, and hear the producer Bob Precht say, 'Oh, my God, did he really say that?' "

Then there were behind-the-scenes goofs when he forgot the blocking. Eddie Brinkman, the show's stage manager for 21 years, recalled in a *TV Guide* interview, "Ed would charge all over the place, and into the audience, and forget that we had to keep up with him on camera." As the show unfolded, floor men would cry frantically, "He's coming out! He's coming out!," indicating that Sullivan had left his fixed spot at stage right and was headed into uncharted territory, like the time he wandered way off-camera to summon ten basketball players onstage for a bow.

More than once, Sullivan crossed up conductor Ray Bloch, like the time he walked into an Ed Ames number just as it started. It was a difficult number that involved counting the bars before he sang. As former Sullivan secretary Barbara Gallagher told me, "Mr. Sullivan walked over and tapped him on the back and said, 'So how ya doin', big guy?' Poor Ed [Ames] didn't know where he was. He totally lost his place, so he just winged it! And the music ended before he did. That was it. But that's what made the show fun. He was a real average guy."

After a Dave Clark Five number got great applause, Sullivan was moved to shout, "Wasn't that great! How'd you all like to hear that again? Let's hear it again!" Ed had forgotten that the audio was on tape and the band had been faking it. "You should've seen the look on Dave Clark's face!" said Gallagher. "They couldn't do it, without backing up the audio. In the control booth, Bob Precht is yelling, 'Close the curtains! Close the curtains!' So they closed the curtains and went to a commercial."

Carol Lawrence told me about a September show Sullivan had to stretch, and that he ran out of things to say, finally signing off with, "And let me be the first one to wish you all a Merry Christmas!" He asked Woody Allen, after calling him over, only to be stuck with nothing to say, "How's your father feeling?" Once, in rehearsal, Ed chatted onstage with singer Jack Jones and asked him, "Wasn't your father [opera singer] Allan Jones?," and Jones replied, "He still is," which got a big laugh, so Sullivan kept it in the show. Except that he mangled the setup line on the air, asking, "*Isn't* your father Allan Jones?" Jones told me he could only say "Yes." Sullivan was livid afterward, blaming Jones for screwing up the bit—"You should have said, 'He still is'"—and didn't book him again for a few years.

Sullivan and Richard Hearne ("Mr. Pastry"), who had performed his "passing out ceremony" sketch 19 times on the show, rehearsed an exchange in which Hearne tells Ed he wants to do another routine but Sullivan talks him into repeating the old bit just one more time. On the air, when Hearn pleaded with Sullivan to let him perform a new sketch, Sullivan replied blithely, "Fine, Dick, go ahead."

Bill Dana, who did the Sullivan show 17 times as his alter ego, José Jiminéz, told me about an incident with Sullivan, whom Dana often used as a stooge: "The big boss was my straight man. And he was a damned good one. *Most* of the time." Once, however, Ed's setup line was, "You know, José, money doesn't buy happiness," and José's reply was: "For three thousand dollars a day, you can rent it." At the Sunday dress rehearsal, even reading it off a teleprompter, Sullivan botched the line, telling Dana, "Money doesn't *bring* happiness." Dana salvaged the joke by ad-libbing, "For three thousand dollars you can send it out," which still got a laugh. Dana recalls, "Then I made a critical error with Ed. I noted that he had read the setup line wrong. 'Ed, it's a "buy-rent" joke. You said "bring" happiness.' There was a pause. Then a look of global freezing, two eyes drilling into my own, placing my entire body in rigor mortis. I said nothing. Corpses usually don't. He wheeled and disappeared."

Dana continued: "I knew I would have to wait till on-air before a live audience and America for my next encounter with him. He introduced me with love and vigor and the routine went on. Big screams." When they got to the ill-fated joke, Sullivan, still reading the teleprompter, said, "Money doesn't *get* happiness." Dana's punch line still got a laugh, but the comic said, "It made no sense. People don't say, 'Money doesn't get happiness.' Ed Sullivan did! He not only owned me but the American language." Sullivan "never liked to be corrected at all," recalled Dana. "It was pure spite, which almost scuttled that routine because I corrected him. Ed was the uncle you don't want to piss off."

The first time Dana met Sullivan, the host was berating the legendary comedy team Smith & Dale over money. "They were cowering" from Sullivan, who was spewing profanity ("I gave you the fucking money. Where the fuck do you get off, coming out here wasting my fucking time?"). Once he became a regular, Dana dined with the Sullivans. "It was like going to Uncle Ed's for lunch on Saturday." After lunch, they would read the routine through with Sullivan as straight man. Dana says Ed gave him twice as much time on camera as most comics, "because I was performing with God!"

Sullivan had flopped on radio because, ironically, nobody could see him. You needed to *watch* Ed shifting uneasily, head jammed into his shoulders, tying his arms into pretzels, as he implored—no, commanded—the audience to respond with hand after rousing hand. A semitalented entertainer won't engage us, but anyone can identify with a stumbling but well-meaning Everyman. Sullivan, like television itself, wasn't larger than life—like movie stars on a 30-foot screen—or smaller than life—like a disembodied voice over the radio. He was exactly life-sized, however jangled and semi-intelligible.

The show was live and so was he, despite jokes like "the Night of the Living Ed." He once said, wisely, "You can't pretend to be spontaneous." He didn't smile for years on TV, because usually he was fretting about how the show was going. The old Port Chester jock couldn't wipe off his game face with a grin. "They kidded my stony expression, but I couldn't do anything about it. I couldn't smile because I wasn't happy on camera." But Carol Burnett told me, "He often appeared upset when he was merely lost in thought. Ed had the kind of looks that, when he wasn't smiling, you thought he might be a little angry. But that's just the way he was in repose."

In 1963, he conceded, "I still can't smile on cue, and I envy a performer's ability to do it. I've never learned to smile while I'm talking. That's a performer's trick. Singers are even taught to smile while they're singing. But the fact that I've stayed in the entertainment business without mastering that stunt has become a sort of trademark for me. The legend that I never smile has become an easy way to identify me." In fact, he smiled a lot, but between grins he could look grim on camera. "I figured it was hopeless to become a polished performer and take diction lessons or have my teeth capped." Ed was authentic and proud of it. In a medium where a toothy grin is vital, he was his own man, even a rebel of a kind. As Marlo Lewis wrote in *Prime Time*, "His 'act' was no act at all, and America found that beguiling." He wasn't being paid to smile. Sullivan explained that he purposely didn't look into the camera because he had been told by seasoned actors Charles Boyer and Charles Laughton that they always played to the left or right of the camera—staring into the red eye unnerved them, too.

An NBC executive, Paul Klein, said (as reported by Martha Weinman Lear in an article she wrote for *Life* in 1968), "People watch Sullivan so they can hate him—it's mass masochism." People never hated him, though they may have laughed at him. Mostly, viewers identified with him—he gave hope to the severely talent-challenged. The public embraced Sullivan as a fellow human, stripped of affectation and showbiz gloss. "Audiences loved that he was himself," recalled Florence Henderson. "He had credibility," John Moffitt commented. "People would say, 'I could do better than that.' Viewers don't like slick people who think they're smarter than they are. Those people don't last on TV. They like to look at people they think are just like them. People loved to say, 'Did he really say that?' 'Did he really try to pull that guy's beard off?' "

It was Sullivan's very amateurishness that eventually was his triumphant saving grace. If a slicker, heartier emcee had fronted a show like Sullivan's—Bert Parks, Ralph Edwards, Art Linkletter—it likely wouldn't have survived long. "If there is one man who has done more than any other to render obsolete the loud, brassy, smirking master of ceremonies of yesteryear, the man may be Ed Sullivan," noted one national magazine, adding that, even though Sullivan had thawed out a little over five years, he did so "without adopting the offensive forwardness that once was every emcee's stock in trade."

Sullivan was the ideal emcee of his show because he *was* the anti-talent, maybe the antidote, to all the artists he threw at us. He was a gray backdrop that allowed the performers to stand out in colorful relief—just as Major Edward Bowes, the glum "Original Amateur Hour" host, was before him. Ed Sullivan was the original amateur.

In "Death of the Salesman," *Time* credited Sullivan with founding a new school of commercial spokesmen: "Most admen agree that the new look in announcers was started by Ed Sullivan on 'Toast of the Town.' Despite his wooden expression and lack of announcer's glibness, Sullivan does the sort of job that makes any sponsor swoon with joy." Sullivan outpaced Godfrey's genial commercial gab by addressing regional Lincoln-Mercury dealer meetings, presiding over the Rose Festival in Portland, giving blood in San Francisco, and crowning the Cotton Queen in Memphis—whatever it took to spread the show's gospel, butter up the sponsor, and seduce more viewers. It was partly to feed his own insatiable vanity, but it was also to meet the people. Like a relentless, obsessive candidate, Ed was always shamelessly campaigning for more votes.

He was forgiven his on-air trespassing during TV's own struggle to define itself and determine who would be permitted entrée into America's living rooms. TV allowed an ambitious galoot like Sullivan to get

I watched it with my family in suburban Philadelphia. Corn was faithfully popped—popcorn and apples and Coke and Ed Sullivan on Sunday nights. My father did the popping, his only kitchen contribution. My father was sort of humorless, but he liked variety shows, and I remember him laughing at both Gleason and Sullivan the way I never saw him laugh anywhere else—at the comedians and other acts. My father loved those overhead camera shots of the dancers. I would have been 12 or 14. To this day I'm not sure how Topo Gigio was done. I certainly remember Sullivan as this dour presence, strange and intimidating, this odd-looking man, oddly compelling, severe, and slightly frightening. He reminded me of my junior high school principal, a similarly severe, intimidating presence who seemed to know a lot more than he was letting on. Sullivan was vaguely contemptuous of the whole process and the audience also. On a certain level he seemed bored and impatient about everything going on—a kind of detachment. He was literally cool, not in the sense of a cool guy, but he was emotionally removed.

Steven Winn, San Francisco

inside your house. If he had arrived after TV had matured, he would have been thrown out the door. But something about the very nature of TV—with its person-to-person appeal, unlike that of the formal theatrical structure of stage, screen, and radio—welcomed "performers" with nebulous skills to carve out careers.

Television's broad canvas had room for Broadway-quality drama— "Hallmark Hall of Fame," "Studio One," "The United States Steel Hour"—but also could accommodate an aging, rumpled, ink-stained newsman with no visible abilities or apparent appeal. "Ed has never lost his appeal," said a TV producer, "because he never had any." A good line but all wrong. While Ed *seemed* one of us, his supposed ordinariness was partly a facade.

Sullivan was the perfect embodiment of Andy Warhol's famous dictum, the major difference being that Ed had much longer than 15 minutes of fame. And despite all the unflattering descriptions hurled at Sullivan during his career, the rotten tomatoes and cream pies somehow, eventually, turned into wet kisses and bouquets.

In his book *Understanding Media,* the media guru Marshall McLuhan deftly summarized Sullivan's lack of charisma as ideal for TV: "Mr. Sullivan has the perfect television countenance—a mask instead of a face. It is a corporate image which contains the entire audience within itself." Ed Sullivan, like Walt Whitman, contained multitudes; via coaxial cable, Ed sang the body electric. Ed was his own audience, a microcosm of the millions of Eds and Sylvias sprawled on their sofas across America watching the show—the people's show. As a *Newsday* TV critic wrote in 1967, "The Sullivan mystique is not skin deep. Its roots lay right smack in the midst of the American psyche. He appeals to our own national tastes and to our imagined national tastes."

It was always a severe mistake to maintain that Ed Sullivan had no personality, as Harriet Van Horne claimed. Nobody as relentlessly mimicked lacks a personality. He just wasn't the traditional, stereotypical broadcasting "personality." Ed's lack of the standard, poised, and polished TV persona *was* his persona—his shtick. He was a superb nonperformer, which made him instantly captivating—unusual, anyway. When the lavish "Colgate Comedy Hour" debuted opposite Sullivan in September 1950 to rave reviews, NBC figured all they had to do was toss enough money at a show to knock Sullivan off TV, but they missed the point— and the point was Sullivan, a sui generis host who transcended his own show. You could always hire a smooth polished host, a Perry Como, a Dinah Shore, a Garry Moore, but there was only one Ed Sullivan.

In time, however, there were legions of Ed Sullivans—mimics and comics who reveled in his strange on-screen persona. Sullivan finally figured that, instead of defending his performance, his best bet for longevity was to encourage the impressionists he booked to take potshots at him as the camera cut to Sullivan breaking up. On one show he referred to "this rigor mortis face." Introducing a deadpan 1960s comic, he said, "As a poker face in good standing, let me present another poker face— Jackie Vernon!"

For years, though, he flinched. Monica Lewis told me, "When Ed said, 'They're making fun of me,' Marlo said, 'Don't listen to it, Ed. Don't pay any attention. They want to be on the show. Let 'em say what they want.'" A case could almost be made for a claim that, after Will Jordan's great groundbreaking 1954 imitation of Sullivan, whom few had even considered impression-worthy, Sullivan became an icon, a figure of good-humored fun, a good-natured punching bag whom just about anybody thought they could imitate. But Jordan "created" him.

Jordan's stylized impression established Sullivan's identity beyond his actual self, elevating him. It sold him to America as a bizarre character, warmed him up, and made him, if not human, then amusing. After Jordan collected and recycled his mannerisms, Sullivan became a certified celebrity (as did Jordan), part of every mimic's standard gallery of impressions. Partly because of his impression, Jordan suspects, the name of the show was officially changed in 1955 to "The Ed Sullivan Show," although everyone had always called it that. "Now, it didn't happen overnight, but that was the beginning of the change," Jordan told me.

Sullivan learned to use his image and parlay it into a trademark showbiz persona as indelible as Cagney's, Grant's, or Bogart's. Ed's accumulated facial tics, deadpan gaze, rolled eyeballs, contorted body language, halting speech, non sequiturs, and snarled syntax were as rich and colorful as any star could wish for.

Many of the imitations were based on, or rudely stolen from, Jordan's concept of Sullivan as a well-dressed gorilla—rolling his eyes, cracking his knuckles, crossing his arms uneasily, fidgeting, tugging on his chin, and speaking in halting bursts and run-on sentences that often ended in a syntactical train wreck. Jack Paar once mused on his show, "Who can bring to a simple English sentence such suspense and mystery and drama?"

Sullivan had always talked funny, even as a boy, he said. "The kids in school used to mimic how I'd talk"—in that peculiar pinched reedy voice in some unknown dialect, the words squeezed between clenched teeth as if through a compressor: "Reet here on ar-r-r stage t'night, we 'ave a reeely big shew fr yew . . ." Nobody ever talked like that, not even Ed Sullivan, insisted Will Jordan, explaining how he took a few gestures and turned them into the surreal caricature we all think of as Ed Sullivan. Ed reveled in the impressions that finally cemented his stature. "I put these comedians on the show to impersonate me," he said, "because I want to let people know I have a sense of humor about myself. When [Jordan] gets going, he breaks me up. He's more like me than I am myself. He's right on the button."

Jordan's creation, a twisted robotic zombie, was an original, finely observed work. But the Sullivan impression imprisoned Jordan and limited his career. "I always wanted to get into other things. I didn't want Sullivan to be the dominant impression." Prior to 1954, Jordan cut "Roast of the Town," a record parody of the entire show in which he imitates Sullivan plus 20 other voices. When he first did Sullivan in 1953, it made no, well, impression. "Sullivan's show hadn't become that important. He still was no big deal. It was a big hit in June of 1954 because of all the new mannerisms—the knuckle cracks, the spins, the 'really big shew,' all the other gestures I developed." Using little makeup, Jordan contorted his face into a virtual Sullivan mask. Sullivan once said, after Jordon finished a performance, "That guy scares the hell out of me!"

Jordan was first booked on the show after Joe Moore, a Sullivan crony and trusted scout, glimpsed Jordan on a local show, "The Will

Ed Sullivan was a Sunday night ritual in our home in Cleveland. The stoop-shouldered, simian-looking, easily mimicked (aped?) Sullivan created a strange sense of assuredness in us as he came on our small-screen RCA Victor TV with its black-and-white cathode pictures and its big dials and, of course, no remote control. Sullivan was our weekly impresario, our ringmaster. He was predictably and comfortably dull, but the outward, unruffled guise he presented put us at ease as we raptly waited for the acts. We welcomed him into our home. We trusted him. We put ourselves under the spell of him and his very big show. We experienced him and his variety of entertainment with rare and dumb wonder as a family together in our own house, part of a younger and sweeter America.

Michael Krasny, Greenbrae, California

Jordan Quiz," in which the questions were impressions. Jordan said that Moore told Ed, " 'You've got to see this guy,' so they booked me." Frank Fontaine and George Kirby had also mimicked Sullivan. "But the first one to steal it was Jack Carter—and that was the beginning of the end for me." Jordon was hurt that Sullivan "condoned" other comics' Ed Sullivan routines by booking them. "People used to say that you had to imitate Sullivan to get on his show, which was insane."

Jordan went on to say, "Sullivan got tired of [my version]. He hired people like Carter, who was a great comedian but also stole my act. He and Jackie Mason did me great harm. See, the thing is, *they* didn't need the Ed Sullivan bit, and I did. For them, it was supplementary," but to Jordan it was a meal ticket. "I didn't get that much out of it, because of Jack Carter, Jerry Lewis, George Kirby, etc." Jordan once spotted Carter in the audience. Flattered, he thought, " 'Gee, isn't this terrific, a famous comedian come to see little old me.' About a week later, I found out why. He came up to me after a show, and he was just bursting. He launched into an impression of me impersonating Sullivan. He *had* to show me. That's when I first sensed how things were going to be." Jordan's calling card, Ed Sullivan, was opening doors for every comic in the land. "I thought I was finished," Jordan said. "My hair fell out, William Morris dropped me, and I lost a girl I was in love with." But his Sullivan impression had launched him, and he went on to make a living doing other voices in commercials, cartoons, and industrial shows.

John Byner's inspired version of Sullivan was less photographic, subtler, than Jordan's. Byner captured Sullivan's flutey voice, clipped speech, and trailing non sequiturs. Bob Precht told me, "Byner gets into Sullivan's head." Jordan said, "Precht put us in competition with one another, which is ridiculous. Johnny is very funny, and I respect him very much, because he's the only guy that doesn't imitate *me*. Byner and [Jackie] Mason are probably funnier than I am," but he alleged Mason stole the spins and cracked knuckles from him. Overkill finally set in. In 1959, a *Variety* critic wrote, "Ed Sullivan should immediately impose an absolute ban on any more impressions of himself. A routine that once was very funny is now being overworked." Columnist Leah Garchik said, "My main impressions of Ed Sullivan were really impressions of impressionists impersonating Ed Sullivan."

Sullivan impressions became an epidemic that Ed never tired of. One of his favorite mimics was Ken Rothstein, a teenage friend of Ed's grandson Rob. Rothstein began doing impressions at age ten, inspired by the black mimic George Kirby, and his specialty was Sullivan. "You've gotta meet grandpa!" Rob would tell him. One Christmas Eve around 1971, Rothstein had his big chance at the Precht home in Scarsdale, he told me, when someone said, "Why don't you come over to the house and meet grandpa?" He was only 16.

As they walked to the house, Rothstein recalled, "I became very nervous. I had this reputation around town of doing Ed Sullivan, never imagining I'd be meeting him." And here he was at last. "Ed was standing there, with characteristic hands on hips, elbows bent, looking well-dressed, standing by the Christmas tree. I'm shaking. One of the kids says, 'Grandpa, this is our friend Ken, who's been making a name for himself performing as you.' So Ed turns around, gives a broad smile, and says, 'Oh, *really?*' I look at Ed and I say [as Ed], '*Really,* Ed.' He broke into a big laugh."

Rothstein adds, "To do Ed Sullivan for Ed Sullivan was amazing, and such an honor. You could say Ed was being polite on the first occasion, but on the third time he asked me to do it, that's not polite. That's Ed really enjoying it. I think he got off on the fact that a teenager, a new generation, was now doing him. Then he would have me go on to impersonate Cagney, Grant, and Bogart. All this was very heady to me. It was a combination of this warm down-to-earth family relationship I had, and then suddenly stepping back enough to realize that this is *Ed Sullivan!*"

When in New York, Ken and Rob would drop by to see Sullivan at his hotel. "Once Ed was in his pajamas sitting on the sofa and he demanded, 'I wanna see me! I wanna see that impersonation of me!' He called Sylvia in to watch. Then he asked me to do a full performance. He was so receptive and amused he had me do 15 minutes of material. He would sit there and enjoy the performance and just laugh. He loved to tell me, 'I think you're the greatest. The only person who may be better than you is Will Jordan.'"

Rothstein never saw an actual Sullivan show, but had a bigger thrill when asked to impersonate Ed for a film demonstrating high-definition TV. To do his impression, he stood on sanctified ground at the Ed Sullivan Theater, on the very mark—a star painted on the stage—where Ed would always stand. Rothstein was surprised how close to center stage it was. He says it was as thrilling as when he went to Yankee Stadium for some location scouting and stood on the pitcher's mound.

When Sullivan did a series of one-nighters in May 1955, Will Jordan toured with the show, along with Sullivan favorites Mata & Hari, June Valli, and Peg Leg Bates. "It was hit or miss," Jordan recalled. "The reason it failed is that people thought it was going to be the TV show, but there were no stars. People said, 'Where are the big stars, and Sullivan said, '*I'm the big star.*'" With no camera to hypnotize him at one-nighters, he mixed it up onstage with performers. Jordan and Sullivan did a bit together onstage, and, Jordan related, "we became sort of friends over the years," but not close. "I don't think anybody ever got close to him. Tony Martin said they went out and picked up broads together, and that may be true, but you never got close to him. I don't think his wife even knew him."

Comedian and sitcom director Dick Martin caught Sullivan's stage show at the Desert Inn in Las Vegas. "He had four or five acts with him. He would just introduce them. He was so popular that people would come to see *him*. They never expected him to do anything," Martin told me. The first Vegas show starred Carol Burnett, Julia Meade, Rickie Layne, and a magician. It was such a hit that he was asked back the next year for four weeks.

Jordan's cartoon Sullivan was more Sullivan than Sullivan, who felt almost compelled to assume Jordan's inflections and gestures. He noted, "Ed had to be onstage with me to make the impression work." He didn't interact with Jordan onstage at first, but then the director put the camera on Sullivan laughing—"the single biggest ingredient" in its success, says Jordan, who added that, when they interacted together, "he could never get it right." Sullivan even had trouble rendering his real self accurately, saying, "As Will Jordan would say, 'We have a *very* good shew.'" Jordan says Sullivan always thought he said "shew." "But he didn't," protests Jordan. "*I* said 'shew.'"

Sullivan told *Saturday Evening Post* profiler Pete Martin in 1958 that his top-heavy build led to his stiff-necked look. "I have a very big neck for a man my size. It's a size 17 and all out of proportion to the rest of me. It's that construction that makes me walk the way I do." Jordan studied every facet of him closely: "He dressed immaculately, every hair in place. But he had very long arms and a very big neck, and he was short. Still, he was not really that bad looking. With his blue eyes, even with the bags and everything, there was still something charming about him."

Jordan was the go-to Sullivan clone for decades, until "Pulp Fiction"— "That movie was the thing that hurt me the most"—in which another actor imitates Sullivan. Jordan said he never received a nickel for imitating Ed Sullivan's voice in the movie musical "Bye Bye Birdie," and earned just $50 a performance during the show's long Broadway run. He commented, "The whole Sullivan thing was a fluke." Jordan retains an affection for Sullivan. "Whatever feelings I have about Sullivan, I will always be grateful to him." He had one major complaint: "He was insensitive to how hard it was on me. On one show he actually had the balls to say, 'I believe Will Jordan was the first.' That hurt me very much. 'I *believe*'? How could you doubt it?"

Early Ed Sullivan shows, a side-by-side mix of the unforgettable and the highly forgettable, are a parade of pop culture. In a typical "Toast of the Town" show from the early 1950s, the show opens with half a dozen June Taylor dancers—"The Toastettes"—prancing onstage over the Sullivan theme song, titled "Sunday Swings," composed by conductor Ray Bloch and music coordinator Robert Arthur. The song was eventually published after a long legal battle with CBS. As she noted in her book, Mina Bess Lewis wrote the lyrics for the jaunty tune:

> Here's the "Toast of the Town"
> The pride and boast of the town!
> The cream of the crops
> From classics to pops
> We have found the tops for you!
> We've looked all aroun'
> Up town and down
> From East Side to West
> To bring you the best
> We've pulled out the stops for you!
> So now come and greet the man
> New York's Ed Sullivan
> He's the host on
> "Toast of the Town"!

In one typical show, Sullivan appears in a gray suit, looking like an undertaker, to tell us how special the show is we're watching. He tells us what great pals he and Milton Berle are, how terrific the upcoming ballet dancers are (with a vintage Sullivan gaffe: "The American Ballet is having such conspicuous expense—*success* . . ."), and the difficulty he had booking singer Gracie Barrie, who then warbles "A Sunday Kind of Love" as Sullivan plays her husband, sitting quietly in a rocking chair silently perusing the newspaper. (He's remembered as a leaden emcee welded in place, but in fact Sullivan was interactive early on as a willing musical prop, magician's helper, athletes' foil, and stand-up comedy stooge.)

Later in the show, stifling a belch, he stares into the camera and delivers a lead-in to the commercial ("Lazen gennulmen, now a word from

Emerson's Rex Marshall . . ."), then returns to introduce some square dancers, claiming, not too persuasively, "Y'know, the square dance is really taking over the country," and adding, "You might never have seen a real square dance caller before!" It's clear that Ed is enthralled by every act, especially old troupers like Pat O'Brien in a mushy reading of "Little Girl" (Sullivan was a sucker for sappy readings) and black vaudeville icon Bert Williams pantomiming a poker game.

Sullivan was a lifetime pitchman, especially for new acts with minor talents and big-time stars ("Let's have a nice New York welcome for a new Hollywood star, Terri Moore!" . . . "The greatest puppet act in the theater!"). He sold each performer rather than simply packaging and presenting it; he was more than "a pointer," in Fred Allen's disparaging phrase. He constantly hectored his audience—"C'mon! C'mon!" he would shout, whipping up the crowd. Polite applause told Sullivan that he had failed to produce the goods; robust applause validated his lifework. After every juggler, tenor, or dancer, he hoisted his arms in salaamlike homage. In the era before laugh tracks, Sullivan provided his own applause track when he asked the audience, shamelessly, "Are you having a good time?" Ed was like a neighbor showing you his vacation slides.

On one typical show, he introduces Victor Borge, mangling his name ("We were fortunate enough to get Victor Bor-gee, a great performer from Denmark"), and confides where he found a performer or where they had just appeared ("I heard this next singer in Covent Garden" . . . "Direct from Bill Miller's Riviera!"). He lauds three New York Yankees, who troop onstage from the audience, and asks a bewildered player, "Which one are you?"

You never knew what was coming next, one of the show's strengths. It might be "England's strongest woman" out in the audience, New York City postmaster Albert Goldman, or Mae West. Or a tribute to the Boy Scouts ("We're so proud to have you in our audience"); actor Monty Woolly *reciting* "Miss Otis Regrets"; a men's chorus singing "Lucky Old Sun" in French; comic Joey Adams and straight man, ex-boxer Tony Canzeneri; or John Garfield reading a letter to Santa from a kid whose father is ill and out of work—but, Ed explains, his sponsor, Emerson Radio and Phonograph Corporation, "is giving him a job." And of course, "now, for audiences all over the U.S. and Canada—Japan's top top-spinner!"

Habitually, Sullivan takes us under his wing, the savvy insider telling us, as Carol Channing takes a bow in the audience, "Carol is heading out to Detroit to appear in 'Hello, Dolly!' Be sure to say hello to Detroit for us!" Of Monty Woolley, he requests, "Bring back my regards to Saratoga Springs, Monty, because my family comes from up there." Stumped for a good-bye, he bids singer Caterina Valente a heartfelt "Happy New Year!"

On one show, Sullivan introduces the Will Mastin Trio with Sammy Davis Jr. wearing his old eye patch, crooning "Hey, There!" and doing several precise impressions—a frenetic 15 minutes of Davis in his early, mesmerizing heyday. Sullivan then brings on one of his proudest catches, the singer Julius La Rosa, reminding us, in cryptic Sullivanese, "He's really a remarkable youngster. Most of us can handle failure, but not everyone can handle success like this young fellow."

And always he keeps things moving. We're privy to a long, classy clip from the movie "Daddy Long Legs," before Fred Astaire himself rises from the audience and canters onstage to perform a few steps just for us. The great dancer chats awkwardly with Ed, who brings out a golf club so Astaire can demonstrate his proficient golf swing while dancing, as in the movie. We see, in a flash, Astaire as audience tourist, megastar, golfer, and dancer. Sullivan then bids Fred good-bye, telling him, "Every good luck on the opening of the picture," and adds, with a large wink, "I'll be there at the opening!"

After Cole Porter takes a bow, in another Sullivan audience, Sullivan builds an unlikely bridge to introduce other audience members: "Cole Porter is from Indiana, and so is the Notre Dame football team. Take a bow, fellas!" He tells us why this is important. "I was out to Notre Dame for their annual football banquet." Ed is everywhere. After Roy Rogers and Dale Evans take a bow, Sullivan reveals, "Dale was once in a vaudeville unit with me, y'know." At *Look*'s annual baseball awards, Sullivan personally handed each player a Benrus watch, turning the moment into a kind of nationwide retirement dinner.

Sullivan brilliantly glommed onto celebrities, leaving no doubt that he was chummy with anyone in show business who mattered ("I want you all to meet a wonderful writer who is out in the audience tonight— and a good friend of mine . . . Jacqueline Susann!" . . . "Father Patrick Payton—my old friend"). A favorite line of comics in those days was, "I gotta do the Sullivan show. I'm not famous enough to be in the audience."

He was an unabashed self-promoter, informing viewers, "We've been getting tens of hundreds of letters about *Look*'s second installment of 'The Ed Sullivan Show' story," before asking *Look*'s photographer to take a bow. After introducing producer Lee Shubert in the audience, he reveals, "As a matter of fact, I just took on the assignment of writing Lee Shubert's biography—so put your orders in now!" (It was never published, nor was his unfinished biography of Arnold Reuben of Reuben's Restaurant and Delicatessen.) He shows clips from the new movie "Giant," throwing out the comment "It was just five years ago that Edna Ferber and I discussed the dramatization of 'The Giant' [not "Giant"] on our stage."

Introducing Dorothy Dandridge, Sullivan cries, "Dorothy Dandridge is opening at the Waldorf-Astoria's Empire Room in our town!" He always referred to New York City as "our town," distinguishing it from *your* nowhere town. "And now from the stunning Persian Room . . . !," he shouts, making you sorry you don't live in his town. Before the "I ♥ New York" bumper stickers, mugs, and T-shirts, Sullivan was the city's unpaid one-man chamber of commerce. The very name of the show, "Toast of the Town," referred to his one and only burg. Long before John Kander and Fred Ebb's New York anthem, the subtext of the show was, "If you can make it here, you can make it anywhere." Sullivan's show was America's showplace, its nightclub, its circus, its Broadway theater, all in one.

Then there were the show's unexpected, even surreal, forays into the unknown—Jim Bailey channeling Judy Garland; Moms Mabley in likely her first national TV appearance; Lord Buckley, the inexplicable comic who spoke in jazz lingo understood by almost nobody except his prize student, Lenny Bruce; a 12-year-old Indonesian girl dancing to "The Flight of the Bumblebee"; some comic accordionists; Rudy Vallee reciting a poetic tribute to taxi drivers; Margaret Truman in her TV debut; and ten pianists on ten grand pianos banging out "The Siege of Saragossa." (Take *that*, America!) On a 1956 show, a boyish Johnny Carson does a deft capsule version of "Toast of the Town," with "The Flying Raviolis," "Señor Blintzes," and impressions of Jack Benny and Ed Murrow. When Ed calls him back for a bow, Carson returns holding two poodles.

The videotapes are little time capsules: when the show reaches the 1970s, Ed Sullivan sports long sideburns and, during a Christmas show with the Mamas and the Papas, dons love beads; Cyd Charisse dances to "MacArthur Park," and pianist Peter Nero plays the theme from "Love Story," backed by 21 violinists (about 20 too many)—a priceless segment that mirrors the 1970s at its cheesiest.

However strange or silly an act might be, Sullivan's implied contract with America was: I am now going to show you something amazing or amusing or moving. I am going to present a person who can do something brilliantly, whether twirling a dozen plates in the air or belting an aria from "La Gioconda." Talent at that time seemed more easy to measure than the talent of today's pop stars, which is often fashioned literally out of electronic smoke and mirrors. Plenty of Sullivan's acts were equally dubious, but many were authentic pantheon material. Edith Piaf, Jimmy Durante, Ella Fitzgerald, and Ethel Merman were built for the ages; whither the Turtles and Rare Earth?

But whether it was dancing bears or Balanchine ballerinas, Ed always felt he was letting us in on something wonderful, something he knew about that nobody else did—he was fleshing out every gossip columnist's classic crowing credo "You read it here first!" On the Ed Sullivan show, you saw it there first.

PART II

How to Succeed in Show Business without Really Talking

CHAPTER 7

From Small-Town Sportswriter
to Manhattan Sport

He was read and quoted by students, faculty, parents, and he
was praised, condemned, defiled, and adored. . . . When Ed
spoke on a typewriter, he was read by thousands.

Jim Bishop, writer

Everything in Ed Sullivan's small-town past led him to June 20, 1948,
steering him toward—and inadvertently grooming him for—his lifework
as television's ruling showman. He had always been a star-worshipper,
first of sports figures and then of stage performers. He grew up in a
house where, as in many homes in the early 1900s, families listened to
opera singers and sang Irish ballads and the hit songs of the day around
the parlor piano, the home entertainment center in the early 20th century.

If upright Steinways, player pianos, and cranked-up Victrolas were
the iPods of 1912—when Sullivan was a boy—vaudeville was its cable
and cineplex, a veritable smorgasbord of entertainment of every sort at
25 cents a show. The bigger towns had two or three vaudeville houses;
Port Chester had none. Sullivan was always praised (and praised himself) for presenting TV shows for the whole family, but in fact Ed was
just entertaining his inner child.

"The Ed Sullivan Show" was truly a boyhood fantasy come alive—a
video theater, a virtual one-man vaudeville circuit, where Sullivan could
not just revel in but also book and chat up any performer he fancied. Not
only that, he could introduce performers in his own flowery language,
praise them before America, and command they sit in his audience and
watch *him*—and maybe afterward dine with him. Sullivan was Charlie in
the chocolate factory, Alice in Wonderland, Shirley Temple on the Good
Ship Lollipop, and Dorothy in a video Oz—as well as the wizard.

Sullivan, a true child of the century, was born September 28, 1901 (though some sources give the year as 1902). He grew up listening to giants like John McCormack and Nellie Melba singing the anthems and ditties of the day—"A Bird in a Gilded Cage," "After the Ball," and the songs of Gilbert & Sullivan. The persistent parade of opera singers on his show was a silent tribute to his parents: "Each time I have a Siepi, a Pons, or a Roberta Peters on our stage, I think how pleased my father would have been had he lived to hear them introduced by his son." In fact, he did. Ed's mother died in 1929, at 55, too soon to see him become a TV impresario, but his father lived to be 90, and Ed's success on TV "never ceased to astonish him." That wasn't the only thing that surprized him. Ed's aging father once asked him, "How do you get in that little box?" Sullivan said, "I tried to explain it to him, but he didn't get it."

The Sullivans lived on the top floor of a large, two-family frame house on Pearl Street with a wide front porch and velveteen-upholstered furniture, in Port Chester, New York. "Someone was always playing the piano in the parlor and singing songs by Victor Herbert or other composers of operettas," he would recall, and his mother's family was full of amateur musicians. "From the time we were kids, we were saturated with recordings by Caruso, Melba, and the opera greats of the day."

Before talkies, before radio, before television, there were limited ways to amuse yourself if you were a kid in Port Chester in, say, 1910. You could sit around the piano or go to the local movie house to catch a silent "flicker" with William S. Hart or Fatty Arbuckle. Or you could dress up and accompany your family to a vaudeville show on Saturdays, to be dazzled by low comics, tumblers, singers, magicians, dancers, and dog acts—the very core of the later "Ed Sullivan Show." It was here that the young Eddie Sullivan first developed his lifelong passion for raw entertainment; anything on a stage that moved, moved him.

Sullivan painted an amber-tinted portrait of his hometown, once writing in Collier's: "Our town, Port Chester, was the rootingest town in the world. The people were modest, sincere, helpful. The village churches of all denominations were crowded each Sunday. Nobody hated anybody. The people had pride in themselves. Your name or color or religion cut no ice. You stood or fell on your own performance."

Edward Vincent Sullivan, the second of nine children, lived the typical, idyllic-sounding life of a boy growing up in a second-generation middle-class Irish Catholic family in New York in the early 20th century. Liberty Square, the town plaza, still provided watering troughs for horses, and traveling medicine shows and gypsies peddled their potions and trinkets. The Sullivan family moved to Port Chester from 114th Street in Manhattan's Harlem, then a dense, crowded, white middle-class neighborhood of working-class Irish and Jewish families. When Ed's twin brother, Daniel, died in infancy, followed soon after by a younger sister, New York City didn't seem a great place to raise children. So when Ed was five, the family moved to this drowsy town between Long Island Sound and the Connecticut border, 26 miles north of New York City and surrounded by well-manicured suburban enclaves like Scarsdale, Greenwich, and Rye, where he later caddied. Port Chester is still mainly a blue-collar town in the center of Westchester privilege.

"I was weaned on vaudeville up there in Port Chester," he told an interviewer in 1967, strumming a favorite family-values theme. "My uncles would come over on a Sunday afternoon and we would all stand around the piano and sing. Out of that background came my kind of show—not evil or dirty in any way. There's never been any filth on my show. I present what's for the family, what's in the public good—the great sports stars, the heroes, the boys from Vietnam."

Sullivan never forgot the family's move from Harlem to the suburban wilds: "I still recall the excitement of Helen, Charles, and me en route to Port Chester, when we first saw cows grazing in the country fields." He grew up on tree-shaded streets, doctors making their rounds in horse-drawn carriages, even a village smithy. As he wrote in the *Collier's* reminiscence, "For a small-town kid, my life has been an incredible thing—the sort of improbable adventure I might have dreamed up while romanticizing over a Horatio Alger book under the cherry tree in our back yard on Pearl Street." Ed's favorite saga, however, was really his own.

His smart, impassioned, but moody father, Peter Arthur Sullivan, had a $12-a-week patronage job as a minor customs house official. He was a man, Ed wrote, "keenly interested in the rights of the laboring man, suspect of the J. P. Morgans and the steel tycoons of the day," a follower of the famous liberal orator Robert LaFollete. Sullivan inherited his father's stubborn, pugnacious streak. "He had nothing but contempt for the politician who appointed him, refused to thank him for it, and wasn't reappointed."

Peter Sullivan, his son recalled, had a sharp mathematical mind and regretted not having gone to college. When Sullivan's college-educated uncles dropped by on Sundays, the brothers would hotly debate issues of the day. "Though my Uncle Florence was a famous New York lawyer and my Uncle Charles and Uncle Dan, who fought in the

Spanish-American War and World War I, were college honor students, my father could always out-reason them. Mentally and physically, he was the most completely fearless man I ever knew." When a neighbor kid stole a rooster from their backyard, Peter Sullivan leaped the fence, walked into the boy's kitchen, grabbed the bird, and cried, "If any of you ever so much as lays a hand on anything of mine again, I'll break all of you in half."

Jim Bishop, in his 1957 newspaper series on Sullivan, wrote, "Ed still aspires to have that kind of physical courage. He hasn't got it. He has moral courage, lots of it. No one can speak disparagingly of another race or another faith in Sullivan's presence." Bishop added, "Ed has never forgiven history for not giving his father recognition for being the great man he was. So Ed has become the substitute for his father. He strives harder and harder to be a noted American, and he wants to be known as an honest and good man. Everything is carefully weighed on Peter Sullivan's scales." The major influences on Sullivan were, in order, father, mother, Sir Walter Scott, sports.

Sullivan once wrote, "My father was, in every sense, the head of the family. But my mother was its heart." They were emotional opposites. "She was always gay, he always stern and introspective, a man of few words." His mother, the former Elizabeth Smith, from a proper, once-prosperous upstate New York family of McNultys and Daileys, dabbled in the garden and daubed floral scenes on canvas. She was a pretty, dark-haired, delicately built woman with an air of fallen gentility. Sullivan described her as "a slender handsome woman who wore her black hair piled high in front and a cheerful smile always on her fine regular features. Through measles, mumps, scarlet fever, and many lean years, she steered the five of us on a true course."

One of his sweetest memories was taking his mother to see the musical "Sunny," with Marilyn Miller, on Broadway: "The colors of the production, the music—these were right down her artistic alley." Despite the family's modest comforts, his mother insisted "the rich are unhappy," which Ed disputed after caddying for "a rich young man who was very, very happy." His mother argued, "He was happy because he was good to the poor."

In a 1939 column written from Hollywood, perhaps during an onset of homesickness, Port Chester's most celebrated native wrote wistfully of growing up there, painting it as a Norman Rockwell village, a veritable "Our Town" "made up of decent hard-working men and women and their children. There are small-town drug stores and restaurants, there are theatres which offer double bills, and on Saturday nights, Main Street is jammed with shoppers and their automobiles." In the town square, horse traders swapped animals and actual snake-oil salesmen set up their stands. Wrote Sullivan, "Their spiels were the finest oratory in our town until William Jennings Bryan once belabored the populace from the back of his train which was supposed to have carried him to the White House." He recalled townsfolk gathered in 1917 to listen to the Liberty Loan war bond appeals of "fire-eating Sgt. Cooper, just returned from France." Cooper turned out to be a fraud, noted Sullivan, "but he sold more bonds than any orator in the country." We're talking prime "Music Man" country.

Sullivan watched silent films at a nickelodeon off Liberty Square—strong, silent, unsmiling cowboys and heroines like Pearl White of the unending perils. He recalled, "The biggest day in Port Chester was the afternoon 'Birth of a Nation' came to the local theatre, and the board of education, in recognition of the event, declared a half-holiday for the schools." Like his siblings, Sullivan attended St. Mary's Parochial School. When he was 16, Sullivan's Aunt Lizzie invited him in from Port Chester to parties at Mount Saint Vincent College in Riverdale with his cousins, but first sent young Ed to a tailor shop at Broadway and 137th Street to be fitted for a rented dinner jacket for events that were then called "the social graces."

Sullivan, being Sullivan, later laid out a moral imperative for readers of those rose-colored recollections, before leaving New York in 1937 for a hitch in big bad Hollywood: "Before returning to Hollywood, it is well to return to the small town from whence you came, because it reminds you, in case you've forgotten, that moving pictures are aimed at the Main Streets of the country, rather than the show-wise residents of Vine and Sunset. . . . Liberty Square and its memories tell you that showmanship is still based on the same principles that the snake-oil spielers employed decades ago."

Ed was preceded in school by a brother, Charles, and big sister Helen, whom he called "disgustingly brilliant"; all through school he heard: "Your sister Helen was such a bright girl." Around town, he was always "Helen Sullivan's brother." A younger sister became a nun and a brother a priest. They all painted, danced, sang, or played violin, but Ed was the scrapper known for his hot head, stubbornness, and athletic skills.

As a boy, he had a bad bout of scarlet fever, and Helen later told an interviewer, "I've always wondered if that might not have had some effect on his disposition. He could be very kind and gentle, but he was quick to anger sometimes." Sullivan himself recalled in a column, "The only thing that distinguished [my] ignoble youth was a brattish temper of such proportions that neighbors suggested a stretch at Dannemora" (a home for delinquents). He claimed to be a "lazy" kid who pulled down what he called "frightening" grades, except in English, where essays flowed easily. He scraped by, scoring half a point over the minimum for graduation (72 percent). An uncle volunteered to pay his way to college, but he preferred to be paid by a local paper to watch ball games.

The first full-length stage show he ever saw, at 17, was the comedy hit "Lightnin'," on Broadway. He and his date, Alma Burnes, took the New Haven train into New York ("a terrific adventure when I was a kid") and found the theater by following a diagram big sister Helen had drawn. "After the play—a tremendously exciting experience," he wrote, "—we went to Lorber's and had sandwiches and milk"; he felt quite the sport.

Until he ran away to Chicago at 16 to join the marines, Ed Sullivan was an obedient boy. While his brother sang in the church choir, the much less lyrical Ed dutifully pumped the pipe organ, earning 25 cents for midnight and Solemn High Mass, 10 cents for regular High Mass, and five cents for Low Mass, all of which his mother insisted he drop in the poor box at Our Lady of Mercy church.

In Port Chester, the main excitement for kids was sitting in the park high above Pearl Street, watching college boys and their dates in raccoon coats whiz by in Pierce Arrows, low-slung Packards, and Locomobiles on the Boston Post Road just below, headed for Yale football games in New Haven. Port Chester, with its ethnic mix of Irish, Italians, Germans, Poles, and Jews, was close enough to New York to feel the vibrations of a vital metropolis but still retain its midwestern flavor and values, unpolluted by dirty, smelly, fast, wicked, highfalutin Manhattan. Had Sullivan grown up in his Harlem birthplace, he might have been a less basic, moralistic guy than he became as a churchgoing, organ-playing, leaf-raking, book-reading son of Port Chester.

In *Christmas with Ed Sullivan*, a 1959 anthology of celebrities' holiday memories (all of which begin, "Dear Ed"), compiled by Sullivan and his daughter, Betty, Sullivan recalled his Port Chester Christmases as "lively and gay," writing that "during Christmas week the house would fairly bulge with friends and relatives. There was a great deal of gaiety at these get-togethers, but I remember chiefly music." He described a merry, pungent Christmas card out of Dickens. "I have no recollection of my part in the music-making, but my sister Helen told me that I frequently sang, that I had a sweet voice, and that my singing of the Christmas hymns the nuns had taught me sometimes would make the family cry (maybe in laughter, who knows?)." That was followed by a round of Irish songs. He remembered his mother as "the moving spirit at Christmastime . . . filling the house with delicious aromas no matter how thin our family purse was at the time. And each year she devised different ways of decorating the house."

Ed was fond of heroic boys' novels, most of all *Ivanhoe,* full of knights and damsels, good and evil, and towering castles—which for him meant New York City. His flair for writing propelled him into a job covering high school sports for the local Republican paper, the *Port Chester Daily Item.* He loved the attention, and was no longer considered "just another high school halfback." Everyone knew who he was, and when he walked through the hallways, classmates acknowledged him—a kick Sullivan was instantly addicted to and never got over.

He set out at ten to supplement his nickel-a-mass organ playing by caddying for 35 cents a round at the nearby Apawamis Club; a fellow caddy was Gene Sarazan, later a champion golfer of the 1920s. Ed became an avid lifelong golfer himself, but he played every sport at Port Chester High, winning 11 letters, distinguishing himself as a catcher. He had badgered the baseball coach to give him a shot, and went on to become team captain. He also played football and basketball and ran sprints, all the while covering sports for the school paper. He twice broke his nose playing high school football, so severely that he said it ruined his sense of smell and made eating a bland experience but kept him trim. For most of his life, he stood five foot ten and weighed 160 pounds, but was described as a "ruddily handsome" high school athlete. After graduation, he caught for the semipro Saxer Catholic Club.

Sullivan's reason for running away from home at 16 involved nothing more than a gesture of teenage independence. He chose Chicago, not New York City, so his parents wouldn't be able to easily retrieve him. It didn't work. After Sullivan cashed in a $50 Liberty bond to get to Chicago, a marine recruiting officer realized the boy was underage, with no birth certificate, and called his parents. Ed was sent home, concluding the most rebellious act of his life (until 1956, when he booked Elvis Presley on his show).

Ed tells the story in a slightly different way. In 1917, America was at war, and he longed to join his pals, many of whom were ambulance drivers. "The farther I got away from home, I figured, the safer I was from my father's anger. I had been so completely obsessed with the idea of getting into the Marines that I never imagined failing in the attempt. When that happened, it seemed almost as if there was nothing to live for. I was a failure; I had no friends; I was broke; and to make things worse the weather was bitter cold."

He considered wiring home for return train fare, "but the idea of my father's wrath at his runaway son stopped me. At 16, I was completely on my own for the first time in my life." He holed up at the YMCA for 50 cents a night, watching sailors from the Great Lakes Training Center come and go in heavy peacoats, knitted caps, and warm clothes while Ed shivered in a light jacket. Looking for work, he spent Christmas Eve at the Illinois Central freight yard, curled up behind crates near a luke-warm radiator. A yard inspector took pity on him and gave him a job working Christmas Day—the most dismal day of his life, he later said. He broke down when he went into a chilly room where perishable freight was stored and saw two puppies huddled together, frozen stiff.

Before going home, still determined to prove himself, he pushed rail-road hand trucks for a few days before taking a less grueling job in a cafeteria. He didn't write home for money but waited until he had a few paychecks before swallowing his pride and returning home aboard a Pullman car, "like a man." When he walked into the kitchen, his father didn't crucify him, as feared, but broke into tears, the only time Ed saw his dad cry.

Upon graduation, he got a full-time job at the *Port Chester Daily Item*, where his big stories included a front-page piece about the Life Saver company opening a factory in town and a story about an exhibi-tion game played by the Russell, Birdsall & Ward Bolt and Nut Com-pany's semipro team against the Philadelphia Athletics. When Sullivan dared to write that the A's had used a third-string pitcher, the local team called Sullivan's publisher and demanded an apology. Sullivan refused ("You Irish!" his boss moaned), convinced it was true. The publisher called the team owner to explain. In Sullivan's plucky account, the bolt-and-nut company mogul told Ed's boss, "Good for him! Tell him to stick to his guns if he's right."

Sullivan's career began in earnest the day he arrived at the tiny (circula-tion 3,900) *Port Chester Daily Item* as a general assignment reporter, at $12 a week, covering not just city hall, courts, and fires but also wed-dings, funerals, social events—and sports. He bagged his first major ex-clusive there—an interview with Babe Ruth in the lobby of the Almanac Hotel when Ruth was in town for an exhibition game, which made the

boy reporter a local hero. When Sullivan left the *Item* at 19, Port Chester's
sportswriters and athletes gave the popular junior journalist a going-
away banquet and a large pocket watch.

He applied for a $50-a-week job at the *Hartford Post* and got it, and
ten days later the paper was sold. Sullivan, afraid to tell his family, took
a job as a gift wrapper in the basement of a Hartford department store.
A week later, a Port Chester colleague gave him a letter of introduction
to an editor at the *New York Evening Mail,* where he was hired in 1922
to write schoolboy sports, turning out stories in longhand until he
taught himself to use a high-tech device called a typewriter by copying
editorials out of the *New York Times.* Barely 20, Sullivan began living
the life of a rakish young New Yorker. He drove a fancy car and became
something of a boy-about-town when he met and got engaged to an
Olympic swimmer, Sybil Bauer, who died before they could wed. By then,
Sullivan had found enough of a foothold to hang on in a city he would
one day toast as his own.

At the *Evening Mail,* he worked under the savvy Hughey Fullerton,
reporting college sports, golf, and tennis. Sullivan strained to write in
what he imagined was a sophisticated New York style. "I was pressing
and getting worse day by day," he told biographer Michael David Harris, "instead of writing the way I did at the *Item.*" Fullerton told Sullivan that he might not have the right newspaper stuff: "Try and remember that our readers are more interested in quotes from John McGraw
than in your personal whimsies"—a credo he took into television, much
later saying, "It's the people and what they do who have kept me on the
air all these years. I'm just here to tell you their names."

Assigned to cover a dog show, Sullivan was miserable. "I figured that
was the end. I'd never been to a dog show and didn't know one breed
from another." Angry and humiliated, and feeling foolish, he figured he
had nothing to lose. So, after overhearing a little girl ask her mother about
a bulldog, "How do they wash their faces with all those wrinkles?," he
was inspired to compose his piece as a series of answers to a little girl's
questions about dogs. On the train ride home, he had dire misgivings
and decided the piece was a huge mistake, but it was too late to retrieve
it. "I became more and more terrified as I imagined what the sophisticated New York sportswriters would think when they picked up this
piece of whimsy."

The next morning, certain his career was over at the *Mail,* he bought
a copy of the paper. "I damn near dropped dead," he recalled. The story
was displayed across two columns under a large headline. Jubilantly, he

hopped the midtown shuttle and rode it back and forth between Times Square and Grand Central about five times, spying on people reading his story of the little girl at the dog show. "I was tempted to nudge the passenger next to me reading the paper and tell him, 'I'm Ed Sullivan.' " He learned a major life lesson that morning—"Be yourself"—which he tried to live by, for better or worse.

Suddenly confident in his new job at the *Mail*, he was determined not just to make good but "to be the best sportswriter in New York." That didn't happen, but he became a diligent worker bee who got some attention when he interviewed Jack Dempsey—his first big New York story. He revealed that Dempsey began fighting five years earlier than writers and fans had thought. It was just a tiny scoop but gave him needed credibility at the paper (and a later encounter with Ty Cobb at dinner didn't hurt). That job, he said, "opened the door to a world more glamorous, fascinating and exciting than I'd ever imagined, for the country was just entering into the golden age of sports." Sullivan wrote daily stories plus a column ("Sidelights of Sports," subtitled "A Bit of This and That"), covering everything from six-day bike races to winter baseball meetings.

Sullivan then lived above Billy LaHiff's Tavern on West 48th Street, a colorful joint whose upstairs renters included Dempsey, Bugs Baer, Damon Runyon, Mark Hellinger, and Toots Shor. Soon he began hitting Times Square clubs and speakeasies—"the first time I'd seen big nightclub shows and all the top people. It was a pretty rough citizenry inhabiting the town at the time." He hung out at the Silver Slipper, watching performers like Ruby Keeler; Clayton, Jackson & Durante; and Van & Schenck.

He began cozying up to stars, boasting in print how "Lou Clayton and I would go out to Flushing [Long Island] for a round of golf first thing in the morning. We'd pick up a milkman to caddy." He was now earning a lavish $75 a week, driving a jazzy Durant roadster, and ordering custom-made suits and shirts. Sullivan, notes biographer Jerry Bowles, was "an outgoing guy [who] made acquaintances easily in those days. He had a habit of immediately getting on a first-name basis with everybody he met, even if it was their first encounter."

In the 1920s, when Sullivan wrote sports—first for the *Evening Mail* and then for two other New York papers that folded under him (he later joked that he had a knack for closing newspapers)—it was the era of dynasties, mythic matchups, and ersatz gladiators: of the New York Yankees and John McGraw's Giants, of Red Grange and Knute Rockne's Notre Dame titans, of Jesse Owens, Jim Thorpe, and Man o' War, of

golf and tennis golden boys Bobby Jones and Bill Tilden, of boxing legends Jack Dempsey and Gene Tunney. Spinning their feats in purple para-
graphs were equally vivid sportswriters, primarily Grantland Rice, who
wrote for the *Evening Mail,* and Paul Gallico. The impassioned sportswriters helped build publishing empires—for Hearst, Pulitzer, Bennett,
Patterson, Luce—transforming mere men into giants who bestrode the
earth—or at least the gridiron, the diamond, and the ring.

Athletic heroes were ritually manufactured in Sullivan's youth, when
people took newspapers seriously, a time of tough-guy journalism later
sanctified in Ben Hecht and Charles McArthur's sardonic Broadway
satire of big-city tabloids, "The Front Page." Here's the film's Hildy
Johnson announcing he's quitting his lurid Chicago paper: "Journalists!
Peeking through keyholes! Running after fire engines like a lot of coach
dogs! Waking people up in the middle of the night to ask them what they
think of companionate marriage. Stealing pictures off old ladies of their
daughters that get raped in Oak Park. A lot of lousy, daffy buttinskis,
swelling around with holes in their pants, borrowing nickels from office
boys! And for what? So a million hired girls and motormen's wives'll
know what's going on."

Newspapers created fame—movie stars, national idols, presidents,
moguls, fads—by tilting public opinion and taste. In 1911, there were
14 daily newspapers in New York City. At the top rung were the *Times,*
the *Herald,* the *World,* the *Journal,* and the *Sun.* The second tier consisted of what was once called the slag heap of New York journalism—
the *Telegraph,* the *Press,* the *Globe,* the *Evening Mail,* and the ancient
Post, founded by Alexander Hamilton; all of the second tier papers but the
Post would collapse within 15 years. The best of the secondary sheets
was Sullivan's *Evening Mail,* which had boasted not only Grantland
Rice but also two other now-gilded names—Franklin P. Adams ("FPA")
of the revered Algonquin Round Table, author of a much-quoted witty
column, and cartoonist Rube Goldberg, of the wacky contraptions and
pointless inventions that still carry his name.

The *Mail* was a literary outpost—Sinclair Lewis, Eugene O'Neill,
George S. Kaufman, Dorothy Parker, E. B. White, Ring Lardner, Robert
Benchley, James Thurber, Ira Gershwin, and John O'Hara had all fought
to get their contributions into Adams's column, "The Conning Tower."
When Rice had joined the paper, the stock of its sports coverage had
suddenly inflated the sweaty world of athletics. Charles Fountain's biography of Rice noted that a blurb heralding his arrival at the *Mail* said,

"The paper has secured the services of Mr. Grantland Rice. . . . If you like sport and intelligent, amusing comment on it, you'll like Mr. Rice's daily grindings."

Sullivan saw that sports could be his calling card to recognition. For the kid from Port Chester, it was a thrill to be working on the same paper that had been home to the great Granny Rice and FPA, and that also boasted the future playwright Russel Crouse and, believe it or not, Robert Ripley. Sports heroes were golden creatures then. In that era, observed author Charles Fountain, "American fans were vastly less sophisticated on the nuances of [sports] than they are today. . . . Fans and newspaper readers knew who was in first place and who was hitting what, and that was about all. Rice and the others brought another dimension to the sports page, the 'why' behind the 'what.' "

Rice personified what came to be called the Gee Whiz Era of American sportswriting, which ruled until the Aw Nuts Era of the mid-1960s; Ring Lardner was a notable, cynical exception to the school of gush during sports' golden age. Ed Sullivan was barely a cloud in the Gee Whiz firmament. Never in the same league as Rice and Lardner as a writer, he was a conscientious second-stringer who attempted to emulate Rice's romantic school of reportage. Jocks now assumed legendary stature through labored press names: "the Iron Horse," "the Manassa Mauler," "the Sultan of Swat," "the Galloping Ghost," "the Big Train." Sullivan himself created a famous nickname: he dubbed tennis champ Helen Wills "Little Miss Poker Face," which later haunted Sullivan, known as TV's famous Mr. Poker Face.

Sullivan, steeped in such tactics, was born and bred in this hero-worshipping, hero-building industry, where, wrote Paul Gallico, sportswriters "protected athletes and kept them reasonably human, decent and heroic in the eyes of the reader. . . . Readers prefer the boost to the knock. The reader wants his too godlike heroes humbled sometimes, but he still wants them heroes. If the writer knocks him down[,] . . . he may someday find himself out of a job. . . . Your job is to please people and sell papers. And you don't please readers by ridiculing their favorites. The sportswriter must feel the public pulse as delicately as the editorial writer." Sullivan later carried out that manifesto every Sunday night on his show.

In Florida in 1924, while Sullivan was covering the winter golf season for the *Evening Mail,* the paper was purchased by the *New York Sun* and folded. Stranded in Florida, the resourceful Sullivan landed a job as a publicist at the Ormond Beach Golf Course, booking exhibition matches and devising PR stunts; on the side, he hustled work as an AP and UP sports stringer. When John D. Rockefeller turned up to play the celebrated millionaire banker George D. Baker, Sullivan wired the New York papers for an assignment to cover the eight-hole match. His story got front-page play around the country and paid him $235, giving him his first taste of how the other half lived, or at least putted. Decades later, scanning the magazine *Southern Golfer,* he saw an ad for the Hotel Ormond that read, "Visit the course where John D. Rockefeller and Ed Sullivan once played."

The mid-1920s was Sullivan's roughing-it period. He was 25 when he quit the golf publicity job in Florida for a sportswriting slot at the *Philadelphia Ledger* at $35 a week. Sportswriters then were as low on the economic ladder as barkeeps and barbers, so many supplemented their salary with an acceptable form of payola—promoting fights, wrestling matches, and exhibition baseball games for an extra $50 a week. It was cheaper for promoters to pay off sportswriters to promote events than to take out an ad.

After the *Mail* collapsed, Sullivan hopscotched from paper to paper—from the *Morning World* to the *Morning Telegraph* to the *Bulletin* to the *Leader,* which was published by the socialist presidential candidate Norman Thomas. During his two-year stay at the *Telegraph,* Sullivan was tipped off to a job writing about sports at the bizarre *New York Evening Graphic* by its sports cartoonist Will Gould, and he eventually joined that paper, in 1927, after first spending some time at the *Bulletin* and the *Leader.*

A few *Graphic* details: the notorious tabloid was a wild and crazy quasi newspaper published by physical culturist and health food advocate Bernarr Macfadden, a zany who exercised in his office by standing on his head, strolled barefoot through the newsroom, and walked 20 miles to work each day—shoeless ("I get magnetized from the earth"). He parachuted into the Hudson River at age 83 and into Paris at 84. Sullivan liked him—"Despite his idiosyncrasies, he was a fine gentleman."

McFadden hadn't made his fortune in health foods but in red-meat romance magazines like *True Stories* and *True Romance.* His empire included 13 magazines and ten newspapers, with a combined circulation of 220 million. The *Graphic,* the lecherous granddaddy of the *Enquirer,* the *Star,* and the sleaziest rag of the 1950s, *Confidential,* was called by a *Herald Tribune* advertising director "the lowest form of newspaper life"—a badge of honor among the city's blood- and sex-soaked tabloids. "Gargoyle journalism," Broadway chronicler John Mosedale labeled it, "the most bizarre daily in the history of New York journalism, a goofy experiment which to everyone's astonishment lasted eight years." A typical front-page scoop, headlined "Rudy Meets Caruso/Tenor's Spirit Speaks!," relates an encounter between Valentino's and Caruso's ghosts, with the faces of Rudy and Enrico superimposed on figures wearing what look like movie togas.

Macfadden, the Larry Flynt of his day, who once decreed, "Sex is the sirloin steak of true living," was arrested for promoting a beauty contest with posters depicting men and women in their underwear. Macfadden was unashamedly candid about his reckless ambitions, announcing, "We intend to dramatize and sensationalize the news and some stories that are not new. We want this newspaper to be human. We want to throb with those life forces that fill life with joyous delight. Gird up your loins!" The *Graphic* was the pulpy start of tabloid media in America, and its headlines sound like old Jerry Springer TV shows: "I Am the Mother of My Sister's Son," " 'Let's Be Lesbians,' Urges Cult Woman," "Three Women Lashed in Nude Orgy."

The aptly named *Graphic,* which Sullivan once called "a step removed from pornography" (many called it the *Porno-Graphic*), lasted from 1924 to 1932, gleefully wallowing in sex tales, gore, and showbiz scandal, usually with an implied moral, plus many first-person articles by betrayed lovers, tear-streaked mothers of killers, and murderous spouses ("I Shot Myself for Love and I Gave Up Love Forever!" "I Killed Him, What'll I Do?"). In its first year the circulation zoomed from 30,000 to 300,000, then collapsed to 78,000 after New Yorkers' curiosity wore off.

The *Graphic*'s most famous alumnus was not Ed Sullivan but Walter Winchell. Winchell had gone from collecting items for a backstage throwaway sheet called the *Vaudeville News* to the sensationalist *Graphic,* where he cut his literary fangs as the paper's drama critic and showbiz snoop in his column "Your Broadway and Mine." He also held the titles of drama editor, amusement editor, and amusements ad salesman—a fourway conflict of interest grand slam. A minor newsroom double cross sparked Sullivan's dislike of Winchell and ignited their lifelong bitter feud. Winchell loomed over Sullivan's early life. Sullivan wrote, "His life has somehow been entwined with mine since I can remember. He was full of beans. He was then a completely likable and human being. I was later to consider the man the complete heel. But I have never denied his talent."

Other than Winchell, the *Graphic*'s most graphic invention was a crazy creation called the "composograph," a tabloid print version of today's TV "dramatizations," in which the paper concocted its own courtroom or bedroom pictures when photographers were barred, pasting heads on cartoon bodies and using models in lieu of the actual figures. The paper morphed make-believe "photos" depicting Valentino's final operation, the king of England scrubbing his back in the royal bathroom, and a bedroom scene from the lewd scandal of the day about the aging roué "Daddy" Browning and his bimbo bride "Peaches," along with her alleged "honeymoon diary." One composograph showed Daddy in pajamas with a cartoon balloon of him barking, "Woof! Woof! I'm a Goof!"

Horrified readers gobbled it up while upstanding journals like *The Nation* wrote somber editorials about the dismal state of journalism. But in its tawdry way, the *Graphic* was a pioneer, inventing the "Lonely Hearts" column, early personals ads, and skin magazine meat markets. Eventually, advertisers fled the scene and readers lost interest and also left. The paper was later prosecuted for endangering public morals.

Sullivan must have wondered how a fine, principled Port Chester lad like himself, from a solid Irish Catholic family, wound up working for such a mud- and blood-stained newspaper, but he made himself heard amid the din. That wasn't hard to do if you worked for the *Graphic*, a gaudy showcase in which a mover like Sullivan could produce quirky sporting events that publicized the paper—and Ed Sullivan. He organized "strong-man tournaments," physical fitness sideshows with bodybuilders exhibiting weird feats of strength, like tearing telephone books in two and pushing a freight car with one's head. Sullivan put on sports banquets that he emceed, rounding up celebrities to perform or just appear—Dempsey, Ruth, Tunney, Sarazan, Jim Corbett, Al Jolson, Red Grange, Sophie Tucker, and so on—a warm-up for Sullivan's television celeb-fest two decades later.

The *Graphic* sports dinners, under Sullivan, became major events. At one show at the Hotel Astor, Rudy Vallee introduced what became Vallee's signature theme, "The Maine Stein Song." You can easily hear the excited Sunday night TV host-to-be in this advance, bylined puff piece by Sullivan in the *Graphic* promoting the dinner he would emcee: "It won't be long now! The long-awaited third annual GRAPHIC Sports Dinner, greatest event of its kind ever held in this country, will get underway at the grand Ballroom of the Hotel Astor. . . . Every sport, every high walk of life, will be represented on that dais, 1200 of the famous stars of competition, professional men and sporting fans who avail themselves annually at this opportunity to view their idols at close range."

In his *Graphic* column, "Ed Sullivan's Sports Whirl," he was a dogged investigative reporter and crusader. In one piece, Sullivan revealed that, to pacify the University of Georgia basketball team, NYU had agreed to bench their top player, who was black. Outraged, Sullivan wrote, "If intercollegiate athletics had sunk to that low a level where the gate receipts were the thing[,] . . . where it was more important to make money on a big game in New York than it was to humiliate one man, whether he was an Irish Catholic or a Jew or a Protestant or a Negro, then I suggest that NYU cancel the game and give up basketball." It was an early indication of Sullivan's passion for civil rights, or for doing the right thing, which he said he learned from his father. Despite a contentious relationship (both were hotheads), Ed tried to emulate Peter Sullivan's sense of justice.

Sullivan's "Sports Whirl" columns of the late 1920s reveal a workmanlike writer, especially in pieces on Knute Rockne's death in a plane crash and an impending Jack Dempsey–Jim Jeffries fight. Sullivan dug deeper and took more seriously the sports events he covered than the Broadway follies he later followed from afar—on the aisle, not in the locker room.

He was elected sports editor but drifted until the star columnist, Winchell, jumped to the *New York Mirror,* followed by Broadway columnist Louis Sobol, opening up a gap that Sullivan was drafted into filling in June 1931, against both his better judgment and his grain. He claimed he took it because it paid an extra $50, but it was a natural progression, as showbiz names had begun creeping into his sports columns. Sullivan much preferred hanging out with fighters and golfers, not singers and comics. But he was incapable of turning down a promotion. By then, said Sobol, Sullivan's sports column "had been denigrated until it was allotted merely a few inches of space. Acquiring the Broadway department gave him a new lift." And a new life.

CHAPTER 8

He's Just an Ink-Stained Broadway Baby

I defy anyone to make any good writing out of the three-dot stuff.

Ed Sullivan

As he began his new *Graphic* column, "Ed Sullivan Sees Broadway" (with Ed depicted staring sternly from under a sincere fedora), Sullivan was grumbling to himself. "I didn't want the job," he later told *Time*, "but it was either take it or be fired. I took it but determined never to rap anybody the way Winchell did. I don't think I had the right to pass final judgment on other people's behavior."

In her 1950s column, "Behind the Bylines," Peggy Mann wrote, "Unlike other columnists who slaved to see their by-line become a by-word on Broadway, Ed Sullivan looked upon his assignment as a distinct demotion." She added, "He knew sports. He loved sports. He excelled in sports. And he had written sports professionally since the age of 15." Broadway was foreign turf for Sullivan, but he simply transferred his gee-whiz awe from sports to showbiz. Not only was he the *Graphic*'s new Broadway columnist, but, like Winchell, he was also the paper's drama critic, despite a gaping lack of theater history. After ripping a production of August Strindberg's "The Father," Sullivan remarked that the playwright (who had died in 1912), ought to rewrite the second act.

It was then a dubious but not uncommon practice for drama critics to double as Broadway columnists. Winchell's yakking gossip column, "Your Broadway and Mine," alternated with his real reviews, published under the heading "Opening Nights" (which he followed with movie gossip, labeled "Flickerettes"). New York theater in the 1920s was considered, even by major Manhattan newspapers, less an art form, an event, than a pleasant pastime—much as TV and pop music are regarded now. Even barely literate writers could pass judgment on the shows opening each week while also batting out backstage babble.

The critic John Leonard, in an article on Sullivan published by *American Heritage,* wrote, "Broadway was invented by *Variety,* the show-biz daily, and by the Runyons and Winchells [and Sullivans] who covered the theater, nightclubs, and crime waves the way they covered sports. The columnists all had been sportswriters, anyway, before they went to Broadway" (many of them). Leonard added, "They reported the neon night as if it were one big game, . . . with its own particular slanguage of ballpark lingo, stage idiom, underworld argot, immigrant English, fan-speak, black talk, promoter hype, and pastrami sandwich. . . . That was Ed's grand buoyant world."

Broadway columnists developed astonishing power and, with it, often bogus credibility. After rendering opening night decrees, they followed up by plugging producers, directors, bit players—and stars. On the side, they blasted what they hated. It led to colossal ethical conflicts. George S. Kaufman, the playwright and director, was also the *New York Times* drama editor until 1930, the year his hit comedy "Once in a Lifetime" opened on Broadway. The *New Yorker* drama critic Alexander Woollcott took over the lead in "The Man Who Came to Dinner," playing a version of himself, and Kaufman later assumed a role in his own hit. Columnists regularly hosted events.

So when Ed Sullivan walked onstage to emcee the Loew's State shows that he had not only produced but also hyped in his column, it was simply show business as usual. Partly to display his displeasure in his new assignment, but maybe, more shrewdly, to make a Winchellesque splash (his TV producing credo was "open big"), in his first Broadway column in the *Graphic,* June 1, 1931, headlined "The Maimed Stem" (a play on Broadway's old nickname "the Main Stem"), Sullivan declared open war on his scandal-mongering Broadway colleagues.

In an incredibly ballsy debut, he wrote his own Times Square *j'accuse:* "I charge the Broadway columnist with defaming the street. I have entered a field of writing that ranks so low that it is difficult to distinguish one columnist from his road companions. I have entered a field which offers scant competition. The Broadway columnists have lifted themselves to distinction by borrowed gags, gossip that is not always kindly, and keyholes that too often reveal what might better be hidden." (Winchell coyly called himself "Little Boy Peep.")

Sullivan quickly served warning that he was raising the bar for any-one who might try to gain entry to his column: "Phonies will receive no comfort in this space," he proclaimed sternly. "To get into this particu-lar column will be a badge of merit and a citation—divorces will not be propagated in this column. . . . In my capacity as drama critic, I pledge you of the theater that if I like the show I will say so without any ambi-guities of phrasing that might protect my *Variety* box score. . . . With the theater in the doldrums, it means a decisive voice, and I promise to supply it."

The night after Sullivan's self-righteous opening salvo, Winchell and Sullivan encountered each other at Reuben's Restaurant and Deli-catessen, where Winchell asked, undefensively, "Did you mean what you wrote today?" Sullivan claimed he was just trying to start off with a bang, and Winchell seemed momentarily mollified, but then Sullivan ex-ploded. As he recounted the incident later, "I got so mad I grabbed him by the knot in his necktie and pulled him over the table, right on top of the cheesecake. 'Apologize to you?' I said—'You son of a bitch, I did mean you, and if you say one more word about it, I'll take you down-stairs and stick your head in the toilet bowl.'" In one version, Winchell stood and "slunk out."

Sullivan, later that same week, wrote, "To my former associates in the field of sportswriting, I must report that THIS [new Broadway column] is a soft touch in an unusually responsive arena." He added, as if again taking aim at Winchell, "While all my columning contemporaries are fuming and fretting at my invasion, one of them has even carried his per-sonal alarm into the two-column measure of his daily piece. This partic-ular fellow has never had much competition. He's got it now." It's hard to know how true these stories are, relayed decades later by Sullivan when he was in power and Winchell was a pale imitation of himself, un-able to retaliate, but Winchell biographer Neil Gabler said the latter tale sounds embellished, if not sheer fantasy: "In 1931, almost no one, cer-tainly not a fledgling columnist, treated Winchell that way."

Gabler quotes Sullivan praising Winchell only weeks after the alleged toilet bowl incident: "Your Monday column still fills me with respectful amazement. It's gorgeous great. Where you get it [items], I don't know, but as I pay better dough I believe your operatives, with the possible ex-ception of Dorothy Parker, will see the error of their ways and get on the Sullivan bandwagon." Was Sullivan just buttering up Winchell (and if so why?), or had his anger subsided? A whole lot of both, it would seem.

Unlike Winchell, Sullivan was uneasy holding grudges; he often made up with his enemies. He was almost overeager to patch things up with Winchell, who had far more massive clout.

When Winchell first went on network radio, in 1932, all the major reviewers cheered and raved, except Sullivan, who was eaten up with jealousy. Still, Sullivan wrote him that, despite their long-standing rivalry, "you are the only one for whom I hold a sincere personal and professional respect." Sullivan was becoming a master at creating conflicted relationships. During a later feud, when Sullivan ran into Winchell's wife, June, and tried to shake her hand to signal he was upset with her husband, not her, she spit in his palm.

Sullivan's opening columns startled Broadway and disgusted his new fellow columnists. More than one viewed him as a pompous prig. Jerry Bowles reports that "a lot of people laughed at the sanctimonious tone. Both Winchell and Louis Sobol, Sullivan's recently departed colleagues, took it as a personal attack."

Macfadden, his publisher, asked if Sullivan was kidding. Recounted Bowles, "Macfadden was assured it was a phase and that no column could exist for long without gossip." Indeed, three weeks later, the lead item in Sullivan's column read, "Grover Cleveland Alexander [the pitcher] is back with his wife and off the booze." He followed up not long after with: "Abe Lyman's sister is returning from the coast . . . without her hubby," and "Jean Malin belted a heckler last night at one of the local clubs . . . All that twitters isn't pansy"—a lame attempt at Winchellese; Winchell never referred to other gossip columnists as competitors, but dismissed them en masse as "my imitators."

Sobol zinged Sullivan with a parody column headlined, "The Ennui of His Contempt-oraries," mocking Sullivan's self-righteous debut. It so riled Sullivan that he tried to beat up the tiny Sobol, a beaky, jug-eared 125-pound bantamweight. As Sobol recalled the incident in 1979: "I was standing in front of a theater when I saw him charging toward me. He was really angry. 'I'll rip your cock off, you little bastard!,' he says. Fortunately I was able to duck out of the way while people held him back."

Sullivan, the new Billy Sunday of Broadway, tried sticking to his vow to clean up the gossip columns. He gave himself a good grade a few months into the job: "Just twice in eight months of Broadway columning have I linked a married man with a girl, both times through sheer ignorance of the tie that binds and both times to my complete embarrassment when I learned of my blunders" (Sullivan was acutely aware of his own fidelity issues). "I believe that I have held fairly well to the resolutions expressed at that time. I guaranteed The Stem [Broadway] a fair break and I have given it a fair break. I abjured the phonies and that still goes. . . . If I have been kind to the theater and its people, they've been more than kind and generous to me."

Basking in his new life, he beamed, "Broadway columning is more varied and more interesting than sports columning." Lustily, he began constructing a bigger and broader platform for his opinions and causes, although he insisted that he still hadn't lost his urge to write sports. Starstruck all over again, he was finding that "the people you meet in the theater and its wings are in the aggregate smarter and more interesting" (than athletes), but he disliked the "office politics" of showbiz, especially in musical theater—unlike the purity of sports, based solely on achievement. As he put it: if you could hit .398, knock out ten opponents, or boot home winning horses, you were a justifiable hero; "how a youngster ever gets to the top in this field [show business] I do not know." In no time, the adaptable Sullivan grew to know, and indeed fawn all over, celebrities, unlike Winchell, who considered showbiz stars simply an unavoidable bother, a way to burnish his own star.

Three years later, Sullivan sheepishly confessed in print that he had been hopelessly corrupted: "My platform against gossip hasn't a single plank left in it, for in the course of a week I run two full gossip columns." He rationalized it: "The reason I do it is because the readers demand it." He called gossip "distasteful to a grown man," but a necessary evil, along with reports about celebrity babies ("you got to run them or be scooped"). Winchell may have had illusions about writing for the ages; Sullivan had none.

In that same schizoid column, he congratulated himself: "Just how well I've lived up to my promises of 1931 is difficult to tell. My resentment of effeminates as performers is just as keen as ever[,] . . . my intemperance of dirty jokes and dirty songs has not tempered, and the show which has toured vaudeville under my name proves that a clean show can be crisp and entertaining without the injection of smuttiness or double meanings."

This was the pious code that Sullivan took with him to television. He was a selective Victorian who often mounted his pulp-lined pulpit to bemoan changing social mores: "It seems to me that well-bred young ladies I meet are becoming more and more fond of telling dirty stories— in mixed company. I'm not puritanical[,] . . . but it is an unhealthy lewdness that adds nothing to a girl's charm. . . . It may be ultra-smart, or cute[,] . . . but to me it is an ugly practice." He would be rolling over in his column today.

The *New York Post,* in its March 1956 series on him by Alvin Davis after Sullivan became a TV star, concluded, "For all his zigzagging between moralizing Broadway and mongering its gossip, Ed Sullivan is at heart a reformer." The *Post* noted that Sullivan was even trying to reform himself, citing a steep drop in scandal items and an increase in birth announcements—17 in one month. Davis wrote that Sullivan's column was "an awkward mixture of copybook preachments and nasty scandal. The accent in his column is: some politics, some show-business chatter, a little moralizing." The paper added that, once his TV show became the focus of his life, he relied on only a handful of trusted press agents and trashed all spicy items. He lived on vanilla-flavored showbiz tidbits.

In 1932, just a week before the *Graphic* went under, "Captain" Joseph Patterson of the *New York Daily News* offered Sullivan a job writing his Broadway column for $200 a week, $175 less than his *Graphic* salary. Patterson hired Sullivan after Winchell's carnal gossip column became a smash hit at the *Mirror.* But, as the Lewises wrote, the two-timing publisher later confided to Winchell, "Anytime you want to come here you're welcome. Ed Sullivan owes his job to you. If you gave up your job [at the *Mirror*] I would get rid of Sullivan."

Sullivan grabbed Patterson's offer and made up the financial gap with a radio program on CBS at $1,000 a week. He stayed at the *News* until his death, 43 years later, in the last 20 or so years cranking out two tepid columns a week, Mondays and Fridays, still earning about the same paltry $200 a week. Sullivan was devoted to the paper—and to seeing his name in print.

He became a Patterson loyalist after receiving a memo from Patterson about a column in which he wrote that Sam Goldwyn's hot new highly publicized discovery, Anna Sten of Sweden (billed as the next Garbo), was a bore. The fatherly memo read: "I do not say that I disagree with your opinion. However, I am deeply disturbed that any writer of mine would recklessly jeopardize the professional career of a young actress." The note so struck Sullivan that he "read and reread the memo. And as the meaning sunk in, I thought to myself: here indeed is a great man." Sullivan liked to say that he never wrote a mean column he didn't later regret, an admission that served as a kind of painless trip to the confession box.

Sullivan totally steeped himself in the Broadway lifestyle and its wiseguy lingo, writing ersatz Winchellisms ("There's a playboy for every light on Broadway and, as Blossom Seeley phrases it, 'Some of them may be hot but they won't be bothered' ").

But Sullivan still cast longing looks at the sports whirl, writing about bumping into "my old friend George Carpentier" (the French boxer) or comparing the two worlds: "Sports offers no parallel to Sime Silverman [*Variety*'s founder], one of the greatest characters in show business." Silverman, an early Winchell supporter, took a paternal interest in the gossip whiz kid, lent him money, and gave him advice. The showbiz bible was the source of nasty Winchell items that *Variety* couldn't run in its own pages.

Sullivan, for his part, treated the raffish *Daily News* as if it were just a big-city version of the *Port Chester Daily Item*. Many of his columns read like the unedited jottings in a small-town weekly written in lazy shorthand, a lifeless litany of birth, marriage, career, and death announcements: "Perle Mesta huddling with McGraw-Hill . . . Tin Pan Alley mourning the passing of Jack Robbins . . . The Dave (MCA) Begelmans expecting . . . Sam Briskin won't be back at his Columbia Pictures desk before Jan. 16 . . . Sen. Wayne Morse's grandson named Nicholas . . . Hank (CBS) Warner's sec'y, Mary Allen, to wed Joseph Ahbruzzee . . . Hal and Candy March expect a February stork."

The bulletin-board flashes were interspersed with Sullivan's occasional sermons and warmed-over public-spiritedness. He blasted Jerry Lewis for "his mimicry of spastic children," shouted "Hooray for de Gaulle! He's got guts," called for repairs to the Major Deegan Expressway, and trumpeted pet causes. He dashed off minieditorials ("Labor unions are playing into the hands of the Commies by urging a 35-hour work week") and sticky odes, like a heart-clogging Mother's Day column that he reran every May, imploring readers to "Render her, on Sunday, a tiny gesture of affection."

In 1937, Sullivan engineered a three-year stint as the *News*'s Hollywood columnist (he was replaced in New York by Danton Walker). During that period, Sullivan—pugnaciously envious of Winchell's power in the industry—nearly accepted an offer from the *Hollywood Reporter*'s Billy Wilkerson, but Patterson wired him: "If you can better yourself permanently, I would not wish to stand in your way. But I want to make it clear I consider you one of our best men and that you can stay with us as long as you want.—J. M. Patterson." Sullivan, who reveled in loyalty, was never again tempted to leave the *News*. "Whenever I felt low, I dug out that wire," said the diehard *News* man.

In Los Angeles, although he gave star-studded parties and tried screenwriting and even acting, Sullivan was a stranger among palm trees and swimming pools. After first resisting Patterson's request that he return to his old Broadway beat, he relented, and Patterson welcomed him as a prodigal son returning to his true home: Broadway. The earlier plan had been for Sullivan to trade places with the paper's Hollywood columnist, Sidney Skolsky, hired to rival the Hearst papers' Louella Parsons. Sullivan had arranged for the switch by telling the editors that Skolsky was too cozy with the people he covered, an occupational hazard Sullivan knew plenty about. Skolsky quit, labeling his recall to New York an insult—and for Skolsky, a famous Hollywood columnist, it truly was a demotion. As *Variety* reported on August 31, 1937, he sneered, "I believe Broadway columns are as passé as Broadway. Therefore I have resigned."

Skolsky was wrong about Broadway but prescient about the Broadway column, which had begun to lose its grip as Parsons and Hedda Hopper began writing excitedly about movies and moviemaking, building on the country's new manic fascination with screen stars over Broadway figures. Theater was becoming old news. Movie faces, along with pop singers, later emerged on TV as Sullivan's own ticket to stardom.

The balance of showbiz power was shifting to Hollywood. By 1968, Sullivan was being introduced on his show this way: "And here he is, live from New York, Ed Sullivan!" No mention of his nationally syndicated column, no reference to the *New York Daily News*.

Perhaps Sullivan had resisted giving up his sports column to tackle Broadway, because it meant going toe-to-toe each day with journalism's champion rottweiler, Walter Winchell, with whom he jousted until the end of his life. (They made up in their final years.) Winchell grew like an ulcer inside Sullivan's psyche, his major antagonist in print and on the air.

Even so, the prospect of taking Winchell on must have been an irresistible challenge to the ambitious, competitive Sullivan. Over the decades, the Sullivan-Winchell warfare left many wounded bystanders. In a nostalgic address at the Friars Club in 1953, Winchell blasted New York columnists; Sullivan later blasted the Friars for giving Winchell a forum. Sullivan further retaliated by banning Gwen Verdon from his show because she had appeared on Winchell's newscast.

But Sullivan knew his limitations. He couldn't match "WW" as a phrasemaker or scandalmonger, let alone as a charismatic celebrity. Sullivan knew he would never be that widely read, that quoted, that loved—and that loathed—for that long. Ethel Barrymore expressed some of the loathing when she sized up Sullivan's rival with an epitaph: "Walter Winchell does not deserve to live." As Sullivan biographer James Maguire wrote, "Ed knew he tapped a wellspring of tacit approval whenever he attacked Winchell." Winchell's word was instantly accepted on any item he ran. When, for example, Bette Davis entered a New York hospital for an operation, Winchell told radio listeners she had cancer, which Davis strongly denied. As Winchell biographer Neal Gabler reported, that night a press agent at Lindy's told a friend, "If Bette Davis doesn't have cancer, she'd better get it!"

Sullivan had reason to fear, admire, and attack Winchell. "Mrs. Winchell's little boy Walter" (as he winsomely dubbed himself) was not only an investigative snoop but also a crack reporter and innovative stylist respected for his ability to reshape the American language daily in Winchellisms. Sullivan was no match for this astonishing stylist who created a new American idiom, coining words like a 24-hour literary mint: "pffft" (split up) and "Reno-vated" (divorced), "Chicagorilla" (gangster), "pash" (passion), "shafts" (legs), "giggle-water" (liquor), "Park Rowgues (newspapermen, whose offices lined Park Row), "Hard-Times Square," "Hardened Artery" (Broadway), "revusical" (musical revue), "moom picture" (movie), "messer of ceremonies" (emcee), "infanticipating" (pregnant), and "whoopee" (sex; Winchell didn't invent the term but so popularized it that it became the hit song "Makin' Whoopee," a musical, and even a movie).

His longest-lasting coinage, "blessed event," became the title of a 1932 movie with Lee Tracy as a fast-talking imitation Winchell in frantic high gear. For years, *Time* had merged words ("cinemogul," "WPAdministrator"), and *Variety* was famous for its slangy showbiz shorthand ("Wall Street Lays an Egg"), so it's hard to say who begat what, but linguists and scribes were impressed by Winchell's dazzling verbal inventions.

Sullivan knew what he was: a competent reporter and passable writer. Winchell's column was copied, republished, quoted, and parodied, but Sullivan's columns died daily after publication. While competing columnists tried not to mimic Winchell, it wasn't easy. Gossipist Hy Gardner once wrote that columnists "involuntarily but obviously patterned our patter after Winchell." Sullivan couldn't shake off Winchell. He echoed Winchell's "Girl Friday" columns in his own crude version ("My Secretary, Africa, Speaks") and in his "Chorine's Letter to Her Ma." Like Winchell, Sullivan printed purported hourly diaries ("The Columnist's Clock"), revealing what a busy guy he was, taking calls from Jeanette MacDonald, Hal Roach, and Mrs. Paul Muni, going to tennis games, cocktail parties, and dinners with Will Rogers, Clark Gable, and Myrna Loy.

Sullivan aped Winchell by writing open letters to politicians, Christmas doggerel, showbiz quizzes, and a popular series of "Listen Kids" columns in a campaign against juvenile delinquency, coming across as wise old Uncle Ed: "As a Broadway columnist I can tell you youngsters that there is very little glamour in jail. I go up to Sing Sing every now and then. Don't let the gang pick you out as a sap." Or: "To all of you kids of high school and college age, I ask you to be good sports on the highways. Let's resolve for 1938 that each of us will turn over a new leaf instead of turning over a car." This was Ed in his role of Father Sullivan, crime-busting columnist.

Another hat he wore was Panglossian optimist, dispensing curbside wisdom ("My experience with life persuades me to believe with the ancient philosopher that this is the best of all possible worlds"). Broadway insiders snickered at his bromide-laced sermonettes from a tabloid pulpit, mocking his daily homilies that came out boldly in favor of religion, safe driving, motherhood, loving thy neighbor, and racial equality.

Sullivan never stopped competing with Winchell, carving out a wartime niche to counter Winchell's in-your-face patriotism. He organized, produced, and emceed scores of hospital, armed forces, and Red Cross shows, and war bond benefits at Madison Square Garden, stuffed with as many stars as he could find—the first step on his road to TV. After the war, Sullivan kept at it, producing shows for the wounded, and prodding celebrities like Jimmy Durante to entertain at veterans' hospitals. He put together all-star shows—an early version of Bob Hope's wartime shows. The comic Jack Carter told a GI audience, "Ed isn't like you guys. He'll never be called up until the Japs are in Radio City."

Sullivan and Winchell were attached at the macho id, if not the hip. They coveted Mob friendships and had a lust for power, patriotism, and girl singers. But they traveled in different nighttime circles. Arty Pomerantz, former chief photographer at the *New York Post,* explained to me that Sullivan "wasn't a guy who hung out at Lindy's," where columnists, agents, and photographers met for pastrami and cheesecake at midnight. "Winchell would be at those places." Sullivan was more of an El Morocco–Copacabana guy.

Jimmy Mitchell, El Morocco's publicist in the 1960s, told me he saw Sullivan "night after night" at the East 54th Street club with the zebra-striped banquettes, paper palm trees, and doormen dressed like French Legionnaires. "I knew him very well. I went out with him a great many times. He was a very powerful celebrity, but very approachable, always very courteous and kind to everyone. He was more of a gentleman than some of the other columnists. He was like a regular person. He wasn't a tough columnist. But he loved his celebrity status."

Winchell's longtime assistant Herman Klurfeld emphasized to me in 2005, "Sullivan was not Winchell's adversary. Winchell was *his* adversary. Winchell couldn't give a damn about him. Nah, he wasn't important. I mean, Sullivan's making $200 a week. Winchell was making $200 a day! Sullivan meant nothing. I thought he was a nice guy. I never talked to him too much. I didn't take him seriously—because Winchell didn't." Klurfeld recalled, "Sullivan wanted me to work for him, and I said he didn't want me, he just wanted to take me away from Winchell. And he said, 'Yes, that's true.' When you work for Winchell, you've got everything. Everybody else is second-rate."

Klurfeld never saw Sullivan at the Stork Club. "He wasn't welcome there, because it was Winchell's nightly headquarters." WW's right-hand man denies Sullivan ever dunked Winchell's head in the toilet or dragged him across a plate of cheesecake by his tie. "That's the type of thing a drunk would do; Sullivan wasn't a drunk. And Winchell would've shot him. Winchell carried a gun."

Many Broadway columnists were closely linked to mobsters like Owney Madden, a former child actor who took over the Cotton Club in Harlem. Even after Prohibition ended in 1933, the Mob ran New York nightclubs as branches of their social clubs. It was a mark of status for a columnist to be on a first-name basis with a gangster. Via columnists, gangsters themselves became celebrities—characters like Madden, "Legs" Diamond, Dutch Schultz, Bugsy Siegel, and Hymie Cohen of Hymie Cohen's Hotsy Totsy Club.

Winchell ceaselessly taunted Sullivan in his column, but Sullivan's counterattacks were, to Ed's chronic frustration, deleted by the *Daily News* copydesk, under orders not to give Winchell and the rival *Mirror* any ink; Sullivan's failure to publicly respond gnawed at Winchell. Sullivan disguised Winchell's name in print, as in a 1932 item from his first-anniversary column: "Most frequently asked question during the year has been: 'Is that feud with Orchidaceous [a sly reference to the "orchids" Winchell bestowed in his column to worthy folks and causes] on the level?' The answer is Yes. He doesn't like me and I don't like him, although at one time we were palsy-walsies." Winchell accused Sullivan of being a no-talent fraud, a plagiarist, and an immoral bum. While Winchell never felt threatened by Sullivan—until the debut of "Toast of the Town"—he needled him whenever possible, just to keep in practice.

With pleasure, Sullivan kept counterpunching. He compared Winchell with Joseph McCarthy and the führer, writing, "Long before McCarthy came into the character assassination racket, Winchell was one of its originators. . . . This small-time vaudeville hoofer who never even got to the Palace . . . has developed into a small-time Hitler. . . . He has capitalized on the Big Lie." He called Winchell a "charlatan" and a "terrorizer." Winchell yawned, telling *Time* from his mountaintop, "I don't engage in bouts with small-timers. I would rather hear what the President has to say to me."

In "The Gossip Columnists," a 1956 analysis by David Cort in *The Nation* of the chattering masters' styles and work ethic, Sullivan comes off the worst. Cort called Sullivan "the most cursory, imbalanced, and generally amateurish. His malevolence is almost buried from sight beneath awesome dullness and ambition." Cort accused Sullivan of "inventing feuds" and possessing an "ignominious lust for power on the TV stage."

Winchell, Sullivan, Dorothy Kilgallen, and company made enough noise to alarm *Editor & Publisher,* proper industry keeper of the journalistic flame, which editorialized about them: "These gossip columnists are the creator of the 'new culture' which circles about the Broadway column, babbles an audacious brand of illiteracy, sets up a new concept of decency in human relations and has as its bugle call the Bronx razz. We may learn just how far a reporter may peek behind the curtains of private lives." *E&P*'s editor, Marlen Pew, stopped short of calling for a code of ethics for gossip columnists, but was "perfectly willing to let Broadway sewage find its own way to the sea."

John Leonard, in his *American Heritage* Sullivan profile, wrote, "Broadway columnists like Damon Runyon, Walter Winchell, Louis Sobel, and Ed Sullivan never went to college—they went to newspapers instead. Newspapers and Broadway: together they were inventing 20th Century American popular culture." Broadway's trade school was gossip peddling, a sleazy, humiliating racket. The very jargon of the press agent's trade—"servicing columnists" and "scoring" with an item—was the lingo of pimps and whores. Yet press agents provided the crucial oil that kept, and still keeps, the pistons of show business pumping. As Neil Gabler observed in his Winchell biography, "The press agents, for all their abasement, were the ants that moved the mountain. Without them, there was no celebrity, no gossip, no mass culture really."

Gossip was a systematic industry, dating back to the 1920s, that manufactured, packaged, and delivered showbiz items to journalists. A critical player was Allan Eichler, who hacked his way through the New York press agent jungle from 1963 to 1969, handling such clients as the Rolling Stones, Dorothy Lamour, Patti Page, Paul Anka, and "The Bob Hope Show." Eichler told me he learned the gossip trade at the feet of flackmeister Lee Solters, who taught him the fine points of a recycling gambit called "rerouting." If columnist X didn't use an item, it went to Columnist Y, and then to Columnist Z. In item planting, he said, "I was taught, 'there's no good writing, only good rewriting.' "

The gossip mills had layers, back channels, and intricate codes of conduct. "There was a social structure, a pyramid," Eichler recalled. "Kilgallen was more gossip than news, Sullivan was more news. Winchell and Kilgallen were the kings. Earl Wilson was important." He explained, "You had to learn each columnist's style. Sullivan was very good at encouraging me to give him items. He was very good at giving plugs to someone opening at a club. . . . He used short, zippy items, an occasional joke. He liked humor." Eichler put jokes in clients' mouths at random. "You could cross out Edie Adams and put in Peggy Lee. It didn't matter who said it." A nasty part of gossipmongering was the practice of including, along with innocuous, made-up "free items" (the real dirt, unattributed), a form of item payola that helped get agents' clients mentioned. "They had to be real," said Eichler, who claimed Sullivan didn't play that wily game, unlike Winchell, Jack O'Brian, and Kilgallen.

The collapse of the Broadway columnists' power coincided not only with the rise of the TV and radio talk shows—and Sullivan himself—but also with the tell-all autobiography and the gossip-drenched tabloids. Suddenly celebrities were unburdening themselves without shame, indeed with great glee, wallowing for fun and profit in their private misfortunes, drug habits, one-night stands, hideous marriages, wretched childhoods, dysfunctional families, illegitimate offspring, and sexual adventures.

Scandalous show business secrets were no longer (a) secret or (b) scandalous. "When people tell on themselves," noted Kilgallen biographer Lee Israel, "the professional tattler is rendered somewhat redundant." When gossip became everybody's business, the columnists who controlled it suddenly were out of touch or out of work—obsolescent. In the new TV age, a star like Jack Paar could, before the entire nation, attack Winchell or humiliate Kilgallen and render them irrelevant tyrants.

Just about the time that the world of the mighty Broadway gossip columnist was collapsing, Sullivan—his survivor's instinct always working—was lucky, smart, and blessed enough to wander into television. The man was nothing if not adaptable. Indeed, Sullivan had easily shed his small-town ways and immersed himself in the glitzy New York nightlife culture. So many shows opened on Broadway in the 1930s and 1940s—often one or two a night—that it was a buyers' market for back-stage gossip. Columnists could be choosy what they ran. "Press-agentry flowered and competed fiercely to achieve breaks in New York's nine newspapers," wrote the *News*'s nightclub man Bob Sylvester in his memoir. "Press agentry had existed since the days of P. T. Barnum and before. But it never flourished as it did in the Winchell era—nor has it since."

Winchell's favorite nest was Sherman Billingsley's Stork Club, the jewel in the nightlife crown, where it was easy in 1948 to spend $100 a night, the equivalent today of $860. It attracted the literati, though the owner wasn't overly well read. When *Post* columnist Leonard Lyons brought Carl Sandburg to the Stork Club, Billingsley asked Lyons, "What does he do?" "He's a writer," Lyons told Billingsley, who said, "Well, tell him to stick in 'The Stork Club' once in a while." Billingsley, who ruled café society from his Stork Club roost, said, "The out-of-towners come to see the natives, who come to see each other." A slick onetime Midwest bootlegger and a celebrity bootlicker, Billingsley bestowed gifts on regulars and parlayed Winchell's plugs into a 1950s TV talk show.

Winchell defended the Stork's unabashed elitism: "The Stork Club discriminates against everybody—white, black and pink," he wrote when a racial incident involving Josephine Baker exploded. "It's a snob joint. But if your skin is green and you're rich and famous or you're syndicated, you'll be welcomed at the club." The host, an equal opportunity bigot, supposedly turned away the dark-skinned maharaja of Jaipur. Ralph Blumenthal, in his book on the Stork Club, noted, "People were always getting barred. There were more of them, it seemed, than guests in good standing"—even Harold Ross, the *New Yorker* editor, was 86ed after the magazine ran a mocking profile of Winchell.

In the notorious Baker brouhaha, in 1951, Sullivan found himself a major warrior. Sullivan's and Winchell's decades-old sniper war erupted in an epic battle when the black entertainer accused the famously snooty club of racism and refusing to serve her and her entourage at midnight. Winchell, whose constant plugs put the Stork Club—where he was treated as house royalty—on the map ("New York's New Yorkiest place on W. 58th"), sided with Billingsley, while Sullivan attacked Winchell for supporting Billingsley's alleged biased practices.

Winchell, like Sullivan, had always proudly displayed his antiracist credentials in print. *L'affaire* Baker was loudly aired by New York radio talk-show host Barry Gray, over whose mike Sullivan delivered a blistering tirade against Winchell, venting a lifetime of personal loathing. Winchell then launched a nasty crusade to drive Gray off the air, labeling him a Communist during the McCarthy era. Nobody ever learned what really occurred that night at the Stork Club. It may have been the club's slow service, racism, or perhaps even a stunt by the flamboyant, publicity-savvy Baker.

Klurfeld, Winchell's assistant, was at the Stork the night of the Baker flap, which he suspects was a Baker self-promotion ploy. "It's a good example of the ingratitude of people," he said. "Winchell made her famous! He gave her money! He did everything for her you could ask. By the time he got through plugging her, she was earning $5,000 a week. So that's Josephine Baker." By the time it all died down, everybody, including the not-so-innocent bystander Ed Sullivan, was splattered with mud—just another day in the Broadway killing fields.

Toast of the Nation

If Shakespeare didn't convince us all the world's a stage, Ed
Sullivan did.

> Kay Gardella, *New York Daily News* television critic

After Sullivan took an abrupt turn off Broadway into television, it took
about two years for "Toast of the Town" to become a nationwide Sunday night addiction. In today's impatient hit-or-flop network climate, it
would have been yanked off the air in six weeks.

When the initial sponsor, the Emerson Radio and Phonograph Corporation, jumped ship after 13 weeks, mostly because of Sullivan's on-
air bumbling, the show was rescued by Ford's Lincoln-Mercury dealers,
which increased Sullivan's weekly talent budget from $375 to a whop-
ping $2,000, enough to keep Sullivan and coproducer Marlo Lewis from
digging further into their pockets to buy the hot names they wanted.

Ford's sponsorship was just the massive vote of confidence that Sullivan badly needed—a major automobile company willing to take a chance
on an unknown no-talent, a fledgling TV personality reeling from withering reviews. Sullivan's usual gung ho spirit was wilting as the nasty
New York critical flock began pecking him to death.

Gratefully, he agreed to become a traveling salesman for Lincoln-
Mercury, revving up dealers across America while boosting the show. Sullivan was one of the first celebrity corporate spokesmen in TV history,
well before Ronald Reagan became a genial front man for General Electric, which launched his political career. Sullivan had no designs on higher
office; he already was well in over his head as a credible television host.

As the Lincoln-Mercury figurehead, Sullivan toured every major U.S.
city to give speeches and attend community events; he sold cars, kissed

infants, and led parades. Later, he brought performers along, and discussed a touring version of the TV show, doing a remote from Philadelphia that helped put wheels on his show. In time, Sullivan brought touring versions to opera houses, colleges, hotel ballrooms, army bases, battleships, beaches, and golf courses. He talked to steelworkers at their blast furnaces in Pittsburgh, landed on Boston Common in a helicopter, and sailed up the Mississippi in a barge before 75,000 onlookers to open the Memphis Cotton Carnival.

Benson Ford, the man responsible for Lincoln-Mercury's decision to sponsor the show, wrote, "Sullivan is a phenomenon. . . . Wherever he goes, women hold up babies for him to kiss, traffic stops, policemen smile. I've even see Ed choke up. Ed is a one-man interfaith council, a chamber of commerce and an unequalled sales force. The crowds love him." This New Yorker with the common touch just might have become an earlier Ronald Reagan had he ventured into politics.

Self-respecting vanity-ridden stars would never have agreed to perform such backslapping public relations stunts. But Sullivan happily did interviews with auto-magazine editors—anything to hype the new show. His quest for fame, his many critical misfortunes, and his ravenous need for adulation had made him a willing candidate for national recognition. Once again, Sullivan's lack of early stardom, plus his need for adulation and his desire to build his TV career, made him a rousing cheerleader.

Joe Bracken was the Lincoln account executive at Young & Rubicam, based in Detroit, the liaison between corporate Detroit and the creative unit in New York, which had hired Julia Meade as their on-air voice. When Bracken worked the show, in the mid- to late 1950s, Lincoln was trying to crack Cadillac territory. "Lincoln was having a hard time getting close to Cadillac," Bracken told me. "The reason we went on the Sullivan show in the first place was, not because the demographics of the show were prospects for our product, but because the audience was so broad they would be the people who would be the car's admirers. 'Oh, look at the person who drives a Lincoln! He must be something.' We knew we had a lot of wasted [demographic] coverage with the Sullivan show. It was a prestige show all the same."

The Lincoln commercials ran every other week (alternating with other big-name sponsors like Kodak, Motorola, and General Foods), with a fresh focus each time. "They weren't your everyday garden variety commercials," Bracken stated, but were set in ritzy locales like the Beverly Hills Hotel, Aspen, Havana, and a diplomatic hotel in Washington, D.C. "They were all special situations where the car was the star." Lincoln even did a live commercial onstage that parodied the movie "Love in the Afternoon"—daring for such a white-shirt, conservative company. Lincoln left the show in 1962, as did Meade, for the usual time-for-a-change reasons.

Bracken never dealt closely with Sullivan. "For the most part, Ed looked the other way. He was much more concerned with the program, the talent, whether the jugglers and dancing bears were doing it right. During rehearsals, he was a hard-driving guy. He was a tough taskmaster. He had good people to keep the thing on an even keel, but sometimes his keel was not all that even." Bracken recalled, "Sometimes during rehearsal he could flare up pretty quickly. He seemed to cool down as fast. It was pretty inflammatory. You didn't have to be a psychic to know what he was thinking."

The Lincoln wasn't built to be the common man's car: it was an elite machine for the extremely affluent and those hoping to be. Oddly, it sponsored an all-American show designed more for Chevy owners. "Using Julia as our spokesperson and doing the kind of commercials we did, we tried to give people the idea that you had to be special to be in this car," explained Bracken. "We wanted the Sullivan show to deliver people who would aspire to the Lincoln even if they never owned one." The car's regal bearing and advertised prestige rubbed off on the show. "It was a nice backlash," noted Bracken, "that the people who bought the Lincoln—and the dealers told us this—really felt that the car and its association with the Sullivan show was gratifying. It was an ego massage."

Sullivan's job was to massage the Lincoln dealers, who were often invited to attend the show and sit in the client booth to watch; this allowed them to tell their friends, families, and foes that they were showbiz insiders. "That was a real treat for them," recalled Bracken. Better yet, dealers might be introduced from the audience like celebrities. "Yeah, it was a real good thing for us. That way they felt very happy and content that the agency was doing a good job." The Lincoln dealers liked being identified as part of Ed Sullivan's TV family.

Sullivan was "a real worker" for Lincoln, recounts Bracken, going out of town to meet dealers and talk up the show. "I don't think he liked doing that stuff," Bracken told me. "I think he did it because he was a smart businessman." It was a close-knit team, he noted, adding that Meade and the president of Lincoln were very good friends. "He kept her in Lincolns comfortably."

When Marlo Lewis, the show's coproducer (who got few public strokes), was skeptical of Sullivan's rah-rah marketing efforts, Ed told him to be patient, that it would all pay off in the end. "Kiddo, have faith. We got a lot of years ahead, and we're moving right along." Many decades later, the prescient Sullivan said, "When I brought the show to television, people would tell me, 'What the hell are you doing on that damned thing?' On our block we had only two television sets, but even then I expected television to become big. And it naturally did, because it was free, it had pictures, and it could present stars in people's living rooms. It was a cinch to develop."

When it began, "Toast of the Town" was available live in only eight cities, connected by AT&T's new coaxial cable, which would take years to electronically unite America; Miami wasn't plugged in until 1954. The rest of the country saw the show on grainy kinescopes (images rephotographed on 16-millimeter film off the picture tube), but even "kines" were expensive, so they were reused and "bicycled" to other cities, often with ripped sprocket holes, jagged splices, and out-of-synch audio tracks; many cities had to wait weeks to get the "new" shows.

Despite technological primitivism and shabby production values, the new Sunday evening variety show immediately caught viewers' eyes—but then so did Roller Derby skaters endlessly circling a track. Entertainers that people had seen only from afar on the stage, in movies or newsreels, or in magazine photos, or had just heard over the radio, arrived right there in their homes—patchy, slanted, snowy, or out-of-synch, but they were there. Not big as life, but six-inch organisms squirming under a living room microscope.

Almost immediately—within weeks, in fact—NBC was forced to declare war on Sullivan's groundbreaking variety show and roll out its heavy artillery: Arthur Godfrey, who debuted on TV with two hugely popular shows simulcast on radio, "Arthur Godfrey's Talent Scouts" and "Arthur Godfrey and His Friends." The following season, 1949, NBC matched CBS with a satirical variety show, Max Liebman's "Admiral Broadway Revue," featuring new faces Sid Caesar and Imogene Coca. A year later, it was renamed "Your Show of Shows," a TV groundbreaker of a very different sort. Although George S. Kaufman famously said that "satire is what closes on Saturday night," it thrived on NBC on Saturday nights with Caesar, Coca, Carl Reiner, and Howard Morris. A few blocks away in New York, Ed Sullivan, the militantly nonperforming un-Caesar, ruled Sunday nights on "Toast of the Town," where satire was nearly unknown.

"Your Show of Shows" had a fanatical following in the urban, affluent, educated East, where its literary and cinematic references were reveled in. But Sullivan's "Toast of the Town" flourished everywhere, marketing new or soon-to-be-new names on TV—Crosby, Hope, Durante, Merman, Horne, Mary Martin, Count Basie, Victor Borge, Helen Hayes, and Marian Anderson. Marlo Lewis argued that "Toast of the Town" "created a new phenomenon—the mass video audience." In fact, Berle really discovered or created it, but Ed Sullivan expanded and exploited it. Ed Sullivan was AT&T to Berle's Alexander Graham Bell.

Sullivan's show and television matured together in the same lab. His and Caesar's massively successful, breakthrough shows encouraged the industry to boost the technology—using high-resolution cameras, zoom lenses, videotape, and special effects (slow motion, instant replays, superimposition, trick shots), much of it played with by Ernie Kovacs on his antic shows but experimented with first on "Toast of the Town."

I remember watching the Ed Sullivan show in Colorado Springs at the house of a classmate, the richest person I had ever met. When he brought me to his large house (three bedrooms was gigantic to me) he opened kitchen cupboards and asked me what I wanted; he had every imaginable can of Campbell's soup. He also had the first TV I had ever seen in a house. Some stores had them in the window, which drew bulging eyes, but I didn't know anybody who owned one. It was an RCA and had a big ball with metal ears on top that everybody twisted this way and that. Pike's Peak and other mountains caused lots of interference, so we had fuzz balls, streaks, herky-jerky images, and sudden blackouts when the screen turned pure gray. It was a comic scene when the image went out and everybody in the room, none of us with any mechanical abilities, tried to twist the damn ball and ears to bring back a juggler, an opera singer, or Stan Musial being introduced. We never thought they would ever perfect TV technology. We were so in awe just to get cloudy patches, so when you could see everything clearly it was a miracle. I thought—that's the price of watching this new thing—to get only snatches of Louis Prima or George Kirby. And one snatch was good enough, better than what I'd had before, which was just photos and newsprint.

Randy Poe, Long Beach, New York

As Marlo Lewis wrote, "The Sullivan show became CBS's testing ground whenever a new electronic device became available. We were the first to introduce any advanced techniques, as our variegated bill of fare afforded the latitude for experimental staging." Looking at those first shows 60 years later is like watching silent films of the first rattletrap Model-T's, but for its time the Sullivan show did some fairly dazzling Industrial Light & Magic stuff—a ballerina pirouetting in a singer's palm, a miniature chorus dancing atop a piano, an acrobat frozen in midair, singers on water skis.

During the show's second season, *Billboard* charged that Sullivan was blackmailing performers to appear on his show for next to nothing, and that they cooperated for fear of retribution or worse: a total snub in his column if they declined to appear. Forever defensive and stung by any hint of unethical conduct, Sullivan paid a quick call at the *Billboard* office with his show's budget and payroll sheet, revealing that neither he nor Lewis was coercing their stars, and that in fact, they not only were taking no salary but also were putting up some of their own money to buy talent. In the show's first weeks, Sullivan said, the most he ever had left over was $180, all of it plowed back into the show.

Billboard may have been easily satisfied, but the radio performers' union, the American Federation of Radio Artists (AFRA; later American Federation of Television and Radio Artists, or AFTRA), was unconvinced. They asked Sullivan to open his books, accusing him of exploiting talent. The union claimed that Sullivan and Lewis were routinely underpaying performers. Sullivan blamed another union, the American Guild of Variety Artists (AGVA), for not insisting their members demand higher payment from CBS. In the end, AFRA and Sullivan joined forces to pry more money from Paley to pay everybody. The union ruckus eventually led to the two producers' first weekly paychecks ($200 per show), and then CBS doubled their weekly budget to $6,000 to $8,000 for performers, out of which Sullivan got $2,000. Everyone walked away happy.

The show was by now a marquee event for entertainers. Any implied or semishady quid pro quo coercion on Sullivan's part—whether applied in print, in person, or on the phone, to badger entertainers into playing the show—ceased to be an issue. Performers lusted, furiously competed, and in time prayed for a single shot on Sullivan. Playing the show was box office gold for a singer's latest recording. Within a season or two, it became CBS's centerpiece show, the so-called Tiffany network's brightest light.

Even so, wicked criticism of Sullivan's on-air hosting fluffs continued, but the wisecracks became increasingly gentler and more good-
humored, and in the end he shared in the joke and wildly encouraged it.
He eventually wore down the opposition just by showing up Sunday after Sunday, year upon year, until the show was in the top five after two
years and never out of the top 20 until the end.

"Toast of the Town" established its credibility early. CBS left Sullivan
and Lewis alone to create shows, without meddling. The Ford agency
urged the host to become even more visible in the show—to perform in
sketches, sing duets, maybe dance; someone suggested he narrate an on-
air gossip column each week. He wisely declined. (Winchell tried just
that a few years later on ABC, looking silly and lost as he clacked away
on his teletype still wearing his trademark hat; the Winchell show soon
was canceled, though Sullivan charitably praised it in print.)

Sullivan was always more than an emcee on the air. When appearing
on a Dean Martin show in the 1970s, he hopped up on a piano, à la
Dino, with a Martinesque "Whee!" On a Flip Wilson show, Sullivan
played Lucille Ball's very gay caballero in a pink shirt and purple vest
and pants; Wilson's "Geraldine" tried to seduce Sullivan with the line,
"Some people may consider you their bread and butter, but to me you're
the toast of the town." On one Sullivan show, dancer Jacques d'Am-
boise tossed a ballerina into Sullivan's waiting arms; on another, Sullivan donned a cowboy outfit and shot up a saloon.

The guy could fool you, as in a rare moment with the McGuire Sisters
when he filled in for sister Dorothy, on maternity leave. In a strong
voice, Sullivan joined Phyllis and Christine in "Together," linking arms
with the girls and even managing a dance step. Only Ed Sullivan, the notoriously untalented host, could make it seem endearing. Seeing him
with the McGuires (or warbling "When Irish Eyes Are Smiling" with
Peter O'Toole), you almost wish he'd performed more. The personal
moments, when he joined a dog act, fed a bear, played straight man for
Topo Gigio, or was taught to swing a golf club by Ben Hogan, shoot
pool by Willie Hoppe, and deliver a punch by Muhammad Ali, humanized Sullivan in spite of himself. It revealed him as our earthbound link
to the glittering celebrity world of poise, glamour, and talent.

After the first season, things were going so well that Lewis quit his
job at the Blaine Thompson ad agency to concentrate on coproducing
"Toast of the Town." So when Sullivan asked Lewis to lunch at the Delmonico Hotel ("We've got a lot to talk about. Things are moving fast.
I'm making plans for the years ahead, and it's important for us to dis-

cuss them"), Lewis was surprised to find Sullivan's lawyer, Fred Backer, also at the table. After regaling Backer with stories of their early financial problems, as Lewis relates the scene in his memoir, Sullivan pulled their original partnership contract from his pocket and said, "Look, I don't want you to misunderstand, but the fact is—I've got star status now. I've worked like a dog and paid my dues . . . and our deal is not equitable. It has to be changed. Lord knows, you've done a great job, and we're a great team. But this old agreement of 50–50 doesn't make any sense anymore."

Backer translated, "What Ed is getting at is that he wants to change the deal. It's no longer fair to him. We want it to read 75% for him, 25% for you. That's it in a nutshell." Though he remained calm and businesslike, Lewis was stunned. He lost, and never fully regained, his respect and affection for Sullivan after that lunch. He told Sullivan, "You certainly deserve extra compensation for your starring role—but I think I've earned my way too. And for a long time neither one of us has gotten much for our efforts. But now, just when this baby of ours is ready to pay off, you want to cut me in half. I'll have to mull this over." Backer said their position was firm.

Sullivan tried to turn on all his persuasive power; he wasn't about to cave. "Come on, Marlo!" he told Lewis, who recalled glaring at the lawyer, blaming him for convincing Sullivan he was an indispensable star, "the hub that held the wheel together." Sullivan clutched Lewis's arm and said, "You're gonna get rich on this show. Don't take it so big. I need you, you need me. You gotta remember, I'm a lot older than you. And without my muscle there never would've been a show in the first place."

Lewis was well aware that Sullivan had gone out on a limb for the show, and had sucked up some harsh personal blows from critics and foes, but was also aware that he had risked a lot, too. What deeply upset him was that Sullivan waited to renegotiate the contract after Lewis had severed his ties to the ad business to devote himself to television. Stewing after lunch, Lewis stalked over to CBS at 52nd and Madison, where Hubbell Robinson, the network's new vice president of programming, saw him and said, "What's the matter? You look as though you've just come from a funeral." Lewis answered, "You could say that. Call it the death of a partnership. I just came from a meeting with Sullivan and his strong-arm lawyer. They want me to tear up our deal and, for auld lang syne, to take the shit end of the stick."

Robinson laughed and tried to soothe Lewis's anger. He advised him not to quit. For Robinson, such showbiz hardball was just another day at the office. "I'm laughing because the network's been through this kind of contract shenanigans a hundred times. A star is a star is a star. In the beginning he's a pussycat, begging to be loved, waiting for tidbits, purring with gratitude. Feed him enough and he turns into a tiger, anxious to devour anything in sight." Robinson went on: "Let's face it—Sullivan's becoming a big star and he's going to get bigger. So he clobbered you. Next time it'll be us. Sit tight for a day or two. CBS needs him; CBS needs you. Act as if nothing has happened. Keep your cool. Trust me."

A few days later, Lewis got a call from Paley's office, on the set, a rare event. Paley's secretary asked if Lewis could meet for lunch the next day at Paley's apartment in the St. Regis with Robinson; Frank Stanton, the head of the business department . . . and Sullivan. Over lunch, in an effort to mollify Lewis and Sullivan and heal their breach, Paley offered Lewis a position beyond his coproducing duties at "Toast of the Town"—executive producer for *all* CBS variety and comedy shows. "I want both of you to make CBS your home and to be an integral part of the network," said Paley. Lewis called the new contract "a triumph of diplomatic maneuvering." The show had been saved by Paley, whom Lewis called "one of the most astute and sensitive negotiators I have ever known."

So the rift was swiftly healed—or rather, papered over with money: a new $15,000 weekly budget gave Sullivan $900 and Lewis $600, plus an escalation clause, which meant that, if they achieved certain goals, their compensation would escalate accordingly. Lewis also got a fancy executive suite to celebrate his new title. Everyone left smiling, especially Sullivan, who told Lewis, "We both got what we wanted, kiddo! With Paley in back of us, the sky's the limit! Forget what happened [the other day]. It's totally irrelevant now." But Sullivan's arm-bending lunch always stuck in Lewis's craw.

In 1954, with the show in its heyday, Sullivan hired the high-profile showbiz lawyer Arnold Grant, who took his client to MCA's razzle-dazzle agent, Sonny Werblin (later owner of the New York Jets), who got CBS to give Sullivan a 20-year contract and a grandiose new $50,000-a-week budget, of which Sullivan got $8,000. Best of all, CBS finally agreed to change the name from "Toast of the Town," and "The Ed Sullivan Show" first aired on September 18, 1955.

The show was still owned by CBS, which had a two-week cancellation clause. (Before that, CBS hadn't been ready to rename "Toast of the Town" as "The Ed Sullivan Show," still worried that the host would retire, die, or, worse, bolt for another network.) Finally, Sullivan would no longer be introduced at the top of the show as merely the "host" of the show. From now on, announcer Art Hannes would bring him on with: *"And now here's the star of our show—the nationally syndicated colum-nist of the* New York Daily News, *Ed Sullivan!"* Sullivan was 53, and his star was atwinkle at last.

CHAPTER 10

It's the World, on Line One

The very first phone call I got after a TV show on Helen
Morgan [that] I did in 1957 was from him. I'd just finished
the show—literally. The red light went off and the phone
rang and it was Ed Sullivan calling. . . . He was on top of
everything.

Polly Bergen

Although on the surface "The Ed Sullivan Show" just looked like vaudeville in a box, that was far too simple a reading of what went on every
Sunday night at Studio 50. The workaholic ethic and authenticity that
CBS's Tony Miner and Ford's Joe Bayne first saw in Sullivan were keys
to the show's success and longevity. The variety acts and the big names
were major parts of the story, for sure, but the nuts and bolts—and major "gets"—largely came from Ed Sullivan. Away from the screen, he
was not your Everyman next door, the stammering tongue-tied talker
unable to finish a sentence. When he wanted to, he could exude warmth,
even emotion. Today, because of his honest yet idiosyncratic persona,
Sullivan might even be considered, yes, cool.

The comedian Orson Bean told me, "He probably made people feel
superior, which is the greatest thing you can give an audience. He was
your uncle that's not good at parties. He was kinda stiff, but he had a basic warmth underneath and he wanted desperately to be liked, which is
why he liked doing stuff with Topo Gigio. He was liked in *spite* of his
attempts to be liked."

He was on a first-name basis with the greatest celebrities in show business, grabbing them by the arm, punching them affectionately on the
shoulder, rocking on his heels as he flung an arm around them onstage,
shaking hands with apparent intimacy, beckoning performers to his side
with that big roundhouse gesture, nuzzling women, always whispering
sweet nothings into entertainers' ears under the applause.

"Yanking stars, then pushing them off stage," Marlo Lewis wrote, "Ed made himself a proprietary, authoritative figure. So there was no need for him to perform." He was a theatrical God, pulling the strings, manipulating the stars, and making miracles happen for an hour every Sunday night.

But hosting was only the tip of this bottomless impresario iceberg. "He was the best producer of his era," observed TV critic John Leonard. "Television is a producer's medium. . . . All Ed cared about was Sunday night on CBS, forever, reinventing his show each new season for a tribe of ghostly millions." Jim Bishop, in his 1957 Sullivan profile in the *New York Journal-American,* commented, "One is led inexorably to the conclusion that this man is too easily dismissed. By all the rules of the theater, this man is a cipher. . . . When he tries to smile, this dyspeptic little man looks like he's trying to swallow a quince whole. . . . [But] he has outclassed all of his talented detractors. They are gone. He is here—and on the top. In his ninth year he can point to the fact that his show has been in the top five longer than any other show. Ed Sullivan, once a sportswriter, is now the King of Television."

Ed was fond of reducing his recipe for success to a formula. "Open big, have a good comedy act, put in something for the children, keep the show clean" was Sullivan's boilerplate line for interviewers, but it didn't probe into *how* his shows were crafted. Sullivan resurrected an ancient formula—variety—but he reshaped it, streamlined it, heightened it, and updated it. He quickly sensed the fickle, impatient nature of viewers; he didn't make audiences wait for the headliners, and all but abolished the headliner mentality. Everybody had near-equal footing on the show, although he was obsessed with Big Names. Later, he admitted that a few of his major botches were due to his overheated newsman's nose for scoops, like trying to engineer Ingrid Bergman's return to America—on his very stage—after an adulterous affair sent her into European exile. "I was thinking as a columnist. She *never* forgave me," he later confessed.

Sullivan always likened his show to a newspaper: "When I was on the New York *Evening Mail* I used to do the makeup. You know, putting in your one-column boxes, cuts [photos] in here and there, you could make the page interesting to look at. My shows were just like a newspaper—it had sports, drama, movies, celebrities." Not to mention the show's most unifying aspect—Ed's keen sense of newsworthiness. "I'm a newspaperman. I view things as a newspaperman." When he telephoned people, he often would announce himself as "Ed Sullivan of the *Daily News,*" not of CBS.

Every performer walked through that same green curtain, each one treated by the host-producer as just another hired hand. The implicit understanding was that everyone on his show was a star or he or she wouldn't be there—if not a star here, then in Budapest or Shanghai, wherever. Even big stars had to earn their way on the show and wait for an approving word from Ed afterward—a ritual that Johnny Carson later formalized by rare engraved vocal invitations to sit on the famous sofa and spar with His Royal Hostness. Sullivan didn't know from sofas. His version of the sit-down chat was a personalized footnote ("I used t'know yer father," "Y'know, I first saw you in 1937 at the old Palace Theatre . . . ," "That's wonderful! Jes' terrific! Where can we see ya next?").

Sullivan labored to induce movie stars to appear in a then-scary new medium, persuading video-shy celebrities to make their TV debuts with him by promising that, "although they didn't need the dough, we could present them in a manner that would add to their prestige, not diminish it." That's how he tallied up endless, famous TV debuts—Bob Hope, Bing Crosby, Dean Martin and Jerry Lewis, Vaughn Monroe, Gloria Swanson, Hedy Lamarr, Cole Porter, Fred Astaire, Richard Rodgers, Margaret Truman, James Cagney, Lena Horne, Lana Turner, and on and on.

Sullivan explained his savvy movie-star MO: "Getting them for one appearance was difficult enough," he said, "but the main idea was to satisfy them so completely, in presentation, photography, music, that not only would they come back a second time but they would persuade their equally famous friends that our show was the proper setting for their TV debuts." He took big stars under his avuncular wing, after they'd been softened up by Marlo Lewis.

Lewis found it easier to entice Hollywood film stars to appear on TV once he had snared Fred Astaire, a firm holdout. Monica Lewis told me that, when Astaire told her brother, " 'The studio won't let me do it,' Marlo reassured him, 'Fred, I'm gonna build you a staircase, and you will walk down it, you will meet Ed and you will greet the audience and he'll ask you about a new picture or something and you will take a bow.' " Marlo told his sister, "This guy walking is better than any other 12 dancers."

The radical notion that movie royalty would unveil themselves on lumpen TV was sealed with an hour-long tribute to Walt Disney. In 1961, Sullivan said, "Hollywood finally recognized that it was safe to enter into an alliance with us." They would have been fools not to. Sullivan so lovingly framed, and drooled over, movie stars that he turned television into a safe house for wary big-screen luminaries terrified of a new, daunting, possibly damaging turf—much as silent film stars had shied away from talkies.

It was one thing to be heard on radio, or to pose for a feature in *Photoplay,* and quite another to let America gaze at them live, scriptless, emotionally naked, and unprotected in fans' homes. Rosalind Russell turned down the lead in a TV version of "Lady in the Dark," saying, "Live television isn't for me. The wrong camera picks you up by mistake and your career can be ruined. No thank you!" Bette Davis said, "No movie queen past 25 can possibly look the same on the home screen as she does on big theater screens"; or to paraphrase Norma Desmond, there were no small actors then, just small screens.

Despite his lifelong affection for Broadway, Sullivan was among the first to recognize the new supremacy of Hollywood over New York. His tributes to studio moguls like Disney, Zanuck, and Goldwyn propelled Sullivan to leap into bed with the movie industry. He was an ex officio Hollywood talent broker, promoting upcoming films in exchange for interviews with film stars. A Sullivan admirer commented that Ed had turned TV from a threat to the film industry into a wing of Hollywood's publicity machine.

By the end of the 1950s, he was a full-time marketing director for the movie academy, plugging movies like "Anatomy of a Murder," "The Diary of Anne Frank," and "Ben-Hur," showing clips and introducing the films' stars in the audience or cooing over them onstage. Appearing in the flesh on TV and not merely, as before, at premieres in newsreels, gave movie stars a reality that, in the end, stripped away their shimmering glamour. Peering at stars up close was a quick thrill, but it reduced the excitement of seeing them larger than life on the big screen. On the little screen, they were reduced to mere human creatures.

Sullivan first struck ratings gold (a 63.4 in the Trendex ratings) with his Disney salute in 1961, which helped pave the way for Sullivan's later, lavish movieland salutes. Disney by then had built his own cozy promotional castle in Televisionland, hosting a hugely successful Sunday night show on NBC, "The Wonderful World of Color." Disney wound up surpassing Sullivan's historic 23 years on the air by four years. Unknowingly, Sullivan had helped create a major rival, a threat, and a hydra-headed cultural behemoth.

The public's conflict-of-interest detectors were less finely tuned in the 1950s and 1960s. Pushing a big new movie on a TV show was considered a legitimate form of reporting the news—and in fact it still is. The TV industry has turned into an incestuous arm of the movie industry. Endless film stars turned infotainers appear on talk shows to push their new product. Today's talk shows, left to their own imaginations, would collapse without a parade of movie stars. All of this shameless showbiz conglomerate logrolling began with Ed Sullivan's seduction of Hollywood.

For the pragmatic Sullivan, it was just a new way to grab big names (that is, ratings) while justifying the trade-off by reporting on a new movie. Today, when even intellectually serious TV or radio hosts like PBS's Charlie Rose or NPR's Terry Gross snuggle up to film stars and directors of new movies, they're stepping into Sullivan's giant footsteps by saluting new films—often before they even open, and often despite critical pans or public apathy. But Ed Sullivan was America's first movie-star stalker.

He often boasted of his many TV firsts, but some were nothing to brag about—such as the entertainment-industrial complex that Sullivan helped erect by shilling for new movies in exchange for reclusive stars' exclusive appearances. That provided the seed for today's Disney ownership of ABC, General Electric's purchase of NBC, and Westinghouse's snatching up of CBS. "Toast of the Town" was simply an early creator of talent software, an entertainment content provider for multiple media delivery systems. Sullivan's was the first TV show to screen scenes from upcoming movies, even though studios had forbidden their stars to show their faces on TV, fearful of promoting television. Once the studios embraced TV as a mass-marketing unit of the movie industry, they realized that a 30-minute sales pitch about the making of, say, "Moby Dick" was a wise investment. Meanwhile, Sullivan leveraged his TV clout for higher viewer numbers. He told *Look* magazine's Eleanor Harris, "When my ratings were down, I felt as if I were watching the blood run out of me. Your rating is the entire expression of your work."

Around 1955, a watershed year for TV, television itself discovered gold in them thar films. Westerns, sitcoms, and detective shows—the industry's bread and butter—all packed up and moved their wagons west to Los Angeles, hauling most of the entertainment industry with them. Four studios—Disney, Warner Bros., 20th Century-Fox, and M-G-M— became producers of major TV series, giving them almost monopolistic power to promote their theatrical movies. Shows like "M-G-M Parade" and "Warner Brothers Presents" became video floats parading new screen releases.

Sullivan, a tasty slice of the studios' business pie chart, dutifully presented hour-long bouquets to Hollywood's founding fathers—Disney, Warner, Zanuck, and Goldwyn. Sullivan's studio-mogul "tributes," which included scenes from soon-to-be-released films, were raw publicity disguised as entertainment news. Sullivan saw himself as a kind of co–movie producer, using TV to sell cinematic popcorn. Once TV and movies married, becoming lifetime partners, it was the end of live TV and, most sadly, of live dramatic shows. Filming sitcoms, westerns, and cop shows was easier, controllable, and cost-efficient; they could also be rerun indefinitely. Television now became just another kind of movie, only much smaller in its scope and its dreams.

Despite temptations to head to California, Sullivan himself remained blissfully rooted in New York. It's impossible to imagine "The Ed Sullivan Show" coming out of Los Angeles, like Johnny Carson's "Tonight" show, which moved there in 1972. Sullivan's show kept its brassy New York edge to the end, refusing to stray far off Broadway; CBS journeyed west to erect Television City, but Sullivan preferred Theater City. By 1960, a New York show was an anomaly. *Variety* wrote, "Today, a live New York origination tailored specifically for TV is becoming an occasion for rejoicing." Television historian James L. Braughman noted, "The critics, certainly those based on the East Coast, regarded the relocation of production in California as a cultural disaster for television, the newest medium."

So TV lost its immediacy, its theatricality, and its individuality, the spontaneously vital creative juices that fueled early live drama and helped lift television off the ground and make it unique. Aging movie matinee idols who had picked up loose change on radio were now extending their lives on TV. Dick Powell, Charles Boyer, David Niven, and Ida Lupino hosted "Four Star Playhouse," taking turns starring in undemanding, often mediocre, half-hour tele-movies. Ralph Bellamy became the "Man against Crime." William Boyd was an aging western star languishing in Hollywood until he became TV's first big (and only silver-haired) cowboy hero, Hopalong Cassidy.

Sullivan, the booster of new technology, seemed to welcome the demise of live TV, perhaps because it made his own live show increasingly rare. He told *TV Guide,* "Films mean rerun revenue, simultaneous showings, better lighting, and a chance to use material from the whole wide world." But he conceded, "Live TV offers that all-important spontaneity, timeliness, and lower production costs." As George Burns put it, "A live show is never seen again. So if I happen to say anything that

strikes you as funny, please laugh now. It's the last chance you'll ever get."
TV's finest young actors (Paul Newman, Joanne Woodward, Robert
Redford, Richard Kiley, John Cassavetes, Ben Gazzara, Eva Marie Saint,
Jack Klugman, Kim Stanley, Grace Kelly, Sidney Poitier, James Dean),
directors (John Frankenheimer, Delbert Mann, Sidney Lumet, Fred Coe,
Arthur Penn), and playwrights (Rod Serling, Paddy Chayefsky, Tad
Mosel, Reginald Rose, Horton Foote) all left nonlive television for
movies, filmed series, or theater.

Sullivan found a way to attract movie-crazed American viewers by
relying no longer on New York stage and nightclub performers but on
film clips and movie stars. As early as 1953, Sullivan was promoting
Hollywood. He signed a pact with 20th Century-Fox to hold "miniature
world premieres" each month of the studio's new films. This was the
first time Hollywood allowed its product—both films and stars—to be
seen on television. The deal gave a huge boost to Fox films like "Titanic," "Gentlemen Prefer Blondes," and "Call Me Madam." The two-
year agreement called for movie stars to make nonperforming personal
appearances to hype their movies on "Toast of the Town," which led to
Sullivan's battle with Frank Sinatra, who bitterly attacked the TV host in
1955 for not paying him enough to appear on the show to talk up "Guys
and Dolls"; a feud ensued.

That same year, reviewing Sullivan's hour-long show about the filming of "Mister Roberts," under a headline reading " 'Mister Roberts'
Rides Free: Sullivan Show Is One Long Ad for Movie," Jack Gould wrote
in the New York Times, "Give Hollywood a little longer and it will be
turning television into a coast-to-coast trailer." He said that the Sullivan
show, rather than providing an insightful history of the studio, was a
60-minute advertisement for the upcoming movie version of a Broadway
hit. Gould later rapped Sullivan's 1954 hagiography of Metro-Goldwyn-
Mayer, calling it, again, "in essence a long trailer for M-G-M" relieved
by some black-and-white clips from classic Metro films. In 1956, Sullivan did an hour-long tribute to John Huston, devoted half a show to the
movie "High Society," and filmed an on-location segment on the making of "Fire Down Below" with Rita Hayworth and Robert Mitchum.
Now actively marketing movies, Sullivan flew to Los Angeles that year
to emcee the premiere of Burt Lancaster's "Trapeze," quite literally becoming a video ringmaster for the movie.

Sensing that he might become a Hollywood tycoon himself, Sullivan
jumped into moviemaking in 1959. He set up a CBS production company to make six pilot films for TV series (partly a tax dodge similar to

one set up by CBS for James Arness to keep him from leaving "Gun-smoke"). Sullivan wanted to produce a dramatic series of famous news-paper stories, but it never happened. Flexing his new corporate muscles, he discussed with CBS selling foreign rights to videos of his shows, giv-ing him half the residuals.

Aware of Sullivan's prowess and his self-booster bones, Jack Warner decided in 1955 to make a biographical movie called "The Ed Sullivan Story"—scratch, scratch—with Sullivan producing and starring in it for $100,000. The film ran aground after Sullivan refused to surrender con-trol of the movie or even to collaborate with the legendary producer. The movie had a $1 million budget—huge for its day—but the auto-cratic Warner, famous for battles with Bette Davis and James Cagney, re-fused to cave in. Two omnivorous control freaks, Warner and Sullivan, were headed for a clash of titanic egos.

Warner politely asked Sullivan for a movie treatment and got back a six-page synopsis that was a patchwork version of Sullivan's show with a biographical narrative, not unlike his own celebrity tributes—a kind of "This Is My Life." Warner saw the movie as a drama, not a documen-tary with dog acts. He hired veteran screenwriter Irving Wallace, who fashioned a script based on Sullivan's life, but Wallace added melodra-matic flourishes: Sylvia leaves Ed when the show's sagging ratings absorb all his time, but, in a climactic scene, she reappears with a Las Vegas singer who is so stupendous that his ratings soar and the Sullivans reunite. Fadeout.

Sullivan was embarrassed by the script, hated it, and asked that it be rewritten. Warner—ever mindful that the finished film would get a huge sendoff on Sullivan's show—ordered Wallace to try again. In the rewrite, Ed comes to his own rescue. Relying on his fortitude and programming genius, he pulls the show out of the ratings doldrums by concocting a brilliant, groundbreaking show that blends jazz and opera. In this draft, Sullivan's producing skills are magnified. James Maguire, in his detailed account, said that the rewrite depicted Sullivan "as a driven, competitive showman who assesses the opposition and out-produces it at every turn"—Ed's own lifelong view of himself.

But Sullivan couldn't quit meddling. He had second thoughts about the depiction of him as a combative, two-fisted producer (which contra-dicted his carefully crafted image as a benign Everyman). He also didn't think the script properly depicted how he had defeated all the critics who had debased and ridiculed him. The movie, he hoped, would validate his professional life. It would be his ultimate vindication. In Sullivan's scenario synopsis, he wrote, "So this is the story of a guy who worked like a bastard in TV and found his employment jeopardized by the critics, some of the network brass, and others." He wanted the script to reveal how he had emerged victorious over all the forces aligned against him and to include interviews with viewers telling why they so loved the show.

Sullivan wanted the film to be factual but was also aware that the truth about his sometimes ornery off-screen self, the embattled producer and critical punching bag, might soil his image as a benevolent TV presence. As Maguire noted, "The Warner Bros. script portrayed the other man, the one behind the curtain, the competitor, the ambition-driven workaholic. This was a more interesting man, surely a better film subject, but . . . it wasn't the persona he wanted splashed on movie screens across the country."

When Sullivan ignored Wallace's version and wrote a third draft, Warner, who had been juggling the film's shooting schedule to accommodate Sullivan's rewrites, threw up his hands and sent an angry telegram to Ed's attorney, saying, "We will have to be a magician to put this together. As you know, this is not like putting on a TV show. People expect to see something. If [Sullivan] is going to try and ad-lib this picture as he does his TV show, it won't come off, nor will we produce it that way." Sullivan, an inveterate last-minute tinkerer on his show, was testing Jack Warner's patience, but the studio boss sent Wallace and two other writers back to the typewriter for another rewrite.

They sent it to Sullivan for his approval—"by phone if possible," as time was running out. Sullivan, undaunted, tore apart the latest script and sent a note to his attorney saying, "I don't think Irving Wallace will ever be able to write the story." Warner angrily canceled the movie the moment he learned that Sullivan was futzing with the script yet again, eight months after the film had been announced. Sullivan explained to the press that he couldn't interrupt his TV producing chores to work on the film, but it was his incorrigible need for the final word that wrecked the movie, one that might still be a compelling film now that the subject is no longer around to rewrite it into the ground.

If the public underrated Sullivan's on-camera power, they were almost totally unaware of his behind-the-camera work as a wheeling and dealing producer, the sturdy mogul behind the on-screen stumblebum. Producers are the least understood operatives in show business. Audiences suspect they have something to do with raising money, but no idea of the artistry, personality, and often chicanery that goes into this fuzziest of titles.

The executive producer is where it all starts and very often ends. He (or she) makes the delicate machine hum—finds the performers, director, composer, and everyone else. He figures out how to budget the enterprise, and hires and fires. A producer is the glue that holds everything together, or watches it fly apart, but he is much more than that. He must be a brilliant tactician, a persuader, a person with vast amounts of charm, guile, and muscle. He must know how to flatter and browbeat, to coo, cajole, bluff, and fast-talk, to anticipate disaster and work every angle, to be cheerleader and both good and bad cop, to create a show and then peddle it to an often apathetic public.

All of these gifts Ed Sullivan had in his bulging bag of tricks. The opposition, even his own network, misjudged him and badly underestimated him at the start. They measured him by his unconvincing on-camera self, a mere decoy for the shrewd, stubborn, tough-minded showbiz wizard who took over the reins from the mumbling host once the red light went off.

Sullivan assessed his genius with unblinking candor: "I am the best damned showman in television. People who work on the show think so too. I really believe, immodestly, that I am a better showman and have better taste than most and have a better 'feel' as to what the public wants because of my newspaper experience. And I know quicker than anybody else on Sunday nights whether we have done a good show or not."

Sullivan's instinct for entertaining people was shaped by all the vaudeville shows he had seen as a boy in Port Chester, and later in New York as a sportswriter and gossip columnist with an unquenchable lust for talent in any form. He rarely had an intuitive eye for raw or unique talent; it first had to prove itself elsewhere. Yet most producers might not have discerned the broad appeal of, say, Topo Gigio and be willing to risk giving the mouse marionette a national spotlight in the network's most glittering showcase.

Sullivan's mimic Will Jordan told me, "Almost everyone who was on the Steve Allen show became a star. The Sullivan show boosted no one's career. They were already established. They had me, they had Topo Gigio, they had Rickie Layne. But compare that to Steve Lawrence, Eydie Gorme, José Jiminéz [Bill Dana], Don Knotts, Tom Poston, Andy Williams." Bob Thompson, the TV historian at Syracuse University, commented to me, "The Ed Sullivan show reacted to the culture much more than it actually introduced. He was a gatekeeper, but by no means a discoverer. The Beatles and Elvis ware perfect examples. He was less an innovator and more a guy who kept his ear to the track on what the innovations were. He seemed to always get people right at the time the break happened, so that when he introduced them it looked like he invented them."

Sullivan once told a reporter he had "found this girl [Barbra Streisand] singing in a Greenwich Village nightclub. No one had heard of her above 14th Street. I saw she was a great talent and put her on the show three times. From there, she was in orbit. But in all the stories about her career, she has never said one word about my giving her that first big break." Maybe because, in fact, Streisand had by then (1962) already broken through in a hit Broadway show, "I Can Get It for You Wholesale," won a Tony nomination, and recorded her first album, and was a must-see sensation at the Bon Soir, where Sullivan saw her. It's unlikely he ever would have put her on his show cold, after one engagement at a tiny Greenwich Village club.

There were rare isolated examples of Sullivan sprinkling star-making fairy dust. In 1961, an unknown group of Irish musicians, the Clancy Brothers with Tommy Makem, appeared on the show and, "by the end of a fiery, 14-minute live performance," Joe Lertola reported in *Time,* they "catapulted Irish folk music into the mainstream." Connie Francis pointed out to me, "When Johnny Mathis was just starting to get a lot of air play with his first hit, 'It's Not for Me to Say,' within a couple of weeks Sullivan had him signed up for five shows. He could sense things nationally, like the Elvis thing. He just knew what to put on." Pat Boone added, "You might call it a genius—he just had this radar for what people wanted to see."

Maybe, but his longtime producer Bob Precht downplayed Sullivan's legendary intuitive genius, telling me, "That was certainly people's impression. I honestly don't know. If someone was in the headlines, he grabbed 'em. Often it was just instigated by a good agent or manager who would say, 'Take a look at this kid.' "

When Sullivan was stirred into action by a performer he'd seen, he would reach for a telephone to book them as if calling in a breaking news story. "He knew how to charm people over the phone to get them," recalled comic Pat Harrington Jr. After catching Polly Bergen in the Helen Morgan tribute on TV, Sullivan called her to say he had just caught the show. It wouldn't be seen in LA for another three hours. Bergen told me he was the very first person to call and say, "You're go-

ing to get an Emmy with this. I want you to come back and reprise the
Helen Morgan songs on my show."

Bergen added, "His was a very powerful eye who really recognized
up and coming stars. He was on top of everything. Nobody treated him
lightly, even if he couldn't remember your name—'Polly Belgram!' 'Patti
Bergram!' It was ludicrous. He could never remember anyone's name,
and there were no corrections—it went on as it went on. His was the
first show I did when I got back to New York. I reprised two songs from
'The Helen Morgan Story,' I got nominated for an Emmy, and I won!"
She noted, "At that point, I was just kind of a middle-rung entertainer, a
run-of-the mill, young, coming-up girl singer. I wasn't even an actress
then. I was one of the better girl singers around, but there were a lot of
them. I was lucky because I was very pretty and good at what I did, but
the Sullivan show kept me in the public eye."

Sullivan's few private producer passions usually meshed with the public's, peculiar though it seemed at times. Exhibit A: Señor Wences, a Spanish ventriloquist with a heavy accent, whose act consisted of brief conversations with a face drawn in lipstick and greasepaint on his fist and
with a head in a box whose entire dialogue was "S'awright!" Even now it
seems an absurd, unlikely act, yet it was irresistibly amusing. The routine
defies explanation if you never saw it. But Sullivan just dug Wences, revealed him to America on December 31, 1950, and put him on the show
23 times; the aging ventriloquist became an institution on two continents.

Other distinctly Sullivan imports and TV coups included Edith Piaf
and Patachou from France, and the Singing Nun (Sister Sourire), whom
he pursued to her nunnery in Fichermont, Belgium, to tape her for two
appearances in 1964. Sullivan had by then grown more efficient at booking far-flung novelty acts: a crew would go to Europe, tape someone,
edit the act, and slip it into an otherwise live show—but viewers assumed all the acts they saw were live. He also brought back (alive or
taped) José Greco and Andrés Segovia from Spain, the Vienna Boys
Choir, British music-hall stars Gracie Fields and Hermione Gingold, the
Dublin Players, a newly defected Russian dance team, and from Israel, a
young violin prodigy. The Sullivans were at Churchill Hall in Haifa
when a twelve-year-old boy on crutches played his violin: Itzhak Perlman. "Ed was very touched," recalled staffer Bob Weitman, "and he
said to me immediately, 'I've got to have that kid on my show.'"

Whenever playing defense, Sullivan would tick off his famous hard-
earned firsts: "Toast of the Town" was the first TV show to feature

hour-long tributes to entertainment icons, which amounted to early live versions of A&E's "Biography" series, and sundry TV "specials" devoted to showbiz legends. The only comparable concept was Ralph Edwards's treacly "This Is Your Life." Sullivan's was the first variety program to do themed shows, like an hour about the Ringling Bros. circus.

Just for the record: Sullivan's show also claimed to be the first to broadcast from outside a studio; to use balcony cameras and rear-screen projection; to turn cameras on the studio audience and introduce celebrities out front; to use a split screen on an entertainment show; to hide cameras in the sets and suspend them from the boom; to present a performer in front of a set in a different city; to present a complete ice show; to have a permanent chorus line; to preview forthcoming movies; to take its own equipment to Moscow and perform an American variety show for the Russian people; and to introduce scores of stars never previously seen on TV, including dozens of opera stars and British megastars like Noël Coward and Vivien Leigh, as well as international companies like the Danish Royal Ballet, England's Royal Ballet, and the D'Oyly Carte Opera Company, with its Gilbert & Sullivan repertory.

Sullivan introduced us to worlds we didn't know or never thought about—my first ballet dancer, Hot Lips Page, Georgia Gibbs, names I'd heard on records but got to see "in person" on the Sullivan show. It made me want to see a real live concert. I was about 14, and one of the first images I remember was seeing Jersey Joe Wolcott, who had a suit and tie on and looked like one of the salesmen who sold auto parts like my father. Later I saw Marciano, Joe Louis, and other famous figures for the first time as normal people in everyday attire. A big letdown. But I remember how exciting it was waiting for the show to begin. I got my first introduction to the real, live Vaughn Monroe, and remember how plain and normal he also looked. It was the first time I saw Vic Damone, Teresa Brewer, Don Cornell, and the Ink Spots doing that close harmony right in the living room! Jack E. Leonard I remember, Phil Foster, Sonny Tufts, and Peggy Lee. It was too much in a way, because I was an addicted reader of newspapers and magazines and knew who all these people were, but didn't know what they looked or sounded or dressed like, or how they moved. That show was like somebody opened a magic box and out popped all these famous people.

Elsworth Quarrells, New York City

It was also the first, and maybe last, show to telecast a variety show from a glacier in Juneau, Alaska, where Jill Corey sang "I'm Sitting on Top of the World." Furthermore, Sullivan's was the first TV show to win two Peabody Awards (one for its "contribution to international under-standing"), and Sullivan himself was festooned with honors and decora-tions from every branch of the military service (in thanks for all the show's presentations of military drill teams) and from many foreign governments—Israel, Italy, and France, to mention three.

Another original idea was Sullivan's hour-long tributes aired between 1951 and 1953, shows that included "The Cole Porter Story," "The Robert E. Sherwood Story," "The Samuel Goldwyn Story," "The Bert Lahr Story," "The Bea Lillie Story," "The ASCAP Story," and "A Night at Sophie Tucker's House." Sullivan wrote the tributes himself, earning the sobriquet "TV's Boswell." It's inconceivable today that a major prime-time network TV show would pay hour-long homages to a Broad-way songwriter, a serious playwright, a movie mogul, a British musical star, or a show business licensing company. The closest we have to Sulli-van's salutes are the Kennedy Center Honors, which squeeze five mini-salutes into two hours, not periodically but once a year. No such showcase exists on commercial TV. Imagine CBS setting aside an hour at 8 o'clock Sunday nights to pay tribute to Stephen Sondheim, Edward Albee, Har-vey Weinstein, and the League of New York Theater Producers.

The modest audience bow, a favorite Sullivan device for staying on top of breaking news, was so identified with Sullivan that no other variety show dared steal it. Unbeknownst to viewers, the carefully placed athletes in Sullivan's studio audience were paid to be there, just as other celebrities were; some, like Rocky Marciano, earned $1,500 to stand up and wave.

Sullivan's sports cheerleading likely led to TV's allegiance to football, golf, boxing, baseball, auto racing, and similar competitions. It was a rare Sullivan show that failed to spotlight a famous athlete or the new cham-pion of something or other, from an archery ace to the American Kennel Club's top dog. Sullivan assumed we were all dying to meet the new wel-terweight champ, the world's best lacrosse team, or Argentina's no. 1 diver. It would have been rude to yawn. He even featured the winning jockey of the Hambletonian Sweepstakes. To most viewers, harness racing was an odd, arcane, geezer event. Did anyone but Ed Sullivan give a damn who won the Hambletonian? But Ed had grown up watching trotters at Yonkers Raceway (he later owned two himself) and was its most ardent publicist; one harness race was even named for him, "The Ed Sullivan Pace."

Sullivan behaved as if it were perfectly normal that Jane Powell, Edward G. Robinson, the Sugar Bowl's game-winning quarterback, the prime minister of Bhutan, or a visiting mayor of Cleveland would be in his audience. It was almost as if Cary Grant, Bette Davis, Mickey Rooney, or John Gielgud had dropped by as a personal favor to Ed, because they were his close chums. Stars were willing to play audience stooge in exchange for Sullivan's plug of their new film, play, or Las Vegas appearance—just as stars do now on late-night TV as the host engages them in make-believe conversation (extended versions of Sullivan's awkward curtain chats), when a wave from the audience would be plenty, and faster. Pop star "interviews" with Leno, Letterman, and O'Brien to plug a new movie, CD, TV series, book, perfume, whatever, are really just long-winded updates of Sullivan's onstage love-ins.

In 1967, a CBS press release estimated that Sullivan had introduced at least 2,000 people in the audience—not just your run-of-the-mill stars and sports heroes but also military leaders, songwriters, directors, authors, producers, military men, religious leaders. "Sometimes," noted the release, "depending on the popular appeal of the celebrity, a bow from his seat will not suffice, and Sullivan will have the person come up onstage for a handshake and to let the viewers at home get a longer and better look at him or her. There can be little doubt that these appearances have become over almost 20 years a unique and titillating TV bit of Americana." No doubt at all. As Robert Goulet told me, "He had everybody up there! The whole damn world was up there!"

CHAPTER II

Sacred Sunday Rite

He never expected to be a national treasure.
                    Monica Lewis, singer

Sunday was no day of rest for Ed Sullivan. For America during the 1950s and early 1960s, it was the day everyone else indulged in family rituals that usually concluded at 8 P.M. with the sacramental viewing of "The Ed Sullivan Show." The show became an anchor for the American weekend, as essential as attending church, washing the car, and going over the bridge and through the tunnel to grandmother's house for dinner. The fact that the show was on Sunday nights gave it a special meaning. "Sunday night on radio had been the biggest night," Will Jordan pointed out to me—it was Jack Benny's and Walter Winchell's night.

The Sullivan show was officially recognized as a joyous American holiday in "Bye Bye Birdie." The family in the musical, backed by a chorus, sing "Hymn for a Sunday Evening," composer Charles Strouse and lyricist Lee Adams's salute to Sunday's secular spiritual leader, Ed Sullivan. Strouse said that the image he had in his head was a chorus of heavenly angels, as in "Song of Bernadette." The composer asked the drummer to use crash cymbals to give the song an ersatz symphonic sound. Sunday night at eight was indeed the showbiz promised land.

It was a masterstroke by Strouse, Adams, and librettist Michael Stewart to seize upon the Sullivan show as the epicenter of America's "youthquake"—the phenomenon that began when Elvis made his 1954 appearance on Sullivan's show and shook the country to its pop roots. By the time "Bye Bye Birdie" became a hit, "The Ed Sullivan Show" was an established hit, but the TV show's own great historic moment was Elvis's explosive TV debut, a 1950s touchstone.

In 1960, when the musical opened on Broadway, "The Ed Sullivan Show" was in the middle of its own long run, just a few blocks north of the Martin Beck Theater, home of "Bye Bye Birdie." The show was an affectionate but spirited satire of the Elvis phenomenon that climaxed with Elvis's appearance on Sullivan's show six years before. It's the musical's pivotal event, revealing just how vital the show was in validating a pop milestone in midcentury American life: appearing on Sullivan's show was video nirvana, or like being summoned to the Vatican, where Sullivan guarded the holy grail of entertainment. (Alan King said he once had been politely requested before a Sullivan tribute not to attack the guest of honor—"It would be like spitting on the flag.")

In "Bye Bye Birdie," America is embodied by the townspeople of Sweet Apple, Ohio, one of whose swooniest Elvis fans, 15-year-old Kim McAfee, wins a date with the Presley character, called "Conrad Birdie" (a sly play on the name of real-life country singer Conway Twitty). Birdie's promoter (Dick Van Dyke) promises Kim that her family will be on the Ed Sullivan show with her, every citizen's fondest fantasy. Kim's father (Paul Lynde) exults, "I've got a wonderful wife, two great kids, a good job—and now this! *I love you, Ed Sul-li-van!*" (whose offstage voice was supplied by—who else?—Will Jordan).

Strangely, Strouse and Adams never heard from Sullivan, whose daughter told me that, after seeing the show, "he didn't say he was pleased, but I knew he was pleased." Strouse didn't even meet his inspiration until he played the song at a Friars Club salute to Sullivan. It's almost the best-remembered song in the score, but Strouse recalls that director Gower

We always watched "The Ed Sullivan Show" as a family [in New York City], the epitome of "family style" entertainment. After I went away to college in 1955, I doubt I ever saw it again. My dad would listen raptly to some singer, or laugh raucously at a comedian. I remember him appearing transfixed. But when the act was over, he would always turn away. "That stunk," he would say. But I knew he had been totally absorbed. Ed Sullivan actually seemed out of place on the show. I wondered why they didn't hire someone more accomplished to introduce the acts. It didn't occur to me then that he was the architect of the show and picked all the acts.

Al Negrin, San Anselmo, California

Champion, who insisted on no ad-libs, blew up when Paul Lynde first ad-libbed a line in the number that got a huge laugh and later became a crucial part of the number: "I love you, Ed Sullivan!" The song struck a nerve, reflecting how people really felt about "The Ed Sullivan Show."

Anyone who came of age during the 1950s and 1960s recalls watching the Sullivan show. It was required viewing. In the 1950s and even deep into the 1960s, most homes had only one large hulking TV set that squatted squarely in the living room (or "family room," "rumpus room," "den," or "rec room"). This was long before people began hiding their TV screens behind cabinet doors and before most kids got their own TV sets. In 1954, when Elvis arrived, television was barely six years old. People boasted of watching television, of owning a set (as they do now with giant high-def screens). It was not yet the great scourge of society and America's favorite all-purpose whipping boy.

Bob Thompson, the pop culture professor, told me, "Certain behaviors get into the culture, like Macy's Thanksgiving Day Parade. Nobody would continue to watch a parade in those numbers unless it was something millions of people had been doing forever. Sullivan became one of the things people did on that evening, and it pretty much stayed that way. He became an institution, which carried him for half of his [TV] life. It was part of the daily rhythm of American life."

Ed Sullivan's two major rivals during his reign were NBC's "Colgate Comedy Hour" in the early 1950s and "The Steve Allen Show" in the mid-1950s. Both gave him a marathon run for his money, often beating him in the ratings when they outbooked him with a superstar, but Sullivan's show had an inclusive format that, in the end, nobody could top on a regular basis. To his family-centered show, Ed could add, if needed, a megastar with firepower, a name in the news, a puppet. He had a huge, multicolored entertainment palette. By the time the Colgate show ended and Allen's Sunday show was discreetly moved to another evening in late 1959, Sullivan owned Sunday night.

Both "The Colgate Comedy Hour" (1950–1955) and "The Steve Allen Show" (1956–1959) were awash in comedy but lacked Sullivan's broad talent mural. Allen's show was more topical and satirical than Sullivan's, and "The Colgate Comedy Hour" could claim some colossal names (thanks to a fatter budget), as well as four rotating hosts each month. That was a new idea, clever and unique, yet the "Colgate Hour" had no regular anchor, no familiar, reassuring, presiding presence—no Ed Sullivan.

"The Colgate Comedy Hour" had a simple mission—to destroy "Toast of the Town." It was yet another brainchild of Pat Weaver, NBC's programming renaissance man, the seer who devised the "Today" show, the "spectacular," and other innovative TV formats. Most of the hosts of "The Colgate Comedy Hour" were, apart from Dean Martin and Jerry Lewis, yesterday's news—Eddie Cantor, Fred Allen, Bobby Clark. Fred Allen was a radio name in steep decline who departed after four shows, utterly defeated by the medium—humiliatingly so when the characters who had been the centerpiece of his radio show, the dizzy denizens of "Allen's Alley," were turned into TV marionettes (on 1950's TV, when in doubt go to puppets); Clark, whose name stretched back to ancient vaudeville, washed out fast; Eddie Cantor was aging and wobbly, slowed by a heart attack after arriving on the show in 1952.

"The Colgate Comedy Hour" later added marquee hosts like Bob Hope, Jimmy Durante, Donald O'Connor, and Abbott & Costello, plus a fat newcomer named Jackie Gleason. But among its regular rotating hosts, only Martin & Lewis—the Next Big Thing—guaranteed the "Colgate Hour" ratings that were able to dent Sullivan's ratings every fourth week, when they hosted (but the white-hot new team quickly departed TV for movies).

William Paley declared war against NBC—he was prepared "to go all the way," in the words of programming boss Hubbell Robinson—that is, spend pots of money. Marlo Lewis noted in his memoir that "a siege mentality had taken over, and I admit that I too had been frightened into thinking that our show would not last beyond the next 13 weeks."

Sullivan sounded undeterred by the Colgate threat. "They'll hurt us a little at first. But once the audience gets a look at Pat Weaver's bunch of has-beens, they'll tune them out and tune us in." Lewis quoted Sullivan saying, "I tell you, it's not gonna make any difference. They've got all the same old clowns doing the same old shtick. Eddie Cantor will clap his hands and sing 'Susie' and talk about Ida and his five daughters. Fred Allen will fall back on his old radio material—Mrs. Nussbaum and Senator Claghorn. Abbott is gonna ask Costello 'Who's on First?' for the umpteenth time. And how many people are gonna get all charged up about Bobby Clark?" He had read the enemy exactly. "Sure, we'll take it on the chin a few times," he shrugged. "Martin & Lewis and Hope will win their rounds the first time out, but I'm not worried one bit about the rest of 'em. We're gonna be here for a long, long time."

Brave talk, and, while ultimately he was proved right, the opposition was far more formidable than Sullivan figured. Cantor sliced Sullivan's rating in half on the debut show, and Martin & Lewis inflicted deep wounds (Jerry Lewis, interviewed on "Larry King Live" in 2008, brayed, "We beat Sullivan 28 times in a row in the seven years we did the show, and we had the largest audience of any of the other performers on the show"). Over time, the ratings battle seesawed, with Sullivan ahead more nights than not in varying degrees. What the Sullivan show had that no new show could rival was stability and a familiar brand name viewers trusted, as reliable as Coca-Cola, Kellogg's, or Kraft. After its shaky beginning, the show had grown into a dominant force in (and a cross section of) entertainment and the arts. Ed Sullivan gave viewers, week in and week out, more bang for their viewing buck.

At the start of Sullivan's third season, "The Colgate Comedy Hour" exploded on the scene—as "Toast of the Town" decidedly had not in 1948. NBC gave the show a lavish send-off, spent $50,000 a week on talent (unheard of then), and in its second season moved the show to Hollywood to be closer to the megastars. But by 1954, Sullivan had begun beating back the splashier "Colgate Hour," whose hosts were no longer always comedians—many were decidedly uncomical names, like Charlton Heston, Guy Lombardo, Ezio Pinzo, and Gordon MacRae. The show even changed its name to "The Colgate Variety Hour," a huge acknowledgment of Sullivan's winning format.

Meanwhile, doctors advised Jerry Lewis, Dean Martin, and Donald O'Connor to take a rest from the exhaustive "Colgate Hour" pace. Many of TV's fevered comedians were wearing themselves out, not to mention their vintage material and their audiences. Milton Berle collapsed from overwork, Sid Caesar took to drink, Fred Allen's weary heart gave out, Red Buttons was leveled by nervous exhaustion, Jackie Gleason checked into hospitals with assorted ailments, and Eddie Cantor went down with heart trouble.

By 1955, Sullivan was back in the top five shows as "The Colgate Variety Hour" sank to 25th in the crucial Trendex numbers. NBC was so desperate that it was considering opposing Sullivan by hiring its own newspaper columnist; nobody could be found. Pat Weaver said in *The Best Seat in the House* that he admired "the guts of the CBS command" for sticking by Sullivan during the onslaught of Colgate's comics; NBC cut ad rates and subsidized the show to batter Sullivan. Weaver wrote in a 1953 memo, "They know what they believe and are willing to fight it out." As a last resort, Weaver tried to steal Sullivan from CBS.

What saved Sullivan was Broadway. Sullivan looted Broadway theaters and sagely counterprogrammed this bottomless talent pool to attack the "Colgate Hour"'s laugh-a-minute onslaught, the best that NBC could fling at him. Marlo Lewis wrote that running live scenes from Broadway shows and musicals became "our most powerful weapon." No variety show had ever recreated actual scenes from Broadway hits, which not only gave Sullivan new stars-in-the-making but also provided ready-made raw material—all right in his own neighborhood. The host was able to trade on the prestige of the New York theater, then still the jewel in the show business crown.

Sullivan forgot all about Eddie Cantor, Abbott & Costello, and even Bob Hope—whom viewers had seen plenty of on TV by 1957—and began presenting prize-winning scenes from "Member of the Wedding," "Wish You Were Here," "Tobacco Road," and "Guys and Dolls," and reviving classic legends, featuring, for example, Eva LeGallienne in a scene from "The Cherry Orchard." Broadway, always publicity-starved beyond New York, was eager to respond to Sullivan's invitations. NBC's variety show had barrels of comedians, but "The Ed Sullivan Show" had moments from gleaming new hit shows.

Ed's other major rival, Steve Allen, was a funny, lively, ingenious counterforce to the famously comatose, sobersided Sullivan. Allen's Sunday night show, which debuted June 24, 1955, was a knockoff of his "Tonight" show, but with more structure and sizzle. Allen was a glib, sparkling host—the un-Sullivan—but just a bit "too smart for the room" as comics say, "the room" in this case being the American living room on Sunday nights. Not everyone in Middle America dug Allen's inside references, wry ad-libs, and sharp, literate, self-deprecating humor.

Allen had conquered late night and felt ready for the main event. "It's called prime time. Late-night is nice, but it's not big time," he told me in 1999. "On a good night, I'd have six million people watching the 'Tonight' show, and on Sunday night I'd have 30 million people watching. Also, the money was five times bigger in prime time, which had a lot to do with it. NBC decided I was the solution to a problem they'd had for years, and that was 'The Ed Sullivan Show.'" Bill Allen told me that his father "didn't lose any sleep over" giving up the late-night show. "I'm sure there were times when he thought, 'Wow, look how long a run Johnny Carson had; I could've done the same thing,' but I never heard him say that and never got the sense that he really thought that."

Steve Allen opened his first Sunday night show by walking out escorted by a gorgeous model, parodying the big 1950s quiz shows, telling viewers, as he noted in his memoir, "Every time I see those $64,000 and $100,000 quiz programs, I always think, Here are people brilliant enough to answer questions that would throw a genius, and they can't even find their way to the middle of the stage without help." Allen was a snappy Sunday night equivalent of David Letterman, an alternative to Ed's comfier, less challenging Jay Leno. Allen was an author, jazz pianist, songwriter, critic, and actor; Sullivan was a dog-eared gossip columnist.

No two people on TV were less alike, although both were Irish Catholic and showbiz savvy. Steve Allen was as comfortable in his skin as any performer, while Ed Sullivan appeared on-screen to be trapped inside somebody else's itchy skin. Allen had an instinctive feeling for TV—he grew up in television; Sullivan was a video alien who appeared to be held hostage in the glass box awaiting rescue. Allen was the fastest ad-libber on TV, while Sullivan could not (to revive an old line) ad-lib a belch at a Polish dinner. Allen's incisive wit appealed more to the press than did Sullivan's homilies.

Sullivan was part of the old-boys variety show network of the 1950s (Garry Moore, Perry Como, George Gobel). Allen was the new boy in town. Ed was the past, Steve the future. Sullivan's show and other traditional variety shows could confirm a performer's stature, but Allen could elevate it and confer hipness upon him or her. *Time* said, "The best thing about the Steve Allen Show is Steve Allen, who has a quiet way of being funny unlike anybody else." Nobody ever said the best thing about Ed Sullivan's show was Ed Sullivan.

Bill Allen recalled, "Sullivan was not a creative man like Steve Allen. He was not in his league as a performer, but Steve was not in Ed's league as a producer. Sullivan had an incredible instinct for headlines and celebrity. He knew what kind of people would draw an audience. Ed would aggressively go after certain talent and book them so they would not appear on Steve Allen"—classic defensive booking. Sullivan took credit for presenting the Muppets first, but Bill Allen disputed that: "Clearly, Steve was first. Brian Henson, Jim's son, is a friend. He sent the largest, most incredible bouquet of flowers to my father's funeral, with a note saying, 'We remember where we got our start.' " The date, said Bill Allen, was November 4, 1956, on Allen's Sunday show.

Bill Allen recalled that his father couldn't consistently outhook Sullivan in getting big names. "Dad would say, 'OK, fine, that guy's not available. Who else is available?' And they would build a comedy sketch or a musical number or a big medley featuring great jazz artists. The main thing Sullivan sold was celebrity." Allen razzed Sullivan's show by introducing folks in the audience—comedians pretending to be celebrities. Bill Allen recalled that his father's problem had less to do with Sullivan's show than with NBC. "He wanted to book people who were more talented than they were famous. Like he'd say, 'Let's do a great songwriter like Johnny Mercer and do an hour of their music.' He'd rather book Errol Garner or Oscar Peterson than Marilyn Monroe." Bill's mother, Jayne Meadows, told me, "The joy for him was in the creation of a new show."

Allen may have wanted to stay above the ratings battle, but he wasn't above yelping when he felt he'd been sucker-punched, as when Sullivan scooped him by presenting a James Dean tribute after Allen had announced a Dean show following the actor's sudden death. Their sole rivalry was their battle for names. NBC told Allen he had to book big names; Allen wanted people he could use comically. Meadows recalled that Garry Moore told her, " 'Steve will deliver an award-winning brilliant show, but Ed Sullivan will deliver the ratings.' And I said why? Garry said, 'It's the difference between a genius talent and headlines.' "

Sullivan publicly taunted Allen: "It gets kind of dull beating NBC all the time by such a big margin. The challenge from Allen will only force me to keep to my knitting." A week before Allen first opposed Sullivan, NBC had a 6 rating to Sullivan's 30; the week after Allen began, NBC scored a 13. In the first season, Allen beat Sullivan 11 times; in the preceding six years, NBC had bested Sullivan only twice. Allen told the *Los Angeles Times* that Sullivan was "the toughest challenge I've ever been called upon to face in show business."

On the opening show he said, "All you folks know Ed Sullivan has a long list of people on his show tonight," then unfurled a lengthy scroll listing hundreds of Sullivan guests. When Allen had the bright idea of opening his new Sunday show as the Sullivan show, Will Jordan was advised not to do it because it would upset Sullivan to appear opposite him. Jordan recalled, "That wasn't true. Sullivan would have loved it."

Allen's best anti-Sullivan weapon of mass-audience destruction was his wit. He recalled once zinging Sullivan by introducing "a man who flew in from the West Coast just to be on our show—Mr. Fred Garber of Hollywood, California! Mr. Garber is the only person in Hollywood who was *not* on 'The Ed Sullivan Show' last week." Another night he mocked Sullivan's ritual of calling over performers and, amid hugs and backslaps, exchanging remarks under the music and applause, out of viewers' earshot. In Allen's parody, he and Milton Berle embrace and, sotto voce, Berle mutters, "That was the worst introduction I ever heard," as Allen mutters, "What do you expect for nothing?" Berle responds (hugging Allen), "I'll never come on your stupid show again," to which

Allen answers (hugging Berle), "Is that a promise?" Berle, with a big smile, whispers, "Drop dead!," kisses Allen, exits grinning, and quietly hisses, "You're a big phony!"

Bill Dana, head writer of the Allen show for many years, told me, "Steve was up for the fight. For him, it [Sullivan's show] was like dropping a red hanky in front of a bull. Steve didn't even feel that the Ed Sullivan show was a show. He just thought it was a batch of acts, one after the other. We were Lord & Taylor, he was Macy's; they were Target, we were Tiffany's. But he did have that lowest common denominator thing, and he realized the low threshold of patience the audience had. He knew what America liked."

Several performers were torn between shows, as performers would be during the Sullivan–Jack Paar feud to come. Julius La Rosa told me he turned down the Allen show out of loyalty to Sullivan, telling his agent, "I can't do that." The agent said, "Julie, this is business! This guy is offering you a job! You take the job! Nobody will be offended!" He took the job, but even now reflects, "I tell you, if I knew then what I know now I never would have gone on the Steve Allen show, because it turned out just the way it looked—that I was an ungrateful SOB. I didn't do his [Sullivan's] show for a couple of years. His affection for me was never the same after that."

Allen's new show got off to a fast start, topping Sullivan's and charming all the critics, as "Toast of the Town" clearly had not done in its beginning—or ever. Critics praised the cheery host's wit, inventiveness, and offhand humor, using words like "fetching," "bright," "personable," "versatile," "casual and easygoing," and "radiates likeability"—not exactly terms used to describe Ed Sullivan. Bob Williams in the *New York Post* even predicted Steve Allen would "supersede Jack Benny as the first comedian of show business."

Allen's Sunday night show, revisited 40 years later, plays as well—as smoothly and satirically nimble—as it did originally; it would easily still get laughs in reruns today. Allen is loose and free-spirited, ad-libbing jubilantly, mocking his own setup lines, in inspired sketches. In one, Allen conducts an interview with Anita Ekberg in a seductive Ekberg setting, on a sofa, his banal questions loaded with innuendo ("Where will . . . you be . . . *appearing* . . . next . . . *Anita?*"). Later, they sing "Tea for Two" in Swedish.

When it was first announced that the shows would be going head-to-head, the genial Allen wired his opponent: "Dear Ed: Would you lend me ten Trendex points till payday? Love and kisses, Steve Allen," to which

Sullivan replied, after being beaten in their initial matchup, when Allen booked Presley: "Stinker. Love and kisses, Ed Sullivan."

Thus began the fake feud between Allen and Sullivan, aided by charges and countercharges about stealing, double-dealing, and false bookings. Most of the sniping was, in fact, between managers and network publicity mills laboring to hype both shows. Sullivan later said, "The feud was just something engineered by the NBC promotion department—a cold-blooded publicity stunt." "There was never a feud," says Meadows. "He liked Ed Sullivan! He was an admirer of talent. When Steve was given the job, the first thing he did was ask Sullivan to go on his late night show. He said, 'Let's shut 'em all up before it starts.' Ed Sullivan turned him down. If CBS hadn't said no, he would have done it, I'm sure. First of all, it would have been good showmanship."

In their one actual dustup, Allen had already planned a tribute to the just-killed James Dean when he heard that Sullivan had announced a Dean tribute that would take place a week before Allen's and would feature clips from the actor's last film, "Giant," and appearances by Dean's aunt and uncle. Author Jerry Bowles wrote that Allen was "furious" and "suspected spies in his camp," and says that Allen protested what he called high-handed "piracy." But Allen told a reporter, "I don't believe it is Ed who's making these unethical, cut-throat moves."

Allen revealed that he had canceled Imogene Coca and Vic Damone in order to do a James Dean salute; Sullivan called Allen a "cry baby" and was appalled at the "ghoulish" sorts who might try to profit by capitalizing on the death of such a "fine youngster." The media reported the weekly skirmish between the two like a heated boxing match between two Irish club fighters—a lumbering 55-year-old veteran and a frisky 34-year-old phenom; one paper reported that Allen had "thumped" Sullivan in early ratings rounds. Sullivan was a seasoned champ, Allen a promising contender, a counterpuncher with clever moves. The smart money was on Sullivan, who finally won on points, but when the bell clanged four years later, Ed knew he had been in a fight.

The press played the Sullivan-Allen Sunday night rivalry as a nasty grudge bout ("The Mugger vs. the Great Stone Face: Which one in the long run?" taunted a *Newsweek* cover line). But after a dispute over an Elvis booking, any "feud" that existed fizzled. Allen was not into feuding, and while Sullivan was always up for a tussle, he respected Allen too much to turn it into a blood sport for the media's amusement. Bill Allen noted, "It was a pivotal battle for the networks." Critic Marie Torre in the *New York Herald Tribune* labeled them "the friendliest of enemies." Sullivan even bought Bill Allen a share of Polaroid stock to celebrate his birth, enclosed with a telegram to Steve, "Welcome, little Billy. If the kid is smart he'll grow up to be a cowboy"—a reference to both shows' mutual foe, ABC's upstart western, "Maverick."

At one point, Sullivan conceded, "This whole thing is pretty silly." *Time* ran a letter from Allen "wholeheartedly endorsing" the magazine for calling it "TV's most boring 'feud,' particularly since there is no such feud," just a "healthy rivalry. What is boring, of course, is the endless talk and press comment about such issues." Yet Allen dumped gasoline on the fire when he told *Editor & Publisher* (which covered the matchup as a major media event), "Ed should reprimand those on his staff who are turning what had been, for my part, a very pleasant rivalry into a two-faced operation where a smile is presented to the TV camera but it's cloak-and-dagger during the week."

Later, there was a flapette over a Harry Belafonte booking, when Allen's manager accused Sullivan of lying—promising he would present the singer with a clip from Belafonte's new movie, "Island in the Sun," but failing to produce either. Sullivan was often charged with promising guests he didn't deliver, as a ruse to rope viewers into tuning in next week. When gossip columnist Earl Wilson tracked Ed down on a golf course, he snarled, "I have no comment on anything those two punks have to say"—after which Allen and his manager went around their office calling each other "punk." The tepid feud got so absurd that writers Herb Sargent and Stan Burns gave Allen for Christmas a framed, staged photo of Allen and his manager with Ed Sullivan, shown handing them money. "Sullivan was a very good sport about it," Sargent told me.

Steve Allen's show relied heavily on its popular "Man in the Street" segment (featuring fidgety Don Knotts, addled Tom Poston, clueless Bill Dana, goofy Dayton Allen, hip Louis Nye—a sort of urban "Steve Allen's Alley"), with sharp satire aimed at the missile program, organized crime, cool jazz musicians, modern ballet, the recession, women's fashions, political scandals—whatever struck Allen's fancy, and nearly everything did.

Allen was never interested, like Sullivan, in the big-tent philosophy of entertainment. Social comment was his meat. If Sullivan had any social or political beliefs, they were rarely to be found on his show. Allen's show was more in the vein of Fred Allen's and Henry Morgan's old satirical radio programs—incisive sketches on prime time during the frightened 1950s, for which it won a Peabody Award in 1959. Peabody or no, NBC finally blinked, starting Allen's show at 7:30 to give him a half-hour head start on Sullivan. (About that time, 1960, Sullivan's new coproducer, Bob Precht, tried to add satirical comedy to the familiar bridge mix—Bob & Ray, "Beyond the Fringe" sketches—but it stumbled getting out of the gate.)

Allen, in his memoir, noted a tad haughtily that it was much more of a chore to put together a comedy show every week than a variety show. "Of course, if I'd elected to do a show in the Sullivan formula—hiring several acts and presenting them one after the other—there would've been no such problem. But we created fresh sketches for our guest stars and regular company." Allen hated scrapping for ratings and marquee names. He preferred the freedom to work free-form as the comic spirit moved him.

He told *Newsweek,* "It is a comparatively easy thing to get a big rating by booking a 'hot' attraction. I did not take over the Sunday spot with the purpose of breaking Ed Sullivan." He ranted about "the neurotic concentration on ratings." Allen was either naive or idealistic, expressing dismay that backstabbing booking coups were common practice. He surmised why Sullivan finally won: "Ed Sullivan, who knew next to nothing about the nuts-and-bolts of creating entertainment, nevertheless had a superb journalistic sense of the human fascination with celebrities," which mirrored his own.

Another reason: every fourth week NBC would bump Allen's show for a "spectacular," making it tough for Allen to regain traction with viewers after a bye week. Also, his show had a top payment of $7,500 per star, chump change to Sullivan. In the end, Allen's Sunday show had less of the swinging, unhinged feeling of the late-night shenanigans. Sargent recalled, "In the late stages of the Sunday show, Steve began to feel the audience wasn't getting it. That's when he started to overexplain sketch setups. He got impatient with people."

A year before he died, in 2000, Allen admitted that the Sunday night show had been a grind compared to the relaxed "Tonight" show, which he called "pure comedy and wild sketches," as opposed to Sunday's show, which was "big sketches, big stars. It was hard work. Every week we had to put on the equivalent of a Broadway musical comedy revue." While Allen fared surprisingly well against Sullivan, he half-gratefully returned Sunday nights to Sullivan. He wasn't wounded. Unlike most funnymen, Allen wasn't insecure or frantic. In Sargent's words, "Steve didn't depend on being a comic. He had other things. He didn't care." In 1960, after three years of banging heads with Sullivan, Allen's show, despite respectable ratings, tiptoed over to 10 P.M. Mondays, safely out of harm's way.

By the time Allen departed Sundays, "The Ed Sullivan Show" was so established in its time slot that NBC and ABC dared not sacrifice other variety shows opposite Sullivan's. They wisely didn't pit Dinah Shore's show against it. Shore's hour ran at various times, including Sundays from 9 to 10, after Sullivan, and survived nine chirpy years; against him, Shore might well have perished in a slow but certain TV death. The long-running "Perry Como Show" also carefully avoided being destroyed by Sullivan, hiding out on Saturday and Wednesday nights for six years. By 1959, the other networks had all but thrown in the towel and awarded 8–9 P.M. Sunday nights to Sullivan, the invincible, still unbeaten heavyweight champion.

Even though he had emerged triumphant over the Steve Allen and "The Colgate Comedy Hour" laugh factories, total acceptance for Sullivan at CBS was slowly, almost begrudgingly, extended. The battle-scarred TV warrior was overcome when, in 1958, William Paley finally showed his appreciation at a luncheon in Paley's office to mark the show's tenth anniversary. After lunch and fond reminiscences of the show's early struggles, as the Lewises noted in their memoir, Paley handed Sullivan a Renoir painting. "Ed," he said, "there's something I know both you and Sylvia wanted. I am delighted we could find a way to show you how much we think of you and how happy we are that you are a part of CBS."

Marlo Lewis recalled, "Sullivan just stared at the painting for about ten seconds, pulled out a handkerchief, covered his eyes, and began to sob." The group of CBS executives was stunned at the sturdy Sullivan's emotional reaction; nobody said anything. Then Sullivan, between sobs, pointed at Lewis and said, "This kid . . . if it wasn't for this kid . . . All of us thank you, Bill." After he pulled himself together, Sullivan took a sip of water, wiped his eyes, shook hands, and left the room alone.

Frank Stanton turned to Lewis and asked, "What was that all about?" Lewis said, "Damned if I know," but he knew. "If Stanton had known Ed as I did, he would have realized that in all our years at the network, Ed had never felt anything personal in his relationship with CBS. The show, on the other hand, was a very personal thing with him and never merely a commercial enterprise. It had been his life, his total dedication.

Thus, when Mr. Paley acknowledged Ed's value on a human basis, Ed was so touched and so gratified that he broke down. What is more, underneath Ed's tough self-reliance, he shared the universal need for approval from an ultimate authority. In Ed's case, it happened to be William S. Paley."

While chastened, the rival networks refused to give up despite the ultimate ratings failures of the Steve Allen and Colgate shows. The shows that clenched their teeth and, kamikaze-like, flew forth to do battle with the Sullivan show over the years, only to experience varying degrees of shame and disaster, included a vast range of the good, the bad, and the goofy: "The Philco Playhouse," "The Big Payoff," "The Amateur Hour," "Dragnet," "Car 54, Where Are You?," "The Tab Hunter Show," "National Velvet," "Pete Kelly's Blues," "Follow the Sun," "Grindl," "The Bill Dana Show," "Branded," "Music on Ice," "Jamie McPheeters," "Buckskin," "Wagon Train," and "Hey, Landlord!" NBC even hired TV's ace playwright Paddy Chayefsky to write an hour-long drama called "The Man Who Knocked Off Ed Sullivan," but it never aired. NBC may have decided that contemplating murdering Sullivan might be seen as a tasteless solution, however tempting.

Sullivan by now had more important things to worry about—specifically, a new ABC western called "Maverick," which threatened to make toast of the former "Toast of the Town." By 1958, there was a stampede of "horse operas," hugely popular series like "Rawhide" (starring a tenderfoot Clint Eastwood), "Wagon Train," "The Rifleman," "Wanted: Dead or Alive," "Tales of Wells Fargo," "Have Gun, Will Travel," "Wyatt Earp," "Sugarfoot," and, to be sure, "Maverick"—a very different breed of horse that featured a sardonic, wisecracking card shark played by James Garner, a wry satire of the square-shooting, guns-blazing western in the weatherworn "Gunsmoke" tradition.

In March 1959, "Maverick" scored a 31.6 Trendex rating, double that for Allen (15.7) and even worse for Sullivan (13.5). Allen announced that he planned to outsmart "Maverick" by booking Marshal Matt Dillon. After two years, "Maverick" collapsed. In *A Really Big Show*, John Leonard wrote, "Like Eddie Lopat, the crafty Yankee southpaw, Sullivan seemed to throw nothing but junk, and still they couldn't hit him."

"Maverick" didn't finish off Sullivan, but it blazed the trail for a later ABC western that helped gun him down—the unstoppable "Bonanza" gang of Cartwrights. Cowboys stampeded TV in the mid-1950s as networks ground out cheapo westerns, rerunning an ancient television genre

(TV's first cowboy star was Hopalong Cassidy), a fad that reached its manic phase with "Davy Crockett" in 1955. "Maverick," a smart, sassy new style of western, knocked Sullivan from the top ten in 1961 and 1962. Ed didn't climb back into the top-ten saddle until 1964, when the Beatles rode to his rescue.

CHAPTER 12

Not Quite All in the Family

[Ed] had girlfriends, but he wasn't as bad as Winchell.
Jane Kean, comedian

While Ed Sullivan wrapped his seemingly invincible and enshrined show—and his public persona—in family values, he was, in his own home life, a peculiar role model. He was tightly bound to his wife, Sylvia, and their daughter speaks of him with affection, but Ed used to say, "Family life is overrated." As it turns out, he had three families—one at home, one at the show, and one at the *Daily News,* plus a circle of girlfriends on the side.

Sullivan's grandson Rob Precht told biographer James Maguire, "He did not, on a personal level, enjoy family life." Maguire observed, " 'The Ed Sullivan Show' was the ultimate family show produced by a man who had little patience for the rituals of familial togetherness," and called it "the central paradox of his life. He was a confirmed loner, distant from the countless people he knew, even removed in family gatherings, yet he was the producer of a program that brought the entire clan together like few others. The master showman, gifted at manufacturing the pixie dust of entertainment, created a convincing fictional image of himself as the ultimate Uncle Ed. He wasn't a family man but he played one on television."

He was a loving (if unfaithful) husband and a supportive (if distracted, distant, undemonstrative) dad, but he didn't jump through all the conventional family hoops. He hated home cooking—mom's apple pie wasn't nearly as good as Danny's Hideaway's. Family values were fine, if you liked that sort of thing, but he lived more by theatrical values. The show must go on, and the family could follow the acrobats. Even the Sullivans' dog, a black poodle called Bojangles, named for Bill ("Bojangles") Robinson, had a showbiz connection.

Except for three years in Los Angeles, beginning in 1937, when Sullivan was sent by the *New York Daily News* to cover Hollywood, and a brief fling at suburban life, the Sullivans resided in hotels, first at the Astor in Times Square and then at the ritzier Delmonico on Park Avenue. This was Sullivan's turf—easy walking distance to the Brill Building (a.k.a. "Tin Pan Alley"), Shubert Alley, Madison Square Garden, *Variety*, the 52nd Street jazz clubs, Carnegie Hall—everything he needed was at his feet when he stepped outside his hotel.

And everyone: Broadway characters, agents, publicists, newspaper cronies, comics, and singers to the right of him, sports heroes to the left of him. Taking a walk was like strolling through one of his columns. It was a veritable scene out of "Guys and Dolls," "42nd Street," and "Gypsy," where chorus girls, comedians, mobsters, and columnists mingled freely. Partly he made the rounds to gather column items and bookings, but he also went out to take sidewalk bows and be kowtowed to as a "big town czar" (the title of the 1939 movie he wrote and appeared in).

The Sullivans ate dinner out every night. Sylvia Sullivan didn't like to cook. His lunch, prepared in a kitchenette and usually eaten at home in midafternoon—consisted of a broiled lamb chop, canned pears, and tea to calm his volcanic ulcer. Breakfast consisted of oatmeal and Postum, eaten while hunched over a coffee table as he read telephone messages. He'd lost interest in food after he lost his sense of smell in his youth, and his troublesome duodenal ulcer further diminished his diet. He told daughter Betty he'd lost his sense of smell, along with most of his sense of taste, in a diving accident that burst his eardrum (but sometimes he blamed a football injury). He spent his life complimenting chefs for meals he could barely taste; he even dumped sweetener into his wine.

Sullivan married at 28 and remained with the same wife all his life, serial affairs notwithstanding. He doted on Sylvia and was dependent on her, calling home after each show to get her candid review. He trusted her gut reaction and instincts. She never saw the show in person, explaining, "I get too nervous." Their daughter, Betty, told me, "She never went to the show. My mother and I were interested in how it came across on TV—the mechanics of it, how it was presented to people watching. We'd have a critique of the show but we were always careful not to say anything too critical. My mother and I were very interested in the ratings the next morning. We had a rooting interest." Sullivan never dissected the show at home.

The show's longtime Lincoln spokeswoman Julia Meade, who knew the Sullivans ("I was friendly with his wife, a divine lady, and his daughter"), told me she believed Sylvia had a big influence on the acts he chose—or didn't invite back. "He'd go home and she'd tell him everything that happened on the show that was good and things that were funny. I think he paid serious attention to her. Nobody had more influence on him." After her death, says Meade, "Ed was really never the same. After the show ended, I guess he was bored, but she kept him active. They'd go to '21' and she'd say, 'Look, there's so-and-so over there.' "

Decades before that, as a dapper young columnist about Manhattan, Ed prowled the nightclubs in quest of gossip and girls, which is how he met Sylvia Weinstein, daughter of wealthy New York builder Julius Weinstein, who later went broke but was bailed out by Sullivan. The old man was strongly against the marriage, but Sullivan's nephew Bob Pitofsky told me, "Sylvia was a very strong-willed person. She was going to do what she wanted to do, and because she cared for him they went ahead and got married. But there was a rift for a period of time. Julius was not happy. At that time, remember, Ed wasn't the Ed Sullivan we know, he was Ed Sullivan, writer for the *Graphic*." As it turned out, Pitofsky said, "Julius couldn't have had a more wonderful son-in-law. Ed did everything in the world to take care of Julius in his later years. He even took him with them to California, and later he set him up in the Mayflower Hotel in New York."

The sure-footed Sullivan eventually charmed the Weinsteins, but his own family in Port Chester didn't rejoice at the idea of a Sullivan marrying a Jew, a likely reason he had little to do with most of his family after he and Sylvia married. According to Mina Bess Lewis, Sullivan was also ashamed of his family once be became a celebrity. Though he spoke nostalgically of growing up in Port Chester, as if to affirm his small-town roots, his siblings were rarely at the show and he seemed all but estranged from them. "My sense is that he wasn't real close to his family," Bob Precht told me, but Ed stayed close to older sister Helen. "Helen was a go-between" between Sullivan and the family, recalled Betty Precht. "Whenever they needed anything, that information would be related to my father and he would do whatever he could" financially. Her father wasn't a churchgoer, she said, and her mother never went to synagogue, which may help explain why the intermarriage worked.

Sullivan had met 26-year-old Sylvia in 1926 at the Casa Lopez, run by bandleader Vincent Lopez, where she was dining with friends. Table-hopping, he spotted the tall, pretty, dark-eyed girl and went over to introduce himself, assuming she would be impressed. Not quite. Sylvia had never heard of him. Ed was newly unattached; his fiancée, an Olympic swimmer named Sybil Bauer, had died soon after they were engaged. Sullivan had courted her avidly, but after her death he never referred to Bauer publicly.

Sullivan was so taken with Sylvia that he asked her for two dates at once, first to see French tennis star Suzanne Lenglen play at Madison Square Garden. "Ed asked me if I liked sports. I said I was crazy about them. He asked me if I liked tennis," she recalled. "Of course, I loved it." So he asked her for another date to see the Jack Sharkey–Harry Wills prizefight at Ebbets Field. "I shuddered but didn't let him see it." She later admitted, "Actually I had never been interested in sports, and knew almost nothing about it. I went home that night and started reading the sports pages. What young girl wouldn't have been excited about going out with Ed Sullivan, sports editor? Ed was very attractive."

The younger Sullivan was striking looking, with black hair and blue eyes that could go from limpid to icy. He even reminded some people of Humphrey Bogart. The TV screen later flattened his face and squashed his long horsey head into his shoulders, almost as if his head had been superimposed on someone else's body, as in an old *Evening Graphic* "composograph."

At 54, he was described by Eleanor Harris in *Look*, in 1955, as appearing ten years younger than his TV self—"a quick-moving man with a spare figure. Everything about him is neat-looking: his features, his dark, curly hair, his compact build." Yet even in a flashy plaid jacket, checked shirt and tie, striped belt, plaid pants and dark blue suede shoes, she said he managed to look "as proper as a banker." TV critic Kay Gardella, a *Daily News* colleague, told me, "He was like what you saw on TV, but he was not as stern. He had a much kinder side. I found he was very giving of himself and his time when I belonged to a woman's organization. If you asked him to do something, he was very willing." He was known to be courtly—seeing visitors to the elevator, standing when a woman arrived, lighting their cigarettes, walking female friends to the door.

Sylvia Weinstein had lived a pampered life in what she later called "the Marjorie Morningstar world of the time," the daughter of a well-off

Jewish family on the Upper West Side. "We went to temple on the High Holy Days. But I think if I had married a manufacturer, I probably would have become a typical 'Shirley' [a matronly Jewish housewife]. I guess he was the first Christian boy I ever really knew. Not that my family was strict, but remember, back in those days 'Abie's Irish Rose' [the long-running play about a Jewish-Catholic couple] was still a comic novelty." The couple stuck it out despite protests from both families, and Sylvia's persistence wore her family down: "I was so emotionally involved with Ed that they wanted me to have anything that would have made me happy."

Sylvia was described by Atra Baer, a New York newswoman and childhood friend of Betty Sullivan, as "a reed slim, sparkly person whose warmth is a near-tangible thing, the sort of woman who would have to be rated too-good-to-be-real if it weren't for her sometimes wickedly acid wit." Marge Champion, the dancer, added, "I always thought of her as having a society background. She was always beautifully dressed, a woman who knew how to direct servants." Many recall her as "elegant." Ed's cue card man Peter Calabrese told me, "She was a society woman," and he only saw her at home "playing mah-jongg with her friends."

Sullivan and Sylvia dated three and a half years, on and off, regularly breaking up with farewell dinner parties. "We couldn't quite decide if we wanted to get married," she said in a rare 1958 TV interview on Hy Gardner's TV talk show, so we'd say next Monday night we'll have a farewell dinner—and then we'd reconcile." Ed said that after two weeks he was lost without her. Her version is that he didn't really want to get married, "but finally I trapped him into eloping"—to city hall in 1930, in a ceremony witnessed by ex-fighter Johnny Dundee. Due to Sullivan's prominence as a *New York Graphic* sports editor, the wedding made the news. A Catholic ceremony in New Jersey followed; Sylvia never considered converting but dutifully helped raise their daughter as a Catholic.

An early Eloise, Betty Sullivan mastered room service and restaurants but developed a taste for a normal home in Beverly Hills during the three years Sullivan covered Hollywood. After they returned to New York and moved into the Astor Hotel, at 44th Street and Broadway, Betty rarely ate with her folks and instead dined most nights at a nearby Child's Restaurant or the Automat with a paid companion, preferring it to the chic bistros her parents frequented. (The Automat, she remembered, "wasn't bad at all. They had the best creamed spinach.") Her dad once asked why she liked Child's: "Because they like me for me," said the insightful 11-year-old girl, "not because I'm your daughter."

1. A tousled young Ed Sullivan during his easygoing sportswriting days in the early 1930s. (Photo: Photofest)

2. Sullivan, now the sporty Broadway columnist, interviewing an unidentified performer in the mid-1930s. (Photo: Photofest)

3. Ed Sullivan as the smiling, dapper host of the Harvest Moon Ball in 1938. (Photo: *New York Daily News*)

4. Making his nightly rounds as columnist and talent-spotter, Sullivan dines at the Stork Club with his wife, Sylvia, and teenage daughter, Betty, in the 1950s. (Photo: Photofest)

5. Singer and comedian Jane Kean, one of Sullivan's favorite entertainers, especially off-camera. (Photo: Photofest)

6. Sullivan with his loyal aide Carmine Santullo, secretary, and pet poodle.
(Photo: Photofest)

7. The show's brain trust: with Sullivan are longtime conductor Ray Bloch, director John Wray, and the show's cocreator and coproducer, the handsome, unflappable Marlo Lewis. (Photo: Photofest)

8. The elegant Julia Meade, the show's Lincoln-Mercury spokeswoman, in 1954. (Photo: Photofest)

9. *(Opposite top)* The lineup of the first "Toast of the Town" in 1948, bookended by an array of Toastettes. Sullivan is at the mike with, in their TV debut and Sullivan's first TV exclusive, Dean Martin (at Ed's left) and Jerry Lewis (arms folded), plus Richard Rodgers and Oscar Hammerstein II (to Ed's right), a classical pianist, a fight referee, and a singing fireman. (Photo: Photofest)

10. *(Opposite bottom)* Sullivan in 1960 with his new son-in-law and no-nonsense producer, Robert Precht, who made the talent run on time. (Photo: CBS/Landov)

11. *(Above)* Sullivan's most definitive mimic, Will Jordan, who created the Ed Sullivan everybody else (including Ed Sullivan) imitated. Sullivan drove comics crazy with his blue pencil, butchering their routines for reasons of propriety and personal whim, but he loved them in his own way, whether they were old-timers like Jack Carter or fresh faces like Carol Burnett. (Photo: Photofest)

12. *(Opposite top)* Sullivan with the beloved storyteller Myron Cohen. (Photo: Photofest)

13. *(Opposite bottom)* Sullivan cracks up at the clean-cut, not-yet-bad-boy Richard Pryor in 1966. (Photo: CBS/Landov)

14. *(Above)* Carol Burnett in a 1958 appearance on the show, which sent her career soaring. (Photo: CBS/Landov)

15. *(Left)* Jerry Stiller and Anne Meara, adored regulars on the show, in 1968. (Photo: CBS/Landov)

16. *(Opposite top)* Canadian comedy team of Johnny Wayne and Frank Shuster, who performed on the Sullivan show more often (58 times) than any other comedy act. (Photo: Photofest)

17. *(Opposite bottom)* Jackie Mason, a Sullivan favorite who later turned foe, with a troublesome finger extended. (Photo: Photofest)

18. *(Above)* Ventriloquist Señor Wences, a signature Sullivan act, with his hand puppet Johnny ("Yonny"). (Photo: CBS/Landov)

19. *(Opposite top)*
Stupendous pet tricks—
"And now something for
yew youngsters"—were a
crucial part of Sullivan's
TV circus. (Photo:
CBS/Landov)

20. *(Opposite bottom)*
World-class bowl-spinner
Eric Brenn in 1959. (Photo:
CBS/Landov)

21. *(Above)* Ventriloquist
Rickie Layne and his Jewish
dummy, Velvel, in 1959.
(Photo: CBS/Landov)

22. *(Left)* The show's
biggest, smallest, and best-
remembered star, Topo
Gigio, one of the few
performers able to make
the boss smile in 1967.
(Photo: CBS/Landov)

23. *(Opposite)* Sullivan's big-tent policy recognized no boundaries, niche markets, or demographics. Talent was his only criteria for showcasing performers, whether pop singers, classical musicians, athletes, plate-twirlers, or dancers such as Paul Draper, shown here in an appearance before the 1950s blacklist caused him to be exiled from the show. (Photo: Photofest)

24. *(Left)* Roberta Peters, who appeared on the Sullivan show 41 times, in a scene from "The Barber of Seville" in 1952. (Photo: Photofest)

25. *(Below)* Teresa Brewer, a tiny, twinkly crooner whose 31 appearances set a show record for pop singers. (Photo: Photofest)

26. *(Above)* The King and his court tear the place up on Sullivan's show in 1956. (Photo: CBS/Landov)

27. *(Opposite top)* Connie Francis and Bobby Darin, a major item then, in a duet on the show in 1960. (Photo: CBS/Landov)

28. *(Opposite bottom)* Richard Burton, Julie Andrews, and Robert Goulet in a scene from "Camelot," during a Sullivan tribute to Lerner & Loewe that saved the musical from closing in 1961. (Photo: CBS/Landov)

29. *(Opposite top)* Jackie Robinson joins the parade of athletes featured by the ex-sportswriter on his show, here giving Ed batting tips in 1962. (Photo: CBS/Landov)

30. *(Opposite bottom)* Itzhak Perlman, a 12-year-old Israeli violin prodigy in leg braces, making his American TV debut on Sullivan's show in 1964. (Photo: CBS/Landov)

31. *(Above)* The McGuire Sisters—Christine, Phyllis, and Dorothy—charming Sullivan in one of their many appearances on the show, in 1964. (Photo: Photofest)

32. *(Left)* Louis Armstrong growling "Hello, Dolly!" yet again, on a 1964 show. (Photo: CBS/Landov)

33. *(Above)* The Beatles in 1964, waiting politely to launch into "I Want to Hold Your Hand" as Sullivan vainly attempts, with his own hand, to quiet a crazed crowd of teenagers. (Photo: Photofest)

34. *(Opposite top)* The sizzling new dance team of Rudolph Nureyev and Margot Fonteyn, on the show in 1965. (Photo: CBS/Landov)

35. *(Opposite bottom)* Mick Jagger singing the Rolling Stones' naughty hit song "Let's Spend the Night Together," which Sullivan insisted be changed to "Let's Spend Some Time Together" for the show in 1966. (Photo: CBS/Landov)

36. *(Opposite top)* James Brown and Ed Sullivan, two of the hardest-working men in show business, find something to say to each other on camera in 1966. (Photo: CBS/Landov)

37. *(Opposite bottom)* Janis Joplin in full throttle on the show in 1969. (Photo: CBS/Landov)

38. *(Left)* Pearl Bailey, one of many black entertainers Sullivan introduced on early TV, when black performers on prime-time television were rare. (Photo: Photofest)

39. *(Below)* Sophie Tucker and Maurice Chevalier, two of the vintage vaudeville stars Sullivan welcomed on his show in their twilight years. (Photo: Photofest)

40. TV's solemn impresario imploring the audience to applaud ever more wildly.
(Photo: Photofest)

The Astor was a fabled Times Square landmark, but it was surrounded by tourists, winos, bums, hookers, and litter—not the ideal front yard. Betty remembers passing strip joints on the way to church. "At 14, I felt penned up in New York," she recalled. "One of the things I missed by living in hotels was getting all the family together for holiday meals. A home to me is wall-to-wall carpeting and holiday dinners."

Of her four years at the Astor Hotel, she said: "We did not have a real kitchen, and my dad would put his milk on the window sill in the winter time. I had to stand in line to get the mail in the lobby. . . . Toots Shor told my dad that a hotel was no place to bring up a child," she added, and soon afterward the Sullivans moved from the commercial Astor (now a Hyatt) to the posher Delmonico, a residential hotel that felt more like an apartment than a commercial hotel. Sullivan expanded their suite to create an office out of the adjoining apartment. His daughter remembered phones ringing in his office, but said their apartment life was utterly normal—no agents or performers negotiating or auditioning in their living room.

One night a week, Wednesdays, Betty ate dinner with her parents. "I could always choose the place, and I always chose Toots Shor's, because the ballplayers hung out there." It sounds like a lonely childhood. "I didn't have friends, possibly because I had a companion, so I guess I didn't feel the need of a friend." Even so, she loved being invited to a playmate's big house at the ocean for weekends.

After Betty turned 14 and was enrolled at Miss Hewitt's girls' school, she began dining out with her parents. For their daughter's graduation from UCLA, they gave her a leather-bound book full of baby pictures and every note her father had written her, which she treasures. As tough as he could be, he was supportive—maybe too supportive: he tried to write all of her compositions, and Milton Berle once wrote a sketch for her school play. Sullivan signed all his notes, "Win, lose or draw, we love you.—Daddy." The scrapbook was embossed, *"Win, Lose or Draw . . . Limited Edition, Love Unlimited."* Monica Lewis told me, "She loved her dad. He was a good dad. Ed had a wonderful relationship with his daughter."

When Betty got engaged to Bob Precht, he recalled, her father readily accepted him. "I admired his inclusiveness," said Precht. "I came from another world; I grew up in San Diego. But when I married Betty he embraced me. He was proud of me, very supportive. When we wanted to get married, he wrote me a long letter trying to persuade us to wait, but we didn't want to. Then he threw this fantastic wedding at the Beverly Hills Hotel."

The Delmonico, where the Sullivans moved after four years at the Astor, was uptown, at Park and 59th Street—now a Trump residence hotel but with no lobby plaque attesting to its most celebrated resident's 30-year stay there. The apartment had four baths and a tiny, barely used kitchen, but no dining room, and a hotel maid maintained the six-room suite; two rooms were later added to serve as Ed's office. If it seems a curious way of life to most, it perfectly suited Ed Sullivan, the consummate Manhattanite-about-town. He was rarely home to watch TV but, if he was, he always tuned in "The Tonight Show"; Johnny Carson was his liveliest rival.

If Ed ate lunch out, it was often roast chicken at Gino's two blocks away, after which he'd wrap up a drumstick to gnaw on later. Gino's is still there, with the same zebra-striped wallpaper; the Zagat guide calls it "cramped and shabby" but "homey"). Long-ago family friend Ken Rothstein told me, "That was Ed's place, almost his kitchen. So much of Ed's New York is gone, so it's wonderful to be able to walk into Ed's restaurant and take it all in as Ed did." Whenever Sullivan's grandson Rob and Rothstein visited him, "Without fail Ed would say, 'Now you're gonna go to Gino's' "—at Lexington and 60th. Sullivan always picked up the tab. "They treated us like celebrities because of Ed."

The family's suite, 1102, was formally but warmly furnished in the French Provincial style popular at the time, and it housed the Renoir landscape CBS had presented to Sullivan on the show's tenth anniversary, two other Impressionist paintings, and an original Disney that depicted Sullivan playing golf with Donald Duck. The shelves contained several biographies, from Hedy Lamarr's to Marshal Tito's, but Betty said her parents read newspapers, not books. The walls were covered with photos of Sullivan laughing with, talking to, and hugging stars, plus signed photos of everyone from Cardinal Spellman to Ella Fitzgerald.

The photos' subjects were also sometimes seen in the apartment. One morning Sylvia made her way to the kitchen to put on a pot of coffee and ran into Yul Brynner. During a Saturday canasta game, the door opened and in strolled Elvis. Al Jolson once dropped by to watch a prizefight. But normally, noted Betty, it was a quiet apartment. Morning was the only private time the Sullivans had as a unit, but Ed often slept late after making the rounds of shows and clubs. He really had two jobs, banging out his twice-weekly column with two fingers in "one hour and 35 years," as he put it, finishing about 2:30 for his 4 P.M. Daily News deadline, with a big assist from his guy Friday, Carmine Santullo.

He liked working on deadline, and he ate at all hours. "If Ed feels like eating at six, off we go," explained Sylvia. "If he wants to nap until ten, we eat at ten." She had to book a dinner date to talk to him. "Ed isn't interested in small talk, so I make it a rule to keep up on all the news and to save amusing stories for dinnertime." Monica Lewis believed the couple had a tight marriage—at least "on paper," adding, "They weren't going to split, although he had talked to me about that, about getting a dispensation if I would marry him." He made similar promises to other crushees.

Polly Bergen told me she remembered Sylvia, as do many, as "a very nice lady—I liked her a lot. She was like a lot of big stars' wives whose lives revolve around their husband. Their job is to make their husband comfortable and happy, to protect and support him. Their life is making his life work." Sylvia could even stand in for him, as when he cut an interview short once to get a shave. After he'd left she turned to the reporter, asked, "What do you want to know?," and helpfully chatted another 20 minutes, listing her husband's accomplishments; her main outside achievement was hospital charity work. "My mother was the perfect wife for my father," remembered Betty Precht. "She never had to cook anything. He didn't want anyone cooking for him, because he couldn't taste anything." Betty said her mother "didn't mind not living in a house—other women might have. He adored my mother. They had a reasonably good relationship. I think she did what she had to do. She was a typical mother, except she didn't have to shop. She played cards, saw her friends"—and, she adds, acted as "a go-between" between Betty and her inexpressive father, whose passions were mostly poured into the show—or at times, spent romancing other women.

Asked to describe him, Betty said, "That's a hard one. He was not a warm, friendly person. He was very stubborn, very ambitious, but these qualities didn't always show. Everything was kept inside him. He was not a demonstrative person—except with sports figures, whom he loved introducing on the show—Mickey Mantle and so forth. His sportswriting days were the happiest days he had. He was Irish, and he had a temper. He was very much the same" at home as on TV—often removed.

She called him "very patriotic. He'd interact with soldiers at hospitals—but it was more of a surface involvement with those people"—as with all people, it appears. "He was almost an introvert. He felt things very deeply but it wasn't noticeable. *Remote* would be a good word, or maybe something a little stronger." But when her parents went to South America on a long vacation, "my father missed me the most—my mother was having a ball—and wrote these very tender letters to me," later fondly bound.

Her emotionally bottled-up father, she went on to say, "helped me in many ways in practical matters. He would do anything for me—he'd help me with a composition, and I'd have to hold him back because he'd want to write the whole paper." Sullivan helped her get into UCLA by writing a letter to Joe E. Brown, the comedian, who had some pull at the college. When a friend of hers couldn't get into Columbia's Journalism School, Sullivan called Dwight Eisenhower (then president of Columbia) and got him accepted. "He was very generous—he didn't care about money. He just wanted to make enough to live the way he lived."

The Sullivan marriage had numerous Jiggs and Maggie moments. "The two of them would get at each other," director John Moffitt told me. "Sylvia was like [in nagging voice], 'Ed, you have to do this, Ed,' and Ed would go, 'Sylvia . . . Sylvia . . . will you *shut up?*' They went back and forth like that; but they weren't nasty to each other. She was always saying, 'Ed, we gotta do this, we gotta see so-and-so, we're going out . . .' And Ed would say, 'Sylvia, I'm trying to work on my column. Please. Be quiet.' He'd have the glasses down over his nose, always trying to work, and she'd come in with something. But other than that kind of thing, they were totally devoted." Mrs. Samuel Lionel, a close friend, pointed out that Sylvia had no influence on him professionally, "but it was a lovely union they had. She was his right arm." Their attorney Ron Greenberg told me, "They very much understood each other. Like long-married couples, they interrupted each other and finished each other's sentences."

Ken Rothstein, Rob Sullivan's boyhood pal, commented, "Even at a young age, I was able to sense this genuine deep love these two people had for each other—like we should all hope to be loved. They loved listening to each other. Sylvia had pride in Ed, and he had a genuine love for her. They were a high-water mark for a long-term relationship."

Even so, it was the show and, before that, the column—not his home life—that was the emotional center of Sullivan's world. In the office in his apartment he haggled with agents over the phone and sometimes interviewed performers. The Sullivans' transient lifestyle made sense to them. "We always believed we wanted to live in such a way that we could walk away from it," Sylvia explained to people who thought their domestic life a bit bizarre. "We didn't want to be possessed by our possessions. That's why we've lived in hotels." For Broadway babies, an ideal arrangement.

Sullivan, born in Harlem and raised a short train ride from Manhattan, was a New Yorker in his bones. He loved the rich lullaby of Broadway— "the hip hooray and ballyhoo, the rattle of the subway trains and taxis, the folks who entertain at Angelo's and Maxie's." It was a mythic world we now know only through Broadway musicals.

John Leonard, in *A Really Big Show*, wrote that they lived a kind of movie life: "Nobody had to wash a dish or make a bed. Ed and Sylvia were children of the Roaring Twenties. Days and nights always had had a floating quality, like the dream life of athletes and gangsters, actors and comics, showgirls and sports, hustlers and swells; songwriters, gag writers, and ragtime piano players; of men who gambled and women who smoked; guys and dolls."

Not surprisingly, Sullivan was unhappy when he lived briefly in Hollywood and then Connecticut, where rustling leaves kept him awake nights. Sylvia said, "We tried the quiet life. Before the first year was out we had more lights burning than 42nd Street. But it was still too quiet. One day I came home and found Ed washing the windows. I said, 'Ed, let's get outta here—fast!' So we left the trees and the squirrels and came back to where we belonged, the big city." Sullivan was a loyal citizen of Broadway. He would begin an introduction on TV: "If you haven't been over to the Mark Hellinger Theatre, you've missed a great show." He assumed we were all New Yorkers, or would-be New Yorkers, but if we couldn't get over to the Mark Hellinger he would gladly bring the theater to us. He made his TV show simultaneously personal and cosmopolitan.

Sylvia became expert in reading his moods and soothing his flare-ups. "Of course, he has a temper and he can be unreasonable," she told an interviewer. "I may say, 'It's a nice day,' and if he's annoyed at something he will say, 'Why?' or some such silly thing. But in our life we have never had an important fight." She dealt with his driving ambition by becoming a trusted copilot. Like his father, he was a brooder; and he feared that, like his father, he might end up a thwarted, angry, bitter man unable to achieve his life goal: fame. On his 30th birthday, he moaned to his wife that he felt he was going nowhere despite his success as a sportswriter and syndicated Broadway columnist.

"It was one of the unhappiest moments of Ed's life," she recalled in 1956. "I'll never forget that day as long as I live. There he was, looking as

if the end of the world had come. He didn't have national prominence—
and that's what he wanted. I was perfectly satisfied with him the way he
was, but he was born with a desire to be a big success. He was big in
New York, and in the cities he was syndicated, but he didn't have national prominence. He was always terribly ambitious, and until he got
the reputation and success he wanted, he was terribly tense. Now that he
has attained it he is much more relaxed."

To those in Sullivan's large Irish family, like Megan Sullivan, the great
man was simply "Cousin Ed." The Sullivans would arrive at Megan's
home in a Lincoln town car, and, while Ed golfed with Megan's dad,
Sylvia would go to the track with David Marx of the toy company
Marxes. "She was really nice, classy and gracious, in a Chanel suit,"
Megan told me. She recalled her family discussing the pair's mixed marriage, then an exotic event. She was ten or so when the Sullivans would
come to their home in Rumson, New Jersey, to pick up her father for a
golf game. Her dad, Sullivan's first cousin, was a Wall Street financier
also named Ed. The two Ed Sullivans played at the Beacon Hill Country
Club; Alex Webster, the football player, and the fighter Dick Tiger often
joined them. Sullivan was a fair golfer in his prime, averaging in the
upper 70s, who liked hanging out with other, less famous entrepreneurs—
stockbrokers, manufacturers, real estate tycoons, bistro owners, your
basic country club set. Bob Precht confirmed that Sullivan had no close
show business friends other than the Jerry Vales. Vale had glowing but
unrevealing things to say of his old friend. As was said of Sullivan more
than once, his best friend was his audience.

David Brown, the movie producer, knew Sullivan well and traveled to
Acapulco with him, but he told me he recalled little about him except
that he didn't talk show business. "We talked about other things. Artists
generally don't talk about their work when they're off-camera. He was a
man of conviction, a very decent and outgoing person. He was just a
jovial guy, but he wasn't a joke teller." Bob Precht agreed—"He talked
a lot about golf and sports generally," but not show business. He had a
cursory interest in politics and what was happening in the world. Precht
said Sullivan was "generally a Democrat."

About once a year, Megan Sullivan and her large family drove into
New York to see the show—usually the 4 P.M. dress rehearsal. "Ed always seated us behind or in front of audience guests," she recalled, "so
we would be on camera. After the show we would all go up onstage to
have our photo taken with living legends" like Buster Keaton. "Ed was a
sweet guy who made a point to talk to the kids. To us, he was just Cousin

Ed who'd become a big celebrity." Sunday nights, the family gathered to see the show. "We *had* to watch him," she said, and remembered being bored by the old-timers but loving the plate spinners and, of course, Topo Gigio. When Megan's sister Laura was in boarding school, she had an 8 P.M. lights-out on Sundays, so Laura wrote Sullivan, who sent a note to the head of the school asking that the curfew be extended to 9 so the girls could watch his show. It was.

The adopted member of the family, Carmine Santullo, was Sullivan's devoted assistant for 35 years, a quiet, sallow, thin, sad-eyed man who worked out of Sullivan's home office; one secretary remembered him as "meek and fragile." Santullo met Sullivan when he was a 16-year-old backstage bootblack at Loew's State Theatre; Ed got to know him while hosting stage shows. Sullivan became his fairy godfather, paying him to deliver his column to the *Daily News* and then later hiring him as a full-time aide—running errands and running down items, working the phones (100 calls a day), opening mail (2,500 letters a week), and taking the column to the paper and proofreading it there. Sullivan also had a secretary who worked with Santullo in a space off the living room.

Sullivan stored most of his awards, plaques, cups, and citations in Santullo's Bronx apartment; Carmine loved to boast that both he and Sullivan were born on East 114th Street. Sullivan gave him his cast-off Lincoln when the sponsor sent over a new model. The fiercely faithful, thick-skinned Santullo, described by intimates as Sullivan's secretary, messenger, confidant, and buffer—indeed, his Nubian slave—was adept at coping with his boss's easily ruffled feathers, but remained mild-mannered. "You can't have a temper of your own around here," Carmine told a reporter. "You either roll with the ball or get out of it. If there's any punishment to be had, you just take it and say, 'Tomorrow's another day.' "

Santullo acknowledged to Jerry Bowles, "He had a temper, of course, and naturally I had many experiences with it, but he would soon quiet down. You couldn't let what happened yesterday carry over." Will Jordan told me he remembered Santullo as "a very, very nice guy" who, after Sullivan died, would call Jordan's parents to offer them tickets to Broadway shows. Oddly, Carmine himself attended the show only a few times during his entire 35-year career at Sullivan's side. He never married ("The Sullivans were his family," noted Bowles), and lived with a sister in the Bronx; on his desk were small pictures of Ed and Sylvia in a two-dollar drugstore frame. Precht remembered, "Carmine was an amazing person. He was bright and energetic, and there was nothing he wouldn't do. If Sylvia wanted a sandwich he'd go get her a sandwich. He worshipped Ed." Staffer Peter Calabrese told me, "He looked like a cross between Jamie Farr of 'M*A*S*H' and Eddie Cantor. Very efficient. This was a guy whom Ed trusted implicitly, and he had to have earned that."

"Carmine was the keeper of the flame," recalled former Daily News entertainment writer Patricia O'Haire, who got to know Santullo in the composing room, where she made up the entertainment pages alongside him. "After Ed died," she told me, "Carmine would call the paper to remind people whenever there was a Sullivan anniversary coming up. He didn't talk much about anything, but he was a very nice man, very good about giving tickets to the printers. He took care of them when the circus came to town." When Sullivan died, Carmine was at his bedside. Said a family friend, "He died in Carmine's arms."

Right until the end, Santullo called him "Mr. Sullivan." Carmine (called "Carmen" by Ed) mainly collected items for "Little Old New York" but at times assembled and even wrote the column, which in its last years was a humdrum laundry list of items batted out with little personality or purpose, full of plugs, kudos, and birth notices, no longer the work of a onetime Broadway boulevardier. In 1971, Sullivan, one of TV's wealthiest men, earned $200 a week from the column, but after the show folded that year it became his main showbiz connection.

Sullivan always considered himself a lifetime member of the larger Daily News family. Even in the 1970s (when I wrote a humor column there), the News had three Broadway columnists—Bob Sylvester, Charles McHarry, and Sullivan, by then a faded newspaper presence who was never seen at the office. But before he was a TV star, he dropped off the column at the News, and is still vividly remembered by the paper's longtime entertainment writers O'Haire and George Maksian, sports cartoonist Bill Gallo, and the late critic Kay Gardella.

"I was a copy boy when he would bring his column in," Gallo told me. "He'd tell me who was in the column and what he wanted, and I'd go to the library and get the photos. This was long before the TV show. But he was already a celebrity. I got to know him when I was president of the boxing writers association. He'd been a boxing writer for the old Graphic, before my time. He loved fighters and he emceed the Golden Gloves. He was well respected, kind of a hero at the News with the young guys here. He was a helluva nice guy—a straight shooter. There was nothing fake about him, very to the point. He'd send me a letter when he liked something I did. A good fella. He never took himself that seriously. Although he seemed like a star—he had that aura, even before the TV show. That was the age when people who wrote columns were stars. Not like now, when it doesn't mean a goddamn thing."

Kay Gardella, the *News*'s longtime TV critic, remembered Sullivan coming into the paper with his column, which then was a double column that ran down the entire side of a page. "He wasn't much of a mixer in the office," she told me. "You never saw him schmoozing with anybody. He hung around the desk and talked to the editors, to check on something in his column." According to her, he wasn't regarded as a star at the *News,* despite being touted for years in the show's intro as "the nationally syndicated *New York Daily News* columnist."

Gardella said the paper "took him for granted. He worked there for a long time before he had the show. TV didn't mean that much to the editors. They didn't have the feeling for it that viewers did. They're on the desk all night, reporting, and the last thing they're worried about is TV. I never heard much raving or carrying on about him. Maybe the column was beginning to bore them—it was just notes." She suspected Sullivan used his column "as a payoff for people on the TV show. It would certainly be a natural thing to drop in an item—you know, one hand washing the other."

Gardella noted, "The editors didn't appreciate the publicity" he got for the paper. "They didn't know what impact he had and what value it had. They could have taken more advantage of it. At that time, they weren't smart enough or interested enough in television to know it was important. I said to someone, 'They didn't know what they had. They didn't make use of the TV connection.' " Some editors might have been resentful, rather than proud, of Sullivan, she said: "If you're getting ahead, there are always people putting you down instead of saying you're valued. That's a common trait in the newspaper business, and I think it's a destructive one."

Lee Silver, onetime arts editor at the *Daily News* who moved into corporate relations at the Shubert Organization, remembered Sullivan at the office prior to his TV life. "I would say he was an egalitarian. At the paper he was another one of the guys on the staff. Even after the TV show, he was still just another guy on the staff, not like *the* Ed Sullivan. He thought his value to TV was that he had a newsman's outlook. He didn't act as if he was a 'television star,' in quotes. He kept repeating, 'I'm a newspaperman.' "

When Sullivan came into the office, Silver pointed out, "he didn't expect special attention, and he didn't get any special attention." He remembered Sullivan as "very reserved, but friendly to everybody in the city room, including the copy boys. He didn't talk down to copy editors. He always wore a jacket and tie; he made phone calls at his desk with his jacket on." He had his own desk at the *News* that nobody used when he wasn't there, reserved for Santullo to review a column before handing it to the copy desk.

Silver confirmed that the *News* copy desk edited out all mentions of Walter Winchell in Sullivan's column. "Winchell found Sullivan to be a threat and began to pick on him. When the *Mirror* was about to fold, Winchell made a pass at getting onto the *News*, but was turned down. He was a star. They didn't look on Winchell as a newspaperman who was a team player." Sullivan remained a *Daily News* team player. If he had an item that should be followed up by the paper, he would tip off the news desk.

Sullivan, who often cozily referred to his wife on TV ("When Sylvia and I were in London . . ."), leaned on her for support and confirmation. "I'm married to a wonderful woman," he always said. "During the lean times she always felt I was a success. When I came home at night she made me feel successful, no matter what had happened during the day."

Nonetheless, Sullivan remained a girl-chaser long after he married. An early infatuation, singer Monica Lewis, told me, "He was pretty Catholic, but he was not a celibate or a priestly man. When he first made a few moves, I thought, 'There's no way I'm gonna be another of his girls,' so I kept ignoring it. I kept treating him like royalty, except the poor bastard fell in love with me. He became quite serious. He was an old man to me, in his late 40s!" Monica was 23.

She recounted, "This went on for about a year, where he continuously paid court, to use an old-fashioned expression, in all the most delicate and decorous ways. He was very lovely to me, and then he courted my mother, my father, my sister, with dinners at Tavern on the Green, that sort of thing. But not in any disgusting fashion. He was always very circumspect, very careful. But I was not going to fall into any categories that were not good for me—as a famous married man's mistress."

She added, "I was pretty damn self-protective and lived with my family. I'd been married for a year, which was a disaster, so I was really leery of anything that could look not right. But he was very, very sweet. I was appearing in Baltimore during a terrible rainstorm, so Ed sent me over,

by courier, an umbrella and a note that said, 'Take care of yourself.' "
The one-sided courtship ended after a year. "I probably fell in love with
somebody. Finally it just dwindled away; it wasn't going to go anywhere."

Sullivan was a far more discreet lothario than Winchell, who, though
also married, flaunted his mistresses on the dance floor and at his favorite haunt, the Stork Club. During their careers, the men's paths kept
crossing—once almost in bed, when Sullivan and Winchell were chasing
the same girl, Jane Kean, a singer and comic who performed with her
sister Betty in an act that both men eagerly plugged in their columns.
After Sullivan gave up, Jane Kean and Winchell had a serious romance.
Kean later replaced Joyce Randolph as Trixie Norton on "The Honeymooners," in 1966.

Kean said Sullivan wooed her when she was barely 18 and was one of
the acts on the Harvest Moon Ball show at Loew's State Theatre that he
emceed. Wrote Kean in her memoir, *A Funny Thing Happened to Me
on My Way to "The Honeymooners"*: "His show seemed like a big break
for me. Being on the bill usually generated publicity, especially in his
columns in the *Daily News*."

In the memoir, she related how persistent Sullivan could be, at one
point forcing himself on her when she resisted him. As she wrote, "At
the end of the Loew's State engagement, Sullivan requested that I play
other theaters with him. Wow! I was on cloud nine." Kean was also confused. "Unaccustomed to so much attention, I was becoming more and
more attracted to him," she said. "In my 18-year-old eyes, he began to
resemble Humphrey Bogart." Kean later told me by phone, "He was a
powerful man, and there's always a certain amount of flattery to have
someone that powerful be attracted to you and come to the door with
flowers and candy and umbrellas"—a favorite gambit.

Sullivan kept offering her rides to and from the show, she recounted in
her memoir. "At the end of every ride he would get affectionate and suggested I feel him in a certain area which shall remain nameless. I declined.
After one show, he invited me to his personal suite at the Delmonico Hotel. I declined again. The closing night of the tour, he suggested I invite
him up for a cup of coffee to celebrate the end of the tour. I didn't think
that would be wise, because my mother was usually there."

But Kean relented and invited him upstairs, to her regret. "Sullivan
wasted no time," she wrote. "He pushed me down on the couch and got
on top of me. He exposed himself and ripped off my underwear. I tried
to fight him off but he was as strong as an ox. He had been a fighter in

his youth and he definitely won this round. I was terrified and ashamed."
When he departed, she said, "He kissed me on the cheek and said 'goodnight.'" Worried she might be pregnant, she told her mother what had
happened, and Mrs. Kean invited Sullivan to their apartment, grilling
him on details of the event. "He assured her he had taken the necessary
precautions," she said. Sullivan didn't back off even then. "He continued to call me and sent me love notes when he went to Florida. He
claimed he was in love with me and sent messages through Carmine."

Kean told me, "Ed never had the reputation as a ladies' man or a
player, but he was. I did not have an affair with him. He attacked me. It
did not go any further than that. I really did not want to get involved like
that. He just was overly aggressive. He professed his love. I was like 17 or
18, a naive kid at the time." She added, "I knew one or two women he
had been involved with. One was a very cute black girl, a singer. But he
pursued me—oh, yes, he did indeed. He was very persistent. But I wasn't
involved with him. With Walter it was a love affair."

Sullivan finally gave up, as he did with Monica Lewis and others he
chased. "As he became more involved with his show, his interest in me
waned somewhat," Kean wrote. "I still continued to hear from him, but
we were both busy, busy, busy." Even after that, Kean agreed to appear on
his show. Sullivan's womanizing continued for much of his marriage,
but no affair ever surfaced or appeared to threaten the couple. As Jerry
Bowles delicately put it in his Sullivan biography, "Sullivan never lost his
eye for the ladies. Throughout his life he maintained his interest in a
shapely leg, and production people recall that he practically had to be
handcuffed whenever Juliet Prowse was on."

Sullivan was addicted to girl singers. One of them, part of a singing
group, who asked to remain anonymous, turned him down because he
was married. "Ed was kind of a player," she told me. "He liked women.
About the third show we did—I'll never forget this as long as I live—he
said, 'Ya know, I'm stuck on you.' I had never heard that expression before. I figured it out." Later he called her up and said, "Sylvia and I are
celebrating our wedding anniversary, and I would love you to come."
She said, "I didn't think that was a very good idea if he's stuck on me, so
I made up an excuse."

She remembered often bumping into Sullivan at a corner phone booth
near both their apartments. "I would call my boyfriend on the pay phone
because I always suspected everything was bugged in those days. And
I'd run into Ed and wait for him to get out of this phone booth. This had

to be in the wintertime, because you could write your initials on the phone booth glass it was so steamy." She added, "Sometimes Ed would wait for me, and I'd say, 'Why are you leaving your hotel to come down here to the corner to make a call? And he'd say, 'The same reason you are!' "

The crooner mentioned an affair Sullivan had with big band singer Jane Harvey that she claimed broke up Harvey's marriage to powerful A&R (artist and repertoire) man Bob Thiele, who later married Teresa Brewer. She said Sullivan "was also involved with one of the Barry Sisters." The singer added, "He was more charming off-camera, but what you saw was what you got. He was a wonderful person to work for, but I wasn't attracted to him at all." Sheila MacRae was another singer Sullivan coveted. "Oh, yeah, but he also liked my talent," MacRae told me, claiming that he was "seriously" in love with her. "He was just crazy about me after I left Gordon."

Sullivan director John Moffitt called his boss's dalliances harmless "office flirtations rather than serious affairs." He told me Sullivan "would chase a secretary around the office, but they always outran him." Jean Carroll, a comedian who played his show 39 times, hoots at the notion of Sullivan the ladies man: "You're joking! Really? I never, ever, ever pictured him as a Don Juan," she told me. "Never! He didn't make any advances—maybe I wasn't his type. But I didn't mix. I did my show, I took my shopping bag, and I went home."

Show staffer Peter Calabrese never heard of any Sullivan dalliances. "I can't say, but I wouldn't be surprised. He was Ed Sullivan when that meant something. He made people's careers, and he was definitely a man. But he was very respectful, very courtly, not the kind of guy who would say, 'Look at the knockers on her.' If he was having extracurricular affairs, he was very discreet about it."

Polly Bergen deftly spurned his attentions, but it took quick, creative thinking: "I always found him very, very nice until one evening when I agreed to do a charity performance at the Plaza Hotel. He asked me if I'd be on it. Of course, you did anything that Ed Sullivan asked you to do. He was the man. So I got my evening gowns and my music charts and went to the Plaza Hotel. His wife, I guess, was out of town. I was getting ready to go on and he kind of sidled up to me—this never happened before. He said, 'I'd love to take you to dinner tonight after the show.' I didn't know what to do! I don't want to go to dinner because *if* he's gonna make a pass and I say no, I'll never do the show again. I don't want to put myself in that position. I don't know if he's gonna make a pass or not. What the hell is he doing inviting me to dinner by myself?"

She went on to say, "I was in my early 20s, and I really panicked. It was the first time I'd seen him as a letch. I said, 'Oh, I'm so sorry, Ed, I'd just give anything to go out with you, but I have a prior date. As a matter of fact he's sitting out in the audience right now. He'll be coming back when I finish, helping me with my gown and my charts, and then we're going to dinner. If I didn't have that date, I'd go to dinner with you in a minute, Ed. Thank you *so* much for asking!' "

Bergen had concocted the entire story. "I ran out to the table that my agent at MCA was sitting at. There were, like, ten of them. I went to my favorite, Jay Kantor, and I said, 'Now, listen, you've got to be my date, honey. You've got to go back and do the gowns and the charts and tell Ed we're having dinner together, because he's coming on to me. Jay said, 'Honey, I can't. I'm meeting my wife with her mom and dad at the 21 Club.' And I said, 'No, you don't understand. This is really important,' and he said, 'I know what—let me ask Freddie [Fields], because maybe he's free.' I said, 'Oh, God, no, don't ask him, I can't stand him.' So Jay said, 'Listen you want to get out of trouble or not?' I said, 'Christ, OK.' He asked Freddie, who said, 'Oh, all right.' To him, I'm just another girl singer. So he comes backstage and gets me into a cab. As we dropped the stuff off, he said, 'Want to grab a bite?' He was just being nice. I felt obligated because he'd gotten me out of this mess. I couldn't stand him. I thought he was a very mean guy. But I said, 'Well, OK, I guess so.' Within a year we were married."

Whatever the strains on the Sullivans' marriage—not just the girls on the side but also his equally hot pursuit of singers and comics for his show and items for his column—divorce was never an option. Wrote Sullivan biographer Michael David Harris (his former CBS publicist), "Sylvia's workaholic husband would reject divorce even if the marriage hadn't been happy." Sullivan was much too seriously involved with the main love of his life: the show.

CHAPTER 13

Extended Family

I was happy to see Topo go. Frankly, I think we wore the little bastard into the ground.

Jack Babb, talent coordinator

Unlike Arthur Godfrey, who had his "friends," or even Steve Allen, who had his "Man in the Street" gang, Ed Sullivan never had a snug on-screen television "family" unit. Over time, however, he adopted a small circle of regulars that viewers eagerly welcomed.

There was Ed's household TV pet, Topo Gigio, the cutesy-pie rubber Italian mouse that Sullivan played straight man to; Señor Wences, whose surreal act consisted of a hand puppet named Johnny (or "Yonny"), Wences's fist turned into a face with lipstick and a tiny blond wig (whose catchphrase was "Deefeecul' fo' you—eesy fo' me!"), and a bearded head in a box that Wences slammed shut after asking, "S'awright?," and the head had growled back, "S'awright!"; and Rickie Layne, whose dummy, Velvel, spoke with a Yiddish accent. Nobody can say why these peculiar acts enchanted America for years, but all three went from zero to stardom after repeat appearances with Sullivan, and all are still remembered today.

Topo Gigio was an acquired taste and made as many people retch as coo over him (her? Some speculate Topo was a gay or maybe unisex mouse). The chatty rubber rodent moved as if animated, but in fact was manipulated by puppeteers' unseen sticks. Sullivan felt his banter with Topo warmed up his famously frozen image—which it did. Marlo Lewis said, "It was a love affair between the two. Topo would say, 'I love you, Eddie.' We thought if the mouse says that, the audience is going to say the same thing. That was Ed's brilliance. Ed told us, 'I got this little mouse.'" Sullivan would assume a gentle Geppetto-like manner with

Topo, whose invariable tag line was "Kees-a-me goo' night, Eddie."
Topo became the world's most famous mouse after Mickey, and one of
the show's major lasting memories. Bob Thompson, the TV historian,
told me, "I've got a memory of that mouse that, once you saw it, would
haunt you till the day you died."

Topo Gigio (that is, Luigi, or Louie, the Mouse) debuted on the Sullivan show April 14, 1963, a day that will live in puppetry. Topo was ten
inches tall, with baby doe eyes cut from foam rubber, a sort of old-world
ancestor of the Muppets. Viewers were thoroughly perplexed about how
Topo Gigio could walk, talk, roll his eyes, wiggle his ears and toes, and
gesture—all at once. Not even Walt Disney could top that then.

The cuddly mousette with the wee voice was more complicated than
he looked, requiring a trio of puppeteers plus a falsetto supplied offstage
by Giuseppe Mazullo, who recited his lines phonetically. Unlike most
puppets, Topo was manipulated with sticks, not strings; to stay invisible
the puppeteers wore black velour against a black curtain, heads covered
by black hoods. Topo's mysterious internal workings were revealed in
the official U.S. patent application submitted by his creator, artist Maria
Perego Caldura of Milan. She controlled Topo's movements by inserting
two fingers in the mouse's legs and, with the other hand, manipulating
rods that opened and closed his mouth. With her remaining fingers, she
pulled cables that rolled Topo's big imploring eyes and curled his toes.
Two other puppeteers moved his arms and hands.

Sullivan said in 1963 that no live entertainer had attracted as much attention during the show's 15 years on the air as dear li'l Topo. "When he's
on my arm, I actually feel that he's a living thing, and that I'm talking to
somebody. I've never had that feeling before with any puppet or dummy."
The staff was less enamored of Topo, because none of the puppeteers
spoke English and it was tricky coordinating the act, which relied on Sullivan not screwing up his lines, as he was wont to do. As Russ Petranto
pointed out to me, "Since Ed seldom said the same thing twice, this was always scary."

Topo Gigio was the absolutely worst thing ever to be shown on a TV
screen. I'd watch a week of "Jerry Springer" before a minute of that rubber rat!

George Garris, St. Paul, Minnesota

Early in her career, the struggling Joan Rivers was hired to write material for Topo Gigio. Aghast, she told her roommate, "Can you believe this? They want me to write Topo the Mouse for Ed Sullivan for $500!" She recalled in her memoir, "I was born corrupt. I said, 'I'll do it, I'll do it.' I lay on the floor and wrote a sketch about this comic Italian puppet mouse, with a little Italian accent, who had become a semi-fad in America. I had him asking Ed Sullivan to explain football. I put Topo in a little football jersey that said ¼ on the back." She put her roommate's name on the script and was hired to write two more. Rivers then realized she could write material for other people—mice, anyway.

The publicity proclaimed that Sullivan had discovered Topo Gigio, when in fact it was Jack Babb, Sullivan's trusty ace scout, who first glimpsed Topo in Italy and sent a film to Sullivan. In any case, Topo appeared some 50 times on the Sullivan show, eventually wearing out his welcome. Babb was happy to see the mouse go, but Topo felt otherwise and later starred in a 1961 Italian movie, "Le Avventura di Topo Gigio," released in the United States as "The Magic World of Topo Gigio." Marketed like mad, he also turned up in cartoons and on trinkets all over Italy. He remains an icon of Italian pop culture, performing at festivals. After his finale on the Sullivan show in 1971, Topo went on a world tour to South America, Spain, and Japan and had a children's TV show in Italy; he is honored in Chicago by a restaurant near the Second City Theater, called Topo Gigio Ristorante. Thus the minimouse lives on, serving up "fusilli Topo" to aging, nostalgia-starved baby boomers.

The endless parade of puppets, ventriloquists, and animal acts was a critical plank in Sullivan's mission to construct a family audience— much of what kept the show running so long. In America in the 1950s, as now, The Family was regarded as the glue that holds the country together (soaring divorce rates, deadbeat dads, working moms, abused children, and dysfunctional families to the contrary). America worships The Family, a kind of state religion.

A case might be made that TV's pandering to youth began with Sullivan's decision to seduce kids—and, when they became teens, to mesmerize them with rock and roll. In those days, grown-ups controlled the set. In the early 1960s, prime-time shows were geared to parents, not kids, unlike today's shows. Sullivan obsessively labored to snare the family audience, enticing tots with chimps, ponies, and puppets. Parents, delighted to keep the kids content, or at least silent, tuned in Sullivan's show to help preserve the already endangered 1950s family unit that was slowly beginning to splinter.

The Sullivan show, again a mirror reflecting America, catered to, if not kowtowed to, "the youngsters," as Ed called them. Bob Precht said, "You've got to appreciate how much he brings to the show by virtue of his own personality [and values]. He must feel that whatever he presents is good clean fun for the entire family. *That's* what makes 'The Ed Sullivan Show.' " Someone in his studio audience once remarked, "Ed is like Howard Johnson's. Wherever you are, there'll always be good food and clean restrooms."

The show's second most popular act—again, with both kids and adults—was Señor Wences. The former Wenceslao Moreno was near 50 when he struck gold on Sullivan's show on December 31, 1950. He died in 2004 at 103. It's safe to say that on no other TV show then would you have been likely to find Señor Wences, Topo Gigio, the Muppets, or even the traditional ventriloquist Rickie Layne. All were on Sullivan's menu as tasty appetizers for his headline entrées. The 1950s and 1960s were a heyday for ventriloquists; they were elevated from birthday party Punch and Judy shows to pop art.

Wences was to puppets what a fellow Spaniard, the surrealist Picasso, was to painting. Wences opened the door to a disparaged form. Only Edgar Bergen and Charlie McCarthy had crossed over into big-time show business in America, with their sardonic radio program and, before that, their performances in clubs, where Noël Coward discovered them. Bergen and McCarthy never translated to television because Bergen was such a famously lousy ventriloquist on radio (the show's running gag); he didn't keep his lips closed even for studio audiences. Talent manager Marty Fisher told me, "Wences was archenemies with Edgar Bergen. According to Wences, Edgar Bergen would stop at nothing to exclude him as a competitor; he spent a lot of time trying to get Wences out of the picture." The ventriloquist star wars of the period could be brutal.

Sullivan gave ventriloquists a glittering new life. Besides Topo Gigio, Señor Wences, and Rickie Layne, Sullivan featured Paul Winchell and

During my high school years in Cleveland, Ed Sullivan was the only person who could lure my brothers and me out of our locked bedrooms and into the living room with our parents. To the world, he was a TV emcee. To me, he was our first and only family therapist.

Rita Abrams, Mill Valley, California

Jerry Mahoney, TV's smartest dummy act; the copycat Jimmy Nelson and wisecracking Danny O'Day (both Winchell's and Nelson's impudent puppets were chips off the Charlie McCarthy block); Shari Lewis and the cuddly Lambchop, a Topo-like mouse in sheep's clothing; and finally, most lastingly, Jim Henson's Kermit the Frog and his fellow Muppets, who played the Sullivan show 25 times, which led Henson to "Sesame Street"—and then led to Emmy and Tony awards and a cottage industry capped by "Avenue Q." Maybe modern puppet stars technically can't trace their roots to Sullivan's show (Howdy Doody got there first, in 1947), but Sullivan boosted ventriloquists into prime time and made them respectable for grown-up viewing.

Wences came to America in 1934 after a brief career as a 15-year-old bullfighter that ended when he was severely gored. He joined a traveling circus in Spain, where he was a bareback rider, juggler, and acrobat, later turning to ventriloquism. Pedro, Wences's man in the box, wore glasses, a mustache, and a beard, and Señor Wences was so skilled at muffling the voice that it sounded as if it really *were* coming from inside the box. Wences lore has it that the bit came about when a full-length Pedro was damaged in a baggage-car train accident and only the head survived. Prior to that, Wences was just another ventriloquist, but the talking head in a box made his name. In another signature bit, Wences stuck a cigarette between the "lips" of his puppet Johnny and somehow blew smoke rings from between his thumb and index finger.

Wences's act had no true punch lines, just absurdist Spanish-accented dialogue that should have bewildered viewers but instead entranced them. Post-Sullivan, Wences toured with Martin & Lewis, did a Broadway show

I was about five when I walked unknowingly into the living room that fateful night (in my footed pajamas, I might add), glanced at the screen and saw that hideous, hideous deformity! This guy would take a fist, draw a crude red mouth on it, glue on huge lifeless reptilian eyes, attach a limp stuffed "body," and, last but not least, add an androgynous blond wig. The result was one of the eeriest television specters ever to be viewed by man, very high on my list of scariest images ever—right up there with the twins from "The Shining" or Linda Blair's head spinning in "The Exorcist." Hopefully all existing footage of this thing has been burned in a studio vault fire to protect the psyches of future children.

Charlene Norris, Miami, Florida

with Danny Kaye, played the White House for four presidents, and appeared endlessly in Las Vegas for a tightly timed 19 minutes plus a one-minute encore, his only props a card table, a cigarette, and a glass of water. Ventriloquists remain in awe of him and of his minimalist act.

Michele LaFong, a New York ventriloquist, met Wences at a tribute to the master on his 100th birthday, and says he gave her Pedro and Johnny replicas from his vintage collection. The fabled ventriloquist is enshrined on a section of West 54th Street in New York named "Señor Wences Way," just around the corner from the Ed Sullivan Theater. LaFong told me, "From the very beginning, I studied Señor Wences and analyzed what set him apart from other ventriloquists. The main thing he taught me was that it's not about the jokes."

She explained, "If you wrote down all of his words from any Ed Sullivan show, it wasn't funny. He made everything funny by the voices—the cuteness of the voices—and the rapid exchanges. He could do it in any country and it didn't matter. He was the only international ventriloquist that ever existed. People just thought he was great, hysterical, although if he was doing his act today, it wouldn't fly. We've all changed. We're so bombarded with images. Cute isn't enough."

Wences didn't like ventriloquists, she noted. "He was very paranoid, because ventriloquists were always trying to rip him off. He would always turn his back on the Sullivan show and not reveal how Johnny is made and how he works, because of the rip-offs that would take place." She recalled a night at the Improv in Los Angeles when Paul Winchell was sitting across from her and Señor Wences. "It was like a dream come true. Winchell acted like such a fan of Señor Wences, asking for his autograph. Wences wasn't as interested in Paul Winchell." In person, recalled LaFong, Wences "was like an overage kid. He would make things out of napkins while we were out to eat—little doves. He always tried to lighten the moment." She called him "Wences," and she remembered that, even at 100, he was still "very sharp, especially in his act. He was able to do his act like a 35- or 40-year-old person." Only offstage did he seem elderly. She added that he never learned much English apart from the lines in his act, but "we made it work."

Wences had many puppets (including a wiseguy chicken) but relied on Johnny and Pedro. Once, LaFong related, Sullivan told Wences, " 'I only want Johnny, I don't want Pedro.' And he said, 'My act—I use both.' Sullivan got mad and paid him off and didn't book him again for many months." LaFong notes that, after Sullivan left the air, all such novelty acts "were forced to go to Europe—it was almost like somebody sprayed Raid." Apart from the Muppets, post-Sullivan ventriloquism in America all but died; only a few acts (like Ronn Lucas) have since emerged. Digital animation has stolen their act.

When Rickie Layne played the Catskills, his Yiddish-accented dummy, Velvel (Yiddish for "Willie"), was born. Although dialect humor was largely passé by the mid-'50s—Myron Cohen notwithstanding—Layne appealed to Sullivan, who grew up with dialect comics, plus it was an opportunity for Ed to interact with yet another puppet, à la Topo.

Layne (born Richard Israel Cohen) was discovered not by Sullivan but by Nat King Cole, whose wife, Natalie, was singing at Ciro's in 1955 on a bill that included Layne. Cole told Sullivan, "There's a guy working with my wife. He's hysterical. He uses a dummy with a Jewish dialect." Cole promised Sullivan that if Layne flopped he would play one show for free. Sullivan, a sucker for dialect comics, was sold. Cole never had to donate an appearance after Layne's debut on the show in 1956, the first of 39 appearances, mostly with Sullivan as foil (it was always wise for new comics to bring Sullivan into the act). To wit: Velvel tells Sullivan he once played for Notre Dame. "Were you a student?," Ed asks. "No, a goal post." Layne got a lifetime achievement award at the Las Vegas Ventriloquists' Festival in 2002; he died in 2006. His daughter Teri is writing Layne's biography.

Sullivan seldom took chances on unproven talent. Performers usually had earned their ticket to his show via radio, stage, clubs, the circus, somewhere. Sullivan was not a high-risk guy, which makes it seem even less likely that he would feature such risky, bizarre acts as an Italian mouse puppet, a Spanish ventriloquist, and a Jewish dummy. But once the show had become a solid hit, Sullivan had the luxury of taking more chances on unusual novelty acts. If they fell flat, the show was insulated by plenty of celebrity padding to absorb any nationwide thud.

Sullivan's feel for pleasing viewers, however, was not totally foolproof. The comedy act that appeared on the show more than any other (58 times), (Johnny) Wayne & (Frank) Shuster, was a clever Canadian team that Sullivan prized (Shuster was a cousin of Joe Shuster, who cocreated Superman). The team's best-remembered routine was the enactment of a baseball game using Shakespearean phrases. But their 58 appearances on the show failed to impress America. The team's cerebral satire never caught on, even though Sullivan initially hired them for 26 appearances and paid them more than he'd shelled out for anyone up to that time (1958), including Elvis Presley. Their literate comedy, with all the Shakespearean references—a "Dragnet" version of Julius Caesar's assassination called

"Rinse the Blood off My Toga"; a Hamlet spoof of "All in the Family" titled "All in the Royal Family"—couldn't be translated by Sullivan's mass audience; Shakespeare was too literate for mainstream America. Dick Cavett
mentioned to me that he told Woody Allen, "Wayne & Shuster are the only
comedy team in which you couldn't say either one is the funny one."

Yet the often inspired, literate Wayne & Shuster were test pilots for
the more sophisticated humor and satire that arrived with a bound on
TV five years later (on the Smothers Brothers show and then on "Laugh-
In," two very different forms of the standard variety fare). Sullivan,
again, was ahead of his time—just as he was sometimes behind it. Reviewer Gary Cruse wrote on his Web site, "Wayne & Shuster's comedy
was low key, soft focused, and slightly baffling to Americans." Certainly
it was baffling to the comedian Dick Martin, of the far more popular
team of Rowan & Martin, who played Sullivan 15 times before landing
"Laugh-In."

Martin never understood Wayne & Shuster's constant appearances
on the Sullivan show—a view possibly colored by professional rivalry.
"Ed thought that, because they were doing bits about Shakespeare, they
were very bright and avant-garde," Martin told me. "He liked the idea
that they were supposed to be very sophisticated. They weren't at all!
They were not a big hit in Canada. Never!"

Sullivan may have been not all that crazy about them either but just
trying to court the vast Canadian audience he coveted. Ed had a thing
for Canada, once proclaiming, "And now for all you youngsters in the
U.S. and Canada—the Rolling Stones!" Sullivan berated Shecky Greene
for a routine the comic did on the show about trapped coal miners at the
same time some Canadian miners were actually trapped—totally unbeknownst to Greene. Greene told me that, backstage afterward, Sullivan
screamed at the hapless, suddenly battered Shecky, "You dirty Jew sun-
ofabitch, you're sicker than Lenny Bruce. You'll never be on my show
again! You lost me Canada!" (Canada loved Ed anyway, so much so that
his face was carved on a nine-foot totem pole by Ottawa's Huron Indi-
ans and shipped to his New York hotel; the pole was then proudly displayed on the show as part of a Salute to Canada week and a Canadian
trade fair in Philadelphia.) Shecky added a postscript: "Years later, I was
in an elevator with Ed at the Fontainebleau Hotel in Miami Beach, and
he turns to his wife and he says, 'Sylvia, why do we hate Shecky Greene?'
And she says, 'The Canadian mine disaster.' And he says, 'That's right,'
and the doors close."

The seductive member of Sullivan's TV family was its fetching Lincoln saleswoman, Julia Meade—part auto dealer, part chic sexpot, as she extolled the sensuous virtues of the new 1961 Lincoln. As on many shows then, the host would do a lead-in to the commercials, so that single sponsors became strongly identified with shows. Meade was an elegant temptress who recited car commercials in evening gowns while "running her manicured hands over the upholstery," to quote Karal Marling, author of *As Seen on TV,* who adds that Meade was "as tastefully turned out as any diva on Sullivan's show."

Providing lengthy five-minute commercials for Lincoln before the era of multicommercial breaks, Meade (born Julia Kunz) was a headliner in the days of loyal sponsor identification, and a demi–TV star. Like Westinghouse's Betty Furness, Revlon's Barbara Britton, Muriel cigars' Edie Adams, Noxzema shaving cream's Gunilla Knutson ("Take it off—take it *all* off"), Top Brass dandruff remover's Barbara Feldon, and other early, comely, commercial pinup girls, Julia Meade parlayed graceful moves and purring salesmanship into a modest off-TV career. Profiling her, *Look* magazine revealed her Yale Drama School background, hopes for a movie contract, and annual salary ($16,000). A faint Broadway presence before her Lincoln days, Julia saw her career blossom after Lincoln stopped sponsoring Sullivan in the fall of 1959. Meade's come-hither car commercials catapulted her into leading lady status, and she starred onstage in "Mary, Mary," "Wait Until Dark," and "Camelot." She told me, "Oh, dear, I got everything! For five years I hosted 'Playhouse 90.' I did 'Your Hit Parade.' I worked every day of the week." Even now, she remains vaguely familiar to aging Sullivan viewers: "I was in a restaurant the other night and a man came up to me and said, 'My God! You look famous!'"

Meade, who still sounds elegant over the telephone, was the prim show's sole sex object. "Maybe so, but I didn't want that," she laughed. She was on the show ten years, from 1952 to 1962, and was neither Ed's "niece," as he liked to joke, nor, she says, his girlfriend, as some (like director John Moffitt) assumed. Meade didn't even meet him for the first three months, while she was working out of another studio. "Before he even met me he called me his 'niece.' He didn't want to say 'She's my girlfriend.' He just got panicky. We weren't related but we had a very, very nice relationship. He was just like a regular guy." Meade recalled Sullivan as "a very hardworking, sincere, intelligent man with a great sense of humor, though nobody knew about it except those of us who knew him. We knew a whole different personality than what was on television. People thought he was very serious, but he really wasn't like that at all. He had a wonderful smile."

Meade was chosen, said Lincoln's onetime account executive Joe Bracken, because "she had very interesting credentials, most of them minor stage things, but her audition was perfect. She was beautiful, she was articulate, she could memorize things in a nanosecond. And Ed liked her. I can't think of anybody who would have done a better job. Things were pretty rosy because people thought the Sullivan show was a class act, and Julia was a class act."

People still believe that Ed Sullivan discovered scores of stars and gave new faces their first break, but in fact, what Sullivan gave polished entertainers was their first major break on *prime-time television*. The national media took little notice of performers until they landed on his show—showbiz's front page. Many of Sullivan's alleged discoveries got their first network exposure with Paar or Steve Allen, not Sullivan, but Ed Sullivan's show was prime-time Sunday night—the biggest window on Main Street, U.S.A.

Sullivan's true prowess lay in finding and giving a final push to entertainers just on the brink of stardom, like Carol Burnett, who created a New York stir when, in a 1957 cabaret revue at the Blue Angel, she warbled a comedy song called "I Made a Fool of Myself over John Foster Dulles," which put her on Jack Paar's show. Dulles's TV adviser called Paar to say the secretary of state had missed it and could she sing it again on his show. She did, that very Thursday. Sunday she was on Sullivan's show. Monday she was a star.

As James Gavin noted in his history of New York cabaret life, "The doors that opened for Burnett because of that song were extraordinary." From the Sullivan show, she joined Garry Moore's morning show in 1957, then nailed the lead in "Once upon a Mattress" on Broadway and joined Garry Moore's nighttime show. Said singer Will Holt, who shared the cabaret bill with Burnett, "I never would have thought she'd become a star. But that's what happened." Burnett told me, "Ed Sullivan was America's taste. When Ed put his arm around you and pulled you over and said, 'She's a really funny little lady,' America said, 'She's a really funny little lady.'" The moment the kingmaker put his arm around her she was home free. Joan Rivers echoed Burnett: "Ed Sullivan *was* America in those days. If Ed Sullivan liked you, he was telling America, 'She's

OK—you can all like her now' "—a fairy godfather role later assumed by Johnny Carson.

Burnett remembered Sullivan taking her and other performers to dinner. Ed was intimidating, she noted, "but he didn't mean to be. It was just because of who he was." Burnett could read him. "He'd say, 'That was very good,' which was like someone else saying, 'That was *fantastic!*' But you never knew what was going to come out of his mouth." Carol Lawrence, who played his show 17 times (and recalled Sullivan as "a shy man, really kind of into himself—not a funster"), told me, "When you did a Sullivan show, you were immediately recognizable to the rest of the country. I got commercials and many other things because everybody knew who I was after that. If he liked you, and if you got into his column, it was a further validation. He reviewed my first act at the Persian Room, and the headline said, 'The Greatest Act I've Ever Seen.' It was enormous. We couldn't get enough tables in the room."

Sullivan can take total credit for giving national exposure to an even earlier female comedian, Jean Carroll, forgotten by many now. She was a major female stand-up pioneer, blazing trails before Phyllis Diller, and was the subject of a 2007 documentary, "Jean Carroll: I Made It Standing Up," narrated by Lily Tomlin, who idolized Carroll. Tucked into a cocktail dress, riffing on shopping and husbands, Carroll played the Sullivan show 29 times after successes at the Copacabana and the Latin Quarter, billed as "the female Bob Hope." Sullivan, with his keen memory of vaudevillians, first met Carroll backstage in the late 1920s, when he was a sportswriter, and decades later brought her to TV when she was an established monologist.

Carroll, still sardonic in her mid-90s, claimed the show didn't help her career that much, but she recalled a classic Sullivan tantrum: "After every show he would go around backstage, grab me, and say, 'That was a really, really, really great show.' But once he didn't think I was so great." She explained she did a routine that mentioned a pretty young girl driving a Cadillac. Sullivan went nuts. It was then common for TV comics to drop in references to specific items—early product placement—and be rewarded with a sample product. Sullivan thought that was Carroll's scheme—to snag a Cadillac—which crossed the line because the show's sponsor was Lincoln, Cadillac's major competitor. Ed was livid.

"It was a hilarious routine," she said, "and after the show I waited for him to congratulate me backstage. When he didn't, I went over and said, 'Hey, where are you?' He said, 'Where am I? Where are *you!*' I said,

'You didn't like what I did?' He said, '*Like what you did? Do you real-*ize what you've done tonight!?' He could have strangled me." He mentioned the Cadillac reference and "lit into me, and insisted I did it deliberately." Somehow he hadn't caught the Cadillac line in rehearsal.

The incident foreshadowed the notorious Jackie Mason finger flap of 1964. Carroll, who had never signed a contract, tried reasoning with Sullivan, who wouldn't listen. "I said, 'You've known me for years. My word is my bond. I don't lie, and I don't cheat. I would never jeopardize your show or my career.' But he was having none of that." Sullivan didn't rebook Carroll for two years. He was angry and her feelings were hurt. But she did appear on the Carson show and others.

When she played a party Sullivan attended, he blithely asked why she was never on his show anymore. "I said, 'I don't want to work for you. You insulted me. You accused me of doing something against my nature.'" He called her husband and ex-partner, agent Buddy Howe, and pleaded, "Buddy, talk to her, persuade her." She played the show again, but says, "He never believed me." Carroll also encountered his absent-minded side when he told her to cut two minutes. "I said, 'How will I know when?' He said, 'I'll cross my arms when you have two minutes left.' So I start to talk, and he crosses his arms. I said, 'What? Already? I just opened my mouth.' He said, 'Oh, I forgot.'" He'd inadvertently crossed his arms. "I wondered how he ever achieved the position he achieved in show business. He was a real enigma."

Entertainers who were catapulted to stardom are well catalogued, but whither the thousand wannabes who finally got five minutes on Ed Sullivan's show, never to be heard from again? Not to mention entire performing life-forms, now totally extinct, like comedy teams and male quartets, dispatched to the showbiz graveyard. Hundreds of acts Sullivan introduced on network TV vanished without a trace—the flip side of the overnight hits. Whatever happened to the Jovers, the Amin Brothers, Bory & Bor, Leny Eversong, the Three Bragazzis, Rita Streich, the Sparkletones, Dick Buckley, Rosella Hightower, Lolita & Montez, and the Kim Sisters—acts you were unlikely to see anywhere else, or ever again, and maybe didn't need to?

And then there were all the performers knocked off the show at the last minute, or who just missed making the initial cut. Consider the plight of the Charles Unicycle Riders, whose ill-fated efforts to get on the Sullivan show typified those of many hungry novelty acts. The black, Puerto Rican unicyclists were managed by hustling 16-year-old

Bill Minson, who hung around TV stage doors in the hope of encountering Garry Moore, Carol Burnett, or Jackie Gleason—or maybe even Ed Sullivan.

Minson struck gold one night in 1965 when Sullivan emerged from Studio 50. "He was going down the street, so I just started walking and talking with him," Minson told me. "He used to go into this bar before the show started Sunday night, a block from the theater. When he came out of the bar, I walked up to him, and he said, 'Now, listen, go see Mark Leddy' " (the show's novelty act booker). Minson, who later sold the act to Ringling Brothers ("their first black act in 99 years," he noted), recalled Sullivan's friendliness. "He was so nice to me, and I was so appreciative that I got one of those little trinkets in Times Square and left it for him at the stage door with a note. Then I got a note back from *him!* I went to the Delmonico, where he lived, and brought photos of the act."

When Sullivan came into the room, wearing a bathrobe, he told Minson, "Oh, this is great!" "So I'm thinking, we're on the show! It's his show! He insisted we audition for Bob Precht. I met Precht for a moment, but there was no warmth there. I still can't figure out why he wouldn't allow the group on the show. We never heard back from him." Precht said part of his job was to be the show's bad-news bearer. Most of the acts that were dumped after the dress rehearsal, due to time or a flat response, were novelty acts, but Precht said it rarely happened. "Ed was tough. If he didn't like something, forget it. That was my job—I was very much the hatchet man. If something bombed or didn't work, it was my job to tell the guy's agent, 'We can't use you.' I'm sure from their perspective it seemed cold and unkind."

The King Charles Troupe, as the act was renamed, is now 40 years old and has appeared at Las Vegas and in Europe, yet they failed to crack the Ed Sullivan show, a seeming natural for a pack of ethnic unicyclists. Even so, Minson's meeting with Sullivan was a life-changing moment. "I figured, if I could talk to Ed Sullivan, I could talk to anyone," recalled Minson, now a minister. As a consolation prize, Sullivan plugged Minson and the act in print.

Larry Wilde, a scrappy young 1960s comedian, finally got to audition for Sullivan at the Delmonico and recalls his own near-miss experience in his one-man show, "Going on Ed Sullivan"—which, in fact, he failed to do, though he came painfully close. Wilde's agent got to Sullivan through a mutual friend, prizefighter Paddy Cochran, who went to the Friday night fights with Sullivan. Wilde's agent convinced Cochran to get Sullivan to give him an audition, which took place in the foyer of Sullivan's penthouse apartment with Sullivan and Cochran sitting in chairs behind fake poinsettias as Wilde did his five-minute routine. "We never even got into his living room," he told me. "We were just out in the hall."

Wilde said Sullivan failed to chuckle even once. "He sat there stone-faced and stared at me. He never laughed or even smiled. I heard later from Jackie Mason and Alan King that he never really opened up and laughed. That was not his personality. He might smile. If he got hysterical he parted his lips. He said thank you and dismissed me. Why Cochran thought it would be good for me to do this I have no idea."

Cochran persuaded Sullivan to let Wilde do the Sunday afternoon warm-up show. "A week later, I showed up to do the warm-up show, ready to go on that night. I was a nervous wreck when I arrived. I stood in the wings, ready to go on, when the stage manager said, 'I'm sorry, Larry, we've run out of time, you'll have to come back next Sunday.' Wow! Another week of sleepless nights. But seven days later, Sullivan brought me out onstage again. I did a five-minute routine that the audience loved. Lots of laughs. Big applause. Sullivan called me back for three bows—and I *still* did not get on the show. My agent called for months, bugging Cochran, who kept saying, 'They're thinking about you, Larry, they're thinking about you—don't worry, you're gonna get on the show.' But it never happened."

What likely did happen is what befell many acts—either Sullivan decided Wilde wasn't good enough for the show, and Ed was just doing Cochran a favor by auditioning him, or coproducer Bob Precht nixed it. Wilde is philosophical about it at 80: "As my mother wrote me, I had a successful life, a happy career, and a happy marriage in *spite* of Ed Sullivan." He said, "I'm still waiting for Ed to call." Conductor Ray Bloch's son-in-law Sherwin Bash told me that "many, many times," if Sullivan felt a comic had fallen flat at the dress rehearsal, he would send someone to the Stage Deli to grab a pastrami sandwich and a replacement comedian to go.

PART III

Inside the Star-Making Machine

CHAPTER 14

Herding Comedians

You want to know the day Christ died? It was on "The Ed
Sullivan Show" and Ed gave him three minutes.

Talent booker Mark Leddy to Jim Bishop,
author of *The Day Christ Died*

From the mightiest diva to the lowliest tumbler, each performer came
equipped with his or her own set of neuroses, needs, idiosyncrasies,
problems, and demands. They all required stroking and often had to be
firmly dealt with. They could be nervous, truculent, childish, paranoid,
and unmanageable—often all at once. Their nerve endings, as well as
their careers, were on the line when they were at last invited to play "The
Ed Sullivan Show."

A performer could be famous in five minutes or dumped back into
oblivion. For Sullivan, it was just another show he had to get through.
He himself was a perpetual nervous wreck, not only worried about how
the show would play and be received but also fretting over his own duties as ringmaster. He too was a star who had to keep proving it every
Sunday night. He left many of the dirty details—such as asking a performer to cut a song or part of a routine, or the whole act—to Marlo
Lewis or Bob Precht.

Ron Clark, a comedy writer, told me Sullivan would ruthlessly decap-
itate acts "without any regard to sequence. He was just like a butcher.
Take two minutes out and that's it. Everybody did it because the show
was so important to them." Sullivan remained totally on the scene and
frenetically fit during most of the show's 23 years, but as he began showing his age in his late 1960s and running out of gas, he reluctantly relin-
quished the bookings to his trusty son-in-law, Precht.

Sullivan still eagerly scouted talent in his nightly rounds of clubs and shows (while also relying on platoons of outside scouts), but Lewis said Sullivan hated dealing with agents. He left that to Lewis unless it was a star whom Sullivan needed to sweet-talk. Some stars were insulted if anyone below Ed called to make a deal. Sullivan loved dialing performers or meeting them at a club. "Whyncha come on arr shew sometime?" he would say as nonchalantly as if asking for the time, sending entertainers into shock.

Precht, laughing, told me he remembered that, "if Ed and Sylvia were having dinner at Danny's Hideaway and some comic came up to him and beguiled him somehow, I'd get a call the next day [saying] that the comic was on the air. And I'd say, 'Jesus, Ed—why'd you do that?' He would do that a lot." Staffer Russ Petranto told me, "In some ways Ed was so unpretentious you couldn't stand it! Ed would go out alone to lunch all the time, and he would do this awful thing. He never wanted a limo, so he'd end up in some coffee shop nearby and bump into a performer and say, 'Y'know, why don't ya come on the show next week?' And you'd go, 'Holy shit!' And they'd book him if they could."

Once, Sullivan was captivated by a puppet show he'd seen in Los Angeles, remembered Precht, "and he booked the whole damn puppet show for an hour! Without talking to me. Oh, God, so now we had to send a crew to shoot this puppet show, and he *knew* I was totally opposed to it." (Precht can't even recall the great act's name now. It was the Obraztov State Puppet Theater.) "The show aired, and he announced, 'If you really liked this act, please write us,' so of course we got tons of mail from people who loved it. All this mail was stacked up onstage on the next show, from everyone who'd loved the act. And Ed said, 'Bob Precht and I want to thank you!' That was Ed's way of letting me know he had done the right thing."

Once an act was booked and in rehearsal, a different Sullivan often showed up. This Sullivan was intense, unsmiling, severe, barking orders, trimming acts, changing the running order, and throwing performers off the show hours before it went on if the rehearsal studio audience didn't respond; the 4 P.M. audience was his personal control group. Jokes, songs, tricks, and entire acts were expendable. He once insisted that an animal trainer cut a middle stunt from his elephant's routine, and the trainer replied, "You tell him."

Sullivan's great unseen talent was not just intuiting what viewers would love but also "routine-ing" it—juxtaposing the acts. In any variety show or revue, the running order is crucial: where a number occurs in a show can spell disaster for the act—if it follows a powerhouse act, say, or is too bold for the top of the show, or too similar to something else near it, or has an emotional wallop better held for the end of the show. "Routine-ing" is seat-of-the-pants staging, the result of having sat in a thousand audiences, as Sullivan had, and developing a feeling for what act fit where. Thus the Sunday afternoon dress rehearsal was, for Sullivan, vital—not just for timing and tech purposes but also for determining whether the girl singer should come before or after the magician. John Moffitt told me, "For many, many years, it was all Ed's gut instinct."

In vaudeville, the placement of acts on a bill was part of a pecking order dependent on salary and reputation. Next-to-closing was the plum spot, reserved for headliners as the show ramped up to a colossal star turn. First and last place on the bill were deadly—throwaway acts that went on while audiences settled in and latecomers arrived or, at the end, as spectators slipped out the door. But those cardinal rules of vaudeville didn't work on TV, and Sullivan recognized the difference—which was the reason his show was more than electronic vaudeville. On TV, the idea was to open big, grab viewers, and close big, using the hottest star in both halves of his show and the novelty acts as hamburger helper.

Ed was notoriously wary of songs with sexual innuendoes and of fleshy female singers with revealing necklines. He ordered them to mask their décolletage with a fringe of tulle, kept on hand to camouflage any overly heaving breasts; the TV camera, he said, emphasized bust lines.

I remember as a child being slightly confused about what burlesque was, what vaudeville was, what variety shows were. They all kind of merged together. There was something about a variety show that felt slightly racy and titillating to me. I remember that sense of glamour—the showgirls, a grown-up aura—watching it as a kid in our suburban Philadelphia home. There were still the last vestiges of a vaudeville show on Arch Street in Philadelphia. I remember my father going with his business associates to the Troc, short for Trocadero, sort of a burlesque club with a strip act of some kind. There was always this sense [on Ed Sullivan's show] of that older generation, with the slightly mysterious ways of grown-up men like my father. Sullivan seemed the quintessence of a grown-up man to me—scary and intimidating, mysterious, and also sort of serious about fun.

Steven Winn, San Francisco

Some performers—Kim Novak, Jeanne Crain, Esther Williams—quietly removed the fringe just before going on-camera, risking later banishment; cameramen were quickly directed to focus on their faces, foreshadowing the later historic Elvis hip-wriggling episode. Ed's battle cry was, "This is television, not burlesque." He felt he was protecting public morals. Whenever a sexy singer crossed the cleavage line, she always heard about it later.

Many of the female crooners—Patti Page, Peggy Lee, Kay Starr, Abbe Lane, Sarah Vaughan, Diahann Carroll, Julie London—wanted to appear on-screen in the same revealing dresses they wore in clubs—"creations designed to expose as much of a woman's charms as the law allows," said one writer. Under Sullivan's law, female charms were carefully concealed. Marlo Lewis's sharp-tongued wife, Mina Bess, recalled in their memoir that she told opera singer Dorothy Sarnoff to wear her gown backward: "Even though you're singing a lullaby, our audience does not expect you to look like a nursing mother." Sullivan told Eartha Kitt to wear pants on the show, because, he explained, "Every time you wear a dress we get letters from Catholics saying you're too sexy."

Ann-Margret once pulled the tulle stuffing out of her neckline after Sullivan pounced on her after a run-through. When she insisted it was her only dress, he ordered her to talk to the wardrobe mistress. The shapely singer peeled off the dress and walked away—and, as an eye witness noted, "there were these huge casabas falling out for all the world to see, so Sullivan grabbed her by the hand and, hoping to shame her, said, 'Look into the camera and say hello to your lovely mother!' "

Polly Bergen, who did the show eight times, never dressed as seductively as she did in clubs or on album covers. "I learned early on, if I had a low-cut gown, I had to fill it in," she told me. "They weren't that low-cut, but it was a family show at eight o'clock. Children stayed up and watched it. I wouldn't have worn anything revealing, like I would do in Vegas—very low-cut, form-fitting gowns. I knew I was good at what I did. I did not have to wear a low-cut gown to do it, you know?"

Sullivan edited and bullied even obedient regulars, like Nat King Cole. Cole once asked to sing his new recording—the first time he'd ever made such a request—and Sullivan, in a cranky mood, resisted. Connie Francis was there. She told me, "Ed said to him after rehearsal, 'You're not doing that song.' Nat was a real gentleman, a sweetheart. He said, 'Why not, Ed?' Sullivan snapped, 'You're not using my show to make a hit song!' " Cole was baffled, recounted Marlo Lewis. Cole told him, "I can't understand why Ed has turned on me. I've always tried to do my best—and he should know I wouldn't do anything on your show I wasn't proud of."

When Lewis intervened, Sullivan exploded, "If Cole doesn't like it, he can get lost. Nobody tells me what to do on my show! Tell that to Cole and tell that to his agents too. I want them all to know that I'm gonna put a stop to all acts who want to use us to launch their wares. The exploitation of us has come to an end!" Sullivan, the leader in hit exploitation, was venting his disgust at the recording industry using his show as a marketing tool for new songs. Cole, humiliated, chose never to appear on the show again. The song that created such distress became one of his biggest hits—"Those Lazy Hazy Crazy Days of Summer." Connie Francis explained Sullivan's behavior: "He didn't want to take a chance on someone breaking in a new record on his show that might go nowhere"— part of the host's ingrained risk-avoidance policy.

But Sullivan often changed his own rules and whims. Francis introduced a lot of new songs, but she had Sullivan eating out of her hand. "Ed allowed me to do whatever I wanted. Whatever I said was OK with him. That's what was so unusual about our relationship. He was a fan, and we trusted each other. He loved my innocence—that I wasn't 'a show business-type person.' When I was about to do Vegas or the Copa I would schedule an Ed Sullivan show just prior to that. I did about five appearances a year. I knew that would get high rollers into the casino. I'd then introduce a song I wanted to sing, or that was already a hit."

Similarly, Nancy Sinatra told me, "If you had a record coming out, you could pretty much count on a chart record. That's why I did the show so often." Music coordinator Robert Arthur pointed out to me, "Generally speaking, the reason Ed had anyone on the show was because they were hot, they were young, and they were hit makers." But Leslie Uggams explained, "You didn't necessarily have to have a hit record. My career was not about recording, so it was great for me." Despite several appearances, Nancy Sinatra never grew jaded playing the show: "We felt we were lucky to have the job. And it was live TV!" She recalled freezing up the night she looked out and saw Tony Bennett staring up at her.

Even a favorite like Francis could create hassles. Typical of the ego battles that Sullivan, Lewis, and Precht fought weekly was a full-scale fracas over a song that Francis planned to sing, "My Yiddishe Mama," from her album of trusty Jewish songs. It became an ethnic turf war when Sullivan also booked Sophie Tucker, who had made the song her trademark anthem. After a tantrum, Tucker got Jerry Lewis, also on the bill, to threaten a walkout. Sullivan, as usual, refused to be dictated to even by megastars, and told Tucker and Lewis, "She'll sing whatever she wants"—and so she did.

Francis, caught in a backstage power play, recalled the skirmish: "After the rehearsal I hear this big harangue going on with Jerry Lewis and Sophie Tucker. Ed Sullivan walks by. Sophie Tucker says, 'She can't do my song on the show. That's my song!' So I went up to her and said, 'Excuse me, Miss Tucker. I have 11 other songs on my album I can do. I don't have to do 'Yiddishe Mama.' And Ed said, 'Oh, no you won't. You're doing *that* song!' "

Pop divas were a constant hazard. For the show's Irving Berlin salute, celebrating his 80th birthday, production assistant Russ Petranto remembered, "They wanted to close with 'God Bless America.' There's only one person to call, so Bob Precht calls Kate Smith. A smart cookie, Kate. She said, 'Oh, goodie! Who else is on the show?' And Bob tells her, 'Well, Bing Crosby, the Supremes, Peter Gennaro, Ethel Merman.' And Kate went, 'You don't need me. You've already got yourself a girl singer.' " (They replaced Kate-the-not-so-great with 100 Boy and Girl Scouts out on the street, and Berlin sang the song himself.)

"People would get such attitudes," secretary Mary Lynn Gottfried told me. "Either somebody at the height of their career, or [somebody] who had been a nobody and [who] would get a chance to be on the Sullivan show, could be so demanding about what hotel they wanted to stay in. I remember thinking, 'You were such a nobody, and you're gonna be such a has-been!' " She noted that often a singer's manager-husband spelled trouble.

Male divas were no easier. On that same tribute to Berlin, Bing Crosby was unable to hit a tricky note during rehearsal. "Crosby couldn't hit a key change," recalled production assistant Petranto. "He couldn't find the note. We stop, and he goes off stage. We try it four times and he can't do it, so finally he basically says to everybody, 'I cannot fucking do this!,' walks offstage, goes upstairs to his dressing room, and slams the door.

"So we're all standing there, and Bob Precht turns to me and says, 'Go get him.' I was scared to death! What the hell am I gonna say to Bing Crosby? I go up to the dressing room, knock on the door, and say, 'Mr. Crosby, my name is Russ Petranto, and I'm the PA on the show, and the reason they've sent me is that they're all afraid of you.' I said, '*Please* come back down, we can make this work, because if you don't come down I'll be fired.' So he opened the door, and he said, 'I'll be right down.' He was not particularly pleasant. Not a mensch. He didn't apologize. Bing Crosby never apologizes for anything."

Staff secretary Susan Abramson told me that Crosby needed cue cards to get through "White Christmas." In rehearsal, he had sung, ". . . and may all your Christmas *cards* be white." Mary Lynn Gottfried recalled, "Even people with their most famous songs still wanted lyrics printed out. It was live!" Secretaries often stood in for stars for lighting and sound checks, earning $10 extra. Gottfried and others got to stand next to Peggy Lee while she spoke her songs (saving her voice for the telecast), and make sure she got the lyrics right.

Peter Calabrese broke into showbiz as an assistant cue card guy, toting the cards and the pen for the head cue card man, but later became a proficient cue card writer and flipper. He recalled, "There were a few people—Alan King comes to mind—who had everything he did on cue cards. He would say to put three dots at the end of every setup line, to indicate how long he would wait before delivering the punch line. He also didn't have great eyesight, so the cue cards were, like, three feet by four feet, and they were heavy. King would have maybe 20 cue cards, and he needed you to point at every line so he could look away; when he looked back, he needed for you to be pointing to where he was in the routine. It was a huge responsibility."

Calabrese goes on: "Cue cards were pretty important to performers. Singers had their lyrics on the cue cards if they didn't know the song. If the cue card guy blows it, that's the end of it. You got kind of close to these celebrities, who were depending on you, and a lot of them were great to work with, and really good tippers. Alan King never tipped. Robert Goulet tipped pretty good. King's agent always gave you a sweater because his family was in the *shmatta* [clothing] business—and it was always stuff you probably wouldn't wear, like sweaters with a sewn-in dickey. Alan King was a piece of work." Calabrese at first wrote the cue cards Saturday night for Sunday, only to have stars like King come in the next day and say, " 'I can't see them, you gotta rewrite them.' Quickly you learned to ask everyone, 'How big do you need these?' "

Connie Francis noted that, while she remembers Sullivan as "a true gentleman, a class guy, a warm guy," many performers found him intimidating. "He was powerful," she recalled, "but I was never afraid to be in his company." She sketches in an enigmatic, contradictory man: "He was like an ordinary guy watching the show, who'd say, 'Hey, I can talk better than that,' " but at the same time "inaccessible." She says he had few showbiz chums. "I was a good friend—he came to my wedding.

Jerry Vale was a good friend. Don Rickles was also a good friend for a time. Other than that, not too many other people." She adds, "A lot of people feared him—performers, agents—because he had such power. There've only been a few shows in TV history that could make a star overnight, and he had the ability to do that. He also had the ability not to be so kind sometimes. But he was not the austere, humorless person people thought."

Lainie Kazan, who was on the show five times, recalled the day that, after the rehearsal, Bob Precht asked her to cut the ending of her song, "What Now, My Love?," right at the crescendo, when it ran longer than planned. Kazan told me she refused. "I said, 'I can't do it. You can't cut it there; it's an acting scene and it isn't over! I'm not going to sing that song if that's what you expect me to do.' He acquiesced to me, but he was not happy. He [Precht] hired me back several times after that, [but] he asked me to sing 'up' tunes, only two of which were in my repertoire, so I did more of those. He seemed to be a very difficult man and had definite ideas. I feel he didn't take art or the performance into consideration. On the other hand, Ed Sullivan was polite and amiable."

Singers generally were more willing than comedians to oblige Sullivan, but he remained a remote figure to Kazan: "He was a strange fellow, very distant. I personally never got to know him. I never felt like he was communicating with me, even on camera." (Eartha Kitt hit a similar brick wall: "You never had any idea if what you said had penetrated or gone over his head. He was a bland man with no sense of humor.") He called Kazan "Lonnie" and "Lennie" and moved her around in the running order. "It didn't make any difference if they put me first, middle, last. I didn't care. I was on the Ed Sullivan Show! It wasn't just another gig. I was very impressed that I was [even] on the show." Susan Abramson remembered the time Kazan was in her dressing room pulling rollers out of her hair as she was being introduced. "When he said, 'Ladies and gentlemen, Lainie Kazan!,' she wasn't there. I guess Ed just vamped."

Leslie Uggams, a Mitch Miller discovery who played Sullivan's show ten times after making a splash on "Sing Along with Mitch," also recalled Sullivan as a shadowy presence. "He kept far away from us. He stayed in his dressing room. He wasn't a greeter." Precht, she told me, was "nice but businesslike" and ran a tighter ship than Uggams was used to as part of Mitch Miller's clubby troupe. "The timing had to be just right. Ed was hands-on but not hands-on to *you*. He watched everything. He didn't miss a thing. But his conversations were all with Precht, who would come to you for a discussion."

Singers are fragile vessels, and opera divas notoriously breakable. Dancers require special handling. Animal acts are disasters waiting to happen. Jugglers and acrobats who don't speak English need constant reassuring. They all require coddling, stars most of all. Any imagined slight can cause major tremors, and nervous wrecks are commonplace. But comedians come with their own set of psychoses; each comedian is a subset of craziness.

Sullivan had no qualms about telling comedians large and small how much to cut and what to cut, blue-penciling routines without apology. Jack Carter told me, "He was tough as hell to work for. He had a right to be. It was his show, and obviously his way worked." After a rehearsal, he might order, "Cut the magician to three minutes. The start of the act was lousy." A singer was told to cut a chorus or maybe add a song. A dance act would be moved from the opening to the end. "Few reasons are given for the changes, and no questions are asked," reported Wayne Warga in a 1967 backstage story in *Life*.

Over the years, Sullivan made life treacherous for even established comedians like Carter, Shecky Greene, Jack E. Leonard, Woody Allen, Jackie Mason, and others. Over time, regulars such as Alan King, Myron Cohen, and Sam Levenson were trusted not to befoul the show's sacrosanct family air. "He kind of adopted me," King told me. "He'd call me in to consult on comedians." But even King hid his script from Sullivan. "Ed had this thing about editing comedians," confirmed talent coordinator Vince Calandra in an interview conducted for the Archive of American Television. A comedian was more vulnerable than a singer. If the act before a comic ended on an emotional high, it could kill a bit as surely as a lavish spectacle, which no jokes can compete with. Good but comfy unshowy singers were a perfect lead-in (the reason major comedians on the road rarely leave home without one), able to warm up the house without overshadowing the star.

When Sullivan didn't know or trust a comedian, he would make him audition in front of a throng of one. Auditioning for Sullivan was often a descent into comedy hell: Sullivan would listen grimly, at times with pencil and legal pad in hand, as the comedian delivered his monologue. It was like trying to pry a laugh out of a statue, the world's most famous living chunk of marble. Even if he'd seen the comic at a club, he wanted to vet every word of his or her TV monologue. When he ordered a comic to delete a joke that had even a slightly suggestive tinge, often it was the very line that drew the loudest laughs in clubs. While Sullivan was church-lady-ish on his show, he could be as profane as the mobsters he once knew. "I never saw him get profane, but I'm sure it happened," said Precht.

Jack Carter knows it did. He told Jeff Kisseloff, "When he called you into the dressing room after your run-through, he'd say [mimicking Sullivan]: 'What kind of fucking shit is that?! You do that shit on my fucking show, you asshole! Fuck you with that shit! How dare you come in here with that cock-sucking shit. I don't need that fucking shit. Don't do that cock-sucking shit on my show. Balls! That's bullshit. Now, take that out. You can't do that.' It was hysterical. When you went on Sullivan, you couldn't say belly button. You couldn't say navel. He said, 'I don't want any navels on my show. That's a fucking hole, you little shit!'" Roland DuPont, a longtime musician on the show, told me that, paradoxically, "Sullivan wouldn't tolerate any onstage profanity even in rehearsal, from either a big drunken film star or a West Point plebe. He would chew them both out."

Sullivan saw any perceived smut as an attempt to destroy the show. "The show was Ed's life," said Carter. "He was concerned with every small act, every detail. He fought you tooth and nail on every joke, every line." One-liner comics like Henny Youngman could painlessly delete three jokes, but storytellers like Danny Thomas had a structure, an arc leading to an emotional payoff. Sullivan's hacksaw approach messed with their rhythm, their pacing, their head, eviscerating keenly crafted knockout lines.

Carter explained the comedians' ongoing dilemma. "The exposure you got from being on Sullivan was unbeatable, but Sullivan was vicious. Sullivan was crazed. That veneer of being very holier-than-thou: 'Hi, there, all you nuns out there, and my dear friends the priests' . . . 'These nice youngsters . . .'"

Singer-comedian Mimi Hines told me she vividly recalls auditioning for Sullivan in the ballroom at the Delmonico Hotel with her partner and husband, Phil Ford. "Ed sat in a chair. The room was empty and bare with mirrors all around it. He wanted to hear what these kids he'd heard about were doing. Don't forget, there wasn't any tape then. There was no way to say, 'Here's what we did last week on Jack Paar's show.'"

Joan Rivers, too, was summoned to the Delmonico to audition for Ed as he listened mutely: "I wasn't at all risqué in those days, but he was very worried about me because I was a woman."

Playing to an audience of one didn't faze Hines. "I wasn't scared, because we had solid material. But Phil and I were mentally hanging on to each other all the way through it." The performance proved to be a breakthrough. After doing the show, the couple went salmon fishing in Vancouver, and upon docking in a tiny isolated town, Hines recalled, "about eight Japanese fishermen started flying out of their boats and surrounding us. They had seen us on their little black-and-white TV set in their fishing boat!"

Comics' primal fear when auditioning for Sullivan wasn't just that they would not get on the show but that he would gut their best material. Said Carter, one of the show's senior comedy survivors: "Ed cut out everything but the punch line and then wondered why you weren't funny. Sullivan didn't know anything about comedy." Orson Bean witnessed Sullivan demolish his prize bit as a snooty sportscaster describing a Harvard-Yale game. Sullivan ordered Bean to wear a raccoon coat, carry a Harvard banner, and don funny shoes. "It just killed the bit," Bean pointed out to me. "If you go out wearing yellow shoes, you better be damn fuckin' funny. Ed insisted on the raccoon coat. I knew it was gonna bomb, and it did. It was humiliating. The routine had already played so well—he had seen it and booked me because of it." Afterward, Sullivan told his agent, "Orson is a comedian with a very limited audience. He's not good for my show." He canceled Bean's next booking.

George Carlin told James Maguire about the terrors he felt performing on the show in the 1960s: "First of all, it was live, which produces a higher nervousness quotient than something that can be done over." Many shows switched to tape in the 1960s, but Sullivan kept his show live, giving it an extra charge of derring-do. Carlin recalled, "The Sullivan staff was notorious for coming to you during the on-air show and saying, 'The monkey skated too much, you have to give us back a minute.' I didn't do things that were chopped up into segments, I did things that had a thread, making it all the more panicky."

Jan Murray played the Sullivan show 14 times, a stepping-stone to his long career as a game show host ("Treasure Hunt"). "Sullivan's was the toughest show," because of that dreaded last-minute sawmill. Murray told me, "If you've got a routine, with a beginning, middle, and end, you edit it as finely as you can—every word counts. Right before you go on, he says, 'Give me two minutes out.' He wanted you to cut while you're onstage. How do you cut it? He didn't understand this. He made comics nuts."

Dick Martin, of Rowan & Martin, told me, "No matter what you did, Sullivan would still want two or three minutes out. He never censored us for words. He wanted minutes, to squeeze in more acts. That's why we were so popular with the show. It didn't matter to us. We could squeeze a bit. It had no structure anyway." As the show grew increasingly successful, Sullivan slashed comics' routines with increasing abandon. Comics who might enjoy a leisurely ten minutes in the 1950s got half that ten years later.

Martin said, "I don't think he knew what was funny. Ed was a bit of a lox—nice guy, but he was strange. If the audience was laughing, you were funny. All TV audiences in those days were just glad to be there. They were seeing a free show, just waiting to laugh. They were duck soup for a good act."

The comedy team of Charley Brill and Mitzi McCall were dead ducks, doubly doomed: not only did they appear (rather, disappear) on the first Beatles telecast, but also they were forced to rewrite their sketch in the dressing room just hours before the show, according to Sullivan's dictates. McCall noted in an interview with Terry Gross on NPR's "Fresh Air": "We didn't know that the dress rehearsal was looked at so carefully and had an audience." Brill added, "We go back upstairs and we hear over the loudspeaker, 'McCall and Brill, Mr. Sullivan's office, please.' We go into Mr. Sullivan's office, and there he is—Ed Sullivan. He's sitting in a chair getting made up, and I looked at the man who could make our entire career. He said, 'The piece of material you're doing is too sophisticated for this audience. There's going to be mostly 14-, 15-, 16-year-old girls in the audience tonight—kids.' He said, 'So show me your entire act.'"

Brill went on to say, "Because we were so new, we showed him our entire nightclub act—everything we'd ever worked on"—30 minutes of sketches. "So he said, 'OK, we're gonna take the first girl in the first sketch and put her in the second sketch, but then you do the other girl in the third sketch.' We went upstairs in a panic." McCall: "It was a nightmare. We just about wanted to kill ourselves." They gamely did as Sullivan ordered—patched together a new routine to replace the written sketch they had fine-tuned. But it was all moot. Nobody noticed McCall & Brill—or any other act—that historic night.

Sullivan could also wreck a comic's routine with overkill. Jan Murray's most famous bit—a father forcing his little girl to eat her Crunchy-

Munchies—ended with Murray shoving the cereal down a doll's throat. "That fucking audience shrieked for five minutes," said Murray. "It was one of my big bits, a classic comedy bit, a smash. Two months later, my agent tells me, 'Ed wants the Crunchy-Munchy man.' I said I already did it. I called Ed up, but he wanted it again, and then again. After the fourth or fifth time I refused to do it. I told Ed, they'll think that's all I know. Each time he gave me the same argument—millions of sets have been sold in the last six months to new viewers who had not yet seen the Crunchy-Munchy man. So I went on and did Crunchy-Munchy, against my better judgment, and the same critics who had loved it before now excoriated me."

Comedian Jean Carroll testified to Sullivan's one-more-time fixation, telling me, "He'd say, 'Jean, listen, I want you to do that "buying the dress" routine.' I said, 'Ed, I did that routine last month!' He said, 'Sylvia wants to hear it.' I said, 'I'll come to your house one day and do it for Sylvia. I'm not gonna do it on the show!' He said, 'Yes, you will, I'm the boss, I pay you.' I said, 'Ed, you can't do this to me. I have a little thing called professional pride.' " He wore her down, and she repeated the dress routine. "Then I'd get all kinds of criticism because I was doing the same old routine."

Apart from Wayne & Shuster, Sullivan's favorite comedy team was Jerry Stiller and Anne Meara (or "Mara," as Ed introduced her, with a proper Gaelic accent). They played the show 36 times, one of the few careers virtually spawned, perfected, and launched on the show. Although they were popular on the New York club circuit, they now began to play major cities and made a series of Blue Nun wine commercials that made them household names.

Stiller & Meara were a grittier, more ethnic, gentler, and cuter Mike Nichols and Elaine May. Their signature routine was a blind date between Stiller's Hershey Horowitz and Meara's Mary Elizabeth Doyle. The scene mirrored Ed Sullivan's own courtship of Sylvia Weinstein (and Stiller and Meara's). Their agent told them Sullivan would never put the sketch on the air because of the show's conservative, churchgoing audience, but afterward Sullivan kidded them: "I love the sketch, but these mixed marriages never work out." Stiller insisted, "Ed Sullivan had a great sense of humor."

But even the favored Stiller & Meara found a way to upset him in a sketch about a maid cleaning up after astronauts in a space capsule. Sullivan called it dirty. Recalled Stiller, "He had always trusted our taste," but now he confronted them after a rehearsal: "How could you bring in a piece like that? Do you know what that sketch is about, Jerry? It's about *shit!*" It's not funny." Sullivan killed the bit, but, savoring the team's drawing power, he had them back six weeks later. Precht said, "He was very particular and puritanical about anything that bordered on risqué. Ed imposed that on himself. It didn't come from CBS." In June 1962, Sullivan explained to *Newsweek* his ongoing crusade against perceived smut. " 'All comics,' he says, and then spreads his arms to indicate the size of the comic conspiracy, 'I have to tell them, this is not only dirty, it's *vile*. That's where I got my ulcer from.' "

Hines and Ford felt the Sullivan hatchet for different reasons, because of their takeoff on "BUtterfield 8," based on a John O'Hara novel banned by the Legion of Decency. Hines recalled, "Ed told us, 'You can't do that because we'll lose Boston.' Boston was a huge market the sponsors didn't want to lose. With all those Catholic families sitting down to dinner, you're not gonna do a sketch by a guy the pope is against."

Allen & Rossi, the poor man's Martin & Lewis and another staple Sullivan team, were on the show 17 times, including the first Beatles broadcast. Unlike other performers buried alive on that milestone show, Marty Allen—the fat, frizzy-haired one—survived by coming out in a Beatles wig and announcing, "I'm Ringo's mother!" He said, "All the kids started screaming. We did very well." Allen told me, "We related to Sullivan right away. We were very close. He never bothered us. He knew whatever we did was gonna be clean and it was gonna be funny. He'd just say, 'What are you gonna do tonight?' And we'd say we're gonna do the blind dancer or the football routine. He trusted us. He knew we'd never hurt the show. But we knew what he wanted. He'd say to other acts, take this or that out, but we never had that problem. And he knew we'd do it within the time he wanted." For them, Sullivan's show was a piece of cake—or apple pie: "We had toured heavily," said Allen, "and this was the American audience. This was middle America."

Even the pristine Woody Allen managed to rile Sullivan with a joke the host considered filthy. Allen presented a frisky routine about his ex-wife, using the phrase "orgasmic insurance." Woody had decided, without telling Sullivan, to change the act that he'd performed at the dress rehearsal—to stay fresh, he claimed. The bit he did for the rehearsal crowd contained the offensive phrase, and Sullivan exploded.

Allen biographer Eric Lax wrote, "When Woody finished, Sullivan, in front of the cast and crew, berated him for his perceived lewdness, threatened to throw him off the show, and accused him of practically single-handedly being responsible for the moral decay of the country, shouting, 'Attitudes like yours are why kids are burning their draft cards!' " Allen considered telling Sullivan to shove it, but diplomatically apologized to the host, who apologized for blowing up. Allen told Lax, "When the storm abated, from that day on, I had no better ally in show business. He had me to dinner, he plugged me in his column, and he had me on the show all the time" (well, four times).

Sullivan often nixed jokes if he didn't get them. Phyllis Diller once quit in disgust after she felt he had filleted her act. "He knew *nothing* about comedy," Diller told me, recalling how she auditioned for him in his suite while he was drinking coffee as his pet poodle nibbled her toes. Jean Carroll agreed, "He really had no great sense of humor. He never said anything funny, never. But I think he had a secret desire to be a comic. The last few years he'd try to get all the comics he booked to do a bit with him."

Jackie Mason told me that, even before their famous falling out, he viewed Sullivan as a heavily wired case. "He was a very, very tense guy when the show was on—full of tension, nervous all the time, very insecure. The closer to the show, the more uncomfortable and nervous he was. He had less patience with someone else's opinions." Even so, "he was very friendly towards me. He would invite me up to his dressing room before the afternoon rehearsal"—a rare honor. "He would say, 'What are you doing now?' He would come to my manager and kibbitz a few minutes before the show."

Sullivan's lust for control was regularly experienced by Mason, who played the show 20 times prior to their historic split. He recalled, "I would win 90 percent of the arguments. He usually backed off. He had some kind of respect for me because, even if he criticized something, he didn't seem to fuck with me as he did with most of the comics. Sometimes he would say, two hours before the show, it's five minutes too long. A guy works out a perfect routine and suddenly he's got to chop off a minute or two? It completely dislodges the guy. Ed would say, 'Oh, that's all right, I'm sure you can straighten it out.' "

Sullivan, he said, changed his approach from comic to comic. Mason, like others, tolerated Sullivan's mood swings: "You couldn't tell what mood he would be in. He treated people differently depending on how much he needed them or how good he thought they were." Mason learned how to dupe him. "I'd pretend I changed something. He didn't know exactly what he had said. I saw comedy was not really his business. He didn't really know what he was talking about."

Mason, despite all, now speaks sympathetically of Sullivan's methodology: "He was insecure and uncertain about almost everything. He was a man with a great amount of drive and ambition, and an intense perfectionist. He tried to be firm and authoritative, but he wasn't always sure how firm to be. He was malleable because he wasn't so sure himself, so he would second-guess himself. It was a sporadic, totally indefinable system. To some people, he came across as arrogant and obnoxious, but I don't believe that. He was just somewhat insecure and trying to do the show as best he could."

Shelley Berman is one of the few top-tier comedians to praise Sullivan for improving his routine, an unexpected admission from Berman, finicky about anything that interferes with his timing. Berman told me, "If there was a problem, you'd hear from him—but sometimes he'd just call you in and say thank you. Usually you waited in your dressing room to see if you're gonna live or die. He was a far scarier presence [onstage] than he was in reality. He was just a guy. He didn't expect you to kiss ass."

Berman remarked, "You're gonna get a lot of stories from people badmouthing him, but to me he was the greatest showman who ever lived. Comedians generally on that show got five, six minutes. Star comedians got seven minutes. I went on with the [classic] father-son routine, which toward the end becomes rather poignant. So I tape the afternoon rehearsal. The spot runs 12 minutes, a full five minutes over the allotted time. Now there's that period where you're waiting in your dressing room for him to call you to his office. And that's a terrifying time!"

He continued, "So I get that call, and I go in and he's muttering— 'Very good, very good, very good.' I thought the axe is gonna fall any minute; he'll emasculate the bit, I'm dead. 'Cause I know it's 12 minutes. So he says, 'You know when the father says to the boy, "Write the letter"? Why don't you have him write the letter to his *mother?*' Sullivan said it would be more gripping, more sentimental. I said, 'Well, I can't just add the line, Ed. I'd have to fulfill that moment, and it might add a minute.' He says, 'Yeah, yeah, go ahead. Have him write the letter to his mother.' He then very firmly *ordered* me to do what he said. It was like: do it or else."

Sullivan turned Berman's bittersweet sketch into a moving soliloquy: "That night as I do the routine, as I'm getting to the poignant section, I feel the lights dimming except for the spotlight. It's perfect for heightening this situation. As a performer, I *feel* it. Toward the very end, I hear one violin"—Sullivan's idea. "He hadn't said a word to me. But as I end the piece, that audience screamed! I mean bravos, cheers, standing. I didn't get that usually. So I added all that and I've kept it in the routine from that day on."

He added, "And this is this man who makes mistakes, this is the man who doesn't introduce properly, who everyone makes fun of. He botched intros—he was not a public speaker—but *God* did he know his business!" Carol Burnett, too, found Sullivan a judicious editor, who cut one line from her breakthrough song, "I Made a Fool of Myself over John Foster Dulles." "It was the last line, which was kind of a punch line he felt was redundant," she told me. "All I really had to do was look blank, he said, and everyone would get it. He was right."

Berman ranked Sullivan "miles and miles above P. T. Barnum. Who else gave us an opera singer following an elephant? He had the most amazing eye and ear for talent. He was very involved in the work of his performers to get the very best show out of them. He wasn't back there judging you at rehearsal; he was back there hoping to make you *better*." When he deleted a joke for taste reasons, said Berman, "frequently he was absolutely right. He was never any kind of dummy." Nonetheless, he added, "Every time I was on the show I was scared to death. That never changed. I wouldn't use the word *fear,* but he could behead you."

Jack E. Leonard feared nobody, not even Ed Sullivan. Leonard, the bald 300-pound insult comic (an earlier, funnier Don Rickles) who wore a panama hat on his head and twirled the hat after each punch line, engaged Sullivan in a steady barrage of backstage bickering over what was funny and why. Leonard took nobody's guff, nor did Sullivan, so when the host tried to edit his material, the air crackled.

Leonard flouted the host by agreeing to delete a line or a phrase only to restore it on camera. An infuriated Sullivan would then refuse to book him, Leonard would complain to the press, be reinstated, only to get banished again. "Whenever he came on our show," recalled Marlo Lewis, "Ed and he would slug it out"—getting into debates on the nature of comedy, vulgarity, and delivery. Sullivan loved Leonard's humor but bristled at his refusal to obey his edicts. Lewis remembered that Sullivan once told the comic to cut his act, asking him, "What can you do in five minutes?" Leonard said, "Boil two eggs."

Sullivan once tried to show up Leonard by telling him he talked too fast for the audience, and bet $1,000 that the rehearsal audience wouldn't laugh at his routine. Unbeknownst to Leonard, Sullivan asked the afternoon audience to refrain from laughing, and the band was also ordered to remain mute. After his act, Leonard attacked the audience: "Good evening, opponents! You're a great crowd. I only wish you were somewhere else. Why don't you all get together and leave?" He called them "Hitler's children" and stalked off.

Sullivan gleefully confronted him, "You see, didn't I tell you your delivery kills your material? Now maybe you'll start listening to me! Go out there and do the same stuff again, and do it slower." Leonard yelled, "All right, Mr. Genius! Mr. Know-It-All! Mr. God! I'll show you how fuckin' little you know about comedy!" This time the audience (per Ed's instructions) exploded in laughter. Afterward, Leonard grabbed Sullivan by the lapels: "You dumb sonufabitch! You think you showed me you know about comedy! All you proved was that you got that bunch of hick freeloaders you call an audience in the palm of your hand!" Marlo Lewis said that, during their backstage battles, Sullivan and Leonard were "as funny a comedy team as any that ever appeared in front of our curtain."

(*Note:* That famous pea green curtain wound up at Notre Dame High School in West Haven, Connecticut, according to alum Mark Kerrigan. The school's lay drama teacher, explained the school's principal Patrick Clifford, was close to Brother Pierre, director of music, who knew a guy in New York, who sent the school discarded sets and the curtain seen every Sunday night for years all across America.)

Staffer Peter Calabrese recalled a conflict involving Rodney Dangerfield: "He had Dangerfield following Alan King, who was, like, the hottest comedian out there, getting top dollar." King was considered first among equals. "So Dangerfield is so nervous, so scared—'How could Ed do this to me? Please! I can't do that [follow a major comedian]. Put on a juggler or something.' I think it was another Sullivan lapse. I don't think they changed it. But the interesting thing is that King didn't do well that night, and Dangerfield came out and killed. So maybe he knew what he was doing after all."

Sullivan would listen to a comic's wounded cries but rarely blinked: "Some of the comics must think they're talking to a lunatic when their routine is slashed," Ed conceded. "They always look as if I've slapped them in the face, but I'm usually right." His philosophy: "Brevity is the soul of wit on television. No performer thinks he gets enough time, but we have a formula and we know how much viewers will take."

He further argued, persuasively, "A comedian who works in a nightclub has perhaps 40 minutes to do his act. His audience is there for the evening. TV audiences have to be won quickly. Viewers can switch to other channels." Even before remote control, he sensed that home viewers had itchy trigger fingers. Sullivan felt he was working in the comic's best interests. "With a live audience, there is no laugh track. The laughs are real. And when the laughs aren't there, that's even *more* real." By 1967, his show was the only prime-time program still telecast live, and without canned laughs. Sullivan refused to sprinkle artificial "sweetening," telling Jerry Stiller, "It isn't honest." Precht said, "Ed did not like laugh tracks," but admits "we experimented with them."

Usually Sullivan watched the 4 P.M. rehearsal on the backstage TV monitor, but sometimes he sat onstage to gauge the audience, not far from the comedian. Audiences eyed Sullivan watching the comedian, to see if the host laughed—or simply stared. Sullivan became an automatic laugh cue for the audience. His habit of plopping himself onstage led to the infamous Jackie Mason "finger" episode, when Mason reacted to a one-minute time cue by flinging fingers in Sullivan's direction, one of which the host interpreted as an upraised middle digit. Sullivan read the finger as not just obscene but blasphemous insubordination (for a blow-by-blow description of the historic event, see chapter 18). Mason was banished from the show for years. Sullivan also kept Henny Youngman off the show for five years when the comic fumed at him for butchering jokes.

"Ed would pick away at comedians, and it would drive them crazy," Precht said. "But the time thing was always an issue." Regarding Mason, Precht disqualified himself: "I was always in the control room, not onstage, so I didn't observe it personally. We had a guy onstage who stood with Ed, with a stopwatch. If a comic was running over, the guy with Ed would give the fingers for the minutes left. Mason is, like, this rapid-fire guy, so he may very well have done it. In any case, it was taken as an offensive gesture."

"I was the guy with the stopwatch," said Russ Petranto, who had a direct line to Precht in the control room and reported if the show was running long, in which case he would tell Ed to cut the intro shorter or to skip chatting with a performer. Petranto wasn't minding the watch the night of the Mason incident, but was in the audience, and recalled, "Everyone's mouth just popped open. Everyone said, 'What the hell was *that* all about?'"

A rare exception to the comedian time constraints, Petranto remembered, was a lengthy Richard Pryor routine—a long semidramatic piece about a wino telling a kid, "Don't turn out like me." It was unusually long, running seven-plus minutes in rehearsal. "It was so brilliant you couldn't stand it," said Petranto, and Precht and Sullivan refused to cut it despite protests from the CBS censor about the raw subject matter.

Peter Calabrese remembered when Sullivan unwittingly sabotaged Norm Crosby. "Crosby's routine was based on malaprops. He was hard of hearing, a lovely guy and really good at what he did using the malaprops, very adroit, but you really had to listen, and to know what the right word was that he was mispronouncing, to get his act." Sullivan first saw Crosby at the dress rehearsal. "You have to understand," Calabrese pointed out, "for the dress rehearsal they would basically get people off the street, maybe some of them half in the bag—you just didn't know. They had a lot of regulars. You weren't getting people from Park Avenue who had written for tickets, or Ed's close friends. That was the night-show crowd."

He continued: "So Sullivan introduced Crosby, but he didn't really go over well. Ed called him up to the dressing room after the show, and he really reamed him—'That wasn't funny! Tell me, where are the laughs supposed to be?'" Calabrese, who was in the room, recalled that Crosby said, "'Mr. Sullivan, with all due respect, I gave your people a setup that you didn't do. You kind of have to tell the audience to listen carefully, and then they'll get it.' Ed said, 'Write the intro, and I'll do it exactly the way you say—and it better be funny.' Norm writes the intro, and Ed does the intro properly, something that says, 'Now you have to listen to my friend Norm Crosby closely because he talks kinda funny . . . Ladies and gentlemen, Norm Crosby!' So Norm comes out and he starts his bit, and people are starting to laugh. Sullivan, standing off-camera a few feet away from Crosby, looks out at the audience and puts his finger to his lips as if to say, 'Shhh! Listen!' Ed literally, inadvertently, almost ruined his act."

In later years, when he was showing signs of forgetfulness, recounted Calabrese, nobody could find Sullivan after a dress rehearsal. "His normal routine would be, after the dress [rehearsal] and the changes were made, to go out to lunch with his friend Joe Moore, the ex–Olympic skater, to a place called the Hickory House. They were never open for lunch, but they would open for Ed. He would sit in this little room with Joe or by himself and watch football on the TV set and eat lamb chops. This one day, Ed's late, he's not at the Hickory House, nobody's seen him. People are really starting to panic. Finally his wife called and said she'd just got home and Ed was asleep on the bed. He'd forgotten he had a show."

Comics tolerated Sullivan's petty rules and peccadilloes because nothing topped playing "The Ed Sullivan Show." In Mason's words, "It was comparable to a nightclub comedian playing the Copa or an opera singer being at the Met." Dick Martin related, "You could say two things in your ads—'Direct from the Copacabana' or 'Direct from the Ed Sullivan Show.' Nothing else meant anything." The show's coast-to-coast sweep was so vast that *Life* once did a five-page photo spread titled "The Short Happy Life of a TV Joke," depicting people laughing at the same joke on the Sullivan show all over the country—in living rooms, trailers, hospitals, dorms, hotels, farms, even a submarine.

Despite Sullivan's meddlesome behavior, there was a scramble among comedians to get on the show that could double their asking price in clubs and guarantee a year's work. Agents hustled Sullivan and his staff for a break. But many gifted comic journeymen did the show once or twice only to return to the nightclub trenches in New Jersey the next day—guys like Lou Alexander, Jack DeLeon, and Jeremy Vernon, comedians who rarely lacked for work but whose single appearance on "The Ed Sullivan Show" failed to turn them into a star, often for perverse reasons beyond their control.

Alexander was booked after Sullivan saw him at the Copa, a major feeder to Sullivanland. Alexander was opening for Tony Martin in 1968. "That night, Ed said to me, 'I'm gonna use you somewhere,' Alexander told me. "He said he'd call me. That week, Richard Pryor canceled and Sullivan said, 'Go get that kid Lou Alexander at the Copa.' I took Pryor's place." At rehearsal, Alexander did seven minutes about contact lenses, and Myron Cohen came over to him afterward and said, "Tonight's your night, kid. That routine you just did, you're gonna kill 'em tonight."

Ten minutes before Alexander went on, a Sullivan aide came to his dressing room and told him to cut two minutes. "So I cut it, and the bit was about a third as good as it was in the afternoon. If I'd done the same thing that night, I probably would have gotten 20 shots [bookings] out of him. But they cut my balls off. I was a monologist. You take out two minutes, you're killing me. I'm doing this in front of 40 million people and editing onstage, and you could see I'm white as a ghost. He still called me over and said, 'Very good job, very nice,' but I knew it was not a tenth as good as what I did that afternoon. That was the end of it; I never went back on."

Compared to appearing on Sullivan's show, playing the Copa was a cakewalk. Consider the unhappy fate of Christopher Weeks, then known as Jack DeLeon, also a Copa veteran. He remembers every detail of what became a horror epic. Weeks/DeLeon did the Sullivan show in 1966, slotted in the middle, a ripe spot. In the afternoon rehearsal, he did his routine, a takeoff of an Italian movie. "Well, it bombed," he told me. "They didn't know what I was talking about! The people who came in off the streets to the afternoon show were like dummies. I was very concerned. I walked around Central Park to get my head together. I dreamed up new lines, readjusted lines. I wanted to vomit. I came back to the theater, and my name was not in the middle of the show. Now it was at the end, at 8:45. Not only that, they put me on after another comic. They were looking to bury me!"

He wasn't even sure he'd have time to do his entire act. But he wound up doing a luxurious seven minutes. "The nighttime audience was very sophisticated, like a Broadway show audience. And I murdered them! They not only laughed but interrupted with applause continually, after each joke. While I was performing, I thought, 'This is it. I'm gonna be the new Danny Kaye. I'm gonna be a star!' It was a special evening in my life, one of those high moments. You only get three or four of them in your lifetime."

He continued: "So I finished to applause, and I turn around and am waiting for Sullivan to come out and put his arms around me. But there's no Ed Sullivan. I walk off. Show's over. Everybody's coming to my dressing room congratulating me, but my manager doesn't come in for 20 minutes. Finally he stands there and I smile: 'Well, where do we go from here?' He says to me, 'You may never do the show again.' I said, 'You're putting me on.' He says, 'You ran over. You ran seven minutes— they couldn't do the last commercial.' I'd run into the commercial spot!" The director hadn't asked him to cut anything because he was doing so well, but the network fumed when a commercial got cut. "I could have cut my act at any point, I was doing that well," he lamented. "William Morris called the next day and said, 'He doesn't want you for a repeat.' It was one of the most disheartening experiences I ever had in my life. It shattered me."

"It was the greatest one-shot I've ever seen," DeLeon's former manager (now a rabbi), Jerry Cutler, told me. "People couldn't stop laughing. It was mass hysteria. I was expecting at least a three-shot deal, probably a five-shot deal." Instead, Precht informed Cutler, "The old man doesn't want him again." Cutler asked, "What do you mean? That's the best shot I've ever seen." Precht: "You're right—it was a great shot. But he ran over—he lost the Lincoln commercial." Cutler said, "I've hated Sullivan ever since. I could not stand the man. It was devastating. But even the afternoon videotape, where the audience went nuts, got him some jobs in Vegas and elsewhere."

According to Cutler, Precht said they were trying to flash the cut sign, but DeLeon either didn't notice or ignored it, and, Cutler went on, "they thought he was trying to screw Sullivan"—a foreshadowing of the Jackie Mason incident. "Jack [DeLeon] was not that used to TV at the time." Cutler recalled Precht as "a wonderful, lovely guy. He was the hatchet man, and we'd struck up a very good friendship by then, so when he came in I took one look at him and could tell. It took a while for him to get it out—he didn't know how to tell me." Cutler said, "It was a great shot, but Precht said there was no talking to him. Sullivan was God. You put a guy who was really a hack in that position—he was the most powerful guy in TV—it goes to your head." He added, "He had no sense of humor whatever."

Cutler delayed facing DeLeon. "He was devastated. He just put his head down low. Jack was always on the brink of getting something great. He did great impressions, smart material, was a good-looking guy, and used his voice a lot—more than a stand-up comic. He did the Carson show and Mike Douglas, but Sullivan was *it*." Cutler—who handled Jackie Vernon, Stiller & Meara, and Stanley Myron Handelman—said he tried to go back to Precht and ask for a second chance, "but it was hopeless."

Comic Jeremy Vernon got booked on the show twice during its last year. Vernon was at the Copa, opening for Al Martino. Sullivan came in, called Vernon over to his table, and said, "You're a damn fine comic, Jeremy. Where are you staying?" A day later Vernon got a call: "This is Ed Sullivan. We want to have you on the *shew* this Sunday.' Biggest thrill of my life," Vernon recounted. But the night he appeared, Sullivan informed the studio audience just before Vernon went on, "Ladies and gentlemen, I understand we've got two and a half feet of snow outside tonight. And now, here's comedian Jeremy Vernon!" "As I'm going on I realize that all of these people in the audience have just been told they're trapped and may not get home." Not only had Sullivan dampened Vernon's act, but as the comedian walked on he was told to cut a minute. "I'm thinking, Am I gonna talk fast? How am I gonna cut it? I had to think on my feet, and it affected my whole performance, my pacing. I didn't bomb but it was nothing as good as the rehearsal audience."

Sullivan's show was such a critical venue that it triggered bitter warfare among comedians who felt other funny men were poaching on their comic terrain. Alan King said that when he started telling family stories, not one-liners, Sam Levenson claimed his home had been invaded. King remembered, "Levenson took umbrage with my talking about my family.

He thought he had a lock on families. I had an ongoing feud with Levenson. He went on the Sullivan show and had a great impact. When I was starting to create a little heat, I heard Levenson was saying very derogatory things about me. He kept me off the show."

King ended up playing the show 37 times. He owed his career to steady exposure on Sullivan's show—his club fee went from $50 a night to $500. "I used to fight with him all the time. Ed was a great friend but a terrible enemy, very vindictive. He wouldn't let Richard Pryor on the show. I said, 'Ed, this kid is terrific.' He said, 'I don't like his attitude.' " Precht told King, "Alan, Ed respects you. Go upstairs and talk him into putting on this kid Pryor." Years later, King finally met Pryor, who said, "I owe you. You went to bat for me years ago on the Sullivan show."

Dick Cavett has his own slightly tarnished 1971 golden memory. While prepping for the show, Cavett asked himself, "Have I got enough good stuff from my club act that's appropriate to use on television? I took out what I thought was the more sophisticated stuff and it worked." Contrary to the reports of Sullivan's fogginess in the show's final years, Cavett told me, "he seemed to be right on, serious, working hard, making a lot of decisions. He was not vague in any way, absolutely certain of what he wanted to do, what he wanted taken out."

After the 4 P.M. rehearsal, Cavett was summoned to Sullivan's dressing room. "He had a paper with notes on it. He'd say, 'OK, youngster, we're gonna take out the Jerry Lewis thing. I don't think you need that.' That's the only line I remember, but I was sorry to see it go. It would always get a huge laugh. I guess he didn't want anything that could be interpreted as negative about Jerry." He laughed. "Or maybe he thought it ungracious of a beginner to knock an icon."

Cavett described psyching himself up for the potentially life-altering event. "I just felt, I've got to start controlling myself three days before, or I'll get into such a bundle of nerves that I'll go out there with a squeaking voice, and with pauses that never end. There was a big dance number ahead of me, and it had that typical black shiny floor that looks like black glass on TV. But it needed mopping. It was dusty. And I thought, Gee, here I've gone through the looking glass and found it oddly mundane. Backstage I can remember thinking: I'm really here. All of the people who have been on the show have been through this door, up this elevator. I kind of envied the elevator operator. He'd had everybody in there from Risë Stevens to Bob Hope."

Cavett recalled, "When the moment came and I heard my name, I just said, 'My God, I *am* on the Ed Sullivan Show!' I wasn't nervous. I walked out, and I think partly it was Woody [Allen] being out there that helped. I just remember thinking, I'm here and I'm doing it. There was a little thing going on in my head saying, 'Now just do what you're supposed to do here. Don't think of other things.' I didn't kill them, but it was a nice appearance." Even if it didn't do anything for his career. Cavett now believes his manager, Jack Rollins, got him on the show "before I was really ready for it."

Onstage, to his shock, Cavett recalled, "Ed is standing right at your ears, five feet away, as you're doing your act. Ed was deaf, according to some, which is the only thing that would explain why Wayne & Shuster were on 15 times" (58, in fact). Cavett only played the show once, but every detail is burned into his brain: "It was strange to be on the show that I had watched hundreds of times in my home in Lincoln, Nebraska, wondering what it would be like to be backstage and see all those stars. I saw it in the 'Toast of the Town' period on my grandparents' television set. We didn't have one yet. I remember as a kid thinking, 'This is a wonderful show, but the host is such a klutz.' Everybody would say, 'How did this guy get this job?' "

An onstage chat with Ed could be a career-making moment, but on the live show he might easily forget to signal a performer over, as he had at rehearsal, dashing hopes. After his routine, Cavett looked for Ed to beckon him over: "I couldn't wait to see what it was he said when he'd awkwardly hold the comic by the elbow until he let the exit applause die and then release the comic to walk off in dead silence—and you'd *hear* his footsteps. Other times he'd just grab them and say something unintelligible." When Cavett sidled over to Sullivan, he thought, "At last I'll hear what he says to the comic. He had introduced me as 'an attractive young man from Yale.' Now he's grinning and he says, 'Nice to have you back, youngster.' Except I *wasn't* 'back.' I remember thinking, '*Goddamn* his stodgy head!' He probably meant to say 'It would be nice to have you back.' But the show ended a few months later, so that was that." (Likewise, when Tom Smothers met Sullivan at a party, hoping it might lead to an invitation, Ed told him, "It was nice having you on the show.")

Cavett added a postscript: "The first time I realized anyone had even seen me on the Sullivan show, I was sitting down at a Broadway play and a very striking, witty-looking woman to my right said, 'Oh, you're the young man who amused me so on the Ed Sullivan program.' I thought she was a British actress. It was Mrs. William F. Buckley Jr. I still remember that phrase 'amused me so.' With all other people it was, 'Hey, dint I see ya on whatchacallit—Ed Sullivan? Yeah, I remember ya.' "

Connie Francis had her own scary up-close moment: "All the performers dreaded being called over by Ed. They never knew *what* he was
going to say. He didn't know either. Nobody knew. No script. Sometimes he would just put you in an embarrassing situation without meaning to, just because Ed was Ed. So at rehearsal—thank God it wasn't
on the show—he called me over to take a bow after I sang 'Yiddishe
Mama,' and he said, 'That was beautiful, Connie. Is your mother still
dead?' Yes! Really!" Nancy Sinatra told me that every time *she* appeared
on the show and walked over to him after singing, Sullivan would say
the same thing: "How's your wonderful mother?"

Bob Precht advised comic Robert Klein to be ready for Sullivan to
call him over for a kind word, but warned him, "If he does that, he's
gonna turn you the wrong way—don't let him." Klein told me, "Here I
am, terrified, and this guy's been doing this thing for 20 years and he
still can't get it right! And sure enough, he calls me over and introduces
me, 'From the Bronx . . .' And he points me here, and I go there, and he
points me here again—it felt like one of those mechanical hockey
games." Sergio Franchi's widow, Eva, says Sullivan once got her husband in a bear hug and wouldn't let him go.

Carol Shaw was a singer, not a comic, and played the show only once,
not long before retiring. Shaw's peak career moment arrived in November 1955 after her hit record "Careless" made the top-50 charts. "I was
21 years old. That show was a big, big, big, big deal." For the event, Shaw
bought a big-deal gown from Patti Page, she told me. "It was an incredible gown. I'd never worried about my voice, but the day I was supposed
to do the Sullivan show, I was, oh, so sick—lady problems. I was so sick
my manager said, 'If you can't do it, you can't do it.' I said I would die
before I would walk away. And so I did it!"

Shaw remembered, "I was on the show with Kate Smith and, I think,
Johnny Carson. Unfortunately, that was the night 'Peter Pan' was pre-
miering on TV, with Mary Martin." Sullivan called Shaw over and said,
"With young people like this, we don't have anything to worry about."
He even got her name right. But that was it. "Truthfully, it didn't have
that big of an impact." She married her manager soon after and had a
child, so Sullivan's show was really her career finale. But she had one
shining memory. "I was wearing this truly elegant gown. I felt like a
queen that night!"

Often Sullivan had to haggle for acts he'd first introduced to TV, like
a dance team called the Szonys, who had accepted $500 for their first
shot on the show but later wanted ten times that for the same act (plus

more bookings). Sullivan was creating monster stars who turned on their maker once they hit pay dirt. Want me, pay me.

Celebrity agents played their crafty agent games—hardball, softball, and dodgeball. Sullivan felt that acts he had made famous on network TV owed him lifelong loyalty. But agents rarely observe such niceties, realizing that Sullivan created the codes of conduct when his was the only game in town. Agents might duck a call from Sullivan about a client and then speedily dial rival shows before phoning Sullivan back, playing him off against other shows—standard agent practice. Ed saw these shenanigans as keeping him from being TV's only sugar daddy. In the early days, he resented agents who tried to get the best deal for clients; he felt the ingrates should be banging on his door in perpetuity.

While Sullivan always bristled at any hint that he used his column as leverage to purchase, promote, or punish acts, one showbiz insider noted that Sullivan was famous for paying off performers by mentioning them in his column without actually referring to their upcoming appearance on his TV show.

"His bitterness toward the agents became a very personal thing," said Marlo Lewis in his memoir, "and grew ever more acerbic over the years." Sullivan once vented his rage at Lewis: " 'Marlo, I'm gonna kill that Joe Wolfson [a William Morris agent]! That slimy bastard lies to me about everything! I get advance tips on a vocalist's record sales, and that prick takes my information and gets double the dough from the "Colgate Comedy Hour"!' His agent diatribes were a leitmotif in our conversations." Sullivan called one agent "a fat-faced bum with soft-boiled eyes." Precht said he never saw any animosity toward agents from Sullivan: "He liked them and had respect for agents." But Vince Calandra maintained, "He had this thing about not liking agents." Peter Calabrese explained that the agents got upset with Precht or coordinator Jack Babb—"They never took Ed on."

Lewis wrote that Sullivan banned all agents from the studio after they became a motley gang that gathered there, almost as bodyguards for their clients. Sullivan finally forced them to huddle outside the CBS security desk, like derelicts awaiting handouts, while a bored guard read *The Racing Form*. Marty Kummer of MCA (Music Corporation of America) christened the barrier the "Wailing Wall," where stars moaned to their agents about the personal humiliation and career damage inflicted on them by Sullivan. Agents and managers danced cautiously along the wall. Lewis said the Wailing Wall was "a show in itself," with agents from competing offices "trying to top one another with smart talk" and regaling each other with tales about Sullivan and his callous treatment of performers. Marlo Lewis referred to the Wailing Wall as "the place where agents prayed that Ed Sullivan would drop dead." Dick Schaap, writing in the *New York Herald Tribune* in June 1962, pointed out, "No one in show business would expect Sullivan to be any different from the kind of person he is—a mixture of schmaltz and stiletto."

CHAPTER 15

Backstage Life (and Death)

I once saw him strike 103 West Point cadets from the show
without batting an eye.

Eddie Brinkman, stage manager

While it looked to viewers as if Ed Sullivan were winging his introductions, in fact he carefully wrote them all out himself, fussing with the wording right up to airtime. During Marlo Lewis's day, a frenzied secretary typed out Sullivan's last-minute changes and ran off new mimeographed scripts, often moments before the red "on air" light flashed.

When the show's running order was shuffled hours (or minutes) before airtime, secretary Susan Abramson told me, there was a low-key madness. "It was a good chaos, with your adrenaline pumping. Excitement! You'd look at your watch and say, 'Oh, my God, we only have three hours to go!' I worked on many a show where it got so crazy you can't stand it and think you're gonna lose your mind. But this was a very well-run show." Even so, prior to airtime, "everyone would have to scramble. This was before computers. There were these ditto machines [churning out last-minute changes], and you'd have purple ink all over you." Her colleague Mary Lynn Gottfried added, "We would be changing things at five minutes to eight! It was *that* close."

Under Precht's more orderly regime, the Sunday show was blocked out with a technical rehearsal Saturday morning, to configure the lights, sound, and camera angles, followed by a rehearsal with Ray Bloch's musicians and the major acts. The 4 P.M. Sunday rehearsal ran nonstop for timing purposes and to ensure that the sets, light, and sound cues were in synch—and, to be sure, to gauge audience response to each act.

But anything could happen, like when jazz pianist Roland Kirk did a five-minute solo at rehearsal, but on the actual show he kept playing . . . and playing . . . and playing. Russ Petranto, clutching a stopwatch, had no way to signal to Kirk he was running over. Kirk was blind. "I'm now in deep doo-doo," Petranto recalled. "Pages are flying and I'm screaming backstage." During a commercial, he ran over to the West Point Glee Club and told them to cut their first song. "So they did one song, Ed said goodnight, and we finished right on time."

During the era of live television, set designers had to plan, build, and maneuver sets for the equivalent of a new Broadway show every week—and the sets had to please Sullivan, Lewis or Precht, and the performers. The pressure was enormous on designers like Grover Cole and, filling in one summer during Cole's vacation, Bob Markell, who had designed sets for such landmark TV staples as "You Are There" and for George Balanchine and Noël Coward. "There were many acts and many sets," Markell pointed out to me, nine or ten sets a week. "It wasn't just designing it; you had to draw construction plans as if you were an architect. You had to supervise construction, plus painting and, finally, the setup in the theater. You had to make sure it was designed and painted correctly. And all on budget. By the time you finished, you were dead." He added, "Saturday we would bring the scenery in and set the show up. They would tell us what the lineup was, and we'd try to sit with Marlo and the director. Sullivan wouldn't get involved in preproduction or anything. At that point it was all Marlo."

Being in television then was like working on Broadway—and, indeed, the Sullivan theater itself was a converted legit house literally on Broadway, not a custom-built TV studio. In the mid-1950s, the networks presented about a dozen original live dramatic shows—"Lux Video Theater," "Robert Montgomery Presents," "G.E. Theater," "The Alcoa Hour," "The Ford Theater," "Studio One," "Playhouse 90," "The Play of the Week," "Four Star Playhouse," "The Hallmark Hall of Fame," and "Kraft Theater," as well as "Matinee Theater," which presented an original one-hour play every weekday. Markell said, "We felt like a branch of the theater. It was live, so when that clock showed 8 o'clock, you were on, and there was nothing you could do about it until the hour was over." He remained in awe of the show's scope: "They chose the most extraordinary things to show the American public—they chose ballet, Virginia Woolf, excerpts from plays. It was amazing. The audience then sat still for culture."

Markell lamented, "The day they found they could put something on film and repeat it and get money for it each time, that's when it all disappeared. It became serious business with repeats. But we were doing 52 shows a year then. You couldn't show kinescopes; they looked terrible." Often on live shows, sets wobbled or fell over, or the wrong set was slid into place, but Markell recalled few mishaps. "They were good, highly creative sets. They hold up very well today. Once in a while I'll see one of the sets on an old TV show and I think, that's not bad!"

Sullivan was at his sullen worst during the hours leading up to the show—tense, uncertain, worried, often in a dark mood; performers dreaded that he might change his mind about them between rehearsal and airtime. He in turn fretted that an act might collapse, and he took every failed act personally. If it bombed, *he* bombed. He got furious if any staffers wandered around the theater during the show. "That was a sacrosanct rule," his former secretary Barbara Gallagher pointed out to me. "He didn't want the audience distracted." She didn't remember that Sullivan was tense, just the performers.

"After the dress rehearsal," recalled stage manager Eddie Brinkman, "Ed would pull the show apart. He was absolutely ruthless. He might rearrange the running order, which meant we'd have to restack all the scenery. Two hours before airtime, he might cut an act that had been rehearsing all week." Director John Moffitt told me, "Ed was an Irishman with a temper, but you wouldn't see it that much. He lit into Sophie Tucker a few times. He prevailed. He was Mr. Big. He was *huge*." Neil Hickey, *TV Guide*'s former New York bureau chief, pointed out, "I never heard anything negative about him, except that he was a grudge holder. If you got on the wrong side of him, he tended to remember it."

Frankie Laine had only rosy memories: "We got along great," he told me. "Ed was supposed to be a curmudgeon, but I never found him to be like that, maybe because I stayed out of his way." But in five appearances on the show with her husband, Louis Prima, Keely Smith couldn't recall Sullivan ever saying a word to her. Comic Christopher Weeks remembered Sullivan as "very removed. There was no real person there, nobody inside," he commented. Robert Klein agreed, "When I walked up the stairs behind him to his dressing room, I don't remember him being particularly cordial. Ed was such a zombie, I tell ya."

Sullivan brooked no nonsense from anyone who questioned his authority—comics, agents, or censors. Peter Calabrese, a weekend staffer for five years, told me, "The CBS censors would go to Bob, but one day there was a new guy who went to Ed, and Ed says, 'Who are you and what do you do?' Ed threw the guy out, but first he got [CBS executive vice president] Frank Stanton on the phone and told him, 'There's a guy here who tells me he's a censor. I'm about to throw him out, and if I ever see another censor here, you won't have me on the network. I've been doing this for how many years now, and you need somebody here to watch my taste?' "

Sullivan was willing to offend anyone except certain megastars he curried favor with. A few performers, like Barbra Streisand and Jack E. Leonard, had the guts to talk back to him. Streisand refused to sing a comedy song from her Broadway show, John Moffitt said, and insisted on a ballad instead. TV critic Kay Gardella commented to me, "Milton Berle always had the reputation of running his show like a lion tamer. I never heard that about Ed, but I'm sure you couldn't have run that show without having an iron hand." Part of Matthew Harlib's job as floor manager on the show in 1950 and 1951 was to tell people to take their positions before airtime. His widow, Dorothy, recalled, "He once had the nerve to go up to Ed Sullivan and tell him where to stand. Sullivan was outraged. You don't tell the star where to stand. After that, he was pushed up the ladder. Ed Sullivan didn't want him there anymore." Comedian Larry Storch testified, "He had a violent temper—everyone knew that."

Jan Morgan, a press agent for many comedians—Stiller & Meara, Rodney Dangerfield, Richard Lewis, Larry Storch—told me, "He was very curt with people who tried to talk to him, if he didn't know who you were. He was not approachable at all. He was not nice to the people who worked backstage. He wasn't mean, like Phil Silvers, just curt. Exactly what you saw on TV is what he was. But if you were associated with someone he really liked, like Anne [Meara] and Jerry [Stiller], he was very pleasant. He fawned over stars."

Performers feared the often deadly Sunday afternoon rehearsal crowd composed of youth groups, professional freebie-grabbers, and oldsters

I remember my father saying, "Those New York audiences will clap for anything." We didn't know about applause signs then. This was one show that the whole family watched in the early '60s. What else was there to see in a small town with two stations?

Gene Monroe, Fargo, North Dakota

who stared mutely or dozed. The audience for the 8 P.M. telecast was better dressed, brighter, full of friends and celebrities, all hyped for the cameras and relentlessly egged on by Sullivan's constant pleas for more applause, more noise—the sort of planned pandemonium that now infects all TV studio audiences, which are prodded like Pavlovian dogs to explode into cheers, whoops, whistles, and applause at any excuse. It's one of Sullivan's lesser legacies, and it began in earnest with Elvis's hyped appearances.

Phyllis McGuire, who with her singing sisters became a Sullivan favorite and did the show 22 times, related how physically tricky it was performing in an old theater not built for TV: "You played the camera and you didn't look away. There was a camera in the balcony, a camera to the extreme left, a camera to the right below the balcony in front. You had to know which camera to turn to." During the early years, the show used four cameras—one on Sullivan, one on a crane, one for angles, and a fourth for low angles to shoot dance numbers and to elongate the dancers' legs.

Denny Doherty, of the Mamas and the Papas, told me he loved the show's big-time theatrical atmosphere. "I never noticed the cameras. It was like live theater. You performed for the audience, as opposed to L.A., where you performed for cameras. The venue was a theater, as opposed to a TV studio, so it was like a concert, like 'A Hard Day's Night' when the Beatles are doing a concert in that old theater. It was like that old theater."

Doherty went on to say, "I'm sure it was like that for anybody on that stage, because the audience was right *there*. It wasn't like they were in the bleachers or way the hell across a soundstage. You were *performing*. Ed hated you coming out and pretending to be performing [that is, lip-synching]. If you were on his show, you had to deliver the goods. You know, 'Let's see what everybody's so excited about here.' " At rehearsal, Doherty remembered, "it was such a circus going on there most of the time. You went to your dressing room and you were called, but when you came down onstage, it was zoo time!"

Robert Klein, who played the show six times between 1969 and 1971, including the last live show before it was canceled and slipped into reruns, was badly thrown by the theater's nerve-jangling configuration. "That theater was very ill-suited to stand-up comedy, because people in the balcony could not actually see you around the equipment. So people looked up at TV sets. Most of the orchestra was filled with sound booths. The orchestra was extremely small and enclosed in glass so they could mix the sound."

He said, "You were on your own! If you looked up, the balcony was very close because the stage came further out, but you'd only see a bank of monitors. You're not really looking directly at anyone, a few heads and faces. It was *extremely* distracting. If you're a singer, that's one thing. But when you're talking for a living, you can't have an open bar around the sides of the theater. It's not a lounge act! You had a spot to stand in. I couldn't prowl the stage like I wanted to do. I was restricted." Meanwhile, "the people would be watching Ed, and he's not even watching you. He's being prepped for the next thing, consulting with someone—all in full view, and guys with earphones running around. So there's all this action while you're on. And it was such an echo-y place. It wasn't until Letterman signed a contract that CBS spent millions renovating it."

Klein recalled, "Playing the Sullivan show was difficult territory, as difficult a program as I've ever done. And Johnny Carson wasn't there to laugh me up." He remembered the chaotic backstage atmosphere: "It was a madhouse. It was a real proscenium theater. I remember the back brick wall, cables, and classical dancers stretching. There was an assortment of background sets, 35 feet long; there were animal acts. There was a European dog act, and the dog took a leak against the wall. These dogs could do calculus, but they didn't know not to take a leak on the wall." Secretary Barbara Gallagher recalled once seeing backstage Robert Merrill, a marching band, Totie Fields, and an elephant.

A few years ago, Klein looked at old tapes of himself on the show. "I was appalled and amazed at how few laughs there were. And yet they invited me back. I was considered to have done very well. The laughs were just smaller than they would be elsewhere. There was no sweetening [laugh track] of any kind. You'd go out there and it was real, as real as can be."

He theorized that "the show fostered the idea of the stand-up comedian. It was this mass exposure of monology—guys 'in one.' What we think of as stand-up comedy is a post–World War II phenomenon carried over from vaudeville and music halls. Lots of important careers were made there—Totie Fields, Alan King, Rodney Dangerfield. King's appearances were key to his whole career." Dangerfield was going nowhere at 44, in his second life as a stand-up after failing to make it as "Jackie Roy," when, in 1967, Sullivan threw him a lifeline—a one-shot on the show, where his sweaty loser's looks and hooks ("I tellya, I don't get no respect") made him a born-again comedian.

Klein said that, when he revisited his Sullivan tapes, "I gained a whole new respect for the show as a performer, because it was an honest test. I had much less respect for 'Laugh-In'—that was a machine and I resented it. On Sullivan's show you had to get *real* laughs. You had to deliver the goods, even if the response was meager—very weak laughs. It certainly was different for 'The Ed Sullivan Show.' I was trying to push the envelope a little. I was a hot kid, and they were trying to keep up with the times. But it was part of the prestige of a career: to do 'The Ed Sullivan Show' and be invited back."

The house orchestra had its own pitfalls. "It was a rule in those early days [that] you could not bring your own conductor," said Phyllis McGuire. "They had this conductor, Ray Bloch, and he would get your tempo so off. He'd flap his arms like wings. Nobody had whatever it took to speak up and say, 'Ed, we have to have our own conductor.' I was young and foolish, so one day I said, 'We will not be able to do the show anymore because Ray Bloch gets our tempos all wrong.' Ed liked us so much that he agreed."

Sherwin Bash, Bloch's son-in-law and a former manager, told me that musicians often complained about tempos. "I've managed many people, from Herb Alpert and the Tijuana Brass to the Carpenters, and I can tell you that I have *rarely* represented any artist who thought that anybody else did anything right. They were the only ones who knew what was right; everybody else was wrong. Steve [Lawrence] and Eydie [Gorme] told many that Ray never got their tempos right."

Often a singer would have recorded a song in a certain tempo that Bloch would try to copy; but in the meantime the performer would have been on the road singing it in a different tempo. "So Ray got into that all the time," said Bash. "After a while, Sullivan said, 'Hey, if they want their own conductor, fine, let them pay for it.'" When the McGuire Sisters became regulars, Phyllis said, the show allowed singers to use their own conductors. But Jerry Vale, also a Sullivan regular, remarked to me, "I never had any problem with the musicians. Ray Bloch's was a great orchestra—the best musicians in the world" (jazz pianist Hank Jones among them).

Bob Arthur, the show's longtime music coordinator (1955–1971), was Bloch's right-hand man. The conductor hired him so that Bloch (busily conducting other shows, like "The Jackie Gleason Show," where Gleason always hailed him as "Ray Bloch, *mm-mmm*, the flower of the musical world!") could walk in on Sunday to conduct after Arthur had done the grunt work. "Ray was just there because it paid well," Arthur joked.

During rehearsals, Bloch was known at times to conduct with his left hand and hold a tiny transistor radio to his right ear, glued to a ball game. Bloch's casual approach caused occasional tempo tantrums. "Sometimes singers would lose their way in the arrangements on the air," Arthur added. "More and more, the big stars had their own conductors. Ray wasn't that thrilled with it, but in a way it was a relief. If Ray had just used a metronome in rehearsal, he could have made life easier on himself. He just never wanted to use a metronome. Sometimes he did miss the tempo. But he wasn't bad. It was a good orchestra. It was a good steady yearlong gig"—a 23-year gig, in fact.

Musicians had to sight-read Saturday and be ready to play the next day on the air. Trombonist Roland DuPont, with the show 14 years, sprang to Bloch's defense. "There was a lot of pressure on Ray," he told me, "because a lot of the acts came in and wanted to conduct the band. So he'd just put his stick down and say, 'Look, I'm the leader of the orchestra. You tell me what you want.' And if they started to conduct, we would stop."

Few performers caused major problems, recalled Arthur—but Kate Smith had a Kate Smith–size ego. "Kate Smith was a bear. She would say things like, 'Is the left side of the orchestra playing the same thing as the right side of the orchestra?' She was tough. . . . There were some other nasty people, but I can't remember them." He added, philosophically, "Most show people have temperaments, all the way down to the acrobats. That's why they're in show business—because they're the most important thing in their eyes. So you put yourself into neutral and just move through it."

Precht told me, "Bob Arthur was really the key guy. He prepped Ray before the show." Arthur hammered out the details—arrangements, keys, tempos—of each number for the band and the singers, and devised song ideas for certain performers. Bloch's office housed three arrangers and five copyists, who arduously wrote out arrangements by hand; filing cabinets were stuffed with arrangements for any and all acts. If a singer said, "Do you have 'Blue Skies'?," Arthur would go to the 'Blue Skies' file and bring out charts in four different keys. At a rehearsal for the Irving Berlin tribute with Bing Crosby, Russ Petranto remembered, "Bob took the arrangement for 'White Christmas' from the movie, and when they started to play 'White Christmas,' Crosby says, 'What the fuck is that?! Are you crazy? I haven't sung in that key in 25 years.' "

Arthur—who wrote theme music for many awards shows and did the score for a live unproduced musical, "The Last Ed Sullivan Show"—described himself as "the house coach for all the singers." When singers were not on just to peddle their latest hit, he created the songs, staging, scenes, sound mix, and medleys for singers, from pop to opera stars; he also worked with the show's choreographers (John Wray, Peter Gennaro, and Michael Bennett in his first high-profile job). "If a singer didn't have a hit, they'd look to me to come up with something fresh musically they could do. Like for Johnny Mathis: I had him do 'Johnny One-Note,' not normally the sort of thing he would do."

Arthur once put together a five-minute medley of 50 Irving Berlin songs for the Supremes. "They were thrilled; they loved it. I did a Fats Waller medley, and they almost didn't know who Fats Waller was. [Motown's] Berry Gordy wanted them to do more standard material—white material. He had me do special numbers for Diana Ross, Fred Astaire–type numbers. He wanted me to devise fancy things for the Supremes. He was full of pep and ideas—a likeable guy. He'd tell me what he wanted me to do, and left it up to me."

For Arthur, rock and roll was an easy transition. "Most rock acts played for themselves. Miking was the big problem—all kinds of trouble. We finally got Ed to let us use stand mikes and hand mikes." Sullivan hated visible mikes, but boom mikes didn't work for rock groups. Did he have any personal dealings with Sullivan? "*Nobody* did!" Arthur laughed. "Except Bob Precht. Ed stayed at his hotel all week, booking acts. The first time we saw him was at Sunday's rehearsal. He didn't involve himself deeply in details. He admitted he didn't know a helluva lot about how things worked. Bob didn't know a lot about music, so he depended on me a lot in that area. Bob was very efficient and pleasant. Marlo Lewis winged it a lot more; Bob wanted things more under control."

Polly Bergen described the show to me as a showbiz conveyor belt: "It was the show to be on, but you never got to know anybody, and you never really hung out together. If you did the Perry Como, Milton Berle, and Andy Williams shows, you all rehearsed together for four or five days. You got to know other people in the show; you became kind of a family. That would not happen on Sullivan's show. The great thing is, it required almost no work at all. You just simply walked on and offered them various songs, and they would tell you which one they'd like you to do. You weren't asked to do anything unusual or spectacular. You just did your number and it was over."

Patti Page, who was on the show 17 times, and who told me she twice filled in for Sullivan as host ("I believe I was the only girl who ever emceed his show"), remembers that Sullivan "was strictly business"—but scary. "He just came in, and they put all the cue cards in front of him. You were never sure if you were going to be on the actual show. If he didn't like someone in dress rehearsal, he would cut it right out." She treasures her personal Sullivan gaffe: After she sang "Eli, Eli," the poignant Jewish ballad, Sullivan called her over and said, "Ladies and gentlemen, in all the years I've been on television, I have never been so moved by this . . . act." He meant to say "by this song." Page laughs, " 'Act!'— like some high-wire act! I was ready for all these accolades. It was so funny."

Sullivan began his own Sunday run-through with his regular luncheon lamp chop, before working on the Monday column. His personal aide, Joe Moore, picked up Sullivan at the Delmonico in his Lincoln (the license plate was inscribed "ES") for the 15-minute drive to the theater across town, where the marquee announced that night's guests.

At the West 53rd Street stage door, Sullivan would emerge from the car wearing buckled loafers and carrying a neatly pressed suit (custom made by Dunhill Tailors). Sullivan dawdled outside the theater signing autographs, then toted the suit bag up to his dressing room, furnished with a sofa, chairs, tables, a typewriter, and a TV set. A door led to a small cubicle with a desk, chair, and bed—the royal dressing room, with a private bath. Sullivan had numbered suits, ties, and pocket handkerchiefs for every show, so that they could be matched with his attire on summer reruns, for which new intros were inserted.

The mood tensed once Sullivan arrived on the premises, as staff and crew anxiously scampered about. There was always more tension when Sullivan was around, remarked weekend cue card man Peter Calabrese, "But there was a lot of respect too. People loved him, but you had to laugh sometimes. You couldn't be around that guy week after week, with all the things that happened—his quirks, forgetting someone's name, and impromptu decisions on air—and not love him." In the early years, Sullivan himself greeted the rehearsal crowd (perhaps the only TV show at the time to have a rehearsal audience). Lincoln spokeswoman Julia Meade told me, "They loved him. Of course, the audience came there wanting to love him." During commercial breaks in the early days, Sullivan schmoozed with the studio audience, dispensing tourist tips on what to do in New York while in town ("Go down the block and see the Hudson River"). He once got entangled in the curtain and came out of the break dizzy and disoriented, stumbling through the next intro.

Sullivan's backstage family gathered after each show at the China Song Restaurant for a laugh-laden postmortem. Calabrese remembered these gatherings vividly: "The great thing about a live show is that, when it's over it's over—no videotape to edit, nothing else to do. For better or worse, at 9:10 much of the staff was next door at the China Song. You let down your hair." The director Tim Kiley, said Calabrese, "had the best impersonation of Ed in the world. Kiley was hilarious," regaling the staff with Sullivan stories. "We almost thought Ed had to rehearse this stuff"—the gaffes—"because he would come up with some of the most incredibly inappropriate comments. Tim would always make an entrance—he'd come in and faint, or have a one-liner. The more everyone drank, the funnier it got. We all made fun of Ed because he was comical at times."

Ralph Paul, one of the show's announcers (there were three—Bern Bennett, 1948–1949; Art Hannes, 1949–1964; Ralph Paul, 1959–1961, 1964–1971), would warm up the afternoon crowd: "I'm here to ask for applause. Sometimes people forget to applaud. That's the sound a performer needs. I'd like you to sound like 50 million people"—not the 700 on hand. Paul would introduce the producer, director, and conductor, go to the end of the stage, and, at 8 p.m., in a booming voice, proclaim, *"Tonight from the Ed Sullivan Theater on Broadway—'The Ed Sullivan Show.' . . . And now, live from New York . . . Ed Sullivan!"*

As John Moffitt described the drill, "It was very, very smoothly run. It was run from the stage, not from the control booth [like most shows]. Even when Bob Precht produced and sat in the booth, he didn't tell Ed what to do. The stage manager told the booth what Ed was going to do." Standing next to Ed, at stage right near the wings, was the stopwatch man.

Steve Blauner, Bobby Darin's manager, told me, "Sullivan was always lurking. But he had very little interaction with anyone. He was uneasy with people. All you had to do is watch him as host. He was a very strange duck. But very opinionated. If he didn't like something, he'd tell ya. It was his world, and you were just passing through. He always talked to Bobby like he was his son—'Keep up the good work, keep your nose clean.'"

Sullivan was aware that the audience was watching his reactions to see what he liked. Michael David Harris, writing in 1968, noted, "He does not reveal very much. It is hard to tell from his face if he likes or dislikes an act, but unless something is off-color he appreciates what the audience enjoys. He carefully measures the mood in the theater and [he may have] a double reaction to a comedy line—first an amused chuckle and then a heartier laugh as the audience responds."

He knew that a big laugh from him would amplify the audience's laughter. A huge ten-foot TV screen in the balcony registered his expressions—grins, winces, frowns, impatience, indifference. Agents learned to read Sullivan's every twitch: "Many of the talent agents consider themselves expert Sullivan watchers and capable of discerning his opinion," reported Harris. "He is supposed to reveal his distaste by drawing back the corners of his mouth very slightly. Agents said that 'a certain pursing of the lips is the kiss of death.' "

After a rehearsal, Sullivan would go over revisions and then break for a late lunch with aide Joe Moore, who never discussed the show with him. "Eddie wants to relax," Moore explained. "He likes to get his mind off the show and think about other things." After eating, he would take a walk, return to the studio around six, and insert any changes, followed by a nap before the 8 P.M. telecast. Just before airtime, people he planned to introduce in the audience might come backstage to say hello. About 7:45, Sullivan descended the stairs but didn't interact with the evening audience until he was introduced, creating more electricity as the crowd awaited the great man's entrance. Even Ed's wife, watching at home, was anxious. "Every program is like an opening night," she said, even after 20 years of Sunday night openings. "I still get nervous before every show."

As with all shows in TV's pretape era, it was an extraordinary accomplishment to get any show on the air in decent shape—comparable to staging a live hour-long musical each week with one blocking, and a technical and dress rehearsal three hours before opening night. "The Ed Sullivan Show" did exactly that, with few visible hitches, for 23 years.

Despite his reputation as a nonperformer, Sullivan loved warming up the audience before shows in the early days, where he could belie his stony reputation. He strolled out to huge applause and asked, "How many are here from out of town?," then recoiled in mock surprise as tourists' hands shot up. "New Yorkers can't even get seats!" Wagging a stern finger at his staff, he would joke, "Heads will roll." He instructed the crowd how to behave. Awed simply to be in his presence, they eagerly complied.

Sullivan was a thwarted ham who didn't let his lack of talent hamper him from taking part once the show was off the ground. In retirement, mocking his image, he played Smiley the Magic Clown on a special called "Clownaround," made up in full Bozo regalia. On his own show, he interacted with the Marquis Chimps and played straight man to comics like Jack Benny, Jack Carter, and Phil Silvers; the latter tried to teach him to sing "My Mama Done Told Me." He donned a Jimmy Durante nose and a frizzy Marty Allen fright wig, and once appeared in full drag in blonde wig and boa, like his old rival Milton Berle, for a sketch with Soupy Sales. He sang with the McGuire Sisters and did a soft-shoe with Durante, Gene Kelly, and Jackie Gleason.

Sullivan was game for almost anything, and far more engaging when goofing around on others' shows than when stuck in cement on his own show, announcing the next act. As usual, his famed clunkiness and our lowered expectations worked in his favor. In 1955, while stuck briefly in suburbia, he appeared in a Connecticut Southbury Players' production of "King of Hearts" as a newspaper publisher, to glowing reviews: "Sullivan fitted the role perfectly," wrote a critic, "showed no signs of stage fright and had sufficient poise to ad-lib on occasion, sending his audience, and cast members, into gales of laughter."

After he began hosting hour-long salutes to showbiz legends, Sullivan's onstage interviews furnished him with his favorite role, that of ace reporter, chatting with Carl Sandburg, Oscar Hammerstein, Josh Logan, Cole Porter, Walt Disney, and others. It was the guise Ed was most comfortable in—intrepid celebrity interviewer and friend to the stars, leaving the impression that he was getting the lowdown when, in fact, it was just standard showbiz palaver, an early version of Barbara Walters's pop star interview love fests. Sullivan wrote the questions and narrative, most of it fan magazine puffery.

Director Joshua Logan broke the cotton candy barrier when, at the end of an hour-long Sullivan tribute to him in 1953, he revealed his long fight against depression and made a plea for more understanding of mental illness. Inaugurating let-it-all-hang-out television, Logan was the first major celebrity to spill his guts on TV, in prime time, leading to today's unending celebrity-in-recovery star turns, soap-Oprah tales of woe and rehab. Gloria Swanson told Ed that her comeback in "Sunset Boulevard" happened because "I believed in God"; Oscar Hammerstein II revealed he refused to quit show business despite eleven years of flops, thanks to the love and encouragement of his wife.

Logan used the show to come out of the closet about his crack-up, telling Sullivan in rehearsal, "Ed, this is turning into one of those boring

slap-yourself-on-the-back routines. It's flattering but of no importance."
The Lewises noted in their memoir that Logan asked to discuss his
breakdown and recovery. Sullivan went along with it and cut a song
from the show, despite his staff's objections. Sullivan overruled them,
and Logan told of his mental collapse in the hope of (in Ed's words)
"comforting families who might be terrified at the thought of mental illness in their homes." Sullivan said the speech drew more mail than Elvis.
Years later he noted, "The things that stay in the minds of people across
the country after a show ends are the things that involve sentiment—not
phony sentiment, something set up as a weeper."

Sullivan became an unwitting TV pioneer in his hour-long tributes,
primitive versions of today's splashy Kennedy Center Honors and Mark
Twain Awards, A&E's "Biography," PBS's "American Masters" and
"American Experience," and other full-length biographical portraits.
The tributes were partly a Sullivan maneuver to counter "The Colgate
Comedy Hour" and other rivals, but also a way to grab more attention
and prestige for the show, often considered a lightweight hour over-
loaded with puppets, animals, and acrobats.

Sullivan's 1955 hour-long Oscar Hammerstein tribute, the first of the
series, was a turning point in the show's upward mobility, lifting it from
the realm of a simple one-cell variety show. Sullivan genuinely admired
the people he honored—Robert Sherwood, Bea Lillie, Helen Hayes,
Richard Rodgers, Samuel Goldwyn—and had the clout to pull in viewers who might have no idea who playwright Robert Sherwood or British
comic singer Bea Lillie were. When Broadway still ruled supreme, Hammerstein, Hayes, Sherwood, and Lillie were theatrical rock stars.

Sullivan celebrated theater, and not just musical theater. If he saw a
serious play he admired that was struggling at the box office, such as
"All the Way Home," he would clear ten minutes of his show to feature
a scene from it—worth millions in advertising. It's hard to imagine a
prime-time TV show today devoting an hour (or ten minutes) to salute
Edward Albee, Tom Stoppard, David Mamet, or even today's counter-
parts to Goldwyn, Hammerstein, Hayes, or Lillie. (Try to conceive of
CBS setting aside an hour to salute movie producer Harvey Weinstein,
Broadway songwriter John Kander, dramatic actress Cherry Jones, or
musical theater star Christine Ebersole.) On one show, Sullivan did a 60-
minute tribute to ASCAP that included an explanation of the legalistic
aspects of how songwriters and publishers are compensated. *Variety*
noted, "It could only have the vaguest meaning for the general public."
But Sullivan didn't care. He thought it was important that viewers know

all about ASCAP. In just such ways was "The Ed Sullivan Show" truly Ed Sullivan's.

Vince Calandra, who worked for the show from 1960 until it ended in 1971, is a major repository of Sullivan show lore and the mechanics of how the thing was hammered together each week. He broke in at 29, after leaving the army, was hired as a gofer, and wound up chief talent coordinator. Calandra worked with Marlo Lewis during Lewis's last season and then with Bob Precht. Ed bonded with this fellow streetwise New Yorker; he liked the Brooklyn boy with (like himself) only a high school education.

"Ed and Bob rolled the dice for me," he remarked in an interview for the Archive of American Television. "The old man really protected me, I don't know why. He'd always say, 'C'mon, kiddo.' He never remembered my name." Calandra said Sullivan called women "honey" and men "Hey, there!" Calandra literally began from the ground up—kneeling by a camera holding cue cards and taping the show's running order to the camera to remind Ed who was on next. Working cue cards for comics was "real pressure, because you had to know when to turn the card, on just the right beat," he told Jeff Abraham in his 2003 interview. "Sullivan really needed those cards—he was very insecure."

Calandra recalled Sullivan as "a sharp guy, but he didn't want to be a slick guy. He wanted to be like the average guy. Never a stretch limo, never an entourage. He took taxis. He'd rather flag a taxi in the street than take a limo. He always told me, 'Don't listen to the chauffeurs; listen to the cab drivers.' He really listened to what people he met told him." Secretary Barbara Gallagher remembered that, when she shared a cab with Ed on the way home, "he would always get the name of the driver and talk to him by name."

After promoting Calandra to production assistant, Sullivan sent him to check out big shows. "He'd say, 'Don't be like a Walter Kerr or some snotty critic when you go to the show. Think of a family in Des Moines sitting in front of their set, and pick out three minutes that *they'd* like.'" Staffer Russ Petranto added, "The genius of the show was that Ed never got sophisticated. He was always the common man."

Sullivan carried his own suit bag into the theater, and when Calandra first went to take it Sullivan waved him off—"Do I look like I need help?" Sullivan, he said, not only took time to sign autographs but asked for hometowns before inscribing personal notes ("To Brian from Toledo"). Once at dinner he signed his name ten times for tourists' kids while his food was cooling. Calandra asked me, "Would Britney Spears do that?" Calandra would have to steer him into a restaurant during a rehearsal break lest Ed spend the lunch hour signing autographs instead of eating. Precht added, "He could be tough at home but was considerate of the audience. He had a caring and a compassion for people. He'd stand onstage and sign autographs till the last person left."

Calandra's tasks included rounding up props for the acts, clearing British rock singers through immigration, and such odd jobs as standing guard outside Richard Burton's dressing room to keep Burton from stepping out for a drink or two or six, or searching every saloon on Eighth Avenue to retrieve Lee Marvin.

Calandra revered Sullivan not just as a producer or as an icon but also as a mensch. "I was still a young guy, and I'd ask Bob Precht, 'Why are we booking some of these people?'—old acts like Smith & Dale and Sophie Tucker and Benny Fields, some of them right out of the motion picture actors' home. That wasn't our audience. I found out why: if he booked them for two appearances, it would pay their hospital, pension, and health plan." Sullivan cherished many an aging, ailing star. "It was payback time," said Calandra. "He really cared about these people." Precht remembered, "He'd bring on someone like Blossom Seeley, someone he fondly recalled from vaudeville. For me, it was like, 'Who's this old lady we got on here?' But viewers loved it. So his thoughts were good."

Bob Pitofsky, Sullivan's nephew, told me, "Ed extended himself to many people he helped financially over the years—ex-fighters or tap dancers, people that had been successful in their careers and, for whatever reason, were not at the top of their game anymore. He tried to help these people, and never took credit for it." Pitofsky recalled that when he got engaged to a radio actress (the lead on radio's "A Date with Judy"), Sullivan called an agent at MCA to see if they could help her.

Sullivan was an especially soft touch for broken-down athletes. "The second week I was a production assistant," Calandra said, "Ed asked me, 'Do you know who Johnny Dundee was?' I didn't. Sullivan explained that, when he came to New York, 'Dundee [a onetime boxing champ] kind of established me. He introduced me to Jack Dempsey and Babe Ruth and was best man at my wedding. Well, you know the old guy who comes in here and *tawks like dis?* Well, that's Johnny Dundee.' I'm sure Ed was paying his rent. He'd tell me, 'I want you to treat him the way you'd treat Sinatra.' So I'd tape off two seats for 'Johnny Dundee and Guest.' After the show, Johnny would come backstage, and

Ed would ask what he thought, and he'd say, 'Oh, I loved that mouse!' or whatever. Then Ed gave me 50 bucks, and I'd tell Johnny, 'Ed really appreciates your input. Why don't you go over to the Stage Deli and get a bite?' Ed had a temper and he'd let you know about it, but Ed was a *very* sentimental guy. He'd cry at the drop of a hat."

When Calandra was elevated to talent coordinator and his salary raised from $100 to $300 a week, he recalled, "that was like a class D ballplayer being called up to the Yankees. I was 30 years old. I didn't know what I was doing, and here I was dealing with cutthroat agents. But people said I had a streetwise sense, and I was a quick learner. I had an instinct." He conceded, "If you had half a brain, you could book that show. Everyone wanted to get on it. They shoulda paid *us* to do the show!" Managers and agents dangled bribes to get their clients a shot— "I was offered money by lots of record companies. They'd offer you anything"—once even a swimming pool for his home.

It was a buyer's market, and Calandra adopted Sullivan's my-way-or-the-highway approach: "Ed had a great attitude. If a group like the Byrds were no. 1, but were a pain in the ass, which they were, he'd just say, 'Let's get someone else.' He didn't even know what the no. 1 record was. All the rock acts knew that, if they did the Sullivan show, it would push them to one million sales."

Even the Rolling Stones were obliged to play the show, and showed up for rehearsal with their surly attitude in place. When Calandra introduced himself to Mick Jagger, Jagger snarled, "Fuckin' Yankee, get outta here!" Janis Joplin refused at first to wear makeup to cover her splotchy complexion, but once she saw herself on camera she changed her mind. The Jefferson Airplane was "a royal pain in the ass," recalls Russ Petranto. After being instructed not to wear anything blue (for color-key reasons), they turned up in blue jeans. "They didn't give a fuck. There was a major fight."

Sullivan was addicted to animal acts despite also being sabotaged by them, like the rude horse that upstaged Frankie Laine, lions that tried to attack trainer Clyde Beatty, and Victor the Bear. Precht thought it would be cute if Ed gave Victor an ice cream cone after a trick, but the ungrateful bear tried to take a nip out of Sullivan's face. In the X-rated Frankie Laine moment, the singer recalled, "I came out dressed as a preacher, the long coat and everything, to sing 'I Believe.' I came out in a buggy with a horse, and he let go onstage!" The audience howled. "The first thing you do is, you look at your fly. It wasn't that. At that moment, I smelled the urine. They switched cameras and got a different shot, so it didn't go out on the air, except briefly. Sullivan stayed out of it. I was only halfway through the song, and he didn't know what I was going to do—and *I* didn't know what I was going to do. I just kept singing."

Julia Meade recalled a Clyde Beatty tiger incident like a bad dream. It happened just as she was about to do a Lincoln commercial: "It was terrifying, because the animals got at each other. They immediately closed the curtain. They yelled, 'Go, Julia, go!' And I had to go out and do a commercial. Behind me it was wild! Thank God, my concentration held; I got through it. By the time I finished, they had things calmed down and got the tigers out the door into cages and a van in the back." To distract the crowd, and escape being mauled, Sullivan skedaddled into the audience, where he rarely ventured, to introduce jockey Eddie Arcaro and Walter Brennan while bewildered viewers heard jungle sounds in the background—roaring tigers and a gun going off. (Meade's second most harrowing moment was being stuck in an elevator with Señor Wences: "He got panicky. It was just me and him and the elevator guy. Wences made him open the door, and he climbed out. He went bananas.")

Other mortal dangers surrounded the show. When Bobby Darin and Connie Francis were dating, against her father's will, her father showed up unexpectedly. Darin's manager, Steve Blauner, recalled, "Bobby was up in the dressing room visiting Connie when her father came in the stage door. Somebody rushed in and cried, 'Her father's here and he's got a gun!'" Darin fled through the front door of the theater. "Everybody was freaked out. Her father was a monster." Another time, recalled comedy writer Ron Clark, one of the Marquis Chimps grabbed a comic's testicles and held on until he beat the monkey away with a guitar. Sullivan saw him bashing the chimp. After the comic struggled through his routine, Ed exploded: "You'll never be on this show again! Anybody who treats animals the way you just did, you're finished."

Looking back, Calandra said, he still had to pinch himself: "I think, 'Did I really work on this show?' On *one* show we'd have Red Skelton, Barbra Streisand, the Rolling Stones, Woody Allen. Amazing! There'll never be another 'Ed Sullivan Show.'" After the Sullivan tent folded, Calandra hopscotched from show to show—John Davidson's, Mike Douglas's, Alan Thicke's, Joan Rivers's—but, he remarked, "where do you go after 'The Ed Sullivan Show'? Being on the Sullivan show was like winning the World Series every week. The Sullivan show had six or seven guys who banded together, and all these other shows were full of all this back-stabbing—no loyalty, and you always had to watch your back. It was just a whole different era. 'The Ed Sullivan Show' spoiled me for everything else."

While he was at college, and even while teaching high school, Peter Calabrese worked on the Sullivan show every weekend for five years, between 1964 and 1969, first as a gofer, before graduating to the job of cue card holder. He made $50 a day plus tips (cue card guys were tipped). "It was fun—it was just a great time to be there. Ed Sullivan started me on the road to my career." (When he taught, his students knew they could get him off the lesson on Mondays by asking what happened the night before on the Sullivan show.) "But for 'The Ed Sullivan Show,' I'd be teaching school." Calabrese wound up as an NBC vice president for specials and late-night and variety series, overseeing "The Tonight Show" with Johnny Carson, "Late Night with David Letterman," "SCTV," and "Saturday Night Live," and as a producer and/or director for Jay Leno, the Smothers Brothers, George Burns, Frank Sinatra, Mike Douglas, Steve Martin, and Bill Maher.

"As a weekend employee, I had a pretty unique perspective on the show," he noted. "I had very little clue what went on during the week." He'd sit in on the Saturday rehearsal, the dress rehearsal on Sunday, and the on-air show that night. He recalled, "I had a real attitude about taking the job. When my friend suggested it to me, I said, 'As a gofer? I was president of my class—what are you talking about?' But $50 a day plus tips was good money then." At the time, he didn't even know what a gofer did.

He said that working for the Sullivan show "was like going to an accounting office, except for the picture on the wall of ballerinas and big stars. It was kind of corporate. Their offices were in the Broadcast Center on 57th Street." He asked his new boss, "How do I know who's important," and was told, "To a gofer, everybody's important." Every Sunday for the next five years, Calabrese sat in the audience and watched rehearsals. "It was a pretty easy day. Mostly I got to see the show come together. For two years I saw every major rock act. Because it was live, no breaks or retakes, everybody was pretty uptight on the weekends."

Susan Abramson, Bob Precht's secretary during the show's last four years, said, "I ruled the roost there; I was a kind of gatekeeper—they had to get through me—but Bob would talk to anybody." She later worked on several Sullivan specials and got involved in the booking—without credit. She said women staffers never were credited. Mary Lynn Gottfried, a production secretary there, remarked, "Instead of a glass ceiling, it was a cement ceiling. There was no way we would ever have been promoted. We didn't care. That's the way it was. But we got so many perks"—like a chartreuse dress with feathers that the Supremes' Cindy Birdsong had worn on the show and that Abramson ended up with.

For Abramson, working on the show was total showbiz immersion: "It was the best time of my working life. We were all young, we were a family, a very small group. We called ourselves the Little Mafia. We were arrogant and proud, and for all of us it was a dream come true. I came from a small town in California. When I was a kid, I'd never miss a Sunday night. My homework had to be done. It didn't matter who was on. I just watched it because it was so exciting. I loved the Broadway shows. I'd never seen a Broadway show. And then—to be able to work there!" She wound up there after a friend said, " 'Let's go to New York and get into show business.' . . . I said, 'OK, that sounds like fun.' Nobody in my family ever really got it. To this *day*, they don't get it."

Abramson went on to say, "There was not a better job in New York. My God, to be right in the middle of everything! I was so happy to be part of such a big thing. It was my home, my family, everything. We would all go to China Song after the show to rehash the weekend. We didn't want to separate. We were each other's support group. It was just the best time to be young, to be in New York, to be working on that show. We could get tickets to anything we wanted to see, all the hottest shows. Even after the show went off the air, it still had that cachet—'Sullivan Productions.' "

To Ed, the secretaries were interchangeable. "So to be safe, he called us all 'girl,' " Gottfried noted. "He didn't know any of our names." She and Abramson have memories of Sullivan in his shirt and tie and boxer shorts outside his dressing room near the office. "Everyone treated him like a beloved grandfather," said Gottfried. "You wanted to protect him. We were so polite. We all called him 'Mr. Sullivan.' " He never engaged in chitchat; it was all business.

Ron Greenberg, attorney for Sullivan Productions from 1962 on, recounted, "He was very human. Here I was, a kid, just out of law school, sort of awed at being with him, and he treated me like I was an important human being. There was a give-and-take. He listened. It was very special to me. From his image I thought that he would be distant, but he was quite warm. He was not a stone face. He didn't posture in any way. He was very direct. It was easy to deal with him. He was quite interested in what I did—'Are you married? Do you have children?' When I met other prominent people later on in life, I never felt awed." Greenberg added, "He was very considerate. If it was my anniversary, he'd have a note in the column about it. My mother loved it! I would really be surprised if anybody who worked with him for any length of time would have anything negative to say about him. It was very much a family situation."

Barbara Gallagher, the show's receptionist before working for Precht, remembered seeing a more playful Sullivan than many when she worked with him on his life story for the *Saturday Evening Post*, typed the lead-ins and lead-outs for the acts and commercials, mimeographed scripts, and so on. "It was interesting—he didn't consider himself, like, 'I'm *Ed Sullivan!'* He always considered himself a newsman. He would always identify himself on the phone as, 'This is Ed Sullivan of the *Daily News*.' That floored me."

Sullivan and Gallagher made a cheery team. "We got along really well, I don't know why, maybe because I was also Irish. He liked to joke with me," she recalled. "He was very cute with me. People were amazed. We just hit it off. He liked long legs on women, and I'm very tall. So he used to call me 'Legs'—'Hey, Legs, get over here!' He once said, 'You can call me Ed.' But I just couldn't. We'd banter back and forth. One day, he came out of his dressing room and said, 'I'm going to dinner—can I bring you anything?,' and I said, 'Yeah, a double scotch.'" He returned from dinner with a double scotch for Gallagher—along with his leftover dinner. She acknowledged, "He had quite a reputation" but made no passes at her. "To me he was like a thousand years old, a grandfather. I was 22! He was in his 60s."

Peter Calabrese added, "Ed was especially fond of Barbara Gallagher. It became a running gag. Whenever Barbara was called over to the hotel, it was, 'Put the track shoes on!' But she's not the type who ever would have done anything. I remember her telling the story of the time Ed was holding her by the arms, close to him, and he said, 'I like you, girl!' She didn't know what to do, but she could feel his grip on her arms, and she said, 'Mr. Sullivan—you're *very* strong!' He was kidding around, but he wouldn't grab. He was all business at the studio; there were no women going in and out of the dressing room—none of that."

Russ Petranto, on the show during its last three years, added, "It was a sensational atmosphere to work in. Bob Precht was the kind of boss everybody dreams about. His attitude was this: I'm going to pay you a nice salary, and I'm gonna work your ass off. Once he brought me to tears, I was so tired. The producer sets the tone, and Bob was a class act. We did a 40-week season, and we worked six days a week. The only night you knew you could make a date was Sunday night at 9:30. It was that demanding. It was great, but it was hard! That's a *lot* of time to be together. That's why many of us are still friends—we had no other friends except each other. Everybody covered for everybody. You never wanted to see anybody go up in flames."

Being at the center of the world helped keep the underlings happy. Petranto recalled standing backstage at a rehearsal of the Irving Berlin tribute. "We were coming up to the lunch break, and Irving asks me, 'What are you gonna do for lunch?' I said, 'I'll probably just go around the corner and grab a sandwich.' And he says, 'Can I come?' Like Ed, he was one of the boys. He was so unpretentious. We're at the Stage Deli, and no one recognized him! I wanted to tell everyone, 'Do you who I'm having lunch with—Irving Berlin!' Well, that's when you know you're in showbiz."

CHAPTER 16

Give My Regards to La Scala

The difference between a Broadway flop and a hit was
20 minutes on the Sullivan show.

Marlo Lewis, producer

The Antarctic had Admiral Byrd, Africa had Dr. Livingston, the Pacific
Ocean had Ferdinand Magellan, and television had Ed Sullivan. Long
before *National Geographic* discovered TV, even before Marlin Perkins
tamed the wild for our viewing pleasure, Ed Sullivan turned viewers into
armchair explorers accompanying him on his daring exploits into the
darkest corners of global entertainment.

Peruvian foot jugglers, Romanian aerialists, Ugandan tribal dancers,
Javanese acrobats, and Korean violin prodigies—all were part of an
early experiment in "cultural diversity" designed by Sullivan. In trying
to please everybody, Sullivan inadvertently created the mass television
audience. He brought major celebrities into the home who, prior to that,
had been only faces in fan magazines, disembodied voices on radio, far-
away figures on movie screens, or printed names in newspapers. Lasso-
ing Sophie Tucker, Joe E. Lewis, and Polish aerialists was one thing, but
corralling Birgit Nilsson, Maria Callas, and Richard Tucker quite another.

Sullivan was an unlikely classical impresario, even for TV. Although
he grew up in a family that reveled in music of all kinds, he wasn't an
opera lover, let alone a buff. He presented opera singers not out of passion but because they gave the show more heft, balancing the kitschy animal acts and lowbrow comics. It added a different element and created
a theatrical food pyramid: opera, like ballet, was vitamin-enriched cultural spinach, which Sullivan knew was vital to our cultural diet. "There

used to be more high culture on television because there was less television, and we would watch almost anything," observed John Leonard in
"The Ed Sullivan Age." "Middlebrows like Ed felt they had some dues
to pay."

Irwin Segelstein, a CBS programming executive in the 1970s, took a
more cynical view of the show's cultural clout. "I think that three or four
minutes of a [classical] performance gave the audience the feeling that
they were part of the culturally elite, just by seeing the performance," he
commented, according to Bernie Ilson in *Sundays with Sullivan.*

Segelstein went on, "The audience did not have to put in the investment of two hours to watch an opera or an Alvin Ailey or Martha Graham ballet, which might have meant boredom to them, but in three or
four minutes they felt like New Yorkers." An aria, a ballet, or a violin
solo was a quick, painless dose of instant high culture. To make the
transition even easier, noted Ilson, the show's publicist during its last
eight years, "attractions such as opera singers performed popular arias
from 'Carmen' or 'Pagliacci,' which are 'tunes' the audience might have
heard before."

Monica Lewis told me, "The opera stuff all came from Marlo
[Lewis]," the show's first coproducer. "Ed had never been to an opera in
his life. Marlo had enormous culture. Marlo did everything. He was responsible for all the hot new young stuff, like Presley. Ed didn't have a
problem with opera singers—just so everybody stayed within their time
frame." Lewis made the tenors run on time. "If you said you did 'Min-
uet in G,' Ed would say, 'Is it really one minute,'" she laughed. "Ed did
not know culture. He knew pop, he knew sports, he knew dog acts."

Opera signified for Sullivan, as for most Americans, the ultimate class
act, revered by people who hadn't ever been to an opera and never intended to see one. On his show, they couldn't avoid it. Opera, along
with ballet and classical soloists, was a piece of his weekly package deal.
If you looked forward to performing poodles, or Blackstone the Magician, or Tony Martin, you had to give up 15 minutes a week and sit
through an aria or a pas de deux or two.

In a 1997 review of the video "Great Moments in Opera" from the
Sullivan show, *New York Times* critic Ira Rosenblum wrote of the "formidable" singers who had paraded across the show's stage—Renata
Tebaldi, Joan Sutherland, Richard Tucker, Franco Corelli, Anna Moffo,
Birgit Nilson ("Ladies and gentlemen—Bridget Nelson!"), Beverly Sills,
and, to be sure, Maria Callas—in what Rosenblum called "great singers
doing great arias from great operas, presented with no frills, reflecting a

time when a close-up seemed like fancy camera work. Most of the performances are done out of costume and without sets. There is no idle chitchat. The focus is, pure and simply, on the singing"—even though idle chitchat was the fun part of the total Sullivan experience.

On the video, Sills recalled, "Backstage we were crammed into small dressing rooms. Everyone was behaving like a prima donna. It was a contest of egos." There was little rehearsal time. "You did the first eight bars, were asked, 'Is this the right tempo?' and that was it." It was "staggering," she said, realizing that in one night "more people would hear you sing than heard Caruso in his whole lifetime." Music critics lauded Sullivan for expanding the audience for opera and popularizing it, making it more accessible to opera-wary Americans. Sullivan was, again, merely following vaudeville protocol, where opera singers were part of the bill, wedged between comics and tumblers.

Bernard Gurtman, a manager and publicist for classical artists, told Ilson, "You have to develop a taste for classical music. And how can you develop this acquired taste when you can't afford to go to the opera and pay $100 for a ticket? During the 1960s and 1970s, there were other variety television shows that presented classical musicians and singers, but the producers of these other shows often treated classical performers in a comedic way or poked fun. The Sullivan show introduced the classical artists as if they were important. They would sing a little aria, or half an aria, and it was presented as an important, and even serious, spot."

Largely because of their appearances on the Sullivan show, Sills, Robert Merrill, Placido Domingo, Luciano Pavarotti, and others were invited on Johnny Carson's "Tonight" show in the 1970s, a practice that ended once Carson split. Johnny had inherited a little of Sullivan's one-size-fits-all approach to the arts, and Sills took the baton from Sullivan to the Carson show—helping to "demystify opera for American audiences," as critic Joshua Kosman remarked in his appreciation of Sills after her death. He noted that Sills, like Ed Sullivan, Americanized opera: "If Beverly Sills sang it on TV, opera was American," read the headline over his piece. "Sills was a diva disguised as a real person." Like Sullivan, another real person, she humanized opera just by standing next to it.

A Sullivan gig gave any classical performer instant street cred. According to Ilson, producer Bob Precht pointed out that "to have these attractions come into your living room with a guy you kind of trusted with your taste, like Ed, was important. . . . That had to strike some people, and even inspire some." And as Samuel Ramey, the Metropolitan Opera baritone who grew up in Colby, Kansas, said, "The first time I ever heard an opera singer was on 'The Ed Sullivan Show.' I'd never been exposed to opera at all before then. I remember seeing Roberta Peters. I just fell madly in love with her."

Sullivan was also the first to present great dance companies to a mass audience on prime-time television—the Sadler's Wells Ballet, Moiseyev Dance Company, Balinese Dance Troupe, and Kirov Ballet. A few other elite TV shows—"Omnibus," "Camera Three"—showcased the classics but were stuck in the Sunday daytime cultural ghetto, not spotlighted Sunday nights at eight with half the country watching. Sullivan's show was not "niche marketed," a concept he would have scoffed at: why grab a niche when you can gobble up the entire supermarket? The world was his niche.

But Sullivan didn't present classical artists because it was a nice thing to do; he was too much the pragmatic showman for such altruistic deeds. He booked divas because they would draw a cultured crowd and also score aesthetic brownie points with the critics. As he said much later, "I was the first to introduce ballet and opera on TV. Before that, a lot of people around the country didn't give a flying you-know-what about opera and ballet." Precht added, "There is another person to take into consideration, and that is Ed's wife. Sylvia liked classical performers, having been a woman brought up going to concerts, and she was always anxious to go to the Metropolitan Opera or a concert at Carnegie Hall. She would go to see the Moiseyev, and get wildly enthusiastic and excited. It had to have had some influence on Ed's thinking on this."

In great part it was Sullivan's quivering nose for news that made him a TV pioneer. Sullivan obeyed both his news sense and his pledge to bring Art to the unwashed when the new ballet team of Margot Fonteyn and Rudolf Nureyev debuted on his show in 1965. It made them house-

Strange as it might sound, my memories of the show mostly involve opera singers. I remember seeing Richard Tucker, Jan Peerce, Roberta Peters, Robert Merrill, Lily Pons. They were all Jewish. And that made it all so wonderful, that Jewish singers were recognized and enjoyed by a huge audience. It truly made us proud. I thought Mr. S. was influenced by his Jewish wife, but it was probably a ratings thing. I also remember Myron Cohen and Sam Levenson. We all laughed so much, and we didn't have to worry about anything being off-color.

Isabel Green, San Mateo, California

hold names beyond the dance world—just as, earlier, when Fonteyn and Moira Shearer appeared on the show in "Sleeping Beauty" and "Swan Lake," or when Sullivan presented excerpts from Jerome Robbins's "Ballets: USA." Likewise, when Sullivan spotlighted pianist Van Cliburn after the young Texan had scored his upset victory in the Tchaikovsky competition in Moscow, it gave Cliburn's career a spectacular boost, as if he were a hot new pop singer. As TV historian Ron Simon notes, Sullivan was "the cultural eyes and ears for middle America[;] he introduced . . . legends into the collective living room."

Sullivan was mocked by highbrows, but few could trash his cumulative record in the arts. The show became the poor man's "Omnibus," the Sunday afternoon salon hosted by poised, erudite, articulate British journalist Alistair Cooke, the very antithesis of Ed Sullivan. "Considered to be the embodiment of banal, middle-brow taste," wrote critic Eric Schaeffer, "Sullivan exposed a generation of Americans to virtually everything the culture had to offer in the field of art and entertainment." TV critic Kay Gardella told me, "The show was like an arts headline in a magazine. If somebody was on the Sullivan show, you knew it was important."

John Leonard, alluding to Sullivan's show, commented, "Celebrity is what a democratic society has instead of aristocrats." After the release of videos of old Sullivan shows in 1991, Howard Reich wrote in the *Chicago Tribune:* "The show flourished as long as it did because it epitomized an unmistakably American, refreshingly democratic, view of culture. On Sullivan's program, a knife-thrower who performed his stunt while standing on a tightrope was as much an artist as a dancer pirouetting in a scene from 'Swan Lake.' This was art presented without pretension as show business." And, he might have added, show business presented as art.

New York Times political columnist David Brooks, in a 2005 column headlined "Joe Strauss to Joe Six-Pack," argued that cultural elitism wasn't sneered at in the 1950s and 1960s but aspired to by the public—before reverse snobbism set in. "Once upon a time, the masses liked art," the column's subhead read. Brooks wrote, "If you read *Time* and *Newsweek* from the 1950's and early 1960's, you discover they were pitched at middle-class people across the country who aspired to have the same sorts of conversations as the New York and Boston elite. . . . They devoted as much space to opera as to movies because an educated person was expected to know something about opera, even if that person had no prospect of actually seeing one." Sullivan's show was a huge part of that crossover cultural nurturing. In 1953, *Newsweek* noted, "Sullivan believes in culture."

In the show's early days, Sullivan had expressed his TV credo: "I don't think there's anything that, expertly done, the public won't go for. I think they're way ahead of us." To make good on his cultural manifesto, he would book an entire hour of Metropolitan Opera singers, present excerpts from verse plays by Christopher Fry, and invite Charles Laughton to read from the Bible; perhaps the most popular of all the loftier acts he featured, it launched Laughton on a national Bible-reading tour.

Roberta Peters, Sullivan's pet diva, was featured on the show 41 times, a record for opera stars and singers generally (runner-up Teresa Brewer checked in a mere 31 times). Sullivan was enamored of Peters (he once told her he'd had a dream about her), perhaps the best-known American opera star before Beverly Sills and, like Sills, a New York–born diva (born Roberta Peterman) who wore well and helped bring opera to the masses. "I did thousands of concerts over my career," she told me, "and every time I went out, people would say they had seen me on 'The Ed Sullivan Show.' That's why I was popular in popularizing opera."

Sullivan's show gave established opera stars a chance to shine anew, on their own. As Bernard Gurtman told Bernie Ilson in 1997, "The Met-

We gathered to watch the show Sunday nights in Dixon, California. If you missed the show, you'd be out of it during discussions in school on Monday. For all the time we spent doing homework, getting to watch the show was one of my parents' few indulgences. Back in the '50s and '60s, very few Chinese were seen on television. When they were, they were usually portraying servants (Hop Sing on "Bonanza") or villains. So when Ed Sullivan featured a young Chinese American girl, Ginny Tiu, at the piano, we noticed. She might have been seven years old, but she played with great confidence. She wore tight braids and had a broad, glued-on caricature of a smile that turned her eyes into little slits. Ed Sullivan must have thought she was Chinese cuteness personified, but we were self-conscious, even horrified, at seeing such a programmed performance. We hated her! I have no memory of what she actually played. I vaguely remember Ginny Tiu being featured in *Life* magazine, and my grandfather showing it to us all. Why couldn't we aspire to that? (Never mind that we had no piano.) Years later, I heard that Ginny Tiu was performing in a lounge. I do wonder what became of her after so much national TV attention so early in her life.

Ellen Leong Blonder, Mill Valley, California

ropolitan Opera directors didn't want a Robert Merrill or a Roberta Peters to stand out from the company. . . . Here [on Sullivan's show] they were in street clothes doing the most popular arias. Even Callas, Peters, Anna Moffo[,] . . . they came on in gowns and tailored clothes. Moreover, these great divas were shown in tight close-ups, so the television audience could really see what they looked like. . . . [It] made them human."

Suddenly, Robert Merrill, in a tux or a business suit, "became a recognizable face," said Gurtman. "The publicity surrounding his appearance on the Sullivan show increased his value as a concert artist. And that is where the big payoff in fame and monetary rewards occurs in the classical field." Merrill's career took off after he became a Sullivan regular: he became one of opera's first crossover stars, and even played Las Vegas with Louis Armstrong (much to the displeasure of the Met's Rudolf Bing), trading places with Armstrong in a bit in which Satchmo sang an aria and Merrill sang jazz. He also turned up in the movie "Aaron Slick from Punkin Crick."

Peters also emphasized that it was Marlo Lewis, not Sullivan, who opened the show to opera. "Ed was not a very educated guy," she said. "He never came to my operas. He was never interested in opera. He didn't even know the names. Luckily for us, he left everything to Marlo, who was able to elevate the public. Marlo had a history of good music, good culture [his father was a classical violinist]. He ran that show and was able to put on people like Risë Stevens, myself, Maria Callas."

Today, she lamented, "there's no interest in opera whatsoever, certainly not on the major channels." Did it bother her to follow, say, Topo Gigio? "Never, never. He had Itzhak Perlman, too." She recalled once singing "The Shadow Song," an aria that requires a flute for the cadenza—"but they didn't get a flute. They had me do it with Al Hirt—a trumpet!" She took a swipe at the show's "orchestra, or whatever you want to call it. I think they were more of a pick-up band." Compared to the Metropolitan Opera band, anyway.

Peters speculated about why Ed's divas were palatable to the TV masses: "I don't think he had on any obese singers." Peters—a pert, sexy diva—helped break the stereotype of bulky, scary Valkyrine heroines. "And now and then I did a popular song. I once sang with Richard Rodgers at the piano, doing one of his songs." Being on the show didn't increase her Met fee but opened up many other commercial outlets.

The show could convert a starchy operatic singer into a pop star overnight, as in the case of Sergio Franchi, who was brought to America by the impresario Sol Hurok. Even though he wasn't regarded as a Met-caliber tenor, Precht told Ilson, "he did sing well, especially the Neapolitan love songs and light classical works. He also was a charming man, and good-looking onstage. Hurok brought him to our attention, and we booked him on the show, and he did extremely well." Franchi wound up playing the show 24 times and starred in a couple of Broadway musicals. The show also was a conduit for other agencies that handled classical singers. "They were aware there was no other market for a classical performer," noted Precht. "We were the major platform for their talent."

Sullivan's initial love affair with opera burned out in 1957, when he presented three segments from the Met that put a nasty dent in his ratings. He tried to cancel a remaining Met appearance. The series had led off with opera's reigning megastar, Maria Callas, in arias from "Tosca," but when that night's Trendex rating dropped six points, Sullivan panicked. It had been too arduous a climb to the top to wreck the show with a few divas. When Callas finally retreated, as Sullivan biographer James Maguire notes, one diva had met an even bigger diva. Elvis had shown Sullivan the path to monster ratings. Ed was more devoted to ratings than to Rossini. "You lose an audience when you put on opera," Sullivan conceded bluntly. NBC's rival "Steve Allen Show" had surpassed Sullivan's show in the ratings in the weeks that Ed presented opera stars. Before he had any real rivals, like Allen, he could trot out a diva every Sunday if he felt like it.

Rudolf Bing, the tyrannical Bavarian Met managing director, was not amused, snapping, "The Met has found it can't compete with Elvis Presley." Bing called on Sullivan to honor his contract for further appearances by Met stars. Callas had sung for 18 minutes, a third of the show, so when Sullivan reluctantly agreed to a final Met segment he insisted it be in concert form, not staged. "I learned that 18 minutes of opera is too much on a [60-minute] television variety show," he said, not unreasonably. Bing argued for actual scenes, pleading, "Please give opera a chance," and criticized Sullivan's decision to bracket opera singers with ventriloquists—missing the whole point of the show. Some ventriloquists may have been equally upset following Callas. "Mr. Bing considered me a real lowbrow," said Sullivan, but Bing reluctantly let his dignified divas became a kind of novelty act. "I was amazed that he didn't object," says Risë Stevens.

For the show's final Met segment, Richard Tucker and Renata Tebaldi planned to do a duet from "La Traviata," but Sullivan demanded a four-minute aria from "La Bohème," because it was "something people know."

That was the beginning of the end for opera on Sullivan's show. But by then, he had featured many of the great opera stars of the day—Dorothy Kirsten, James Melton, Eleanor Steber, Mimi Benzell, John Charles Thomas—all equally visible on "The Bell Telephone Hour" and "Voice of Firestone." Sullivan ended his contract with the Metropolitan Opera in February 1957, reported the *New York Times*.

Risë Stevens remembered how exotic television itself was, let alone divas in your living room. "In those days, you didn't have television so handy. I remember traveling throughout the United States doing concerts, and when we went to certain towns, if you wanted to see 'The Ed Sullivan Show' on Sunday nights you had to sit in the lobby with all of the guests." Stevens—whose first name Sullivan regularly mispronounced as "Ree-zay" and "Ryza" (rather than "Ree-suh")—was amused to appear between bell ringers and jugglers, but it helped sell opera to the masses. "The fact that we were on that show—the most important show of the time—publicized the opera, and people came to the opera who had never, ever been there. That was wonderful, what he did with opera. Amazing!"

Precht told Bernie Ilson, "I think that Ed liked the classical arena, and he enjoyed the feedback. And I certainly did. It was great to be part of the [classical] culture. You felt somehow that you were doing something that had some importance to it. I am sure he liked that. From a social point of view, I think he enjoyed the cultural world—and the opera

I particularly dreaded the opera singers—Helen Traubel, Patrice Munsel, Risë Stevens. To my ears they were just shrieking, all the worse if they attempted to warble some pop tune. But more vivid than the show was the scene at our home in Brooklyn. My grandparents, who owned the only TV set in our two-family house, would regularly watch what my grandmother called the "Ed Solomon Show." So as not to wear out the living room furniture, they kept a set of folding lawn chairs in one corner of the living room, [which they] set out in the middle of the floor. Only adults got the real chairs. And my grandparents probably liked the opera singers best of all, particularly because they had a good likelihood of being Jewish. Every time Richard Tucker appeared, I would be told that he had appeared at some nephew's bar mitzvah. We had some remote connection to Richard Tucker. Nobel Prize winners? Feh!

Leah Garchik, San Francisco

singers. It enabled him to have lunch with Sol Hurok"—two impresarios basking in each other's serious luster. Precht pointed out, "Let's be
candid about it. Hurok looked at the Sullivan show as a powerful promotional device."

Sullivan was regarded as such a conscience of television culture that
in 1961, after FCC commissioner Newton Minow's jeremiad against
TV calling it a "vast wasteland," he was summoned before federal in-
vestigators to deliver his own indictment, presumably to confirm Minow's industry-shattering blast. But Ed crossed them up. Donning his
diplomat's hat, he testified on June 23, 1961, "There always will be, of
necessity, a TV wasteland." He thought TV was just great as was, a luxury he could comfortably afford as the industry's cultural commissar.
Vincent Donehue, the director of prestigious TV dramas and the famous
"Peter Pan" special, called Sullivan's apologia "a defeatist view."

Perhaps self-servingly, Sullivan said he found no fault with the ratings
(his own were always in the top tier), which are "dictated by the
people." He added, "TV, by and large, does a remarkably fine job, day
in and day out, 365 days a year, from 6 A.M. to 1 A.M., producing
10,950 hours of programs. By contrast, all the Hollywood studios produce 200 pictures for 600 hours of entertainment annually. [TV] has,
for some time, been the favorite whipping boy of the nation." He quoted
Will Rogers's line about violent crime shows on radio: "I just ain't got
sympathy for anybody too lazy to turn the radio off."

The FCC hearing was an ideal forum in which to become a true industry leader, but Sullivan steadfastly defended the status quo—as usual,
feathering his own hard-won nest. Arguing with convoluted logic, Sullivan testified that, because "companies spend huge amounts of money"
for ratings, the numbers "present an accurate picture of what the people
preferred"—neglecting to notice that the network menu of sitcoms,
westerns, and cop shows might be a bit limited. Sullivan attacked TV
critics for their "hypocrisy," and claimed that the *New York Times* had
never given advance notice of opera singers on his show, nor reviewed
them. (Not true, the *Times* proved in rebuttal.) He said that critics
who demanded opera on TV "would be bored to death by it"—perhaps
a rationale for his recent diva downsizing.

Though clearly no opera fancier, Sullivan was fiercely addicted to musicals and went out of his way to promote them. If he loved a new musical, he would devote a third of his show to it, as he did for "Do Re Mi"
in 1960, with Phil Silvers and Nancy Walker, or "Annie" (he gave it
23 minutes), and others, such as "South Pacific," "Call Me Madam,"

"West Side Story," "Man of La Mancha," and "My Fair Lady." " 'The Ed Sullivan Show' was the most important showcase for the Broadway musical," Julie Andrews commented in Michael Kantor's three-part PBS series "Broadway: The American Musical."

He imported not just scenes from musicals but also scenes from serious plays like "Member of the Wedding" and "Dark at the Top of the Stairs," whose ten minutes on his show created a sudden demand for tickets. "We saved 'All the Way Home,' " he boasted. The first dramatic scene he ever presented, on October 8, 1950, was from "Member of the Wedding," with Julie Harris, Ethel Waters, and Brandon DeWilde, followed weeks later by David Niven in a scene from "Journey's End," Helen Hayes in "Victoria Regina," and Alfred Lunt in "There Shall Be No Night."

"Moments like these simply can't happen again," said Sullivan with a sure sense of theatrical history. A lesser visionary might have coasted with comics, magicians, puppets, and pop singers, but he felt obliged to aim higher, aware that he had assumed, if by default, the job of national curator, bringing live to his stage the world's greatest performing artists. "In the old days, people had no such golden opportunity," he said in 1963, looking back with justifiable pride on 15 years of presenting the best the culture had to offer—and not just America's.

Over those first 15 years, viewers who might not otherwise ever see a Broadway show could get an advance peek at contemporary and classical dramas, everything from Henry Fonda in "Mister Roberts" to Rex Harrison and Audrey Hepburn in "Anne of the Thousand Days." Sullivan created, as well as rented, theatrical moments—presenting original readings by Carl Sandburg, Bette Davis, Charlton Heston, Judith Anderson, and more, from Henry Fonda reciting the Gettysburg Address to Lauren Bacall intoning "Casey at the Bat." Marlo Lewis noted in his memoir, "Sullivan alone succeeded in breaking down the barriers Broadway had initially erected against TV"—the first time Broadway producers saw a value in parading their precious wares on TV. It gave New York actors sudden national exposure they had never enjoyed; their taped appearances became audition reels.

Noël Coward narrated "The Carnival of the Animals," accompanied by the New York Philharmonic, and in 1961 Salvador Dalí appeared in what Sullivan called "a historic moment in art" (and TV), when the artist fired a pistol loaded with paint pellets at a canvas, which he then signed. You wouldn't see *that* on "The Perry Como Show."

The show not only featured Broadway musicals but often salvaged them. After Sullivan spotlighted a number from "Wish You Were Here," a modest success, the musical took down its closing notice. There are endless examples of Sullivan rescuing shows on the verge of collapse, most famously "Camelot." The Alan Jay Lerner and Frederick Loewe musical was mired in a sluggish run after the John Kennedy assassination months earlier, but after Julie Andrews and Richard Burton sang two duets on Sullivan's show, a long line formed the next morning outside the Majestic Theater.

Precht commented, "David Merrick [the Broadway producer] used the Sullivan show as much as we enjoyed having the attractions. They got the national exposure, and we presented a wonderful scene from a Broadway show. But looking at it realistically, where else could a producer go with a Broadway show on television?"

The 1950s and 1960s were the last period when musicals truly mattered in America, when they were a springboard for major careers and a mirror of what American entertainment was all about then. Discussing the 2005 movie version of the musical "The Producers," film critic A. O. Scott of the *New York Times* observed, "Once upon a time—the hazy '50s New York golden age in which 'The Producers' seems to take place—musical theater was the class of American pop culture, a source of democratic delight and artistic ingenuity. Now, many musicals represent the lowest common denominator: theme park attractions for tourists."

Yet there was once such deep rivalry between theater and TV that director Jerome Robbins refused to allow any scene from "West Side Story" to be seen on TV for a year. The show's original Maria, Carol Lawrence, explained to me, "He figured if people saw you on television, they wouldn't want to see the show." Just the reverse occurred after Robbins relented and she and Larry Kert performed the show's balcony scene, singing "Tonight." Afterward, she said, "it was just lines around the block" (even though Sullivan introduced the scene as "a ballet"— not "a balcony scene"—from "West Side Story"; and he called Kert "Larry Kent."

Even if that theatrical golden age still existed, there is no place on TV now for scenes from hit plays and musicals to air regularly. So Sullivan's show was far more than a cultural turning point in America: it was a theatrical Smithsonian, a sprawling video museum of all show business, including rare theatrical moments. What did Tito Gobbi look like? How good, really, were Bert Lahr and Carol Channing and Rudolf Nureyev? Now you can find out by watching old Sullivan shows at the Paley Center for Media in New York City and Los Angeles, among other broadcast museums.

Sullivan's show provided the first, best, and last platform for most of America to see what all the shouting was about on Broadway. Sullivan presented rare time-capsule moments for posterity. In 23 seasons, he introduced an astonishing number of Broadway musical excerpts—some 400 in all—which amounts to a spectacular display from the American musical's gilded age. Documentaries like Kantor's "Broadway: The American Musical" in 2004 heavily relied on it. Vintage tapes and early kinescopes of excerpts from Broadway musicals on Sullivan's show are a mother lode of archival moments that existed before Lincoln Center's Library for the Performing Arts.

Nobody realized it at the time, but Sullivan did not just oversee a popular television show. He was a major archivist of the arts, the cultural curator of the 1950s and 1960s. Before it was built in 1966, Ed Sullivan was Lincoln Center.

CHAPTER 17

Elvis Has Entered the Building

Elvis Presley is the greatest cultural force in the 20th century.
It's not even close.

Leonard Bernstein

In 2006, the History Channel named Elvis Presley's appearance on Ed Sullivan's show as one of the "ten days that unexpectedly changed America," along with the Battle of Antietam in the Civil War, the discovery of gold at Sutter's Mill, and Einstein's letter to FDR explaining the atomic bomb. Pretty fast company for a TV variety show.

If you believe in the Big Bang theory of pop culture, the moment Elvis first set blue-sueded foot on "The Ed Sullivan Show," life in America—in the world—exploded, and everything was forever changed. But like most huge historical moments, it almost didn't happen. Sullivan originally had passed on Presley. Ed was still smarting from a 1955 run-in with Bo Diddley, the blues-rock singer. Bo had demanded that he be allowed to perform his namesake hit, but Sullivan told him to sing something else, along with an old slave song Diddley had actually planned to perform after his signature "Bo Diddley."

"I got cussed out for it," he related in his biography by George White. "They said I was only supposed to do one number, 'Sixteen Tons,' but I was there to do 'Bo Diddley.' If I'd a did 'Sixteen Tons' that would've been the end of my career right there. So Ed Sullivan got pissed off and told me—these were his exact words: 'You're the first black boy that ever double-crossed me on the show.' I was ready to tag him, 'cause I was a little dude off the streets of Chicago, an' him callin' me 'black' in them days was as bad as sayin' 'nigger.' "

He went on to say, "My manager an' all these other dudes there grabbed me and says, 'That's *Mr.* Sullivan!' I says, 'I don't give a shit about *Mr.* Sullivan!' I didn't know who the hell Sullivan was. All I knew was this cat was sayin' this to me, and to me it was an insult. He don't talk to me that way. I didn't call *him* no names!' I says, 'You ain't gonna get away with this, buddy.' An' so he told me, 'I'll see that you'll never work no more in show business! You'll never get another TV show *in your life!'* It scared the hell out of me! And we didn't have much to do with each other after that."

When Bo launched into his hit song, it enraged Sullivan, confirming the host's innate dislike of rock and roll—or "race music," as it was labeled by record executives and much of white America. Diddley was forever resentful that, a year later, Presley got all the attention he felt was rightfully his. "Elvis Presley didn't invent rock 'n' roll," he said, implying that he had; Bo also resented that his revolutionary style and beat were uncopyrightable: "I am owed, and I never got paid." He might have, had things gone smoother with Sullivan.

Elvis Presley's act posed its own cultural dilemma for Sullivan, secure in his belief that he knew what constituted good entertainment. Presley and his music clashed with Sullivan's gut newsman's instinct for what was hot, what people were yakking about: Elvis. Never before had the public's taste collided so loudly, so threateningly, with his own. As the irresistible force (rock and roll) ran into an immovable object (rock-solid Ed Sullivan), he did what he always did when he sensed defeat: Ed blinked.

Like most 54-year-old Americans in 1956, Ed Sullivan had to be dragged kicking and screaming into rock and roll. Rock produced a cultural-demographic midlife crisis in America, and Sullivan's show helped trigger the nation's so-called youthquake. Even if he knew what music the public liked, the definition of what constituted "music"—or even "the public"—was shifting.

The aging showman was bewildered. Pre-Presley, everyone in America pretty much agreed on popular music; the show "Your Hit Parade" was a reliable barometer of pop taste. "Your" meant all of us; a "hit" was clearly marked by numbers and accepted by everyone. Parents, grandparents, teenagers, and kids pretty much all felt that "Mr. Sandman," "Hey, There!," "If I Give My Heart to You," "Secret Love," "Misty," and "Three Coins in the Fountain"—all of them mid-1950s blockbusters—were certified all-American hits. Nearly everyone knew the lyrics, sang and hummed them, and heard them on jukeboxes or on their 45-rpm player, spinning them endlessly.

Presley, with major help from Bo Diddley, Bill Haley, Chuck Berry, Johnny Cash, and Jerry Lee Lewis, was invading the nation's musical comfort zone—a suddenly vulnerable area. After the vital 1940s era of stirringly romantic wartime songs, many of which were now classics, came a flood of sappy, sticky pop music ("Love Letters in the Sand," "If I Give My Heart to You," "The Tennessee Waltz") that bored, or gagged, teenagers aching to rebel against their parents' fairy-tale musical tastes. Whatever the reason for the rebellion, Elvis was its anointed leader, an oily-haired Pied Piper leading the children astray, down the garden path headed straight for Sodom, away from home and hearth, where Ed Sullivan's show was a family meeting ground. That Sullivan's sanctified show was the staging area for a musical revolution was not just unlikely; it was un-American, even un-holy.

As historian David Halberstam wrote, "Sullivan's show provided a pleasant, safe blend of acts, including some performers of exceptional talent. There seemed to be a guarantee that nothing would happen that was at all threatening." Ricky Nelson's occasional singing appearances on "The Adventures of Ozzie and Harriet" (as unlikely a rock-and-roll petri dish as the Sullivan show) didn't change TV in the late 1950s, but, as veteran rock critic Joel Selvin wrote, Nelson "first demonstrated the incendiary potential of mixing rock 'n' roll and television." Slick, cute little 16-year-old Ricky—the sitcom's lovable wisecracking kid brother— caused his own malt-shop uprising in 1957 and 1958 (when Elvis was in the army), singing "I'm Walking" on the family sitcom; it was a shy suburban version of Fats Domino's rollicking hit.

By 1958, Ricky was the hottest act in popdom, but Ozzie wouldn't let him play Sullivan's show (he appeared there late in his career, in 1967, when his stardom was ebbing). Like Ed Sullivan, Ozzie and Harriet assured viewers that nothing going on was as bad as it might appear. If there was a pop, or other, revolution, they could contain it and freeze it in the living room. Wrote Selvin, "Ricky Nelson brought the subversion of rock 'n' roll safely into America's '50s living rooms disguised as family entertainment"—a crucial part of rock archaeology.

Sullivan could neither stand nor understand rock and roll, and like most of the showbiz establishment he viewed it as a goofy fad that would burn out in due time, even if it was momentarily titillating those crazy teenagers. Some Americans, stubbornly happy with "Secret Love," "Misty," and "Hey, There!," are still waiting for it to go away. Selvin told me, "The whole relationship of television and rock was problematic from the very beginning. Television really ill-served the music. First of all, in the sound quality. Also, the media didn't understand rock and roll at all. There was total disrespect by the media."

Selvin also noted, "There was a real ham-fistedness about dealing with rock and roll. They had sound guys who were switching football games on Sunday doing this stuff, like they'd cut to the keyboard player during a guitar solo. Television was an older, adult medium. Rock was just a fuckin' thing they were throwing teenagers—here's a little bone for the kids." With Sullivan's slavish devotion to pleasing "the youngsters," and with his proud instinct for seizing on anything newsy, he was quick to book performers like Bo Diddley and Elvis Presley, which Ed considered novelty acts, like puppets and monkeys. Sullivan didn't make a big distinction between Bo Diddley and Topo Gigio.

While Sullivan is credited with bringing rock to the masses, the simple act of bringing Elvis on his show *three* times fed a raging rebellion that was razing radio. The mighty network programs that had dominated the airwaves for decades (comedy shows, cop shows, westerns, quiz shows, variety shows, soaps) were now in their dotage, dying softly, steadily being destroyed by television—by shows like Sullivan's. Forced to become new and creative, radio went regional. Local stations began creating stars out of home-grown news, talk, and disc jockeys. They played new tunes and, between spins, hyped songs—often for under-the-counter cash in a rampant pay-for-play system that had always covertly existed but was growing into an industry.

The DJs, learning fast how to bait, trap, and create vast new devoted teen followings, could conjure a hit overnight. The key was replaying a song until it was seared into listeners' brains and loins. Presley was on TV only a few times, but his songs throbbed hourly on radio. Television impresarios like Ed Sullivan and Arthur Godfrey were slowly being augmented by local DJs, the new power brokers of pop music in the mid-1950s—previously unknown guys like Alan Freed, Murray the K, William B. Williams, and Jim Lowe in New York, Don Sherwood and "Big Daddy" Tom Donahue in San Francisco, Hunter Hancock in Los Angeles, Howard Miller and Dick Biondi in Chicago.

Many DJs were efficiently bought off by record companies' promotion people—if not in actual cash, then in lavish gifts, trips, drugs, and girls. The payola scandals of the 1950s, which led to congressional hearings and headlines, confirmed that smash hits could be manufactured out of vinyl and vice. New York DJ Alan Freed (credited with inventing the phrase *rock and roll*) testified he had taken $2,500 in payola, was fired, and quickly fell into oblivion. Even TV's deodorized boy emcee, the clean-cut teen tycoon-next-door Dick Clark, became tainted and was forced to sell his record company interests.

DJs co-opted by record labels in the 1950s helped create the teenage demographic that eventually wagged the pop culture dog—not just the music but also the social changes fueled by sex, drugs, and rock 'n' roll. This demographic even changed comedy and theater. The steady decline of the Broadway show tune—once fertile ground for emerging pop standards-to-be—can be traced to the rise of Elvis and the Beatles. These upstart adolescent hit-makers were christened the children of Ed Sullivan.

When Leonard Bernstein declared that Presley was the greatest cultural force in the 20th century, *Time* editor Richard Clurman asked if he meant bigger even than Picasso. Bernstein said it wasn't even a contest. "No, it's Elvis. He introduced the beat to everything and he changed everything—music, language, clothes, it's a whole new social revolution." John Lennon decreed, "Before Elvis there was nothing." Before Sullivan, Elvis had been relegated to the fringes, somewhere between country and R&B, out there in rockabilly Appalachia.

With undisguised delight, the press dissected the Presley-Sullivan alliance and Ed's shocking capitulation. He too had been bought off, but by ratings points, not cash. A July 14, 1956, story in the *Los Angeles Times* reported, "Ed Sullivan has succumbed to teen-age pressure and inked Elvis Presley." According to the *New York Times,* "Ed Sullivan joined the crowd beating a path to Elvis Presley's agent yesterday. In announcing the transaction, Mr. Sullivan said that he had received thousands of letters from teen-agers asking him to have the singer on his show." The *New York World-Telegram* chuckled, "Ed Sullivan today did a flip-flop that makes the gyrating Elvis Presley look like an amateur." The $50,000 that Elvis got topped the record per-show fee of $13,000 that Sullivan paid ice skater Sonja Heine in 1952. Had Ed acted faster, he could have got him for $5,000 a show.

Rock drove a dagger into the heart, and changed the very meaning, of "entertainment." Nearly all other existing music was shoved to the sidelines and off the charts. Classic pop songs by Gershwin, Porter, Harry Warren, and Johnny Mercer were patronizingly labeled "easy listening" on radio and in record stores (presumably opposed to rock's "hard listening"). Music with massive followings—folk, country, jazz, standards, big band—was marginalized on radio, relegated to the furthest reaches of the dial, way out there with the evangelists, ethnic fare, and farm reports.

While Sullivan was rock's most conspicuous godfather, he was actually late to the rock 'n' roll party. Before his historic show, Presley had quietly debuted (at $1,250 a show) on the Dorsey Brothers' summertime "Stage Show" (the Dorseys supposedly threatened to quit in protest). Twice Elvis was on Milton Berle's show, where Berle, with only two shows left, had nothing to lose and let him twist and shout. Both shows drew huge ratings. Before all that, though, Elvis had failed to make the cut on "Arthur Godfrey's Talent Scouts" (as had Buddy Holly). Even Presley's six appearances on "Stage Show," Jackie Gleason's summer replacement, made barely a ripple.

Presley got booked by the unlikely Dorsey Brothers (the last stand of 1940s big band music) only after Colonel Parker, his inventive manager, sent a glossy photo of Elvis to Gleason with a note saying, "JG: This is Elvis Presley. About to be Real Big . . . —Colonel." Parker and Gleason were old pals. Gleason carried the photo into a production meeting and told his staff, "If this guy can make any kind of noise at all, let's sign him up." When the shrewd Gleason saw a photo of a sullen Elvis, he said, "Look, this guy is Brando with a guitar. He has that same sensuous, sweaty animal magnetism that made Brando a star. But first, let's find out if he can sing." Quickly convinced he could, the Great One commanded, "Sign him up." Gleason had no qualms about unleashing the guitar-strumming sex machine's hips and legs, snapping at a nervous CBS executive that the censors could go to hell.

Bellowing "Shake, Rattle and Roll" in his first national TV appearance, January 28, 1956, he sneered, writhed, and wiggled through what many still call his best TV performance. Gleason, in the control both, reportedly cried, "Wow! Run down there and have him sing another song. That thing about 'I got a woman downtown.' Or uptown. Or wherever. He'll know what I mean." Gleason booked him for five more appearances.

Colonel Parker sent the tape to Milton Berle, who booked him for a show on the flight deck of the USS *Hancock* in San Diego Bay, before hundreds of horny young sailors Presley's age. The Berle show, April 3, 1956, was seen by 40 million viewers—and by Buddy Rich, the drummer with the Harry James Orchestra also on the show. Rich rolled his eyes and sneered, "This is the worst." On that show, Berle did a comedy sketch playing Presley's brother "Melvin Presley." On the next Berle show, Elvis sang a new Jerry Lieber and Mike Stoller song, "Hound Dog," which he told a friend was "dangerous stuff."

New York Times critic Jack Gould agreed and was aghast, writing that Presley had "a tin ear" and dressed badly, to boot. He noted, as quoted by Larry Rohter and Tom Zito in the *Washington Post*, that "Mr. Presley has no discernible singing ability. . . . He is a rock-and-roll variation of one of the most standard acts in show business: the virtuoso of the hootchy-kootchy. . . . The gyration never had anything to do with popular music and still doesn't." Presley replied, with mock innocence, "My arms and legs just follow the music." He pointed out that another of the show's guests, Debra Paget, "had on a tight dress and wiggled more than I did. She bumped and pooshed all over the place . . . talk about sex! But who do they say is obscene? Me!" The idea of male sexuality had never before reared its greasy head on TV.

Steve Allen, in his first month on NBC opposite Sullivan, scooped TV's master impresario by booking Presley, for $5,500, soundly thrashing "Mr. Sunday Night" in the ratings, 20.2 to 14.8. Allen's widow, Jayne Meadows, told me, "They had a meeting and invited us wives, and we all sat there discussing whether to sign this guy. By then the ratings had come in, and they went boom!" Parker was asking $10,000 but that would have meant that he'd have to pay stars like Bob Hope and Sinatra that much.

Allen wanted Elvis, but on his own comic terms, deftly reshaping Presley to higher satiric purposes. He played against the singer's sexuality—indeed defused it—by dressing Elvis in a tuxedo for one song and later using him in a comedy sketch to warble "Hound Dog" to a basset hound. As he noted in *Hi-Ho, Steverino!*, Allen told Elvis, "You're certainly being a good sport about the whole thing." According to author Jake Austen, Allen considered Presley "talentless and absurd," but Allen's son Bill told me this was not at all the case. "Steve liked him, even went over to Paramount's office in New York to look at footage of Elvis' new film. He said, 'That kid's got something,' and wrote a piece for *Cosmopolitan* about Elvis." Allen booked Presley because he was a pop curiosity: "I found his strange, gangly, country-boy charisma, his hard-to-define cuteness, and his charming eccentricity intriguing. I told my staff to find out who he was and book him for our Sunday show."

Steve Allen had a history of kidding rock and roll (such as reciting deadpan dramatic readings of "Splish Splash" from a music stand). Allen even roped Elvis into doing a sketch with him, Imogene Coca, and Andy Griffith, playing a cowboy named Tumbleweed in a parody of a country music show. Bill Allen says, "They used him brilliantly. Elvis got real laughs! He was very cute with the lines; he read them beautifully.

And he and Steve sort of ad-libbed together. You could see he was having a good time. You could see him breaking up." (Actually, he looks
pretty embarrassed.)

Some Elvisphiles claim Presley was conflicted about the whole thing
but went along with the gag to please Parker, telling his backup musician Gordon Stoker, "Oh, hell, man, let them have their way. I'm not going to argue with them." Experts differ widely over whether Elvis was
amused or abused. Stoker said, "Elvis was always running scared when
it came to Colonel Parker. Elvis was afraid if he gave him any back talk
or any trouble all the success would vanish. Elvis despised that show. He
never wanted it mentioned again. And he never ever watched the tape
they sent him. He was hurt deeply by the slurs on his background. He
knew they were laughing at him and it hurt bad."

"Total crap," countered Bill Allen. "There's so much misinformation
about this. These were rock-and-roll people who resented the fact that
Steve used to read rock lyrics and make fun of them. My mother [Mead-
ows] will tell you [Elvis] was a great friend of my parents, and when they
would go to Vegas to see him he would talk about them from the stage,
about what a break Steve gave him. You have to remember, Elvis was in
real trouble from a previous appearance he'd made with either Berle or
the Dorsey brothers. And no one would touch him. Ed Sullivan said
some very negative things about him. Dad said, 'Oh, come on, he's just
swiveling his hips, for God's sake. Let's give him a shot.' Elvis appreci-
ated that." When Elvis appeared with Allen to sing "I Want You, I Love
You, I Need You," the comedian held up a petition signed by thousands
of fans who wanted to see him back on TV, as if Elvis's appearance was
a public service.

But Allen's playful hound-dog gambit failed to amuse large numbers
of teen viewers. Some picketed NBC, charging Allen with slanderous
bad taste for making jokes at Elvis's expense. "Bring Back the Grinds,"
read one sign; another said, "We Don't Like the 'New' Elvis, We Want
the 'Old' Presley." Somebody hadn't gotten the joke. By 1956, as Elvis
worship was gaining momentum, one toyed with Elvis hysteria at one's
peril. Presley went along with Allen's gag, maybe against his better judgment. Earlier, Allen had been quoted saying, "Elvis is a flash in the pan.
He won't last a year." In his *Newsweek* column, John Lardner blasted
Allen for his effort to "civilize" Elvis, "to mute and frustrate Presley for
the good of mankind. Allen's ethics were questionable."

Bill Allen responded, "The truth is, if Elvis hated being dressed up with
a hound dog, he never would have given Steve the option of having him

back. I had lots of conversations with my father about this. Remember, Sullivan may have seemed the bigger show, but Steve Allen with Presley beat him handily in the ratings. And you could reach more people on the Steve Allen show because it was a younger crowd. Steve had been willing to have Elvis on when he was in trouble early in his career, and Sullivan was not! Parker turned down Sullivan two or three times. He said no, no, no. The only reason the Sullivan show offered him $50,000 was they knew Ed had offended the kid. It was the only way to get him back. Presley was the hottest thing on television."

For Sullivan, the fifty grand was a form of protection money. After he relented and rolled out the green carpet for Elvis's milestone appearances, he defended his change of heart by saying he'd been misled by those who claimed that Elvis was the devil incarnate. "I'd been told this guy was disrupting the morals of kids, that his whole appeal was sensual, that he did bumps and grinds and rubbed his thighs when he sang." After viewing Presley on the Berle show, he was almost disappointed: "I saw a guy who was a pale replica of Johnny Ray, who came on our show a few years ago and shouted and got down and beat the floor and frothed at the mouth." Next to Johnny Ray, Elvis looked tame and tasteful. Ed called the attacks on Elvis "a frightening evil thing. I didn't know what the fuss was all about."

Sullivan was far more shocked to learn that Steve Allen hadn't instantly locked up Presley with an exclusive deal after he'd put a nasty dent in Sullivan's ratings. But Allen was playing a different, funnier game and was told Elvis would rather not do comedy sketches. By then, Allen figured he'd used up his best Elvis gags and allegedly told Parker to accept Sullivan's offer. Later Allen announced, "I hereby offer Ed Sullivan $60,000 for three appearances on my show, and if he accepts, I assure my viewers he will not be allowed to wiggle, bump, grind, or smile."

Sullivan beat himself up for turning down a chance to book Elvis months before, not eager to shell out $5,000 for a hillbilly guitar player. He had told a reporter that Presley was unsuitable for family viewing, that he had better taste than to book such a lowlife, and that some people would do anything for ratings. And Ed Sullivan was one of them: days after speaking to the reporter he called Colonel Parker and booked Elvis for three shows for $50,000, an exorbitant price then. This was right after Sullivan snorted that he wouldn't have Presley on his show "at any price. . . . He's not my cup of tea." Which the *New York World Telegram* interpreted as: "He didn't care to have people accuse him of having lunatics on his show, and he didn't believe Elvis would help him sell cars."

Just prior to booking him, Sullivan had said, "Though I wouldn't want to have him on our show, I'd be happy not to have him on against me." Now he crowed, "I guarantee we'll have the biggest audience in our eight years when he comes on." Good call. The show, September 9, 1956, was seen by a record 60 million people, representing 82.6 percent of the TV sets in use, one of the largest TV audiences in history. By comparison, the "Dallas" finale, "Who Shot J. R.?," pulled a paltry 41 million viewers. Sullivan surrounded Elvis with harmless fare, as if to reassure viewers that their host had not totally lost his marbles: an acrobatic team, Dorothy Sarnoff singing "Something Wonderful" from "The King and I," and the Vagabonds, musical cutups.

After all the great hullabaloo over signing Elvis, and all the press it generated, Ed was not even there to host the historic occasion. He was recovering from an auto accident. The guest host was the even less likely Charles Laughton. The distinguished British actor intoned, "Mistah Presley, if you ah listening in Hollywood, may Ah address myself to you: It has been many a yeah since any young perfahmah has captured such a wide and—as we've heard heah tonight [slight chuckle]—devoted audience." Then Laughton cried, "And now, away to Hollywood to meet Elvis Presley!" That night, Steve Allen threw in the towel: NBC ran a film opposite Elvis. After Presley sang "Don't Be Cruel," "Love Me Tender," and "Ready, Teddy," a bemused Laughton said, wryly, "Well, what did someone say? Music hath charms to soothe the savage breast."

Presley sang two songs without unleashing his much-feared pelvic choreography. The cameras locked onto his upper torso but the teenage girls in the studio audience, eyeballing his full lustful body, yelped their orgiastic accompaniment. After sending Ed best wishes for a speedy recovery from the car accident, Elvis soberly declared, "As a great philosopher once said . . . You ain't nothin' but a hound dog!!"

Then Elvis did his Elvisy thing—appendages flying, face curled into that practiced feral snarl. He awakened female sexual desire in living rooms across the nation. Frantic reports from the hinterlands recalled manic reactions to Orson Welles's "War of the Worlds" radio broadcast 18 years earlier. Listener Mae Zeoli threatened, "The few studios that welcome rock and roll and vile characters should be warned that a license to operate a TV station is a privilege that can be taken away by the authorities." Lester Jacobson, now a San Francisco cardiologist, once mentioned to me that his family in New Haven was shocked by Elvis's gyrations—"Nobody in New Haven ever did *that*." Israel banned Presley, fearing he would corrupt its idealistic youth.

Sullivan's loyal auto sponsor, Lincoln, got squeamish. Lincoln's ad agency man Joe Bracken told me, "There was all kinds of controversy about whether Sullivan should do this. There were a lot of people who thought it was not an appropriate act for a family show." The Lincoln hierarchy, he said, "kind of went along. Whatever Sullivan was going to do, they figured it was the right thing. We didn't have any trouble from Lincoln." Bracken recalled, "That night, we were in the sponsor's booth when Elvis did his gyrations. The camera had to shoot from his waist up. It was suggestive, but not, you know, lewd. It was a great show and wildly received. He was motivated by the controversy. That was an interesting show. Lots to talk about in the office the next day."

The easily outraged TV press was mortified at the sight of Elvis enshrined in TV's family values headquarters. Bessie Little, in *TV World* magazine, was appalled that Sullivan had betrayed his ideals by booking Presley for mere ratings, writing, "This is the man who once inspired the youth of America[,] . . . who is safe now because his own beautiful daughter is past the age when she could be influenced by the sexual gyrations of an Elvis Presley. Other parents are not so fortunate."

Chronic Sullivan antagonist John Crosby wrote that Presley's performance was "unspeakably untalented and vulgar," and Ben Gross in the *Daily News* said that the singer "gave an exhibition that was suggestive and vulgar, tinged with the kind of animalism that should be confined to dives and bordellos." The *Journal-American*'s conservative columnist Jack O'Brian—who was first the paper's TV critic and later its Broadway gossip columnist—sneered that Presley "added to his [performing] gamut (A to B) by crossing his eyes," and reported that the New York audience "laughed and hooted." He condemned Elvis's "display of primitive physical movement difficult to describe in terms suitable to a family newspaper" and described Presley's "ridiculously tasteless jacket and hairdo (hairdon't)."

That last needle really hurt, because Elvis had gone shopping for snazzy duds at Lansky's on Memphis's Beale Street, which catered to a black clientele. He had told Bernard Lansky he would be going on Ed Sullivan's show and needed fancy apparel. Along with a gold lamé vest and a midnight blue shirt, he bought an oversize kelly green sports coat with black flecks, a checked coat accompanied by a matching shirt with contrasting checks, three pairs of black trousers with a black stripe down one side, and two pairs of two-tone, black-and-white shoes. His mother had been appalled at the ensemble, but he'd argued, "Mama, this is *Sullivan!*"

Sullivan was concerned not about Presley's wardrobe but about what might be beneath it. Examining clips of the singer on Berle's show, he supposedly pointed out to Marlo Lewis that Elvis appeared to have a foreign substance jammed into his trousers. "He's hanging some kind of device in the crotch of his pants, so when he moves his legs back and forth you can see the outline of his cock," Ed is said to have told Lewis. Sullivan thought it might be a Coke bottle and said, "Do what you have to do to fix this." So when Sullivan dispatched Lewis to Los Angeles to oversee Elvis's final taped appearance in 1957, it wasn't—as legend insists—to keep the cameras off his hips but to make sure he didn't jam anything down his pants. Sullivan's decision to shoot above the waist was, as *Washington Post* critic Tom Shales put it, "one of the most strategic pieces of publicity the singer ever got."

Jack Gould wrote, "When Presley executes his bumps and grinds, it must be remembered by the Columbia Broadcasting System that even a twelve-year-old's curiosity may be over-stimulated. Over the long run, however, maybe Presley is doing everybody a great favor by pointing up the need for early sex education." During the shooting of the singer's third appearance, Lewis did push a camera to one side to mask Presley's gyrations. Sullivan video producer Andrew Solt told me, "They relied on long or side shots to blunt the sexuality." It all looks surprisingly tame now, hardly worth all the anguished hand-wringing at the time.

By bringing Presley on his show three times, Sullivan legitimized not just Presley but rock and roll itself. As a final thumbs-up, Sullivan went out of his way to praise Elvis as a darn fine boy, shocking parents more than Presley's actual performance. Sullivan played the surrogate father that folks trusted, thinking that maybe rock and roll's reputation as devil worship was exaggerated. Bob Greene, the columnist, at a party in Las Vegas thrown by Frank Sinatra, paid scant attention to Sullivan, who was there with stars like Burt Lancaster. Greene was on assignment to write about Sinatra, and afterward he recalled, "Not until much later did it occur to me that Sullivan was probably the one person at the party about whom I should have been most curious. Maybe the reason that being in the same room with Sullivan didn't affect me more—as the memory of it does today—is that he seemed sort of like my own father. It was Sullivan who brought Elvis Presley and the Beatles into my home. And my dad was always there, like a chaperone. It was as if Sullivan was saying to my dad (and to so many other American dads): 'This is Elvis Presley.

He's only going to bother you for a few minutes. He's a little strange, but your kids may like him.' "

When Ed took the onus off rock, he became (after Elvis) one of its most significant influences. TV historian Ron Simon wrote, "His introduction of rock 'n' roll . . . brought the adolescent subculture into the variety fold." Because rock so blankets pop culture today, it's easy to forget how far out of the mainstream rock and roll was in 1956, and that it was rarely heard on TV. On September 10, 1956, rock entered the mainstream, the American bloodstream. By Elvis's third appearance, notes Simon, Sullivan had discovered a vast new audience, later called baby boomers.

Steve Allen, reflecting on it all, calmly assessed the Elvis phenomenon: "Some singers are born with the ability to make a naturally pleasing noise with their vocal cords—Frank Sinatra, Ella Fitzgerald, Perry Como, Bing Crosby. Elvis was not. But his lack of a good 'instrument' turned out not to matter. . . . What his millions of young fans responded to was Elvis himself[,] . . . precisely the same way that young women have, for decades, reacted to [sexy] film stars." Elvis *was* the instrument, more important than anything he was singing. Allen pointed out that many great pop stars were "freak personalities" like Presley (and like James Cagney, Mae West, Jean Harlow, Marlon Brando, Marilyn Monroe, Jack Nicholson, and Woody Allen), entertainers "just offbeat enough to be fascinating. It's the extra electric-plus that makes all the difference, granted the breaks. And Presley has it."

The 1950s historian David Halberstam contended that Presley's true goal was Hollywood, not Nashville; he wanted to be a movie star, not a rock icon. Halberstam said that Elvis "spent hours in front of a mirror working on that look"—part sullen sideburned hood, part mama's boy, the sensitive brute embodied in films by Brando and Dean, brothers under the leather. Sam Phillips of Sun Records said Elvis saw himself as a country Dean Martin, although Presley claimed he modeled his singing style after country balladeer Eddy Arnold.

By Elvis's second appearance on the Sullivan show, the shock-and-awe factor of his sexual tease had begun to dissipate. In his Presley opus, Peter Guralnick zoomed in for a close-up of the seminal moment. "It was a relaxed, confident, and very much at ease Elvis Presley" who turned up for his encore. "Gone were the explosive nervous energy, the involuntary mannerisms, that had dominated his television appearances of just a few months before; even the self-abashed, somewhat shambling manner of his Sullivan debut had been replaced by a good-natured, almost studied and bemused *playfulness*. . . . It was as if for the first time he really took it all as his due." Opening for Elvis was what James Maguire called "pure virtue—an Irish children's choir, 30 kids singing a sweet Gaelic folk song[,] . . . with many close-ups of their angelic faces." Sullivan joshed, "People wonder if that little boy in the kilt is Elvis Presley—it's not."

To further temper the climate, Sullivan set up Elvis's next song, the theme from his forthcoming first film "Love Me Tender," by explaining that it takes place in a scene when "his three brothers come home from the Confederate armies[,] . . . and he sings this song to his mother and his young bride." He adds that the song is based on an old Stephen Foster ballad, as if to reassure his fretting TV faithful that rock had early-American roots. After Presley sang, further calm was restored by Señor Wences.

When Elvis returned for his second appearance of the evening, Sullivan made light of the madness—in an effort to bridge the still-unnamed generation gap that threatened to split his audience asunder—saying, "I can't figure this darn thing out. He just goes like this" (Ed shook his hips) "and everybody yells." He praised the maddened teenage throng on their fine behavior and awarded them a gold star: "I wanna thank all you youngsters. You made a promise you wouldn't yell during his songs, and you're very, very good—you haven't." They had in fact gone berserk, but at least they hadn't stormed the stage and torn Elvis to shreds. To help maintain order, Sullivan brought out Joyce Grenfell, a sophisticated British comic in white gloves, followed by a rousing chorus number from "Most Happy Fella." The host's implicit message: See, folks, it's still the good old harmless Ed Sullivan show.

God-fearing skeptics at Elvis's second coming on the Sullivan show may have been converted that night. Presley was a rebel, yes, but he was such a *nice*, polite rebel; he "Sir"-ed and "Ma'am"-ed his elders. The second appearance didn't pull the same monster rating as the first, but Sullivan beat the big rival show—a TV version of "Born Yesterday" with Mary Martin and Paul Douglas—two to one. For his third and final Sullivan appearance, January 6, 1957, Elvis wore his Memphis gold lamé vest over his blue velvet blouse from Lansky's that, says Guralnick, made him look like a Middle Eastern pasha.

Elvis's third live appearance was historical for (a) the famous waist-up camera shot and (b) Sullivan's semi–mea culpa after Elvis wrapped up the last historic performance: "Ladies and gentlemen, inasmuch as he goes to the Coast now for his new picture, this will be the last time that we'll run into each other for a while. But I"—here he quiets the audience screams and holds up his hand—"I wanted to say to Elvis Presley and the country that this is a real decent, fine boy, and wherever you go, Elvis, we want to say we've never had a pleasanter experience on our show with a big name than we've had with you. So now let's have a tremendous hand for a very nice person!" Sullivan meant it, but he was also justifying Elvis's presence, as if to say: if he's on my show, he can't be all bad.

Bob Thompson, the TV historian, told me, "Sullivan completely took the teeth out of him. Elvis was an unstoppable force who represented all that postwar alienation stuff"—but Sullivan sort of tamed him by shooting him from the waist up and by showing the Miami audience. "Instead of screaming girls ripping off their blouses, the cameras were going to these octogenarians really digging it. It helped to ease in, to lubricate, the entrance of rock acts into the mainstream and stripped them of any kind of truly revolutionary, dangerous power they might have. It was a cultural detoxifying process." Backup musician Gordon Stoker added, "Sullivan provided just what Elvis needed at that particular point in his life, to push him forward and make him a truly great star."

Ed's brief farewell curtain speech evolved into the Gettysburg Address of rock 'n' roll's civil war. "He appears genuinely taken with the young man," said Guralnick. "And Elvis for his part is just as genuinely thrilled—he says as much to friends—to have received recognition and validation from someone so widely respected, so experienced in the business." Commented Andrew Solt, "That speech came directly from Ed's heart. It was not rehearsed. He had been surprised, in the end, that he had such tremendous liking for this young man." Carol Lawrence, who was on that first Elvis show, told me she recalled "a screaming bedlam of young girls. We were all standing downstairs backstage next to a football player, an opera singer, and a chimpanzee. But Elvis was the most shy, sweet young man. He won Sullivan over."

Sullivan's pro-Presley remarks, wrote Halberstam, "appeared to be the generous speech of a man receiving a surrender, while in fact it was the speech of a man who had just surrendered himself. Market economics had won. . . . This was a visceral democratic response by the masses. The old order had been challenged, and had not held. New forces were at work. . . . The young did not have to listen to their parents anymore." In a TV interview that same night, Sullivan reiterated to Hy Gardner, "This is a nice boy and I want you to know it. He could so easily have had his head turned by all that's happened. But he hasn't." Sullivan was again conferring his lay version of a papal blessing.

But Elvis was not yet home free. Pockets of grave concern remained. Congressman Emmanuel Celler, whose antitrust subcommittee was investigating payola, stated that, while "rock 'n' roll has its place" and gave "great impetus to talent, particularly among the colored people," Presley's music and "animal gyrations . . . are violative of all that I know to be in good taste." Dirty dancing was wrecking the republic. Celler's remark rose from dark apprehensions about Presley being given such prominence on America's leading family TV show—a white man singing "colored people's" music, which threatened not just pop music, and even pop culture, but also American society itself. "It was becoming all too clear," noted Guralnick, "that rock 'n' roll now served as a lightning rod for a more and more sharply divided society."

When Sullivan embraced Presley and gave him his little benediction, long-buried fears of a "mongrel nation" stirred, not just in the South, but also among practicing rednecks everywhere. As Elvis's patron Sam Phillips has often said, "We needed a white singer who could sing the black songs." In Elvis Presley, "colored people's music" had crossed over. So when Elvis played the Sullivan show and received an official salute from Ed—the official arbiter of pop culture—a major bridge had been crossed into white America.

Rock had replaced comic books in the mid-1950s as the leading corrupter of American youth, those very youngsters whom Sullivan had labored so long to beguile. But were they about to leave him? Would the acrobats, jugglers, magicians, and animal acts no longer hold the kids enthralled? "Now Elvis was working the American home," remarked Halberstam, "and suddenly the American home was a house divided." Indeed, for teenage America, Presley's appearances on Sullivan's show, and his approval by the host, was a declaration of their independence, a shot fired across the generation gap. It was intergenerational warfare, fathers fighting sons, and mothers battling daughters, teenagers openly denouncing their parents' accepted notions of music, entertainment, and sexual values.

Before Presley, "The Ed Sullivan Show" was a haven for songwriters who wrote great romantic ballads and witty lyrics: the Berlins, Gershwins, Porters, Harold Arlens, Rodgers & Harts, Rodgers & Hammersteins, Hoagy Carmichaels, Johnny Mercers, and Cahn & Van Heusens. But they were all dead, aging, or irrelevant. Sinatra, Crosby, Como, Fitzgerald,

Clooney, and Shore still ruled the charts, but their sales were stagnating. Rock was swarming into their cozy, largely white-bread habitat, led by the first Elvis impersonators—Ricky Nelson, Fabian, and Tom Jones.

The country had a new teen elite with deep pockets for single records. A former subculture was an emerging dominant economic force. Elvis was a pop Paul Revere, awakening the country to the start of the revolution led by rebels with and without causes and attitudes—Brando, Clift, Dean, and Monroe in movies; Mort Sahl, Lenny Bruce, and Dick Gregory in comedy; Pete Seeger, Joan Baez, and Bob Dylan in folk music; Andy Warhol, Jackson Pollock, and Mark Rothko in art; and Norman Mailer, J. D. Salinger, Jack Kerouac, and William Burroughs in literature.

The big new unasked question was: what is "talent"? Before Elvis, it was whatever Ed Sullivan said it was, but nobody was quite sure anymore. "Pop music was no longer edifying, and not even harmless," noted John Leonard. "Elvis, the Beatles, and the Doors signified the confusion to come of politics and culture. The juvenile delinquents had their own tribal music, and it wasn't 'Sentimental Journey.' "

In 1957, a year after Elvis's first appearance on Sullivan's show, Dick Clark established his own teenage beachhead in Philadelphia on "American Bandstand," a sort of "Toast of the Teens." Clark was a pop power broker, cashing in on acts that had played Sullivan's show. As pop music critic Joel Selvin said, "Dick Clark was MTV. He was on three hours a day and an hour on weekends! He was an after-school babysitter." Clark quickly felt Sullivan's heat, recalling in his memoir, *Rock, Roll & Remember*: "[Sullivan] was a miserable bastard in those days. He tried to do us in, to kill the show. He tried to put clauses in his contracts [saying] that if an artist did his show the artist couldn't appear on [our] show. He couldn't understand how artists like Tony Bennett did my show for $155, then hit him up for $5000 to $7000 for an appearance on his show. He was convinced I put a pistol to Tony's head. Sullivan didn't understand that 'Bandstand' with their huge teenage audiences sold records."

Sullivan beseeched AFTRA, complaining that Clark was strong-arming entertainers to appear on "Bandstand," much as Sullivan had been accused of doing on his own show. They wouldn't have taken much pressuring, since Clark created a hugely efficient showcase for new records, just as Sullivan had. Clark asked Sullivan to cease and desist ("I wanted his acceptance and his blessing"). In 1978 Clark tried to spin off his own Sullivan-like variety show, using three former Sullivan staffers, but it never caught on.

Selvin told me that rock acts presented themselves differently for Dick Clark's all-teenage audience than for Sullivan's older crowd. "If you're Jackie Wilson, you want to do your ballad on the Ed Sullivan show. If you're the Beach Boys, you want to do your big hit and then cover a standard. Rock and rollers didn't know whether to seek respectability or to be what they were." For performers, moreover, said Denny Doherty, of the Mamas and the Papas, " 'Bandstand' was pantomime, but Ed Sullivan was live."

Even the Beatles tried to work both sides of Tin Pan Alley when they sang an actual show tune on their first appearance—"Till There Was You" from "The Music Man," which most kids just assumed was a Beatles original (its writer, Meredith Willson, considered rock and roll an abomination). Clark's audience was wall-to-wall teenagers. He courted them but never made attempts to seduce their parents. Even his Saturday night prime-time specials were musical teen sleepovers.

Just as Sullivan's credo of "family entertainment" was being tested, so were families themselves. Myron Cohen, Bert Lahr, Bea Lillie, and Bing Crosby were Egyptian relics to teenagers in the 1950s and 1960s. While old vaudevillians were taking victory laps on Sullivan's show— Bert Lahr appeared four times a year to stay alive—teenagers were in their bedroom chortling over *Mad* (which ridiculed all traditional pop culture) until their parents called them into the living room to watch "Bob [sic] Diddley."

But teens were selecting and erecting their own icons—Elvis, Buddy Holly, Brenda Lee, Marvin Gaye, Jerry Lee Lewis, Chuck Berry, Little Richard—which included an endless parade of irresistible black doo-wop acts like the Platters, the Penguins, the Temptations, and the Four Whatevers. White crooners Pat Boone, Georgia Gibbs, Teresa Brewer, and Bill Haley were colliding with each other to remake black hits, bleached-out ghetto favorites like "Tweedly Dee," "Ain't That a Shame," "Dance with Me, Henry," "Tutti Frutti," "Shake, Rattle and Roll," and "Rock around the Clock."

With Presley now duly blessed and anointed, the Sullivan show rocked—rhythm and blues and Motown, then light punk and heavy metal. CBS wove new welcome mats for the Animals, Janis Joplin, the Lovin' Spoonful, Gerry and the Pacemakers, the Dave Clark Five, the Beach Boys, Freddie and the Dreamers, the Mamas and the Papas, the Fifth Dimension, Credence Clearwater Revival, and the Young Rascals.

Conveniently, the Sullivan show was broadcast from a pulsating building at 1697 Broadway that, in the 1960s, housed many major music companies, right in the thick of New York's pop life. As the 1960s rocked on, rockers didn't need Sullivan as much as he needed them in order to appear contemporary. Talent coordinator Vince Calandra noted in his interview recorded for the Archive of American Television, "Ed, in his characteristic desire to take advantage of the popular idiom, turned more and more to rock 'n' roll entertainment. To me, frankly, it was all a bore."

Rock acts used Sullivan's show as infotainment ads for new records, as they did with shows hosted by Tennessee Ernie Ford or Arthur Murray: Buddy Holly played the Murray show and the Everly Brothers did the "Tennessee Ernie Ford Show." Selvin commented, "So there were other variety shows, but they didn't have the Sullivan audience. Those shows were fighting for audience. Letting in rock-and-roll acts was a dicey thing for them. The Rolling Stones were on Ed Sullivan every time they had a new record, every time they came to America. There were very few options. There was no 'Shindig.' There was no 'Hullabaloo.' Those came in '66 and lasted a very brief time."

Among the viewers of Presley's milestone Sullivan shows were rock legends-to-come like Buddy Holly in Texas, who played the show a year later as Sullivan stood off-camera, crying, "Go, Tex!," during "Peggy Sue." Afterward, Sullivan called Holly over for a quick curtain chat, his highest accolade. Holly biographer Philip Norman said the moment "reeks of metropolitan condescension: let's give this hick a break and see if he can string two words together."

Even for rockers like Holly, Sullivan's show was slippery terrain. Holly's big hit "Oh, Boy" got him and the Crickets invited back by Sullivan for a second shot, but Sullivan nixed "Oh, Boy" as too "raunchy," dealing with a boy's greatest orgasm. When Holly told Sullivan they had no backup song, Ed capitulated but, according to Norman, "took revenge

My father hated Sullivan's crusty personality and scoliotic posture, but watched anyway for the acts. He and my older brother (born in 1954) would fight endlessly over the rock acts. My homophobic father hated the mere sight of young men with long hair and foppish clothing; my brother worshipped them. They actually got into a knock-down-drag-out over the Rolling Stones' 1967 appearance on the program. Everyone could find something to love and hate equally.

Jud Wiltner, Boise, Idaho

in characteristic fashion," bringing them on as "Buddy Hollered and the Crick-cuts." Holly countered by playing an unscheduled chorus at fever pitch and adding a final banshee wail. Norman reported that Sullivan, "amid the audience's delighted applause, smiles with the conviction of a man whose toenails are being extracted with red-hot pliers." Nonetheless, the response was so great that Sullivan invited Holly back, but he'd had enough. When Sullivan doubled the offer, wrote Ellis Amburn, "Buddy told them to shove it."

Sullivan's favorite new pop group, the Supremes, played the show 15 times, concluding with their farewell appearance as a trio September 21, 1969, with the girls all wrapped in gold lamé and fluffy chiffon. It was a fitting place for their swan song, "Someday We'll Be Together," after which Sullivan announced, matter-of-factly, "Diana Ross will continue her career as a solo star." And then they were gone—just like that. Ross was once chastised by Motown producer Berry Gordy for a careless comment in *Look* about "bein' pushed on and off the Sullivan stage as if we're nothin'." "What are you, *crazy?*" scolded Gordy. "Talkin' 'bout Sullivan like that? You know how tough it is to get you on his show?"

Selvin summed up the Sullivan show's impact on rock: "In 1956, television was still new. It really hadn't been established as a nationwide phenomenon. Networks had run political conventions, but they hadn't really sensed that the entire country was hooked up until Elvis appeared on Ed Sullivan. So it's not just celebrating the entrance of rock and roll with those broadcasts, it actually signified the nation being hooked up to this new network where everybody is meeting Elvis Presley on the same night at the same time."

Elvis helped to reestablish Sullivan as much as Elvis's appearance on the show legitimized him and rock and roll. Bob Precht said Sullivan considered Presley and the Beatles mere "highlights" of his reign, and was prouder of the show's variety. The old impresario today would be stunned, maybe traumatized, to realize that the thing he is now most remembered for is introducing rock and roll to the nation and making Elvis Presley safe for America.

CHAPTER 18

Newspaper Wads at Fifty Paces—
A Few Off-Camera Feuds

I'm a pop-off. I flare up, then I go around apologizing.

Ed Sullivan

By the time Ed Sullivan came to TV in 1948, the celebrity radio feud had become a cherished tradition: Fred Allen took on Jack Benny, Charlie McCarthy duked it out verbally with W. C. Fields, and Walter Winchell did mock battle with bandleader Ben Bernie. Those were all in jest, but Ed Sullivan's TV feuds—with Winchell, Hedda Hopper, Arthur Godfrey, Frank Sinatra, Jackie Mason, and Jack Paar—were for real. Ed never ran from a real fight, and he provoked several.

Sullivan had long trained for his showbiz feuds, coming out of an era in the 1920s and 1930s when gossip columnists were always mixing it up in print, taking potshots at each other for sport—and for added readers. Columnists even had ugly intramural sniping matches—Dorothy Kilgallen versus Jack O'Brian, Hedda Hopper versus Louella Parsons.

Armed with an Irish temper and thin skin, Ed brought to his feuds a hunger for combat fed by his coverage of, and devotion to, boxing. He loved prizefights, lustily wrote about them, and hung out with ring heroes and their underworld pals (he covered the fight scene with affection), mugs like mobster Owney Madden and even Copacabana toughguy owner Jules Podell. So when Sullivan found himself in feuds with entertainers over showbiz niceties—bookings, fees, and so on—even Frank Sinatra seemed a flyweight to him, and bums like Godfrey, Paar, and Hopper were barely contenders.

Sullivan attacked Marlene Dietrich in print for walking out of a Broadway show at intermission ("Well, what can you expect from one

296

of Hitler's cuties?"), Kate Smith on grounds of snootiness ("She is cordially disliked because of her attempts to ritz the crowd who started her off"), and Joan Crawford for declining to appear on his show ("Nobody has gone so far in this business with so little talent"). In response, Crawford sent an open letter to a fan magazine accusing him of forcing her into a "newspaper publicity stunt" she labeled "cheap, tawdry, gangster journalism," adding that she couldn't understand papers that "permit journalistic lice to stink up their pages."

There were also behind-the-camera squabbles, like one in 1963 when Mary Tyler Moore threatened to sue the show for $15,000 after two appearances were canceled. Sullivan had learned at a dress rehearsal that Moore planned to lip-synch lyrics. It went to arbitration, and she got a $7,500 settlement fee, but Sullivan had made his point. (Ron Greenberg, Sullivan's attorney, told me, "There were a couple of disputes from time to time, but remarkably few. There was nothing I can recall that was really bitter or acrimonious. It was remarkable how little acrimony existed—people liked coming on the show, and Ed really enjoyed having them there. It was an experience everybody wanted.")

The old Loew's State Theatre host prized live performance. His show might not always be sensational, but it was always alive with the sound of flesh and blood. "Mostly we were live," Bob Precht explained to me, "and occasionally live to a backup [tape] track, but it wasn't an issue. We prided ourselves on being live. There may have been some exceptions, but rock groups were expected to perform live. If someone wanted to come in and lip-synch, it was trouble. That became an issue on a few occasions. We stayed live until the end." Well, mostly.

Sullivan later regretted all the feuds; it was easy for him to apologize after inflicting damage. "No writer has ever done a story about me that hasn't made me sound belligerent and pugnacious," he told Pete Martin of the *Saturday Evening Post* in 1958. Sullivan insisted he hadn't started most of the hostilities. He admitted that he was "eager to tangle with Winchell because I've never liked the guy much, but with the others I was an unwilling participant. . . . I get sidetracked into talking about the feuds that have been forced upon me—the brawls and the name-calling. Although such distractions bring in carloads of publicity." His wife often tried to intervene, telling him, "Why did you have to start something again?"

Nearly two decades after beginning the show, he confessed, "I've had maybe half a dozen feuds in 20 years. That's not so bad, is it? And to this day I don't know what some of them were about." He was quick to take on anyone who implied he paid off people for doing the show by plugging them in his column. Such rumors, he claimed, were "started by a lot of malicious little bastards. There was a lot of jealousy. Newspapermen were saying, 'What the hell? Sullivan's in our business, and now he's making a lot of money in TV.'"

Ed's feuding history begins with Hedda Hopper. In 1952 he accused the Hollywood gossip columnist of "using her syndicated Hollywood column to get stars to appear for her NBC show ['Hedda Hopper's Hollywood,' opposite his] at reduced fees"—as he was accused of doing when his show began. Sullivan savaged Hopper as "this woman who used to hang around the fringes of show business. She's no actress. She's certainly no newspaperwoman. She's downright illiterate. She can't even spell. She serves no higher function than playing housemother on junkets"—a veiled reference to rumors that she procured girls for Conrad Hilton at his hotel openings. He added, "She's established a reign of terror out there in Hollywood." He asked two actors' unions to investigate her. She said, "He's scared to death I'm going to knock him off the air."

Sullivan's 1953 feud with Arthur Godfrey stemmed from Godfrey's jaw-dropping on-air firing, in October of that year, of the show's most popular young balladeer, 23-year-old Julius La Rosa, whom Godfrey had discovered when La Rosa was in the navy. After La Rosa began drawing more fan mail than the host, Godfrey closed him down, informing him and the audience simultaneously, at the end of a show, "That was Julie's swan song." La Rosa was so innocent he had to ask one of the show's writers, Andy Rooney, who later became a "60 Minutes" essayist, what a "swan song" was ("Does that mean I've been fired?").

Godfrey famously cited La Rosa's "lack of humility," which, translated, meant that the singer had quit kowtowing to Godfrey. To protect his career, La Rosa had hired a manager and publicist (displaying too much ambition for Godfrey). He also had refused to attend ballet lessons that Godfrey insisted the cast attend with him; for Godfrey the lessons were therapy after a hip replacement. La Rosa had also dared to date one of the McGuire Sisters, Dorothy, which the philandering Godfrey resented because "his girl was Phyllis," La Rosa later said. Godfrey saw La Rosa as committing a form of celebrity incest. "He wasn't pleased I was dating Dorothy. I dare to say he thought of the ladies on the show as part of his domain."

The incident ripped the mask off Godfrey, showing the public that he was something less than the genial TV papa—indeed, was a man capable of tyrannical, vindictive, even cruel vengeance. That marked the beginning of Godfrey's slide, dashing his folksy image forever. But it was a huge boost for La Rosa, who said he had expected to be fired. "I broke the rules! I got an agent! It was like telling him, 'Up yours, you son of a bitch!' What I didn't expect, nor would any sane person expect it, was the public event and humiliation." La Rosa's firing was a seminal moment in TV history, with front-page headlines for weeks and outraged letters to the editor and righteous editorials. "I couldn't walk down the street" without being hailed, "and [there were] people calling my home"; he still lived with his parents in Brooklyn.

Sullivan, in one of the shrewdest producing moves of his life, parlayed the raging controversy into a colossal bookings coup when he signed La Rosa the day after his firing to sing on "Toast of the Town" the following Sunday (and contracted with him for added appearances). Sullivan earned his salary that day, and also his reputation as a scoop-crazed newshound. Once he'd heard of the La Rosa firing, Sullivan had moved fast, inviting the singer to his Delmonico Hotel suite and offering him $5,000 to sing on the show (La Rosa brought a lawyer and, for good measure, a priest). That was a pot of money for Sullivan in 1953, but he promised, "He'll be worth it. Wait and see"—as indeed he was. La Rosa's appearance on October 25, six days after being fired, drew the biggest rating in "Toast of the Town" 's five-year history, a whopping 76.6, later surpassed only by Elvis and the Beatles.

La Rosa told me, "I went up to his office at the Delmonico, and he saw I was a scared kid; and he said, 'Don't worry, everything is going to work out fine.' " Playing the Sullivan show, La Rosa recalled, was like playing the Palace. "I was the new kid on the block, and [the media] had just kicked him in the ass. God bless the American people—invariably they're always for the underdog. Here was this big important man picking on this new young kid who had a hit record. [Godfrey] had every right to do what he did, because I broke a rule, but his big mistake was his method."

Godfrey took the Sullivan booking personally, but as Sullivan said, "If Arthur were fired, I'd book him, too" (and Godfrey later admitted he would accept). Sullivan, rubbing it in, also booked Godfrey regulars Pat Boone and the McGuire Sisters, and when singer Marian Marlowe was fired he snapped her up too. Hoping to prevent Sullivan from further ruffling the feathers of CBS's golden-egg layer (Godfrey's many sponsors helped keep the network afloat), executive Hubbell Robinson asked him to quit raiding Godfrey's nest.

To prove he had no animosity toward Godfrey, Sullivan hosted "the old redhead"'s show when Godfrey was laid up. Ed warbled along with Frank Parker and a zither player and did a charming soft-shoe. As biographer James Maguire observed, "His own show was too important, too much of a high-stakes struggle, for him to enjoy himself. The self he displayed on the Godfrey show was closer to his Broadway columnist persona, capable of clowning around, comfortable with spontaneity and humor. But that side of Sullivan was stowed backstage when he hosted 'Toast of the Town.'"

La Rosa was dismayed years later to learn Sullivan had "come to my rescue" not as an astute talent scout but as a hungry headline hunter. "Ed said, 'Hey, I'm first and foremost a newspaperman. I put La Rosa on the show because he was news,' not because I was such a good kid or a good singer. I thought, 'Gee, I thought it was because he liked me!' That really burst that bubble for me. But I was a 23-year-old innocent. I don't remember what else he said, but it was always with a great compassion and a great sense of understanding and a recognition that he was dealing with a nice kid."

Sullivan saw the La Rosa coup as just doing his job as TV's celebrity ambulance chaser, an early inroad into tabloid TV (his years at the *Graphic* hadn't been for nothing). After a *Washington Post* music critic blasted Harry Truman's would-be diva daughter, Margaret, provoking an angry letter from Truman, Sullivan quickly signed her for the show, later exploiting the flap by telling viewers that the president had called Margaret after the show to congratulate her on her appearance and had also praised Sullivan for presenting his daughter so nicely—and without once mentioning her old man.

Sullivan's cozy deals with the film studios' marketing machinery played a part in his bruising feud with Frank Sinatra. It sprang from Sullivan's 1955 tribute to Samuel Goldwyn, which included clips from M-G-M's forthcoming "Guys and Dolls," plus onstage interviews with Sinatra costars Marlon Brando and Jean Simmons, who got a modest sum. Sinatra wanted $25,000 to appear live onstage, which Sullivan rejected, saying the stars' appearances were part of M-G-M's promotion for the film, thus Sinatra's beef was with Goldwyn, not him. When Sinatra turned it into a cause célèbre and appealed to the Screen Actors Guild to intervene, Sullivan wrote Walter Pidgeon, head of the guild, saying, "What I particularly resent is Sinatra's reckless charge that 'Toast' does not pay performers. To date we have paid out over $5,000,000 in salaries and, incidentally, rendered substantial benefits to motion pictures, motion-picture artists, studios, and theater operators."

Sullivan also took out a full-page ad in the *Hollywood Reporter* that mentioned Sinatra's low TV ratings (an added thumb in the eye): "P.S.: Aside to Frankie boy: never mind that tremulous 1947 offer: 'Ed, you can have my last drop of blood' "—a pointed reference to the time Sullivan rose to Sinatra's defense in a column when the singer belted columnist Lee Mortimer, and Sullivan had written, "Basically, Sinatra is a warm-hearted, decent person and I think it's about time they stopped kicking him around." Sinatra had sent him a gold watch and an IOU for his last drop of blood. In answer to Sullivan's *Hollywood Reporter* ad, Sinatra's full-page ad in the movie trades read: "Dear Ed: You're sick. — Frankie. P.S.: Sick, sick, sick!" Like most Sullivan feuds, it ended in a draw and hugs when Sinatra volunteered to replace Sullivan after the host's auto wreck. Told that Red Skelton had been hired, Sinatra said he would appear anyway—for free.

A year later, Sullivan got into a shameless squabble with Ingrid Bergman when he invited her to appear on his show, urging her to return to America after her seven-year exile in Italy following an adulterous front-page affair with Roberto Rossellini. To buttoned-up mid-1950s America, Ingrid was a fallen woman whose films were condemned by the Catholic Legion of Decency, and who was vilified in the press for what would now be no more than a one-night item on "Entertainment Tonight." Sullivan in the role of priestly father confessor presented her on TV in connection with the release of her new film, "Anastasia." Sullivan, by then a quasi religious figure, seemed to feel that if Bergman came on his show she would be cleansed of her sinful past.

He addressed viewers in his finest rambling style: "Now the film has been made. It seemed to me that this thing should be left up to the American audience because . . . you decide everything. I was planning to use the film on our show at some time—she [Bergman] doing a scene with Helen Hayes" (a sainted stage personage). "Now I know that she's a controversial figure, so it's entirely up to you. If you want her on our show, I wish you'd drop me a note and let me know to that effect, and if you don't, if you think it shouldn't be done, you also let me know that, too, because I say it's your decision and I'd like to get your verdict on it. . . . A lot of you think that this woman has had seven and a half years of time for penance."

A *New York Times* TV critic, J. P. Shanley, was appalled, writing in August 1956 that "Mr. Sullivan has been guilty of a lapse in taste and judgment," and that his reference to "a period of penance" sounded "like the sanctimonious dogmatism of a modern-day Pharisee." Shanley added, "Anyone taking such a position would be assuming the right to pass judgment on the personal affairs of another. Such an assumption is repugnant to all who believe in justice and fair-mindedness." He asked, "Incidentally, when is Ed Sullivan up for re-election?" Ed had really stepped in it this time, but again donned virtuous robes—just as he had when, in his first Broadway column, he chastised his fellow gossip-mongers for their lowly deeds. In 1967, Sullivan conceded that, yes, he had pandered to his viewers: "Ingrid never forgave me for what I had done—and she was right." Yet again, Sullivan exploited somebody self-righteously, to his TV congregation, only to repent himself.

The Great Sullivan-Paar War of 1961 exploded on the cover of *Life,* which depicted Sullivan and Jack Paar as sparring marionettes. The cover line read, "Puppets Parody Flyweight Feud," with a four-page pictorial spread portraying the feud as a Punch and Judy show. The battle was over fees for guests: Sullivan said he would no longer pay big money for people who agreed to perform on the Paar show at union scale ($320), vowing that any guest who appeared on Paar's show for $320 would receive the same amount from him. Most big names were paid several thousand dollars to grace Sullivan's stage, but Sullivan insisted that "Paar has enough sponsors to pay the going rates."

In his memoir, Paar charged Sullivan with "instituting a boycott and dictating how other shows should be run." The "Tonight" show was famous for paying union scale rates, which it justified because it was on 90 minutes every night and could never afford to pay stars what Sullivan did on his weekly show. Sullivan said if the performers just chatted with Paar, he wouldn't protest—only if they performed.

Paar's budget was $52,715 for nine hours a week; Sullivan's was $110,000 for one hour. Sullivan's fee breakdown was $7,500 for top acts (Tony Bennett; Alan King, who said five minutes on the Sullivan show paid for his house); $5,000 for second-tier stars (Myron Cohen, Sam Levenson); $3,500 for medium-priced attractions (Corbett Monica, Pat Harrington); and $2,500 for novelty acts (magicians, jugglers, animals).

Paar read an open letter to Sullivan on his show in his usual wounded puppy voice: "Dear Ed: I don't think you could have struck any blow that would injure the medium that glorifies you more than the ultimatum you gave television talent today. I am appalled that you raised the question of money and that you challenge me to pay performers what you pay them. Ed, I don't have money to pay performers. This show is a low-budget freak that caught on because performers want to come on and want time to entertain people without the monkey act and the Japanese juggler waiting in the wings." The audience, predictably, roared its approval.

Paar's letter accused Sullivan of "economically frightening performers off this show" and claimed that Paar had discovered many performers (Shelley Berman, Carol Burnett, Pat Suzuki, Phyllis Diller) who had gone on to bigger fame on Sullivan's show—that, in fact, Sullivan *needed* Paar: "Where are you going to find the Bob Newharts we brought to television, or the next Mike [Nichols] and Elaine [May] you first saw here? . . . It's the $320 here that made the $5,000 dollars possible," he argued, fairly.

Paar offered to debate Sullivan, a favorite Paar tactic. "It would be fun, Ed. C'mon, old boy!," said Paar on the air, jubilantly issuing a challenge. Sullivan rashly agreed to debate the issue with Paar on his "Tonight" show, where many a Paar adversary had been dismembered by the host. The polished late-night feuder gleefully had taken on his critics, specializing in Broadway gossip columnists—he had called Walter Winchell "a silly old man" and Dorothy Kilgallen "the chinless wonder." (Even I was once invited on Paar's show to debate him—after my negative review of his return, to a weekly 1973 prime-time show, ran in the *New York Daily News*; I declined, knowing I would be red meat tossed to a ravenous Paar audience.) A practiced provocateur, the Paaranoid host accused the press of ganging up on him because he had dared to take on a newspaperman: "Ed Sullivan is a columnist, and if you say anything about a columnist, even gently correct him, it's like shooting a cop in New York. Everyone comes down on your head."

Paar was a fearless but often foolish and quirky personality who led with his chin and was proud of the battles he had waged in the past, even titling a memoir *My Saber Is Bent*. After Sullivan accepted Paar's gauntlet, the debate got snarled in procedural ground rules over everything from audience involvement to the meaning of the word *debate,* much like the Nixon-Kennedy TV debates of the time. Sullivan insisted on a debate without a studio audience, knowing it would be stacked with Paar freaks. Paar claimed Sullivan insisted on no commercials, no reaction shots, no applause, no talk about the debate before or after, and that the tape had to be destroyed immediately after one airing. Ed also demanded, said Paar, his own makeup man, lighting man, director, and cue card man, as well as his producer and lawyer.

"Paar plays his audience like an organ," countered Sullivan, no minor audience virtuoso himself, as *l'affaire* Bergman had revealed. Sullivan wanted to speak to "the intellect of your millions of TV viewers," not to a studio audience that responds to "skillful cues with cheers or boos. [Paar] would commit suicide before an audience."

Paar replied, "I wanted to talk to the people he had conned, about how he beat people over the head with his column to appear on his show." Bennett Cerf, the respected Random House publisher and long-time "What's My Line?" panelist, was asked to moderate the event, but finally gave up in exasperation ("I have a publishing house to run"). Sullivan argued that he was "protecting performers against their own instincts"—appearing on TV too often and using themselves up. "We've tried to husband their resources by not putting them on too often," he explained in earnest.

Performers were trapped between two wrestling showbiz bears. No longer able to appear on both shows, artists were forced to choose sides in a no-win TV war. The comic Myron Cohen, a $5,000-a-night Sullivan favorite, canceled a Paar appearance, and comedian Sam Levenson, a $7,500 Sullivanite, apologized to Sullivan when he appeared in a late-night rendezvous with Paar. Said Phyllis Diller, also caught in the squeeze, "I feel like leaving town. I feel really indebted to Paar. And I'd really have to be out of my mind not to want to appear on the Sullivan show. The only thing I can do is take the $320 on the Sullivan show. I'd rather have friends than money." Paar loyalists included Buddy Hackett and Joey Bishop, who said, "I've been on this show for two years and I have one gripe. You told me Sullivan paid only eighty dollars. I thought *this* was the big money."

Mimi Hines who, with husband Phil Ford, made breakthrough appearances with Paar, never felt cornered. "It was more of a media thing," Hines explained to me. The team owed their career to both men—discovered by Paar, then given a prime-time spotlight by Sullivan. Hines gushed unabashedly about Ed: "To be asked to play for Ed Sullivan was like playing before a dignitary! It was a command performance."

The hyped-up Sullivan-Paar debate never occurred. Each claimed the other had chickened out. "Jack Paar has just called off the debate," announced Sullivan. "Paar is a welcher. He told me I could make the ground rules, and now he's trying to tell me what they should be. When Paar was notified, he immediately choked up and started to pull his crying act." Paar snarled on his show, "Ed Sullivan has proved to be as honest as he is talented." Sullivan answered, "He's brave when alone," terming Paar's on-air performance "a frightening display that ranged from paranoia to slander." Jack Gould of the *Times* dismissed it all as "a highly distasteful brawl[,] . . . a sickening disgrace" full of "cheap outbursts," and suggested that "both men might profitably shut up."

In Paar's memoir, he insisted it was a fight over important principles, adding, "I had always liked [Ed] and considered him something of a national institution—like the faces hewn out of Mr. Rushmore, which he resembles." Forgetting his own embattled history, Paar commented, "He has a long history of public brawls and figured to be a formidable foe." Finally he argued, "I won the debate by default," but "I came off in the newspapers like Jack the Ripper."

Sullivan conceded to *TV Guide* that Paar had outmaneuvered him. "If that means I lost the propaganda battle, that's tough." But he contended that Paar rigged the game, shifting it from a head-to-head debate to a "discussion," freeing Paar to control both the pace and the content. "I've never pretended to be a comedian, quick with the gag line. Paar's a very good comedian. In any minute discussion, he would kill me." Paar had his writers devise anti-Sullivan cracks for when he appeared on attorney F. Lee Bailey's talk show, such as, "NBC has its peacock and CBS now has its cuckoo. . . . Who but Ed Sullivan can introduce a basketball player with the reverence once reserved for Dr. Schweitzer?"

Sullivan most regretted that, to cram for the debate that never was, he had given up tickets to the Patterson-Johansson fight in Miami Beach, but the Paar-Sullivan prematch was almost as bruising. Years later, Sullivan dangled an olive branch when he got Paar's daughter a coveted ticket to the Beatles' first appearance on his show.

Sullivan's 1964 pitched battle with Jackie Mason was career-threatening and bloodied both combatants. Did Mason really flip Sullivan off on TV? And was it on- or off-camera? Nobody knows for sure even now. Sullivan, who patrolled his show for offensive language, salty innuendoes, and overstuffed necklines and crotches, was already agitated that night because the first ten minutes of the show had been preempted by a Lyndon Johnson speech—a crucial part of the incident rarely mentioned. Peter Calabrese was holding the cue cards during the notorious Mason incident. He had the best view of the famous incident of anyone—"the biggest flare-up" he witnessed in his five years there. Calabrese told me, "Sullivan didn't want to cut anyone from the show, so he decided to cut almost everyone, not just Mason, taking a song away from a singer, telling a comedian he hasn't got eight minutes, he has six."

Mason was a 33-year-old comic on the brink of breaking through from the Catskills small-time to the bigs. It was suicidal to give the boss the bird, but Sullivan's gesture, telling Mason how much time was left, had distracted the studio audience from laughing at Mason's routine. Panicked, the comic feared viewers would think he was bombing, so he began ad-libbing feverishly ("I just thought I'd generate some laughs by making fun of him," he explained to me). When Sullivan (or an aide) signaled Mason that he had a minute remaining in his six-minute monologue—a charade that unnerved comics—Mason momentarily went nuts.

Thumbing his nose at Sullivan, he nattered in his singsong delivery: "What are you showing me, *fingers?* Who talks with *fingers* in the middle of a performance? You think they come here to watch your *fingers?* If your *fingers* are such a hit, why do you need me? Why don't you come here and show your *fingers?* I'm getting lots of *fingers* tonight!" Then he looked off-camera and pointed fingers at the audience, crying, *"So here's a finger for you . . . and a finger for you . . . and a finger for you!"*

Calabrese said that, during a show, "Ed never left the stage. He would stand onstage right with Ken Campbell, the producer's assistant, who held the stopwatch—he was the guy who kept the clock. He had a phone to the control room [to producer Precht], and Ken would call them and say, 'Ed wants . . .'

"So I'm holding these cards for Mason, and he's doing OK; but he starts to go over, and Ed starts moving toward center stage like he's waving at Jackie to give him a cut signal, and Jackie kind of ignores him. Ed pretty much wound up standing next to me, pointing to Jackie and putting the finger across his throat to say, 'Cut.' That's what set him off." Calabrese could tell Sullivan was fuming. "You never had to guess when Ed was mad." Mason was rushed out of the studio afterward. "Ed wanted to fight him. He was looking to punch him out. He was pissed."

Sullivan was first stunned, then apoplectic. After the show, Mason recounted, "Ed came over to me and blew his top. He said, 'Who the fuck are you to use these filthy gestures, you son of a bitch—on national TV! You did dirty things on my program.'" Mason told Sullivan he was trying to be funny, not offensive, but Sullivan, "wound up and furious," vowed, "I will destroy you in show business—I'll hurt you in every way I can"—which Sullivan denied ever saying. He clearly felt Mason had flashed him a middle digit, humiliating him publicly (and privately). Mason, on edge, was just being his irreverent, combative comic self, but

Sullivan viewed Mason as a heretic. Overreacting, as he often did, Sullivan said in a later interview for the *New York Times,* "I was furious and sick to my stomach."

The press played Mason as a finger-flipping rebel tilting at the mighty, magisterial Sullivan. Critics and Sullivan scholars, examining the video footage as if studying the Zapruder tape, debated whether it was merely an up-thrust index or a vile middle finger. Talent coordinator Vince Calandra said Mason wasn't being dirty, and that viewers couldn't see it anyway because his hands were out of camera range. Sullivan charged Mason with performing "lewd gestures, offensive conduct, insubordination, and gross deviation from material agreed upon for the telecast tonight." You would have thought Lenny Bruce had invaded the show.

Mason remained mystified: "To this day I have no idea what he thought, except that he thought I made a filthy gesture," he told me. "I didn't even realize that's what he thought when he blew his top at me after the show. I had no idea what the screaming was about. He said, 'I'll wipe you out if it's the last thing I do, you son of a bitch! Who the fuck this, who the fuck that . . .' Filthy screaming, out of his mind in a violent rage."

Mason, who was banned from the show and lost his next five Sullivan appearances, said, "I had no obscene thoughts in my mind. Ed was so full of venom. His hate was too much to explain, but that doesn't make him a bad person. He had been ten times nicer to me than he had the average person on the show. But he didn't give me a hearing. What was an innocent joke to me was vulgar and indecent to him. And when Sullivan made up his mind to disagree, it was almost impossible to find some way to accommodate him. It was a terrific problem trying to read him. Each time you were on the show you wondered, How soon will he holler? How quick will he dump me?"

Mason—who was raised in a family with three brothers and is an ordained rabbi, like all his brothers and father—only rebelled in nightclub life. He painted his past as a sheltered, semimonastic world. "I had no idea there was such a thing as a dirty gesture. I didn't even know what that gesture meant at the time. People find that hard to believe. It's not at all hard to imagine if you knew what yeshiva boys act like. I was a rabbinical student who was very, very underexposed to the real world. I was thoroughly unaware of any obscene type of gesture. I never knew such people. I never heard a dirty word in person. When I played a nightclub, it was the first nightclub I ever saw from the inside."

Mason filed a $3-million libel and slander suit against Sullivan, whom he charged with saying that he "should be run out of the entertainment business" and with telling him, "I'll hurt you in every way I can." The suit claimed Sullivan had called him "a variety of four, ten, and eleven-letter words of Anglo-Saxon origin, dealing generally with the subject of sex and perversion." Mason's lawsuit was intended to paint Sullivan with the same tarred brush Sullivan had swung. The judge, remarking that he regularly watched Sullivan's show ("although I don't know why"), ordered that the tape be replayed in court. But he ruled that the language in the tape revealed "nothing offensive or obscene that would offend anyone."

Mason's lawyer advised him to pursue the case "all the way," but his manager was afraid of provoking an even nastier public battle with Ed Sullivan, who was, says Mason, not just powerful but "a symbol of American purity and decency." Most of his friends advised Mason to give it up. They told him (in Mason's paraphrase), "You're the little guy and, not only that, you're the Jew, and why give the Gentiles an excuse to dump more hate on another Jew? Better not to look like I vanquished Ed Sullivan. And this way, I'll look humble, the best thing to do."

He went on to say, "So I followed their advice because I didn't know better, and it turned out to be the worst, most stupid mistake of my life. I should have continued, because if I'd won the case I would've looked like a hero. Besides which, I probably would have made 2 million dollars. Instead, the image I had was [that of] an out-of-control character who couldn't be trusted on television."

The suit came to a fuzzy end, called off on account of indifference. The judge, who had also seen Mason perform in the Catskills, decided that his gestures were simply part of his act. Mason says that, though he kept working, the incident damaged his career just as it was taking off. "I was definitely making a good living. But it curtailed completely the climb my career was making. I was moving up toward the stars, and now, instead, I was starting to flatten out and move downward a little. He kept me out of the big time for 20 years." Today the incident would send his career soaring, he said—"Performers now try to come up with a new filthy way to behave every ten minutes."

Contrary to public myth, Mason wasn't banned from TV, as Sullivan threatened. "For about a year or two," he said, "I did certain peripheral shows like Merv Griffin, but I was not able to get any major prime-time shows for two years. Right before that, I was one of the hot young comedians in demand for all of the major prime-time shows—Garry Moore, Dean Martin, Perry Como." He doesn't think Sullivan tried to keep him off TV, but suspects a blacklist existed by gentlemen's agreement.

Two years later, when they ran into each other at the Las Vegas airport, the adversaries shook hands and made up. As Mason told it, Sullivan was deeply apologetic. "He said he never forgave himself for doing that to me and felt terrible he had done it." Sullivan informed viewers at the end of a September 1965 show that, the following Sunday, "highlighting the show will be an old friend of mine and yours, Jackie Mason."

Sullivan choreographed Mason's return with his usual newsmaking aplomb: after the announcement tease, Sullivan brought Mason on for a surprise grand reunion. They shook hands "warmly and compliment[ed] each other," wrote the *New York Times,* reporting the historic event like MacArthur's return to the Philippines. It was one of Sullivan's quasi-magnanimous gestures. He said they were old pals—news to Mason, who never got a repeat invitation. Sullivan enjoyed publicly burying old hatchets almost as much as flinging them. The incident, in any case, has become a major piece of each man's legend, as ingrained in television lore as Arthur Godfrey's firing of Julius La Rosa on the air, the Oscar night streaker, and Janet Jackson's pop-up nipple.

Mason's behavior got mixed reviews from his cronies. Comic Orson Bean noted that the whole thing might have ended had Mason apologized. John Byner told me that Mason "turned his firing into something that was Ed's fault—shame on him." Robert Klein commented to me, "Mason used bad judgment. But he was just being funny." While the feud made Mason momentarily famous, as feuds will, he was an object of curiosity until he returned in grand fashion with a one-man show on Broadway in 1986 (a deft repackaging of his stand-up act). "Being controversial gives you a lot of publicity," Mason said, "but it also leaves you a questionable product so far as a sale to a network is concerned."

When Mason returned to Sullivan's show, he performed a funny, original, mischievous, even taunting Sullivan impression. Sullivan may have invited Mason back on the show just once to prove he wasn't vindictive, or perhaps to keep Mason from suing him again. "I don't think he gave it all a second thought," said Mason. "It didn't seem to make any difference—the damage had been done." Mason sounded forgiving: "I never felt any hostility. I realize what motivated him wasn't anything but his own self-preservation. It was a total misunderstanding, but he didn't give me a chance to explain myself. It was inconceivable to him that somebody would do such a thing—and if I ever had tried to explain, he would not have heard me."

Some still think the fracas perversely helped Mason's career, but he said, "It didn't become a benefit in any way. If it was a David and

Goliath thing, then I would not have been an outcast in show business for 25 years. There was no compassion for me that I could find anywhere. My earning power was cut right in half after that." He concluded, "I never really worked my way back until I opened on Broadway in '86. It was so many years later that, by that time, people either forgot about it, or they weren't concerned with my image and just came to see me as some name they vaguely remembered from the past. Most people probably thought I'd passed away by that point, and they couldn't care less. To them, I was just a forgotten guy from the old days."

CHAPTER 19

Embracing Blacks, Caving
In to McCarthyism

[Ed Sullivan] thought he was the fuckin' pope of show business!

Anne Meara

To me at that time, he was like Martin Luther King.

Vince Calandra, talent coordinator

Ed Sullivan's old-fashioned up-by-the-bootstraps values were constantly at war with his populist sentiments. He was an FDR liberal but a show business conservative and something of a cultural mongrel: a middle-class Catholic wed to an upper-class Jewish woman, with an Italian ex–shoeshine boy for an assistant. In awe of black athletes and entertainers, he raised money to help pay for dancer Bill Robinson's funeral and was on call to emcee benefits for any worthy causes promoting all races and creeds. The built-in subsidiary cause, of course, was promoting Ed Sullivan.

In print, Ed flashed his liberal credentials at any hint of bigotry. The racially inflamed Josephine Baker incident at the Stork Club was an ideal forum in which to expound on his equal-justice-for-all philosophy, when he attacked the club in print and on the radio for bias against Baker and assailed Walter Winchell for defending the Stork's presumed racist owner, Sherman Billingsley.

Broadcasting's leading historian, Eric Barnouw, wrote, "Radio had been close to lily-white, but implicitly. Television was explicitly and glaringly white. A seeming mirror of the world, it told the Negro continually that he did not exist." Television was much trickier, slipperier terrain than radio. Sponsors and the network were always peering over your shoulder. It was easy to champion liberal causes in print and risk offending readers—unlike on TV, where 100 offended viewers can send a network scurrying for cover and threaten a show whose policy is to make everybody happy. Controversy is courted—even fanned—by most newspaper editors, but feared by easily cowed commercial TV executives (at least those beyond Fox, MSNBC, and MTV). It's less true now than then, of course, but even in today's anything-goes social and cultural climates, the political-correction police patrol the airwaves for excessive social and sexual infractions.

Most TV variety shows welcomed acceptable black superstars like Louis Armstrong, Pearl Bailey, and Sammy Davis Jr. But in the early 1950s, long before it was fashionable, Sullivan was presenting the much more obscure black entertainers he had enjoyed in Harlem on his uptown rounds—legends like Peg Leg Bates, Pigmeat Markham, and Tim Moore (the Kingfish on TV's "Amos 'n' Andy"), strangers to white America. Sullivan showcased the Harlem Globetrotters on six shows before most Americans ever saw them in person or anywhere else on TV.

"He rekindled Pigmeat Markham's career," sitcom director Howard Storm told me. "I know that as a fact because my first cousin was married to Pigmeat Markham." Mel Watkins observes in his definitive history of black entertainment, *On the Real Side,* that Sullivan's "uninhibited display of friendship and admiration for performers elicited numerous irate letters from white viewers, many of whom labeled him a 'nigger lover.' But Sullivan never backed away from his liberal approach."

It could get ugly, as Eddie Cantor learned when he casually wiped Sammy Davis Jr.'s brow on a show. "Vicious, racist mail poured in," wrote Cantor biographer Herbert Goldman, such as that from a viewer who demanded, "How dare you mop that coon's face with your handkerchief on national TV?" Mary Lynn Gottfried, a Sullivan secretary who answered fan mail, told me, "A tremendous amount of mail came in every day, and some of the letters were scary, even threatening." Some were so hostile ("Don't put those niggers on!") she turned them over to CBS security.

Sullivan's show had an open door, through which anyone of any ethnicity might walk—the only passport required was talent. A leading black newspaper, the *Pittsburgh Courier,* observed, "Sullivan's video offering has, from the beginning, back in 1948, offered opportunities without restriction to persons of talent. Sullivan presents Negro entertainers as an integral part of his show, knit well into the proceedings, with never a hint of bias." Blacks felt so at home on the show that the comic Godfrey Cambridge once snuck up behind Sullivan on camera, slipped an Afro wig on his head, and declared Sullivan "an honorary Negro."

Sullivan told *Ebony* three years into his TV run, in 1951, "If there has been a generosity, television has received it from the Negro. In the first place, you just can't have great programs unless you integrate the Negro performer into the show. In the second place, it has never been pointed out that the Negro has been a great friend to television. I personally know that, without his generous help, the early days of TV would have been a nightmare."

Mel Watkins added, "Compared to what followed in the '50s and '60s, the late '40s were banner years for blacks on television"—not just on Sullivan's show but also on Milton Berle's, Arthur Godfrey's, and Ted Mack's "Original Amateur Hour." In 1948, five months before his TV show debuted, Sullivan received a plaque from the Negro Actors Guild of America for his service to the organization. He had worked to convince advertisers to support the group's efforts to prevent Communist influence on television—in effect helping to keep unfairly tainted black actors employed in TV.

In 1955, Sullivan devoted an entire hour to black performers, hosted by New York disc jockey Tommy Smalls, a.k.a. "Dr. Jive," featuring R&B performers Bo Diddley, LaVern Baker, and the Five Keys. It was, said Marc Weingarten in a book on rock 'n' roll and TV, "a joyous, blithely untethered celebration[,] . . . a groundbreaking event, the first time a popular mainstream variety show had devoted an entire broadcast to race music."

That same year, Sullivan spotlighted Bo Diddley (born Elias McDaniel), whom Ed had seen at the Apollo Theater but was uncomfortable introducing. Pop critic Joel Selvin told me, "He saw this thing at the Apollo, and he said, 'We gotta get some of that.' But black people on Sunday night on TV? Dicey. So he brought on a black DJ. He brought Bo Diddley to network TV but wouldn't introduce him. He said, 'This is Dr. Jive from the Apollo Theater—he'll explain this to you.' You could see he's trying to distance himself." Selvin added, "It's a phenomenal performance [Bo's], just raw. It's like going through a rabbit hole and coming back with something from another world. White people hadn't touched this. It's absolutely transported from the jungle."

While Sullivan wasn't racist, he played the race card close to his vest, shielding himself from any racists who tuned in, CBS honchos and sponsors included. After Bo Diddley, he hosted pioneer appearances by the Platters and Louis Jordan in 1957, Brook Benton in 1959, Jackie Wilson, and Fats Domino. Vince Calandra, Ed's longtime talent aide, admired Sullivan's progressive racial attitude, recalling in the interview for the Archive of American Television: "I remember once he sent me to Harlem to see these six elderly black tap dancers at the Apollo. They really kicked ass. My wife and I were like 'Wow!' I told Bob Precht they were absolutely sensational but their wardrobe was dated, so Ed sent me out to buy 'em new tuxedos. That's what made the job so worthwhile— seeing the expressions on performers' faces when you could help them out." Decades later, Motown's Berry Gordy came over to Calandra's table in a restaurant and said to his (Gordy's) wife, "See this guy? He's the one who helped make it happen.' "

Sullivan had to fend off his hard-won sponsor, Ford's Lincoln dealers, after kissing Pearl Bailey on the show and daring to shake Nat King Cole's hand. It was Cole's appearances on "Toast of the Town" that led to his being offered his own network show, the first by a black entertainer, which many southern affiliates refused to air. The show was canceled when no sponsors could be found, even after white performers agreed to appear on it at union minimum. Cole bitterly attacked the network's ad agencies: "They could have sold it if they'd wanted to. They sell much worse."

Southern salesmen who peddled radios and TV sets for Sullivan's first sponsor, Emerson Radio and Phonograph Corporation, asked him to "drop Negro stars" from the show, saying it would ruin their business. CBS's Jackson, Mississippi, affiliate routinely censored shows that included appearances by blacks (just as distributors of musicals shown in Dixie movie houses often cut out scenes with black singers like Lena Horne). Sullivan said, "I told them they were wrong[,] . . . that you can't put on a topflight show without the talents of a Nat King Cole, a Pearl Bailey, a Louis Armstrong, a Lionel Hampton, a Sammy Davis Jr." The critic John Leonard put it simply in "The Ed Sullivan Age": "There wasn't

After Sammy Davis Jr. did a number once, he and Ed embraced. My grandmother went insane! She said, "Oh, mah God! Ah cain't believe it!" I'll never forget it, because her reaction was so disgusting to me, even as a little girl of 12. My grandmother was from North Carolina, nowhere near as racist as the deeper South. She watched him all the time. He was really [blazing] a path, with all of Middle America watching: if Ed Sullivan was so unbiased, then white viewers had to think twice.

Bettina Devin, Terra Linda, California

an important black artist who didn't appear on Ed's show." Marian Anderson made her TV debut on his show in 1952.

Orson Bean was the house comic at the Blue Angel in New York from 1950 to 1959 and also a familiar TV face. He explained to me that, on TV shows, "if we had a black performer on, we would be told, 'Don't touch this performer. If your shoulder so much as brushes the shoulder of the black performer, we will lose stations across the South.' When Pearl Bailey appeared on the Sullivan show, he said, 'Pearly Mae, how ya doin'?,' and threw his arms around her. And all across the South TV station phones lit up. What happened? He touched a Negro!"

It wasn't just southern bigotry. According to biographer Jerry Bowles, Sullivan once had a Ford executive from Detroit thrown out of the theater when he suggested that Sullivan stop booking so many black acts. And a dealer in Cleveland told him, "We realize that you got to have niggers on your show. But do you have to put your arm around Bojangles Bill Robinson at the end of his dance?" Bowles wrote, "Sullivan had to be physically restrained from beating the man to a pulp." One viewer wrote in, "We enjoyed Ella Fitzgerald right up to when you had to make the point of hugging her right there in our living room!" Sullivan wrote angry replies to many racist letter writers.

After Leslie Uggams was discovered by Mitch Miller and featured on "Sing along with Mitch," Sullivan snatched her up. She was well aware of his special place in TV. "It wasn't one of those shows where once in a while you would see a black star," she told me. "It was practically every week. Even on the Perry Como show, which was on way after that, there was a whole thing with Lena Horne when Gary Cooper touched her hand. It's like when I was on the Mitch Miller show: Mitch was constantly being told, 'Can't she be in a separate segment?,' so they could cut me out" when the show aired in the South.

Not until the birth of the Motown sound, which Sullivan dug, were black singers allowed to sing the blues on TV. Black entertainers on TV, according to comedian Dick Gregory, were instructed not to sing romantic ballads (just up-tempo ditties or gospel), because presumably blacks didn't have serious love lives. The Supremes became the first Motown act to appear on the Sullivan show, on December 27, 1964, perhaps because of their carefully staged girls-next-door image that Berry Gordy constructed—as black McGuire Sisters.

Ross biographer J. Randy Taraborrelli wrote, "In the McGuires' ensemble, Phyllis, the leader, was the only one who came alive during a performance, but each of the Supremes had animated personalities."

Motown's house choreographer, Cholly Atkins, who had once worked with Ethel Waters and Lena Horne, was responsible for the trio's stylized, Broadway-influenced choreography that reminded Sullivan of performers he had loved and plugged at the Cotton Club and the Apollo.

Mary Wilson told me Sullivan grew fond of them. "At first, being young, there was a little distance, but he became very close to us when he found we were kind of, you know, *nice* girls. He really liked that." She added, "He wasn't an overly friendly person, pretty much like he was onstage." Wilson recalls rehearsing all week with Atkins, but her most vivid memory is encountering the show's makeup person at dress rehearsal. "The makeup was so horrible because the makeup artist really didn't know how to make up black people. We weren't really used to being made up. We were still very young and didn't wear makeup. We didn't need it. We wore only eyeliner and a little mascara, all Maybelline and lipstick, right?"

She goes on, "We got on the show and here they come, slapping on all this pancake makeup. They put it light on Florence because she was very light-skinned. On me and Diane they put it on heavy—caked it on. We came out and we looked like . . . clowns, like masks. We couldn't believe it. It was horrible. We came back to our room and we looked at it. It was the biggest day of our lives! We were thrilled to be on 'The Ed Sullivan Show' that we had watched all our little lives—but after rehearsal we started trying to scrub that stuff off our faces. We were just crying we were so hurt." They went onstage as is, wearing only untinted natural skin tones. A staffer recalled, "There was always a drama when the Supremes were on"—about wardrobe, makeup, something—but few cultural clashes. (Another Motown performer, James Brown, was also a handful, a secretary on the show told me. "I never liked him. He was very mean to me.")

Motown's innovative Gordy targeted the Ed Sullivan show early as a primary platform for his singers, and he found in Sullivan a willing accomplice. "Gordy was always around," Susan Abramson told me. Ed may have hated most rock and roll, but, as an old Harlem habitué, he loved doo-wop and R&B. To him, Motown was a snappy mix of gospel and Tin Pan Alley. Some of the grittier black groups were sanitized for the show. John Leonard noted, "For the longest time, even entertainers like Nat King Cole and Leslie Uggams sounded as pink and squeaky clean as Pat Boone."

Joel Selvin explained, "The Sullivan show was a real pipeline for Motown acts. Ed Sullivan was their homie. In the mid-'60s, when the soul music thing happened, blacks discovered that they were their own audience. They directed their music toward their culture; you see that in James Brown. Motown is not for black people. Motown is black music for white people—very specifically. This is not Aretha Franklin. This comes from Jerry Wexler, producer of Aretha Franklin and Ray Charles, who said he made Aretha Franklin records for steelworkers in Birmingham, and Berry Gordy made Motown records for white teenagers."

Gordy—whose first record was "Gimme Money, That's What I Want"—was, Selvin went on to say, "into music for vast, broad mainstream American success. It was not a black cultural thing. Gordy was a philosopher-king, a visionary who worked on the assembly line at Ford and saw a methodology he could transfer to the music business. He had songwriter-producer cells, creating the material, and then they'd bring in different artists—Temptations, Jackie Wilson" to fit a particular slot. It was early niche marketing for the white masses, like Americanized Chinese food.

Selvin added, "Gordy insisted songs be written about everyday people, not extraordinary people. He was looking to make rock-and-roll records that sold to the white teenage market. He cleaned up the rhythm and blues, which was much funkier, much more sexual, more of the mud of the African American community. He washed off that mud and cleaned it up, made it safe. You can see how that philosophy segues perfectly into the Sullivan show. He and Sullivan were almost partners in many ways over that period. Berry Gordy kept bringing these extraordinarily exciting acts to Ed Sullivan." Groups like the Temptations had such dazzling Cholly Atkins–designed moves that, said Selvin, "they were just a marvelous visual experience that connected with the broadest part of Sullivan's demographic, versus a Herman's Hermits kind of thing, which he had to [force] his adult audience to sit through. But they liked the Motown sound."

Sullivan's credentials as a champion of black athletes and artists dates back to 1926, when he wrote his *New York Evening Graphic* sports column about a black New York University football player who would be benched when the team played a game against the University of Georgia—in New York. "For the next week," as he recalled in the *Daily News* in 1958, citing his history of supporting black causes, "I castigated NYU's immorality and suggested that their Hall of Fame be torn down and transferred to some other university with a higher regard for a boy's dignity."

Sullivan routinely booked black entertainers in the pre-TV stage shows he produced. In print he had promoted blacks as viable air force pilots during World War II (because of their "lightning reflexes"), and defended outspoken black actor Canada Lee, a target of anti-Communist slurs. Most prominent was his effort to raise money for Bill Robinson's funeral through his column; he also had flags lowered on Broadway after the dancer died and produced the memorial service as he might a stage show. He arranged for stars like Danny Kaye, Milton Berle, Jimmy Durante, Ethel Merman, Jackie Robinson, Louis Armstrong, and W. C. Handy to sit in the front row of the church; some 500,000 people attended. Vince Calandra said, "He turned it into a national event."

In 1942, when he had coproduced with songwriter Noble Sissle a black revue, "Harlem Cavalcade," the critic Burns Mantle led off his rave with a prescient line: "You couldn't keep Ed Sullivan out of show business." What's more, Sullivan regularly boosted shows at the Cotton Club and booked black performers on his early radio shows. Sissle told Sullivan, "You have been a great friend of the Negro."

Sullivan once explained, "As a Catholic, it was inevitable that I'd despise intolerance, because Catholics suffered more than their share of it. As I grew up, the causes of minorities were part and parcel of me. Negroes and Jews were the minority causes closest at hand. I needed no urging to plunge in and help." He claimed he introduced Bill Robinson in Miami to the first mixed audience in the South. The leading African American newspaper, New York's *Amsterdam News,* wrote in 1974, after Sullivan's death: "Ed Sullivan discovered the compelling magic compounded by blacks long before there was such a thing as television. And he did it in a tough, cynical world, jaundiced with jimcrow and bigotry. Bucking the establishment is never easy, and in those days that was not only unpopular, it was practically impossible."

In the late 1920s (as the *Pittsburgh Courier* recalled after his death), Sullivan was the only white sportswriter who wrote about a black basketball team that challenged the Boston Celtics. No Boston arena would rent to them. Sullivan helped find them an armory to play in. The night of the game the place was packed, thanks to what the *Amsterdam News* called "a brash young sportswriter." "In those not so good old days," Alvin E. Wright said in his *Courier* tribute, "there weren't too many Ed Sullivans around. But he was a pretty good teacher and the lessons weren't wasted on those who followed. Sullivan had many enemies and he had many faults[,] . . . but Ed Sullivan was a man unafraid." Ed even instructed blacks on their own cultural history—right on his show. He asked a member of the all-black Fifth Dimension to name the first great black superstar, and a singer guessed Bojangles Robinson. Sullivan said, "No, it was Bert Williams—and don't you forget it!"

In 1958, an editorial in the *Montgomery (Alabama) Advertiser* asked readers to boycott the Sullivan and Steve Allen shows for showcasing black entertainers, claiming, "Sullivan's show has lost considerable popularity of late [in the South] due to the prominence it gives Negro performers." To rednecks, it was all "mongrel music." Sullivan insisted his show hadn't suffered at all in southern markets: "Our ratings in the South have always been way way up. It would be impossible to do a show without availing one's self of Negro talent. If the time ever came when I couldn't exercise complete freedom on the talent I'd selected, I'd get the hell off. In booking acts, I've never thought in terms of religion or color. I'm looking solely for fine performers who have something on the ball." Steve Allen commented in his book, "Talent is color blind."

As early as 1951, Sullivan wrote a piece in *Ebony* called "Can TV Crack America's Color Line?," in which he said, "We need to do nothing special for the Negro in television or in any other phase of American

It was definitely different for blacks watching the Sullivan show. Back in those days, it was a big event in the black community to see any blacks on television. When I was growing up in Youngstown, Ohio, among many working-class people, not everyone had a TV set in their house in the mid-1950s. TV came much later to Ohio. So I would go to a friend's house to watch the show, particularly if we knew any blacks were going to be on. We'd watch Ed Sullivan often, because he'd have people on you just didn't see elsewhere on TV, like Sarah Vaughan, Sammy Davis Jr., the Mills Brothers, Sam Cooke, Jackie Wilson, Nat King Cole. People like that we'd rush to see. I remember once, before we had a TV set, looking in a showroom window to watch a black performer on the Sullivan show. "American Bandstand," "The Nat King Cole Show," and "The Ed Sullivan Show" were the only shows I remember that really had blacks on, on any kind of a regular basis. It was noticeable. It was a date every Sunday in our house. It was an amazement, because blacks were invisible then on American TV, like Ralph Ellison's Invisible Man. There basically were no blacks on TV before 1955, when I was 12. We tended to listen to radio more. We'd listen to "The Shadow"—the closest thing to a black person on radio! The only other TV show with blacks was "Amos 'n' Andy," which came later, and we watched it with the same enthusiasm we had for "The Ed Sullivan Show."

Mel Watkins, Hamilton, New York

life. As I see it, the Negro neither wants nor needs special consideration but only the decent and full opportunity every other American merits and should enjoy." Ralph Bunche, the revered African American ambassador to the United Nations, proclaimed, "Ed Sullivan *lives* democracy."

Sullivan saw his showcasing of black artists in blunt civil-rights terms, commenting that only TV was able to take the black struggle for equality "into the living rooms of America's homes, where public opinion is formed." He felt that kids, especially, might be influenced by exposure to great black performers, saying it was the next generation "who will finally lay Jim Crow to rest." It might not have been totally a matter of his liberal sentiments, for Sullivan was utterly pragmatic when it came to the show: "Ed was about hits," Joel Selvin told me. Hits were their own justification. Hits trumped racism.

Sullivan and Steve Allen were ratings rivals but equal-opportunity hosts, as J. Fred MacDonald pointed out in his book *Black and White TV:* "Few personalities except Ed Sullivan and Steve Allen had the conviction and leverage necessary to withstand these pressures"—from nervous white sponsors (one of whom, Pillsbury, was accused by bigots of selling "nigger flour," whatever that meant). In 1959, Sullivan featured such artists as Eartha Kitt, Lionel Hampton, Dorothy Dandridge, Johnny Mathis, Della Reese, and the Platters. With the 1950s rise of rock and roll, it would have been foolhardy, indeed fatal, for any variety show's sponsors, however racist, to ignore black singers.

Harry Belafonte said he preferred to sing on Sullivan's show, where he made his TV debut in 1956, because of its record of booking black performers. In 1974, Belafonte remarked, "Ed doesn't worry about the [John] Birchers or the South." Belafonte, who had once been rejected by Pat Boone's sponsor, took TV to task for not taking Sullivan's lead: "Are any Negroes doing specials? Does any Negro have a series? And what about Negro TV writers? We're tired of being told 'Be patient,' 'Be good' and 'Wait.' You can't wait forever." For black artists on Ed Sullivan's show, there was no waiting.

Sullivan flinched from booking black entertainers only when they were said to have Communist connections. The word *Communist* was more lethal than all colors combined, severely testing the limits of the host's liberal instincts. Anything that threatened his show was avoided. Sullivan was enmeshed in the Red-scare terrorism of the 1950s and eager to display his all-American stripes to CBS's trembling hierarchy. The net-

work was terrified of being labeled friendly to anyone charged with tilting toward "red."

Jeff Kisseloff of the *New York Times*, writing about the era in 1999,
said that CBS was a more brutal enforcer of the blacklist than any other
network. CBS demanded that employees take loyalty oaths. Sullivan trumpeted in his column that he had fought the Commies he said were "trying
to take over AFTRA," the broadcasting union, adding for good measure,
"The Negro performers always voted solidly with me to defeat them."

Paul Robeson was a third rail for both blacks and lefties like African
American folksinger Leon Bibb. Bibb had been on Sullivan's show about
half a dozen times but, after 1965, was never invited back because he
had performed at a controversial Robeson rally. Sullivan, like most of
television, deserted Robeson, an avowed Communist and such a lightning rod that any performer glimpsed in his vicinity was blacklisted.
Liberal blacks were encouraged to denounce Robeson just to save their
own skins.

The far-right *New York Journal-American* tried to have Lena Horne
barred from the Sullivan show, until she had "made her peace" with
Counterattack by meeting with the anti-Red bulletin's editor, Theodore
Kirkpatrick. "She's been given a clean bill of health," happily announced
her manager, as if Horne had been pronounced cancer-free, and he promised, "She'll try to avoid groups even *called* subversive." Horne, Robeson's friend, was blacklisted, but later credited Sullivan for "helping get
me back on TV."

Suspect blacks like Horne, Bibb, and Belafonte were reviled, attacked,
and monitored constantly by Red-hunting vigilantes. Belafonte couldn't
be signed to star in the movie "Carmen Jones" until he had been
"cleared" by militant Red-baiters. The singer was fingered by a member
of the House Un-American Activities Committee after putting his fist
through a car window when Belafonte learned that the Supreme Court
had rejected an appeal by Julius and Ethel Rosenberg, the convicted Soviet spies. Some felt Belafonte had named names, which he hadn't, but
one night in a Harlem bar he was saved by Sidney Poitier from a guy
who came after him with a knife, thinking he had ratted on other blacks.
Said Belafonte, "He thought, how could I have possibly gotten on 'The
Ed Sullivan Show' unless I finked?"

Sullivan, who brought more black performers to '50s and '60s prime-
time TV than any other showman, soon began canceling performers
who had been scarred by Red-hunting conservative groups and listed in

broadcasting's blacklist house organ, *Red Channels,* which pledged to "purge" the industry of anything even remotely pink. The publication's cover logo showed a dark hand about to strangle a microphone.

Any mention in the little witch-hunting journal (subtitled "The Report of Communist Influence in Radio and Television") could wreck a 40-year career overnight—stars as well as journeymen radio and TV actors, like Philip Loeb. Loeb (the papa on "The Goldbergs"), despite his denial that he was a Communist ("I oppose Communism in all its forms and am heartily in sympathy with American principles," he told Jack Gould of the *New York Times* in 1952), was replaced after General Foods canceled the show's sponsorship until he left. If a sponsor decided a show was considered friendly to certain red-tinged artists, the star could be pushed off the air.

The most insidious part of the blacklist was that many, like Loeb, were never accused of anything except being a "controversial personality." Once his name appeared in *Red Channels* Loeb was swiftly unhired by a show on which he'd been a mainstay for many years. Gertrude Berg, creator and star of "The Goldbergs," backed Loeb until General Foods dropped the show, but finally, reluctantly, capitulated. She offered Loeb $85,000 to quit so the show could continue, but he told her, "I'm sorry, I have no price."

Loeb changed his mind after appealing to Actors Equity, and in 1952 settled with the network for two years' salary ($40,000); Equity put the show on its own "Unfair" list. The actor called the settlement "very good," but he stated, "I'm still blacklisted." After a few small acting jobs, Loeb checked into the Taft Hotel and committed suicide at 61. His story and the rancid McCarthy-era climate were detailed in "The Front," in which Woody Allen plays a front man for blacklisted screenwriters— one of whom, Walter Bernstein, wrote the script. Zero Mostel, himself blacklisted, plays a ruined comedian who kills himself by jumping out a hotel window (Loeb died of a sleeping pill overdose).

Bernstein, whose book *Inside Out* is a definitive look at this anguished period and his part in it as a blacklisted screenwriter, told me, "Sullivan was good for black performers. As for the blacklist, I don't know where he stood there. I don't believe he would have been allowed by the network to hire blacklisted people, no matter how powerful he was, and I don't know if he hired anyone under the table. His reputation was that of an anti-Communist, but that club was not an exclusive one." Of all the mass media, TV was the most "timorous," said TV archivist Thomas Doherty. Blacklisting in the radio-TV industry began in 1947 and lasted until 1954, when Joseph McCarthy was condemned by the Senate; but the equally notorious kangaroo court, the House Un-American Activities Committee, kept prying into people's pasts until the 1960s.

Sullivan went to the mat a few times, notably for dancer Paul Draper and jazz harmonica player Larry Adler, both besmirched in *Red Channels* as Communist sympathizers (and both of whom later fled to Europe to continue their careers). Sullivan caved in on Paul Robeson and others. In 1958, he canceled the appearance of Arthur Leif, conductor of the Moiseyev Dance Company, after Leif refused to say if he was a Communist before the House Un-American Activities Committee.

Some 151 performers were listed in *Red Channels,* many of whom had appeared on "The Ed Sullivan Show"—Horne, Judy Holiday, Burl Ives, Lee J. Cobb, Alfred Drake, Jack Gilford, a list that TV historian Eric Barnouw called "a roll of honor." To be cleared by *Red Channels,* you had to jump through several hoops, vowing your Americanism and proclaiming your loathing of all things crimson to self-appointed guardians of the American Way like Ted Kirkpatrick, one of the three former FBI agents who published *Counterattack.*

Sullivan tried to intercede on behalf of Draper and Adler, but in time—more for self-serving than political reasons—he "began to turn more and more to Kirkpatrick for guidance," according to Jerry Bowles. In a June 1950 column, Sullivan wrote, "Kirkpatrick has sat in my living room on several occasions and listened attentively to performers eager to secure a certification of loyalty. On some occasions, after interviewing them, he has given them the green light; on other occasions, he has told them, 'Veterans' organizations will insist on further proof.'" Old soldiers in VFW caps were now passing judgment on major artists' patriotism and theatrical viability. Sullivan walked a razor-thin line during that period, at one point insisting that *Counterattack* was doing "a magnificent American job." He was still busily protecting his own behind.

"One might ask why Sullivan allowed himself to be duped by Kirkpatrick," Bowles said, and theorizes that Sullivan was insecure about having not served in World War II and, to compensate, became "a fervent anti-Communist"—even though, as Bowles notes, Sullivan was the first to present many great acts from the Soviet Union. Larry Adler told Bowles, "Sullivan thought he was being extremely patriotic, I suppose," and the host had promised Adler he would book him if he named names.

"It was the difference between working and not working," said Adler. "But, for me, anyway, the price was just too high." Even so, noted the harmonica virtuoso, "I must say that Ed was not as vicious to me in his column as were Winchell and the Hearst columnists." On a visit to Stockholm, Sullivan and his wife went to see Adler and took him to dinner. "It was kind of courageous of him, being seen in public with a notorious 'Commie' like me. He told me that he thought I had had a raw deal."

The charitable Adler added, "I think he was under the influence of Bishop Sheen and Cardinal Spellman a lot during this period. He really, honestly, thought he was being a good American." Sullivan's own church turned up the heat. A 1952 letter from the Catholic War Veterans warned that Sullivan's position as a powerful Catholic TV producer was being exploited in order to, in effect, "clear" suspected Communist performers (such as Danny Kaye) by presenting them on his show.

Eric Barnouw said Sullivan's effort to book Draper was "to an extent a courageous act." Draper and Adler issued a statement declaring they were not Communists and swore their allegiance to the United States of America and the Constitution. It wasn't good enough for the anti-Red posse. But Sullivan booked Draper (who pointedly danced to "Yankee Doodle Dandy") despite attacks by conservative Hearstlings George Sokolsky, Jack O'Brian, and Westbrook Pegler, who demanded that the Ford Motor Company withdraw its sponsorship of "Toast of the Town."

After Draper's performance, 1,294 letters and telegrams of orchestrated protest came into CBS, forcing Sullivan to write William Lewis, president of the sponsor's ad agency (in a letter released to the press): "Dear Bill: I am deeply distressed to find out that some people were offended by [Draper's appearance] on the show. You know how bitterly opposed I am to Communism and all it stands for. You also know how strongly I would oppose having the program used as a political forum, directly or indirectly." He said the point of the show was to entertain, not offend, people, and that he was sorry if anyone took offense. "I just want 'Toast of the Town' to be the best show on television."

Sullivan, picking his words carefully, failed to defend Draper's appearance but made sure everyone knew he was in no way an accessory to the crime of giving an alleged Commie sympathizer a stage for his subversive dancing. Sullivan was doing his usual tap dance under fire, letting everyone know that, "hey, I just work here." Ed explained that he and "government agencies had made a thorough investigation to determine whether Draper is or was a Communist. Draper voted for [perennial Socialist presidential candidate Henry] Wallace, but that doesn't necessarily mean he's a Communist. I've been battling Communism vigorously right along, but it would be awful if we reached a state of mind where performers were not hired because of unsubstantiated rumor." By then (1958), that state of mind had long since spread across America.

Anti-Red guardians like Vincent Hartnett, Hester McCullough, and Laurence Johnson would personally call on advertising agencies and threaten negative publicity and boycotts. "The ploy was very successful," wrote Lewis J. Paper in an article on the era published in his book *Empire:* "Ed Sullivan, for one, refused to allow anyone on his show who had not won a silent vote of approval from Aware"—yet another gang of Red-busters.

Robin Morgan, who played the young daughter Dagmar on "Mama," the hugely popular 1950s TV version of "I Remember Mama," and who grew up to become editor of *Ms.* and a leading feminist writer, said in her memoir of the show and the period that Aware was really "a shrewd protection racket." Any actor, director, or writer listed in *Counterattack* as "unacceptable" or "uncleared," she noted, could buy his or her way to political acceptability for a onetime appearance fee of $7 "per clearance."

Morgan claims that sponsors like Borden's and Procter & Gamble kept their own blacklist of "obstreperous" actors. The beloved star of "Mama," Peggy Wood, was actively involved with Aware, and, at a 1965 reunion of the show's cast and crew, Wood attacked Morgan for daring to run for a union post in AFTRA, calling her an antiwar pro–civil rights "pinko." But at Wood's memorial, Morgan had the last word, remembering Mama as a fervent blacklister.

Bob Precht told me that, when he arrived at the show, "I experienced some of that. There were people in the late 1950s you just didn't use— Jerome Robbins was one," even though Robbins had named names. In 1950, Robbins was a fast-emerging ballet star and a Broadway and classical choreographer booked to appear on Sullivan's show on Easter Sunday, only a few months after Senator Joe McCarthy's infamous tirade against alleged Communists in the State Department. In her 2006 biography of Robbins, *Somewhere,* Amanda Vaill wrote that the dancer's agent, Howard Hoyt, got a call from Sullivan canceling the appearance. "We checked on Robbins," she quoted Sullivan telling Hoyt, "and we found out that the FBI has a long record on him"; Sullivan cited *Counterattack* as his source. "We must cancel him off our show." (In earlier testimony before the House Un-American Activities Committee, actor Larry Parks had named Robbins.)

The incident unmasks Sullivan as a Red-buster more intensely involved than indicated by previous accounts. Vaill wrote, "For Sullivan was at the very least a facilitator, if not an informant, for the FBI and the House Un-American Activities Committee in their efforts to enforce the blacklist in the entertainment world." Sullivan, eager to prove his patriotic colors, donned his witch-hunter's hat and, alleged Vaill, offered Robbins a deal: if the dancer met with him and disclosed the names of people who had attended a "cause party for Soviet-American friendship" at Robbins's apartment, hosted by Lena Horne, he would let Robbins concoct an excuse for canceling his appearance on Sullivan's show, ostensibly because music rights had not been cleared. James Gavin, author of a 2009 biography of Horne, said he doubted this party occurred, but Robert Silverman, Robbins's cousin, told Vaill there was such a party.

Vaill wrote, "Sullivan vowed to ruin his career by printing in his column the allegation that Robbins was both a Commie and a homosexual," which in 1950, as she pointed out, "could have landed him in jail on sodomy charges." He mostly feared being outed as gay. Vaill stated that Robbins, terrified his career hung in the balance, met with Sullivan, who "confronted Robbins with his party membership as well as a string of trivial accusations": his support of a left-wing legislator, his work for a world peace conference at the Waldorf Hotel, his part in a May Day parade. Robbins denied none of it but refused to give Sullivan any names—names, she said, he "would surely have printed in his column."

Sullivan then suggested Robbins explain it all to Counterattack's Kirkpatrick, who asked Robbins for a signed statement "all about his Communist activities—names, dates, everything." Vaill said Kirkpatrick warned him that, if the Russians dropped an atom bomb anywhere, "Robbins would be one of the first people the G-men would round up for questioning." Such was the manic mood of the moment.

Donning the robes of fierce anti-Communist agitator, Sullivan went after Robbins in a column that ran on March 24, 1951, in the Philadelphia Inquirer—but not, interestingly, in his own Daily News. Robbins's lawyer, stated Vaill, managed to keep his name out of the New York newspapers, but it appeared elsewhere in syndicated versions.

Under a Philadelphia Inquirer headline reading "Tip to Red Probers: Subpena [sic] Jerome Robbins," Sullivan wrote, "I accuse. I'd suggest that the House Un-American Activities Committee subpena [sic] ballet star and choreographer Jerome Robbins. . . . In my office not long ago, Robbins revealed that he had been a card-member of the Communist Party. . . . Robbins can give the Committee backstage glimpses of the musical shows which have been jammed with performers sympathetic to the Commie cause. . . . He has a wide familiarity with Commies of all hues. In accusing him, I also call upon him as an American to aid the Government in identifying conspirators who hide behind the music racks, ballet bars and musical comedy billing." Pretty nasty stuff—a major low point in Sullivan's career and character. Robbins's indictment was handed down just days before "The King and I," choreographed by Robbins, opened on Broadway.

For three years, Vaill said, Sullivan and the FBI pressured Robbins to testify, but he resisted until, playwright Arthur Laurents related, "he panicked. He wanted to be in the movies." To clear his name, in a brief, hour-long grilling by the House Un-American Activities Committee he named eight people, among them Zero Mostel and Laurents, as Vaill noted in a March 2009 documentary that aired on PBS. None of it made a dent in Robbins's later career, though it scarred him for life, but the incident clearly sullies Ed Sullivan.

Now officially cleared, if scorned by the colleagues he outed and by much of the liberal theatrical establishment, Robbins, along with his company, Ballets: U.S.A.—after a triumphal tour of Europe and the Soviet Union—in 1958 was invited by Sullivan to appear twice on the show. The host proudly declared to viewers how the company had "conquered the world and [had done] so much good for America with all typical American kids dancing." Thanks in part to Ed Sullivan, America was now safe from any Communist-tinged, left-leaning dancers.

The Red scare was over by 1963, but a lingering antileft scent was in the air. In 1963, CBS censored a song that 21-year-old Bob Dylan planned to sing on Sullivan's show. In "The Talking John Birch Society Blues," a satirical ditty ridiculing the virulent anti-Communist group, Birchers are depicted searching all over for Reds, even in the refrigerator, until the Reds are finally nabbed by a mailman.

Sullivan was "puzzled" as to why CBS forbade the number, because the John Birch Society had become a handy punch line for comedians. Dylan departed after the dress rehearsal when a CBS censor nixed his song. "So I just left," he said. He refused to sing something else. Sullivan suggested a Tommy Makem tune, probably assuming Dylan was Irish. Dylan took a long walk that ended his Sullivan-show career. He filed no grievances, but news of his refusal to bend only enhanced his rebel reputation. "We fought for the song," Sullivan told a *New York Post* TV critic. "We pointed out that President Kennedy and his family [are] kidded constantly by TV comedians, Governor Rockefeller is also kidded, among others. But I said I couldn't understand why they were being given such protection. But the network turned us down." The Dylan incident foreshadowed CBS's canceling of the Smothers Brothers in 1969, when their political satire got a bit too bare-knuckled for the network.

In 1963, Lee Grant, Jack Gilford, and Pete Seeger were still "unhireable" on CBS, according to Robin Morgan. The network's program practices department, she claimed, told writer Ernest Kinoy to switch the topic of his script about TV blacklisting to the movie industry. Morgan contended that CBS denied there had ever been a significant TV blacklist.

Orson Bean is one of many who can dispute that. Bean was blacklisted for, he said, having a Communist girlfriend and for being active in union politics. "Just after a union election," he recalled, "I was booked for another appearance on the Sullivan show, and Ed himself called me up and said, 'I got some bad news for you. Have you seen the latest issue of *Counterattack?* You're in it, and I'm afraid the booking for next Sunday is out—as a matter of fact, I won't be able to use you at all again.' I could feel the blood draining out of my face. He said, 'I'll help you when I can.'"

Bean reflected later, "I don't blame him. He sensed that there were maybe some people in the business who were dangerous. I certainly was not one of them. He clearly saw I'd been swept up along with a brush that swept a lot of people up." Bean had played the show six times when his career came to a screeching halt. "I went from being the hot young comic at CBS to being persona non grata. Fortunately I got a Broadway show, 'Will Success Spoil Rock Hunter?,' which ran for a year. Broadway was never affected by the blacklist; most Broadway customers don't give a shit about anybody's politics. There were no sponsors on Broadway. There were a few TV shows I could still go on that didn't have sponsors. Burl Ives had a show; Ives himself was blacklisted."

Bean added, "Almost a year to the day after he'd called, Ed called me back and said, 'I think the pressure is off enough that I can book you again.' And he did. He caved in, but he was calling me back, keeping his word. I'd pretty much given up on being a stand-up comic at that point. People made fun of Sullivan, but he had a basic decency about him."

PART IV

Rescued by Rock 'n' Roll

CHAPTER 20

The Son-in-Law Also Rises

[Bob] Precht was young, ambitious, and—by most accounts—
nearly as cold-blooded as Sullivan himself.

Jerry Bowles, biographer

"The Ed Sullivan Show" splits neatly into two distinct eras, Before Precht
(1948–1959) and After Precht (1960–1971), when Sullivan's new son-in-
law, Robert Precht, replaced the show's departing cofounder and coproducer, Marlo Lewis. After Precht, the show took on a decidedly more
contemporary flavor: more rock and roll, edgier comedians, less opera and
dance, and far fewer of the old-time vaudevillians that Sullivan and his
original, but now late-middle-aged, audience so cherished.

Although Precht brought a younger sensibility with him, Sullivan still
ran the show and followed his own increasingly encrusted instincts. It
took Precht a few years to gain both Ed's and the staff's confidence, but he
slowly became the show's chief mover and shaker. Some who were there
at the show's creation, the Lewis loyalists, both resented and dismissed
Precht—not just because he was relatively untested on prime-time TV,
with little of the showbiz savvy (or available charm) of Marlo Lewis, but
also because he was the boss's son-in-law. It was a classic situation ripe for
disaster. To Precht's credit, however, he didn't instigate a palace coup and,
to Lewis's even greater credit, the takeover was relatively bloodless. Sullivan's daughter, Betty, recalled the transition: "One day Marlo came in and
said to my father that he had just had enough and he'd really like to move
on. My husband was sort of waiting in the wings."

Lewis exited quietly and buried any bitter feelings. In his memoir, he
seemingly shifted easily from the Sullivan show to other triumphs—
creating or producing shows with Phil Silvers, Red Skelton, Jackie

Gleason, Dinah Shore, Red Buttons, and Perry Como—with nary a whimper during what must have been a partly painful departure. Lewis always claimed he was ready to leave, burned out and weary of the tension and headaches, the haggles with Sullivan over booking rock acts, and dealing with recalcitrant performers, agents, and managers. Lewis wrote, "It seemed that we had moved into a grinding routine, a strict presentation of vaudeville acts and a pandering to the nation's preoccupation with youth culture."

Rumors about why Lewis left were rampant: he had a terminal illness; he and Ed had had a terminal quarrel; he'd accepted an irresistible offer from another network; he'd made millions in the stock market. "The truth—that I was tired after 12 years of a marathon run and wanted to work at my own pace, away from network pressures—was just too simple to be considered. I was a lunatic. I was working seven days a week. It was mad. Exciting. Inventive. But too much. I had seen a $400-a-week experimental show called 'Toast of the Town' grow into a $14 million-a-year bonanza. I had watched an infant industry become a giant. The whole thing had been a 'Reeeely Big Shew!' But I was not sorry to ring down the curtain." After its golden age, TV was no longer run by instinctive showmen like Sullivan and Lewis but by market researchers, Nielsen surveys, focus groups, accountants, and guys with MBAs who had no gut instincts for raw talent.

While everyone seems to have loved and respected Marlo Lewis, Bob Precht was viewed as everything from a sharp, driven but decent young guy to a brutal, calculating usurper. Lewis is described as a likable, cultured, classy, easygoing fellow whom everyone was sorry to see go. As singer Carol Lawrence told me, "He was very charming, sociable, friendly. You felt if you had a problem you could go to Marlo and he would fix it." Precht was a 20-something navy veteran out of the University of California, a lanky, blonde San Diego boy who had worked five years in TV on daytime shows ("Winky Dink and You," "The Verdict Is Yours") before learning the ropes alongside Lewis, his mentor. His actual plan was to get into TV news. Precht's tanned, surfer-dude look made him seem automatically suspect to the show's pale New York–centrics.

Precht was smart and sensitive enough, however, not to make any sweeping changes or bold declarations at first, easing himself into Lewis's large, comfy shoes. He joined the show in 1956 as a production assistant. It soon became clear that, if Precht was ready to assume more responsibility, something, or some*one*, had to change. "I'm not sure I forced Marlo out," Precht told author Jerry Bowles, "although I obviously felt I was ready for the job. When you're 29 you think you can do anything. I got along well with Marlo; he helped me a great deal. There might have been some bad feeling between Ed and Marlo over the change, but I was not directly involved in it." (The Lewises and the Sullivans "never had a social connection or had dinner together," Precht told me.)

Monica Lewis asserted that her brother wasn't eased out because of Precht. "No, no, no. He trained Precht. There was no animosity or jealousy. Marlo just wanted to get the hell out of there." Precht "did a nice job," she told me. "Marlo thought he'd be totally adequate, because by then the show ran itself. Marlo's techniques were incorporated into a huge staff. Precht kept the people Marlo had hired. They all knew what they were doing."

But Precht, now retired in Missoula, Montana, with his wife, has his ardent fans. Jerry Vale remarked to me, "Bob Precht was a great guy, a sweet man. He was very nice to me. He was very fair." Dick Cavett told me he liked him—"very nice fellow, which is probably most people's reaction to him." He later worked with Precht on an ABC summer show. John Moffitt, who, like Vince Calandra, owes his early career to Precht, told me, "Bob was charming, couldn't be nicer. Bob pushed me ahead of so many people waiting in line at CBS [to direct]." Moffitt was only in his 30s. "I was scared to death, but he did that for me. That's not all he did for me."

Peter Calabrese, the show's weekend gofer and cue card man, commented to me about Precht: "I liked Bob, but he had to deal with Ed, and sometimes that was difficult. Bob wasn't a bad guy, and everyone understood he was just passing things on [from Ed]. Ed usually talked to Bob and his secretary, and everything got disseminated from there. While Bob could still be one of the guys, and we could say things in front of Bob about Ed—he was in on the joke—he was also Ed's son-in-law. He was a really good producer who took the job very seriously. He was a total pro. When he had to be tough, he'd be tough."

Roberta Peters, the opera singer, a Scarsdale, New York, neighbor of Marlo and Mina Bess Lewis ("We were really good friends," she told me. "They lived around the block from us, and our children socialized"), wasn't fond of Sullivan and felt he had betrayed Lewis at the end. "There was friction when Ed brought his son-in-law in." Peters's husband, Bertram Fields, chimed in, "There was family pressure on Sullivan to let Bob take over the show. He had no qualifications for it.

It was a deliberate slight to Marlo." When Peters and Fields visited the Lewises' home in Palm Springs, Peters said, "Ed Sullivan was almost an obsession. They constantly talked about him—what he did to Marlo and how Marlo was so much better than Precht." She said of Precht, "I found him very cold—businesslike." "Impersonal," added Fields. Sherwin Bash, conductor Ray Bloch's son-in-law, called Precht "the son-in-law from hell" and worse. "He just wasn't a pleasant guy. We lived a few blocks apart in Beverly Hills."

One of the show's pioneers, director John Wray, was no fan of Precht, who fired Wray in 1961 and hired 34-year-old Tim Kiley to replace him (Sullivan made sure Precht canned Wray when Wray was out of town). Wray told Jerry Bowles, "Precht and I did not get along at all. He was willful, irresponsible, and given to violent rages. Bob Precht was strictly from amateur night. He would have been lucky to get a job in the mail room if he hadn't been the boss's son-in-law."

Bowles wrote, "Tempers were frequently short in those days, and Precht clashed often with old-timers. He was careful not to antagonize Sullivan directly." Had he, says an aide, "Ed would have chewed him up and spit him out." Rip Taylor, the comedian, remarked to me that Precht was "tough, tough, tough. Sullivan just did everything he was told to do; he read the cue cards. You'd go in and rehearse with Precht. You didn't see Sullivan until the show itself. He never hung out with the acts."

James Maguire wrote that Precht "would not be the minor tyrant Ed could be, and not prone to Ed's competitive rages, yet he could be headstrong." Precht told me, "If I was to do that job, I didn't just want to take orders and put the cameras out." Julia Meade, the show's Lincoln spokeswoman, explained to me, "Bob was kind of a tough guy, but Ed liked him a lot. Marlo was a very social guy, a lot looser. Bob was much more serious, but Bob moved into a spot that was tough." Precht said, "Whatever changes or tweaks I made, I went about with some delicacy, and it wasn't always easy." Sullivan once noted that, besides doing his job, Precht "has to labor under the burden of being my son-in-law."

Bowles noted that, when Lewis left, "the show Precht inherited had become an antique," and that Precht refreshed and refurbished it. He gave the show a modern look, used more sets so most acts no longer performed in front of a plain curtain—the way older viewers still remember the show. Designer Bob Bohnert remarked to me that when he told people he designed sets for the Ed Sullivan show, they would always reply, "Does it have sets?"

Bohnert was responsible for recreating the Broadway and opera scenery and giving the show a more "mod" 1960s look. Bohnert recalled, "Ed would book an act at the last minute simply because they happened to be in the news, and we would have to create a set overnight. It was like working in a state of permanent controlled crisis. Your adrenaline was flowing all the time." His most famous set was for the Beatles debut show, but his first design was rejected—a black backdrop with "BEATLES" cut out for colored lights to shine through a scrim. Sullivan rudely nixed it in front of everyone. Bohnert's next idea—a semicircle of large carved arrows aimed at the singers, as if to say: the Beatles are right *here*, on "The Ed Sullivan Show"—became his best remembered design.

Whether Lewis was nudged or jumped is hard to say—maybe a bit of each. Friends advised him to leave, while Sullivan cronies whispered to Ed that Lewis was highly dispensable. After the show became a CBS centerpiece, Sullivan was wooed by NBC's Pat Weaver. Jack Van Volkenburg—the same hard-nosed guy who, early on, had offered "Toast of the Town" to sponsors "with or without Sullivan"—now took the star aside and, Iago-like, tried to convince him he didn't need Marlo. In his book, Lewis quoted a network lawyer as saying, "What is Sullivan? Just an inept emcee."

Precht told me that the division of labor between himself and Sullivan became their big issue. "A continuing bone of contention for a long time was the booking. It was a conflict between us because that was Ed's domain. It was hard for him to give that up. The agents and managers always had direct access to Ed, and now they had to go to his son-in-law. That was a pain for them. It never worked out completely to my satisfaction."

He explained, "The booking at that time was done totally out of his office. I wanted to be part of that. It's one of the things I lobbied for and eventually got—but it didn't happen overnight. I felt that the guts of the show was certainly the content, and that had to do with booking. It was something I cared about. I wanted to be part of the process of who was booked. Ed was used to doing it all himself and didn't want to be interfered with. It was an ongoing, almost daily thing. It was a turf war, if you will. Ed felt that booking was *his* thing."

Precht once said, "I just felt that if I was going to be the producer, then I wanted to have the job as well as the title. I felt some of the bookings were detrimental to the show. I mean, how do you use Jack Carter six times in a season? Ed finally agreed, and he was pretty gracious about it." Precht learned how to manipulate Sullivan into agreeing with him, wrote Bowles, and finally told Sullivan that he didn't want to be just a coproducer, like Lewis, but the sole producer—in a subtle sense, nudging Sullivan aside.

"Generally, we worked pretty well together," said Precht, choosing his words diplomatically. "We consulted constantly." (He worked out of CBS's West 57th Street office, Ed out of his home and office on East 59th Street.) "I had been in the military, so I knew that he was my commanding officer. I was chief executive officer and he was the captain. I didn't screw with that. I knew how to manage that setup. But we did have occasional differences of opinion on things. He was tough; he was opinionated."

Sullivan and his son-in-law struck a workable détente. Precht described Sullivan as "a complicated, interesting, certainly ambitious guy. But I was an ambitious guy myself, and I wanted to establish myself. I didn't want to be the son-in-law flunky." He said, reflecting on it all, that his TV career was almost an accident. "I never felt I was cut out for the entertainment world. I always looked back on 'The Ed Sullivan Show' and my whole time in TV as [that of] a navy guy who got lucky."

Precht had no tricks for dealing with Sullivan, but commented, "The good thing about the relationship, and deep down the reason he trusted me, was he knew I'd never do anything to hurt him. I'd never undermine him. I was there to support him. We read each other pretty well. Sure, we had differences, but if we had differences we tried to talk it out together. And of course we shared his daughter—that was an unspoken bond." If Precht didn't share Sullivan's enthusiasms, Precht would hear about it. "We lived in Scarsdale, and one time, for whatever reason, I didn't go to the Supremes' opening at the Copa. Ed called me: 'Why weren't you at the opening?' Well, we had somewhere else to go. But he was angry I hadn't jumped on the Supremes as he thought I should have."

Designer Bob Markell, like most of the staff, was shocked when Lewis left and Precht entered. "Everyone was surprised that a guy with this much inexperience took over," he explained. "Marlo was very positive, and he encouraged creativity. He knew pretty much what Sullivan liked, so he wouldn't let you go down the wrong track. He was a wonderful producer, very special, very easygoing. He made it all easy. It was just a very nice atmosphere." Connie Francis recounted an early appearance on the show, when one of the trumpet players at rehearsal moaned, " 'Oh, this fucking song!' Well, I started to cry. I had never heard anyone use that word before; I was just 20 and very, very sheltered. I told Marlo, 'I'm not coming back,' " so Lewis asked the musician to apologize to her.

Francis says of the chaotic Lewis era, "There was more tension" than on other shows "because there was less preparation. If you were doing the Perry Como show, you would come in at least a day before, do an orchestra run-through, do a camera run-through. And finally do the show. With Sullivan, you'd get up in the morning, have lunch, then you're in front of an audience. That's just the way Ed liked it. How he managed to put that show together in one day is a miracle—people flying in from all over the place to do the show." The dancer Marge Champion found playing the Sullivan show much easier than other shows: "In shows like Dinah Shore, or Perry Como," she said, "you rehearsed for a week with Dinah and the other guests, and it was all integrated. But Ed's was much more a variety show you might have picked up at the Palace or some place like that. It wasn't a problem for performers if you're doing all the numbers you've done before."

Precht is credited with and blamed for pushing Sullivan to entice teenage viewers with hot rock bands—maybe not the calculated demographic move it seemed. Monica Lewis told me, "That was the world then. *Demographics* wasn't even a word in those days. Big bands were gone, and the little, individual artist singing in a beautiful nightclub was gone, and all of those god-awful folksingers strumming guitars on street corners and singing protest songs. That happened with the Beatles much later and [with] heavy metal rock. You had better go that way, because that's what was happening. It had nothing to do with choice. It was the world changing. Rock would have happened, no matter what—unfortunately."

Precht agreed, saying, "We just followed what was happening. We followed the music charts, and the comics playing in the Village—that was our food and [what] kept us going." Sullivan went along. "He didn't fight it. Sometimes he didn't relate to it. We stayed with what was happening. If an act was big enough to play the Copacabana, we nailed 'em."

Calandra noted in his interview for the Archive of American Television, "Precht changed the look of the show drastically—he ran a tighter ship. We started doing Saturday rehearsals. Before that, the show was really thrown together on Sunday. Bob had more of a game plan. He brought in satire and rock and roll. The show became more controlled, more produced." Precht explained, "It had always been so rushed. This gave us more time for rehearsal. We were more ready for the Sunday dress rehearsal show. I felt the show required some freshening up."

But he never tried to clean up Ed's rambling, garbled introductions, mispronunciations, non sequiturs, and snarled syntax. "No way. That was him. He wrote it, read it off the cue cards, and if he garbled it he garbled it. That's part of why people liked him." He added, "I think the malaprops have been overblown." Precht changed the rhythm of the show by having Sullivan interact more with performers. Ed conceded, "I had been putting too much emphasis on getting acts on and off quickly. I decided to go for more talk, for a more human relationship between me and each act." He began chatting up more performers after they finished their act.

John Moffitt moved up from his position as lowly production assistant to that of director thanks to Precht, working from 1962 through the final show in 1971. "When I came on the show, it was on 52 weeks a year. Until the very end, it was never preempted. The joke was that the only one who could take vacations was Ed, because if you took a vacation and came back, you'd have been replaced" (as director John Wray was). Despite the built-in backstage shuffle, Moffitt explained, "in our business, a lot of people are really pricks and bitches and awful, unsavory people, but there was not a lot of that on the show. It's a different era now than it was then. There was more decency."

In the mid-1960s, when the show had a virtual monopoly in its time slot, Precht began experimenting with visual razzamatazz—pretaped semipsychedelic mirror effects, and "electronic ballets," like a floating space station for the Fifth Dimension's "Going into the Sun." Sullivan was confused by the mix of live and tape, said Moffitt. "In dress rehearsal, Ed would introduce the act live and then say, 'Where the hell are they?' Bob had to explain we'd already taped them. He didn't quite get it. He didn't understand videotape. So what we decided to do was, in order for Ed to see something, we'd have the act come out onstage and lip-synch the song while the audience watched the tape. Because he couldn't quite figure out where the act *was* if it was on tape. They were taped live but they faked it so Ed would think they were there."

Moffitt recalled, "The other thing was the red light." If Sullivan often looked like a stranger on his own show, it's because he was never sure where to look. Moffitt explained, "When Bob Precht took over, he said, 'Ed, whenever we come back from a commercial you're looking over to the right. What are you looking for?' 'I'm looking at the monitor to know I'm on,' Ed said. Bob told him, 'Ed, just look at the red light on the camera! When that goes on, you're on!' Ed: 'Oh, that's wonderful. Oh, that's fine, that's great, Bob.' Guess what? The next week: same thing. Ed's looking over the other way. Ed could *not* get the idea of the red light." To train Sullivan to look in the right place, a small TV set was hung below the camera, and a teleprompter above it. Once Ed could actually see himself on TV, he knew he was on and where to look. "He got that," said Precht. It helped keep his eyes from wandering around the stage, as if searching for the nearest escape.

In 1964, to spice up the show and make it more relevant, Precht talked Sullivan into injecting political satire into the mix under the umbrella title "What's Going on Here?," a segment directed by Jonathan Miller of the comedy revue "Beyond the Fringe." But topical satire was wildly at odds with the show's traditional vaudeville flavor—and with a Sullivan audience who wasn't sure what was going on there.

Just about that time, the sassy satirical revue "That Was the Week That Was" (inspired by the British original) made a splash on NBC. Precht replied by booking new satirical troupes from England, "Beyond the Fringe" and "The Establishment," as well as America's own sudden surge of satirists—Mort Sahl, Bob Newhart, Nichols & May, Dick Gregory. On one show, Bob Elliott and Ray Goulding parodied TV newscasts ("Sports item: Alabama has moved ahead of Mississippi in the race race, with more arrests to come . . ."), Godfrey Cambridge did a racial bit, and two British satirists performed a double-talk sketch parodying a John Kennedy press conference. Sullivan unwittingly sabotaged the bit by announcing beforehand that the White House had provided the press conference tape, as if to let viewers know it was not unpatriotic to laugh.

"I was really into [satirical comedy]," said Precht, "and I persuaded Ed we should have it on periodically and do sketches. It was a little cutting-edge for our audience, so we had to drop it." Adding Bob & Ray to Sullivan's show was like Tom Lehrer doing a guest shot with Lawrence Welk. Lehrer was once considered for Sullivan's show. "When I was at the Blue Angel," he told me, "the people from 'The Ed Sullivan Show' came in, and they said, 'Oh, we really love your act. If you ever have anything we can use, let us know.' I think that summed it up."

In TV's predawn, pre–Jon Stewart/Stephen Colbert/Dennis Miller/Bill Maher mid-1960s, American viewers were not ready for prime-time topical satire. Still a few years away was "The Smothers Brothers Comedy Hour" (1967), "Laugh-In" (1968), and "Saturday Night Live" (1975). Satire may be what closes on Saturday night, as George S. Kaufman famously declared, but at CBS it closed with a bang on Sunday night.

Sullivan's natural twitchiness, his travel urge, convinced him to bring his showbiz gospel to entertainment-deprived nations—a major change in the show's second life under Precht. America had been conquered, but there were many lands for Sullivan yet to invade. The restless host was always searching for ways to expand his domain, to become impresario to the world. He wanted not just to exploit American culture but to export it.

By 1957, the world was his onstage oyster. When it became routine for him to book the world's greatest you-name-it from Tokyo or Tasmania, he became a traveling road company—first taking a version of the show to the Brussels World's Fair in 1958, and then to Las Vegas, against the wishes of the Ford Motor Company's advertising agency and CBS's cautious Frank Stanton, who frowned on the idea. Sullivan went anyway.

Most of the acts on his show played Vegas, he reasoned, so why not him? Las Vegas enticed Sullivan to lend his all-American endorsement to Sin City, which even then was out to attract plain folks and shed its image as a sandbox for divorcees, gangsters, gamblers, hookers, and boozers. Sullivan played the Desert Inn with a G-rated extravaganza—Esther Williams, Carol Burnett, and the Kirby Stone Four. On the television show, Ed also began running home movies of his travels as showbiz ambassador to Hong Kong, Istanbul, Hawaii, and Alaska.

Writer Atra Báer said Sullivan hoped to be "the Lowell Thomas of show business"—the intrepid showman as foreign correspondent. To forge a bridge to the CBS news department, he even tried to involve Edward R. Murrow, who quickly turned down an opportunity to become one of Ed's performing seals. Sullivan planned a series of travelogues for CBS, to be called "Sullivan's Travels," in which he would not only display the splendor of Vienna, Rio, and West Germany but also deliver in-depth reports and commentary from world capitals—sans comics, crooners, and chimps.

When CBS told him to forget it, Sullivan pouted and whined to Marlo Lewis, "Why the hell not? I've had 30 years' experience as a reporter. When it involves the news they won't call me. But when they hold their drunken station-owner conventions and want to look impressive, they call on me to put on a show." Again like archrival Walter Winchell, Ed saw himself as a journalist first, entertainer second, and yearned to use both professions to strut upon a global stage—host to the world!

To prove to CBS that he was a crack reporter, not just a producer and emcee, Ed booked his most unusual novelty act—Fidel Castro, a literal headliner. Sullivan figured that by snagging Castro for his first American TV interview he would force CBS to recognize him not just as a TV host but as a hustling correspondent. In the middle of the Cuban revolution, Sullivan plotted to scoop his own network and, on the sly, hired a CBS cameraman to round up a crew to accompany him to the Dominican Republic to talk to Rafael Trujillo—Sullivan's sham cover story.

Castro was frothing at the opportunity to speak directly to the American people on a major show that was not a newscast. Sullivan came home with an hour-long scoop he was sure would convince CBS News to let him become a roving reporter, covering major stories and shedding his image as mere carnival barker. But CBS News scooped him, if only by a few hours. It broadcast an interview with Castro on "Face the Nation" that same day. Sullivan edited his hour-long session with the Cuban dictator down to a six-minute act and dropped it into the show alongside Alan King, Tina Louise, the Little Gaelic Singers of Ireland, and Professor Backwards.

In 1961, furiously determined to be a roving reporter, Sullivan began a "See America with Ed Sullivan" series, saluting one city a month. He saluted Chicago and San Francisco before ditching the plan as too costly and too taxing on the staff. After his trip to Moscow, in 1959, he scheduled trips to Brazil and Argentina ("I think it would be a fine goodwill gesture"). One feature story called him "Television's Marco Polo." After his ulcer was removed, he was more relaxed traveling overseas, able to eat what he liked.

In 1958, deep into one of his sour nobody-appreciates-me funks, and responding to a speech to the Radio-TV Directors Association by Murrow (who suggested that Sullivan give up a Sunday night show and devote the hour to "a clinical survey of the state of American education"), Sullivan groused to *TV Guide*, "*Enlightened* TV! Doesn't Ed Murrow ever look at our show? Don't *any* of these people ever look at our show?" He offered the Moiseyev Dance Company as just one of his triumphal culture-to-the-people crusades. "And what about our Maurice Chevalier and Sophie Tucker show, and our Wayne and Shuster shows? Wasn't that 'enlightened' television?"

Now steaming, Sullivan bubbled over: "These people should know that we invented practically everything that is on TV today. Enlightened television? On our very first show, we flew Eugene List, the pianist, in from Potsdam. . . . Opera? Who gave them the Met, but I never got any kind of support from the critics. Ballet? The American Ballet Theater, the Ballet Russe. . . . Shakespeare? We brought them 'The Tempest' and 'Julius Caesar' from the festival in Stratford, Connecticut."

He next cited all the Broadway shows he'd featured and the Castro interview. "I'm tired of these guys crying about the lack of public service. If we haven't been giving them public service TV on 'The Ed Sullivan

Show,' I'd like to know what you'd call it." In his harangue, he didn't mention his show telecast from the Brussels World's Fair, with the Ukrainian State Dance Group, a Jacques Tati pantomime, and the London Symphony Orchestra playing a "Lohengrin" prelude.

The next year, Sullivan went head-to-head with cultural czar Sol Hurok when he took the show to the Soviet Union. Challenging Hurok's pedigree—in importing European artists to the United States—Sullivan delivered as many Russian dancers as he could scrape up, along with American performers. He told Muscovites, "Thank you and good evening. My name is Edward Petrovitch Sullivan"), and rolled out a platoon of only-in-America talent: the Barry Sisters, accordionist Dick Contino, a modern dance by Nora Kaye, a Hawaiian tenor, Risë Stevens, Marge and Gower Champion, a black tap dancer, and a harmonica player serenading the crowd with "Moscow Nights."

The extravaganza, which didn't end until midnight, "was the first time Russians had ever seen an American variety show," gushed an embedded *McCall's* reporter. The natives were both awed and bewildered. "There was much they didn't understand about the show and why it was the way it was." Many were disappointed that Sullivan hadn't brought along three adopted Soviet musical heroes: Louis Armstrong, Ella Fitzgerald, and Bing Crosby.

Until Sullivan wrote an effectively angry protest to Premier Khrushchev, his show nearly didn't get telecast. Government officials had unreeled miles of red tape, threatening to kill the show on delivery. But compared to a mutinous tiger, TV critics, and union bosses like James Petrillo, Nikita Khrushchev proved to be a pushover.

It was an impressive coup, all right, but nothing compared with what would take place on Sullivan's stage the following February 9, 1964.

CHAPTER 21

"And Now—the Beatles!"

America is at our feet.
Brian Epstein, Beatles' manager

If people remember nothing else about "The Ed Sullivan Show," they vividly recall seeing the Beatles—even if many eyewitnesses weren't born yet. The Beatlecasts are such deeply entrenched landmark moments in the nation's psyche that revisiting them is like watching replays of the Kennedy assassination or Bobby Thomson's 1951 home run.

When you go back and retrace the events that led up to the night of February 9, 1964, the show behind Sullivan's first Beatles show reveals more than the old tapes themselves, which continue to be replayed ad infinitum in documentaries, movies, and pop tributes tracing a by now well-trampled path through the mid-1960s. Less well traveled are the back roads that ended with the Beatles' worldwide detonation on "The Ed Sullivan Show."

A fond legend that many Americans still believe is that Ed Sullivan discovered the Beatles and made them a hit. In fact, Sullivan played a vital but almost peripheral part in the phenomenon on which his own legend now happily rests. Sullivan, crucial cog though he was, is something of an innocent bystander in the ultimate event. Other names were equally, if not more, important in bringing the Beatles to his attention and to America.

Sullivan still gets most of the credit, but by the time he got involved, the Beatles' eruption on his show was a fait accompli. It was so minutely organized that it would have been impossible for the Beatles *not* to explode on the Sullivan show, thanks to the work of footnote names like producer Sid Bernstein, talent scouts Jack Babb and Peter Prichard, fan Marsha Albert, DJ Carroll James, and an anonymous British Overseas Airline stewardess—each one hugely instrumental in making it all happen the way it did.

By the time the Beatles landed at John F. Kennedy International Airport on February 7, 1964, they were famous in England and across most of Europe (only Belgium was strangely immune). For weeks leading up to their arrival in America, radio stations had been pushing their songs; Beatles singles and albums had already sold millions of copies. The stately "CBS Evening News" had even reported their maniacal following abroad, and news producer Reuven Frank noted in his memoir that NBC's valuable London man Eliot Frankel "was sending us material on the Beatles long before they were recognizable names in the United States; we did a long report on them before their more famous appearance on 'The Ed Sullivan Show.' "

Chet Huntley somberly told viewers of NBC's "Huntley-Brinkley Report" that the newscast had no choice but to cover the event: "Like a good little news organization," he said, in his dour deadpan, "we sent three cameramen out to Kennedy this afternoon to cover the arrival of a group from England, known as the Beatles. However, after surveying the film our men returned with, and the subject of that film, I feel there is absolutely no need to show any of that film." Good night, Chet. And hello, John, Paul, George, and Ringo. Other TV newscasts chronicled their voyage and their touchdown in New York. Local DJs urged listeners to greet the Beatles at the airport, joining a gaggle of 200 gaga newspaper, radio, and TV news people who recognized a big story.

The sound and the fury were orchestrated and micromanaged by a massive $50,000 financial campaign and a ruthless promotional push by Capitol Records. The aim was to Beatleize America and create a virus called "Beatlemania" before the group landed. Their official coronation would occur on "The Ed Sullivan Show."

The marketing mogul behind the coup was Sir Lew Grade (dubbed "Sir Low Grade" for his series of B movies). He bought what amounted to the Beatles' immediate future when their manager-guru, Brian Epstein, sold 80 percent of the Beatles' music publishing company, Northern Songs, after the Beatles produced four hits in England in 1963. The tunes made them a national brand, soon to be a national treasure and global economic export, surpassing anything like them in Great Britain since Gilbert & Sullivan. Grade's purchase instantly captured the limited attention of Capitol honchos, who had previously turned down Epstein and his four lads without a flicker.

In *The Beatles Are Coming,* Beatles expert Bruce Spizer quoted Alan Livingston, one of the Capitol executives who rejected the Beatles three times: "I'm sitting in my office one day, and I got a call from London from a man named Brian Epstein, who I didn't know. And he said, 'I am the personal manager of the Beatles, and I don't understand why you won't release them.' And I said, 'Well, frankly, Mr. Epstein, I haven't heard them.' And he said, 'Would you please listen and call me back.' " Livingston's wife, Nancy, told him, after listening to "I Want to Hold Your Hand": "A very nice title. But the way they sang! I want to hold your *ha-a-a-a-a-a-a-and!*' I said, 'Alan, that's the worst thing I've ever heard.' "

Pop critic Joel Selvin filled in some blanks: "So Grade buys this publishing company, and now major corporations have a vested interest in the Beatles' success in America," he told me. "Grade turns around and shoves the Beatles down Capitol's throat and backs it with an unprecedented $50,000 promotion campaign. I first heard the Beatles were coming from [mock] newspapers hitting my junior high school campus. Nobody had ever put 50 grand down on a pop act before."

As to how Sullivan happened upon the Beatles, several stories vie for history's attention. The favorite oft-told tale is that the Sullivans were at Heathrow Airport, returning from London on October 31, 1963, when they noticed mobs of teenagers. Ed claimed he asked what the ruckus was about and, when told, allegedly replied, "Who the hell are the Beatles?" In one version, he thought it was an animal act. He then allegedly leaped into action to book them on his show. In an excited *New York Times* account, he "signed them for an appearance on the spot." The airport myth has hardened into fact, and even the Beatles buy it: Ringo, in a 2008 TV interview, repeated the story and improved on it: "They signed us right there!" Stop the presses—and the music.

The actual backstory of how Sullivan stumbled across—rather than discovered—the Beatles is more complex, nuanced, and intriguing, if less dramatic. Peter Prichard, Sullivan's British eyes and ears, loyally remarked decades later of Sullivan's reported Beatles airport sighting, "Well, as I always said, it's a great press story. What can I say? In real life, if it would have happened [that way], he would have had a photograph of himself there. [But] I wouldn't argue with my boss after all these many years. If that's what he said he did, then, hey, I would never say aloud that Mr. Sullivan was wrong."

Sullivan, who read clips from the London papers, was in fact aware of the Beatles as a hot group; biographer James Maguire even had him perusing headlines and calling out to his wife, "Sylvia, there must be something here." Ed's talent coordinator, Jack Babb, sniffed out European acts for the show during summers abroad, guided by Prichard, the man responsible for tipping Sullivan off to Topo Gigio and arranging for him to film the guitar-playing Belgian nun Sister Luc-Gabrielle (Sister Sourire; née Jeanine Deckers) at her convent.

Associate director John Moffitt told me, "No matter what anyone says, it was Jack Babb who initially brought the Beatles to Sullivan. Ed ran the show, but one person booked that show then, Jack Babb." When Brian Epstein, the Beatles' manager, first took Babb to see the Beatles in 1963, Babb was unmoved. No British group had ever made it in the United States (including Brit pop stars Cliff Richard and Adam Faith). In fact, in September 1963, "She Loves You" was played on Dick Clark's "American Bandstand" and stirred nary a ripple.

By the time Prichard took Babb later that year to see the Beatles again, the group had spent two or three years strumming their way through small Liverpool and Hamburg clubs like the Cavern and the Indra, where Epstein had chanced upon them, known then as the Quarrymen, and then neatly repackaged them in look-alike Edwardian stovepipe trousers, high-heeled boots, and cute identical haircuts. Selvin dismissed Epstein: "He had lead in his ears. He was a homosexual who just thought these guys were cute—dressed 'em alike and got 'em to do their hair. They were his little boy dolls."

Around 1960, they changed their name to the Beatles, in homage to Buddy Holly's Crickets, after calling themselves the Holly, the Moon Dogs, the Rainbows, the Three Tunes, the Beat Boys, and the Silver Beetles. John suggested the "Beatles" spelling and later explained, "Brian was trying to clean our image up. He said our look wasn't right, that we'd never get past the door at a good place. We respected his views." Told the group was America-bound, Ringo Starr had his doubts, telling a Liverpool paper, "They've got everything over there—will they want us, too?" Quincy Jones, Epstein, and Lennon bet $100 the Beatles would be a hit in the United States, but Paul, George, and Ringo bet against themselves.

Beatles archivist Marc Weingarten compared Epstein to Ozzie Nelson, who masterminded his son Ricky's virginal forays into rock 'n' roll: "Epstein, whose genteel urbanity masked a brash, bullying perfectionism not unlike Ozzie Nelson's, had proven to be as canny a packager of youth culture as Dick Clark. By replacing the band's leather jackets—that charged symbol of teenage ruffianism—with fitted suits and ties, he had turned the Beatles into an even more user-friendly product than Elvis."

Epstein, a dandy who wore polka-dotted foulard scarves, had a clear vision. "From his first sight of them at the Cavern," wrote Martin Goldsmith in a moment-by-moment account of the Beatles' discovery of America, "Epstein thought that The Beatles needed smartening up. He began sending them notes about their stage deportment"—no more smoking, eating, drinking, or chewing gum onstage. "Then, drawing upon his stage background, he determined that the boys needed a new, almost virginal, look to attract a wider audience." He outfitted them in neatnik suits and ties and instructed them in how to take a bow in unison. Prepping them for the big time, Epstein got the boys on small-time British radio and TV shows, and by 1963 they had their own BBC radio show, "Pop Go the Beatles," about the time when their "yeah, yeah, yeah" became a trademark yelp of optimism—despite McCartney's proper dad, who tried to get them to change it to "yes, yes, yes."

Their producer, George Martin, created a concept album, much like Frank Sinatra's themed LPs but a radical idea in rock. Martin sent recordings to Capitol and said, "This group is fantastic, you've got to sell it in the States," only to hear a clueless rejection from executive Alan Livingston: "We don't think the Beatles will do anything in this market." The only English singer on American charts was Laurie London, with "He's Got the Whole World in His Hands." McCartney told Epstein, "We're not going to America till we've got a Number One record," insisting "it would make all the difference."

In the United Kingdom, they got their major TV break on "Val Parnell's Sunday Night Palladium," a sort of British Ed Sullivan show that the Beatles headlined October 13, 1963. Bruce Spizer wrote, "The bedlam caused by the group both inside and outside the theater caught the attention of British news editors, who elevated the Beatles from a successful entertainment act to a national news phenomenon. The *London Daily Mirror* described the hysteria as 'Beatlemania.' The name stuck." The airport scene that Sullivan reportedly witnessed occurred two weeks later, by which time the Beatles were the biggest thing in Britain, with record sales grossing $17.5 million—excluding U.S. sales. Four years earlier, they had been performing at $20 a night in Liverpool.

The next rung was a Royal Command Performance (dubbed the "Royal Variety Show"), a milestone appearance on November 4, 1963, that "drew more attention than the arrival of the Royal Family," says Spizer. The queen's official reaction was: "The Beatles are most intriguing." A Capitol press release quotes a blurb from Her Majesty (but it sounds more like her swinging sister, Margaret) calling them "young, fresh, and vital."

They were seventh on a bill of 19 acts and sang "She Loves You," "Till There Was You," "From Me to You," and "Twist and Shout," after which John Lennon told the well-heeled crowd, "For our last number, I'd like to ask your help. Would the people in the cheaper seats clap your hands? And the rest of you, if you'll just rattle your jewelry?"—all part of the plan as well. Earlier that night, Lennon informed Epstein he would ask the Royals to rattle their "fookin' jewelry" but cleaned it up for the box seats.

His brash comment made news, a tryout for their cheeky wisecracks to come. The repartee was fizzily bottled in the movie "A Hard Day's Night," released later that year, directed by Richard Lester, firmly transplanting them in American soil. The film captured their rapport with fans and the jubilant experience, the exuberance, of being a Beatle; in the film the lads seem as caught up in Beatlemania as their fans are.

After the queen's gig, Epstein flew to New York the next day with pop singer Billy J. Kramer, a protégé he was peddling, but Epstein also wanted to find out why the Beatles had not yet fully conquered America. Prichard told Epstein not to talk with anyone until he'd first met with Ed Sullivan. When Prichard called Sullivan, Ed said he needed an "angle" to justify booking an unknown British rock act. Prichard offered him a tempting news hook: the Beatles, he said, were the first long-haired rock act to perform for the queen of England. Sullivan suddenly felt better about the whole idea—he had a solid news angle. At the time, comments James Maguire, Sullivan's audience—if not Sullivan himself— "viewed rock 'n' roll as akin to a social disease."

Sullivan intended to book the group once, but agreed to meet with Epstein. Sullivan feared the Beatles were a flash in the pan and told Babb, "It's not the money, but who's gonna want to see them three times?" He met Epstein for dinner the next night at Delmonico's to seal the deal, but when Sullivan proposed the one-shot idea, Epstein was dismayed. Foxily, he persuaded Sullivan to give them three shows at $3,500 per shot (the top fee then was $10,000 for showbiz royalty). "Even for an unknown act," Bob Precht told me, "that was about the least we could pay."

Epstein, every bit a negotiating match for Sullivan (a Capitol exec claimed that Epstein had ice in his veins), kept arguing that the Beatles

deserved top billing, which Sullivan said he would "consider." Both he
and Precht were stunned by Epstein's unprecedented demand for three
shows plus air fare. They finally settled on two additional shows and a
fourth, taped appearance. Newly emboldened, Epstein went to Capitol
and prodded them to release "I Want to Hold Your Hand," claiming
that it had been produced with an "American sound." That was a pitch
to deflect the bad vibes Capitol thought it was getting from British rock
groups and to flatter their all-American hearts.

Precht was irked that he hadn't been consulted by Sullivan. "I was
called over to the hotel, and Ed was there with Epstein, and I was told
more or less what the deal was. I was not privy to that deal, and obviously I didn't like that. I liked to be in on what was going on. I thought
[the money] was excessive and I told Ed. I don't know what his thinking
was. He just sensed there was a lot of excitement going on and he better
be in on it." Precht later placed an urgent call to Sullivan saying he was
having severe second thoughts. He protested, "Ed, Jesus, nearly $4,000
bucks [per show] for some unknown rock-and-roll group? And three
shows?" But Sullivan—his eyes on the headlines—had convinced himself they were worth the expense. He later said, "I made up my mind
that this was the same sort of mass hysteria that had characterized the
Elvis Presley days."

"Sullivan didn't care much for rock 'n' roll, but he knew crowds,"
Jerry Bowles wrote. Decades later, Precht revisited the event: "We all
knew that the Beatles were big, but we didn't know how big they would
be. I had a rather jaundiced view of the whole thing because I felt they
were just another act. But we had a tiger by the tail."

Enter here Marsha Albert, a 15-year-old from Silver Spring, Mary-
land, who innocently engineered a major PR push. After watching the
Beatles on the CBS evening news, she wrote a letter to WWDC radio in
Washington. She asked, "Why can't we have this music in America?"
Her plea resonated with WWDC DJ Carroll James. He asked a station
staffer to call a stewardess friend at British Overseas Airlines and have
her smuggle "I Want to Hold Your Hand" aboard her next flight, like
valuable contraband.

The rest is straight out of "Bye Bye Birdie": James invited Marsha to
the station to introduce the song and asked listeners to call in with their
instant reactions. Albert's simple request, and DJ James's fevered huck-
stering, overloaded the WWDC switchboard even before the song
ended. James turned down the volume midway into the record to proclaim, "This is a Carroll James exclusive," to keep rival stations from

bootlegging it. But a UCLA researcher, D. L. MacLaughlan, found playlists from other stations that predated James's claim by ten months, as the *New York Times* noted in James's obituary, in 1997.

Meanwhile, Capitol Records, meticulously plotting a Beatles invasion with the care and urgency of generals in the D-Day war room, demanded that WWDC stop spinning the record before its scheduled release on January 13, 1964. Capitol's attorneys, joined by Epstein's lawyer, made ferocious litigious noises. Carroll James had a better legal argument: "You can't stop me from playing it. The record is a hit. It's a major thing." Capitol, not wanting to stand in the way of an unstoppable phenomenon, ceased, desisted, and capitulated, immediately shipping a few thousand copies of "I Want to Hold Your Hand" to Washington, D.C., record stores.

Capitol's promotional people went into full-assault mode, issuing specific instructions to DJs and record stores, distributing 5 million "The Beatles Are Coming" stickers and "Be a Beatles Booster" buttons. Seventeen press agents were assigned to their U.S. tour. A Capitol marketing man tried in vain to bribe a University of Washington cheerleader to get the rooting section to display "The Beatles Are Coming" placards at the Rose Bowl. In brief, by the time the Beatles landed in New York to perform on Ed Sullivan's show, their triumph was a lock.

A Chicago DJ and another in St. Louis played the song, further nudging the inevitable Beatles avalanche. Capitol caved in a week before Christmas, normally a dead season for new records, and moved up the release date to December 26. In the first three days, it sold 250,000 copies; by January 10, more than a million. All of this frenzy occurred a full month before the Beatles actually appeared on "The Ed Sullivan Show."

The histrionics behind the Beatles had many godfathers besides Sullivan. One was Sid Bernstein, a rotund booking agent who marketed singers and had a sensitive nose for new vibrations. He had produced a multitude of eclectic voices (Judy Garland, Tony Bennett, Miles Davis, Muddy Waters, Ray Charles, Fats Domino). His early hunch about the Beatles got them booked at Carnegie Hall—"the linchpin in the deal to get them over here," said Selvin. "The Carnegie Hall show is what brought them here."

Bernstein was taking a class in British democracy from Max Lerner at the New School when he first read about the Beatles. "Our teacher told us to study the British way of life by reading the British newspapers. That was how I first heard what the Beatles were doing over in Europe," he explained to me. Bernstein called Epstein about a year before Sullivan ever got involved, and Epstein said, "You're the first man from America calling. Why would you want to commit suicide? They don't mean anything in America." Bernstein brazenly told him, "They'll break here," but later confided, "I really didn't know. I hadn't ever heard their music." Epstein, cautious, said, "I don't want my boys playing to empty houses. We fill every music hall in Europe. We get top dollar—$2,000 a night per show." Bernstein says, "I just ad-libbed—and I don't know where I got the figure from—'I'll give you $6,500 for two shows in one day,' an offer he couldn't refuse."

Bernstein told me, "Brian was one of the very few guys in the history of the pop music business you could make an important deal with and know it was gonna come out the way he said on the phone—an extremely honorable man." There was no formal written agreement, Bernstein recalled. "We never signed anything—it was all verbal. No contract." He instinctively trusted Epstein. "He never changed a dot over an *i,* or uncrossed a *t.* He was a very serious, ethical young man. It was all done on the phone." Ron Greenberg, the attorney who handled Sullivan's contracts, pointed out, "Many of the entertainment industry transactions in those days were just agreements to go ahead, and after the fact you'd paper it. They weren't contracts in the formal sense—they were general understandings. For a young lawyer—I was 26—it was a little scary."

Bernstein, who had helped guide Judy Garland's dramatic comeback tour and first brought Tony Bennett to Carnegie Hall, convinced himself that the Beatles could be transplanted to America. He backed up his faith by coughing up $6,500 months before their first hit here, "I Want to Hold Your Hand." He shrugged, saying, "I'm a hunch player. I was just glad to get this group I'd been reading about for months. I had to convince Carnegie Hall and my financial backers to take a chance on this unknown group. But I was fascinated by the hysteria that surrounded them." (He also helped produce their famous post-Sullivan Shea Stadium concert, and later brought the Rolling Stones to America.)

Bernstein went on to say, "It was a bit of a chance. I saw what they were doing, and I had four sons of my own. I thought, well, their ages are the same as the Beatles, the language is the same. So I figured, what the hell could I lose? I wanted to be the first. I booked 'em and sweated it out for about a year before they started to break" with their first hit. "Brian had said to me, 'I will not book them until they have airplay.'"

Ed didn't move on the Beatles until well after the hubbub at Heathrow. Still wavering on whether to book them, Sullivan sought Bernstein's counsel. Though they knew each other, Sullivan didn't even bother to speak with him personally about the Beatles. Ed's secretary called Bernstein, he said, and asked just one question: "What do you think of them, Sid?" Bernstein recalls, "They assumed that I'd heard them. They didn't ask me that, and they didn't ask me to qualify it. That was it." He told Sullivan's secretary they were a "phenomenon." That was all Sullivan had to hear.

A British reporter said to Bernstein in a 2001 interview, "'Phenomenon'—that's a word you can use but it doesn't mean anything," and Bernstein said, "Exactly! I also said it to the Polish lady who booked Carnegie Hall." After he'd told her about the Beatles, she'd said, "Vat are dey?" "I knew Carnegie Hall would never allow a pop concert to happen in its famous auditorium. When I told her, 'They're a phenomenon,' she said, 'Oh, a *phenomenon*,' assuming they were a European string quartet."

The Beatles' U.S. debut was a one-two media punch: "Sullivan had the band on Sunday, and I had them the following Wednesday at Carnegie Hall, Lincoln's birthday, when I knew the kids were out of school," Bernstein went on. "Talk about good luck." He reflected, "I was called a genius, but I was not a genius—I just happened to make the right phone call at the right time." The day the Beatles checked into the Plaza, Bernstein said, "I came down there early that morning, and I saw 1,500 kids outside the hotel singing their songs. Nobody recognized me. I thought, 'Shit, *I'm* responsible for bringing them here!' "

Precht commented, "Like [with] any success story, everyone wants to take credit. My take on the whole thing was that it was Epstein who really engineered everything. It was largely his doing—the promotion and radio exposure and where he wanted the Beatles to go. That was all his maneuvering." Sullivan forgot about the booking until he saw the CBS news report on the Beatles and realized he might have caught a far bigger fish than he had thought. He asked Walter Cronkite, a crony, what he knew about "those bugs, or whatever they call themselves." He was reassured that, if Cronkite had cleared precious airtime for the Beatles, they were, if nothing else, newsworthy. Three days later, in a February 3, 1964, press release, CBS announced the coup: "The Beatles, wildly popular quartet of English recording stars, will make their first trip to the United States Feb. 7 for their American television debut on 'The Ed Sullivan Show,' Sunday Feb. 9 and 16."

Although Sullivan's old rival, Jack Paar, scooped Ed by a month, on January 3, when he ran a BBC clip of the Beatles at the Royal Command

Performance, he did it to snicker publicly at the galloping teenage madness, noting later in his memoir, "I didn't know they were going to change the culture of the country with music. I brought them here as a joke." He introduced the clip by telling viewers he was "interested in the Beatles as a psychological, sociological phenomenon." While the film showed teenage girls going bananas, Paar deadpanned, "I understand science is working on a cure for this," adding, "Does it bother you to realize that in a few years these girls will vote, raise children, and drive cars?" After "She Loves You" and the requisite shots of screeching teenage girls, Paar said, "It's nice to know England has finally risen to our cultural level."

Capitol kept rolling out its heavy PR artillery to assure America that the Beatles were indeed a phenomenon. Memos commanded the marketing staff to wear their "Be a Beatle Booster" buttons (the CBS press release instructed them to "offer them to clerks and disc jocks"), and ordered, "As soon as the Beatles wigs arrive—and until further notice—you and each of your sales and promotion staff are to wear the wig during the business day! Get these Beatles wigs around properly. Offer some to disc jocks and stores for promotions. You'll find you're helping to start the Beatle Hair-Do Craze that should be sweeping the country soon."

Trendy Hollywood hair stylist Gene Shacove created a Beatles coiffeur, and his first celebrity client was Janet Leigh. Shacove, spurred by Capitol, pushed a three-step styling process to ensure the Beatles look and what the CBS press release had called the hairstyle's "ease of handling" that "gets the hair off the neck." A British company called Seltaeb ("Beatles" backward) was in New York weeks earlier arranging licensing deals for sweaters, headbands, sneakers, bracelets, boots, tie pins, dolls, pens, bow ties, and even Baskin-Robbins Beatle Nut ice cream. The *Wall Street Journal* estimated sales of $50 million in Beatles tchotchkes, from edible discs to masks.

Marketing agents were told via a CBS internal memo to literally plaster " 'Beatles Are Coming' stickers on any friendly surface," until they became as ubiquitous as "Kilroy was here" stickers ten years before. Capitol printed a mock tabloid newspaper filled with Beatles features and delivered it to teenagers in schoolyards in major cities. Paul Russell, Capitol's national album merchandising manager, exhorted his troops in a nagging in-house directive: "The message is certainly clear—there are a lot of people who are putting up big money to ensure that The Beatles are the biggest thing yet in America. We should be fully prepared to take every possible advantage of the Beatles snowball." An AP photographer snapped oil tycoon J. Paul Getty wearing a Beatles wig at a kids' party in England; *Esquire*'s June 1965 cover depicted Ed Sullivan in a Beatles wig, which by then had become the rock 'n' roll version of Davy Crockett's coonskin cap. The cover line reads, "Do today's teenagers influence the adult world?," to which Ed replies, "Ridiculous!"

Capitol gave out the details of the Beatles' New York arrival time and itinerary so that on February 7, when Pan American flight 101, carrying its precious cargo, finally set down at Kennedy airport at 1:20 P.M., thousands of teenagers were jumping up and down. Pop music stations in New York cut into weather and traffic reports to issue countdown bulletins on the plane's progress.

Paul McCartney later recalled the trip: "I remember the great moment of getting in the limo and putting on the radio and hearing a running commentary on us: *'They have just left the airport and are coming towards New York City. . . . They're out over the Atlantic Ocean headed for New York' "*—as if Orson Welles's radio Martians were about to land in New Jersey again. Ringo Starr recalled, "On the plane, flying into the airport, I felt like there was a big octopus with tentacles grabbing the plane and dragging us down into New York." The boys clamped transistor radios to their ears to hear the feverish coverage of their arrival.

At the airport, one of the most theatrical and beguiling press conferences in the history of airport press conferences was staged by Capitol. The press lobbed questions by the dozens at the four singers, including some planted by the record company. The Beatles had mastered this medium, and they overpowered the press in what turned into a preconcert warm-up comedy act, with reporters serving as willing stooges. The repartee:

"What are you going to do about the bumper stickers in Detroit that say 'Help Stamp Out the Beatles'?" George: "We're printing some that say 'Stamp Out Detroit.' " Q: "How do you find America?" Ringo: "Go to Greenland and turn left." Q: "What don't you like about America?" George: "Well, I don't much like your tie." Q: "What do you do when you're cooped up in your rooms between shows?" George: "We ice skate . . ." Q: "Who writes the music?" John: "What music?" The jaunty cracks were calculated to disarm the press and America, and they did just that, though to some it sounded prefabricated, lip-synched in a sense. A *London Evening Standard* writer said, "Either they're employing the most marvelous concealed gag man or Bob Hope should sign them up right away."

The Beatles checked into the Plaza Hotel under their own (but still obscure) names. Jerry Bowles noted, "Management had no idea it had agreed to lodge a social phenomenon." Teen fans took cabs to the hotel and posed as guests. Outside, groupies chanted a parody of the Conrad Birdie song from "Bye Bye Birdie"—"We love you, Bea-tles, oh, yes we do-ooo!" That night, the Beatles watched themselves on the CBS news in their ten-room mansion on the 12th floor, giggling at radio stations playing their songs. They heard Cronkite, in a rare droll mood, intone, "The British invasion this time goes by the code name Beatlemania. B-Day has been common knowledge for months, and this was the day. The invasion took place at New York's Kennedy International Airport." Then Walter said goodnight with his signature, "And that's the way it is, Friday, February 7, 1964."

So the stage was beautifully set for the Beatles when Ed Sullivan faced the camera February 9 and said, as if delivering the minutes of the last meeting: "Now yesterday and today [screams] our theater has been jammed with newspapermen and hundreds of photographers from all over the nation. And these veterans agree with me that never has this city witnessed the excitement stirred by these youngsters from Liverpool [screams] who call themselves the Beatles [screams]. Tonight, you're going to be entertained by them right now, and then in the second half of our show." Dramatic pause, then, finally: "*Laze and gennulmen—the Bea'les! Bring 'em on!*" (blood-curdling screeches). Marlo Lewis wrote that the Beatles screams were recorded and used on later shows, which Precht firmly denies. In any case, some 41 million people watched, later eclipsed by the 50 million who tuned into the "M*A*S*H" finale; the Beatles shows now rank only between the 20th and 30th most-watched TV shows.

Sullivan had earlier reminded the audience that other acts on the show deserved the courtesy of their attention. "If you don't keep quiet," he warned, "I'm going to send for a barber." After the Beatles' first set, Sullivan again quieted the crowd and said, "Something very nice just happened that they [the Beatles] got a big kick out of. We just received a wire from Elvis and Colonel Tom Parker wishing them a tremendous success in our country. And I think that was very nice." Very nice indeed, since Elvis and the Colonel were mortified at the thought that the Beatles were about to steal their golden spotlight, which is precisely what they did. But it was a sweet public relations ploy by the King to extend a southern-fried welcome to the four aliens from abroad.

Soft rock dominated the charts in 1963—"Surfin' USA," "Sugar Shack," "Hey, Paula," "He's So Fine," all of them hits. In Liverpool, very young Beatles-to-be were gorging on American pop music fast food. John Lennon later said, "America was a big youth place in our imagination. We all knew America. Every movie we ever saw as children, whether it was Disneyland or Doris Day, Rock Hudson, James Dean or Marilyn, everything was American: Coca-Cola, Heinz ketchup. And all the big artists were American. They wouldn't even make an English movie without an American in it." He said, "Liverpool was 'cosmopolitan.' It's where the sailors would come home on the ships with the blues records from America."

Devin McKinney, in *Magic Circles: The Beatles in Dream and History,* wrote about how the Beatles "listened to American music and lived on fantasies of everything their culture lacked"—part of which was "The Ed Sullivan Show." As the Beatles ground out music in sweaty rock clubs as the Quarrymen, their style superbly advanced American pop. McKinney contended, "The group echoed the sound of America back on itself, only louder, newer, with more screams"—what he called "a squall of unmediated adolescent emotion." It was an earthier squall than

We often watched "The Ed Sullivan Show" as a family on Sunday night in Los Angeles. I remember we made gentle fun of his accent—none of us had ever heard anyone say "shew" before—and mannerisms. He was somewhat eccentric, but a soothing presence in an avuncular way. I remember thinking, even at the ripe age of ten, that Topo Gigio was the dumbest thing I'd ever seen on TV. But I loved Shari Lewis and Lambchop. Most of all, I loved watching the singers, especially the glamorous girl singers like Keely Smith, Connie Francis, and Patti Page—and of course the great Ella. But the most exciting and memorable show was, for me, as for so many other adolescents, the debut of the Beatles. Up until then we'd enjoyed the show as a family. But on that fateful night, a rift occurred between the generations. Suddenly we were plunged into rebellion, along with a whole generation, and for us, long hair and "Yeah, yeah, yeah!" won out. Well, not a true rift but a watershed event, as it was the first time my parents were aghast at a rock group, while my sister and I were cheering and getting caught up in the excitement of Beatlemania. [After that], my father referred to "our" music (Bob Dylan, the Beatles, the Stones, etc.) as "noise."

Cherie Zaslawsky, Menlo Park, California

the sounds their mothers had wailed in the 1940s at the Brooklyn Paramount, shrieking "Frankie!"

The Sullivan show was thrown into a pandemonium unseen since Elvis first arrived eight years earlier, like Napoleon marching into Moscow. By the wintry February week in 1964 that the Beatles occupied New York, "The Ed Sullivan Show" had settled into a groove, an efficient, humming entertainment machine. CBS Studio 50 seated 703 people, about 49,397 fewer than there were ticket requests for the February 9 show.

The crew knew something was afoot when Sullivan made a rare appearance at Saturday's rehearsal, which he normally avoided. One of the people ensnared in the Beatles frenzy was Vince Calandra, who recalled in an Archive of American Television interview recorded for the 40th anniversary of the Beatles show, in 2004: "The hubbub over Elvis Presley was nothing close to the Beatles."

Calandra first met the quartet that Saturday after emerging from the subway at 52nd Street to find 4,000 screaming kids, streets closed, and cops on horseback trying to keep order. Inside, he noted, "There was *lots* of negative attitude from the band, who were great musicians. Like, 'Why are they carryin' on so?' " Conductor Ray Bloch was unimpressed: "The only thing that's different is the hair. I give them a year." Calandra said, "Everyone felt this was just another English group we'd never hear from again."

Calandra quickly changed his mind: "These were not, like, just four young kids—they were really serious. We rarely let anyone into the control room, but we let them in." He was astounded that they asked to hear the playback of their songs. No other group had ever wanted to listen to their playback. In all other rock acts," he explained, "the music was the predominant thing. But the Beatles wanted the guitars and voices in equal balance, so the lyrics could be heard—not the usual mix where the music was more dominant than the lyrics. That told us they were no-nonsense guys." He added, "They came in very polite, no demands—not like today. They had such a likable attitude: 'Can we do this?' 'Can I suggest that?' They were so respectful and pleasant."

Calandra was appointed the boys' caretaker. One of them, George Harrison, was cooped up at the hotel with bronchitis (regular news bulletins informed America of the status of George's throat), so Calandra stood in for him, clumsily clutching a guitar. "Paul told me his life's ambition was to be on an Ed Sullivan show. John asked me if this was the same stage Buddy Holly and the Crickets had performed on. Ringo thought we were all nuts, us Americans. They thought this sort of thing happened all the time."

Gofer Peter Calabrese's first day at work on the show was historic—the night of the Beatles' first appearance with Sullivan. "I'd come over from New Jersey," he told me, "and the only thing I knew about TV was that I watched it. I get to 53rd and 8th Avenue and the street is blocked off. There's wall-to-wall people, sawhorses blocking off the street, and I don't know what's going on. All I know is that I've gotta get to the stage door."

He was turned away at the stage door because he had no ID card yet, but someone waved him in, and he was introduced to Eddie Brinkman, the stage manager with an ever-present cigarette dangling out of his mouth. "He was the guy who got the show on and off the air," said Calabrese. Brinkman asked him what size sports jacket he had on—a 38. Calabrese: "He walks over to the Beatles, in rehearsal, and brings the jacket to Ringo Starr, who had on a white satin shirt that was driving the cameras nuts by reflecting the lights. Brinkman gave Ringo the jacket. After three minutes I'm now in show business." His jacket was, anyway.

Come Sunday, Calandra said, "there was even more pandemonium than the day before. Paul was the calmest, John was the most nervous, George was quiet, and Ringo was immune—it was a party to him." Celebrities were calling all week for tickets to the show for their kids. Calandra recalled how "pushy" Leonard Bernstein was, viewing seats for his kids as an entitlement. Walter Cronkite's daughters got in; so did Julie Nixon. Sullivan's erstwhile foe Jack Paar tried to cadge a seat for his daughter, and Ed found one for her. For his own mysterious reasons, he told perplexed viewers, "Those first three Beatles songs were dedicated to Randy Paar, Johnny Carson, and [columnist] Earl Wilson."

Sullivan was abnormally antsy about the show and covered his trepidation with banter, telling the berserk teens, "If you're not quiet I'll take your names and tell the principal." Before the show, when the scrupulous Brian Epstein saw Sullivan writing out an introduction, he said, "I would like to know the exact wording of the introduction," and Sullivan snapped, "And I would like you to get lost." The fledgling British control freak was bested by the master. There was an unwritten but severe rule: one never interrupted Sullivan while he was writing his intros.

Four cameras were judged totally inadequate to capture the Beatles in all their Beatletude. Director Tim Kiley added a special camera to catch the frenzied teenagers in the balcony. At one point, the camera singled

out two young girls licking their lips "in a manner," according to one reporter, "that surely confirmed the worst fears of every disapproving par-
ent tuned in that night." Kiley choreographed all the camera angles by
following the song sheets. Moffitt told Marc Weingarten, "Tim meticulously laid out a shot list for every segment. He knew the bar count of
each song, so we would know when an instrumental break happened,
when there was a bridge and a chorus, and so on. It gave us a lot of freedom to try different approaches."

The Sullivan show used traditional boom mikes. "It never occurred to
anyone to put a mike in front of a performer, or in a performer's hand,"
music coordinator Bob Arthur explained to me. "As rock on TV progressed, it got louder and louder. We struggled with ambient noise for
years." All of their intricate planning was nearly useless because of the
roars and wails. Later, when other rock stars appeared, the crew used
headphones from the sports department, which was accustomed to
screaming fans. "All went fine until airtime," said Moffitt. "No one was
prepared for the pandemonium." Amplifiers were overloaded, and the
singers couldn't hear their own voices. "The soundmen also couldn't
hear anything."

Recalled Arthur, "The crowd is screeching, just screeching, at the top
of their lungs. They were beside themselves. Ed tried to hush them, but
it was just no use. In those days we all used these little Mickey Mouse
radio headsets with no padding. None of the cameramen could hear
Tim's directions." But the crew followed Kiley's detailed shot list, and
all went smoothly despite the chaos, with no serious glitches during the
mythic 13 minutes, except for the fact that John's mike cut in and out.
The songs were virtually mouthed above the din.

The sparse collection of boys in the audience sat befuddled and mostly
silent amid girls in urgent need of an exorcist. Not all the screaming,
though, was as spontaneous as it looks. Nancy Cronkite, the newscaster's
daughter, who was there, recalled, "Your friends were screaming so you
screamed too." In her book *Where the Girls Are,* Susan Douglas said
that teen girls were drawn to the Beatles because of their nonsensual vibrations: "The Beatles channeled sexual energy away from where Elvis
had located it, in the male crotch, and moved it through safer, nonsexual
parts of the body—their feet, their legs, their heads, their hair. Like electricity, it arced to the audience, where it surged safely through female
limbs and faces."

This debut show, like the next two shows, became an abstract collage
of sobbing girls and bobbing mop tops. It was like watching a silent movie

with dubbed musical accompaniment and unruly mob roars. Viewing it 40 years later, *Rolling Stone*'s David Fricke wrote that the 13 minutes looks starkly beautiful: "Today, against the hypertensive editing and Technicolor computer graphics that pass for music television, the black-and-white simplicity of the Beatles' *Sullivan* debut seems antique, like a moving daguerreotype."

Except for the quartet from England, it was a routine Ed Sullivan show, featuring Georgia Brown and the cast of "Oliver!"—including, as the Artful Dodger, Davy Jones, later of the Monkees, the Beatles TV knockoff sitcom band. Jones later recalled, "I watched the Beatles from the side of the stage. I saw the girls going crazy, and I said to myself, I want a piece of that." Also on the bill: mimic Frank Gorshin, the comedy team of Mitzi McCall and Charlie Brill, magician Fred Kapps, acrobats Wells & the Four Fays, and Tessie O'Shea, the roly-poly British banjo-whomping music hall singer whose signature song was "Two-Ton Tessie (from Tennessee)." O'Shea perfectly embodied the pre-Beatles Ed Sullivan spirit.

Frank Gorshin (later the Riddler on "Batman") remembered, "I didn't know who was going to be on the show with me. I'm up in my dressing room, I look out my window, and I see thousands of kids." While in the wings waiting to go on, Gorshin heard the screams. "I'd never witnessed that kind of adulation. I was consumed with the idea that they could get this kind of reaction. The kids kept screaming, right through Ed's introduction of me. When I walked on I was already getting screams. I went through all my bits, and they just kept screaming. I finished up and those kids were still screaming."

McCall & Brill, a husband-and-wife comedy team, recount their doomed debut on the Sullivan show that night in wrenching detail, a story they've dined out on ever since. In 2004 they retold it to the *Washington Post,* Terry Gross of NPR's "Fresh Air," and any reporter who couldn't resist a juicy showbiz horror story marking the 40th year since the Beatles' Sullivan debut.

"We were sitting at home starving," Brill told Gross, "and the phone rang and our manager said, 'Guess what? I've got you on "The Ed Sullivan Show"'!—and we let out a scream because that . . . was . . . *the* show. This was the ultimate. If you had a shot on Ed Sullivan, you had a shot at stardom!" Their manager had added excitedly, "And guess what—you're gonna be on with the Beatles," but it didn't register with the couple. "We were cheering! When our manager said, 'It's with the Beatles,' we said, 'Oh, OK.' We weren't really sure who they were."

The team wrote a special routine and told everyone that they would be on "The Ed Sullivan Show." "I skywrote it over Hollywood," Brill recalled. "We were on our way!" They were newlywed 26-year-olds, soon to be seen coast-to-coast, stardom within their grasp. They knew that Gorshin, hot and in demand, would be on the show. Brill: "So we go to rehearsals in New York, and we see thousands of people in the streets clamoring, cordoned off. I look at Mitzi and I said, 'God, all of this for Frank Gorshin!' "

The team was toiling away in a dressing room after Sullivan had ordered them to revise their sketch for the show ("We were in a daze," said McCall), feverishly rewriting, when someone knocked on their shabby dressing room door next to the Coke machine. Brill: "We opened it and there's this weird-looking kid with strange hair, and he said something that sounded like, 'Give us a ko, glove.' We didn't understand him, so he said it again, and we started to laugh, and the third time we finally realized he was saying [in clear Liverpudlian], 'Give us a Coke, luv.' "

They asked the kid in, and he turned out to be John Lennon, who doodled a sketch of McCall and Brill on a napkin, which they tossed out. Brill: "We just wanted this kid to go so we could put the sketch together. Our careers were at stake here!" Lennon finally left and they heard an announcement on the backstage speaker, "McCall & Brill, McCall & Brill, onstage for the show." Sullivan introduced them, the last act before the Beatles returned. They did their sketch in a blur. Brill: "It was an out-of-body experience. I know we were onstage, and I know we were doing something, but that's it." McCall: "We did it by rote"; she recalled someone out front shouting, "Get 'em off!" Brill: "I think *I* said it."

They might have been forgotten even without the Beatles' help, but their big moment was buried in the rubble of history being made. All that night's surrounding acts were just bubble wrap for the Beatles. After the sketch, the couple looked at Sullivan, hoping he'd call them over. He didn't. McCall: "We knew—into the toilet!" The most embarrassing five minutes of their careers, recorded for posterity to enjoy. They didn't want to go home, so Gorshin took them to Sardi's to console them, "Don't worry—it's not the end of your life." One writer called it every comic's darkest nightmare: "McCall & Brill had committed the unthinkable: they had bombed on the Ed Sullivan show."

But when the comics finally watched the tape 40 years later (they claim never to have dared look at a video of their painful five minutes—available on a DVD, "Ed Sullivan Presents the Beatles and Various Other Artists"), Brill noticed, to his astonishment, they got decent laughs,

most loudly at his ad-lib about "stepping on some Beatles." "You know
what? We were a hit," declared Brill.

If it had been any other Sullivan show, McCall & Brill might have
been launched rather than reduced to a pop history curiosity. People still
beg them to relate their experience of being eaten alive on Sullivan's
most memorable show. When Brill met Larry David, David wanted to
hear all the gory details of the team's brush with fame. Now when they
meet people and remark offhandedly that they were on the Ed Sullivan
show at the time of the first Beatles appearance, everyone says, "Oh, my
God, you're famous!"

Elvis Presley felt seriously threatened by the Beatles. When Colonel
Parker told Elvis that the Beatles wanted to meet their idol, Elvis snickered, "Hell, I don't want to meet those fucking sons of bitches." But
Parker, on his own, sent the Beatles gifts "from Elvis"—cowboy suits
and ten-gallon hats—and told Epstein that the King was far too busy to
grant an audience.

The two managers later maneuvered their rival cultural forces into a
pop summit. It was convened at Presley's home on August 27, 1965. The
Beatles showed up, utterly awestruck. Elvis finally drawled, "If you damn
guys are just gonna sit here and stare at me all night, I'm gonna go to
bed. I just thought maybe we'd sit and talk, maybe play a little, jam a little." That broke the ice. One Beatle asked Elvis how he dealt with hysterical crowds. Elvis said, "If you can't take the crowds, you're in the
wrong business."

Even after the Beatles' massive coup de television, Sullivan staffers
were not thinking Historical Moment. Moffitt told me, "Nobody realized the impact to come, how momentous it would be. We didn't talk
about making history. It was more like, 'What are we going to do *next*
week? Not only are we doing this again—we're on location.' "

Precht also was unaware that the Beatles debut was a landmark event
in the making: "We realized something big was going on," he said, "and
it was exciting and people were going crazy. But my job was to get 'em
on and get 'em off. I was less concerned with all the excitement and
what was going on than with 'How do we deal with it?' Getting them in
and the security. I kept thinking of my navy days. I was the executive officer, and my job was to make it happen." (More thrilling to Precht was
producing a follow-up Beatles concert at Shea Stadium with 60,000
people and eight 35-millimeter cameras.)

By the Beatles' second appearance, in Miami Beach on February 16,
Sullivan had settled back into his old groove, giving the top spot to

musical star Mitzi Gaynor. He burbled to the TV audience how excited the Beatles were to see Mitzi: "The greatest thrill for the Beatles—and we got a big kick out of it—is the fact that they were going to meet Mitzi Gaynor tonight on our show." Once again Sullivan was reassuring the grown-ups that the Beatles were just reg'lar fellas (who likely never had heard of Mitzi Gaynor). In a ballsy effort to cross over to older viewers, Paul McCartney dryly announced that their final song, "From Me to You," had been "recorded by our favorite American group, Sophie Tucker"—a line he had used playing before the queen. But poking fun at the rotund Tucker, a Sullivan stalwart, went over nearly everyone's heads.

After the Beatles arrived in Florida, the *Miami Herald* sneered, "For the information of the young and deranged, these wailing weirdies will disembark from National Airlines Flight 11 at 3:55 P.M." By then, the Beatles had touched an exposed nerve beyond pop music: at the Dade County airport, a near-crazed cop fumed, "This is disgusting! If I ever caught my kid out here, I'd beat the hell out of her."

When the Beatles left town after the telecast, the *Miami Herald* heaved a sigh of relief: "The plague of the Beatles has lifted. After an eight-day local infestation, the Liverpudlian lads caught a jet from Miami to New York and London, as 500-odd adolescent females here bid them a blubbering bye-bye." Once Miami and the siege of New York were all over, George Harrison reflected, "I didn't think beyond the moment during that U.S. trip. We just enjoyed the novelty of 'conquering America.'" In a 1970 *Rolling Stone* interview, Lennon strutted: "We knew we could wipe you [Americans] out. When we got here, you were all walking around in fuckin' Bermuda shorts with crewcuts and stuff in your teeth." In 1987, McCartney said, "Luckily, we didn't know what America was—we just knew our dreams of it—or we probably would have been too intimidated."

Newsweek, in its cover story on November 18, scoffed, "They wear sheep-dog bangs. They are The Beatles, and the sound of their music is one of the most persistent noises heard over England since the air-raid sirens were dismantled. . . . Beatle music is high-pitched, loud beyond reason, and stupefyingly repetitive." CBS's man in London, Alexander Kendrick, sniffed that the Beatles were "the modern manifestation of compulsive tribal singing and dancing"—once again, as with the old uproar over Elvis Presley, invoking the dread specter of jungle "race music." The *New York Herald Tribune* snickered that they were "seventy-five percent publicity, twenty percent haircut, and five percent lilting lament."

Missing the boat in every respect, the *Washington Post* labeled them "asexual and homely." A *Washington Star* editorial, under a headline reading "They Bug Us," huffed, "Their musical talent is minimal. Their weird hairstyle is merely a combination of the beehive and the Hamlet, or 'little moron,' hair-do. Months ago, the *Star* editorially expressed thanks that we had nothing like the Beatles in this country. We may never have produced a Shakespeare. But we never produced a Beatle either." *Washington Post* critic Laurence Laurent called them "imported hillbillies who look like sheepdogs and sound like alley cats in agony." And Dr. Joyce Brothers, analyzing the pesky creatures, observed: "Beatles might look unappetizing and inconsequential, but naturalists have long considered them the most successful order of animals on earth."

One favorite theory to explain Beatlemania was that the group arrived on the Sullivan show less than three months after John Kennedy was assassinated and jolted America out of its doldrums with their joyful, uplifting music. On the 40th anniversary of the Beatles' triumph, Fred Kaplan dashed that sentimental notion on Slate.com: "A slew of clueless scholars and columnists have mused, over the decades, that the Beatles caused such a sensation because they snapped us out of the gloom brought on by the Kennedy assassination, which had taken place the previous November. This is silly sociology."

The Sullivan show's audience hysteria was equaled by the pop music media's hysterics. Music writers developed sinister underlying causes and effects to explain the Beatles. In the *San Francisco Chronicle,* jazz writer Grover Sales, a horrified observer, advanced a theory that the Beatles were actually "a gleefully calculated parody of rock 'n' roll. It is evident that the Beatles are savoring to the full the delectable irony of being taken at face value by all of pubescent America." He compared the hysteria to "scenes suggestive of the classic Nazi propaganda film 'Triumph of the Will.' " The much less uptight *London Daily Mirror* editorialized, "You have to be a real sour square not to love the nutty, noisy, happy, handsome Beatles!"

Due to an absence of serious rock critics in 1964, the *New York Times* dispatched their classical music critic, Theodore Strongin, to comment on the Beatles' musicianship. Wisely, in his February 10 report, he first noted the more relevant, cogent, succinct remarks of his 15-year-old daughter: "You can tell right away it's the Beatles and not anyone else. The Beatles are different, and we have to get rid of our excess energy somehow. We haven't had an idol in a few years. It's just that English rock 'n' roll is more sophisticated."

Classical tongue firmly in cheek, Strongin wrote, "The Beatles are directly in the mainstream of Western tradition; that much may be immediately ascertained. Their harmony is unmistakably diatonic. A learned British colleague has described it as pandiatonic, but I disagree. The Beatles have a tendency to build phrases around unresolved leading tones. This precipitates the ear into a false modal frame, momentarily suggesting the Mixylodian mode. But everything always ends as plain diatonic all the same." He ended on a philosophical note: "The longer parents object with such high dudgeon, the longer children will squeal so hysterically."

New York Times TV critic Jack Gould, one of Sullivan's constant nags, weighed in on February 10 with pure disdain: "The Liverpool quartet, borrowing the square hairdo used every morning on television by Captain Kangaroo, was composed of conservative conformists." He claimed that the group "hardly did for daughter what Elvis Presley did for her older sister or Frank Sinatra for her mother"—but the Beatles had done precisely that.

Gould praised the group's marketing skills over their music: "In their sophisticated understanding that the life of a fad depends on the performance of the audience and not on the stage, the Beatles were decidedly effective." He nominated Sullivan for "chaperone of the year." The critic concluded with a yawn: "Televised Beatlemania appeared to be a fine mass placebo, and thanks undoubtedly are due Britain for a recess in winter's routine. Last night's sedate anticlimax speaks well for continuing British-American understanding. The British always were much more strict with their children."

Israel banned the Beatles, claiming, "The Beatles have an insufficient artistic level and cannot add to the spiritual and cultural life of the youth

My memory concerns a famous show that I watched in the junior common room at Lady Margaret Hall, Oxford, England, which was filled with ardent, student Beatles fans. This amazed me, as "Oxford women" at the time were supersmart and serious bluestockings, not known to be frivolous. The object of their swooning surprised me, too: adorable boys in cute suits singing songs, some of them pallid versions of hits by Chubby Checker and Elvis. So prim. I was sure the group wouldn't go over in the U.S., where you could listen to the real thing.

Judy Gingold, Los Angeles

of Israel." Forty-three years later, in September 2008, the country changed its mind (the newspaper *Haaretz* said the original embargo was due to a rivalry between impresarios) and welcomed Paul McCartney to a concert in Tel Aviv when a benefactor put up $8 million.

Pop sociologist Vance Packard noted in the *Saturday Evening Post* that the boys' "amiable impudence" wasn't nearly as threatening as Presley's raw, steamy sexuality—they weren't roughnecks but "rather loveable, almost cuddly imps." He added that the Beatles had taken over from Presley, Brando, and Dean: "Surliness is out, exuberance is in. Sloppiness is out, cleanliness is in. Self-pity is out, whooping with joy is in. Pomposity is out, humor is in." The Beatles, he added, tapped into the secret desires of young girls: "The subconscious need that they fill most expertly is in taking adolescent girls clear out of this world. The youngsters in the darkened audiences can let go all inhibitions in a quite primitive sense when the Beatles cut loose. They can retreat from rationality. Mob pathology takes over, and they are momentarily freed from all of civilization's restraints." Another writer a bit more bluntly observed that teenage girls "both wanted to mother the Beatles and screw them."

The *Saturday Evening Post,* of all unlikely publications, nicely nailed their popularity: "The Beatles displayed an ingratiating quality, all too rare in show business. They refused to take their 'talent' or themselves too seriously" (note the snarky quotes around "talent"). The *Post,* bastion of U.S. middle-class taste, put them on its April cover with a cover line vowing to divulge "The Secret of the Beatles" and promising "an intimate account of their American tour and a probing analysis of their incredible power to evoke frenzied emotions among the young." It sounds like a report from a spy that had infiltrated a bizarre religious cult.

The Miami Beach television broadcast opened with what looks like a commercial for the swanky Deauville Hotel before zooming in on Sullivan boasting, "Last week in New York, the Beatles played for the biggest audience that has ever been assembled in the history of American TV"—nearly 74 million viewers, a lot but not the record (for example, "Cinderella" on CBS had 107 million viewers in 1957, according to *Variety*). "Now from Miami Beach, the Beatles face another record-busting audience! Here are four of the nicest youngsters we've ever had on our stage—*the Bea'les!* Bring 'em on out here!"

Ed, of course, had also characterized Elvis as a "nice" fella. "Nice" was how you behaved on Sullivan's show, and it counted a lot with him— "nice" was the highest compliment he could extend to a performer.

Niceness had a secondary impact: it restored confidence among his worried flock that, rock revolution or no, it was being led by some extremely fine young chaps. It also justified his booking rebel rockers, and, lastly, it signaled the nation's grown-ups that all was still well in Sullivanland.

To relax the faithful, he produced yet more certification from the musical establishment—a wire from the durable center of mainstream popular culture, Richard Rodgers. Sullivan eagerly announced to the Beatles, "Richard Rodgers, who is one of America's greatest composers, wanted me to tell the four of you that he is one of your most rabid fans. . . . And that goes for me, too!" If Beethoven were alive, Ed would have solicited a handwritten rave from the old master saying that Ludwig grooved on the Fab Four. Rodgers represented the spirit of pop music past, far from ready to pass the torch to the Beatles but at least willing to acknowledge their presence.

In Rodgers's heyday, America led the world in groundbreaking pop music—from Tin Pan Alley, to Broadway, to Hollywood musicals, to New Orleans–Chicago jazz and blues, to Nashville country-western, to Appalachian folk music, to Detroit Motown, to San Francisco rock and roll, to Los Angeles surfer anthems. But now, out of nowhere, four Liverpool whippersnappers had seized the baton and the moment. The Broadway musical was in a deep coma by 1964 (Richard Rodgers wrote his last show in 1979, the failed "I Remember Mama," but his last hit was "No Strings" in 1962). Even film musicals were passé and the reliable "Hit Parade" was history, top-heavy with rock, doo-wop, and R&B.

Prior to the Miami show, Sullivan's battle-scarred staff had met with the police chief to discuss extra security. John Moffitt told me that the chief had explained to him, "We've done this kind of thing before, don't you worry." But even then a teenage Hurricane Katrina was building, and the cops were totally unprepared. Kids had invaded the hotel, pushing every doorbell, gambling that a random Beatle would open the door. Police had formed a flying wedge to get the Beatles through the Deauville lobby into the Mau Mau Room, site of the telecast; they barely made it on time.

As Moffitt recalled, "We're on the air and someone is signaling to Ed, 'They're not here!' Ed mumbled some ad-libs, then went to a commercial," whereupon the Beatles burst through a door, skipped down the aisle, and hopped up onstage. The Miami show's actual audience, however, was suddenly devoid of manic teenage girls. The rollicking balconies of ecstatic New York Lolitas were replaced by a classic winter crowd of courteous, tired, tanned retirees. When it panned the audience for writhing females, all the camera could find was one attentive little girl.

After the wild week was over, a farewell dinner was thrown for the foursome, and Moffitt was seated with two Beatles. "Ringo seemed kinda morose. I said, 'What's wrong, Ringo?' He said, 'Oh, well, this is it for us. It can't get any better than this. This is our moment. This has just been the most brilliant week. How in the world are we ever going to top this? I'm sure it's all going to be downhill from here.' He was sad! We always think of Ringo as the least sensitive one, yet he was the most melancholy about it."

By the third show, February 23, 1964, Sullivan was smiling more easily as he reeled off the other acts the audience would be seeing that night besides the Beatles—Cab Calloway, Gordon and Sheila MacRae, British comics Morecambe & Wise, jazz clarinetist Acker Bilt, comics Dave Barry and Morty Gunty, and life-size marionettes—a cow, a worm, and a bird singing "You Must Have Been a Beautiful Baby." Good sturdy Sullivan fare.

On the final live telecast (the fourth performance, taped and shown September 12, 1965, was interlaced with comments from Sullivan to make it appear live), after the Beatles had finished their last song ("I Want to Hold Your Hand"), Sullivan sauntered out and said, in his best rambling fashion: "Y'know, all of us on the show are so darn sorry that this is the third and last show of the Beatles, because these youngsters from Liverpool, England, and their conduct over here, not only as fine professional singers but as a group of fine youngsters, will leave an imprint over here with everyone who's met them—and that goes for everyone on our show." Moffitt summed up the Beatles' jubilant, groundbreaking week more simply: "They were like kids in a toy store."

The director added, "Ed really did like them. The later rock music acts Ed didn't like very much, but he knew it got ratings. He knew they would be here this week and gone the next, so he never got close. But he truly loved the Beatles. He was really proud of them. It was almost like he was their godfather—Uncle Beatle. Clean-cut kids, they came to rehearsal, they called him 'Mr. Sullivan,' they played live. The Beatles, he really took to heart. You gotta remember, Ed's kind of music was Louis Armstrong, Ella Fitzgerald, Duke Ellington."

After his farewell speech, Sullivan also complimented his unruly audience, as if relieved he had survived the whirlwind and the rapture: "I want to congratulate everyone; you've been a fine audience despite severe provocation"—even if, at one point, he had yelled at the madding crowd, *"Now, be quiet!"* As the Beatles trotted out, he pumped their hands individually. "I want to congratulate the four of you for the way you've handled yourselves. They're a bunch of nice kids, and we're gonna miss 'em."

Well, sort of. There was no need for Sullivan viewers to adjust their set, for the next week's show would return to its regularly scheduled programming, with a vintage Sullivan lineup: George Raft, Rickie Layne, Anita Bryant, and sketches from a musical revue. After bidding the Beatles farewell, Ed said to the camera, "Good night, and to all of you in the audience, drive safely!"

The Beatles telecasts reverberated for the rest of the show's life span. Paying him a backhanded compliment in the *New York Times* in 1965, on his 18th anniversary, Jack Gould called Sullivan "really one of the fathers of rock and roll," but added a sharp elbow: "The screams of girls over boys in long hair are the contemporary barometer of success in TV, and Mr. Sullivan is content to ride the tide[,] . . . a telling reminder of how much Mr. Sullivan has had to compromise to retain his lofty seat. When the chips are down on an important Sunday night, when the ratings are taken, he has virtually abandoned his original concept of rounded popular family entertainment."

While acknowledging Sullivan as "one of the medium's great intuitive showmen," Gould, protecting the mom-and-pop franchise, advised sternly: "He undoubtedly has an obligation to keep the youngsters and teenagers in mind when he plans his show, but perhaps he will also see the wisdom of not disenfranchising other members of the family too regularly, if only because they are the ones who have somewhat larger allowances to spend with advertisers." Many of those older "disenfranchised" fans continued to rail that their show had sold out to The Youngsters.

In late 1964 the network, Sullivan, and Precht addressed the show's rising decibel factor, which parents were fuming about. For CBS, the problem was that audiences were packed with teenagers holding tickets that their well-connected parents snagged for them. The tickets stipulated no one under 16 would be allowed in the studio, and ushers were now alerted to enforce the rule, never before a problem. When a rock act was scheduled, half the ticket holders were teens. "I don't know where the kids are getting all the tickets," said Precht in a *New York Times* story. "The whole show is being colored by the kids' reactions."

The AP's Cynthia Lowry, quoted in the *New York Times,* wrote that "the adult viewers have had it with the bedlam created by rock acts on his show." TV critic Ben Gross, viewing the issue as a marketing stunt, charged that much of the audience's "barbaric yowling" was planted by record companies, DJs, press agents, and fan clubs "manipulating the hysteria of the kids for only one purpose—to collect more dollars." But Joel Selvin hooted, "They didn't have to plant that. You see those girls today, they're in sexual ecstasy!" But Gross made a compelling argument for the prerock generation: "As for the kids having the right to enjoy their 'own music,' no one disputes that. But most of the r 'n' r aficionados aren't satisfied with this. They seem determined to wipe every other form of music from the air."

Many traditional acts were infiltrated by residual racket from the rafters. Alan King grew visibly annoyed during a routine, facing balcony screechers left over when the Dave Clark Five departed the stage. "We have made efforts," said Precht, "to turn down microphones that pick up audience reaction to reduce the din going out on the air." Asked if he might book fewer rock acts to maintain order, Precht backed off: "That's a possibility, but we feel strongly that rock 'n' roll is a part of the entertainment scene. Such groups are selling records like mad. We don't want to be a rock 'n' roll show, but we can't ignore an important trend in our business."

Sullivan, the once sure-footed impresario, was juggling two opposing forces, attempting to offer wildly popular new voices without alienating original viewers. It was a basic fight for the soul of the Sullivan show— and of Sullivan. Overnight, pop music had become intensely political. Sullivan was appealing to rival factions while straining, like any candidate, to stay true to his base. Mainstream entertainment had been one of the few areas of American life uninfected by politics, but now the left and right wings of show business attacked each other like sniping political parties. Moffitt told me, "Bob Precht kept pushing the button—'Ed, that's the future, we gotta have these music acts on.'" But Precht says Ed needed no pushing, happy to follow the herd. As Mina Bess Lewis observed, "The show was becoming trendy rather than contemporary"—a keen distinction.

The fierce new culture clash had racial and social undertones driven by the Beatles' deep affection for American singers like Buddy Holly, Little Richard, and Chuck Berry, all of them major pop influences. Martin Goldsmith wrote, "It is likely that more white kids were introduced to African-American music by the Beatles than by the original artists."

Said Selvin, "They were white people playing black music. The Beatles were a white English representation of American working-class music, which was African American. They contained all that excitement, but they had a sexual component because the teenage white female American audience identified with these guys in a way [in which] they couldn't identify with Bo Diddley. They were reaching white pubescent sexuality."

Many say that the Beatles would have triumphed in America without the Sullivan show, but Selvin argued otherwise: "It's really hard to imagine the Beatles emerging in America without that piece of dynamite at the Ed Sullivan show blowing up at that moment. They had tremendous difficulty convincing American Top 40 radio to play their records." Mainstream AM radio was opposed to early rock, so the FM stations became outlaw outposts for rabid rockers. "Radio was *not* open to it," insisted Selvin.

After their final Sullivan show in September 1965—also the last black-and-white Ed Sullivan show—glimpses of the Beatles on live TV were rare. In 1970 Sullivan recycled the Beatles in a show devoted to their songs performed by traditional names—Steve Lawrence and Eydie Gorme, Peggy Lee, Dionne Warwick, Duke Ellington. In 1965, he filmed a live concert at Shea Stadium that was televised and sold to ABC in 1966 and later boxed in videos, in 1991. The Beatles' entire crazed week in America was documented by David and Albert Maysles in their 1964 film, "The Beatles in America," a raw, grainy, muddy-sounding total-access account that might be a draft of "A Hard Day's Night"; and Eric Idle made a deft mockumentary of the entire fantasia, "The Rutles: All You Need Is Cash."

In retrospect, Ed Sullivan needed the Beatles more than they needed him. If they hadn't played Ed Sullivan's show, they might well have been snagged by Perry Como or Dinah Shore, but neither of the latter possessed Sullivan's scoopmeister mentality. As James Maguire observed, "The meeting of these two major entities, the life force of the Beatles with the national institution that was 'The Ed Sullivan Show,' produced a kind of nuclear fission, an inestimable spark of change."

After the Beatles, the Sullivan show was a haven for countless British rock groups that came calling—Gerry and the Pacemakers, the Animals, the Zombies, the Dave Clark Five, Herman's Hermits, the Rascals, Chad and Jeremy, and Freddie and the Dreamers—but they were usually bands deemed safe for family ears. Selvin makes a telling distinction:

"Even the Animals, who started out playing tough R&B, were sanitized by the time they appeared. You never saw the Kinks, the Yardbirds, or the Who on his show. Sullivan wouldn't have allowed them to break their instruments on his stage."

Selvin remarked, "On the one hand, Sullivan is the absolute figure of authority who represents the antirock forces, a real issue in the entertainment world in those days. You had to take sides. You had the infidels outside the door, as far as the entertainment establishment was concerned. All of a sudden these jerks with dirt under their fingernails are totally running the hit parade, totally dominating the charts, and the old-time music businesses are going, *'What the fuck is this?!'* "

The Byrds and the Doors were two hot rock bands considered too raunchy for the show. For disobeying the adults, the youngsters were sent to their room by Sullivan. A major exception was the career-savvy Rolling Stones, who famously capitulated when Sullivan asked Mick Jagger to change "Let's spend the night together" to "Let's spend some time together." But Jagger prevailed, signaling to fans in his performance that the Stones were appearing under duress. "Jagger really minces it up," laughed Selvin. "He's really pissed off, and he wants to let everybody in America know that he's being fucked with. So he goes, 'Let's spend some *t-i-i-i-i-me* together.' He really lays it out." According to Selvin, Elvis, watching Jagger prancing on the show, hooted, "Look at that motherfucker! Doesn't he look like a faggot?"

Selvin went on to say, "In those days, the Ed Sullivan show was America, and here's Jagger, a real rock-and-roll punk, using that stage to reach a secondary audience. There are people out there that are his people. He's talkin' to *those* people. That's the thing about Ed Sullivan's show then—he was putting on these bands that had a subversive element to them and attracting that audience, but trying to keep it all between the gutters. All those acts, for the most part, were happy to play ball with Sullivan for the exposure."

Even rock's bad boys (and girl) Jimi Hendrix, Eric Clapton, Stephen Stills, Carlos Santana, and Janis Joplin were stirred into the Sullivan blend, along with the seductively mellower Mamas and Papas and the Fifth Dimension. If Sullivan said no, it drew a line in the cultural sand. Culture-watcher Bob Thompson pointed out to me, "You knew that, if Ed Sullivan could not contain them, they were really dangerous forces to be reckoned with."

The Doors refused to comply with Sullivan's rigid code of behavior. Asked to alter "girl, we couldn't get much higher" in their signature song "Light My Fire"—to erase the illicit "higher"—they double-crossed Sullivan. Although the band "nodded their assent," said rock writer Ben Fong-Torres in his Doors book, the group did the song as written, without fear—their sound guys were running the board. When they failed to excise "higher" they were banished for life, less for the offending word than for blatant insubordination. Secretary Susan Abramson recalled the "phones ringing off the hook with people complaining about 'Light My Fire.' It was just crazy."

After that show, Precht told the group, "Mr. Sullivan wanted you for six more shows but you'll never work 'The Ed Sullivan Show' again," to which Jim Morrison coolly replied, "Hey, man, we just *did* 'The Ed Sullivan Show.'" The Doors' Ray Manzarek recalled that Precht reminded them, "You said you weren't going to use the word 'higher.' So we're all just looking at him. I say, 'Hey, man, we're just *boys*. I guess we got excited and forgot. Sorry.'" He added, "It didn't matter to us. We got the Number One song in America. What the hell is another appearance on the Ed Sullivan show going to do for us? We blew it. We said 'higher' on national television." And the republic survived. Fong-Torres wrote that, before the Doors went on, the notoriously sullen Sullivan had come into their dressing room and, having watched the band in rehearsal, advised, "Y'know, you boys are really handsome. But you'd look a lot better if you'd smile more." Morrison replied, "We're kind of a sullen group."

Whether they were sullen or cheery, playing the Sullivan show was a major deal for American rock 'n' rollers who had grown up watching the show as kids. It had a revered place no matter how unhip it may have seemed to hyperhip rockers. Michelle Phillips of the Mamas and the Papas, just 21 when they performed, was oblivious to its significance. "To tell you the truth, I didn't actually realize how important the show was," she explained. "'The Ed Sullivan Show' was not my kind of fare. We'd never had a television in our house; my father wouldn't buy one. So I was kind of surprised at all the hoopla surrounding us being on the show. As far as I knew, it was just another show. I really don't even remember doing the first show." She adds, "Sullivan didn't have any idea what kind of singers we were. I thought he was one of the strangest people I'd ever met, with that funny dialect of his."

Denny Doherty, her cohort, remembered every detail of the group's first appearance. A year before his death, he told me, "Ed didn't mind us. I guess we were a little bit mellow, not like the Rolling Stones with their Nazi SS uniforms. He knew what the masses were going for and what he was going to get—and that was ratings, ratings, ratings." Doherty recalled Sullivan coming up to the trio and saying, 'My daughter really digs your stuff. You got anything you could sign for her?'"

For Doherty, playing the show was a transcendent event, certifying that the Mamas and the Papas had truly made it: "*Elvis* did the Ed Sullivan show, man! On the West Coast, there were 'The Hollywood Palace' shows that we'd do, but this was the Sullivan show, this was New York, this was the Great White Way! This was the ultimate, as far as doing American television—Ed Sullivan's 'Toast of the Town'! I was 16 years old when I watched the show, and then, you know, ten years later I'm 26 and I'm doing 'The Ed Sullivan Show!' It was just another show for everyone else that night, but for all of us it was . . . *the fuckin' 'Ed Sullivan Show'!*"

CHAPTER 22

The Showman without a Country

Ed, what are we going to do on Sundays now?
                    Sylvia Sullivan

Sullivan never again came close to approaching the exalted Beatles moments that became a generational touchstone. As someone wrote, the Beatles programs were a last hurrah for Ed Sullivan. His show never regained the prominence that the Beatles brought him, nor would so much attention from the entire nation again be focused on his doings.

The Beatles changed "The Ed Sullivan Show"—elevating it, transforming it, then indirectly diminishing it. They altered all forms of pop music life: outdoor arenas became the new concert halls, rock journalism gained respectability, and concept albums were a sudden rage. Post-Beatles, the entire school of white soft-rock had to race to keep up. Martin Goldsmith wrote, "Pop stars who enjoyed great success in 1962 and '63—Neil Sedaka, Del Shannon, Bobby Vinton, Bobby Vee, Dick, Dee-Dee and the Dixie Cups—were has-beens by the end of '64, prematurely bound for the oldies sections in record shops." Jerry Lee Lewis proclaimed, "The Beatles cut 'em all down like wheat before the sickle."

After four Ed Sullivan shows, the entire pop landscape shifted, and aftershocks rocked every TV variety show. Cozy hours hosted by Perry Como and Dean Martin were passé. Network executives scrambled to put together all-rock shows, and came up with "Hootenanny," "Shindig," and "Hullabaloo," which led to variety shows with a rock sensibility—"The Smothers Brothers Comedy Hour," "The Sonny and Cher Show," and shows starring Tony Orlando, the Captain and Tennille, Johnny Cash, and Helen Reddy.

"Variety shows had turned into something different," pop artist manager Sherwin Bash told me. "There was Carol Burnett, Sonny and Cher, Tony Orlando, people like that. But it wasn't like Sullivan, where it was one act after another. Carol, Sonny and Cher, and Orlando were doing comedy sketches, which young recording artists wanted to throw up at. It was just a whole different perspective. Young recording artists never thought of themselves as being entertainers."

After the initial Beatles cyclone subsided and the boys went home, the Sullivan show tried to settle back into its familiar routine. But the Beatlecasts had pointed pop culture—all entertainment—in a radical new direction. Show business was changing, television was changing, America was changing, and Ed Sullivan was changing—and aging.

In 1965, Ed was 63 and showing signs of TV decay, partly brought on by undiagnosed dementia and partly showbiz burnout. He'd been booking TV shows for 18 years. "The Sullivan show limped on, a kind of living antique," wrote Jerry Bowles. "Bob Precht tried to walk the high wire that separated young from old. It was an impossible feat." Sullivan was still nominally in charge. When CBS sent around its annual form asking what he planned for the coming season, Sullivan said, "Fuck 'em. We'll do the same thing we did last year." Hardly. Ed had no more Beatles up his sleeve.

All at once, television was crowded with a convoy of amiable variety shows all trying to suck the last gasp of oxygen, and performers, out of the Sullivan show. Where it had once cornered the market on A-list performers, the show now had to share the talent with struggling new lesser rivals. As one writer noted, there was no such thing as fresh talent anymore.

Throughout the show's uncertain twilight years, Sullivan increasingly felt unappreciated by CBS. Nobody in the executive suite, he thought, ever praised him sufficiently. As Marlo Lewis pointed out in his book, neither Bill Paley nor his underlings could grasp Sullivan's historic success. His popularity especially bewildered Paley, who labeled it "magical—beyond explanation." To which Lewis said, "What I find truly inexplicable is Mr. Paley's inability to understand the simple formula that

"The Ed Sullivan Show" didn't get better or worse. At the end of its run, it was exactly the same as always.

Brigid O'Lunney, Bangor, Maine

worked so well for 23 years. That his audience did not demand that their host do an act should not have been so mystifying. Ed was a weekly Santa Claus bringing a bag of marvelous things into American homes."

Fed up at last, years of resentment finally boiling to the surface, Sullivan released his rage at the CBS hierarchy in a 1967 *Life* profile: "With the exception of Jack Schneider, I consider every president of CBS television—and I've been through seven of them—ungrateful, impolite people. I've never heard anything vaguely approaching 'thank you' or 'good job.' I never even heard from Frank Stanton on the show's anniversaries. And when you consider the money I've made for CBS!"

He ranted on: "We've kept their Sunday night supremacy going for years. The strength we've provided for the programs that precede and follow us, the performers who worked here first and went on to their own CBS show. It's selfish and bad manners. At first, I was hurt but now I don't give a damn. I know them for what they are, and my relationship with CBS is strictly business. Thank God Bill Paley isn't at all like the rest of the jerks in that mausoleum."

Life's interviewer, Wayne Warga, commented, "His tone is not vitriolic, just indignant and, in spite of his protestations, hurt. He is secure enough to be publicly sore at the boss and still have a job." Sullivan had once asked Stanton's advice on how to invest his money. "He practically invented CBS so he knew how to make money," Sullivan told Warga. "The guy was ice cold. He just looked at me. He's a success as a machine but sort of a hopeless case as a human."

CBS took the hint and, on December 10, 1967, momentarily humanized itself by officially recognizing Sullivan's legacy and changing the name of CBS Studio 50 to the Ed Sullivan Theater. It was a news event, with Mayor John Lindsay rechristening the landmark theater as Sullivan was escorted inside to the sound of Irish pipe bands. This was the first (and so far only) Broadway theater named for a TV personality, which is only fitting, in that Sullivan had presented, indeed preserved on tape, major scenes from Broadway shows, from "Hamlet" to "Hair."

Yet nowhere in a 21-inch *New York Times* story by Bill Carter about the David Letterman show moving into the Ed Sullivan Theater in August 1993 is there any mention of its famous former longtime inhabitant. However, in an earlier story that month on the move, *Times* reporter David W. Dunlap praised the *building* as the most ornate TV studio in America, describing in detail its "four-story high, apse-like recesses flanking the main stage, luxurious plasterwork flora and 18-foot-high window bays topped by quatrefoil traceries inlaid with cobalt, ruby, and emerald stained glass" that depicted characters from operas Oscar Hammerstein produced in the early 1900s. In a series of New York City afterlives, the building, which opened in 1927 as Hammerstein's Theatre, briefly became Billy Rose's Music Hall in 1933, and then was called Manhattan Theatre in 1936, before CBS signed a long-term lease and converted it into the CBS Radio Playhouse.

In 1950, it was rechristened Studio 50, the network's major broadcast space; on September 19, 1965, it broadcast the first Sullivan show in color. The theater was built as a memorial to Hammerstein, the Ed Sullivan of his day, by his son Arthur, father of Oscar II, the lyricist. The architect of the rebuilt house commented on the restoration: "Our job is to protect the ghosts." As David Letterman's "Late Night" crew moved into the gothic theater after its $4-million renovation, on August 30, 1993, Ed Sullivan's ghost watched from the wings.

While the Sullivan dynasty played out its final years, the critics began lauding the show's hard-won stature in TV history. Not until 1969, however, did Jack Gould finally ease up, 21 years after his first attack on the show, publicly digesting in his *New York Times* column large slices of critical crow: "Of all the Broadway columnists, now a vanishing breed, Sullivan alone saw the potential of TV. He is unquestionably one of the medium's great intuitive showmen." He noted, "Without fuss, he was the first important headliner to make room for visits by Negro artists on prime time, long before it became a major issue."

Yet Gould couldn't resist a little jab at Sullivan's on-screen flaws: "Despite all the gags, he is living proof that an absence of a vivid personality is the best insurance for longevity on the home screen." The burst of gratitude ended with: "The why and wherefore of Mr. Sullivan's accommodating changing tastes, without really changing his show, is one of the most incredible sagas of the entertainment world. But there he was Sunday night, after a whole generation had been born, grown up, educated and married, a one-man feat for anyone in show business let alone an individual who would be the first to disclaim being a performer."

Critics everywhere joined Gould in genuflecting to the acknowledged emperor of Sunday night. *TV Guide* said that "The Ed Sullivan Show" "had joined the pantheon of American verities—mother, the flag, and apple pie." Capping everything, he was given the Television Showman of the Century Award (30 years before the end of the century). In 1997, *Life* enshrined him as TV's "only institution." As Sullivan left television, critics who had mercilessly ridiculed him now jumped aboard the posterity bandwagon, praising Sullivan for his great foresight, wisdom, and showmanship, but for Sullivan it was a belated hug. Marlo Lewis said, "I don't think he ever forgave the savagery with which his confreres had first attacked him, or the way they had overlooked the real pioneering spirit he had brought to the new medium. I know he never forgot."

Even so, all the belated flowery bouquets soon wilted. Precht and other senior staffers knew the show was living on borrowed time: instead of the traditional 52 new shows a year, there were now only 39 and then 24 new shows, padded out with reruns. In the final two seasons, Precht and Sullivan put on a brave front by producing several splashy tribute shows that captured critical attention and generated fresh ink—a tribute to golden oldie Richard Rodgers at the Hollywood Bowl, a Muppets Christmas Special, an ice show from Las Vegas, and a tribute to the United Nations. But the show was costing more and more, and in its last season, 1971, it spent upward of $60,000 for sets per show (big money then).

It's hard to pinpoint a precise moment when the Sullivan show changed its old guard and true colors, but a night in 1966 will do—when Bert Lahr appeared one last time at the tag end of a bill that included the Dave Clark Five. Lahr was winding up a half century on stage, screen, radio, and TV, but was best known then (as now) as the Cowardly Lion in "The Wizard of Oz" (and in 1966 for an impish Lay's potato chip commercial: "Betcha can't eat just one!"). If ever any performer personified Sullivan's world it was Bert Lahr, a classic vaudevillian now on his last legs, just like Sullivan was.

As John Lahr describes it in a biography of his father, Bert was worn, weary and showing all his 72 years that night. He found just enough gas left in his rusted tank to reprise his ancient routine, "The Cop Act," but most of the crowd was there to see the new British rockers. Sullivan sauntered out and, like a drama teacher at a high school assembly, instructed the young crowd: "Look, kids, we've got the Dave Clark Five on tonight. Now I don't mind if you carry on when they come out, but remember there are other acts on the bill." Respect your elders! As the lights went up, and the show began, he announced the evening's marquee, but neglected to mention Bert Lahr, who was set to close the show.

When the vintage vaudevillian appeared, the cameras closed in on his face, losing most of his patented comic gestures. He was forced to hurry through the sketch because the show was running behind; he couldn't wait for laughs. "On stage," wrote his son, "the atmosphere is cramped and antiseptic; linoleum floors, white light, the audience stacked up on raked seats." Lahr got his laughs but the act was just an on-screen blur. Told afterward that Sullivan forgot to announce him, Lahr was forgiving, saying resignedly, "Oh, this guy is like that. We're all absent-minded."

Still wearing his makeup, he left the dressing room, thanking Sullivan on the way out, where people huddled about. Lahr spotted a young girl standing shyly to one side. "Little girl—miss—did you want my autograph?" He signed her pad, headed for the elevator, and outside was met by older kids rushing toward him screaming. His pen wouldn't write, so one girl said impatiently, "Just put an X," eager to get her notebook back to snag a Dave Clark Five signature when they emerged. Back home, Lahr's wife, Mildred, said, "Bert, you weren't even billed—it's disgusting," and Lahr again excused Sullivan's oversight, repeating, "Maybe he just forgot." Then Lahr checked the TV listings for the show with a magnifying glass and saw that his name was missing there too. "Well," he sighed, "I just got the booking last week. At my age, I'm in this business for the money. Anyway, who cares now?" The old lion died a year later.

Seasoned Sullivan observers trace the demise of the show to the 1968–1969 season, which featured the Doors and their sensual lead singer, Jim Morrison, with his long curls and skintight black leather garb. The Doors represented yet another tectonic shift, persuading Sullivan to book bands like Steppenwolf, Sly and the Family Stone, Blood, Sweat & Tears, and the raw, edgy, gritty Janis Joplin, whom Ed introduced as hailing "from Joplin, Missouri" (not Port Arthur, Texas, her actual hometown).

The melodic Beach Boys were now singing acid-laced love songs like "Good Vibrations," and even Supremes songs were heavy with sexual relevance, like "Love Child"; James Maguire wrote, "Hearing the 67-year-old showman enthusiastically shout . . . 'And now, here's "Love Child"!' only reinforced the idea that something profound was changing." Sullivan featured the hallucinogenic "Hair" and its let-it-all-hang-out anthem, "Aquarius/Let the Sunshine In." But not even Broadway musicals on the show could sweeten the rock 'n' roll mix and rescue Sullivan.

"There was a little conflict between Bob and Ed because Bob had new ideas and Ed was the old dog," John Moffitt explained. There were still some elements of the old show, but reliable Sullivan hands—John Davidson warbling "Didn't We?," a banjo group strumming "Take Me Out to the Ball Game," the Muppets, comic Norm Crosby—now seemed like door prizes for loyal viewers. But the balance of power had shifted.

Russ Petranto, onetime production assistant, recalled, "When I came aboard in 1968, the show was run by Bob Precht. Ed had very little involvement. He would come over on a Saturday, and he'd write the 'goes-intas' and the 'goes-outas' [the segues]. But Bob did it all. Bob would say to Ed, 'Here's who's on the show this week,' and Ed would say, 'Who's the Jefferson Airplane?,' and Bob would say, 'Trust me, you want them on your show.' Ed would go, 'OK.' At that point, Ed wouldn't fight anything. They're dealing with rock acts and Janis Joplin and Ed doesn't know from all that. With the theater bookings and the Steve and Eydies, he was fine."

Precht's secretary Susan Abramson only knew the older congenial Sullivan: "By the time I met him, Ed's personality had kind of mellowed," she reminisced. "Bob was really running the show. His dressing room was upstairs, and across from that was our production office. Ed used to come out in his underwear and say hello. It was all small talk—'Hi, sweetie,' 'Hello, honey.' He never knew my name, but he was very, very kind to us. I never heard him being harsh with anyone. In those days his temper was not as out there as it once was. Sometimes he'd yell at the teleprompter guy."

While hard-edged pop music acts still sold their soul to be on the Sullivan show, and Ed had mortgaged part of his own soul for their ratings, rock royalty now considered the show embarrassing, even beneath them. Sherwin Bash, who managed Neil Sedaka, Herb Alpert, Neil Diamond, and the Carpenters, maintained that TV and pop music were natural enemies. A TV series was the kiss of death for most pop recording artists, and, after the Beatles, rock performers and their fans rarely looked to TV. The Rascals issued a statement in 1969 that they would no longer appear on the Sullivan show or any other "establishment shows." For rock acts, which he had midwifed, Sullivan was now politically incorrect and passé. As James Maguire noted, "Watching 'The Ed Sullivan Show' meant enduring an hour with one's parents."

In the 1969–1970 season, the show dipped to 27th place, provoking outraged letters from loyal scorned viewers like Beatrice Rapp, who

I'll never forget my parents' stunned faces watching 15-year-old Janis Ian singing "Society's Child."

Lois Franks, Omaha, Nebraska

wrote to the *Philadelphia Sunday Bulletin*, "Whatever happened to 'The Ed Sullivan Show'? It was a good family show until recently." She was offended by the "suggestive dancers" and "the disgusting display of that character Tiny Tim."

That old winning blend of something for everyone now suddenly seemed like a travesty, self-parody, a bizarre mishmash: Santana followed by Henry Mancini, Douglas Fairbanks Jr. in an excerpt from "My Fair Lady" countered by Credence Clearwater Revival's antiwar "Fortunate Son," and the Rolling Stones bashing out "Gimme Shelter" alongside Ella Fitzgerald's lush "You Better Love Me." The show was always a strange mix, but a tasty cocktail. Now it was oil and water. Toward the end of 1971, its 23rd and final season, the show was clinging for life in 43rd place, which was midrange among the mediocre masses, but deadly for the mighty Sullivan show. It might as well have been in last place.

By 1971, CBS was operating in full crisis mode, its dominance finally threatened by NBC, which, at long last, crept ahead in the season ratings. When CBS decided to cancel such 1960s icons as Red Skelton and Jackie Gleason, the handwriting was on the cue card. Precht candidly conceded to the *New York Times* in March 1971, "I have no reason to be optimistic. I do not believe we will be renewed." The show still produced respectable ratings (23 million viewers), but they were middle-age and older, scary specters to sponsors on a rampaging crusade for the youth demographic.

On March 17, CBS president Bob Wood called with the bad news. "I had a sinking feeling as I walked to the phone," Precht recalled. "I knew this was it." Wood nattered on a bit about the show's "grand tradition" but quickly got to the point: CBS wanted "a more relevant 'now' " image." Wood said, "We're awfully sorry, Bob, but in view of all the many considerations for the new season, we're going to have to drop the old format." Then he scattered a few crumbs: "We don't want to lose the Sullivan production team, and you have a commitment to do six to ten specials."

Ed was in sterling company: his fellow corpses included "Lassie," "The Andy Griffith Show," "Hogan's Heroes," "Green Acres," "Petticoat Junction," and one of CBS's most beloved sitcoms, "The Beverly Hillbillies." Sullivan's main audience was judged to be largely small town, or rural "Beverly Hillbillies," viewers. His fan base had always skewed old despite the landmark Presley and Beatles shows, and the show's subsequent playing to younger viewers seduced by rock bands had driven away a core constituency. He who lives by the Nielsens . . .

"It was a painful decision," said Wood, "and from an emotional point of view, one you'd hope not to have to make." Many of the same people Sullivan once booked exclusively were now available on morning, afternoon, and late-night talk shows, not just performing but babbling freely, often baring their tortured souls and eagerly displaying dirty laundry. Gone too were the big exclusive news hooks that Sullivan had dangled to lure audiences to his show each week.

When Precht called his father-in-law at the Delmonico, Sullivan said, "Well, I'll be a son of a bitch. After all we've done for the network over the years. You'd think they'd let me go to 25 [years]." It seemed to confirm his feeling that CBS never really loved him, never knew what it had. For 23 years, he felt he'd been living week to week. The veteran booker Mark Leddy said, "Rock and roll and reruns, that's what killed the Sullivan show," but it may just have been the times. Despite Ed's final appeal to Paley, it was over. The show's Bob Spitzer said, "I just couldn't believe it. I thought it would never end." Vince Calandra recalled in his Archive of American Television interview, "It just all ended so fast." Designer Bill Bohnert remembered watching wistfully as garbagemen piled old Sullivan show sets and props into trucks and carted them to a New Jersey junk heap. That was the week they canceled Sunday.

Precht told me, "Ed was resigned to it, I think. But his cycle was a weekly cycle, and his moment was 8 o'clock Sunday night, and for that to just be taken away . . . The love from the fans continued, but he didn't have that sustaining thing anymore. I felt that a lot, too." Sullivan put on a brave front for interviewers, telling John Mosedale, "The show was becoming a millstone around my neck." The now-and-again specials partly salvaged Sullivan's ego and reputation. He told *Women's Wear Daily*'s Chauncey Howell, "Well, thank Christ, CBS didn't throw us out on our asses entirely." But he conceded to Howell, "The string had run out on variety shows for TV. I outlasted them all. I don't think I'll live long enough to see variety shows return to favor. When our ratings first dropped, I thought, 'Well, maybe it's the weather.' When we dropped to 27th in popularity I knew it wasn't the weather."

During that bleak period, as the show dwindled away, Moffitt had dinner with Sullivan in Los Angeles. "He was kind of quiet when we picked him up at his hotel. We went to Chasen's, and he was humming a little bit, but he was really kind of down. We tried to talk to him. He didn't want to say anything. We got there, got a table, and Dave Chasen comes over. Chasen was a Broadway comedy star before he got into the restaurant business. Ed had reviewed him for the paper years before.

They knew each other very well." Chasen invited them all to his private
bar after dinner—walls full of photos—"and the two old-timers are
talking about all the people on the wall and recalling the scandals and
stories. But a lot of them were dead. We took Ed home, and now he's
singing in the car! He said, 'I want you to know, fellas, I was really down
tonight before we went out. But I feel great tonight. I had a great evening. Thanks a lot. Nice to be with you guys.' He got out of the car, and
we looked at each other, and somebody said, 'You know why Ed feels
great? Because he and Dave Chasen outlived all those people. That's what
made him so happy!' "

Old family friend Ken Rothstein told me he recalled Sullivan remi-
niscing about the show after it had been canceled. "There was a sparkle
in his eye when he talked about the legendary guests he'd had on the
show, almost as if he was taking stock of his legacy. For me, as just a
kid, it was such a heady experience to hear it all coming right from Ed."

Sullivan, his spirit broken, stopped booking new shows. He went to
reruns from April to June; the last all-new "Ed Sullivan Show" was telecast March 28, 1971. "He was crushed," producer and video packager
Andrew Solt remarked. After the announcement, Jerry Vale met Sullivan
at Toots Shor's and noticed tears in his eyes. "How about that?" he told
Vale in disbelief. "After all these years, they canceled me."

Sullivan's physical and mental decline couldn't be masked any longer.
The master showman began to forget crucial things. Precht told me,
"There was the beginning of some level of dementia—something was
happening that we became aware of and concerned about in the last couple of years. We dealt with it carefully, the way one does. I tried to be as
supportive as I could, but it was apparent to people." James Maguire describes Sullivan then as "feeble" and "shaky," "haggard and unsteady,"
with "a timeworn, hollowed-out look." Betty Precht told me, "At the
end of my dad's life, he might have had Alzheimer's, though they didn't
know about it back then." Russ Petranto recalled, "He could be very
forgetful. During a commercial he'd ask me a question, and 30 seconds
later he'd ask me again."

Moffitt remembered, "He was pretty sharp for many, many years, but
he was getting weaker, and his mind . . . I don't know if it was senility or
what, but when you get like that on camera, that's when people start to
tune out, to realize maybe Ed wasn't the showman anymore. Maybe he
was just reading the teleprompter and they didn't believe what he said.
People saw a change." Joan Rivers first got booked on the show thanks

to a Sullivan senior moment: "When I first went on, May 22, 1966, I went on by mistake. I don't know if it was early Alzheimer's, but he was a little foggy sometimes. Right before the show they had been pitching singer Johnny Rivers to him, and he went out and said, 'Next week, Joan Rivers!' "

Mary Lynn Gottfried, the show's weekend production secretary from 1967 to 1970, worked in the office outside Ed's dressing room. "He was extremely forgetful," she told me. "He wouldn't know who was on the show until he got to the studio. I would give him a list of who was going to be on. He didn't know too much what was going on. He would say, 'What time is the show gonna be on tonight?,' even though it had been on at 8 P.M. for 23 years." He once turned up backstage an hour before the show and asked Vince Calandra where everyone was.

Gottfried filled in the blanks for Ed's introductions—who was singing what and where they were appearing. She remembered that he wrote his intros in pencil in a little notebook, later transferred to a teleprompter. Stars might pop in to say hello. "Sometimes I could tell he wasn't sure who they were. *They* all thought for sure he knew who they were. When they'd leave he'd ask, 'Who was that?' Bob Precht knew so well how to handle him. Bob really knew how to explain why we had to change the running order or drop someone or drop a number. I never saw them arguing. Bob was always just one key. I never saw any temper [from Sullivan], or the dynamo that he had once been."

Peter Calabrese recalled an incident involving the Supremes. Sullivan "blew up when the staff was very careful to make sure of the wording in an intro as precisely as Motown insisted—'Diana Ross and the Supremes.' He said, 'I don't want to hear this anymore. What do you think—I'm a moron? I get it.' So he was backing everyone off. That night on the show, somewhere in the midst of his intro, he kind of went off on his own, and then he had that deer-in-the-headlights look and he just said, 'Here they are—the girls!' "

Another time, as Sullivan was leaving to go to lunch, he came out of his dressing room and handed Calabrese a piece of paper and said, "Tell Bob I changed my mind, and I want this to be the running order of the show." Calabrese relayed the message and new list to Precht, who sighed, "He's got Robert Goulet on the show twice, and he's got two full sets back to back without a commercial break [to strike one set and slide a new one into place]. Bob said, 'Find Ed and tell him we need to keep the running order we agreed on—this doesn't work, and I'll explain why later.' By then I'd been on the show four years, and Ed had just seen me a half hour earlier. So I knock on the door of the Hickory House. Ed's in this private room watching the football game and having lunch. I said, 'Hi, Mr. Sullivan, sorry to interrupt—' and he takes the paper out of my hand and takes out a pen and gives me his autograph. I just took it and left. I told Bob, and he just got hysterical." In retrospect, Calabrese mentioned possible Alzheimer's and added, "People would just say, 'He's hard of hearing' or 'It's hardening of the arteries.' "

Precht's secretary, Barbara Gallagher, remembered, "Ed was getting vague when I was leaving, but we all protected him. He had earned that respect. He was an icon! I couldn't believe my luck I was working there, sitting in Ed Sullivan's apartment taking dictation. I liked Ed, I really did. I was amazed he did what he did—to stay on top all those years." She had grown up watching the show: "We'd switch back and forth between the Sullivan show and 'Colgate Comedy Hour.' I always thought he looked like Frankenstein—how he would grease back his hair, and it was all in black and white. He was much more handsome in person—big blue eyes and reddish-brown hair."

John Moffitt noted, "He was a little more frail than he'd been before that ulcer operation. They'd cut out part of his stomach. He didn't get excited very often now. He had run the show until then. When I first got there, he really ran the show." In the final years, "he had everything on teleprompter; he couldn't ad-lib anything." Sullivan would drift in and out of alertness as the show progressed, seeming more of a first-time guest on his own show than ever.

He tried to stay hip or at least look hip, sporting unlikely sideburns in the 1970s; he no longer slicked back his hair, and even colored it brown. He seemed increasingly lost, Maguire reported. "After he delivered his introduction his face might go slack and detached before the camera had cut away." Bob Thomas, the longtime AP Hollywood correspondent who interviewed Sullivan for a Winchell biography, said, "His final years were rather sad. He seemed to be just going through the motions. He was kind of out of it. He was a little vague about some things. His son-in-law was covering for him."

Denny Doherty remembered the night Sullivan shut down completely. He said he recalled Sullivan between acts "leaning up against the wall in pain." When it was time for him to go on, he would come to life. "He'd just sit back with his arms folded leaning against the wall. He had this apparatus, like a World War II stretcher laid flat against the wall, with arm rests built into the side posts. He'd sorta lean into it and hang onto the wall."

The night Sullivan came to a dead stop was the Mamas and Papas' last of three appearances on the show. Doherty recalled, "We did the show to sort of tell everyone we weren't breaking up"—contrary to rumors—"but just going off on a little vacation. Ed wanted to be the one to tell the world on his show we weren't breaking up. The producer told us, 'Ed's going to come over at the end of your number and ask you about the breakup. He'll say, "We're all broken up about the story you're splitting up and blah-blah-blah."' OK, great. Rehearsals worked great. We did 'Monday Monday,' Ed came over, and it's all flowers and smiley faces."

But on the show itself, Doherty continued, "we did our song and here comes Ed, and I think he'd taken his medication for the pain between rehearsal and showtime, because when he came over and sat down, you could hear him groan. It hurt. He just sat there for like one beat . . . two beats . . . three beats. Dead air! Red light's on, and I'm going to myself, 'Oh, my God, oh, my God, oh, my God. America is watching! What's he doing?' And I look over and he's just twiddling this little flower! It seemed like an eternity! And finally I had to go, 'Uh, well, Ed, I suppose you've heard about a breakup?' And that jogged his memory. He realized where he was and was supposed to have asked the question. If you see a video of the show, Cass [Elliot] jumps in and says, 'No, no, we're not going away, we're OK, everything's fine.' When he realized that he wasn't on cue, he looked over at me and, through clenched teeth, went, 'Take it!' Ed Sullivan is telling *me* to 'take it'! He forgot where he was! He came over and just froze up. Brain fart. But in those few seconds, my life was flashing in front of me."

After the show folded, Sullivan was asked to do a few lead-ins to CBS's "Entertainer of the Year Awards," but he had trouble reading the intros in rehearsal. Moffitt recalled, "He had not been on camera for about a year. He had had an illness. We would cue him and Ed would try to get through the copy, all the opening and closing lead-ins. We struggled with Ed to get through it. We got maybe half of them, but it got worse and worse. Halfway through, Bob Precht said, 'John, let's forget it. He's run down.' We were hoping he'd get a good night's sleep."

Sullivan bounced off the ropes the next day. Moffitt: "So the night of the show, there we are: Caesars Palace, full of people, packed house. The music starts, and then the announcer: 'Ladies and gentlemen, the columnist of the *New York Daily News, Ed Sullivan!*' " The crowd cheered. "Applause, music. Out comes Ed, walking across the stage—I'm in the booth directing—and his shoulders are back, he's standing up straight, big steps, he walks over, puts his hands on the podium and says in a big voice, 'Good *evening, ladies and gentlemen! Tonight, from Caesars Palace . . .*' And my God, it was the old Ed! For one last show, the war-horse got it together. The adrenaline began flowing to his brain. He got through it like a champion. Lots of tears in the booth. The crowd had brought him up. All of a sudden this weak old man was the old Ed Sullivan for one hour."

No matter what Sullivan might have done at the end, it probably couldn't have saved the show because of the unbridgeable divide between pop music of the 1960s and the classic television variety show format. The birth of rock and roll was the death of the variety show, which always relied on a heavy musical element.

Variety shows were considered square by new pop standards. Sherwin Bash remarked, "Something happened in the business [in the 1960s] that Sullivan could never grasp. The big stars on his show came out of a different generation. They came out of vaudeville, variety, radio, and night-clubs and even early TV. The big stars in the 1960s came out of the recording industry. They really weren't entertainers. They made records."

Bash noted, "NBC kept trying. They had Dean Martin, but when you talked about Dean Martin you couldn't talk about him in the same breath as the Mamas and the Papas or whoever was hot. The audience for people like Dean Martin and Dinah Shore was older. Their idea of a contemporary musical act would be Harry Belafonte." Indeed, it's hard to think of a single rock group that ever appeared on Johnny Carson's "Tonight" show, which survived for 30 years without catering to pop demographics.

Once the variety format was altered—or polluted, according to older viewers—the core of the show was fundamentally changed. Pop scholar Bob Thompson told me, "Rock and roll became such a historic cultural break along generational lines that that kind of fragmentation made variety shows very, very difficult to do. Once upon a time, those kids would sit still for the acts that would get them to the Beatles and the Stones. By the time you get to '68, many of those kids are 22 years old, baby boomers from '46, and they're not sitting still for that. It had forced you to watch things you didn't think you were interested in, because there was no choice."

Thompson pointed out, "These pop artists weren't interested in going on TV and having Ed Sullivan tell them, 'That song goes four minutes and 20 seconds—cut it down to three.' [And] if you were a big recording artist and the networks offered you your own television show, you could kiss your recording career good-bye. It was absolute death." TV collapsed the recording careers of Glen Campbell, Sonny & Cher, and the Captain & Tennille, Joel Selvin maintained. "TV was mass culture, and rock was counterculture. Three years on the charts in the '60s was an eternity. There was a sense of, 'You gotta get out of TV before [your pop career] is over.' " Johnny Cash was a rare exception, but his summer replacement, the Everly Brothers, didn't last into the fall.

"So many rock singers stayed away from TV," Bash added. "Older people watched television, younger people listened to music on radio and went to concerts." Selvin noted, "Records were sold by radio. Your life and death depended exclusively on radio. TV was not a huge factor. A few big groups, the Beatles and the Stones, might deign to be taped to kick off a new single with an appearance on Sullivan."

Bash believes that not even additional live Beatles appearances could have saved Sullivan. "The first time the Beatles went on Ed Sullivan, it was unique. But if they did it again each month that first year—and I'm sure Sullivan would've wanted them to—it would have been a giant turnoff. What would Sullivan give them? Five minutes? Six minutes? Eight? They took that much time between numbers—just to walk around onstage, pose for the audience, and kibbitz. It was mixing two concepts that didn't mix well. Rock performers not only didn't need TV; the new recording artists that became very important didn't want any part of TV." Not until MTV in 1981 did TV and pop music finally marry in a blessed, nonshotgun wedding.

Fred Silverman, CBS-TV's longtime programming head, was a pallbearer when Sullivan's show was laid to rest. He took over the job in 1970, just before the demise. "It was regarded as a declining show when I got there," he told me. "It was reaching a very old, very rural audience. [Sullivan] became one of the victims of the 'hillbilly purge' "—when

Sullivan might bring on young rock performers, but he had ways of keeping them in hand. I remember Ed tousling Bobby Darin's hair while he was taking bows, as if he were a little kid. Even with Elvis it was, "Yes, sir, Mr. Sullivan." The Beatles changed all that. For once, the act was actually bigger than the show. The performers ceased to kowtow to Ed, because they knew the show was no longer the top but only a stepping-stone to the top.

Jason Kraft, Lansing, Michigan

shows like "Beverly Hillbillies," "Green Acres," and "The Andy Griffith Show" were replaced by sophisticated city dwellers Mary Tyler Moore, Bob Newhart, and "All in the Family."

The reason, noted Sally Bedell in her Silverman biography, is that the canceled shows were "proven successes that happened to appeal to the viewers with the least amount of money in their pockets." Silverman says Sullivan's show "was trending down. But more than that, the [Sullivan show's] bookings started to thin out; they weren't as good as they used to be." With the pragmatic coolness of a veteran TV executive, Silverman added, "That's life. Things come and things go. And his time had really gone."

Silverman dealt not with Sullivan but with Precht, whom he credited with keeping the show alive a few seasons longer than it may have deserved. "We had discussions [about canceling the show] for a couple of seasons before that," he told me. "If it weren't for Bob Precht, they wouldn't have got the show on every week. It's one thing to book the talent. It's another thing to get 'em on. That was Precht's job, and he really did it terrifically." Precht blamed a change in administration at CBS for the cancellation, but he pointed out, "The Sullivan show was also getting expensive, something not talked about much. Ratings weren't what they once were, but they weren't bad." Moffitt said, "Bill Paley loved the prestige of the show" and gave it up reluctantly, bowing to the numbers.

Axing the show was tough, Silverman recalled, because of its unique cachet and because it had enhanced CBS's "Tiffany network" image for two decades. "That's why it lasted as long as it did," he said. "If it were just another cops and robbers show, it probably would have been canceled a year or two earlier." He appended a valedictory: "The Sullivan show made an enormous contribution to television, particularly the history of CBS." Silverman thinks that the show resonates even half a century after it left the air, and cited as evidence three Elvis-on-Ed-Sullivan DVDs he was given a few years ago for Christmas.

The show's end was inevitable, said Bob Thompson: "Rock and roll was the real wedge, but if rock didn't do it, the show was finished off by the fragmentation of the rest of the culture." It happened in comedy as well as music: "There was comedy for parents, and there was comedy for young people. There was no reason to sit through something you weren't already interested in. A generation raised on vaudeville was used to that. To a generation raised on TV it could be really, really irritating." He went on to say, "The show's greatest glory—bringing everybody to the table—was also aesthetically one of its problems. Sometimes you didn't want to see all that stuff. You really were tolerating it, just sitting through it. He mitigated that by the way in which it was broadcast—nothing ever went on too long. He got you in and out. You never got too alienated. You could almost resist even nails scraping on a chalkboard."

There was no farewell show, no grand finale. Sullivan didn't feel up to making a splashy exit. He departed just as he had arrived 23 years earlier, quietly and almost unheralded. The last regularly scheduled "Ed Sullivan Show," on June 6, 1971, was a repeat of a February 7 show that year—a definitive lineup of Carol Channing, Jerry Vale, Caterina Valente, Robert Klein, Pat Henry, Peter Nero, Gladys Knight, Sandler & Young, and, to be sure, Topo Gigio; Sullivan gave him a farewell smooch as Topo whimpered one final "Kees-a-me goo' night, Eddie."

"Vaudeville has died its second death," Sullivan told the press after the show was killed. *Entertainment Weekly*'s A. J. Jacobs, in a fond retrospective, wrote, "No doubt about it, Sullivan was a relic of TV's infancy. In these days of geek chic, the terse, awkward host seems almost cool."

What made it all worse is that, while CBS babbled about going for "a new look" at 8 P.M., Sullivan's old show was replaced with—old movies ("The CBS Sunday Night Movie"). That was an ironic twist, because movies killed vaudeville the first time around, and doubly ironic because Sullivan broke into show business by staging shows between films. Somehow CBS felt that old movies would enhance its urban image, ratings, and demographics, and the films ran in Sullivan's slot opposite "The F.B.I." on ABC, and "The Wonderful World of Disney" and "The Bill Cosby Show" on NBC. (In 1969 and 1970, the time slots of the latter two overlapped: Disney was on from 7:30 to 8:30 P.M., Cosby from 8:30 to 9. In 1971, Disney and "The Jimmy Stewart Show" overlapped Sullivan's show.) Not until the mid-1970s could CBS justify having sacked Sullivan, when it came up with truly groundbreaking hits: "All in the Family," "The Mary Tyler Moore Show," and "Columbo."

The promise of producing an occasional special on CBS wasn't enough to sustain Sullivan, but after his show left the air, he said valiantly but wistfully, "Maybe I can still prove to CBS that they are wrong." In a darker mood, he conceded to an interviewer after the show was dropped that its demise was "long overdue." But Sullivan never copped out and blamed the ratings system on which he had feasted so long: "The ratings game is legitimate," he said. "Saying that TV shouldn't cater to public taste is like saying let's give up the presidential election because public taste has picked so-and-so."

In an October 1971 profile of Sullivan in *Show* magazine, Robert La-guardia commented, "His manner appeared nostalgic, full of pauses and prolonged glances, and with a wee touch of sadness." Ed said, "I feel empty now that the show's over. Very empty. It was the excitement, the fun of it, that I miss[,] . . . meeting celebrities, going out after the show with stars. It was the sudden thrill of going out onstage in front of a live audience every Sunday at 8 P.M. All of a sudden it was over, and there was nothing." Moffitt recalled, "Ed was used to working on a schedule. That's one of the things that killed him. Even though it was cancer, it was also the inactivity."

After the show ended, Sullivan felt vestigial spasms. "I went on think-ing that I was still doing the show. You see, I had put a big part of my life into it, and I don't think it was just conceit. No, it was a terrific letdown, the news [was] like getting a slap in your face from your teacher. I brood about it. I do a lot of walking." When the show was canceled, Sullivan's daughter recalled, "he got really introverted, but you could tell he was hurt. We didn't ever speak about it."

Sullivan told Laguardia, "I think more about the old days than I did be-fore. My wife, Sylvia, tells me I think too much about it. It was an excit-ing past, especially those early newspaper days when I was running around meeting all kinds of new people." Bill Gallo, the *New York Daily News* sports cartoonist, told me, "I saw him walking along Broadway not long after he'd lost the TV show, and his wife had died, and he looked very forlorn, sad, and puffy. He had nothing. Believe it or not, no one recognized him."

A few did: "If I'm out and a cab driver stops me and says, 'Hey, Ed, what have you got on Sunday night?,' what can I do but just laugh?" Sometimes he didn't feel like laughing, and avoided fans because they re-minded him of the glory days. One night, Sullivan was leaving an Italian restaurant with his teenage grandson Rob when he spotted fans waiting for him outside. "My grandfather very abruptly turned to me and said, 'I'm not going to deal with them,'" Rob told James Maguire. Sullivan felt he was a has-been, stirring up the same glum, long-ago worries he'd had as an aging columnist, before he got into television. Another night, two hookers came toward Sullivan and his grandson, walking along Park Avenue, and Rob intensely engaged him so the old man wouldn't be em-barrassed by a confrontation, but as the women came closer, Sullivan called out brightly, "Hello, girls, how are you?"

In a postmortem of the show in the *Daily News*, Ben Gross summed up the national loss: "The passing of the Sullivan show is a landmark of

TV history. More than any other offering on the channels, it served as a bridge between the early days of programming and the programming of today. When next September comes and by force of habit many of us tune in CBS-TV Sunday nights at 8, something will be missing."

During the show's heyday, and even after, Sullivan did cameos on scores of TV shows and films, from "General Electric Theater" to "The Singing Nun" and "The Right Stuff." Shots of the show in the background of a film like "Marty" instantly establish the period, telling you where you are, serving as a kind of cultural GPS. He popped up on shows like "I Love Lucy," "The Phil Silvers Show," "I've Got a Secret," "What's My Line?," and "The Jack Benny Program." His appearances were always welcomed with yelps of delight and surprise at seeing this perennial fish out of water. For decades, Sullivan had always seemed so bolted in place Sunday nights on his own show that finding him in an alien context was like bumping into Henry Kissinger at Wal-Mart.

After his show died, and soon after that, his wife, Ed felt totally abandoned. Sylvia Sullivan, robust and sparkly at 69, looked ten years younger and had never been seriously ill. After entering the hospital for a routine procedure in 1973, she had ordered a TV set to watch a special that night, "Ed Sullivan's Broadway." But that day she died unexpectedly of a ruptured aorta. "Ed fell into a bottomless grief," said James Maguire, who reported that, when Sylvia was in the hospital, she told Carmine Santullo, "Take care of Mr. Sullivan." Their daughter told me, "My mother was his anchor, and when she died he just folded."

After her death, Carmine and Sullivan, two highly unlikely pals, servant and master, drew closer. "When Sylvia died and the show went off, he was a beaten man," Jerry Vale recalled. He was so worried about Sullivan that, after Ed turned down his invitation to an event, Vale drove to Danny's Hideaway, where Ed regularly ate, waited for him to come out, then followed him home in his car to be sure he made it back to the hotel. A close friend of the Sullivans', Mrs. Samuel Lionel, told me Sylvia was "a fabulous woman, very strong. She was really his partner." Joan Rivers (Sullivan was godfather to her daughter, Melissa) said, "She took care of him like a hawk. She was his Nancy Reagan." Bill Gallo recalled the time Ed gave Sylvia a Sullivan-produced birthday gift—her favorite song, via special delivery. It arrived one Sunday morning. When the bell rang and she opened the door, there stood Ezio Pinza singing "Some Enchanted Evening" to her.

Nearing the end, Sullivan mended his lifelong rift with Walter Winchell, by then a toothless king of the gossip jungle. They ran into each other at

Dinty Moore's when Winchell was dining with his girlfriend, Jane Kean, who told me, "Ed was on the other side. They hadn't spoken for years. And Walter went over to him and said hello in a friendly way, like he wanted to mend his ways. They patched it up"—even exchanged photos of their grandchildren—and Sullivan told him they shouldn't let another 35 years go by without speaking. On one of his last shows, Sullivan invited Winchell to take a bow in his audience, and praised him. AP's Bob Thomas explained to me, "He was quite conciliatory to Walter. I think he always felt a little sorry for Winchell because he hadn't been able to make a go of it in TV. And Sullivan had, in a big way."

Finally, when he was 73, Sullivan's rebellious digestive tract claimed him, long after he had had his ulcer removed. He was sent to Lenox Hill Hospital in May of 1974 and was kept there until the end of the month. Afterward, he had orders to see his doctor every day, but Sullivan decided once a week was enough. (A rare churchgoer, he was meanwhile seen praying at St. Malachy's.) On September 6, an X-ray revealed he had esophageal cancer, inoperable. When he got back to his hotel, the Prechts were called and given the dire news. Sullivan went back into the hospital that day. Carmine came by every morning, and then went back to the hotel to assemble Sullivan's column. He returned to see Sullivan after delivering the column to the paper. Often he stayed with Sullivan until 11 P.M., unable to conceive that his boss and benefactor was nearing the end. Sullivan wasn't told how ill he was, and, as Precht told Maguire, "right up until the day he died, his spirits were fine and he believed he was going to get well."

To keep his mind active, Maguire noted, Carmine brought Sullivan items, notes, and press releases. He was still writing, or at least assembling, the column from his hospital bed. "When are we going home?" Ed kept asking Carmine, who kept saying, "Maybe tomorrow." Sullivan's 73rd, and last, birthday (September 28) was celebrated in the hospital. He had two separate parties, thrown by friends and the nurses. On October 13, when Carmine visited the hospital around 7:30 that night, the Prechts were just leaving. "I was sitting at his bedside always looking at him to see how he's doing," he recalled. "I'm sure he knew I was there." But a few hours later, with Carmine watching over him, Sullivan died. Aptly enough, it was on a Sunday night. Noted Maguire, "Shortly after 10 P.M., as the evening's program would have been finished, and Sylvia would have been picking him up for dinner at Danny's Hideaway, he stopped breathing."

Sullivan's last "Little Old New York" column, which ran the day after he died, was a typical menu of showbiz trifles (*gossip* is too sprightly a word) of the sort he had been cranking out for 42 years, written in old-timey dot-and-dash Sullivanese: "Dionne Warwick packing Chicago's Mill Run Theater . . . David Frost and Lady Jane Wellesly a London duet . . . Mia Farrow OK after appendectomy . . . The Jimmy (Stage Deli) Richters fifth ann'y . . . Richard Zanuck and Linda Harrison derailed . . ."

Amid falling rain and black umbrellas, television's most revered host had a quasi-state funeral at St. Patrick's Cathedral, where an SRO crowd of 2,000 mourners turned up. Mayor Abe Beame was there on behalf of Sullivan's beloved New York City. Cardinal Cooke presided. The mourners included figures from every wing of show business—Risë Stevens, Toots Shor, Ray Bloch, Van Cliburn, Walter Cronkite, and William Paley, who eulogized him as "an American landmark."

Cronkite, who had known Sullivan from before World War II, remembered him in the *New York Times* obituary of October 17, 1974, as "a great advocator of New York as a center of entertainment . . . [who] fought hard to keep the city in its pre-eminent position. Ed had a remarkable quality of toughness in pursuing what he saw as right. He was an Irish grabber, and I think that's admirable." He was buried next to his wife at Ferncliff Cemetery in Hartsdale, New York, 11 miles from Port Chester. Most of his rather modest $450,000 estate (plus later deferred CBS payments) went to his daughter; Carmine only got $10,000, little more than any of Ed's siblings. At Sullivan's death, Carmine still owned the 1959 Lincoln Continental "Mr. Sullivan" had given him. He kept the car, too costly now to maintain, in his Bronx garage like a treasured heirloom.

The *New York Times* obituary the next day rendered unto Sullivan what Sullivan always believed he deserved but rarely got: "Ed Sullivan Is Dead at 73; Charmed Millions on TV." *Charmed!* There it was, at last, a word rarely ascribed to Sullivan but one that would have coaxed a smile from him. The obit was his ultimate triumph over all the TV critics and comics who had painted him as so drab and charmless for so long. Describing him as "a rock-faced Irishman with a hot temper, painful shyness and a disdain for phonies," the obit writer got it right when he explained that only TV gave Sullivan "what he wanted most out of life—national recognition."

Ed would have been especially cheered by the obit writer's assertion that, at one time, "he was the proudest possession of the Columbia

Broadcasting System," even though CBS paid him only $164,000 a year. The *Times* noted that "the basis of his appeal was an ephemeral thing that baffled those who tried to analyze it. He was not witty, he had no formal talents, he could not consciously entertain anyone. He was bashful, clumsy, self-conscious, forgetful and tongue-tied. And there were times when he was painfully, excruciatingly sentimental."

The fact that, even so, Sullivan had won over most of America in the end was underscored in the death notice: "He was an excellent judge of entertainers. He was sincere in his enjoyment of their work. And he was so honestly ill-at-ease that viewers came to be affectionately sorry for him." The obit writer added that "he despised bigotry, fraud and irresponsibility. And he had the greatest respect for the power of words." Bob Sylvester, Ed's longtime *Daily News* columnist page-mate, wrote an appreciation for the paper that began with a typically semi-intelligible Sullivan quote: "I never said I did it the hard way, but you can bet your last dollar I did it the Ed way."

For years after, Will Jordan wrote and purchased a boxed advertisement in *Variety* every October 13 on the anniversary of Sullivan's death. It read: "Ed, it's just not the same without you."

CHAPTER 23

Echoes and Afterimages

You figured, hey, we're all one country, and this was the one
place where we could all converse and come together as
Americans and be entertained.

    Murray Horwitz, of the American Film Institute

Ed Sullivan, gone now 46 years, still remains on people's minds. He's a standard reference point in any discussion of mid-20th-century Americana. When a selection of excerpts from the Sullivan show played on XM satellite radio in 2008, with actual Sullivan intros, it was billboarded: "Ed Sullivan is still alive!"

Like many a lost piece in the nation's vast cultural puzzle, "The Ed Sullivan Show" was badly missed once it was gone, and it remains a phantom presence in most attempts to capture its essence. In routine tributes to "The Ed Sullivan Show," such as PBS's "The Pioneers of TV" series in 2008, the show's fabled moments are dismissed with a fast-flip montage—Elvis, Beatles, Topo Gigio, Señor Wences, plate spinner, leaping dancer, Sullivan waving his arm—that reveals little about the show. What is meant to be a fond salute feels more like a patronizing pat on the head. The hurry-up clip-and-paste collages rarely dig up the compelling details that gave the show its scope, depth, originality, and richness. None truly depict Sullivan accurately. We never hear him speak beyond the obligatory "really big shew" sound bite, as if that were his major contribution. We get no insights into the show's cultural vitality or lasting importance.

"It was, by almost any measure, the last great TV show," proclaimed David Hinckley, *New York Daily News* TV critic, when the first Sullivan videos were released in 1991. "In the almost two decades since Ed went off the air, the phrase 'Ed Sullivan' has become a sort of running gag. But it's one of our fondest, dearest pop culture memories." On the show's 50th anniversary, in 1998, David Bianculli, another *New York Daily News* TV critic, wrote, "Before MTV, Sullivan presented rock acts. Before Bravo, he presented jazz and classical music and theater. Before the Comedy Channel, even before there was 'The Tonight Show,' Sullivan discovered, anointed and popularized young comedians. Before there were 500 channels, before there was cable, Ed Sullivan was where the choice was. From the start, he was indeed 'the Toast of the Town.'"

The show finally received official U.S. government–sanctioned iconic status when the Postal Service issued an Ed Sullivan commemorative stamp August 11, 2009, part of a 20-stamp "Early TV Memories" series that also included "Alfred Hitchcock Presents," "Twilight Zone," "You Bet Your Life," "Howdy Doody," "The Honeymooners," and "Perry Mason."

Tom Donnelly, reviewing "The Sullivan Years," a 1975 TV tribute hosted by Dick Cavett, wrote in the *Washington Post*, "To be sure, any lapse into expertise would most likely have eroded Sullivan's popularity. A multitude of fans rejoiced in his almost ostentatious ineptitude; it just showed that, in a democracy, a clumsy, tongue-tied Mr. Malaprop could become a star. When some glib, self-assured performer such as Eve Arden took over as guest emcee, the program suffered." *Show* magazine's Robert Laguardia observed, alluding to Sullivan's peculiar, secret, nebulous genius, "Talent can be an indefinable thing, a product that emerges from some strange doings between the mind and heart of a man and those of the people watching. Sullivan was the perfect antidote to the sugary Dinahs and the too-suave Dinos."

Variety, reviewing a mother lode of Sullivan videos, called the show "one of the more complete histories of the tastes of the times. The standards of Ed Sullivan and the American public coincided." Lisa Schwarzbaum wrote in *Entertainment Weekly:* "Unspool an old episode today, and it's not retro nostalgia that captivates; it's the unjaded tastes of a man as unfazed by hipness as by elephants dancing on his stage." TV critic Kay Gardella told me, "You only had to turn on Ed Sunday nights to know what was happening. Sullivan stayed miraculously on top of all breaking stories in show business."

Sullivan, a one-man cultural army amid a tripartite TV dictatorship, has a resting place all his own, forever. TV guru Bob Thompson, discussing the show's legacy, commented to me, "Ed Sullivan is still something of a household name, especially after the 2004, 40th anniversary

of the Beatles shows, when he was all over the place. Its lasting significance is the significance it had on the culture when it was around. It was
the epitome of the three-network-era cultural trough from which everybody fed. 'The Ed Sullivan Show' is as good an example of that as you're
going to get."

A second legacy, Thompson said, is the idea of one man, Sullivan, as
the show business gatekeeper: "You had to get through that door to
reach a certain status. He set the standard. He was the place to go. He
was the cultural clearinghouse." As John Moffitt put it, "Just about
everyone stepped through those doors at the Sullivan show.' "

Thompson pointed out, "It seems obvious that a juggler follows a
ballet dancer follows a dog act, but it was a lot more artfully done than
most people give it credit for. The show really had that format down."
He placed it in his most significant TV shows of all time, right up there
in the video pantheon with "I Love Lucy," "All in the Family," "The
Andy Griffith Show," "Sesame Street," and "Hill Street Blues"—"not
for quality or political importance but for influence and significance," he
explained, and also for "its flow, its organic quality, its alchemy."

The Beatlecasts revived the Sullivan show and turned it into a major
platform for rock, a big part of the legacy but hardly the whole of it.
Elvis opened the door a crack, but the Beatles tore the door off its hinges.
In his fervent pursuit of ratings, Sullivan became a victim of his own
Beatlemania. In providing a safe haven for rock, the show was rebuilt as
a staging area for pop protest.

"All the social and cultural explosions of that period, the 1960s,
were to some extent domesticated by television," Thompson contended,
"because it would tame them to some degree. The news would show the
chaos. The hottest subcultural stuff that made it to TV then was on the
Smothers Brothers show, or 'Laugh-In,' which is about as tame as you'll
get. The three networks really helped contain some of the centrifugal en-
ergies going on culturally then—[such as] an unstoppable force like
Elvis Presley, who represents all this change and postwar redefinition."

To say that Sullivan legitimized rock 'n' roll for America overstates it,
Joel Selvin remarked to me. "Ed Sullivan was a legitimizing forum—if

The show was truly vaudeville's last gasp, and the same format would
blow lots of the current garbage on the screen out of the water.

Matt Gibb, Orlando, Florida

you were on the Ed Sullivan show, you were in the bosom of mainstream American entertainment—but that didn't *make* you mainstream American entertainment. It just put you on that platform where you could be seen by a vast mainstream audience."

He continued, "In those days we had a mainstream audience. We don't have that anymore. *Mainstream America* is a code word for 'white middle class.' The Sullivan show was just a tunnel into middle-class America. The pop culture sought the approval of the mainstream audience, whereas in a couple of years, '67, '68, who gives a shit? We don't care. We don't need it. We don't care if Iron Butterfly is on Ed Sullivan. Jefferson Airplane played the Sullivan show, but the Grateful Dead didn't." Plenty of lesser rock groups were still desperate to play the show. The Strawberry Alarm Clock would send strawberries and alarm clocks every week to Sullivan, but they still never got booked. ("Badgering never worked," the show's receptionist Mary Lynn Gottfried said.)

Despite all he did for pop music, Ed Sullivan lacks a statue or a plaque at the Rock and Roll Hall of Fame and Museum in Cleveland (it displays only an honor roll of inductees' appearances on his show). There is no recognition of him, the hall's chief curator, Jim Henke, conceded to me. "Ed Sullivan's role in rock and roll is shaking hands with the Beatles," said Selvin flatly. "The rest of his contributions we can gradate—a lot of exposure for Motown black acts, people like James Brown. There's no question the show had an impact on the culture at the time and an effect on people's careers. But if you're talking about the history of rock 'n' roll, and you're trying to take a quick scan and see where Ed Sullivan shows up, he's there standing next to the Beatles shaking hands." That's it? "That's it."

But after the Beatles, his single greatest coup, Sullivan was trapped in a culture war of his own making. The entertainers he had so long championed, and understood, were fading, and a new kind of entertainer—younger, less polished, coarser, who sang sentiments he couldn't understand, literally—eclipsed his beloved entertainment heroes. Booking Elvis, the Beatles, and the Stones was a thrilling but increasingly dangerous game for Sullivan: while the rockers inflated his ratings and boosted his legacy, they ultimately sealed the show's larger fate when it became top ten–heavy with second-rate rock groups. Sullivan's single, unwavering standard had always been quality—but how could he judge the quality of a rock group he didn't like or fathom? Now, suddenly, he was forced to take music acts on faith off highly suspect pop charts.

At the same time that he was giving new life to pop music, Sullivan was the funeral director of his own era. In his book on America's most socially significant TV shows, Steven Stark wrote that Sullivan "presided over a bygone era of Really Big Heroes, Really Big Networks, and Really Big Government. Not to mention 1087 Really Big Shows. . . . His show was perhaps the best symbol of an era in which television provided a national and cohesive culture in the midst of our disunion. Has anyone taken Sullivan's place? The answer is: *we* have." Stark added, "In the cable age, we don't need benign autocrats such as Sullivan or Walter Cronkite telling us who is really big, or that's the way it is. Flipping channels, we program for ourselves."

The few meager efforts to resurrect Sullivan's big TV tent failed: Howard Cosell's 1975 ersatz Sullivan show, "Saturday Night with Howard Cosell," replete with celebrities in the audience, scads of stars onstage, the requisite British rock band, an animal segment from Las Vegas (Siegfried & Roy via satellite), and cranked-up Sullivanesque hyperbole ("The greatest singing star on the international scene—Shirley Bassey!"). It had one fatal problem: Cosell was the anti-Sullivan—a verbose camera hog who, in his incessant attempts to be funny, laid oversize ostrich eggs. One critic said: if Sullivan could do it, maybe Cosell (another TV wild card) could too. But he couldn't. Others have tried riding Sullivan's large, slippery coattails, even the infantile Howard Stern. As he launched his naive move into late-night TV on CBS in 1998, Stern crowed, "I am the savior of the Tiffany network. I'm Ed Sullivan on acid." In 2009, in her *San Francisco Chronicle* column, Leah Garchik quoted dermatologist Seth Matarasso proclaiming, "Oprah is the new Ed Sullivan."

The most recent effort to recapture and bottle Sullivan's unique formula was a disastrous NBC special hosted by Rosie O'Donnell, called "Rosie Live," that aired November 26, 2008, and was immediately pronounced dead on arrival by critics. In an advance piece the day before in the *New York Times,* Brain Stelter wrote, "The Thanksgiving Eve audience will see an attempted revival of the variety show format. . . . Taking pages from Ed Sullivan, Carol Burnett and Sonny & Cher, the show will serve up Broadway dancers, celebrity appearances, musical acts, and comedy sketches." He quoted Mike Darnell, a Fox president of alternative programming, who said, "The entire industry has been trying to figure out a way to bring back variety in some way." This was not the way. *Times* TV critic Alessandra Stanley wrote that O'Donnell had used the

show to take potshots at her critics, and said the show had "a hard, contemporary edge to what was intended to be a corny, heartfelt homage to
variety shows of yesteryear." O'Donnell, in her usual buttinsky manner,
broke Sullivan's cardinal rule: stay out of the way of the acts.

Nobody could ever reconstitute Ed Sullivan's magic elixir except Ed
Sullivan. In 1980, Robert and Betty Precht's Sullivan Productions pro-
duced "The Best of Sullivan" for syndication—six one-hour shows (also
released in a 30-minute format), hosted by John Byner. In 1990, Andrew
Solt—a producer-director-writer whose credits include feature films
("Imagine" about John Lennon, and "This Is Elvis"), 50th-anniversary
specials (for CBS, NBC, and the TV Academy), videos on the Rolling
Stones and rock 'n' roll, plus TV specials on Jacques Cousteau, Bob Hope,
Jackie Gleason, and Walt Disney—purchased the entire Sullivan archives
from the Prechts for between $5 and $10 million: 1,087 shows, from
grainy black-and-white kinescopes to 1970s shows in Day-Glo colors.

The tapes had been rotting away in a New Jersey warehouse for 16
years when CBS simply handed the rights to all the Sullivan shows, past,
present, and future, to Ed Sullivan in a 1964 contract negotiation. Solt
revealed, "Bill Paley said, 'We don't rerun these old shows. They have no
value. Give it to him. Who cares?'" Many did. It was one of the few
classic shows to slip through any network's fingers. Solt said, "It's the
most valuable asset Ed left to his daughter." Many of the tapes can be
viewed at the Paley Center for Media in New York and Los Angeles, and
in other broadcast archives, and can be acquired from SOFA Home
Entertainment.

Once he'd purchased the tapes from the Prechts, Solt put together a
two-hour special, "The Very Best of Ed Sullivan," and sold it to CBS.
Hosted by Carol Burnett in 1991, it was the season's second-highest-
rated show, after the Academy Awards, and was later released to home
video. Burnett refused to fly to New York for the taping, which took
place soon after 9/11, and instead narrated the show from inside the vintage Wiltern Theater in Los Angeles, which stood in for what viewers
assumed was the Ed Sullivan Theater. Using the reruns required Solt to
track down and get permission from every act on every show, a daunting
task.

The Burnett special ignited a sudden Sullivan revival. CBS ordered
three more two-hour Sullivan specials: a 1991 sequel to the first very-
best-of show hosted by a sheepish, out-of-place Burt Reynolds (who
confesses he was never on the show), "Holiday Greetings from the Ed
Sullivan Show" in 1992 (hosted by Bob Newhart), and "An All-Star

Comedy Special from the Ed Sullivan Show" (hosted by Mary Tyler Moore, though a more apt choice might have been Alan King or Shecky Greene, among others; Solt says CBS insisted on using Reynolds, Newhart, and Moore).

All of this was followed by still more vintage Sullivan—"Rock 'n' Roll Revolution," "Ed Sullivan's 50th Anniversary," and "Rock 'n' Roll Forever" hosted by Michelle Phillips and Graham Nash. To squeeze in more acts on each special and video, some of Sullivan's idiosyncratic intros and aimless chitchat, which gave the show much of its flavor, were shortened or deleted to give it what Solt called "a contemporary pace."

Most historically crucial of all, Solt bottled his uncut crème de la crème: "Four Complete Ed Sullivan Shows Featuring the Beatles" and "Elvis—The Ed Sullivan Shows," preserving some of television's golden pop landmarks. In 1992, Solt further sliced and diced the Sullivan shows into 115 half-hour cut-down versions ("The Best of the Ed Sullivan Show"), 52 episodes of which were syndicated in the United States. In 1995, 81 Sullivan show episodes launched the TV Land channel. The series later ran on PBS from 2000 to 2003—it was getting hard to avoid running into Ed all over again.

And there was still much more to come: Starting in 1999, Vh1 presented 36 half-hour, Solt-produced "Ed Sullivan's Rock 'n' Roll Classics" hosted off-camera by Jay Thomas, with a trivia track of forgettable pop factoids at the bottom of the screen ("Karen Carpenter got her first set of drums in high school"). Solt also offered a cornucopia of vintage DVDs: "The Best of Broadway from the Ed Sullivan Show," hosted by John Raitt; the classic "Great Moments in Opera," which was unhosted; and "A Really Big Show: Ed Sullivan's 50th" (anniversary) in 1998, hosted by the Smothers Brothers.

If that wasn't enough to satisfy a craving for Sullivaniana, there were also the DVDs "Topo Gigio and Friends," "Muppet Magic," "Inspirational Treasures," "Fabulous Females," "The Sweet Sound of Soul," "Smash Hits of the Sixties," "Bad Boys of Rock 'n' Roll," and, to be sure, "Ed Sullivan Salutes the Red, White, and Blue"—Kate Smith belting "God Bless America," Carl Sandburg reciting Lincoln, Vietnam vet Barry Sandler warbling "Ballad of the Green Berets," and Roy Rogers singing a feisty anti-anti-Vietnam War anthem ("If you don't love it, leave it / If you're running down our country, / you're walkin' on the fightin' side of me"). Not to mention "Amazing Animal Acts" and "Outrageous Moments," the latter of which, alas, lacks any of Ed's own most outrageous goofs, easily worth a separate video.

Entertainment Weekly, reviewing some of the DVDs, wrote, "Solt crams in so many acts that quality sometimes gets sacrificed to quantity," and noted that major moments are so truncated that it can "make a viewer feel cheated out of history. Andrew Solt's deconstruction is a pleasant memory tickler. It could have been so much more. Solt's defense is that the show's pacing [was] too languid for modern times, which is probably true but beside the point."

Even so, remarked critic Ty Burr, "Truncated or not, almost every moment here works as pop epiphany, mile-high camp, or some inspired combination thereof. Because 'The Ed Sullivan Show' cut such a wide swath through American culture, these tapes are far more than just pleasant nostalgia. They're a profuse, bottomless archeological dig." The oldest recovered "Toast of the Town" relic, Solt told me, is a November 28, 1948, kinescope; finding it was like retrieving the bones of the first *Homo sapiens.*

The "Best of Sullivan" videos were part of an early-1990s TV retro craze. *New York Times* critic John J. O'Connor noted in 1991 that, in Sullivan's day, "there was no palaver about appealing only to men or women, to under- or over-25s. There was only the basic concept of good entertainment. How, one wonders, did 'Gone with the Wind' or 'Casablanca' or 'Citizen Kane' ever become gigantic successes without audience research? These excursions into the past convey a message about the present. If there is an underlying sense of loss, it has less to do with innocence than a sense of community."

Where else in the TV world can you see stars at some of their best and worst in early parts of their careers? Like [in the] reruns of Lawrence Welk that preceded the Ed Sullivan show in my city, many acts make me laugh out loud hysterically, and some make my mouth drop open and [make me] wonder what were they on when they cooked up that set design. I have numerous favorite bits, but some that stand out for me are: Petula Clark in a tent dress doing "Elusive Butterfly"; Lainie Kazan in *huge* hair, earrings, and a wild, one-sleeved chiffon caftan doing "Have I Stayed Too Long at the Fair?"; the Supremes in billowy pink "Endora" dresses singing "My Favorite Things"; Vicki Carr singing in front of purple, glowing, giant "chess piece" moldings; the Benedictine nuns singing "Kumbaya"; and on and on. Priceless TV Americana, gone forever!

Susan Molinsky, Madison, Wisconsin

One kick in watching the videos is witnessing giants taking their first toddler steps, and rediscovering (or discovering) long-lost performers. These lesser acts are vintage 20th-century showbiz, closer to the spirit of the show than the overexposed Beatles and Elvis clips—milestones but anomalies. Here is a last chance to see the cheesy and the classy side by side—comics like Morty Gunty and Dave Barry jabbering at double speed to jam as many jokes as possible into five fleeting minutes; Cab Calloway reprising "Minnie the Moocher" from his 1940s prime; Gordon and Sheila MacRae in a skillful parody of the Garry Moore show ("A musical tribute to the months!").

Reviewing two Sullivan TV specials, *Entertainment Weekly* observed, "Nothing today compares with 'The Ed Sullivan Show' for sheer impact. A few minutes on Sullivan Sunday night and you were a watercooler star Monday morning." As James Maguire wrote, Sullivan "was a man of the moment—that week," and the show was "a curio snapshot of its moment."

"The Ed Sullivan Show" touched almost every performer, major or minor, in its time. Entertainers who never appeared on the show desperately longed to be on it or were inspired by performers they saw there. Tom Smothers told me he was turned around while watching the Sullivan show with his grandparents on their black-and-white set in 1954. "A guy named George Gobel talked about his bowling ball. I said, 'That's what I want to do.'"

The world probably can live without Swiss bell ringers and Peruvian foot jugglers, but we remain in dire need of sublime tap dancers and incisive impressionists, once-vital entertainment genres now on the endangered species list, like other major performing life-forms once taken for granted: comedy teams, singing trios and quartets, ventriloquists. All were kept alive by Sullivan and flourished on his show.

In our cool, hyperironic 21st-century ways (the David Letterman and Jon Stewart postmodern sensibility), we may chuckle at the hodgepodge of weird novelty acts that played the show—the magicians, torch jugglers, spoon players and double-talkers, the Professor Backwardses, crack Marine drill squads and Irish crooners, the master plate spinners, like Eric Brenn, the puppeteers and stilt walkers. But they gave the show its unique folk-art texture. Steve Gottlieb, who produced a CD cross section of Sullivan highlights, says, "People's perspectives may have been distorted. When they think of Ed Sullivan, they focus on the Beatles and Elvis and don't realize the variety and depth of the whole catalogue."

Indeed, the performers who catapulted to stardom are well catalogued, but many acts that finally got their seven minutes of fame on Sullivan's show vanished without a trace. Several landed in circuses or carnivals or on cruise ships and never again found a place to dazzle a nation like Sullivan's showcase. The program spotlighted performers who, however bizarre, trivial, or transient, could actually *do* something—clever, original, loony, something you hadn't seen before and might never see again (or maybe want to), even if was just a slicker version of Stupid Pet (or Stupid Human) Tricks, now presented to us with a detached condescending snicker. Yet even the corniest act held people's attention. Sullivan's show, whatever its excesses, was talent central.

Ed Sullivan's cornucopia of acts spilled out into our living rooms every Sunday. Each week, he showcased what used to be called "showmanship" (itself now a slightly suspect term). Sullivan, until pop forces caused him to veer away, presented irresistible entertainers built to last, unlike many of today's charm-impaired pop stars. Sullivan's show pumped up the era of rock star worship, of teenage fans' ritual screeches. Earlier pop icons—Vallee, Crosby, Sinatra, Garland—had had screaming fans, but the Elvis and Beatles frenzy was of a mightier, scarier magnitude, closer to a Pentecostal gathering.

The very thing that audiences of Sullivan's generation loved about performers of the Jimmy Durante–Maurice Chevalier–Edith Piaf–Al Jolson–Fanny Brice–George Burns era was considered crusty and corny, if not bogus, by the rock generation. The new pop stars doted on indifference, arrogance, and attitude verging on open hostility. A few rock performers were engaging entertainers—Elvis, Bobby Darin, Gene Vincent, Jackie Wilson, James Brown, Jerry Lee Lewis, Little Richard, Tina Turner—but precious few.

If the rock-and-roll sensibility demolished the classic variety show, "reality TV" may have replaced it for now, rebuilding the format out of chewing gum and chicken wire. Cultural columnist Steven Winn told me, "Instead of being talented, you have to be ordinary and just do something that is particularly outrageous or self-degrading, or that you're *not* good at, like on 'Dancing with the Stars.' That's all very much a part of the culture today. Anybody with a computer terminal and a hookup can be a star. It sort of obviates the whole Sullivan aesthetic. *Entertainment* is a meaningless term now."

In Sullivan's day, you had to know how to do something. "There was an attempt to entertain," Winn went on to say. "Now, just being alive is entertainment. There are a million examples of people who have become famous for no good reason other than that they caught the wave." If a variety show like Ed Sullivan's were ever resurrected, he contended, "it would have some stupid reality show component. Jugglers would be out on the street dissing each other."

Bob Precht, assessing Sullivan's lasting contribution, pointed to Ed's "good sense of the family, and concern with the family audience and how to entertain a broad swath of people and not get too specialized." He told me that Ed "brought all that along from his vaudeville days. That's what was unique about him. I think he'd like to be remembered as someone who worked hard to provide quality entertainment for the whole family." Sullivan's grandson Rob told James Maguire, "He had a sense that he was talking to Americans, he was watching out for them. . . . If he were asked what he wanted to be remembered for, I would not be surprised if he would say, yes, fame, but also bringing people together."

There is, believe it or not, a resurgent if still latent hunger for family shows on TV now. In a review of "American Idol," critic Tim Goodman commented in the *San Francisco Chronicle* that the show's great success (30 million viewers—"unheard of in this fragmented, multi-channel universe") is partly due to the fact that "it's one of the few shows that families can watch together anymore." After a 30-year trial separation, families are also being thrown together again to watch "Dancing with the Stars," "Top Chef," "Project Runway," and "Extreme Makeover: Home Edition"—examples of so-called aspirational reality TV, which allows families to root together. Those long-lost tap dancers, jugglers, and mimics have given way to dancing fullbacks, juggling sous chefs, and supermodel impersonators. Mort Sahl once joked that someday everybody would have his own talk show, but it's almost come to pass. With cable, camcorders, and YouTube, anyone can become an impresario—the producer, director, writer, and star of his or her own ordinary life.

Marlo Lewis, looking back in 1980 on the groundbreaking show he coproduced for 12 years, was sure an Ed Sullivan variety program would never rise from the dead again. "Times have changed," he said. "Today what people find exciting on television is the self-confessional, the kiss-and-tell talk on the talk shows. Following the revelation about his or her sex life, the performer gets up and does a song or something. That's what's attracting an audience now."

Asked about an upcoming 1980 NBC variety program, "The Big Show," whose title not coincidentally echoed Sullivan's "really big show!" rallying cry, Lewis replied, "We've got an overentertained public today.

They're fickle. And they've seen all the great acts on TV already. In recent years, Howard Cosell, Dick Clark, Dick Van Dyke and Mary Tyler Moore all tried to bring back the variety show and all failed dreadfully. That's why I think NBC will fail, too." And fail they did—NBC's "The Big Show" (90 minutes long) lasted only eleven months in 1980 despite high ratings and six Emmy nominations.

"The Smothers Brothers Comedy Hour" followed Sullivan's show its first year and was really the last major network variety show. While the Smothers show was hot, Sullivan's was rapidly cooling off, a measure of how far the "variety" concept had traveled between Sullivan's up-with-America spirit and the Smotherses' down-with-the-establishment attitude. It was still variety, but far more self-aware.

Tom Smothers insists that you very much *can* go home again—and should. The performers are there, he says, but they have no place to go. "I still believe it's re-doable, that the concept Sullivan had for television" would work today. "There are more performing artists—the jugglers and the plate spinners. Just do it straight-out—no sketches, just straight-out performance. There's no longer a stage in America for that. I just miss all that great junk stuff in three minutes—world's fastest juggler, hand-balancers, all that stuff." A few street performers found homes in places like the musical "Sugar Babies," fringe festivals, and subterranean clubs. David Letterman stages ventriloquist, impressionist, and magician weeks. Perhaps all these reborn entertainers need now is someone to corral them, tame them, and present them in a new TV showcase—someone like a young, hustling, driven neo–Ed Sullivan.

Murray Horwitz, director of the American Film Institute's Silver Theater and Cultural Center, and National Public Radio performer and commentator (a man of eclectic tastes ranging from ragtime to rap, and cocreator of the musical revue "Ain't Misbehavin' "), loved the Sullivan show because, he told me, it created a "cross-cultural understanding"— often against our will. "If you were a teenager, you may have hated it when this 12-year-old kid with polio [Itzhak Perlman] started playing Mendelssohn, because you wanted to hear rock 'n' roll, but at least you understood this was a cultural phenomenon. This was important on some level. You didn't have to understand a word that Edith Piaf sang, but you knew that, for some reason, she was important!"

He went on to say, "You were waiting just to see the Lovin' Spoonful or Albert Brooks. But Mom and Dad, who loved Itzhak Perlman, would sit there and watch Albert Brooks's routine where he's imitating Marcel Marceau; they might not get it, but Mom and Dad had to deal with it.

They had to deal with Elvis. People like Eddie Cantor, Billy Daniels, Rosie Clooney, and Nat Cole existed side by side with Presley and Bo Diddley. And with its grand mix of things, it gave you a sense, for that little period on Sunday nights, of what it meant to be an American in 1957 or 1967."

People never thought of the Sullivan show as "multicultural," a term not yet in vogue. It was just your weekly minimum artistic requirement. Sullivan's cultural blindness actually worked to the viewers' benefit. "Probably he didn't give a shit whether it was Bo Diddley or Pat Boone," Horwitz added. "He was part of the variety aesthetic—if it grossed $125,000 last week, it was very good." He recalled watching the show with his parents and grandparents in Dayton, Ohio: "I was probably seven or eight years old, but I vividly remember seeing W. C. Handy being wheeled out onto the stage of 'The Ed Sullivan Show.' I mean, I saw W. C. *Handy* on television!"

As Horwitz pointed out, "By the end of the '50s, early '60s, people were eating dinner on TV tables and not speaking to one another." The family was together, but not communicating. Television was hogging the conversation. TV shows became the country's new lingo. Still, he said, "most people were watching the Sullivan show, and the next day at the watercooler were talking about it."

He noted, "We hear much today about how uncivil our society has become, about how there is no level plane on which Americans of all stripes can converse and deal with one another in a kind of gracious, generous manner. We're just so divided. At least my parents knew who the hell the Beatles *were!* They knew who Frankie Lyman and Chuck Berry were! They didn't like them, but they knew what was going on. They certainly knew, when they saw Richard Pryor on television, or Jonathan Winters and Lenny Bruce, that there was a new style of comedy. They thought it was sick, but they knew what it was."

Horwitz concluded, "I bet a majority of people my age or older, 50 and above, don't have a clue who Outkast is." Answer: Winner of Record of the Year in 2007 at the Grammys—"a major, important hip-hop group," he said, "that gives those of us who believe in music a little bit of hope; but nobody our age knows who Outkast is. Even if you only know Britney Spears from her Pepsi commercial, most people really don't know any of her music, what she sounds like. People don't really know who Eminem is and what his aesthetic is, but it's remarkable. It's important for you to at least know what it's about—even if you can't stand his music." "The Ed Sullivan Show" was one-stop cultural shopping.

For the show's 15th anniversary, director Joshua Logan wrote a moving tribute titled "What Ed Sullivan Has Done for the American Theater." He stated that the maestro not only had presented the lively arts but also had invested heavily in their future. "He caught the imagination of many artists yet to come. The birth of a career takes place during some shining moment of discovery while a young man or woman is watching the work of an actor or listening to the words of a playwright. Some voice within him says, 'I could do that—I could do better than that. That's what I want to do.'"

Logan noted that "in small towns there are no touring companies. Personal contact with first-rate theater artists is seldom available to our potential writers, actors, directors, or producers. Ed Sullivan has saluted the art of America. It is time we learn what many countries have known for years—that art is the personality of a country. Often it has more influence than politics, or even high-level diplomacy. And there is where Ed has made his greatest contribution. Ed Sullivan is recruiting for the performing arts."

"The Ed Sullivan Show," which stood at the crossroads of massive social changes, was a bellwether of the culture and, for years, the result of certain long-held assumptions about entertainment. As "The Ed Sullivan Show" went, so went America, whether it wanted to or not. Until a performer succeeded on the show, he or she failed to register on the country's cultural radar, languishing in the Catskills or in small clubs or on late-night TV shows, teetering on the brink of big-time stardom.

Sullivan was able to crank out celebrities, to turn show business itself into a belching national industry. The engine that drove this churning talent dynamo was the host's pure passion for entertainment, his bullheaded certainty in his own taste, and his clear belief in his ability to recognize what would entertain his fellow citizens. He was as much of a visionary of his day as Henry Luce, another major celebrity molder. Luce led Time, Inc.; Sullivan ran Talent, Inc. Famously, Ed himself lacked "a talent to amuse" (to quote a Noël Coward song), but he had a huge talent for finding amusement and focusing a spotlight on it.

His small-town youth—and a mind-set stirred by a boyhood adoration of the heroes and heroines he soaked up in books by Horatio Alger and Sir Walter Scott, and then later the athletes he worshipped and wrote about—is what first sparked him to pursue, promote, and enshrine the entertainment heroes and heroines of his own romantic era.

Sullivan's ego, ambition, and stubbornness, sometimes hard for others to deal with, wouldn't allow him to quit until he had broken through on the national scene, as he had failed to do as a sportswriter, screenwriter, radio host, or gossip columnist. He always felt embattled by the critics and underloved and taken for granted by his own network, and was forever determined to prove himself, long after he had. Sullivan craved mass recognition, and desperately needed it for his own self-worth.

Part of his success as an impresario was instinct, but much of it was due to sheer doggedness and combative daring. Nobody was more scorned or laughed at in his chosen field than Sullivan, but an unyielding faith in himself kept him burrowing forward, however wounded by critics and caricatured by comics. He was flawed and vulnerable, but invincible. For years he smarted under the attacks—and dared to slap down critics who jumped him, breaking the first showbiz commandment: thou shalt not offend the media. He winced but he never ran. He answered his foes by refusing to go away.

Ed Sullivan was able to bend with the times, even if it meant bending his own aesthetic rules—if it assured the show's survival. The show came before anything—friends, family, or fortune. He had fought too hard, and waited too long for personal glory, to be undone by show business whim. Battling himself, going against his own sturdy grain of traditional entertainment values, he brought rock and roll to television.

While he never grew to love the emerging pop music (apart from an affection for Motown and the Beatles), he realized it was not leaving anytime soon; nor was he. Despite his basic conventional standards, he helped turn such unconventional curios as Señor Wences, Phyllis Diller, Will Jordan, Carol Burnett, Jackie Mason, Moms Mabley, the Muppets, and Topo Gigio—and, to be sure, Elvis Presley—into major stars.

Ed Sullivan invented the TV variety show. He blazed the trail and led the way for similar but less grandiose shows that dominated the early days of TV: "The Perry Como Show," "The George Gobel Show," "The Dinah Shore Show," "The Garry Moore Show"—all versions of Ed Sullivan's variety formula yet nothing like what Sullivan did. Other variety shows presented expected, established stars in a familiar mode: singers, comics, sketches, dance numbers, plus forgettable banter between host and stars to glue it all together. Sullivan revitalized, and streamlined, not true vaudeville, but the vaudeville *concept*—something for everyone, every age, every ethnicity, every taste.

Privately, Sullivan remained two people, battling his demons and angels. He was a man with big appetites (for celebrities, for adulation, for girl singers) who had little appetite for financial gain, familial duties, or even actual food. He was a puritan who came down hard on performers, especially comedians who breeched his ironclad code of propriety: if anyone crossed that line he would mow them down in a profane tirade.

He was a guardian of family values who strayed regularly from home in pursuit of outside female entertainment. He was known to most of his TV guests as a remote, cool, even chilly host, but when moved he could click on the charm for a star he wanted to book or for anyone with an autograph pad. Beyond his signature, he gave handouts to aging, needy ex-stars and fading athletes in the form of seven minutes on his show.

To friends, even his family, he was unknowable, retreating into glum silences. He was a star-worshipper who avoided stars in real life and had few close show business pals—or close friends at all, beyond golfing buddies. He wrote heartrending odes to the large family he grew up with in Port Chester, New York, but almost never saw his family after moving to Manhattan, marrying out of his faith and mingling with celebrities instead.

Ed Sullivan fed America's—and his own—insatiable hunger for celebrities. Television could serve them up more intimately and efficiently than any other medium. Movie stars were at a distant remove from us. Theater was doubly remote (although Sullivan helped keep theater alive with scenes from Broadway shows). Radio, for all its intimacy, deprived the eye that craved entertainers in the flesh. Only TV had the power to not just create stars overnight but also deliver them at our doorstep. Sullivan kneeled at the feet of celebrities, and then he asked us to kneel at his Sunday night altar of entertainment.

In the end, television's greatest star-maker was perhaps its most peculiar star. Ed Sullivan seemed a living rebuke to show business glamour. Yet set against his plain on-screen persona, the talent of other performers shone more vibrantly. Ed appeared to be a random television viewer who, like Mia Farrow in "The Purple Rose of Cairo," had been pulled out of his easy chair, pushed before a camera, and given access to any performer in the world. It took 23 years, but television's supreme star-maker, and its least likely host, ultimately became his most celebrated act.

Bibliography

The sources that most candidly revealed Ed Sullivan and his show to me were my interviews with some sixty performers, plus another sixty interviews with members of Sullivan's staff and family who were on, or intimately connected with, "The Ed Sullivan Show"; a list of these interviewees follows the bibliography. I also consulted a shelf-load of books of the period (1948–1971), including two biographies of Ed Sullivan and three of the show itself: *Impresario,* by James Maguire; *A Really Big Show,* edited by Claudia Falkenburg and Andrew Solt, with text by John Leonard; *A Thousand Sundays,* by Jerry G. Bowles; *Always on Sunday,* by Michael David Harris; and *Sundays with Sullivan,* by Bernie Ilson. Other valuable sources were videotapes of Sullivan shows I viewed at the Paley Center for Media (formerly the Museum of Television and Radio) in New York City and Los Angeles; interviews with longtime Sullivan talent coordinator Vince Calandra and director John Moffitt, part of a series conducted for the Archive of American Television by the Academy of Television Arts and Sciences and posted on the Web; and the Web site Bluegobo.com, a cornucopia of memorable scenes from Broadway musicals performed on Ed Sullivan's show and now preserved forever.

Of the hundreds of newspaper and magazine articles I read, those that yielded the richest nuggets include an in-depth, multipart newspaper series about Ed Sullivan by Alvin Davis, which appeared in the *New York Post* in March 1956 ("The Ed Sullivan Story"), preceded a week earlier in the *Post* by Sullivan's own weeklong version of his story, beginning March 26, 1956; the *Time* magazine cover story "Big as All Outdoors"; and a helpful if somewhat worshipful series by Jim Bishop that appeared in the *New York Journal-American.* Equally insightful were lengthy profiles in *Life* magazine by Wayne Warga, *Look* magazine by Eleanor Harris, *Vanity Fair* by Nick Tosches, and the *Saturday Evening Post* by Pete Martin, as well as a Sunday profile by Helen Dudar in the *New York Post.* Also useful were an article full of keen insights by Martha

Weinman Lear in the *Saturday Evening Post*, another by Joan Barthel in the *Sunday New York Times*, and a postmortem of the show with Sullivan conducted by Robert Laguardia and published in *Show* magazine. Nothing gives a truer, more stinging sense of the critical brickbats Sullivan dodged and endured than columns by the *New York Herald Tribune* radio and TV critic (and regular Ed Sullivan antagonist) John Crosby, and by the *New York Times* radio-TV critic Jack Gould.

For the industry's view of Sullivan and his show over its 23-year reign, I consulted reviews and articles in *Variety*, the encyclopedic show business bible, which provided a kind of running account. Other detailed accounts that I read include Ed Sullivan's first-person "My Story" in *Collier's* magazine. Invaluable for capturing the day-to-day feel of Ed Sullivan's pretelevision life are his early sports columns and long-running Broadway column ("Little Old New York"), many of them archived at the *New York Daily News* and in the Billy Rose Collection at Lincoln Center's Performing Arts Library. Ed Sullivan's papers are housed at the Wisconsin Center for Film and Theater Research, and comprise several boxes of personal and business letters, photos, awards, scripts, and other Sullivan miscellanea.

Perhaps the best, most thorough and compelling book available on the early days of television is Jeff Kisseloff's *The Box*, an oral history of the origins of TV programming recalled through the voices of its pioneers—actors, writers, directors, and producers. For a perceptive, critical, knowledgeable, and thorough account of television throughout the years, with succinct capsule views of what show was on when and why, see *Watching TV: Six Decades of American Television*, by Harry Castleman and Walter J. Podrazik, an essential go-to guidebook.

Getting a close-up view of the dynamics of the show's earliest days would have been nearly impossible without an indispensable memoir by two crucial people there at its creation—Marlo Lewis and Mina Bess Lewis. Their book, *Prime Time*, a sort of diary of how the show was born and its bumpy road to posterity, is told in the voices of both Sullivan's trusty cocreator and unflappable original coproducer and his astute, astringent wife.

BOOKS AND MAGAZINES

Allen, Steve. *Hi-Ho, Steverino! My Adventures in the Wonderful Wacky World of TV*. Barricade Books, 1992.

Amburn, Ellis. *Buddy Holly: A Biography*. St. Martin's, 1995.

Barnouw, Erik. *Tube of Plenty: The Evolution of American Television*. Oxford University Press, 1975.

Barthel, Joan. "Says Mrs. Sullivan 'Ed Makes Nice Money': After 19 TV Years, Only Ed Sullivan Survives." *Sunday New York Times*, April 30, 1967.

Baughman, James L. *Same Time, Same Station: Creating American Television, 1948–1961*. Johns Hopkins University Press, 2007.

"Beatlemania," *Newsweek*, November 18, 1963.

Bedell, Sally. *Up the Tube: Prime-Time TV and the Silverman Years*. Viking, 1981.

Bianculli, David. *Teleliteracy: Taking Television Seriously.* Simon & Schuster, 1992.

"Big as All Outdoors." *Time,* October 17, 1955.

Bishop, Jim. "The Inside Story of Ed Sullivan." *New York Journal-American,* March 17–22, 1957.

Blumenthal, Ralph. *Stork Club: America's Most Famous Nightspot and the Lost World of Café Society.* Little, Brown, 2000.

Boddy, William. *Fifties Television: The Industry and Its Critics.* University of Illinois Press, 1993.

Bowles, Jerry G. *A Thousand Sundays: The Story of the Ed Sullivan Show.* Putnam, 1980.

Brown, Peter, and Steven Gaines. *The Love You Make: An Insider's Story of the Beatles.* McGraw-Hill, 1983.

Brown, Peter Harry, and Pat H. Broeske. *Down at the End of Lonely Street: The Life and Death of Elvis Presley.* Dutton, 1997.

Castleman, Harry, and Walter J. Podrazik. *Watching TV: Six Decades of American Television.* Syracuse University Press, 2003.

Clark, Dick, and Richard Robinson. *Rock, Roll & Remember.* Thomas Y. Crowell, 1976.

Cort, David. "The Gossip Columnists." *The Nation,* October 13, 1956.

Crosby, John. "The Amateurs Take Over TV." *Saturday Evening Post,* November 8, 1952.

———. *Out of the Blue: A Book about Radio and Television.* Simon & Schuster, 1952.

Davis, Alvin. "The Ed Sullivan Story." *New York Post,* March 1956.

Davis, Lee. *Scandals and Follies: The Rise and Fall of the Great Broadway Revue.* Limelight Editions, 2000.

"Death of the Salesman." *Time,* January 31, 1955.

Doherty, Thomas. *Cold War, Cool Medium: Television, McCarthyism, and American Culture.* Columbia University Press, 2003.

Douglas, Susan J. *Where the Girls Are: Growing Up Female with the Mass Media.* Times Books, 1994.

Dudar, Helen. "Ed Sullivan: Always on Sunday." *New York Post,* June 16, 1963.

Eels, George. *Hedda and Louella: A Dual Biography of Hedda Hopper and Louella Parsons.* Putnam, 1972.

Falkenburg, Claudia, and Andrew Solt, editors; text by John Leonard. *A Really Big Show: A Visual History of* The Ed Sullivan Show. Viking Studio Books, 1992.

Fields, Sydney. "Only Human." *New York Daily News,* April 11, 1968.

Fisher, John. *The Columnists.* Howell, Soskin, 1944.

Fountain, Charles. *Sportswriter: The Life and Times of Grantland Rice.* Oxford University Press, 1993.

Frank, Reuven. *Out of Thin Air: An Insider's History of Network News.* Simon & Schuster, 1991.

Frankel, Haskel. *Milton Berle: An Autobiography.* Delacorte, 1974.

Fricke, David. "Forty Years of Beatlemania: A Look Back at the Beatles' Debut on 'The Ed Sullivan Show.'" *Rolling Stone*, September 19, 2008.

Gabler, Neal. *Winchell: Gossip, Power, and the Culture of Celebrity*. Alfred A. Knopf, 1994.

Gallico, Paul. *Farewell to Sport*. Alfred A. Knopf, 1938.

Gavin, James. *Intimate Nights: The Golden Age of New York Cabaret*. Grove Weidenfeld, 1991.

Goldman, Herbert G. *Banjo Eyes: Eddie Cantor and the Birth of Modern Stardom*. Oxford University Press, 1997.

Goldsmith, Martin. *The Beatles Come to America*. John Wiley & Sons, 2004.

Goodman, Walter. "Vaudeville: Ed Sullivan before Ed Sullivan." *New York Times*, November 25, 1997.

Gould, Jack. "Milton Berle Appears on Star Theater—CBS Offers 'Toast of the Town.'" *New York Times*, July 4, 1948.

———. "'Mister Roberts' Rides Free: Sullivan Show Is One Long Ad for Movie." *New York Times*, June 20, 1955.

Gray, Barry. *My Night People: 10,001 Nights in Broadcasting*. Simon & Schuster, 1975.

Greenfield, Jeff. *Television: The First Fifty Years*. Harry N. Abrams, 1977.

Gross, Ben. *I Looked and I Listened*. Random House, 1954.

Guralnick, Peter. *Last Train to Memphis: The Rise of Elvis Presley*. Little, Brown, 1994.

Halberstam, David. *The Fifties*. Random House, 1990.

Harris, Eleanor. "That 'No Talent' Ed Sullivan." *Look*, April 5, 1955.

Harris, Michael David. *Always on Sunday: Ed Sullivan—An Inside View*. Meredith Press, 1968.

Hart, Jeffrey. *When the Going Was Good! American Life in the Fifties*. Crown, 1982.

Heldenfels, R. D. *Television's Greatest Year: 1954*. Continuum, 1994.

Hopper, Hedda. *The Whole Truth and Nothing But*. Doubleday, 1963.

Ilson, Bernie. *Sundays with Sullivan: How the Ed Sullivan Show Brought Elvis, the Beatles, and Culture to America*. Taylor Trade Publishing, 2009.

Israel, Lee. *Kilgallen: An Intimate Biography of Dorothy Kilgallen*. Delacorte, 1979.

Jefferson, Margo. "Some Books Are Worth Giving." *New York Times*, December 21, 2005.

Kean, Jane. *A Funny Thing Happened on the Way to "The Honeymooners"* . . . *I Had a Life*. Bear Manor Media, 2003.

Kehr, David. "The Jazz Singer." *New York Times*, October 16, 2007.

Kisseloff, Jeff. *The Box: An Oral History of Television, 1920–1961*. Penguin Books, 1995.

Klurfeld, Herman. *Winchell: His Life and Times*. Praeger, 1976.

Laguardia, Robert. "Ed Sullivan: Where, Why, and How Has He Gone." *Show*, Summer 1971.

Lahr, John. *Notes on a Cowardly Lion: Bert Lahr*. Alfred A. Knopf, 1970.

Lax, Eric. *Woody Allen: A Biography*. Vintage, 1992.

Lear, Martha Weinman. "Let's Really Hear It for Ed Sullivan!" *Saturday Evening Post*, April 20, 1968.

Lehman, Ernest. *Sweet Smell of Success: And Other Stories*. Overlook Press, 2000.

Leonard, John. "The Ed Sullivan Age." *American Heritage*, May–June 1997.

Lertola, Joe. "Milestones." *Time*, August 9, 2007.

Lewis, Marlo, and Mina Bess Lewis. *Prime Time*. J. P. Tarcher, 1979.

Lewis, Peter. *The Fifties: Portrait of a Period*. J. P. Lippincott, 1978.

MacDonald, J. Fred. *Black and White TV: African Americans in Television since 1948*. Nelson-Hall, 1983.

———. *One Nation under Television: The Rise and Decline of Network Television*. Pantheon, 1990.

Maguire, James. *Impresario: The Life and Times of Ed Sullivan*. Billboard Books, 2007.

Marling, Karal Ann. *As Seen on TV*. Harvard University Press, 1994.

Martin, Pete. "I Call on Ed Sullivan." *Saturday Evening Post*, February 15, 1958.

McKelway, St. Clair. *Gossip: The Life and Times of Walter Winchell*. Viking, 1940.

McKinney, Devin. *Magic Circles: The Beatles in Dream and History*. Harvard University Press, 2003.

McLuhan, Marshall. *Understanding Media: The Extensions of Man*. MIT Press, 1994.

Metz, Robert. *CBS: Reflections in a Bloodshot Eye*. Playboy Press, 1975.

Mosedale, John. *The Men Who Invented Broadway: Damon Runyon, Walter Winchell, and Their World*. Richard Marek, 1981.

Nachman, Gerald. *Raised on Radio: In Quest of the Lone Ranger, Jack Benny, Amos & Andy, the Shadow, . . .* Pantheon, 1998.

———. *Seriously Funny: The Rebel Comedians of the 1950s and 1960s*. Pantheon, 2003.

Navasky, Victor. *Naming Names*. Viking, 1980.

Norman, Philip. *Rave On: The Biography of Buddy Holly*. Simon & Schuster, 1996.

———. *Shout! The Beatles in Their Generation*. Simon & Schuster, 1981.

Opotowsky, Stan. *TV: The Big Picture*. E. P. Dutton, 1961.

Paar, Jack. *My Saber Is Bent*. Trident Press, 1961.

Paley, William S. *As It Happened: A Memoir*. Doubleday, 1979.

Paper, Lewis J. *Empire: William S. Paley and the Making of CBS*. St. Martin's Press, 1987.

"Plenty of Nothing." *Time*, October 13, 1967.

Rivers, Joan. *Enter Talking*. Delacorte Press, 1986.

Rohter, Larry, and Tom Zito. "Rock Idol Elvis Presley Dies at 42." *Washington Post*, August 17, 1977.

Shales, Tom. *On the Air!* Summit Books, 1982.

Shulman, Arthur, and Roger Youman. *How Sweet It Was: Television, a Pictorial Commentary*. Bonanza Books, 1956.

Silverman, Al, and Brian Silverman. *The 20th Century Treasury of Sports*. Viking, 1992.

Slater, Edward. *This Is . . . CBS: A Chronicle of 60 Years.* Prentice-Hall, 1988.
Smith, Sally Bedell. *In All His Glory: The Life and Times of William S. Paley and the Birth of Modern Broadcasting.* Simon & Schuster, 1990.
Sobel, Louis. *Longest Street: A Memoir.* Crown, 1968.
Spitz, Bob. *The Beatles: The Biography.* Little Brown, 2005.
Spizer, Bruce. *The Beatles Are Coming! The Birth of Beatlemania in America.* Four Ninety-Eight Productions, 2003.
Stiller, Jerry. *Married to Laughter: A Love Story Featuring Anne Meara.* Simon & Schuster, 2000.
Stuart, Lyle. *The Secret Life of Walter Winchell.* Barricade Books, 2003.
Sullivan, Ed. "My Story." *Collier's*, September 14 and 28 and October 12, 1956.
Sullivan, Ed, with Betty Sullivan Precht. *Christmas with Ed Sullivan.* McGraw-Hill, 1959.
Sylvester, Robert. *No Cover Charge: A Backward Look at Nightclubs.* Dial Press, 1956.
"Talk of the Town." *New Yorker*, July 14, 1962.
Taraborrelli, Randy J. *Call Her Miss Ross.* Birch Lane Press, 1989.
Thomas, Bob. *Winchell: The Man and the Myth.* Doubleday, 1971.
Time-Life Books. *The Patriotic Tide: 1940–1950 (This Fabulous Century).* Time-Life Books, 1969.
"Toast of the Town." *Time*, June 25, 1951.
Tosches, Nick. "Mr. Sunday Night." *Vanity Fair*, July 1997.
Trav S. D. *No Applause—Just Throw Money: The Book That Made Vaudeville Famous.* Faber and Faber, 2005.
Vaill, Amanda. *Somewhere: The Life of Jerome Robbins.* Broadway Books, 2006.
Von Schilling, James A. *The Magic Window: American Television, 1939–1953.* Haworth Press, 2002.
Walker, Stanley. *City Editor.* Blue Ribbon Books, 1934.
———. *The Nightclub Era.* Johns Hopkins University Press, 2004.
Warga, Wayne. "He Really Comes to Life Off Camera." *Life*, October 20, 1967.
Watkins, Mel. *On the Real Side: A History of African American Comedy.* Simon & Schuster, 1994.
Weaver, Pat. *The Best Seat in the House: The Golden Years of Radio and Television.* Knopf, 1994.
Weingarten, Marc. *Station to Station: The Secret History of Rock and Roll on Television.* Pocket Books, 2000.
Wenner, Jann S. "John Lennon: The Rolling Stone Interview." *Rolling Stone*, December 1970.
White, George R. *Bo Diddley: Living Legend.* Castle Communications, 1995.
Wilk, Max. *The Golden Age of Television: Notes from the Survivors.* Moyer Bell, 1989.
Winchell, Walter. *Winchell Exclusive: Things That Happened to Me—and Me to Them.* Prentice-Hall, 1975.
Winship, Michael. *Television,* companion book to the PBS series. Random House, 1988.

Yust, Walter. *1949 Britannica Book of the Year: Events of 1948.* Encyclopaedia Britannica, 1949.

ARCHIVES AND OTHER MEDIA

Archive of American Television. Academy of Television Arts and Sciences Web site. Online interviews.
"Broadway: The American Musical," directed by Michael Kantor. 3 pts. PBS Home Video, 2004. DVDs.
"Ed Sullivan and the Gateway to America," produced by Owen McFadden. BBC, aired August 7, 2008.
"The Ed Sullivan Show" collections. SOFA Home Entertainment. DVDs.
Paley Center for Media, New York City and Los Angeles.
"Pioneers of Primetime," directed by Steven J. Boettcher. PBS Paramount, 2005. DVD.

Interviews

Susan Abramson (5/20/08), Anna Maria Alberghetti (4/24/08), Lou Alexander (6/12/04), Bill Allen (6/13/04), Marty Allen (9/1/05), Steve Allen (6/2/99), Robert Arthur (5/22–24/08), Sherwin Bash (1/28/08), Orson Bean (9/14/07), Polly Bergen (9/14/07), Shelley Berman (6/5/04), Sid Bernstein (5/29/08), Walter Bernstein (2005), Leon Bibb (6/2/04), Steve Blauner (3/27/08), Bill Bohnert (2008), Joe Bracken (7/1/05), David Brown (10/6/07), Carol Burnett (7/27/05), Peter Calabrese (1/6/09), Jean Carroll (1/6/08), Jack Carter (12/14/99), Dick Cavett (10/13/04 and 11/1/07), Marge Champion (6/16/05), Ron Clark (7/23/05), Patrick Clifford (2007), Jill Corey (10/18/05), Jerry Cutler (2/5/09), Bill Dana (6/10/04), Mike Dann (2004), Merle Debuskey (6/21/04), Bettina Devin (6/10/04), Phyllis Diller (6/6/04), Denny Doherty (6/7/05), Roland DuPont (6/3/04), Allan Eichler (7/13/05), Max Eisen (6/21/04), Bertram Fields (7/26/05), Marty Fisher (8/4/05), Ben Fong-Torres (2008), Eva Franchi (1/6/08), Connie Francis (6/16/05), Neil Gabler (2005), Barbara Gallagher (5/28/08), Bill Gallo (6/15–16/04), Kay Gardella (6/1/04), James Gavin (3/14/09), Mary Lynn Gottfried (5/21/08), Robert Goulet (6/8/05), Ron Greenberg (6/2/08), Shecky Greene (12/14/99), Chris Griffin (6/15/04), Pete Hamill (2004), Jim Henke (2008), Neil Hickey (7/6/04), Mimi Hines (10/1/07), Murray Horwitz (6/22/04), Will Jordan (10/6/05), Lainie Kazan (8/10/05), Jane Kean (8/5/05), Mark Kerrigan (2007), Alan King (2/1/00), Jane Klain (3/16/09), Robert Klein (10/15/07), Herman Klurfeld (10/6/05), Michelle LaFong (8/4/05), Frankie Laine (7/7/05), Julius La Rosa (7/5/05), Carol Lawrence (7/29/05), Teri Layne (2007), Tom Lehrer (4/20 and 8/4/99), Mina Bess Lewis (7/23/05), Monica Lewis (11/6/05), Mrs. Samuel Lionel (5/31/05), Sheila MacRae (7/23/05), George Maksian (6/22/04), Bob Markell (9/1/05), Dorothy Harlib Marshall (11/8/05), Dick Martin (6/30/05), Tony Martin (6/28/04), Jackie Mason (6/13/04), Phyllis McGuire (10/28/05), Julia Meade (6/8/05), Jayne Meadows (6/23/05), Alicia Mecner (5/24/08), Rev. Bill Minson (10/8/07), Jimmy Mitchell

(5/31/05), John Moffitt (6/10/05), Phil Morehead (6/15/04), Jan Morgan (3/24/08), Jan Murray (12/8/99), Bobbe Norris (2/8/08), Patricia O'Haire (6/21/04), Patti Page (9/15/04), Roberta Peters (7/26/05), Russ Petranto (2008), Michelle Phillips (4/1/08), Bob Pitofsky (6/18/04), Arty Pomerantz (7/15/05), Betty Sullivan Precht (4/24/08), Robert Precht (4/15–23 and 5/10/08), Sy Presten (7/9/04), Andy Rooney (10/12/04), Ken Rothstein (5/6–8/08), Harvey Sabinson (2004), Herb Sargent (6/25/04), Joel Selvin (11/29/07 and 2/20/08), Carole Shaw (7/14/05), Lee Silver (6/22/04), Fred Silverman (1/30/08), Nancy Sinatra (4/24/08), Keely Smith (3/21/08), Liz Smith (2005), Tom Smothers (6/15/04), Andrew Solt (6/25/04 and 3/24/08), Lee Solters (6/25/04), Risë Stevens (7/26/05), Howard Storm (7/9/04), Charles Strouse (2/11/08), Lyle Stuart (8/10/05), Megan Sullivan (2005), Rip Taylor (3/31/08), Bob Thomas (6/6/05), Robert Thompson (9/23/05), Ed Trinka (10/17/07), Leslie Uggams (8/15/05), Amanda Vaill (3/16/09), Jerry Vale (6/17/04), Jeremy Vernon (7/2/04), Dionne Warwick (5/17/08), Mel Watkins (12/2/08), Christopher Weeks (6/12/04), Larry Wilde (12/17/07), Mary Wilson (6/15/04), Steven Winn (1/25/08).

Acknowledgments

I'm grateful for anyone who was willing to talk to me for five minutes about "The Ed Sullivan Show," or about Sullivan himself, but certain people deserve a singular gold star for their special help or for leading me to other people. As on two earlier books, the major literary assist was provided by Randy Poe, a friend and steadily cheering inspiration. He gave the book a close reading and a cleansing first edit, suggesting cuts and a hundred other things that helped streamline the text and wrestle the original monster to a manageable size; without his ruthless eye and gentle touch, this would be a different, and much heavier, book. My second literary lieutenant was Rodi Ludlum, who transcribed the taped interviews (inserting her own wry running parenthetical commentary), checked scores of elusive facts, and chased down weird data, as did, briefly, at an earlier stage, Wesla Whitfield. Lots of other folks, for lots of other reasons, lent a generous helping hand. They include:

My agent Amy Rennert; archivist Jane Klain at the Paley Center for Media; Cathy Nyhan at the San Francisco Public Library; librarian Johnny Miller at the *San Francisco Chronicle;* comedian Ronnie Schell; man for all cultural seasons Murray Horwitz; writer and CBS go-to guy Gary Paul Gates; columnist Liz Smith; computer wizards Mel Margolis, Jerry Hyman, Sharon Bobrow, and Matt Bell, who, during many dire moments, patiently pulled many a cyberchestnut out of the fire for me; master *Playbill* profiler and pal Harry Haun; celebrity headhunter Mark Kerrigan; comedy impresario Mark Pitta; mimic Will Jordan; comic (and deft Sullivan mimic) Jeremy Vernon; comedian Bill Dana and former archivist Jenni Matz of the Emerson College Comedy Archives; my former editor Robert Gottlieb and agent Martha Kaplan; producer and "Ed Sullivan Show" video producer, packager, and syndicator Andrew Solt and his assistant Greg Vines; Owen McFadden, who helpfully provided a tape of his BBC tribute to Ed Sullivan; Ricky Layne's daughter Terri; principal Patrick Clifford; photographer Pauline Tajchman; former colleagues Joel Selvin, Ben Fong-Torres, and

Steven Winn; Steve Allen's helpful son Bill; Monica Lewis; photo archivists Cornelia Schnall, Shawn O'Sullivan, Ron Mandelbaum, and David Haberstich; ex–Sullivan show assistant Susan Abramson; and, to be sure, my UC Press editor Mary Francis, who responded at once to my proposal and carefully shepherded the book into actual print; her patient, sharp-eyed confederates, editors Dore Brown and Bonita Hurd; and book designer Lia Tjandra, for her eye-catching jacket design. Special citations are awarded my personal cheerleading squad—Jeff Abraham, Rita Abrams, Morris and Sharon Bobrow, Jane Mc-Dougle, Lotte Lundel, Carla Ruff, Bob Sarlatte, Susan Stone, Michael Krasny, Leah Garchik, Dana Rodriguez, Al and Pat Negrin, Jerry Hyman, Wendy Lu, Don Miller, Izzie Green, Mary McGeachy, and Ron Miller—who politely listened as I bent their ears with hair-raising tales of the book's zigzag path over the manuscript's four-year run. Let's really hear it for 'em!

Index

Text: 10/13 Sabon
Display: Bodoni Bold Condensed
Compositor: Westchester Book Group
Indexer: Sharon Sweeney
Printer and binder: Maple-Vail Manufacturing Group